D1410591

Integrative Document & Content Management

Strategies for Exploiting Enterprise Knowledge

Len Asprey & Michael Middleton

IDEA GROUP PUBLISHING

Hershey • London • Melbourne • Singapore • Beijing

Acquisition Editor:	Mehdi Khosrow-Pour
Senior Managing Editor:	Jan Travers
Managing Editor:	Amanda Appicello
Development Editor:	Michele Rossi
Copy Editor:	Lori Eby
Typesetter:	Amanda Appicello
Cover Design:	Integrated Book Technology
Printed at:	Integrated Book Technology

Published in the United States of America by
    Idea Group Publishing (an imprint of Idea Group Inc.)
    701 E. Chocolate Avenue, Suite 200
    Hershey PA 17033
    Tel: 717-533-8845
    Fax: 717-533-8661
    E-mail: cust@idea-group.com
    Web site: http://www.idea-group.com

and in the United Kingdom by
    Idea Group Publishing (an imprint of Idea Group Inc.)
    3 Henrietta Street
    Covent Garden
    London WC2E 8LU
    Tel: 44 20 7240 0856
    Fax: 44 20 7379 3313
    Web site: http://www.eurospan.co.uk

Library of Congress Cataloging-in-Publication Data

Asprey, Len, 1949-
  Integrative document and content management : strategies for exploiting enterprise knowledge / Len Asprey and Michael Middleton.
    p. cm.
  ISBN 1-59140-055-4 (hardcover) — ISBN 1-59140-068-6 (ebook)
  1. Business records—Management. 2. Text processing (Computer science) 3. Information storage and retrieval systems. I. Middleton, Michael, 1947- II. Title.
  HF5736 .A767 2002
  651.5—dc21   2002014270

British Cataloguing in Publication Data
A Cataloguing in Publication record for this book is available from the British Library.

NEW from Idea Group Publishing

- **Digital Bridges: Developing Countries in the Knowledge Economy**, John Senyo Afele/ ISBN:1-59140-039-2; eISBN 1-59140-067-8, © 2003
- **Integrative Document & Content Management: Strategies for Exploiting Enterprise Knowledge**, Len Asprey and Michael Middleton/ ISBN: 1-59140-055-4; eISBN 1-59140-068-6, © 2003
- **Critical Reflections on Information Systems: A Systemic Approach**, Jeimy Cano/ ISBN: 1-59140-040-6; eISBN 1-59140-069-4, © 2003
- **Web-Enabled Systems Integration: Practices and Challenges**, Ajantha Dahanayake and Waltraud Gerhardt ISBN: 1-59140-041-4; eISBN 1-59140-070-8, © 2003
- **Public Information Technology: Policy and Management Issues**, G. David Garson/ ISBN: 1-59140-060-0; eISBN 1-59140-071-6, © 2003
- **Knowledge and Information Technology Management: Human and Social Perspectives**, Angappa Gunasekaran, Omar Khalil and Syed Mahbubur Rahman/ ISBN: 1-59140-032-5; eISBN 1-59140-072-4, © 2003
- **Knowledge and Business Process Management**, Vlatka Hlupic/ISBN: 1-59140-036-8; eISBN 1-59140-074-0, © 2003
- **IT-Based Management: Challenges and Solutions**, Luiz Antonio Joia/ISBN: 1-59140-033-3; eISBN 1-59140-075-9, © 2003
- **Geographic Information Systems and Health Applications**, Omar Khan/ ISBN: 1-59140-042-2; eISBN 1-59140-076-7, © 2003
- **The Economic and Social Impacts of E-Commerce**, Sam Lubbe/ ISBN: 1-59140-043-0; eISBN 1-59140-077-5, © 2003
- **Computational Intelligence in Control,** Masoud Mohammadian, Ruhul Amin Sarker and Xin Yao/ISBN: 1-59140-037-6; eISBN 1-59140-079-1, © 2003
- **Decision-Making Support Systems: Achievements and Challenges for the New Decade**, M.C. Manuel Mora, Guisseppi Forgionne and Jatinder Gupta/ISBN: 1-59140-045-7; eISBN 1-59140-080-5, © 2003
- **Architectural Issues of Web-Enabled Electronic Business**, Nansi Shi and V.K. Murthy/ ISBN: 1-59140-049-X; eISBN 1-59140-081-3, © 2003
- **Adaptive Evolutionary Information Systems**, Nandish V. Patel/ISBN: 1-59140-034-1; eISBN 1-59140-082-1, © 2003
- **Managing Data Mining Technologies in Organizations: Techniques and Applications**, Parag Pendharkar/ ISBN: 1-59140-057-0; eISBN 1-59140-083-X, © 2003
- **Intelligent Agent Software Engineering**, Valentina Plekhanova/ ISBN: 1-59140-046-5; eISBN 1-59140-084-8, © 2003
- **Advances in Software Maintenance Management: Technologies and Solutions**, Macario Polo, Mario Piattini and Francisco Ruiz/ ISBN: 1-59140-047-3; eISBN 1-59140-085-6, © 2003
- **Multidimensional Databases: Problems and Solutions**, Maurizio Rafanelli/ISBN: 1-59140-053-8; eISBN 1-59140-086-4, © 2003
- **Information Technology Enabled Global Customer Service**, Tapio Reponen/ISBN: 1-59140-048-1; eISBN 1-59140-087-2, © 2003
- **Creating Business Value with Information Technology: Challenges and Solutions**, Namchul Shin/ISBN: 1-59140-038-4; eISBN 1-59140-088-0, © 2003
- **Advances in Mobile Commerce Technologies**, Ee-Peng Lim and Keng Siau/ ISBN: 1-59140-052-X; eISBN 1-59140-089-9, © 2003
- **Mobile Commerce: Technology, Theory and Applications**, Brian Mennecke and Troy Strader/ ISBN: 1-59140-044-9; eISBN 1-59140-090-2, © 2003
- **Managing Multimedia-Enabled Technologies in Organizations**, S.R. Subramanya/ISBN: 1-59140-054-6; eISBN 1-59140-091-0, © 2003
- **Web-Powered Databases**, David Taniar and Johanna Wenny Rahayu/ISBN: 1-59140-035-X; eISBN 1-59140-092-9, © 2003
- **E-Commerce and Cultural Values**, Theerasak Thanasankit/ISBN: 1-59140-056-2; eISBN 1-59140-093-7, © 2003
- **Information Modeling for Internet Applications**, Patrick van Bommel/ISBN: 1-59140-050-3; eISBN 1-59140-094-5, © 2003
- **Data Mining: Opportunities and Challenges,** John Wang/ISBN: 1-59140-051-1; eISBN 1-59140-095-3, © 2003
- **Annals of Cases on Information Technology** – vol 5, Mehdi Khosrowpour/ ISBN: 1-59140-061-9; eISBN 1-59140-096-1, © 2003
- **Advanced Topics in Database Research** – vol 2, Keng Siau/ISBN: 1-59140-063-5; eISBN 1-59140-098-8, © 2003
- **Advanced Topics in End User Computing** – vol 2, Mo Adam Mahmood/ISBN: 1-59140-065-1; eISBN 1-59140-100-3, © 2003
- **Advanced Topics in Global Information Management** – vol 2, Felix Tan/ ISBN: 1-59140-064-3; eISBN 1-59140-101-1, © 2003
- **Advanced Topics in Information Resources Management** – vol 2, Mehdi Khosrowpour/ ISBN: 1-59140-062-7; eISBN 1-59140-099-6, © 2003

Len wishes to dedicate this book to the memory of
Emily May Asprey, 1905–1991 (Proverbs 31:13),
and to his family.

Michael dedicates this book to the girls:
Sue, Kathryn, and Alison.

Integrative Document & Content Management
Strategies for Exploiting Enterprise Knowledge

Table of Contents

Foreword

I am delighted to write the Foreword to this book, as its scope and content provides commercial and government enterprises with the essential ingredients for implementing and managing document and Web content systems. Whether the systems are associated with office documents, email management, Web content management, drawing management, or similar applications, they provide crucial support for developing and implementing knowledge strategies within enterprises. The integrative approach is particularly welcome.

These systems play a vital role in assisting enterprises with the complex document control systems required to achieve and maintain ISO 9000 accreditation. They are important elements in reducing risks of noncompliance with regulatory or legal requirements. They also help to support e-business strategies, manage Internet and intranet Web content, provide transactional support for end-to-end business processes, manage administrative documentation, and underpin continuous business improvement strategies.

In my role as President of the Association for Information and Image Management (AIIM) International, I am able to have firsthand experience with commercial and government personnel who are seeking professional guidance on the implementation of document and Web content management systems. I believe that these people will benefit from reading this book for its extensive analysis of requirements.

The book merges the academic and the hands-on knowledge of the authors, to assist organizations in gaining benefits from both perspectives. It offers the practical knowledge derived from the implementation of document technologies, based on the wide-ranging consulting and project management fieldwork of Len Asprey, and the extensive academic research and consulting assignments that have been performed by Michael Middleton in the discipline of information management.

We often hear vendors and consultants in the document technologies industry make the statement that business users need to "define their requirements" for document and Web content management systems. However, these types of statements may not always be clear, because the users may never before have had to plan and specify requirements for document and content management technologies. They may not have a detailed understanding of the scope and level of definition involved in conducting requirements analysis and preparing specifications, and may not have been exposed to the complexity of cultural implications and change management requirements for these projects.

This book cuts through much of the hype and panache associated with marketing of document and Web content management solutions to help address this conundrum. It provides a thorough examination of business contexts that influence the ways that document systems are managed. It goes on to provide a framework for requirements analysis, along with examples to assist with analysis and specification of document and content management solutions. It also provides extensive checklists and sample templates in parts 2, 3, and 4 to assist organizations with the analysis and specification of requirements.

The book offers a project life-cycle framework for implementing document management systems from business conceptualization of a requirement through to go-live operations of the system. It is effectively a recipe or cookbook that develops the essential ingredients from the initial conceptualization of the requirement for document and content management, through the various phases of planning, feasibility analysis, requirements specifications, package selection, and implementation.

This book will help not only the enterprises that are implementing document and content management systems but also the vendors, in positioning the planning and implementation of the systems within a project life-cycle methodology. This emphasizes feasibility analysis, specification, package selection, and implementation planning strategies that minimize risk. It provides practical guidance that may help organizations to implement document management solutions that facilitate the achievement of overall business plans, support e-business, and underpin continuous business improvement, in a secure managed environment.

It is a vital business primer for organizations that wish to embark on document or content management projects, and those that have initiated or are about to initiate knowledge management strategies, or quality management systems, and view document and content management as a core component of their strategies. It is also a most useful reference for organizations that were early adopters of document technologies, perhaps as pilot projects, and are now considering upgrading their systems to implement increased functionality. This book will help those organizations to progress the implementation of the next generation of systems.

When asked what he thought of Western civilization, Mahatma Gandhi is said to have replied, "I think it would be a very good idea." I think that the same may be said of document management systems. We have them now, but we are as yet some way off what they could really be. This book shows us the way.

I am pleased to be able to commend this book to readers, be they those looking for substantive material on knowledge strategy, those looking to understand an important aspect of information management, or those about to implement or upgrade document or Web content management systems. For this last group in particular, I wish you the very best successes with the implementation of your systems.

John Mancini
President, AIIM International
October 2002

Preface

This book blends theory and practice to provide practical knowledge and guidelines to enterprises wishing to understand the importance of managing documents along with presenting document content to facilitate business planning and operations support. The book introduces strategies for Integrative Document and Content Management (IDCM).

OBJECTIVES

Our overall objectives are as follows:

- Enhance the understanding of systems that provide for the organization and management of business document collections, where the documents are a combination of digital and physical documents, and Web content collections that generally involve a combination of multimedia objects.

- Describe the characteristics of how documents and Web content are typically administered within enterprises, and review how the mismanagement of document and Web content collections impacts decision making. We also examine insights into how a well-managed document and Web content environment supports business planning.

- Address the potential benefits of a document and Web content management policy framework, which is a suggested prerequisite or corequisite to the implementation of IDCM, and the types of policy requirements that enterprises may wish to develop.

- Provide an information systems planning framework for the planning, specification, acquisition, development, and implementation of IDCM solutions.

- Offer insights into typical IDCM applications within enterprises and into how feasibility analyses are a suggested prerequisite for analyzing the operational, technical, and financial viability of IDCM.

- Provide a framework for determining and analyzing the functional and technical requirements for IDCM, and provide functionality checklists that enterprises may find helpful when discerning requirements.

- Show how related systems, such as drawing management and content management, may be embraced within IDCM.

- Review package selection and implementation strategies that enterprises may find useful when proceeding with the selection of an IDCM solution, and the subsequent implementation of a preferred solution.

BUSINESS CONTEXT

The setting for the themes addressed is a commercial and government business environment, of which the following can be said:

- Documents in some form are used to support virtually every business process in the enterprise, and they are prone to mismanagement due to the volumes of documents being processed and the diversity of document types and formats.

- Document mismanagement may have deleterious affects on efficient and effective business processes and may impact an organization's capabilities to deliver timely services to customers or business partners.

- Document mismanagement may impact an organization's capability to comply with legislative and administrative regulations, and it may expose the organization to the threat of litigation or brand damage.

- Email volume is increasing greatly, as organizations choose its convenience to interact with customers, business partners, and internal staff members, often without adequate management controls.

- Many organizations are publishing Web content to Internet and intranet sites without adequate management controls, potentially exposing the organization to risks, including litigation.

- Enterprises in many countries are faced with the challenge of implementing privacy legislation but have yet to implement an appropriate model of policies, practices, and systems to meet the requirements.

- Public enterprises that are required to satisfy Freedom of Information (FOI) legislation, or private enterprises with similar requirements to satisfy independent regulators, often have difficulty in finding, retrieving, and assembling relevant information, due to poorly managed document collections.

- Organizations that have not implemented adequate risk management strategies for securing important business documents and Web content may be vulnerable to exposures and threats that impact business continuity.

- Information systems professionals who enforce constraints to maintain the integrity of data in databases seem powerless to implement the same types of integrity controls over enterprise collections of digital documents.

- Governments may mandate information or recordkeeping standards and associated systems within public authorities. However, the authorities might not recognize the scope and extent of the project resources requirement or might not be funded adequately for implementation.

- Organizations may see the solution in relatively simplistic terms, like buying "off the shelf" software, without recognizing the need to develop a solution within an overall strategic management framework.

- Information disciples, who seek to implement document and content management solutions as part of recordkeeping practice, may encounter impediments when using "best practice" reasons to argue business cases.

- Project champions are often faced with the difficulties of obtaining funding for document and content management projects, because management may not have been given a full appreciation of the benefits. There will always be higher priorities if the requirement and solution options are not aligned with business planning imperatives.

- Organizations frequently develop completely inadequate specifications for document or Web content management solutions, then become frustrated when the solution fails to meet expectations, or the costs and time frame for implementation far exceed budget estimates.

- Document management systems (DMS), which have been available to implement management controls over digital document collections for over a decade, have not been taken up to the extent predicted by industry pundits.

- DMS projects and their rates of success in terms of operational, technical, or financial outcomes are open to conjecture, with documented evidence and a significant degree of anecdotal evidence of ineffective implementations.

- Organizations may simply not realize that they have a document problem, or if they do, they cannot understand it, see it as a priority, or identify a strategy to address it.

- Industry projections that were made for DMS are now being made for systems that manage Web content, although it is too early to assess the outcomes of the industry's performance against projections.

When these circumstances are recognizable in business environments, effective problem resolution may be hampered because of the following:

- Document and Web content management products generally only address a part of an enterprise's document and content management life-cycle and rely on integration with third-party suppliers to provide a holistic solution.

- Integration between products that might make up a holistic solution can be complex from a perspective of usability, functionality, or architectural integration. This can lead to time and cost blowouts, redundant functionality, and lack of transparency to the end user.

The problems can be intensified when:

- Information systems such as DMS and Web content management products are implemented without due regard to a management framework that encompasses planning, policies, procedures, standards, and guidelines.

- Enterprises fail to align their document or content strategies with key business planning imperatives, or fail to plan and implement solutions within the context of revitalizing business processes.

- Technology solutions are implemented without adequate attention to elements of organizational culture and behavior, such as workgroup dynamics, and fail to utilize adequate change management strategies.

Executives that fail to address the mismanagement of documents and Web content within their enterprises may be condoning an environment that:

- Exposes the organization to the risk of noncompliance with mandated regulatory requirements;

- Reduces the effectiveness of the organization case during litigation or fails to comply with required documents under discovery processes, which can be particularly embarrassing if the other party can produce the organization's documents;

- Risks damage to brand by applying inappropriate document and content management policies and practices and unsupported systems;

- Hampers strategic business initiatives such as e-business and other Web-enabled initiatives, such as Supply Chain Management (SCM) and Customer Relationship Management (CRM);
- Impacts the organization's capability to implement and sustain quality management processes; and
- Makes it difficult to improve productivity through business process redesign, due to the reliance on documents that may not be managed.

In effect, instead of understanding that information needs to be managed as a resource, executives that condone mismanaged document environments might be abrogating their responsibilities to shareholders (or the public, in the case of public agencies).

This book aims to address the problems that may be facing enterprises that are coming to terms with document and content management and tries to help business managers and information professionals develop and implement workable solutions for managing documents and Web content.

We propose an integrative planning model, which we call Integrative Document and Content Management (IDCM), for the development and implementation of solutions that embrace document and Web content management. The IDCM model offers a planned, methodical, and integrative approach that combines two themes:

- The development of an IDCM Management Framework that encompasses the following:
  - Strategies for aligning business and technology solutions with enterprise planning imperatives;
  - Development of relevant policies covering document management and Web content management to provide the governance framework for implementing business and technology solutions;
  - Review and development of procedures to give effect to the policies;
  - Adaptation and application of relevant information management principles, standards, and best practice;
  - Application of recordkeeping principles to relevant documents and Web content; and
  - Definition of Change Management Strategies and Communication Plans to assist with managing cultural changes within the enterprise.
- The definition, development, and implementation of information systems to support the overall document life-cycle and management of document content. This implies a holistic IDCM Systems Architecture, embracing subsystems that provide *management* of the following:
  - Digital office documents;
  - Email;
  - Physical office documents;
  - Drawings and technical documents;
  - Document images;
  - Document indexing, using recognition facilities, such as barcode and character recognition technologies;

- Business processes using automated workflow management systems for managing document and Web content life-cycles;
- Web content management (Internet and intranet), including multimedia objects;
- Reports output from business operational and support systems.

Support for recordkeeping requirements should be planned, specified and implemented as an integral component of IDCM systems and subsystems, as required.
The IDCM systems environment may include integration with strategic business systems, such as:

- E-business systems;
- Enterprise Resource Planning Systems;
- Supply Chain Management Systems;
- Asset Management Systems;
- Contract Management Systems;
- Other horizontal business applications; and
- Vertical applications relevant to the specific line of business.

The IDCM systems may also interface with technologies such as:

- Knowledge Portals;
- Geographical Information Systems; and
- Data Warehousing.

Given the extent of business and government operations, and the diverse range of applications, we do not attempt to cover every type of business purpose that may be applicable for IDCM projects. Our intention is to provide an overall management framework to facilitate successful implementation of practices and solutions for effective IDCM.

This book addresses the many types of issues that may arise during the development and implementation of an IDCM project. It discusses techniques derived from project management theory and practice that relate to implementation of IDCM solutions. Enterprises may find these techniques useful when embarking on document and Web content management projects and implementing IDCM solutions.

We exclude an evaluation of the functionality of specific products that may support IDCM. This is because of the extensive range of products and their rapidly changing functionality and integration capability that cause evaluations to quickly become out of date. It is also because suppliers may have alliances with other suppliers to provide functionality that may not be inherent within their own product set. Instead, we provide functionality checklists relevant for software that is contributing to IDCM solutions.

INSPIRATION

We were inspired to write this book because of the following:

- **The requirement to manage documents and their content is not going to magically disappear.**
Our ancestors captured information on a variety of recordable media, including cave walls, tortoise shells, and bark. We still do a bit of that but now have a tendency to use

digital mechanisms for recording documents and publishing their content onto Internet and intranet Web sites. New formats may emerge in the future, and they might not be referred to as "documents" or "content," but the container, whatever it is called, will still need to be managed.

- **Mismanaged document and Web content collections represent a level of risk to the enterprise.**

  The impact of mismanaged document collections on an organization's performance might not have been immediately apparent to an external observer. However, enterprises now have the penchant for making documents available on internal or public Web sites, and content is typically not managed. The fact that content may have been derived from unmanaged or mismanaged digital document collections exacerbates the problem, and the staging process from document creation through to publication generally relies on manual processes that can be prone to error. Consequently, outdated or incorrect information on Web sites might be more easily detectable for external observers (like customers), and published content may indeed be subject to litigation processes.

- **Mismanaged document and Web content collections may impact the success of quality management programs.**

  The delivery of timely products and services within a quality management program is becoming increasingly important in the present competitive environment. Customers not only want *timely* products and services, but they also require *quality* products and services. The ISO 9000 series provides a framework for quality management systems. Document control is a vital component of seeking and maintaining quality accreditation and providing products and services within an acceptable quality management system. Mismanaged document collections can have dangerous implications for an enterprise's quality management program, and have been known to lead to an enterprise's cessation of trading until document control systems are managed.

- **Document and Web content management is an integral part of an enterprise's capacity to develop knowledge management strategies.**

  The increasing awareness of the importance of information as an organizational asset has led to many commentaries on information resource management as a discipline. In the last decade, these have been associated to some extent with the embryonic notions of knowledge management, which concerns itself with knowledge in intangible and documented forms. The requirement for document and Web content management should play a pivotal role during the development of an organization's knowledge management strategies. Document and Web content management solutions provide the foundation by which organizations are better able to manage, share, and retrieve information held in document repositories or published on Internet or intranet sites.

- **Document and Web content management systems integrated with workflow collectively provide an integrative environment for business process redesign.**

  The use of workflow management software, combined with document and Web content management systems, provide management controls over all stages of a business process, and the information elements relating to that process. The use of an integrated solution for automating processes, while maintaining controls over information, may offer a compelling environment for business process redesign, and may help organizations make better use of corporate knowledge.

- **Threats to business continuity may represent a high risk.**

  Much of today's business documentation continues to be managed in paper form, where is it exposed to physical security threats, including fire, theft, loss, replication, or unintentional misplacement. As more documentation becomes digital and is used for business decision making, the same security threats apply, and they can be actioned with ease. There is high potential for vast quantities of digital documentation to be lost maliciously or unintentionally. For example, the equivalent amount of paper that could fill a number of pantechnicon trucks can now be held on executives' laptop computers. Given the mobility of laptops, there are risks such as loss or theft, easy transfer of company information to unauthorized parties, or just plain mismanagement of documented information, such as lack of synchronization of files with enterprise file systems.

- **Project failures represent a social cost.**

  We observed that many DMS projects, though initiated and developed by well intentioned document or records management enthusiasts, have undesired outcomes or are terminated for reasons such as lack of project ownership or failure to align the project with business objectives. We mentioned that documented evidence supports the view that DMS projects have not always been effective. Anecdotal evidence would suggest that the overall success rate of DMS is not very high, based on evaluation of outcomes against stated objectives. There is a deprivation of shareholder value if projects are not successfully implemented in the commercial sector, and there is a direct cost to taxpayers if document or content management projects are not successful in the public sector.

- **A collaborative approach to managing document and Web content is important.**

  We wanted to bring together principles from a number of disciplines within a business management framework to address the requirements for document and content management. The framework provides an organized reference for improving the management of documents and Web content. We wished to provide guidance for those enterprises introducing systems where professional expertise, though convergent from a number of areas, is yet to be expressed within an overall framework.

APPLICATION CONTEXT

For our purposes, any documented knowledge is information. A document is effectively a container for information, and the document or container may be represented in multiple file formats and may be stored on multiple types of storage media from paper to disk. We are concerned with the processes for recording the information, particularly digitization, the management of document-based information including Web content files, and the application of relevant recordkeeping requirements.

Electronic systems for organizing and retrieving information have been developed in a variety of communities. Disciplines such as records management, archives administration, librarianship, business analysis, Web site architecture, and data administration have made contributions to their evolution.

A range of information management systems has emerged. Instances can be summarized as follows:

- *Records Management Systems* were developed as processes and finding aids for systematization of physical (hard-copy) documents.

- *Document Management Systems* emerged to address the requirements for managing digital documents.

- *Web Content Management Systems* emerged to manage published (Internet/intranet) Web content.

- *Electronic Records Management Systems* offer functionality for managing digital documents and physical documents as records.

- *Email Management Systems* offer management of digital email.

- *Drawing Management Systems* offer management controls over collections that involve drawings and technical documents.

- *Document Imaging Systems* provide repository management for storage of digital images, or film-based collections.

Many enterprises have implemented these types of systems as "point solutions" to a specific business problem with varying degrees of effectiveness. If these systems have been implemented without an integrated information architecture, they may exist as "information silos," and not support knowledge-sharing strategies.

An organization's document and content management requirements must be considered within the range of an enterprise's document production and publication programs. Consequently, today's requirements are for integrated solutions, which must now accommodate hybrid collections of physical and digital documents (including multimedia), and implement recordkeeping practices that satisfy relevant requirements.

The types of products available to assist enterprises in implementing solutions for managing all types of documents and content are emerging as part of the gradual evolution of these systems. However, the challenge is only partially addressed by software, and the overall requirements need to be addressed within the context of an integrative planning model, which we term IDCM.

Reproduced with the kind permission of Jim Watson.

The IDCM planning model offers an integrative methodology incorporating a management framework and systems approach to planning and implementing document and Web content management solutions and meeting recordkeeping requirements. The scope and requirement for IDCM solutions must be aligned with business planning imperatives and must be viewed within the context of how documents are used to support business processes.

We are concerned with optimizing the management of documents and Web content within an enterprise so that the corporate memory remains readily accessible to authorized users who may require it for foreseen and unforeseen purposes. The implementation of effective IDCM solutions for managing documents and Web content will support business decision making and enable information sharing and reuse. IDCM is a key to achieving excellence in business administration and provides the foundation for enterprise knowledge management strategies.

INTENDED AUDIENCE

We see this book as being useful to the following readership.

Business Managers

- Managers of vital business documents, such as tenders, contracts, leases, awards, minutes of meetings, and regulatory compliance reports, who require a method of storing and quickly retrieving relevant information.

- Engineering managers, engineering services personnel, and draftspersons who are required to improve the management of engineering drawings, specifications, manuals, and similar technical documentation as part of engineering processes.

- Quality assurance, safety, and risk managers required to manage ISO document collections and meet the documentation requirements for an integrated management system.

- Managers responsible for accountability, who must ensure that there is documentation of decisions and actions and an associated framework of accessibility.

- Managers of legal practices and investigators required to better manage document collections as part of the process of assembling document exhibits for litigation purposes.

- Web content managers required to better manage content in the form of digital objects (e.g., images, viewable and downloadable files) and HTML/XML Web pages and associate Web content with other publication programs in an enterprise.

- E-commerce project managers required to improve the management of back-office processes to support e-commerce initiatives.

- Project managers in business and government sectors who are seeking an appreciation of an overall framework for scoping, specifying, selecting, and implementing IDCM solutions.

Information Professionals

- Information managers (including document controllers, records managers, librarians, and archivists) within enterprises who are responsible for implementing and managing systems for organizing and disseminating documents to facilitate knowledge-sharing, for managing content on Web interfaces, and for ensuring that documents are managed in a way that meets regulatory requirements.

- Information systems auditors who are responsible for reviewing organizational effectiveness and accountable management.

- Vendors who wish to gain a wider appreciation of document management requirements and issues within enterprises and confirm the value of an information systems life-cycle approach to the implementation of IDCM applications in business and government sectors.

Students

- Students in information management or information technology courses who have had an introduction to information management and systems work and are now examining specific business applications.

ORGANIZATION OF CONTENT

The book is structured in four parts, followed by a part devoted to appendices:

- Part 1: "Business Context" assists business and government enterprises in gaining an appreciation of the role of documents within the context of business planning and operations. It reviews the evolution of documents from antiquity through to today's document paradigm and the emergence of document technologies. It considers typical business planning imperatives, and provides scenarios representative of a current enterprise document environment. It provides a conceptual overview of characteristics of IDCM systems and typical applications within enterprises that can help reduce the negative impacts on business planning that occur due to fragmented and mismanaged document environments.

- Part 2: "Preliminaries" assists business and project managers in applying information systems life-cycle planning techniques when initiating and progressing an IDCM project. It emphasizes the importance of change management and the need to develop a change management strategy at project initiation and implement the strategy throughout the project life-cycle. It introduces the requirement for a document management policy as a key subset of an information policy and recommends the rigor of the feasibility study approach to determine operational, technical, and financial feasibility of an IDCM opportunity. The feasibility study helps clarify the project scope and is a logical precursor to a full requirements analysis study. It is also a useful prerequisite to building the business case, which is another vital aspect of the project life-cycle that is detailed in this part.

- Part 3: "Requirements Analysis and Definition" reviews the necessity to analyze and define the requirements for IDCM and provides insights into the types of analysis and definition required. It provides a specification framework to help enterprises focus their analytical efforts and resources for document management applications and produce specification deliverables within a structured context. The framework incorporates user and system requirements and examines the functional requirements for an IDCM solution in terms of the standard range of document authoring tools within organizations. The functional analysis also includes a series of checklists to assist with compilation of Requirements Specifications.

Figure: IDCM Framework.

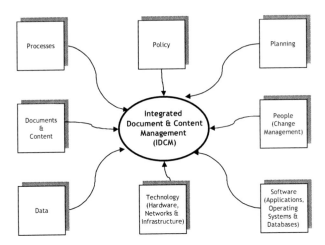

- Part 4: "Package Selection and Implementation Strategies" covers the processes involved in acquiring software to support an IDCM solution and methodologies for conducting evaluations of various solutions and making a selection. We include tips that enterprises may find useful during contract negotiations with shortlisted suppliers or a single supplier. This part also covers the implementation planning phase of an IDCM project, including suggestions for project execution planning, the importance of well-defined design, development, and testing regimes, and system changeover and migration strategies. We reemphasize the importance of change management, which is key to the successful implementation of IDCM.

In Chapter 4, we explain some discrete differences between general information systems and document and Web content technologies, primarily the document-centric nature of the requirements analysis and systems environment involved. However, IDCM involves the same types of components featured within any information system, and these are represented in the figure above, titled *IDCM Framework*.

We structured this book to deal with each of these aspects within the overall IDCM framework, but we do so within the context of a system-based project life-cycle approach to the management of an IDCM project. This approach includes understanding the overall requirement within a business context, the planning process involved in initiating and progressing an IDCM project, the focus on detailed requirements analysis and specification, and the strategies for package selection and implementation. During the life-cycle context, we will examine how each of these key components is relevant to the implementation of successful IDCM. The discrete parts of the book include component chapters as follows:

Part 1: Business Context

In Chapter 1, "**Introduction**," a brief historical perspective on the evolution of document types is provided. In it, a new document paradigm that has emerged with digitization is introduced, and the overall context of documents in organizations is considered. A review of the contributions made by various disciplines to our understanding of DMS is then provided. Other conceptual approaches to document management that are expressed in terms such as content management, are also introduced.

In Chapter 2, "**Business Planning Frameworks and IDCM**," a synopsis of the contemporary business environment is provided and some internal and external factors that influence enterprise planning are reviewed, with particular reference to document role. Several business sectors are considered. Some of the information systems and technologies available on the market to support planning initiatives are examined. The relevance of managing documents and their content is discussed in the context of planning, taking into account matters such as regulatory compliance and commercial processes.

In Chapter 3, "**Characteristics of Enterprise Document Environments**," a review of how business and government enterprises that have yet to embark upon IDCM may be managing processing of different document types is provided. A generic description of functionality and limitations is provided based on the assumption that organizations can apply relevant elements to their specific environments. Specific sections are devoted to digital documents in general, as well as email, physical documents, drawings, and technical documentation and Web content.

In Chapter 4, "**Characteristics of IDCM Systems**," the subsystems available as elements of IDCM solutions, and the types of functionality available to support an enterprise's information management strategy by improving the management of documents, are examined. The characteristics of contributing subsystems (including workflow) are described to enable an appreciation of how the management of documents can be improved by using IDCM.

In Chapter 5, "**Business Systems Interfaces and IDCM Opportunities**," the appraisal of the characteristics of IDCM systems is concluded. In the beginning of the chapter, IDCM opportunities in the context of their capability to interface with business operational and administrative systems are reviewed. We relate these to document and Web content management in order to illustrate how IDCM can support other lines of business systems and their applications.

Part 2: Preliminaries

The information presented in Chapter 6, "**Project Life-Cycle Planning and Methodologies**," deals with the planning aspects of a document or content management project, including scope, feasibility, and life-cycle development of the project. The typical project deliverables that may be used during the planning and subsequent phases of a project are reviewed.

The information presented in Chapter 7, "**Policy Framework for IDCM**," deals with the development of a framework that enables an enterprise to articulate its policy for managing documents and content, the general principles that support the policy, and the strategies for effective implementation of the policy.

In Chapter 8, "**Feasibility Study**," the relevance of the feasibility study as a key component of life-cycle management that may be used when embarking on an IDCM project is examined. It may be used to conduct a preliminary investigation of requirements and to determine the operational, technical, and financial feasibility of such a project.

In Chapter 9, "**Building the Business Case**," the development of a business case for the implementation of an IDCM strategy is developed. It provides insights to assist managers faced with having to acquire executive management commitment and budget funding for IDCM.

Part 3: Requirements Analysis and Definition

In Chapter 10, "**Requirements Analysis and Definition Framework**," a framework for requirements analysis to assist enterprises when conducting IDCM projects is discussed. It examines the types of analytical processes and specifications used to capture the overall requirements of IDCM, as a strategy to reduce the risks of acquiring a solution that does not meet requirements.

In Chapter 11, "**User Requirements**," the type of structure and content of a user requirements specification that might be suitable for an IDCM project within an enterprise is examined. It includes system changeover, backfile conversion of hard-copy documents, and migration of data and documents from existing files and repositories to an IDCM system, along with material on archival management, preservation, security, and storage requirements.

Chapter 12, "**Functional Requirements — Digital Office Documents**," is the first of several chapters in which requirements analysis and definition for functional requirements are reviewed. In this chapter, aspects that may be applied to digital office documents in general, are reviewed.

In Chapter 13, "**Functional Requirements — Email Management**," functional requirements engineering that may be appropriate when compiling a specification for managing email using either the direct capture method or save to DMS are examined.

In Chapter 14, "**Functional Requirements — Physical Office Documents**," the functionality of managing physical office documents using IDCM technology is addressed.

In Chapter 15, "**Functional Requirements — Document Imaging and Recognition Technologies**," requirements for scanning and conversion of physical documents to image format are considered, and requirements for recognition technologies, such as barcodes and character recognition, are included.

In Chapter 16, "**Functional Requirements — Workflow**," the discussion of workflow that was introduced in Chapter 4 is extended in order to review functional requirements when integrating workflow with document repositories in an IDCM context.

In Chapter 17, "**Functional Requirements — Engineering and Technical Drawings**," the functional requirements for using the capabilities of IDCM solutions for managing engineering and technical drawings and automating engineering change management processes, are examined.

In Chapter 18,"**Functional Requirements — Web Content Management**," functional requirements for integrating document management and Web publishing and workflow tools to provide end-to-end automation of processes for distributed development of Web content and a managed Web content environment that is cohesive, are considered.

In Chapter 19, "**Nonfunctional and Domain Requirements**," a requirements determination and analysis is provided that is useful for defining the nonfunctional requirements for enterprise IDCM, including system sizing, architecture, and performance requirements. We also include in this chapter a discussion on system administration requirements and domain requirements, such as the information technology environment.

Part 4: Package Selection and Implementation Strategies

In Chapter 20, "**Package Selection**," the typical procurement processes for selecting an IDCM solution are covered, and useful techniques for validating various solutions against requirements and negotiating a contract with a supplier are provided.

In Chapter 21, "**Implementation Planning**," guidelines for implementation planning are provided, along with techniques that can be used during the implementation process to facilitate a successful project outcome. This includes satisfying the operational, technical, and financial objectives of the project, and providing guidelines for postimplementation review.

In Chapter 22, "**Conclusion**," the main themes of the book are summarized and the challenges facing business and government enterprises with managing document collections and Web content are recapitulated.

Part 5: Appendices

The appendices start with a glossary (Appendix 1), followed by a complete list of text and sources referenced in this book (Appendix 2). Useful Internet sites are then provided (Appendix 3), followed by a representative list of software solution providers (Appendix 4). A final appendix (Appendix 5) provides a brief overview of digital storage hardware.

Acknowledgments

The authors would like to express their sincere appreciation to the independent referees for their comments concerning refinement of the book.

We thank the following industry professionals who contributed to the development of content, and gave of their valuable time to review specific sections of the book: Barbara Clay, Eric Taylor, Guy Lanyon, Margôt Tesch, Michael Rosemann, Milton Tilbrook, Noel Rath, and Peter Elford.

Our particular thanks go to Jackie Bettington, Dennis Connell, Kylie Jones, and David McAlpin for their valuable and constructive comments on the work as a whole, or on complete parts.

We also thank Sylvia Willie and Guy Gable for their supervision of the Len Asprey research thesis at Queensland University of Technology. This thesis provided a foundation for the document imaging components of the book.

We wish to thank Michele Rossi, our Development Editor from Idea Group, for her support during this project. Thanks also to Carrie Stull Skovrinskie and Megan Matzner, Assistant Marketing Managers with Idea Group, for facilitating marketing strategies. Our thanks to our Managing Editor, Amanda Appicello, for facilitating the final product. And, our thanks to the Copy Editor, Lori Eby, and the Assistant Managing Editor, Jennifer Wetzel, for proofing our project.

Our thanks also go to William Almaguer (Gartner Group) for assistance with Gartner Group publication processes and some relevant documents. We are grateful to the Workflow Management Coalition for granting permission to reproduce the Workflow Reference Model.

We gratefully acknowledge the assistance provided by the Queensland University of Technology with facilities and technical support.

Finally, we would like to thank the many customers and business associates who provided insights into problems encountered within enterprises relating to managing documents and Web content, who offered ideas and suggestions, or who otherwise came forward with topics that needed to be covered in the book.

PART 1

The Business Context

The chapters in Part 1 are designed to do the following:

- Provide a brief historical perspective of the emergence of documents and related technologies, review the role of documents in organizations today, and introduce the concept of the IDCM planning model.

- Review planning imperatives within enterprises, and consider the potential impact of inadequate management of documents and Web content on strategic, tactical, and operational planning initiatives.

- Review the characteristics of current document environments within enterprises, covering digital office documents, email, physical documents, drawings, and Web content, and consider the limitations of how these categories of documents are managed.

- Consider the characteristics of integrated document and Web content repository management systems as the core architecture for implementing controls over documents in organizations. We also consider integration opportunities with business operational and support systems.

- Discuss some typical applications of IDCM within businesses that might provide useful solutions for enterprises seeking to facilitate the achievement of planning objectives using document and Web content management solutions.

- Provide examples of how applications within enterprises help to reduce the negative impacts on business planning that may arise from fragmented and mismanaged document environments.

Chapter 1

Introduction

OVERVIEW

This chapter provides a brief historical perspective on the evolution of document types and introduces a new document paradigm that has emerged with digitization. It reviews the role of documents in the overall context of today's business world.

The review then covers the contributions made by various disciplines to our understanding of the evolution of DMS and the emergence of solutions for managing content of documents, particularly for Web presentation. This chapter also introduces the benefits of an integrative approach to document and Web content management solutions.

Our objectives are to:

- Provide some historical background and show its influence on contemporary approaches to document management.
- Examine the way a "document" is presently understood and how this may vary according to disciplinary background.
- Review technological developments that have impacted on the evolution of document formats and methods of registering documents.
- Review the development of DMS and show how the consideration of systems for managing documents and their content has been heavily influenced by the emergence of digital documents.
- Consider the emergence of Content Management Systems (CMS) within the overall evolutionary development of document technologies.
- Introduce an integrative approach to planning and implementing solutions for document and Web content management, depicted in an IDCM planning model.
- Cover the high-level features of the IDCM model, which comprises a management framework and conceptual systems architecture.

THE EVOLUTION OF DOCUMENTS AND REGISTERS

Antiquity

Our glimpses through the mists of antiquity tell us that after humanity developed writing, we found a need to systematize what had been written. Prior to the evolution of writing, our ancestors relied upon the individual and collective memories of tribal communities, in the form of genealogies, myths, and legends, embodied within poetry and songs, to recall and share information about past important events and the deeds of famous people. The earliest "documents" recording memories are the depictions fading on rock and cave walls in various parts of the world.

From at least two millennia prior to the common era (BCE), documents were created on a variety of media as far afield as Sumer, Egypt, and China. Most notably, the media of documentation were the clay tablet or papyrus. However, there were many alternatives, such as inscribed bones and tortoise shells, some Chinese examples of which have remained in existence for over 3000 years.

The organization of such documents was developed in order to maintain effective custody of records in courts and temples. For example, records were kept of court appointments, proclamations, military campaigns, and exchanges of goods. These archives were used to support management of labor provision for military campaigns and public works as well as levying taxes. Perhaps if the illiterate masses had been aware of their existence, they may have regarded them as a tyrannical instrument of the state, maintained by bureaucrats, or scribes, as they then were.

Those who recognized the power of organized document collections posed more of a threat. For example, the emperor Ch'in who unified the Chinese feudal states in 221 BCE, ordered destruction of many documents in order to try to standardize writing and measurements styles, and to stymie subversive thought.

Augustus Caesar, on having assumed the office of Pontifex Maximus (chief priest) in ancient Rome, is recorded as having selectively culled documents that may have contained views contrary to his own political aspirations.[1]

It is evident that the destruction of records by Roman emperors may not always have been to the public detriment, as is evidenced by the actions of Emperor Adrianus (Hadrian) in canceling Treasury debts:

> Hadrian canceled a countless sum of money owed to the fisc (Treasury) by private debtors in Rome and Italy, and also vast sums of arrears in the provinces, and he burned the records of indebtedness in the Forum of the deified Trajan in order to strengthen the general sense of security.[2]

His actions may have strengthened a general sense of security, but no doubt, they also bolstered the emperor's popularity during quite a volatile period. A contemporary example would be a President or Prime Minister canceling our obligations to the taxation collectors. Heads of government please take note — Hadrian's strategy left a lasting impression — a relief struck in honor of Hadrian's actions is available for public viewing in the Roman Forum to this day.

If a business strategy works well, then it is probably worth persisting with it, and a later emperor (Marcus Aurelius) followed the example set by his predecessor:

> Marcus Aurelius remitted all debts incurred by anyone to the imperial fisc or to the state treasury over a period of forty-five years in addition to the fifteen years of Hadrian, and he ordered all the records relating to these debts to be burned in the Forum.[3]

Destruction of documents in an unauthorized context is still practiced today by certain types of corporate executives and government officials, but the outcomes are not for the benefit of the organization's customers, shareholders, or the general public. The latter half of the 1990s and the early 2000s has witnessed the collapse of major companies, including businesses in the financial, insurance, telecommunications, resources, and energy sectors, in dubious circumstances. During investigations of these types of collapses, one of the recurring key issues detected during legal discovery processes has been the destruction or loss of documents.

However, the *information* recorded in documents is not so easy to destroy because of the extent of replication and organization made possible by digital systems. Also, our present mechanisms for dissemination of information make the process of destruction more available to scrutiny by a more literate public. A recent case in point concerns the matter of destruction of documents of significance to the collapsed Enron Corporation in the United States, purportedly involving the policy (Arthur Andersen, 2000) of an associated consulting firm.

Historical Advances

The development of paper and then the means to print upon it, moved us from the age of inscription to the age of replication. However, the wooden blocks for printing that were initially developed in Korea and China lacked the flexibility of discrete use of characters that we now take for granted. The development of individual metal type for characters during the Goryeo dynasty in Korea, then a couple of centuries later by Gutenberg in 1453 in the West, provided the means for large-scale reproduction of documents and the fostering of greater literacy.

We now had a significant mechanical device that enabled mass distribution of information. Prior to the advent of the printing press, each publication was copied by hand, often an undertaking performed by monks. Consequently, publications were rare and expensive, and, therefore, the prerogative of the privileged few. The printing press enabled publications to be produced at a faster rate and at much less cost.

Where previously it had been arduous to share ideas, and access to recorded information had been available only to a minority, now there was a mechanism for disseminating knowledge. Great value continued to be placed upon what had been written down, and the range of applications was great. For example, Gutenburg understood the enormous profit-making potential for his invention, particularly the market potential in selling indulgences.[4]

Mechanical processing of information continued until the mid-1800s, when inventions such as that of Jacquard in France, who developed punched cards to increase production of rugs, introduced the era of electromechanical data processing. Variations on this punched card principle were still being used to capture programs for computers in the mid-1900s.[5]

In 1884, Ottmar Mergenthaler invented the linotype, a mechanized-type casting machine that used a keyboard similar to a typewriter to perform the line composing operations. A subsequent development saw the emergence of the teletypewriter, which enabled composition to be recorded on punched paper tape. The perforated tape could then be converted into electrical signals and promulgated to multiple locations over the telephone system. Similar in principle to punched cards, punch paper tape was still a common form of communication exchange in the mid-1900s.

Photocopying seems to have its origins around the turn of the 20th century, with the advent of copying machines that required liquid chemicals. Beidler patented a dry-plate camera in 1906, and an American physicist, Chester F. Carlson, invented electro-static photocopying in 1938. The first electrostatic machine was too slow, and it was not until 1959 that the first Xerox copier was produced with an output of seven copies per minute. The application of principles of static electricity was to provide the foundation for the development of today's photocopying industry. Modern businesses continue to make extensive use of photocopying facilities for reproduction of business documents.

Facsimile transmission devices, which are used to transmit images across telephone lines, did not appear as common business tools until the late 1980s, although the development of the technology can be traced to the 19th century. Until the 1980s, facsimile machines were fairly cumbersome, expensive, and difficult to operate, and it appears that it was not until Japanese companies entered the market in the 1970s that facsimile machines emerged that were faster, smaller, and more efficient. Notwithstanding the advent of email, there is still extensive use made of facsimile machines to transmit information in the form of business documents.

The Business of Documents

As the numbers of documents proliferated, there was increasing demand for the systematic approaches to filing and classification that had germinated for written documents in the era prior to printing. Hitherto, scholars had managed the organization of the material. It increasingly became a specialist task. For example, bibliography was concerned with the descriptions of documents; records management and archives work was concerned principally with unpublished documents created within enterprises; librarianship focused on creating and maintaining collections of published material; and documentation was concerned with recording the topical contents of documents, particularly the component parts within printed documents, such as articles in journals.

In the early part of the 20th century, scholars paid some attention to the nature of documents, particularly as a result of the work of Paul Otlet, who reasoned that graphic and written records are documents that represent objects or ideas. Further, that the objects as such (archaeological finds, educational games, etc.) may also be considered to be documents if people are informed by observing them.

Although some scholars took a view of documents as being essentially textual records, others took a more encompassing view. This anticipated the way we have defined the term "document" in the standards we use today.[6] We look at ISO document definitions later in this chapter and consider the terminology of document management in Chapter 4.

We are now at a point in time where the different specializations that have developed for handling documents are being challenged in a digital era. This era blurs the distinct roles that may have been responsible for published as opposed to unpublished documents, organization of external as opposed to internal documents, and even production of format as opposed to content. Therefore, we will consider some of the disciplines that are seen as being concerned with the matter of documents and their content through various applications of information management.

Disciplines Concerned with the Document Business

Information professionals approach document management from a variety of perspectives. In some respects, this contributes to confusion in understanding the terminology in the field. In other respects, it should give more substance to formulation of a set of principles underlying document systems. We consider that those groups that have contributed most to the development of principles are as follows:

- *Document managers* provide experience in the requirements of handling a combination of different media in a coordinated manner. Their understanding of issues relating to conversion between formats, and preservation in different formats, combined with management of transfer and storage is important for an enterprise. They are capable of explicating what Sutton (1996) calls a document management architecture. This means that they should be able to identify and eliminate superfluous workflow, and describe pathways, accountability, and authority.

- *Records managers* contribute a well-defined set of principles for describing documents through the continuum of their use in business processes from creation to disposal. In particular, they provide approaches to description and content analysis that enable finding aids to be created using metadata (descriptions of documents), and document organization using file naming and sequencing principles.

- *Data administrators* typically come from an information technology (IT) background. They have an appreciation of the constraints of database administration and can marry the naming techniques of records managers to database support applications. These applications emphasize maintenance of information quality using data validation techniques such as data dictionary or information repository principles, version, and permission control, all to assist with data maintenance.

- *Business analysts* are more concerned with subject content from sources external to the enterprise or investigation of scenarios using internal databases, than the management of the documents that contain the source information. However, as primary users of many types of documents, they have key input to such processes as information auditing that identifies, among other things, organizational document sources of information, and the appropriate organization of retrieval systems.

- *Imaging technicians* contribute expertise to the appropriate conversion and compression of files, to the maintenance of the integrity of information during text conversion or graphic reformatting, and to estimates of file sizes for data administrators.

- *Librarians* contribute expertise in systems of classification, in information retrieval, and in collection management. Although collections have in the past focused on documents obtained externally from organizations, the increasing digitization of collections is diminishing the division between external documents produced by others and internal working documents.

- *Archivists* bring an appreciation of historiography to enable the supervision of judgments about the retention times of documents, and the management of enabling tools such as retention schedules that record judgments concerning why, how long, and where documents should be retained. They may apply this framework using information repositories or data dictionaries in a digital document environment.
- *Publishers* identify, select, and promote content, then mold it through editorial and presentation procedures to validate and enhance subject matter and make it more accessible.
- *Web managers* are responsible for establishment and maintenance of Internet or intranet World Wide Web (WWW or the Web) sites and company portals. They may bring a fusion of computing, design, and information skills, and may have a background in one of the disciplines above. They are concerned with the mechanics of the way an enterprise's information resources are made available.
- *Content managers* may embrace a Web management role, and their orientation can be more along the lines of a publisher, even though the "publishing" may be confined to an intranet. They are particularly concerned with the provision, currency, and quality control of required source materials for internal use, and beyond that, the partition of this material and that which is made available externally.

  Document collections are increasingly becoming hybrid accumulations of physical and digital documents, with a blurred distinction between published and unpublished. A role of content management in such circumstances becomes one of creating an information architecture of organized access points for the different types of material, possibly termed a portal, which may transparently point to an enterprise's internal documents in whatever form, as well as provide access to relevant external material.

One of the key reasons for this book is to develop insights into the principles applied by the various disciplines so that businesses and government are able to understand the different perspectives of each discipline. Successful project management for implementation of a document or Web content management system may well require consultation with and input from each of these disciplines, if they already have organizational roles.

Technological Development
Business Computing

Early computerized systems that were introduced into business and government were large "mainframe" computer systems that (aside from scientific research projects) supported transaction-based processing such as automation of payroll and bookkeeping functions. Due to the expense involved in acquiring computing systems, and the level of technical expertise required to program and operate the systems, there was an initial tendency (circa 1960s, 1970s) for business and government agencies to utilize centralized bureau services for batch processing and online transaction information systems (IS).

These systems evolved during the era of Management Information Systems (MIS[7]) (circa 1970s) to make a significant penetration into much more complex managerial decision-making processes. This period witnessed the rapid increase in memory and storage capacities as well as improved processing and networking capabilities. Computing technology was becoming more affordable for business and government enterprises, due to technology innovations and competition. In addition to more affordable larger-capacity systems, this period also saw the advent of mid-range computers, which were used to address specific business needs, at that time still primarily transaction based.

For our purposes, it is relevant to note that the electronic files used and manipulated by these systems typically adopted a single file format that was proprietary to the host system, and these systems were typically acquired from one supplier. With the evolution of desktop technology, business and government users now have access to a wide variety of complex application systems that generate different types of file formats.

It is also relevant to note in the context of this book that much output from MIS, mainframe or mid-range computing systems, was and generally continues to be in the form of hard-copy reports. Where MIS systems remain in place, these reports may be produced as a result of batch processing and are printed using high-speed line printers or similar devices. These reports can be quite voluminous and often take up significant amounts of storage.

Film-Based Systems

The advent of film-based systems, such as microfilm, microfiche, and aperture cards can be traced to the mid-1800s. Dancer, a microscope manufacturer in England, reduced daguerreotypes (tintypes) about 160 times, combined that process with a then emerging technology of transparent, collodion wet plate process, and produced microfilm (Smith, 1978, pp. 1-2). In France, Dagron[8] was apparently granted the world's first microfilm patent and later was awarded seven patents for microfilm equipment.

The use of microfilm as a technique grew in popularity for concealment and communication during the wars and conflicts that persisted in Europe through to the 1920s. At that point, it seemed that microfilm might be a wartime technique that lacked a peacetime application (Smith, 1978, p. 3), until a U.S. banker decided to use the technology to prove the existence of canceled checks, and built the first rotary microfilm camera to support the application. Different opportunities were then identified. For example, between 1927 and 1935, John D. Rockefeller Jr. provided gifts of US$490,000 to the Library of Congress to replace its existing foreign document copying activities with a microfilming program (Saffady, p. 14).

Until the 1950s, film-based technology was viewed as being beneficial for storing inactive records as archives. It was not until the 1960s that the market began to apply film-based technologies for rapid retrieval of information in active files, and a number of applications developed during the 1960s and 1970s to support rapid retrieval of documents held on microfilm to service current business processes (Saffady, p. 19). The introduction of computer-assisted microfilm retrieval systems to facilitate quick retrieval of microfilm frames, saw microfilm industry pundits claiming that the age of the "paperless office" had arrived.

Technology developments with film-based imaging led to the innovation of Computer Output Microfilm (COM) in the late 1950s. COM technology was designed to output reports from computing systems into microform, instead of these systems producing voluminous quantities of paper. The output can be viewed using a reader, and excerpts can be printed as required. It also has the advantage that microform output reduces the storage space required for paper output.

The state of utopia of the "paperless office" has not been achieved with the advent of microform technologies, although film-based systems continue to make significant headway into providing low-cost storage and retrieval tools for documents, particularly those with long-term archival requirements. Microfilm technology has now been integrated with desktop scanning systems, so that images can be viewed on display monitors and digitized copies distributed via computer networks as required.

Records Management Systems

The era of MIS during the 1970s and 1980s heralded the development of mainframe computer-hosted Records Management Systems (RMS). These systems provided automated registries that enabled enterprises to index, search, and retrieve information pertaining to records.

The RMS typically enabled users to implement a file classification system (or file plan), register files using the classification structure, and register and link documents to a set of files. The systems enabled users to search index data using a single inquiry key or combination of keys (including file and document titles and keywords), and return results. The systems also provided facilities for tracking movements of files or documents, and typically provided a history of relevant transactions for audit and reporting purposes.

However, RMS as a term may have been applied deceptively to this technology development, because it is unlikely that these systems manage all types of records in an organization. For example, a crime report might have been managed in a crime information system, a patient record in a patient information system, an insurance claim in a claims history system, and a drawing register used to keep a record of drawings. Each of these examples demonstrates a business "record" that may not be managed in a specifically designated RMS.

Many RMS were ported to a client/server architecture in the 1990s to take advantage of the Windows user interface and to take advantage of the then common strategy to distribute processing between client and server computers.

Digital Imaging

The concept of the "paperless office" was again strongly promoted in the 1980s. The evolution of imaging and database technologies led system designers to feel that they could produce solutions to software support for managing documents. However, as is so often the case with the overstatement accompanying computer system capability, there was insufficient attention to understanding workflow and management processes, the degree of integration of paper, and digital workflow required.

Digital imaging systems in high-production environments have been integrated with enterprise lines of business information systems for a wide range of applications. These include insurance claims processing, check processing, patient records, and many other transaction processing systems. Imaging systems have also been integrated with RMS, in mainframe and client server environments, to enable users to conduct searches, then quickly retrieve an image or images of documents registered in the RMS.

All types of documents may now be digital. These range from spreadsheets, to drawings, to scanned film, along with versions of these aggregated with text, which may be termed compound documents. The challenge for document management is to be able to deal with these in a seamless manner, and in a manner responsive to the differing needs of those who work with distinctive documents. Later in this chapter, we look at the nature of different documents in more detail.

Like the technology developments that saw the emergence of COM, the advent of digital imaging saw the development of Computer Output to Laser Disk (COLD). This technology is designed to output reports from business computing systems onto laser disk, and not microform, or paper. It offers the advantage of digitized storage of reports or historical data onto optical media. The terminology now being applied to COLD technology is Enterprise Report Management (ERM).

Desktop Computing/Networks

Most business and government enterprises implemented Local Area Network (LAN) systems in the 1990s to enable users remote from each other to share files in secure folder structures authenticated by the operating system. The networks also enabled sharing of devices such as printers and media such as CD-ROM. Many enterprises also provided a Wide Area Network (WAN), effectively extending individual LAN segments, to enable multiple sites to share files and devices.

Concurrently with the implementation of LAN and WAN systems, most enterprises also deployed personal computers as productivity tools by means of which users could exchange files, utilize desktop authoring tools, such as word-processing systems, spreadsheets, presentation tools, drawing tools, and electronic messaging systems. The volume of digital documents grew rapidly with the deployment of these types of desktop tools in a LAN environment.

The document paradigm that emerged in this type of environment included digital document types such as formatted and unformatted text, drawing formats, graphic formats, sound files, and digital video. Nevertheless, physical documents continued to proliferate, primarily due to the behavioral aspects of printing documents for review, temporary or permanent storage, and for records of transactions (e.g., signed contracts and approvals on business forms), but also because of material received from external to the organization.

The RMS applications that were developed in the era of MIS, many of which were later ported to client/server architectures, were not intended, and therefore did not support, an architecture to meet the demands of managing digital documents.

Some organizations tried to register the file system path name and document title as a record in the RMS. However, such attempts typically failed, because any change (e.g., rename, move, and delete) to the folder path and document title on the file system resulted in a loss of data integrity in the RMS.

The requirement to implement management controls over the proliferation of digital documents, represented in multiple formats and storage media, was to provide the impetus for the development of electronic DMS.

The late 1990s and early 2000s has witnessed the development of the wireless application protocol (WAP), and the evolving interactive television technology, each of which enables access to information resources and to Internet sites. This type of technology poses challenges for enterprises, because users will have an expectation that the information will be available literally at their fingertips. Enterprises need to ensure that they have the capability to provide the right information in a timely manner to the end user. In this regard, we note that short messaging services (SMS) for interpersonal and business communications are being adopted rapidly, and there will be greater expectations on the capability to access information from interactive devices.

Drawing Tools

The development of desktop computing tools to create digital drawings emerged with gusto in the 1990s and heralded a major transition in the engineering design and drawing office. The technology had a significant impact on the skills of draftspersons and engineers involved in the engineering change processes of design, review, and approval.

Essentially, there was a major transformation from an environment focused on manual preparation of drawings, manual redrawing of design changes, and review and approval processes, to a digital environment. With the development of Computer Aided Drawing (or Design) (CAD) tools, drawing templates were provided in digital form, standard symbols and objects were provided to save time, and redrawing was simplified by reusing an existing digital version of a drawing to make enhancements and modifications.

These developments laid the foundations for digitized transmittal of drawings using electronic messaging and distribution tools, and later the Internet and extranet technologies for sharing and collaborating during the design processes.

The requirement to manage the increasing volume of digital drawings and associate these with physically controlled copies of drawings provided the momentum for the development of drawing management systems. These tools were designed to place management controls over drawing objects, and the automation of specific aspects of the engineering change management process.

Internet/Intranet

During the mid-1990s, development of the Internet, which had been available for many years for military and academic purposes, began to accelerate. It continues to grow at a great rate. The Internet, as an essential means of communication, collaboration, and resourcing information, has virtually become ubiquitous, at least in technologically advanced countries, and to an increasing extent, in less-developed countries.

Whereas the Internet provides an outward focus of an organization's operations to the global community, intranet technology is rapidly being adopted for internal business and government operations for collaboration, communication, and information sharing. Intranets use similar software and interfaces to those on the Internet, but they are confined to LANs and secure WANs within enterprises.

The impact of the Internet and intranet on the document paradigm that emerged from desktop productivity tools and LAN systems is a greater range of new digital document formats. While the *lingua franca* of the Web to date has been Hypertext Markup Language (HTML), there are many other formats that have emerged, including Web-capable versions of preexisting document formats, and new formats to take advantage of Web technology. In particular, eXtensible markup language (XML) is emerging as a framework for defining documents. It is based upon the markup principles of Standard

Generalized Markup Language (SGML) used for publishing markup from electronic documents that preceded the Web.

The Internet has increasingly adopted the procedures of publishing. After all, that is where the markup languages originated in support of computer typesetting. Now, these languages have been utilized for publications that are available in print and digital form, or in some cases, are simply digital. These include trade publications, promotional material, many digital reference works such as encyclopedias and dictionaries that can be readily updated, periodicals as ejournals, and a myriad of desktop publishing initiatives. Internal company documents may be produced with similar diversity and facility or intranet distribution.

The Web also provides a primary example of complex document relationships. If an HTML page contains embedded links to another object (say an image in JPG format), then it is essentially a compound document like those that we describe when discussing the nature of documents in a following section.[9]

DOCUMENTS IN CONTEMPORARY ENTERPRISES

Role of Documents

The State, by means of government, continues to support many and varied systems for organization of documents. It has been joined by commercial enterprises, which are in many cases larger than individual state jurisdictions, and which must also manage large numbers of regulatory, legal, financial, and administrative documents.

Both state and private enterprises strive to maintain their corporate memory through organized approaches to storage and retrieval of information. Their information may be recorded from data in transactional databases, from business forms, from correspondence (hard-copy and electronic), and from the multitude of other document roles such as research, marketing, and policy needed to oil the wheels of commerce. It is complemented by records management procedures that describe this information and use the devices of classifying and indexing to create databases and finding aids for successful retrieval.

Nature of Documents

Later, we will look specifically at standard definitions of "document," but here, we will consider how technology has affected the way documents are understood.

Our society's traditional understanding of a document is that it is along the lines of something written on paper that provides information or evidence. More generically, we can say that a document is anything that makes use of marks to symbolize a person's thoughts. Therefore, the marks may range from pretextual records, such as those on the tjurunga or stones used by Australian aborigines for recording spiritual totems, through to the pits burned by lasers in optical media to represent digital code.

Now, instruments such as computer disks comprise a significant proportion of the media used for recording information, and encoding is via electronic or magnetic digital representation. There is a multiplicity of file formats, and the information that is recorded may be easily updated or manipulated. The concept of a permanent record on a physical medium has changed markedly, as many of the business transactions in today's society occur electronically. The information society is upon us.

From the viewpoint of a modern enterprise, our documents are most likely to be paper-based or in digital form. The symbols that express a person's thoughts may be represented as numerical data, text, drawings, design, mapping and other graphics, sound, or video. The documents may be created digitally and spend their entire life in digital form. They may have been created on paper, and subsequently digitized, using character recognition or imaging technology.

The concept of a document in a fixed format that can be described as an object in a particular medium is now more tenuous. Document description languages (such as SGML, HTML, and XML) enable documents to be created with emphasis on their content, but then repeatedly utilized wholly or partly using different presentation forms and structures. Format and content are now much less codependent.

The content may also be continually changing. This may be a very dynamic process, as is the case of a database, or a less frequent, but still periodic process, as is the case with policy documents or manuals. Versioning is necessary to identify the successive representations of a document.

The management of these documents requires additional documents. The metadata used for categorizing the documents, identifying versions and responsibilities, identifying routing requirements, and scheduling backup, retention, approval, and other administrative aspects, must be recorded and maintained per medium of records management and archival procedures. So, we have documents of metadata, which it is probably more correct to call metainformation, in forms such as finding aids, catalogs, and data dictionaries, which provide the organization and control for the original documents.

Recordkeeping procedures are influenced by the regulatory environment within which an enterprise functions. For example, business operations may have inspection requirements imposed from outside, such as reporting pursuant to legislation, the need to meet industry standards, audit requirements, or evidence for courts.

Some documents facilitate the creation of others. For example, most enterprises use business forms in order to generate and support transactions. These forms may support procedures as diverse as insurance claims, drug administration, application to study a course, or taxation accounting. In print or digital form, they also require management of formatting, versioning, and structuring for workflow.

Other documents are created in a transitory manner. They are constructed at the time of viewing from separate component documents. Sometimes called compound documents, they may embody one or several formats (for example, text, video, and graphics), or the compound relationship may consist of linkages between multiple document sets.

Some commentators point out that document management has just had a transition, and that it has effectively been absorbed into "content management."[10] There is debate on whether the terms "document management" and "content management" mean the same thing, with a variety of supporting and opposing views being expressed.

Our view is that the debate about the terminology does not greatly matter. The technology used to create markings that represent content, as well as the formats and media used, have changed ever since antiquity, and the latest developments are merely part of that evolutionary development. Effectively, a document is a container for information that may be represented in multiple formats, which includes "content" published as Web pages.

Table 1: Text and Audiovisual Creation — Comparison of Annual Outputs.

Medium	Titles	Terabytes
Books	968,735	8
Newspapers	22,643	25
Journals	40,000	2
Magazines	80,000	10
Newsletters	40,000	0.2
Office documents	7,500,000,000	195
Cinema	4,000	16
Music CDs	90,000	6
Data CDs	1,000	3
DVD-video	5,000	22
Total		285

Documentation Production

Some idea of the amount of business documentation in relation to all documentation being produced may be gained from a project underway at the University of California (Lyman et al., 2000). There, they have made estimates of the amount of information being represented in documents in the world. Among the findings are the following:

- Ninety-three percent of the information produced each year is stored in digital form. Hard drives in stand-alone PCs account for 55% of total storage shipped each year.
- If all printed material published in the world each year were expressed in standard digital format, it could be stored in less than 5 terabytes (a terabyte being a million megabytes). This is well within the capacity of present storage systems.
- Over 80 billion photographs are taken every year, which would take over 400 petabytes (1024 terabytes, or 2^{50} bytes) to store — more than 80 million times the storage requirements for text.

We have adapted their comparison of text and audiovisual creation to provide a summary that is illustrated in Table 1.

Clearly, there is a prodigious volume of business documents being produced, most of them digital. Among the key issues facing business and government with this explosion in documents are:

- Management of the phases of document use;
- Effective utilization for meeting compliance and standards requirements;
- Storage and preservation; and
- Organization for retrieval.

Knowledge Management

In the last decade, the business community has become more attuned to identification and making use of the intellectual capital embodied in personnel and the processes that they undertake. There are many cases of how the intellectual capital within an enterprise is regarded as a resource (Middleton, 2002), such as:

- Recognition that many products now have a significant knowledge component; for example, household appliances, such as washing machines, include a range of software controls that may add more value from the manufacturer than do the components of the physical product.

- Assistance to customer-relationship management by maintenance of databases of preferences and purchasing patterns that may in turn be used to control inventories.
- Individual characteristics of personnel not directly related to their current work, such as languages spoken, hobbies, or associations with institutions, may be brought to bear for the benefit of the enterprise when recorded in human resources databases.
- The difference in market value and book value of many knowledge-based enterprises. The value of their physical assets as recorded on balance sheets, is often only a fraction of what the company is valued at by the market.
- Service industries make use of a wider range of decision possibilities, for example, the travel industry can associate route and transport possibilities with customer preferences and profiles, by making use of geographical databases.

The transience of the knowledge resource has led to approaches to managing the intellectual capital of enterprises. These, in turn, have encouraged the knowledge management movement. Organizations that consider their knowledge workers[11] to be a primary asset, want to retain at least some of the asset, seen to be tacit knowledge, as the employees move on to other organizations. They also wish to keep tapping that asset should the employee be moved to a different role within the organization.

There have been objections to the term knowledge management, usually along the lines that knowledge, being something in peoples' heads, cannot be managed. Once the knowledge is made explicit, often in documentary form, it becomes information until it can be assimilated as knowledge by those taking it in.[12]

Knowledge management looks for ways of explicating how the tacit knowledge may be shared more widely within an enterprise, by processes such as tutorials, analysis, apprenticeships, computer-assisted instruction, or lessons-learned databases. In so doing, the extent to which the tacit material may be written as information for learning can be established. The writing may take many forms appropriate to the circumstances. These include:

- Graphic representation of workflow for a process;
- Reporting retrospectively, possibly via a debriefing process that may be taped;
- Questionnaires, often elaborated by follow-up interviews;
- Filming of a task as it is being performed (in context);
- Oral tape recording of reports on events; and
- Structured database input of lessons learned in relation to procedures.

The tacit knowledge may also be made explicit for the corporate memory through teamwork. Business units comprising small teams with expertise brought together for relatively short time periods enable knowledge-sharing through the structured approach of project management. The pooled knowledge may be shared though normal face-to-face meetings and can also be expanded upon through computer-supported cooperative software. For example, proposal development, task scheduling, message sending, joint viewing of text and diagrams, and report writing can all be carried out jointly to assist overall productivity and effectiveness, even if they are less efficient in the short term.

From examples such as these, it can be seen that if knowledge is to be managed, it is going to depend in great part upon recorded information. The various media in which the information is recorded all fall within the purview of documents in the sense that we have used the term earlier in this chapter, and the way in which we use the term throughout the book.

For this reason, we think that this book is about strategies for the leverage of enterprise knowledge. We consider that an IDCM provides a fundamental infrastructure for knowledge management, and that the analysis and processes described in the following chapters, with effective implementation, help to make effective use of an organization's intellectual capital.

DOCUMENT MANAGEMENT SYSTEMS
Early Developments

The proliferation of digital documents created by the widespread implementation of desktop authoring tools and LAN/WAN technologies witnessed the emergence of systems that implemented repository-style management services over digital document collections.

Early models were implemented using the Disk Operating System (DOS) and later Windows 3.x (with some offering Unix and Macintosh) user interfaces. They managed digital document collections residing on network operating systems. These early systems typically implemented a two-tier client server architecture model. The model was characterized by centralization: featuring centralized index, documents, and administration.

The two-tier architecture model meant that most of the computer processing associated with repository services functionality was managed at the PC desktop, interacting with a database management system (DBMS) for storage of metadata. Typically, each instance of metadata that described each document in the repository pointed to a digital document object that was stored on a networked file system. The file names on the document objects were encrypted to deter people trying to access the documents through the file system.

Workflow and Documents

Taylor, sometimes called the father of scientific management initiated scientific analysis of work design (Taylor, 1909).[13] His methods including techniques such as analysis of work design and timing of work, produced an alternative to the "rule-of-thumb" approach, where workers used practices and tools suited to their own way of working.

Taylor's studies were major contributions to the understanding of work design and contributed to the development of techniques such as Time and Motion Study, Work Study, and Work Measurement. These were common practices used to analyze work processes in business and government sectors in the 20th century for improving business process using structured techniques.[14]

Meticulous application of scientific methods and tools for improving industrial processes and work methods came into question when the outcomes of the so-called Hawthorne experiments were published,[15] in which attention was paid to the social system within a group of employees. These experiments were a turning point in understanding the social psychology of industry and initiated new research into social and managerial psychology (Fincham et al., 1999). Adequate consideration of the environment of workgroups therefore became an important aspect of understanding document transfer associated with workflow.

An example of workflow analysis in the document management environment is investigation of the use of document transfer slips by records administrators using "routing slips" to accompany physical documents or files being transferred from one action officer to another. These slips were intended to be completed by action officers and returned to the records department, at which point the organization's records management system could be updated with the new file or document location. Deficiencies in this type of manual system became evident when action officers forgot to complete slips and return them to the records administrators, or physical files and documents were lost.

By the 1990s, the focus of an emerging automated workflow management industry was on the high-volume transaction environments in the financial services and insurance sectors. Initial workflow projects may have been related to managing the flow of paper within a business process, but now, workflow was aligned with document image processing technology. In Chapter 4, we return to this in more detail when we consider workflow management systems.

Growth of LAN/Desktop Tools

By 1993, there had been a comprehensive take-up of LAN and desktop authoring tools within enterprises, with the outcome that there was a rapid explosion in the creation of digital documents. At about that time, there had been further enhancements made to the functionality of repository services offered by DMS. As a consequence, industry pundits were predicting that document management would become the most important service on the LAN after connectivity. Furthermore, during a period that also witnessed vigorous marketing of business process reengineering principles and practices, some analysts were suggesting that organizations might be required to make substantial business process changes in order to capture the benefits of integrated document management.

Evolving Integration

Technology developments saw the introduction of the integration of DMS with full text indexing software, giving users the choice of searching for documents based on metadata in the DBMS or using full text searching or using a combination of both.

Scanning and imaging technology could also be integrated with DMS to enable images and text captured during scanning or Optical Character Recognition (OCR) operations to be imported directly into the managed digital document collection. Consequently, document management products that did not feature imaging as part of their core functionality met emerging enterprise requirements for a cohesive solution by developing alliances with third-party providers of imaging software.

Workflow, which had a close relationship with imaging systems during the early 1990s, was viewed as the vehicle by which digital documents could be distributed and managed. Again, where this functionality was not offered as core document repository services, alliances were developed with providers of workflow. Consequently, the concept of the "integrated" DMS emerged, with the recognition that organizations might benefit from the further use of document assets stored in managed repository services, using tools such as integrated messaging or collaboration systems or integrated workflow.

Enterprises were also starting to seek a single solution that would not only manage multiple types of office documents, but would also manage the complex relationships between CAD drawings. Drawing requirements included further complex relationships between documents, such as cross-referencing of digital CAD files and embedding of objects within CAD drawings. Many document management products had not developed drawing management functionality, and vendors generally met the challenge of providing that functionality by entering into alliances with third-party providers of drawing management software.

The concept of the integrated DMS evolved to embrace the use of interfaces (some of which are based upon standards) that enable association of the DMS with authoring tools, as well as to the use of application programming interfaces for integrating with core business systems, such as Enterprise Resource Planning (ERP) systems. Some DMS vendors sought strategic alliances with the providers of ERP systems to offer what was being termed at one stage as Enterprise Resource Management solutions that integrated the business systems environment, including integration between ERP and DMS.

Other alliances were also developed for the integration of DMS applications with enterprise tools, such as Geographical Information Systems (GIS), Asset Management Systems, and a range of horizontal and vertical applications that supported business planning and operational and support systems.

Development of Three-Tier Client Server Architecture

During the second half of the 1990s, consistent with emerging requirements for a simple interface to access multiple distributed repositories and simpler systems administration, the functionality of Web browser technology was growing rapidly. There was a business demand for thin client architecture using a Web browser as the interface to application systems. It was recognized that the functionality of two-tier architecture systems might have limitations when considering deployment on an enterprise basis. For example:

- There was a requirement for organizations to invest in substantial memory and processor capacity for each PC to enable adequate performance of the DMS. Hence, the development of the term "thick client" to describe the complexity of the application that was required to be installed on the PC.
- Competition for memory and processing power at the PC became more intense, with increased functionality being provided in desktop applications such as spreadsheets and also the widespread implementation of memory-hungry email systems.
- There was a requirement for organizations to manually install software upgrades on PC desktops, making the installation of patches and new releases a time-

consuming and costly process. This situation was exacerbated as document management technology (and other computing systems) became more widely deployed within enterprises, involving more innovative ways of managing client computing upgrades.

- Compatibility issues between desktop applications increased due to the wide proliferation and variety of applications deployed on computer networks.

It was recognized that systems that featured a three-tier client server architecture model were more suited to managing the complex relationships that by this time could exist between digital documents. This was due to technology developments such as Common Object Request Broker Architecture (CORBA), and the open software architecture of the Component Object Model. This model has been subsequently evolved by Microsoft to Distributed Component Object Model (DCOM).

The three-tier client server architecture model features three components in the structure of the system:

- The first layer is an application at the PC desktop that provides the user interface to the document repository services. The interface is typically delivered in the Windows environment (with browser interface developments occurring in the late 1990s).

- The next layer is an application services layer that manages document repository services at the server level, thus removing much of the processing from the PC desktop.

- The third layer is the DBMS, which is typically accessed from the application server layer; individual PC desktops did not have to connect directly to the DBMS, reducing processing times.

Emergence of "Enterprise" Document Management

Many enterprises had the requirement to manage digital document collections in distributed locations throughout the organization. This type of capability may have included the requirements for the DMS to manage distributed documents, using a centralized or distributed DBMS for management of metadata. Documents that had to be managed included multiple types of document formats, including multiple text file formats, images and graphic files, sound files, and digital video fragments.

Enterprise systems also needed to have the flexibility, scalability, and extensibility to support the management of all types of organizational documents across multiple geographical locations, typically with limited telecommunications bandwidth. Evolving enterprise-capable architectures, typically based on the three-tier model, offered increased functionality for managing multiple distributed document repositories, replication services, and improved systems administration functionality.

The development of three-tier client server architectures that suited the complex requirements of enterprise DMS deployments enabled vendors to market DMS solutions as being fit for enterprise deployment. The term "enterprise" document management was consistent with other key "enterprise" developments, as witnessed by the use of the term to describe ERP systems.

Vendors marketing "enterprise" solutions attempted to distance themselves from DMS that had a particular vertical market focus, by claiming that their systems had a horizontal focus featuring the capability to manage documents in multiple repositories, covering diverse business requirements within an organization. The different marketing and promotional tactics adopted by vendors created a situation that was quite confusing to enterprises. Industry analysts attempted to help resolve the confusion for their subscribers by publishing vendor differentiation statements that covered aspects such as market segments, product capabilities and development, vendors' service delivery capabilities, and strategic alliance relationships.

Subsequently, given the business requirements for integration of core services and the requirement for information systems to be "enterprise" capable, the concept of an "enterprise"-integrated DMS was developed. The concept that was envisaged by the Gartner Group (Popkin, 1996) involved the deployment of the DMS to all desktops where there was a requirement for document management. It also embraced the concept of end users being able to access all of the repositories across the enterprise, where so authorized.

The enterprise concept did not necessarily entail that a single vendor's product was used to construct the enterprise DMS. However, the Gartner Group (Popkin & McCoy, 1998) published a list of ten reasons why a single integrated DMS should provide a solid economic foundation, reduced complexity, and lowered support, training, and maintenance costs. These factors were concerned with issues such as reduction of staffing and training costs and software distribution problems; consolidation of service provision and purchasing arrangements; and optimization of workflow and computing architecture.

A key business trend in the 2000s is organizational transformation from decision making based on functional hierarchy and "information silos" to customer-focused business processes, with the specific aim of streamlining service delivery. There has been significant market impetus given to the deployment of software to manage customer relationships — including specific CRM systems — and integrated business process management software and workflow that support this type of transformation.

WEB CONTENT MANAGEMENT

The development of Web technology and the benefits of a Web presence witnessed a rapid take-up of Internet sites by commercial organizations and government agencies, as a strategy to realize commercial benefit or deliver information and customer services. The Web grew with such pervasiveness that many enterprises were committed to developing Internet and intranet Web sites for strategic advantage.

Tools to support the rapid delivery of content to Web sites emerged to meet enterprise demands for a Web presence, and once embryonic sites had been developed, much of the emphasis transferred to graphical design techniques to help organizations obtain competitive advantage by attracting and maintaining visitors to Web sites. While the tools used to develop content were useful in rapid design and format conversion processes, they did not address the management controls that were required over the large volumes of content that were being published to Web sites.

Enterprises have been dedicated to developing and publishing large quantities of Web pages, on Internet and intranet Web sites. The staged or life-cycle processes involved in delivery of Web content may continue to rely upon traditional review and approval methods. Unfortunately, these methods may entail printing drafts, applying manual review and approval processes, and using cumbersome techniques for staging the transfer of authored documents to Web servers, or for conversion and formatting processes prior to publication. Lessons learned from staged management of publication development in the electronic publishing industry may yet be taken up.

Furthermore, the content that has been published to Web sites has not always been well managed due to the volume of content and the complex relationships that exist between components of content pages published to Web servers. Outdated or otherwise incorrect content has been published to Web sites. The incorrect versions of whole Web sites have been published to the Internet. Customers that by now would expect to have a seamless experience within enterprise Web sites are consistently frustrated due to broken hyperlinks and poor navigation options. The capability of managing navigation and hyperlinks, as well as providing management controls over Web content, has become extremely difficult for many sites due to the large volume of content, and links between content or other Web sites.

The market saw the emergence of a range of tools in an attempt to address the complexities associated with managing Web content. Early solutions initially provided the functionality to manage content on fairly static Web sites, but many of these products have been developed to provide much richer functionality, including the management of dynamic content. The early solutions also included products from DMS vendors, which offered repository management services, and integrated Web publishing or workflow services to provide a managed environment for developing and publishing Web content.

Further, the evolution of Web content management has led to attempts to produce seamless transitions from document production to Web publishing, bound together by an information architecture designed to organize production of documents, render documents to Web formats, and publish them. Many of the DMS vendors now have product offerings that cover document and content management solutions or an integrated repository system for managing both.

The collapse of the Internet bubble at the turn of this century, which reduced the market capitalization of many companies that offered Web content management solutions, has been one key influence that has heralded a convergence in the industry. A second pressure has been the saturation of the market, which has forced heavy discounting. Consequently, the industry has witnessed traditional DMS vendors buying out content management providers or building competitive products. The Web content vendors are building DMS functionality, are being purchased (or are purchasing DMS functionality), or are shutting their doors.

As knowledge is disseminated about the buildup of Web content management as a technology, customers are also becoming more informed. Many have realized that document and content management are two sides of the same coin. The back-end functionality is much the same, the primary differences being in how the authors interact with the development of documents and content, and the methods by which content is deployed (or published).

The requirement to manage Web content is compelling, because expected productivity gains might not be achieved if organizations simply provide a polished dynamic Web interface for customer interaction, while the back office information management framework is in chaos. It is imperative that organizations review their current business and information practices when Web-enabling customer services, otherwise, as one industry observer commented to the Boston Consulting Group (2000), it is like "putting lipstick on a pig" (with our due respect to pigs).

INTEGRATED DOCUMENT AND CONTENT MANAGEMENT

The many capabilities and opportunities offered by information systems that have been developed for managing documents and Web content attracted the authors to produce this book. We wanted to share our research and experiences and to help business and government enterprises understand the benefits of the technology, which has evolved from relatively simple beginnings to solutions offering rich functionality.

However, we see that the mechanisms needed to make management of documents and Web content work require much more than associating document and content management software with business problems. It requires an integrative strategy that pursues an IDCM solution by strategic and systematic analysis of business processes, the documents that support them, the documents that they produce, and the distribution and publication of documents or Web content.

Principles for IDCM Planning Model

Document management implies control of documents through the stages of what has been traditionally called a life-cycle, but for which the term *continuum* is becoming more prevalent. In cases where documents are specifically the evidentiary material of interest in recordkeeping, continuum is used to indicate the interdependent nature of records management and archival management. It is also used to emphasize a proactive approach to managing records such as designing recordkeeping systems, being actively involved in strategies to ensure the creation of records to satisfy recordkeeping requirements, and dovetailing records and archives management.

Web content management is yet to be described in terms of a commonly accepted set of principles. However, the digital objects that carry the content can be regarded as documents. They might be word-processed documents; files marked up according to markup languages such as SGML, XML, or HTML; digital spreadsheets; digital sound or video files; or image files. They too pass through stages from creation to destruction or archiving, and need to be organized and managed for access and retrieval.

If an enterprise is able to manage the various stages of design, creation, storage and retrieval, and disposal of documents, then it is contributing to the management of its own knowledge. The more effectively this can be done, the better that knowledge documented as information may be reutilized.

The agenda of handling documents through their stages has been developed into a set of principles by records managers and archives administrators. This framework is now embodied in an International Standard 15489 (International Organization for Standardization, 2001) that provides sections on responsibilities, strategies, control, appraisal and disposal, and storage for the discipline of records management.

ISO 15489 defines a *document* as recorded information or object that can be treated as a unit. It sees *records* as information created, received, and maintained as evidence and information by an organization or person in pursuance of legal obligations or in the transaction of business.

As yet, the standards that relate to Web content management tend to be internal to the organizations producing the content, similar to the way in which these organizations manage forms for design consistency and currency. However, there have been attempts at technical standardization emanating from the computer managed instruction (CMI) environment, which is concerned with the development of digital learning objects. For example, in the United States, the Advanced Distributed Learning (ADL) specification group involves a collaboration between government, industry, and academia to create a learning environment in which distributed learning tools and course content can be used together.

Through the Sharable Content Object Reference Model (SCORM), ADL seeks to define requirements for content accessibility, interoperability, reuse, and stability, thereby providing what is considered to be a content aggregation model for learning objects (Advanced Distributed Learning, 2002).

The acquisition and implementation of an information system to manage documents and Web content should not be undertaken without preplanning, which takes into account the statutory and regulatory environment impacting the capture, management, and access processes associated with documents within the enterprise. Such aspects as admissibility of evidence, accessibility of information, confidentiality, and security of document collections require consideration. Furthermore, it is also necessary to have a clear definition of vital and important documents that are relevant to the organization and a good understanding of how documents of all types are used within business processes.

Enterprises also need to consider information principles, standards, and guidelines that may impact the management of documents. Furthermore, there is a need to take into account policies, practices, and procedures of the organization and how documents are used. Much preliminary work has to be done to ensure that an IDCM project does not just focus on the information system and technology aspects of document and Web content management, because successful solutions are not delivered in a void.

These aspects need to be considered as part of an organization's document and Web content management (and probably within a broader approach from the viewpoint of information management) framework, and we deal with them in more detail in Chapter 7.

IDCM Planning Model

Figure 1 provides a conceptual schema of an IDCM model that addresses enterprise challenges for managing document and Web content.

The concepts embodied in Figure 1 are as follows:

- The *overall diagram* depicts the model's conceptual framework, which associates business planning and strategic business applications with an underpinning IDCM solution architecture. We examine planning imperatives in more detail in Chapter 2.
- The *IDCM solution architecture* represents an integrative approach that includes a management framework and a range of solution options for managing document and Web content.
- The *IDCM management framework* consists of the relevant policies, strategies, procedures, and project management methodologies that are needed to provide the

governance framework for implementing IDCM business and technology solutions. We examine these types of management strategies in Chapter 6.

- The key *IDCM subsystems* show the types of technology solutions that may be applicable to assisting enterprises in delivering an IDCM solution that satisfies business imperatives. We review the functional aspects of these software options in Part 3.

- *Recordkeeping requirements* depict the requirements to apply recordkeeping principles, policies, standards, and best practice to IDCM solutions.

- The *information technology infrastructure* includes the desktop computers, servers, networking systems, databases, and messaging and collaboration systems to support the implementation of IDCM systems.

- The *security* layer demonstrates that the deployment of IDCM solutions needs to take into account the requirements of information security policy and strategies, which need to provide a comprehensive security framework that protects the organizational information assets and systems.

- The *security* layer also embraces *digital signatures* that might be used for authentication purposes using any number of the identified IDCM subsystems. The capability might be met by autonomous software (i.e., a specific product for digital signatures), featured as a core part of an operating system or built into a messaging system.

Figure 1: IDCM Model: Conceptual Schema.

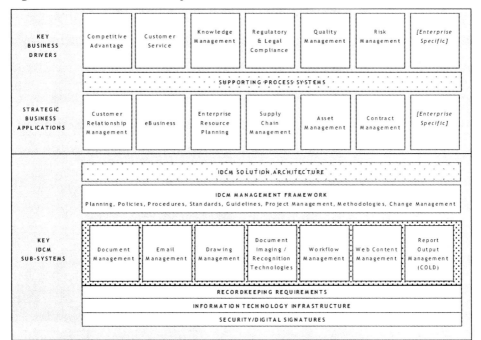

IDCM Model Rationale

The implementation of document and Web content management requires the rigor of a structured approach to problem solving and solution delivery, because the requirement for document and Web content management should not be considered in a vacuum. The requirements for document and Web content management must be viewed as an integral part of the business processes that support the planning imperatives of the enterprise.

Furthermore, document and Web content management projects are typically complex, particularly when reviewed in the context of enterprise requirements, primarily because documents (and Web content) play such an important part in everyday business processes. Documents comprise many of the records that evidence business transactions by enterprises, and there have always been problems associated with managing these types of documents, even before the advent of widespread desktop authoring tools. Many organizations have held document management in low regard and have failed to provide adequate systems and resources to manage documentation.

The problems associated with managing documents are now exacerbated, particularly with the ubiquitous use of email and attachments in business decision making. There are also problems associated with quick delivery of dynamic content to Web sites, and the requirement to manage Internet and intranet content. Web content may consist of large volumes of multiple formats of documents, together existing in multiple compound relationships. Content published on Web sites also need to be maintained as a record of an enterprise's activities, which is difficult using manual processes, or without adequate software and resources.

The introduction of practices, techniques, and tools that introduce management controls over documents is too often seen by end users as an imposition. End users often equate the requirement to manage documents as an additional responsibility over and beyond their responsibilities of achieving the business objectives and outcomes. The end users are too busy getting the "real work" done, and although they acknowledge that document management is a "good thing," they "don't have time to be doing registry work" and give short shrift to document management as a tool.

This problem is exacerbated, because it is often the case that well-intentioned information practitioners are the champions of "document management projects," because they realize that enterprise document collections might be "out of control." They want to do something about it and for all the right reasons. However, unless the requirements for document (and Web content) management are closely aligned with business objectives, processes, and outcomes, then the probability of success is low.

We believe that an integrative approach to document and Web content management projects is an essential requirement to help align the requirement for document and Web content management with business planning imperatives. The practitioner needs to understand business planning imperatives at the strategic, tactical, and operational levels of the enterprise, and develop business and technology solution options that align with these planning imperatives.

Benefits of IDCM Model

The IDCM model provides practitioners with the management framework in which to develop plans, policies, and procedures and adopt methodologies and approaches to align business and technology solutions with enterprise planning imperatives. The model also provides a range of software solutions that can be integrated to provide solutions to real business problems, rather than trying to develop a business case based only on "just good practice" ideals.

The model will help practitioners better understand the nature of document and Web content management projects. It will help enterprises to understand that the solution to document and Web content management requirements embraces more than "buying an off-the-shelf" solution. It will help practitioners convince their management that document and Web content is more than just buying a package.

The model will help project champions to develop compelling business cases for document and Web content enabled solutions that deliver real business outcomes, and support an enterprise's future planning strategies. It will help the organization to manage their vital business records that are in documented form.

Practitioners that have limited experience with defining requirements for document or Web content management systems will be in a position to analyze requirements and develop specifications based on the structures and templates provided by the IDCM model. They will have a better understanding of the extent of effort that may be required when asked to "define their requirements" for document and Web content management systems.

The IDCM model is designed to assist commercial and government enterprises in planning and implementing effective document and Web content solutions, thus arresting the potential reduction in shareholder value or loss of taxpayers' money on projects that are not well implemented, or worse still, fail. Success breeds success, and knowledge exchange facilitates success, and the IDCM model might fill some voids in an enterprise's knowledge of document and Web content projects.

We review the benefits of the applicable IDCM systems when we discuss the characteristics of IDCM systems more fully in Chapter 4, and we provide examples of typical IDCM solution applications in Chapter 5.

SUMMARY

We introduced the features of IDCM that we propose to examine in more detail in following chapters. We have done this by providing an overview of an IDCM model that features a management framework and systems architecture that provide enterprises with a range of solutions that might be relevant to their document and Web content requirements.

This has been prefaced by a historical overview of document and Web content management, including the disciplines that have engaged with it, so that we have a better understanding of the role of documents and Web content in modern business environments.

The legacy of different disciplines developing techniques for handling physical documents in various forms, then digital documents, strongly influences the way contemporary systems are managed. We will see throughout the book how standards and principles have been created from the tenets of such legacy systems, and continue to influence attempts to integrate disparate aspects of document (and Web content) management.

ENDNOTES

1   He advanced his religious policy of an alliance between throne and altar, thus: "…Augustus collected whatever prophetic writings of Greek or Latin origin were in circulation anonymously or under the names of irresponsible authors and burned more than 2000 of them, retaining only the Sibylline Books and making a selection even among these…" Suetonius, Life of Augustus, xxxi, 1–4, cited in Lewis, N., & Reinhold, M. (1966). *Roman Civilization, Sourcebook II: The Empire* (pp. 55–56). New York.

2   "Historia Augusta," *Life of Hadrian*, vii, 6, cited in Lewis, N., & Reinhold, M. (1966). *Roman Civilization, Sourcebook II: The Empire* (p. 150). New York.

3   Dio Cassio, "Roman History," lxxi, 2, cited in Lewis, N., & Reinhold, M. (1966). *Roman Civilization, Sourcebook II: The Empire* (p. 150). New York.

4   Indulgences were written slips that offered written dispensation from sin. These slips were sold to fund crusades and major building projects, which expanded the dominance of the Church during this period. The sale of indulgences became so predominant that it was not uncommon for 200,000 to be printed during a press run.

5   It was during the mid-1800s when the typewriter, a development that had its origins in writing machines, embossing, and typography devices, made its appearance in organizations. The typewriter as a device supported the then popular organizational notion of division of labor and provided new opportunities for skill development and employment. As we ponder life while accessing our desktop computer, we might note that the same type of keyboard developed for the typewriter 150 years ago is a part of our "modern" computing environment.

6   Buckland (1997) reviews the historical debate of what constitutes a document. He notes the contribution of Briet, *Qu'est-ce que la documentation* (Paris: EDIT, 1951), which starts with the assertion (as translated) that "A document is evidence in support of a fact," and that it may be any physical or symbolic sign, preserved or recorded, intended to represent, to reconstruct, or to demonstrate a physical or conceptual phenomenon.

7   MIS are computer-based systems that provide summary information to management from different enterprise areas such as marketing and human resources. As the capability to consolidate material and present it in dynamic and interactive form has developed, the terminology has changed to Decision Support Systems and Executive Information Systems.

8   A Paris chemist, Rene Prudent Dagron, who appears to have been quite prudent, lived up to his middle name and seized upon the opportunity by turning his laboratory into a commercial microfilm business.

9   In effect, information management disciples might see the Internet (or intranet sites) as a massive compound document.

10   Content analysis has been used in the past to describe the description and organization of subject matter within documents. With the advent of the Web, "content management" has been enlisted to encompass this along with the use of the software for managing the documents that hold the content.

11   Knowledge workers are those involved in continuous scanning and learning of new material and creating, analyzing, interpreting, transforming, organizing and repackaging information.

12   Davenport & Prusack (1998) characterize knowledge management as beyond management of the information captured in documents and repositories. Understanding and controlled direction is also necessary for an enterprise's processes, customs, standards, and cultural application of practice, with knowledge being described as the fluid mix of framed experience, values, contextual information, insight, and grounded intuition.

13   His analysis of coal-shoveling efficiencies at the Bethlehem Steel Works led to a reduction in the number of people shoveling coal from 500 to 140.

14   Given that such techniques were typically the tools of trained specialists such as "Work Study" consultants, detractors often observed that it was easier to "study the work" than to actually "do the work." Nevertheless, these tools evolved into techniques such as Industrial Engineering, Methods Analysis, Organization and Methods (O&M), and Management Systems Review.

15   The experiments involved an investigation of lighting factors affecting worker productivity in the Western Electric Company's Hawthorne plant near Chicago, commencing in 1927 and lasting for 12 years. The studies demonstrated that changed lighting conditions did not improve or adversely affect the output of the workgroup.

Chapter 2

Business Planning Frameworks and IDCM

OVERVIEW

This chapter provides a synopsis of the contemporary business environment and reviews some internal and external factors that influence enterprise planning, with particular reference to document role. Several business sectors are considered. Some of the information systems and technologies available on the market to support planning initiatives are examined. The relevance of managing documents and their content is discussed in the context of a strategic planning framework that takes into account matters such as regulatory compliance and commercial processes.

Our view is that effective application of IDCM strategy cannot be undertaken unless attention is paid to the general context of an organization's business processes and the IT environment in which they operate.

Our objectives are to do the following:

- Outline the enterprise business planning framework.
- Consider the commercial landscape and review some of the issues that may impact on business planning.
- Consider the regulatory landscape and review some of the legislative, administrative regulations, and standards that may impact on business planning.
- Reflect on the IT landscape and the implications for business planning.
- Discuss at a conceptual level the role of document management systems as a key enabler of business planning.
- Consider the overall implications of fragmented and mismanaged document environments on business planning.

BUSINESS PLANNING

Business and government enterprises generally embrace a planning framework that represents three tiers:

- The first tier is a Strategic Plan or similar document that defines the enterprise's long-term vision, strategies, key result areas, and performance measures, typically with a three- to five-year horizon.
- The second tier generally consists of Tactical Plans that are designed to give effect to the strategies identified in a Strategic Plan, with a mid-term horizon (say one to two years).
- The third tier represents Operational Plans that are aligned with the other tiers and that support the day-to-day activities of the organization.

The specific types of planning strategies developed by commercial and government organizations depend upon the particular nature of the business or administrative activity. For example, a legal practice may strive to earn and maintain a reputation as a leading provider of services, meet customer requirements, and improve profitability. In government enterprises, the general focus is to meet the statutory requirements imposed upon the organization, to operate efficiently, and to deliver services to customers, in this case the public, through innovative and responsive service delivery models.

In either case, the identified mission of the organization can be brought about through strategies that express what it intends to achieve over a relatively long term, and how it intends to go about it in the short term given the environmental, resource, and organizational constraints.

Document management may not be identified explicitly in strategic plans. However, enterprises that identify strategies relating to areas such as quality systems, process reengineering, customer relationship management, or knowledge management will find that effective operation of these must take into account document management.

Therefore, it is likely that tactical and operational plans concerning records and document systems need to be developed in order to provide a backbone for strategic planning. Planning for document management systems associated with workflow should help to accomplish this.

COMMERCIAL LANDSCAPE

Today's commercial landscape represents a jungle in which the "survival of the fittest" principles apply without fear or favor to every type of business organization. The commercial scene is beleaguered with company takeovers, amalgamations (which in some cases are effectively takeovers), bankrupt businesses, and organizations struggling to compete in a volatile business world.

For example, at the turn of this century, we witnessed the demise of many start-up companies that had great ideas, typically embracing the Internet Web technology. However, with some exceptions, these so-called dot.com companies did not have the marketing, production, and distribution infrastructure to compete against more established companies with the same types of products.

The landscape is characterized, among other things, by an increasingly competitive commercial environment, which is a key driver for improving organizational productivity. There are growing customer expectations concerning the quality, standards, and means of achieving service delivery. In the complex product development and supply chain models, there is a need for businesses to develop mutual understanding, respect, and a close working relationship with business partners and service providers.

Commercial enterprises are required to invoke new ideas and develop new strategies designed to increase market share, maintain and improve competitive advantage, deliver new products, align products and services with customer needs, and provide delivery models that satisfy or exceed customer requirements. Strategies may also be developed to meet requirements such as improving production capacity, reducing time for delivery of products to market, reducing costs, and other procedures designed to help the enterprise remain competitive in highly volatile global markets.

The strategies that have emerged recently are many and varied. Some have been discussed, analyzed, and described to the extent that they have reasonably widely understood concepts. These include knowledge management and customer-relationship management.

Knowledge Management

Profitability continues to be the key indicator of private sector aspirations. However, the "information society" has led to growing realization that an enterprise's capital is more than its financial and physical capital. It is also its intellectual capital. This is supported by recent analysis that attempts to provide approaches to valuing corporate knowledge, for example, works by Skyrme (1998) and Boisot (1998). The value of corporate knowledge is one reason why some companies change hands for so much more than the book value. The purchaser is placing a much higher value on the intellect of the personnel than on the other resources of the purchased organization.

This same realization has led to more focused attempts to capture this intellectual capital — that is of course assuming that the individuals in whom it is embodied wish to share it. Knowledge management is a term used to describe these attempts. However, as we noted in the first chapter, it can reasonably be argued that you cannot manage knowledge — what you can manage is the information that is documented to convey knowledge.

Perhaps a more suggestive phrase for utilization of knowledge in an enterprise is "developing procedures to sustain the corporate memory." This is an orientation that is adopted by writers like Brooking (1999), who uses it with respect to identifying intangible assets and approaches to knowledge-sharing and how these are affected by organizational culture; and by Megill (1997), who uses it with respect to information resources management.

Customer-Relationship Management

The requirement for enterprises to provide information or service customer requests in a timely manner intensified when businesses began to utilize the Web. Customers expect quality information and rapid provision of services, and they expect organizations to deliver within the constraints of quality management systems. Consequently, many enterprises are identifying that a traditional organizational hierarchy, based on business function, may be inadequate to service the information or supply chain to meet customer requirements.

Many enterprises are implementing or examining more flexible structures, so that customer demands for rapid delivery of information and services can be met. The revised arrangements include the implementation of flatter structures with a higher degree of delegation of decision making, or outsourcing specific functions to business partners or service providers.

The use of task-oriented workgroups or project teams organized to achieve specific outcomes, as a strategy for assuring customer satisfaction, is increasing, as predicted by Drucker some years ago. He observed that "specialists brought together in task forces that cut across traditional boundaries" would do the work in future organizations (Drucker, 1998).

A strategy being adopted by enterprise executives is to transform organizations from a rigid structure based on functional departments to a more flexible "market-driven" process-oriented organization. Organizational design and resource allocations are centered on the end-to-end processes of specific types of interactions with customers, with the primary outcome being customer satisfaction.

Innovative use of information systems and technology is a key enabler for delivery of customer services, as they provide the customer with the convenience of bypassing traditional bureaucratic supply chain structures, and using new innovations such as self-help information, electronic bill paying, and online usage analysis techniques. However, they also run the risk of alienating customers through insensitive application of call center interfaces, poor response times from interactive systems, and depersonalization of customer relationships.

BUSINESS SECTOR CONSIDERATIONS
Commercial Challenges

The following challenges are probably applicable to most industries. They are a requirement to:

- Research potential opportunities for the development of new products and services and to maintain competitiveness in an innovative and dynamic market.
- Maintain a relationship with customers, retain existing customers, and attract new customers.
- Deliver new products and services to market in a timely manner.
- Interact with business partners and service providers in a timely and effective manner to facilitate development, production, and distribution.
- Review opportunities offered by e-commerce applications to provide a consistent interface to customers instead of the traditional functional (or "channel") approach to products and services.
- Make effective use of the intellectual capital embodied within the organization.
- Provide support, particularly in the case of international organizations, for multi-lingual services for communication with shareholders, customers, and community.
- Provide effective mechanisms for managing legal discovery processes.

We now look briefly at some of the challenges that face enterprises within specific industry sectors, where workflow has particular document management implications.

Banking and Financial Services

Industry deregulation and technology developments, combined with customer empowerment, have created increasing competition in the financial sector on a domestic basis and on a global basis. Banks and financial institutions are intensifying their efforts to develop strategies that retain existing customers and attract new customers.

The banking sector, for example, has recognized that customer account fees and charges are but one factor in customer retention strategies, and that more emphasis needs to be given to service levels and identifying and understanding customer needs. Service can be the differentiation between competing financial institutions, and the relationship between a customer and bank personnel is also a key factor.

Financial institutions need to create a compelling reason for customers to keep their business with the institution, and the strategy to build an enduring relationship with the customer is viewed as a vital ingredient in customer retention. One of the strategies being adopted is to deliver tailor-made solutions to meet customers' needs and help to build the enduring relationship.

However, the industry has a long history of being product rather than customer focused, and the substantial number of mergers and acquisitions means that there may not be an integrated record of experiences with a customer due to the diversity of information systems that store and manage customer information.

Customer experience is frequently unsatisfactory due to the multichannel nature of banking and financial services. Limitations with the multichannel approach arise when a customer resupplies the same information, receives marketing materials that are inappropriate (e.g., a service may have been cancelled), and endures similar frustrations because of the fragmented information environment within the financial institution.

Financial services companies are required to maintain profitability across business product lines, meanwhile meeting social and community obligations to deliver products and services in a fair and equitable manner to the consumer. This may become quite politically complex, when financial institutions close nonprofitable branch offices that impact upon customer services, particularly in rural communities.

Traditionally, the financial services sector has invested in technologies that help manage the large volumes of transactional (typically forms-based) documents that support the operational business processes. Document imaging and integrated production workflow systems have been implemented to manage check processing, loan applications, and signature verification. These systems have supported fraud mitigation strategies and helped to improve security and competitiveness.

However, while there has been strong emphasis on managing transactional documents within the sector, banking and financial service institutions may not have implemented effective systems for managing the large volume of day-to-day administrative documents used as part of business decision-making processes. The industry is beset by the same problems encountered by other major enterprises: the use of electronic documents has thrived since the introduction of desktop computers, the integration of LANs and WANs, and the training of staff in the use of desktop authoring applications.

Furthermore, email and attachments (as with other industry sectors) may not be managed appropriately to comply with requirements for evidentiary recordkeeping. The sharing of documents across the organization and with business partners facilitates collaboration. However, without adequate management controls, different versions of the same document may be stored in multiple repositories across the organization. Staff members cannot then rely upon the integrity of a digital document for decision-making purposes.

This type of unmanaged document environment poses risks to the financial sector's capacity to satisfy regulatory and legal compliance, particularly in terms of evidentiary support for business decisions and discovery processes. There is also the risk of damage to business brands due to conflicting messages (because of document integrity issues) between the financial institution and its customers or business partners.

The adoption of e-commerce applications within the financial service sector may be slower than desired, potentially due to Internet security concerns, and other priorities including mergers and acquisitions. For example, there is the capability to integrate Internet and Web-based technology for accepting mortgage loan applications so that applications are integrated with workflow technology to reduce transaction cycle times and develop opportunities and capabilities for new business.

The slow take-up of technology may have implications for delivery of services to mobilize users who wish to access banking services via WAP and interactive television.

However, there is a compelling need to manage the document continuum supporting e-commerce strategies, to ensure that information published on the Internet is correct. This strategy may help to maintain high service levels, support personalization for tailor-made solutions to meet customers' needs, and thus help to build an enduring relationship between the institution and the customer.

Pharmaceuticals and Health

Health care industries are being profoundly influenced by technological support for matters such as remote diagnosis, information sharing via networks, and medical records availability. These have contributed to increasing pressure on drug companies to reduce costs and the time to deliver product to market. The processes involved in the drug approval process are highly regulated, and each step of the processes involved in developing and testing drugs must be documented, which generates large volumes of data and documentation.

The submission for a drug approval is voluminous, with supporting documentation that may consist of tens of thousands of pages. An example is the biostatistical analysis of data for clinical trials. The submissions for drug approval may have to be reassembled to meet the specific criteria of those different countries into which the drug is to be marketed. The processes and documentation must support the requirements of the various regulation authorities.

Internal quality management systems must also be supported, and a Standard Operating Environment (SOE) may be expected to include a central repository with version control and distribution and publishing mechanisms.

However, the carriage of internally produced digital records through to electronic regulatory submissions remains problematic. As McLain-Smith (1998) pointed out, there is yet to be agreement on the detail of formats among different national agencies.

Digital data formats are also an issue in hospital records systems. Health care may require the bringing together of digital diagnostic imagery from procedures such as computer-based tomography or magnetic resonance with drug prescription and patient record files, which may be in a mix of digital and physical forms. In addition to the forms and data formats differing, there may also be a variety of indexing or taxonomic schemes used to categorize the information.

Manufacturing

There is intense competition in the manufacturing sector to deliver quality products to market to gain competitive advantage. The delivery of product to market on time has the complexity that the product may comprise a large number of discrete parts. The process for developing the discrete parts and formulating the whole product may involve multiple revisions of drawings and specifications.

Companies in the manufacturing sector may need to interact with business partners and service providers in a timely and effective manner to facilitate development, production, and distribution. This requirement may mean that manufacturing companies are required to simplify supply chain processes and interact with partners or service providers via e-business solutions.

In some cases, this may involve procedures for effective access to literally millions of documents: drawings, service report forms, CAD files, inventories, electrical plans, machine servicing documents, maintenance support, and the like. An imperative is the development of user interfaces that make retrieval and use of such documents straightforward. The interfaces should be tailored to workflow to the extent that end users may concentrate on the content and take the process of consulting the documents for granted.

Engineering and Construction

As is the case in manufacturing industry, the engineering and construction industries must deal with the range and extent of documents mentioned in the paragraph above. There is particular emphasis on engineering drawings, parts specifications and operating procedures, along with contract management.

Contract development means that the industry must carry out effective proposal management. Proposals need to be prepared in a professional and timely manner, to help position the company with the best opportunity for securing new projects. Once a contract for a project has been awarded, there is pressure to complete projects on time and within budget and meet quality management system requirements. Saffady (1996) gives examples of document imaging systems that were being applied at the time of his exploration. Although many of the products that he provides are now superseded, they effectively illustrate the range of document management applications that continue to apply in different industry sectors. For example, in the petroleum industry, he gives many examples of the tracking of engineering drawings, of invoicing, and of accounting document management.

Internal organizational knowledge transfer should be assisted by making the best provisions for sharing information and enabling reuse. This includes provision for effective contract management, including the contracts with customers, and the management of subcontractors, and management of risks.

Professional Services — Legal

Legal practitioners represent the legal interests of clients in a professional manner, and they may represent the client on a number of matters. They have a requirement to assemble evidence and prepare statements and court briefs and a myriad of other legal papers.

The traditional form of document management within law firms has been paper-intensive, with filing typically organized by boxes classified by the client and particular matter. In these circumstances, locating documents can be labor intensive and time consuming.

These limitations can be exacerbated when law firms grow in size, or where there are multiple locations for law offices, or where the firm has taken over or merged with another legal practice.

Enterprises may have the requirement to enable lawyers to access documents quickly at their desktop at any time during the business day without relying on support services, and to focus on billable work.

In Chapter 1, we made reference to the association between document and knowledge management, and the way in which intellectual capital may be made more available by effective document management. Legal practice has been among the areas that has shown most interest in developing principles for knowledge management. There has been recognition of how easily the expertise of professionals is lost to the enterprise should they move on. Therefore, firms have increasingly provided incentives for professionals to document their knowledge so that as information, it may be referenced by others.

Utilities

In many cases, utilities used to be public bureaucracies with an operational, not market-oriented focus. Enterprises in the utility sector are often government-owned corporations that are required to compete in the open market for customers. Challenges within the utilities sector may include the following:

- Realities and challenges of operating in a deregulated market — one that provides consumers with choice, and allows the market to determine pricing for commodities, such as electricity, gas, and water; and
- Competition, not just on price but also on serving their customer needs better than anyone else. Consumer choice is likely to force prices to the lowest plateau, at which point, customer service is a key differentiation.

Therefore, power, water, electric, and telephone companies seek efficient ways to minimize overheads related to the processing of documents. Among these are the following:

- Utilization of electronic forms for capture of meter readings so that these may be passed automatically to accounting systems;
- Online processing of complaints management by service providers so that call center operators have recourse to precedents and may record current information using as much existing client and categorization data as possible; and
- Drawing management systems that may overlay maps of line installation with digital cartographic data provided by mapping authorities.

Government

Government departments and agencies are not immune to the pressures of the current business world. Government enterprises have the requirement to fulfill the legislative obligations imposed by their various enabling legislation and to identify how best to meet the requirements of government and the communities being served.

Governments from the national level to the local level, are faced with communities of people that not only want, but also demand a whole range of services, and expect that the services will be provided using cost-effective, customer-focused mechanisms — and quickly. The implication for governments is that if they are slow to address demands, then the electorates that they represent will speedily show their disfavor through the ballot box.

Furthermore, government departments and agencies also face the specter of alternative service delivery models, such as privatization, corporatization, and outsourcing. Many people in government services see these as a menace to government regulation, which they had viewed as being protected from the pressures of market forces.

Those governments that have implemented FOI legislation have precipitated a need for procedures that enable controlled public access to internally produced documents. This adds complexity to DMS and amplifies the insistence for fast and effective retrieval mechanisms supported by well-developed descriptive taxonomies, or business information classification schemes and syntaxes.

Library and Information Services

The perspective of libraries on document management has been different from other organizations, because in most cases, they have principally been concerned with externally produced published documentation.

However, in recent years, their orientation has moved from collection building to access. This means that they are endeavoring to provide seamless access to a combination of digital and physical material through online catalogs. The digital material comprises anything from networked databases to Web sites to ebooks to digital copies of rare books. Because of their experience with digitization programs, they may well contribute to wider project management for migration of print to digital documents in corporations. This applies particularly to the conversion and assigning of metadata.

Librarians have great experience with content metadata (or what continues to be termed classification and indexing). It is this that has led them to drive many of the Web approaches to metadata development, such as Dublin Core that we make reference to in later chapters. This same metadata development through standard schemas and controlled vocabularies is influencing the development of regimes for document description applied within the framework of markup languages such as XML.

The boundaries between library, records, document, and archival management systems are diminishing. This has become evident particularly in corporations, where it has been seen as desirable to consolidate the information services role. In this respect, there has been a move to consolidate administration of repositories of internal and external information and procedures for distribution of content from the repositories, usually via an intranet. The aspiration has been seamless desktop information provision from all sources.

REGULATORY LANDSCAPE

In addition to commercial and environmental factors, enterprises also face a highly regulated market that features legislation and administrative regulations covering a business's external relationships (i.e., with its customers, its interaction with the environment, and availability of information) and internal relationships (such as the health and safety of its employees).

Boards and chief executives must constantly monitor the economic, political, and regulatory landscape, quickly identify new trends and opportunities, and if necessary, develop new product lines, new marketing initiatives, or make significant organizational changes, perhaps to the extent of reinventing their organizations. In some cases, the monitoring process is formalized through procedures such as environmental scanning that may require structured approaches to the consolidation of external information with internal information in order to enhance the knowledge within an enterprise.

Executives also face the threat of exposure to litigation arising from obligations such as duty of care, and importantly from a document management perspective, need to manage vital and important business documentation and other types of records to respond quickly to challenges such as quality audits and "legal discovery" processes. This requires management that is capable of balancing protection of information with the ability to make it available when required, according to the constraints of prevailing legislation such as privacy laws.

Legislation is gradually being modified with language that accommodates digital documents and recognizes electronic transactions. The requirements to produce paper-based evidence of transactions are diminishing.

Government departments and agencies are required to provide and administer regulations that are responsive to ever-changing social conditions. If there is maladministration, or administration of regulation is not timely and relevant, then a department or agency may also face punitive action from its customers, i.e., the community, and this is generally experienced through ministerial or parliamentary representations. Accountability remains a bastion of democracy. The following of due process, the documentation that supports the process, and the recordkeeping that provides transactional and regulatory access to the documentation, all sustain the accountability.

This accountability associated with responsibility for authenticity of information (and errors in it), should foster information accuracy and credibility. In association with this, governments have increasingly concerned themselves with privacy and accessibility. In the case of privacy, this has been to deal with sensitive information about people and their associations that they wish to withhold from others, whether the information is held in the public or private sector. In the case of accessibility, it has been to uphold the privilege of access through mechanisms such as FOI legislation. To expedite this effectively, recordkeeping and document systems must be responsive and able to deal flexibly with ad hoc queries.

Increasingly, the private sector is also establishing procedures which themselves regulate conformance with imposed regulatory measures or of manufacturing and service procedures. Examples range from service level agreements (SLAs) of the type used extensively in the public sector, to local applications of the international quality assurance standards that incorporate documentation of procedures.

Enterprises increasingly work beyond national borders, and must, therefore, be able to accommodate or respond to regulations in different countries that may have regulatory environments at odds with each other. In the case of commercial enterprises, this may require representations to government in order to facilitate trans-border information flows and transactions.

INFORMATION TECHNOLOGY IMPACT

Today's business environment has been, and will continue to be, impacted by rapid developments in technology. IT is evolving rapidly and changing the way in which all organizations manage and operate their businesses.

There is a compelling requirement for enterprises to interact with other businesses and key stakeholders and utilize new technology to keep pace with the information demands placed on them by stakeholders.

Key stakeholders, such as clients and service providers, develop expectations that IT systems will support acceleration of product to market, improve market share, and enhance customer services.

We will briefly examine some of the implications of the technology evolution on business planning.

Telecommunications

The advent of modern communications with its standards, and protocols provides the foundation by which businesses collaborate and share relevant information with external clients, business partners, and other key stakeholders, thereby facilitating cooperation and coordination and improving service delivery models.

Telecommunications development gave businesses the ability to speed interaction with stakeholders. If they did not embrace electronic data interchange (EDI) for inventory financial transactions when it first became available, then many businesses at least became involved in file transfer and mailing systems.

The advent of the Internet, and particularly the Web, accelerated the opportunities for EDI and provided a much wider platform for what is now termed electronic commerce (or e-commerce). The Web is becoming ubiquitous and is destined to become the preferred means by which organizations are able to exchange information, and by which the stakeholders (including business partners and customers) can access information.

Since the development of the Web browser, there has been a strong international movement toward using the Internet (public domain), often in association with intranets (organization domain) as the means by which organizations can communicate and share information with customers and provide access to information within the organization. Some organizations have adopted extranets to enable communication and information sharing between the enterprise and its business partners, service providers, and customers.

These and other telecommunications developments, such as WAP referred to in Chapter 1, also increase user expectation of distributed messaging capacity.

Information Systems

Business and government enterprises generally adopt information systems and technology solutions that enable organizations to gain a competitive edge, along with improving customer services and customer relationship management. For example, information systems and technology may help organizations develop and deliver products to market, maintain and strengthen existing assets, and streamline manufacturing, supply, and distribution processes. The information industry provides a great range of information systems and technologies to support business and government enterprises.

These systems and technologies may be conceived of as "vertical solutions" or "horizontal solutions." Vertical solutions are designed to meet the requirements of a specific type of industry (e.g., airline reservation systems, plant control systems, local government rating systems, and land information systems, to name a few). Horizontal solutions are designed to meet the general requirements of business and government enterprises (e.g., ERP systems, financial management, accounts payable, employee relations, asset management systems, and GIS).

Information Sharing

Enterprises typically deploy a LAN, consisting of interconnected database servers and file systems, for print sharing and file storage across the organization. Some organizations have the requirement to integrate multiple LAN segments, which may involve interconnecting sites in different geographical regions, possibly on a global basis, thereby forming a WAN. Typical network operating systems include Microsoft's NT and Windows 2000 server, Novell's NetWare, and Unix.

A key component of modern networking systems is the provision of collaboration services, such as Microsoft's Exchange, IBM/Lotus Notes, or Novell's GroupWise, that provide users with services such as messaging (email), diaries, scheduling, and other types of functionality. Additional modules may be offered as part of the set of products, including workflow and the provision of basic document management services.

Today's computer networks typically provide the platform for a wide range of document authoring applications, such as word-processing systems, spreadsheets, presentation graphics, Web authoring, drawing tools, and a variety of similar applications at the computer desktop. They also provide the foundation communications platform for implementation and operations of information systems that support business planning imperatives.

We mentioned that there is a transformation of enterprises from traditional functional hierarchies to process-centric organizations, with the specific aim of streamlining the supply chain from customer request to the supply of information and services. A consequence of this organizational evolution is a growing demand for tools that automate and manage processes in the business environment. Workflow management technology (alternatively called business process management software) is increasingly being recognized as the enabling technology for facilitating organizational transformation from functional rigidity to flexible customer-centric business processes.

Schäl (1998) makes the observation that workflow management technology combines electronic data processing procedures and organizational procedures with process management and exception handling, and also supports the integration of previously separate information systems. The importance of utilizing workflow technology to support business process management from beginning to end is recognized, so that workflow functionality is now being embedded into enterprise packaged information systems, such as ERP systems.

IT the Panacea?

The rapid advancements in technology and the potential impact on service delivery, such as development of new SCM and service delivery paradigms using Internet Web-enabled technology, are a major issue for boards and chief executives. Predictions abound about the future impacts of the Internet on businesses that are not "Web-enabled" or planning to embrace Web technology quickly. Some observers anticipate that companies that are unable to match IT services offered by their more proficient rivals may enter a period of slow decline and may be taken over for their market share.

There are intense marketing campaigns mounted by suppliers of information systems and technology to secure new customers. Often, they relate their marketing activities to the opportunities created by their products for helping organizations to achieve strategic business objectives, such as obtaining competitive edge, managing existing assets, and improving relationships with customers. The Internet and Web browsers are tools that provide new opportunities for suppliers to deliver innovative business solutions based on IT.

Unfortunately, the IT landscape is also characterized by a great deal of industry jargon and hyperbole, much of which is designed to support the marketing strategies of particular suppliers. This leads to significant levels of confusion in the minds of purchasers, both business and government, as lack of shared understanding of terminology leads to disenchantment with underachieving software or software purchased as a panacea for business processes, when the processes have yet to be articulated properly.

For example, the application of "knowledge management systems" to help organizations manage their intellectual capital during the latter part of the 1990s and into the 2000s is one area in which there was a high degree of market activity. Many vendors of document management, imaging, and workflow solutions marketed their products during this period as "knowledge management systems."

Meanwhile, scholars were pointing out that knowledge management was not an "information system," but a management and behavioral concept and philosophy. The term "knowledge workers," which found a great deal of empathy during the late 1990s, was in fact, a term coined by management pioneer Peter Drucker decades earlier. Drucker has continued with his discourse on knowledge work. For example, he sees the key to productivity as being cognitive science rather than electronics (Drucker, 1999), and that the social position of knowledge professionals must change to include social acceptance of their values.

However, knowledge work is not knowledge management — and what work is not knowledge work?

Information technology does not provide the magic potion for business competitiveness. There is growing appreciation that the management of the information that is carried by the technology, and the way that information management complements knowledge creation and sustenance, are also necessary for a vigorous enterprise.

BUSINESS MANAGEMENT SYSTEMS

The development and implementation of integrated business management systems is an important strategy to assist a business in remaining competitive and in providing quality services to its customers. For example, enterprises that follow the international standard on environmental management systems (International Organization for Standardization, 1996) along with quality systems standards (International Organization for Standardization, 2000) to achieve best practice in business management systems, generally map their critical processes in a structured and prioritized manner, as a strategy toward achieving accreditation.

This will be accompanied by documentation establishment and control practices commensurate with the extent of the enterprise. If environmental management is integrated with the enterprise's overall management system, then its documentation will be integrated into existing documentation in order to:

- Identify occupational health and safety policy and objectives.

- Describe how such objectives should be met; explain roles, responsibilities, and procedures.

- Show that the health and safety elements appropriate for the enterprise are implemented.

- Point to related documentation and other aspects of the management systems.

Documentation control is undertaken within the context of establishment of procedures and identification of responsibilities for document creation and maintenance. This includes review and approval for adequacy by authorized personnel as part of an issuing process. Issuing is controlled through procedures for identifying the current revision and ensuring availability to avoid use of obsolete versions. The obsolete versions approved as necessary for retention, perhaps for administrative history or legal purposes, must be appropriately identified.

There is also increasing government and community awareness of the fragile nature of our environment, and there is a growing interest in protecting the environment. Business strategies now need to embrace statements of the organization's interrelationship with its regional environment. For example, an electricity generation company may have a strategy that focuses on providing environmentally responsible energy solutions.

A business that is sensitive to its setting in relation to the natural world may formalize this to the extent of creating a mission and objectives that take account of such matters as sustainability, land planning, waste handling, or energy consumption within its general philosophy. This, in turn, may lead to information management objectives that must connect external intelligence obtained from environmental scanning with internal corporate knowledge.

Business planning and management also involve risk identification and mitigation. Risk management standards, for example, IEC 62198 (International Electrotechnical Commission, 2001c), provide a strategic and operational planning framework for establishing a risk management process. An enterprise typically develops a risk management strategy to assist the organization in achieving more effective strategic planning, in better managing cost controls and resource utilization, and in enhancing performance by minimizing losses and maximizing opportunities.

Organizations may also wish to enhance their operational capabilities by developing practices and behavior that support the generation and sharing of useful knowledge.

There is a growing body of case work and best practice formulation taking place in this area (Rollo & Clarke, 2001).

BUSINESS DOCUMENTS AND THEIR CONTENT

Organizations today may view documents simply as source objects for entry of content into information systems. The information is captured from the source document (which may be a physical document) and registered into the computer system. If these documents are not digitally created through forms, then they are usually filed in cabinets or folders, microfilmed, or perhaps scanned and converted to electronic images. The data in information systems may be subject to review, in which case, the physical source document may be retrieved for scrutiny, and it provides an important record.

The completed documents need to be managed, but so do the shells that shape how the source documents are created — the templates for document format and the forms for data capture.

Forms management is a significant aspect of data management. Barnett (1996) goes to some length to show the significance of forms to an enterprise. He draws attention to the following:

- The actual costs of form usage — a small percentage for design and printing, and a major percentage for clerical handling procedures and file maintenance;
- The importance of form design for maintaining data quality;
- The high costs of correcting or regathering that arise from incorrect form completion; and
- The need for organizational focus on forms management.

The support of planning, operations, and administration within business and government enterprises is enhanced if there is understanding by management that documents, including forms, are crucial to this support. Documents give evidence of business transactions, and as such, form part of an organization's essential recordkeeping functions. They are the foundation stones for managing and developing assets, by providing vital business information in the form of drawings, technical specifications, leases, tenders and contracts, and other types of commercial and regulatory documentation.

Document availability empowers users to make the most of the knowledge within enterprises. Enterprise Content Management (ECM) means that the diverse requirements of internal personnel, business and contract users and affiliates, as well as customers and the general public, are addressed in a directed way. This requires provision of internal distribution and external publication of content selected according to purpose, which is validated, accurate, timely, authorized, and meeting recordkeeping requirements within a managed framework.

Documentation plays a pivotal role in the development and implementation of a risk management strategy, because data in information systems, reports, and other documents (both hard-copy and electronic) can represent significant vulnerability. The storage of information in a secure, managed environment provides an asset that can assist an organization in achieving its strategic objectives.

DOCUMENTS AND BUSINESS ACTIVITY

Since the deployment of computer networks and desktop authoring systems, the volume of information held in digital form within enterprises is growing rapidly. Management of extensive electronic document collections is problematical, as is integration of these with the physical document collections that have preceded them and are likely to be running in parallel.

Typically, electronic documents that support an enterprise's key business processes (including word-processing, spreadsheet, presentation graphics, and drawings) are stored on shared file servers, but they may also be stored locally. There is a significant security exposure, primarily the loss of vital business documentation, when electronic documents are stored on local hard disks or floppy diskettes.

A typical method for "managing" electronic documents is to print and perhaps register the documents and maintain them as hard-copy documents in physical files, which is a process that is very labor intensive. Registers may be used to index details of electronic documents that have been created, or they may point to a copy of the file in a cabinet or folder. Registers may be provided as a "corporate records system," but workgroups tend to maintain their own document registers (based on databases, spreadsheets, or word-processing tables).

Archival and disposal practices might be in place for physical documents stored on physical files, which in this context, are usually termed records (being used as documents that have evidentiary value). However, records of business transactions must embrace more than just paper documents stored on physical files — they may also be electronic documents. Regrettably, we run into terminological confusion here, because a record in the sense used by a database designer does not account for the concept of evidence or of document and is more about the structural relationship of individual data elements (see Appendix 1: Glossary).

In fact, many organizations fail to apply archival and disposal authorities to electronic documents stored within virtual folders. This is despite the fact that guidance is now available for implementation of electronic recordkeeping strategies. For example, the DIRKS approach to managing information developed by the New South Wales Archives Authority has been promulgated in the Australian federal government sphere (National Archives of Australia, 2000).

DIRKS promotes an eight-step approach that comprises actions that are now embodied in ISO 15489 (International Organization for Standardization, 2001):

1. Preliminary investigation to identify resources, define boundaries, and establish housekeeping functions and associated issues;
2. Analysis of business activity, including stakeholder identification, risk assessment, and development of a business classification scheme;
3. Identification of recordkeeping requirements;
4. Assessment of existing systems, including gap analysis;
5. Development of strategies for recordkeeping;

6. Design of a recordkeeping system, including:
   a. Establishment and maintenance of recordkeeping
   b. Assignment of responsibilities
   c. Design or redesign of work processes, documentation, guidelines, and operating procedures
   d. Design of electronic or hybrid systems for records creation, capture, and control
   e. Development of a training plan
   f. Development of an initial system implementation plan;
7. Implementation of a recordkeeping system, including the selection of implementation strategies and management of the process; and
8. Postimplementation review, including the collection and analysis of performance data and the identification of corrective action.

Although this stepwise approach is oriented toward recordkeeping systems, many of its elements are covered in some detail with examples in later chapters, where we examine requirements analysis and implementation strategies for document systems.

Despite the availability of such frameworks, we have observed approaches where organizations apply "archival and disposal" practices to electronic documents, either by adding more magnetic disk storage capacity, thereby exacerbating rather than resolving the problem, or "deleting" documents. There is often no overall strategic approach to the management of electronic documents that takes into account legal and operational business requirements.

Effective management of documents and their content plays a fundamental role in assisting organizations in exploiting their knowledge, because business and government enterprises have knowledge expressed explicitly as information stored in documents, files, and other types of information containers. However, the provision of Internet, intranet, or extranet does not, in itself, provide such capability. The mechanisms for structuring and delivering information must be developed that are sensitive to workflow, user needs, the operational framework of enterprise systems, and organizational culture.

IDCM will help enterprises to develop as knowledge organizations, whereby information is shared with key stakeholders, and the risk of rework being performed on a project-by-project basis is significantly reduced. The system will also support knowledge management strategies by enabling organizations to gain rapid access to relevant information that is held in digital and hard-copy forms, managed by access security. It also provides the basis for sharing relevant information between employees, business partners, and service providers. Increasingly, as the sharing of information is facilitated by intranets or the Web, document management must embrace a content management strategy — a managed approach to the processes of authoring, organizing, and distributing digital documents.

This may be carried out with the aspiration that an enterprise's intellectual assets (content) and document systems can be effectively linked to business processes for effective utilization, that is, ECM.

Document management systems will also support an enterprise's transformation from traditional functional hierarchy to a customer-centric business process-oriented organization. An IDCM solution has the capability to support end-to-end business processes by managing transactional documentation (such as claims, vouchers, customer requests), received in physical or digital formats, and general administrative documentation (such as business templates and office documents).

Typically, workflow provides the technology for automating and managing business processes, administering the information flows, and providing mechanisms for managing exceptions, while an IDCM solution maintains management controls over the documentation during the workflow process.

The business processes may be handled by an ERP system, which provides essential information management and business process automation architecture that will support the back-end processes for customer service and e-commerce initiatives. While ERP systems generally offer document registry functions, and perhaps hyperlinks to documents stored on file systems, the current evolution of ERP systems is such that they typically do not offer document repository management capabilities.

The opportunity exists for organizations to integrate ERP systems with an IDCM solution to manage documentation associated with the process. This type of integration enables organizations to utilize the functionality of ERP systems to manage the database-centric aspects of the process. An IDCM connection enables ERP users to quickly initiate or retrieve documentation that is relevant to the business process.

An IDCM solution may also be used to implement repository controls over drawings and technical documentation during the engineering change process. Depending on the business environment, engineering design and drawing offices (for example, in the construction sector) are required to deliver new drawings, specifications, and revisions to clients to meet stringent target dates.

This enables drawings and technical documentation to be managed through all stages of drawing life-cycle processes, enabling users to have the assurance that they are accessing the correct revision of documentation. It provides organizations with a managed repository to facilitate exchange of CAD drawings and associated documentation, using tools such as extranets and integrated workflow.

OVERALL IMPLICATIONS FOR BUSINESS

Many organizations have a highly fragmented documentation environment with limited association between principles or policies, standards, business processes, metadata, information objects, and technology. This fragmentation may have occurred due to a combination of past factors, such as organizational changes, the deployment of networked desktop computers that enable authors to create documents quickly, and low priority for document management.

This fragmented document environment leads to potential business integrity threats. Disjointed registration scenarios for physical files, reports, and electronic documents mean that users are unable to determine the precise location and status of these types of information objects by accessing the one database.

Consequently, knowledge workers within an organization cannot be assured that they are accessing all information relevant to a particular matter, because document objects (with the possible exception of drawings) are typically not defined by searchable properties and are stored in diverse physical and electronic repositories. Other integrity threats include the multiple stores for the same document, and the threat posed by simultaneous updates being performed on the same electronic document.

SUMMARY

In this chapter, we have drawn attention to some general aspects of the business environment that have an effect on managing documents and their content. These aspects include commercial imperatives, regulatory constraints, the perceived role of information in society, and the impact of IT developments.

We extended this to consider challenges that apply in several specific business sectors, where the role of documents has particular pertinence.

We introduced the business form as an example of content creation, then considered document management with respect to elements of business activity, such as recordkeeping, knowledge management, and workflow.

We also briefly considered the applicability of using an IDCM strategy with integrated workflow or ERP systems to facilitate the transformation of organizations from functional hierarchical structures to customer-centric process organizations.

Chapter 3

Characteristics of Enterprise Document Environments

OVERVIEW

We now review how business and government enterprises that have yet to embark upon IDCM may be managing processing of different document types. We provide a generic description of each type on the assumption that most organizations can apply relevant elements to their specific environments.

Because of the complexities in describing the typical document environments, we structure the review into the following sections:

- Digital office documents for such documents in general;
- Electronic mail (email);
- Technical and engineering drawings;
- Document imaging;
- Web content; and
- Physical documents.

Our objectives are to provide a description of the functionality that applies in each of these environments and to provide an indication of the limitations that apply for each of the document types.

Therefore, at the end of each section, we have included a brief generic checklist. The checklists avoid expressing limitations with respect to specified types of business. We do not endeavor to be exhaustive or prescriptive. The checklists are provided to provoke readers to undertake further research and identify limitations with their own enterprise document environments and to build their own lists of limitations.

We begin by describing typical methods used for managing electronic or digital office documents in general.[1]

DIGITAL OFFICE DOCUMENTS

We recognize that email, digital drawings, digital images, and Web content are digital documents and could be described in this section. However, each has unique characteristics that warrant individual attention, so we will discuss these characteristics separately in following sections.

Document Authoring Tools

The types of PC desktop authoring applications that are available within enterprises generally comprise word-processing, spreadsheet, presentation graphics, and email facilities. They may also include more specialized tools such as project management software, drawing tools, Web authoring tools, and specific types of desktop publishing tools, to nominate representative types.

Enterprises may also have provided users with particular types of desktop authoring tools that are designated for specific purposes. For example, mathematical calculation tools and other types of scientific analysis tools, which may not be widely distributed on enterprise desktops.

Document Creation and Receipt

Digital office documents are typically created using desktop authoring tools in the following manner:

- Create new document from a template

  Many desktop applications, such as word-processing systems, provide the facility to create templates. Templates are files that contain formatting to allow a document to be created for a specific purpose (such as reports; specifications; and correspondence items, such as memos, minutes, agendas, facsimiles, and letters).

  Typically, standard templates are stored in a template folder on a networked drive. The author keys the required data into the template document, using predetermined captions within the relevant template as a guide. Some templates are configured to help standardize the presentation of documents, for example, by generating header and footer information, inserting objects such as logos, and providing page numbers and copyright notifications.

- Create new blank document

  Desktop authoring applications provide the facility to create a new blank document. In reality, the blank document is usually based on the application's native blank-document template.

- Reuse digital document

  The author opens an existing document and either (a) saves the document as a new document, or version, and then edits the document; or (b) edits the document, then saves it as a new document or version.

  Existing documents may also have electronic notes added to them without actually modifying the original, but creating a new digital object.

- Generate database reports

  Digital documents may also be generated as reports from database applications. These reports are often saved as part of the application system storage module or

are exported to desktop tools, such as a spreadsheet or a word-processing document, then saved in a nested folder on a local file server.
- Scan documents to image format
Imaging technology may be used to capture digital documents. This is discussed later in the "Imaging" section.

Electronic documents may be received as email messages, as attachments to emails, or by copying files from removable media. Documents received as email messages or attachments are dealt with in a later "Email" section.

Documents received on diskette, CD-ROM, and other media may be captured by simply transferring the files to a networked drive, personal drive, or removable media. Users characteristically achieve this functionality by using standard operating system file management tools such as Windows Explorer.

Metadata Registration and Validation

Many enterprises have no standards for identifying and recording digital document metadata (the information about the documents that helps to identify and manage them). One aspect of metadata is a concerted approach to file naming. Its importance in the systems development environment has been recognized by organizations such as IBM and Philips. It has also been described in detail by writers such as Brackett (1994), who has elaborated schema for naming.

However, it has proved difficult enough following naming conventions within systems teams, let alone realizing them with end users. Various groups, for example, *OpenACS* and *Filesystem Hierarchy Standard Group*, have promulgated file naming conventions on the Web, and these may be of some use with document naming conventions. Some organizations have a standard whereby document names, which may include path names, are inserted into document footers, and there may be directives concerning how these names should be formed.

Naming metadata are essentially application dependent and may be captured automatically by the desktop authoring application. Most enterprises have not developed and implemented document-naming conventions. The usual situation is that authors give file names to saved documents, but typically, there is little rigor applied to naming. Many authors do not make full use of the long file name capability offered by desktop operating systems and frequently describe documents with file names that are almost meaningless.

Some government agencies developed guidelines for document naming when operating system environments do not cater for long names. For example, in its *Government Recordkeeping Manual*, the New South Wales archives authority makes suggestions (State Records of New South Wales, 1997) such as:

Select the first four characters of the document's two main keywords
Example: **NAMECONV.xxx**

Use the full key word if it is eight characters or less
Example: **NAMING.xxx**

Use agreed abbreviations
Example: **NAMCONVS.xxx**

Use consonants only — omit vowels, double consonants, spaces, and plurals
Example: **NMECNVNT.xxx**

Another aspect of metadata is the additional descriptive information provided. We give some examples of this in the following chapter, where we make a distinction between metadata describing the subject content of a document or the functions it supports, and metadata that deal with the document as an agent that carries content, for example, who is responsible for creating it. Some of these metadata may be captured automatically, but mechanisms must also be provided for addition to them by the creators, reviewers, classifiers, and modifiers of documents.

In Chapter 2, we made reference to DIRKS. For functional metadata, this approach to information management makes use of the *Keyword AAA* thesaurus. This vocabulary is designed to enable the consistent classification, titling, and indexing of records using controlled terminology about the common administrative functions of an agency.

Save and Storage Regimes

When a document is created or updated, the author adds content, and the document may be saved to the local file server, hard disk, or removable media, or be printed, or discarded without saving.

Digital documents are usually stored in the authoring application's native format (e.g., .DOC for MS Word) in nested folders contained on shared logical network file server drives, personal network drives, local hard drives, or removable media.

The many desktop authoring applications that are available in the market save files in their own file formats, though many make provisions for saving in alternative generic or proprietary formats.

Typically within enterprises, users are encouraged to save documents to the appropriate logical network drive. However, documents may not always be saved to a managed drive. They might be saved to drives on personal workstations (removable hard disks), diskettes, or other types of removable media. They may be printed and then discarded without saving.

Version Control

A number of scenarios may apply to version control in organizations that have not implemented a DMS. It is difficult to identify all of these, but the following examples may help enterprises identify those that are used in their own situations:

- Version controls may be applied to certain controlled documents (such as drawings or contract documents).
- There is usually only limited or no version control applied to standard templates, which are the guides used to create important business documents.
- There are generally no business rules for identification and control of document versions on the majority of documents.
- Individuals or workgroups may apply simplistic version control measures to their own documents.

The following types of methods can be used when version control is applied without the benefits of a DMS:

- Allocate a file name and then a numeric or alphanumeric code (e.g., 0.1) to a file name, then increment the code when a new version of a document is saved.
- Manage physical copies of the documents as the primary version ("controlled copy") of the document.
- Use software such as a spreadsheet or manual register to store version details, in which case, the register provides a simple listing but no management.

Where enterprises apply version controls without the benefits of a DMS, the controls are usually managed manually by designated user(s) within the enterprise, and therefore, they are prone to human error.

Renditions

Documents may also be stored as a rendition of the native format or in an additional form. For example, this may be a PDF or HTML object rendered from a word-processing document, particularly where it is planned to publish content to the intranet or Internet. Another example is a document rendered to Rich Text Format (RTF) for exchange with an external party, or a JPG image rendered from BMP or TIF file formats.

Therefore, an individual document may have multiple versions, and each of these may be in several different renditions.

Compound Documents

Compound documents within the office environment enable document creation using embedded fragments of other documents. For example, they may be produced and managed through the use of component object technology like CORBA or DCOM. This technology allows the development of complex compound documents but must be extended to managing the versioning of embedded or linked documents.

Increased use of intranets for document publishing and distribution has increased the need for managing compound documents (e.g., one Web page object containing a mix of HTML/XML, JPG, PDF, TIF documents) and maintaining explicit linkages created between parent and child documents.

When preparing compound documents, inappropriate document authoring techniques can result in large file sizes and ineffective document management behaviors. For example, take the case where a document is created that contains a range of embedded images. The image formats embedded within the arrangement will impact the file size of the arrangement when saved, which may be larger than the sum of its individual fragments.

Such a file may take up a large quantity of storage space. Given that the arrangement is in digital format, it might also be easily copied for reuse as another arrangement or stored again in a separate directory on the file system, thus exacerbating the consumption of space. Space problems may be caused by imaging processes that use unnecessarily high resolution.[2]

If these types of files are stored on a network file system within enterprises, the file will also be backed up to tape or other media. These large file sizes, which could have been reduced significantly by sharing and compression techniques, have an impact on backup capacity. Backup capacity has to increase in order to absorb larger digital document collections, and backup and recovery of data files is time consuming.

Hyperlinks

Enterprises use hyperlink functionality to navigate to documents or specific content references within documents. Such links are facilitated by providing anchors or pointers associated with text that is highlighted. Users may move to linked material simply by using a pointing device (typically a mouse) to activate the link. The linked material may be within a document and established using bookmarks or may be the name of an external document. This is regularly the case with HTML pages developed by enterprises for deployment of content on their Internet or intranet Web sites.

Document Routing

Generally, a number of scenarios apply to document routing within enterprises:
- Physical copies of digital documents are used for manual review and approval processes.
- Workflow technology may be used to varying degrees for document routing and review and approval processes.
- Digital documents may be dispatched as attachments by email, and more experienced users will route links to documents (as shortcuts) instead of attachments, thus enabling users with access to a shared folder to access the document via the link.
- The routing slip functionality offered by some word-processing packages may be used, but if so, it is generally to a limited extent.

Finding Documents

Users may employ the following types of search and retrieval tools for finding and locating documents:
- Browse folders using file management software to locate a document. This is useful if the user has a reasonable idea of which file directory area to examine.
- Use a Search or Find tool in file management software to search attributes that describe the document. This is a useful technique, providing that attributes, such as the Document Title, Author, etc., are known. Due to poor document naming conventions at a corporate, department, or workgroup level, the search may not produce the desired result.
- Restrict the Find search to a specific folder or set of folders. This capability restricts the scope of the search, but it relies upon the user to know, or have a good idea, that a document is contained within the nominated folder(s).
- Initiate a search on the contents of documents, with the option to include a search on document attributes. This search may also be restricted to a folder or set of folders. It may increase the number of candidate documents that meet the search criteria, but it does not help much if the document is an image, as there is no "text" content to search. It may also be slow, because without the benefit of full text

indexing software installed, the operating system has to search each document seriatim.

- Search a digital or physical register to find documents. Many administrators have support staff to maintain documents (word-processing, spreadsheets, or data-bases) to register other digital documents. These registers may prove useful if maintained correctly, but they are not much help if the path or name of the document was renamed or the file was moved or deleted.
- Search an RMS (that does not store the digital document), where such is used to record the file system path name and document title. Again, the automated register is not much help if the path or name of the document is renamed or the file was moved or deleted.
- Use a specific content searching tool (full text indexing package) to locate documents typically across a set of folders. This has the benefit in that selected or all-text documents are pre-indexed to facilitate rapid searching. However, this approach still presents problems if images are sought, unless they are textually described. It can also produce retrieval results that are too large to be useful.

Viewing Documents

Enterprise users may view documents by launching the native authoring application for the relevant document. MS *Quick View* is generally available for viewing certain types of file formats, and Adobe *Acrobat Reader* is available for viewing PDF files. MS *Photo Editor* and Kodak *Imaging Application* are available for viewing images in some versions of MS Windows. Images may also be opened within Web browsers, such as Netscape Navigator or MS Internet Explorer.

Printing Documents

Enterprises provide networked or stand-alone printers for producing printed copies of digital documents. Typically, the environment consists of laser printers and inkjet printers, and may feature the capability to print in color as well as black and white. Enterprises may use an external service provider to produce multiple copies of a document, where the volume of printing required is high.

Many printed documents are managed outside the control of an RMS, for example, in public relations or marketing units.

Security

Security over documents on networked file systems is managed via the networked operating system. Limited security is generally applied over documents stored on local hard disks, including those in laptops, and virtually no security is implemented for removable diskettes and other media, unless they are locked in a safe.

Many organizations and users underestimate the implications of storing documents on local hard disks or removable media. This type of activity represents security vulnerability for critical business documents. The media may of course be stolen, but they may also be temporarily removed, copied, then replaced, which is likely to have a more significant effect on an enterprise.

Scheduling and Disposal

Enterprises may not have implemented retention and disposal regimes for digital documents. Sometimes, a simple procedure is in place but is based upon the age of the material rather than appraisal of its value.

Many organizations tend to solve the archival management issue with electronic documents merely by providing more magnetic, optical, CD, or DVD media with which to store the documents. This is as opposed to having management metadata that establishes for different types of documents the period and form in which they should be retained and the extent to which archival renditions should be produced. Mere provision of more storage capacity is not managing the document environment.

Table 1: Digital Office Document Management Limitations Checklist.

- A document may be generated from a superseded template. This can occur when a staff member reuses a document that has been created using an earlier (now out of date) template.

- Templates are quite often stored on each user's hard disk drive. There may not be any mechanism (manually, electronically, or written procedure) in place to ensure that most templates are updated at the users' local drives to synchronize with the new updated "controlled copy" of the template.

- Templates may be stored on laptop computers to allow users to work while not connected to the LAN. Again, there may be no mechanisms in place to update the templates with the latest version, and users could be relying on an out-of-date template for creating documents.

- When users need to create a document based on a template, they may have difficulty identifying the template required. This can be due to poor naming and classification conventions; lack of retrieval tools; and perhaps the large number of enterprise-, departmental-, and workgroup-specific templates. This may result in creation of a new blank document, cloning an old document, or using an incorrect template.

- There may be no management controls over save regimes, which may be a problem when authors reuse existing material to create new versions, and save the new contents with the same file name or version.

- Important digital documents may be stored on personal network drives, due to a nonsharing culture often maintained by an individual, workgroups, and even organizations. These documents are effectively inaccessible to other authorized users that may be searching for a document.

- Document integrity and security issues may arise when local hard drive or removable media (A:\drive) are utilized for storage (even temporary storage) of digital documents.

- Manual version control processes are typically ad hoc and provide ineffective versioning control. Users may forget to increment the manual version number. A diverse range of individual versioning techniques may be applied, and users may not understand another staff member's technique.

- The flaws in manual version control processes mean that users cannot be assured that they are accessing the correct version of a document.

- There may be a high risk of integrity problems in maintaining relationships between linked documents, due to the limited capabilities for managing linked documents in a compound document relationship.

- There may not be any sophisticated search and retrieval tools for retrieving documents from the current storage systems. The capabilities provided via the operating system may provide options, but they may be limited due to (1) poor file names, (2) types of documents involved, and (3) document collection size.

- The capability to browse and search folders may work sufficiently within small workgroups, provided there are good folder structure and naming conventions applied, but the capability may not be sustainable at departmental or enterprise levels.

- The lack of naming conventions, nondescriptive file names, and lack of document property information may make it complex for enterprises to access or retrieve documents quickly and in a simple manner.

- Geographically dispersed users that require access to important documents held at an enterprise's corporate office may copy these documents to local file shares in order to improve speed of access. This uncontrolled copying is a data integrity issue, because users may access superseded documents.

- The classification for digital storage on file systems is often inconsistent with the classification scheme in recordkeeping systems used for managing physical documents.

Limitations — Digital Documents

A checklist of limitations that are common with the management of digital document environments is given in Table 1.

EMAIL

The characteristics of digital documents described in the previous section encompass email, and specifically, email attachments. However, the messaging role of email warrants its own attention.

Desktop Authoring Tools

Most enterprises provide personnel with an email client. Email accounts are stored in a server environment (such as MS Exchange, Lotus Notes, or GroupWise). Some users also access other email accounts with Internet Service Providers (ISPs) or free Web email accounts via the Internet, possibly for work use. This usage can occur when users email work documents to their ISP or Internet account so they can work from home or for communication with work from other locations.

Document Creation and Receipt

Email messages are typically generated at the desktop within enterprises using email software that may be termed an email client. However, source content for generated emails may come from other documents within the enterprise's standard office suite, the Internet/intranet, other email messages, or text documents.

Emails are addressed to one or more recipients. Recipient email addresses can be other internal email accounts within an enterprise, group distribution accounts, service support accounts (e.g., Switchboard), or external email addresses. Most messaging systems enable accounts to be selected from an enterprise-wide list of account-holders or from a contact list, such as departmental or workgroup. They may also provide for distribution to lists maintained by the sender or as named groups in a central registry.

Emails may include one or more attachments or shortcuts to documents. They may include hyperlinks to documents stored on logical file shares or the Internet/intranet. Emails can have additional features activated, such as sensitivity, importance, tracking options, delivery options, voting buttons, expiry time, and category.

Staff within enterprises can generate email messages by responding to emails received. This action may involve replying to the sender only, replying to all recipients, or forwarding the email to a third party. When replying to or forwarding email, the email client software typically prepopulates the email response with the contents of a received email, which allows the user to add additional content, or remove content, as part of the response.

Email messages can be initiated from the menu of many desktop applications by a "send" or "send to" function, which will send the contents of the current file in that application to recipients, through the email client. A new email dialog box is presented to the user, with the file attached and sometimes the subject filled out, allowing the user to add the recipient, subject, and any text before they send it.

When the email server receives email messages, it typically checks against the out-of-office or other messaging rules configured by the recipient. The system may have the capability to generate an autoreply to the sender(s) and apply rules. The rules allow emails to be forwarded, replied to, moved or copied to folders, or deleted.

Emails can be created and received as a meeting request, allowing the user to accept, tentatively accept, or decline the meeting. Resources for meetings such as rooms and equipment can be booked as part of the meeting request process. Emails can be created and received containing user-specified voting buttons, allowing the user to choose a response from the buttons provided.

Metadata Registration and Validation

The minimum information a user is required to enter on a created email is the recipient email address(es). The email client automatically registers the metadata about sender email address, time and date sent, and message identification. Other fields that can be filled out are Subject and CC: (copies to) recipient email address(es). Other less-used features, where provided by the email client, include BCC: (blind copies to), sensitivity, importance, tracking options, delivery options, voting buttons, expiry date and time, and category. Recipient email address(es) within an enterprise are validated to ensure the address exists. However, the subject fields in email addresses are not validated and may contain low-value descriptive information about the content of the email.

Some email systems permit metadata about recipients to be stored in associated databases that record contact details and interests.

Save and Storage

An email user may store messages in logical folders within the email application, archive emails to personal folder files, or save emails or attachments from the email system to a user-specified file location. They may be stored in formats such as the email message format, template format, TXT, RTF, or HTML.

Generally, single emails can be saved while they are being viewed. Single or multiple emails can be saved, regardless of whether they have been read or not, from the email systems list view. Multiple email messages may be saved to a single TXT file or to RTF.

Emails saved to text files have no record of attachments. They can be opened by any application that supports text files, such as MS Notepad. Emails saved in RTF may contain a link to attachments. They can be opened by any application that supports rich text files. The associated application is usually the word-processing application. Emails saved in message format of the mail client contain a link to any attachments. The associated application is the client application.

Unsent emails can be saved in the email application and so remain until they are sent. Once the email is sent, the saved (draft) copy is normally discarded automatically.

Email attachments can be saved separately from the email. One or more attachments can be saved at one time. Attachments can be saved while they are being viewed or, in some cases, from a tabular view of message listing.

Importing and exporting functionality is generally supported by the email application. Emails can be exported to a user-specified file location in various file formats. For example, email may be exported to a personal file folder in formats such as Comma

Separated Values (CSV), various supported database and spreadsheet formats, and tab-separated files.

Emails can be moved or copied into folders within their client mailboxes that are structured for business needs, as well as into personal folders. Enterprise users typically have folder structures within their email applications. Emails are generally inserted into these folders by "drag and drop" techniques. Emails can be manually or automatically archived into personal folders.

Generally, it is possible for users to change and save an email that has already been sent, or received, without the system recording any change to the email's metadata.

Version Control

Sent and received emails are stored with a time stamp to indicate time sent and received. The combination of time stamp, sender, recipient(s), subject, and content represents uniqueness in email.

There is generally no version control of saved unsent emails in the email application. When a user makes changes to a saved email and saves it again, it is saved over the old saved email.

Emails can be re-sent, which is a manual form of version control. A re-sent message will have a time stamp different from an original message.

Compound Documents

Where emails contain embedded attachment(s), or a link to a stored document, then these combinations represent forms of a compound document. In this case, the combination of time stamp, sender, recipient(s), subject, and content, together with attachment(s) or links, represents uniqueness in email. The email with attachment(s) may be stored as a compound document.

Viewing

Emails can be viewed through the email application. Emails saved to file are viewed through the associated desktop application. Attachments to emails can be viewed while viewing the email or after email has been closed. Attachments can also be viewed from the table (as mentioned in the "Save and Storage" section above), regardless of whether the email has been read. Attachments saved to a file location can be viewed by double-clicking the document in applications such as MS Windows Explorer, thereby opening the document with its associated application, provided the application is resident, or opening the document from within an application. Attachments are viewed in the associated application for the document type.

Printing

Emails may be printed directly from the email application. Emails saved to file are printed from the application associated to their file extension. Single emails are most commonly printed while viewing them, but single and multiple emails can usually be printed from a list view, regardless of whether they have been read or not. Printed emails may be used for review and approval processes, including approvals involving manual or digital signature. Printed emails may be filed in physical file folders, particularly where the email is a record of a business transaction.

Security and Audit

Enterprise email systems generally secure each user's email in a mailbox. The mailbox owner and any other user with permission can access a specified mailbox. Emails archived, saved, copied, or exported to a personal folder, or any other file, are stored in the network file system and are subject to normal file security. There may be no audit rules for email.

Archiving and Disposal

The email systems used in enterprises may provide facilities where users are able to archive emails automatically based on some predefined rule, such as archiving all emails older than 30 days to a specific personal folder (generally stored in network file systems). These settings may be preconfigured by systems administrators or configured individually by users to meet their specific needs.

Users may have a range of other personal folders set up for automatic archiving. These folders may reside on the user's personal network drive, other network drives, local hard drives, or removable media. Users can typically initiate a manual archival of email into specified folders. Users can also manually move or copy selected emails to a specified folder.

Automatic or manual archiving moves email messages from the Inbox to a personal folder. In some circumstances, email coming via a mail server to personal folders on local machines is stored on both the server and the personal machine. System administrators will normally set file size and retention time limits on the files that are duplicated at the mail server.

When a user deletes email, it is generally placed into a folder for deleted items. System administrators or users may configure the folder for deleted items so that it is emptied when a user exits an active email session. However, a user may modify the setting so that deleted email is retained in the folder for deleted items until the user accesses the folder and deletes the messages permanently.

Notwithstanding the user deletion of an email, a separate instance of the email may be stored on an enterprise email server, and registered in transaction logs. Copies of these

Table 2: Email Management Limitations Checklist.

• Email containing important business decisions (and documents) may be left in the user's mailbox or archived to a personal folder; the transaction, unless printed and registered on a file or otherwise recorded, is not known to corporate memory.
• There are no disposal rules for emails. Users delete emails without any type of management controls.
• Employees may delete email containing important business decisions (and documents) due to poor information management practices.
• Email files that are stored on networked drives, local drives, or removal media may contain a large volume of "redundant" information. For example, a sender and receiver may archive the same email message. These messages may contain one or more attachments.
• The "subject" field in email messages often lacks descriptive information about the content of the email.
• Metadata are limited and uncontrolled.

messages may be created under legal discovery processes and have significant ramifications.

Limitations — Email

Table 2 is a synopsis of limitations that may exist with the management of email documents.

TECHNICAL AND ENGINEERING DRAWINGS

As they are often handled by software different from creating general office documents in an organization, we deal with drawing documents separately here, though the characteristics of digital documents in general do apply to them.

Desktop Authoring Tools

Many business and government enterprises will make use of CAD tools, including products such as AutoCAD and Microstation, to develop and modify drawings. These products are generally restricted to those users with a specific need to create and edit drawings.

Some organizations also provide users with additional tools, such as software for converting raster images to vector (see Appendix 1: Glossary). Typical cases involve replacement of all or part of raster image(s) with vector object(s). Once the drawing modifications have been completed, the vector object(s) may then be converted to raster image(s) or composite (Raster CAD).

The extent of use of CAD and similar supporting tools within an enterprise will depend on the nature of its business and how it sources drawings that are required for functions such as asset management and planning. For example, an engineering services company will have an intrinsic focus on drawing and associated engineering change management processes. However, other organizations may simply outsource the development and modification of drawings to an external contractor.

Document Creation and Receipt

Digital drawings are typically created using CAD authoring tools in the following manner:

- Create new drawing from a template

  CAD authoring tools often provide the capability for enterprises to create templates to help standardize drawing formats. The templates include predefined layouts for borders and title block content within drawings. The templates may also include preset header and footer definitions, logos, page numbering, and copyright information. (They may also include other information such as a safety message or instructions such as "do not scale".) As with digital documents in general, the templates are stored in a template folder on a networked drive (or perhaps on a local hard disk).

- Create new blank drawing

  CAD authoring tools enable users to create a new blank drawing based on its own preset template.

- Reuse digital drawing

  Drafting officers may open an existing drawing and (a) save the drawing as a new drawing, version, or revision, and then edit the drawing; or (b) edit the drawing, then save it as a new drawing, version, or revision.

- Scan drawings to image format

  Imaging technology may be used to convert physical drawings to digital format. For further details on scanning physical documents to digital image, see the "Imaging" section.

- Convert drawing to TIF or PDF

  A drawing may be rendered to TIF or PDF formats, for example. (See the "Renditions" section.)

Drawings may be received from external sources in digital format or physical format, or both, which is particularly evident where an enterprise has outsourced its drawing functions to a service provider or has contractual relationships with a third party that involve the preparation of drawings.

Metadata Registration and Validation

Enterprises tend to use a number of methods for registering drawings, depending on the complexity of the requirement and the volume of drawings involved. The following types of document registers may be applied for drawings:

- A package solution for "drawing control" that provides a register for drawings but does not place management controls over the digital drawing objects (The digital drawings may be stored in multiple folders on a file server and may be distributed over multiple file servers.);
- A developed solution that provides document registration capabilities;
- A module of an ERP system that enables drawing information, including revision numbers, to be registered;
- Networked or personal database or spreadsheet files that are used to record drawing information register details of drawings;
- Adapted shareware or freeware applications for drawing information; and
- Manual registers.

Each organization generally has its own requirement for registering information about its drawings, but where drawings are to be shared with a service provider or business partner, the organization may need to collaborate on the registration information held.

Typically, a unique drawing number is the key characteristic that identifies a drawing. Enterprises may have a range of different drawing number formats, based on their specific business requirements. The drawing number is the key that provides quick access to drawings, which may be filed in one or more formats, i.e., digitally in network file systems, on microfilm, or physically in cabinets.

Some CAD tools enable attributes to be registered for each drawing, but these attributes are generally used within the application to provide title block information.

There are a variety of standardization initiatives for spatial metadata that have bearing on the way organizations may define their own metadata. These include the *Content Standard for Digital Geospatial Metadata* initiated in the United States by their Federal Geographic Data Committee in 1994 and incorporating in excess of 200 data elements, and the ANZLIC metadata guidelines for geographical data in Australia and New Zealand. An international standard is being developed by ISO's Geographic Information Technical Committee using a set of metadata elements that support discovery of data, determining data fitness for use, data access, and use of data. Identification elements deal with extent, quality, spatial and temporal schema, spatial reference, and distribution of digital geographic data.

Save and Storage Regimes

When a drawing is created or updated, the drafting officer adds content, and by invoking the "save" command in the CAD tool, the document is saved to a file system, local hard disk, or removable media. It may also be printed.

When a draftsperson is working on a drawing, it is not uncommon for the working copy to be saved to local hard disk, rather than to a network file system, because the speed of retrieval of the drawing object from the hard disk is quicker than from the network. However, the risk is that the drawing may not be secure on the hard disk if another user logs onto the same computer. There are also risks associated with the dependability of the disk system, because if the hard disk malfunctions, the drawing may be lost, unless backed up to a file server. There is also the risk that another drafting officer could access and edit the version of the drawing stored on the network server, unaware that another colleague is already editing it or plans to edit it.

Many enterprises have adopted the strategy of storing copies of their drawings in microfilm image format, including the use of roll microfilm and microfiche, but primarily utilizing 35 mm aperture cards. Drawings are generally microfilmed at the "as built" or "for construction" stage of a project and should be secured in a fireproof container. The microform is given a unique identification, typically the drawing number, and it is generally filed numerically in drawing number sequence order, thus enabling quick retrieval. The microfilm location might be referenced in a drawing register (database or spreadsheet).

In some organizations, access to such material has in the past been accomplished with the aid of mechanical or electromechanical storage and retrieval equipment. It may be necessary to accommodate an interface between such a legacy system and a digital retrieval system.

Revision Control

A number of different scenarios may apply for revising drawings within enterprises that have not implemented an effective DMS (or drawing management system). There are usually only limited version controls applied to standard drawing templates. Individuals or workgroups may apply simplistic version controls when saving digital drawings. However, enterprises typically implement the concept of revision (version) control for drawings in the engineering change management process. The first release of a drawing may be issued as Revision A, 0, 1.0, or blank, and when the drawing is revised, it might then be released as Revision B (or another revision identifier).

Renditions

Drawings may be stored as a rendition of its native CAD format. For example, a digital CAD drawing may be rendered to PDF or to TIF file formats for distribution via an intranet or publication at an Internet site to facilitate collaboration between workgroups, service providers, or business partners. The rendition may also be used to store the "as built" drawing as a permanent (nonrevisable copy) record.

Compound Drawings

Complex reference linkages may be created between parent and child engineering drawing objects. For example, one drawing may be a parent of a number of children drawings and may itself be a child drawing of one or more other parent drawings. Figure 1 provides an illustration of these types of relationships. It demonstrates that drawing A.1.1.3 is the child of two other drawings (A.1.1 and B.1.1) and is the parent of three drawings, namely, drawings A.1.1.3.1, A.1.1.3.2, and A.1.1.3.3.

Drawing Transmission

Drawings may be sent between business units, workgroups, and people within an enterprise, and between an enterprise and its business partners and service providers. Typical methods may be (a) email with attachment(s), (b) workflow (controlled electronic authorization/audit trails/distribution), or (c) physically by postal or courier services.

A transmittal note typically accompanies drawings when exchanged with external sources, and often when exchanged within the enterprise. Its purpose is to act as a record of the transmission and receipt of a drawing between business entities.

It may register the exchange of one or more drawings in either digital format or physical format. For example, a transmittal note with accompanying drawings might be exchanged digitally via email and then a hard-copy sent with physical drawings.

Figure 1: Complex Drawing Relationships.

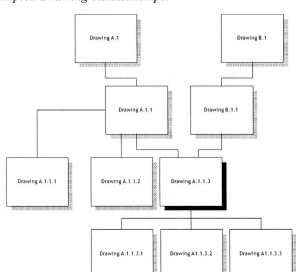

During the engineering work management process, drawings may be moved through a number of states, including states such as *submitted for approval, approved for specification, approved for construction*, and *as built*. These transition states are typically recorded in the drawing register to reflect the current status of a drawing.

Searching Drawings

Metadata may be stored in a drawing register (digital or manual) that provides the capability to search on a particular attribute (property) or set of attributes (properties) that describe a drawing. The register generally provides users with a drawing number, which enables them to find the drawing object on the file server. The same register may provide a link to paper copies of drawings or drawings held in microform. Where a drawing register is not used, users can browse the drawing objects on the file server or utilize the facilities of the CAD authoring tool to provide recent drawings accessed.

Viewing Drawings

Digital drawings may be viewed using the native CAD authoring tool, provided it is in a compatible file format. Drawings that have been scanned to image format (e.g., TIF) may be viewed via the default image viewer available on desktop computers, or if in PDF format, may be viewed through the Adobe *Acrobat Reader*. Organizations may also make use of shareware tools or free or low-cost viewers provided by the suppliers of drawing authoring tools. Microfilm copies of drawings, such as drawings on aperture cards, can be viewed through a microform reader.

Printing Drawings

Drawings in document size ranges A4 to A3 are typically printed on the same types of networked printers that are used for digital office documents. Plotters (including diverse types such as color inkjet plotters) are typically used for printing large format drawings. Alternatively, large format drawings may be referred to a commercial third-party service bureau for printing.

Security

Metadata registered in a drawing register is managed by the security of the computer system or networked file system (if the register is maintained using a local database or spreadsheet application). Digital drawing objects stored on file systems are secured by the network operating system. If the drawing register is maintained on a local hard disk, there are access and physical security vulnerabilities, and the same vulnerabilities apply to any digital drawing objects that are held on local disks.

Archiving and Disposal

Drawings need to be accessible over long periods of time, and enterprises may not have applied retention and disposal regimes for the management of their drawings. Most organizations do, however, archive earlier revisions of drawings, but these may also need to be retained for inspection to support discovery processes. Often, drawings are archived to CD or DVD, particularly backup copies of *as built* drawings that may have also been rendered to PDF or TIF formats. Backup copies of drawings on CD, DVD, tape,

Table 3: Drawings Management Limitations Checklist.

• Drawing processes, tools, and registers may not be standardized within an enterprise, which may mean diversity of CAD authoring tools.
• There may be multiple drawing numbering systems, primarily due to mergers and acquisitions, laissez-faire management style, or other factors.
• There may be duplicated drawing numbering systems.
• There may be a duplication of drawing registers, particularly if drawings are being managed in diverse workgroups, geographical locations, or company subsidiaries.
• The data stored in drawing registers may be inadequate for requirements, or it may exceed requirements.
• Technical documentation, other than drawings, may also be registered in the drawing register(s), while copies of the same documentation may exist in digital form in file shares, and physical copies of the documentation may also be registered in an RMS.
• There may be multiple codes systems for description that require rationalization by being combined into a single overall approach.
• There might be multiple naming conventions with different names for the same item of plant or equipment.
• TIF images, if held, may be difficult to read, due to poor quality imaging during scanning processes, and have incorrect attributes due to poor quality metadata capture during scanning.
• TIF images may be out of date, particularly where physical copies have been marked up and used as "controlled" copies without synchronized update of the relevant TIF images.
• TIF image(s) may be stored in multiple file shares. An integrity issue may arise if the drawing is modified without all copies being updated, presenting difficulties if there is no register of distributed copies.
• Microfilm copies of drawings may not be readable or otherwise usable.
• A drawing register typically does not implement management controls over the drawing objects.
• Search and retrieval for drawings may be slow, because there is a need to (a) first search the drawing register to find the location of the drawing, and (b) then find or browse the folder system to locate the digital copy.

microfilm, or originals should be stored remotely from an operational site, potentially 50 km away, depending on the nature of the industry and level of risk (given the state of global unrest).

Limitations — Drawings

Table 3 provides an overview of limitations that may exist with the management of drawings within organizations. The same limitations that apply to digital office documents (e.g., lack of management controls over digital objects) typically also apply to the management of digital drawings.

DOCUMENT IMAGING

Most enterprises have implemented, or plan to implement, document imaging systems to manage the conversion of physical documents to digital format. There are different types of document imaging applications within organizations, as we see in the following chapter on integrated applications. Suffice to say that for our general review in this chapter, we are not focusing on production level imaging systems, where there are high volumes of images involved. Production imaging applications by their very nature implement controls over the processes associated with image management. Our review in this chapter focuses instead on ad hoc imaging within the enterprise systems, where image management techniques may be less apparent.

Imaging Tools

The types of image capture devices include scanning hardware, facsimile gateways, and digital cameras. The software includes a wide range of imaging conversion or recognition software such as OCR, as well as capture software with digital cameras.

Image Capture

Digital images are typically captured using the following processes:

*   Scan a document or photo into a digital image.

    Scanning devices and software are used to capture office documents or photos into a digital image. Some organizations have acquired photocopying systems that have the capability to scan images. Specialist scanning equipment might also be used to convert large-size format drawings and plans to digital images.

*   Capture inbound facsimile transmission.

    Facsimile gateways may be used to capture incoming facsimile transmissions in digital form, and imaging and workflow systems may be used to route images to action officers.

*   Take a digital photograph.

    Digital cameras may be used within the enterprise to store images on a diskette within the camera or output images to a card and then download them to a computer via cable and specialist software.

*   Convert microform images to digital images.

    Conversion devices might be used to convert (analog) microform images to digital images to enable workgroups or enterprise users to quickly access documentation from a desktop computer.

Document Scanning

Where enterprises have installed document imaging tools for scanning low to medium volumes of ad hoc physical documents, the configuration characteristically includes one or more scanners with imaging software, integrated with a desktop computer that is either stand-alone or may be networked to shared file storage.

The types of document scanning capture scenarios that may exist for ad hoc image capture within an organization are described in Table 4.

Fax Gateways and Digital Cameras

Some organizations use integrated photocopier and facsimile and scanning stations for scanning documents. Other organizations may capture images directly from facsimile gateways or digital cameras.

Recognition Software

The imaging environment may also feature recognition technologies, such as bar code recognition, or OCR technology that converts a document into a single file of text. Intelligent Character Recognition (ICR) and Optical Mark Recognition (OMR) technologies are less likely to be involved within the workgroup category of ad hoc imaging.

Table 4: Image Capture Scenarios.

User Profile Setting	Description
Self-service	Employees access the imaging tools themselves to scan their own documents to digital image. They may not have received formal training in scanner operations or imaging functions. If trained, they may not have retained operational knowledge.
Informal group dynamics – the "specialist"	Employees within the workgroup recognize that one in their group knows how to use the scanner and rely on the "the specialist" to scan most of the documents. The "specialist" may not have received training or may have retained training knowledge.
Formal group structures – scanning operator	Scanning operator(s) is appointed to image the workgroup documents, in a full-time or part-time dedicated role, or as part of a service provided by another internal service group. Then, the assumption is that training is provided and knowledge retained.
Outsourced	Scanning is outsourced to a bureau service for conversion of workgroup documents to digital image. Then, the assumption is that the enterprise has determined that the bureau service provider has knowledge and techniques to deliver effective images. The service may be subject to a formal service agreement. It may be based on a service specification that defines the scope of work to be performed, the scanning requirements, and the quality assurance methodology through the imaging cycle.

Metadata Registration and Validation

In imaging environments that are not production level, metadata registration for images captured by scanning, facsimile gateways, or digital cameras is much the same as metadata for digital office documents. There may not be any standards for identifying and recording metadata that describe an image. There are often no naming conventions, and there is generally little rigor applied to naming of documents. Authors generally give random file names to images when saved.

However, there are published lists of controlled vocabularies that are used for describing image data, such as the *Art and Architecture Thesaurus* and *APT: The Australian Pictorial Thesaurus*. Although these controlled vocabularies have been developed principally for library pictorial images, they may be adaptable to indexing of internal graphical material.

Save and Store Regimes

Images captured via document scanning may be saved in multiple graphic file formats, such as TIF, BMP, PCX, JPG, or PNG, and this list is by no means prescriptive. The types of formats supported depend upon the imaging software used during scanning operations. Documents may also be scanned to PDF format if the imaging software supports integration with software that outputs PDF from a scanning operation.

Scanned images may also participate in an OCR process, which then typically means that two document objects may be saved, i.e., one in an image or PDF format, and the other in formatted or unformatted text. As with electronic office documents, digital images (and OCR text output) may be stored on network file systems, local drives, or other removable media.

Again, reminiscent of the way in which inappropriate document authoring techniques can result in large file sizes, inadequate imaging software or scanning techniques can also influence file sizes. The imaging software needs to support the following:

Table 5: Imaging Management Limitations Checklist.

- Existing scanners and software may be unsuitable to meet emerging requirements.
- Installed imaging software may not support an adequate range of resolutions for the scanning requirement.
- Staff that are not adequately trained or have inadequate experience in scanning and imaging techniques may undertake scanning. This may result in poor-quality images and large file sizes.
- Large file sizes created through ineffective scanning operations impact on storage space, network capacity, and backup and recovery.
- Inadequate file names may be given to images, which may hinder and slow the finding of documents.
- No digitization guidelines are established for image formatting, for example, thumbnails, archival quality, or Internet availability.

- Suitable resolutions to capture clear images yet maintain a reasonable file size;
- Effective compression algorithms that reduce the size of the image; and
- File formats that are fit for purpose, e.g., capability to save to JPG, a format suitable for publication to a Web site, or exchange via messaging systems.

We are aware of instances where poor scanning capability, knowledge, and techniques have resulted in inappropriately large file sizes.[3]

An added complexity is that the scanning operators and workgroups may not realize that this type of file size, resulting from ineffective operation, represents a problem. As with compound documents, significant storage space may be necessary. There may be repeated copying, worsening the problem. If on a network system, it is an example of the requirement to compress and back up documents.

Limitations — Image Processing

The checklist of Table 5 gives a synopsis of some of the limitations that may exist with existing imaging installations.

WEB CONTENT

The use of the Internet is now ubiquitous in those societies that have modern technological infrastructure for their citizens. Since the advent of the WWW and its rapidly evolving technologies, many enterprises developed an Internet and intranet presence. Early Web sites were characterized by simplicity in design and were "passive" in that, with some exceptions, there was little or no interaction with the consumer.

While many sites appear to be still in their embryonic phase, other sites are quite advanced with Web strategies that are designed to target consumer markets and make innovative use of the Web for business partnering or service delivery. Enterprises are now developing Web-based strategies featuring interactive Internet sites to meet the following types of imperatives:

- Going beyond a Web presence in order to give an enterprise a profile, so that visitors may at a minimum provide feedback or ask questions;
- Developing e-business initiatives for interaction and collaboration between businesses, government agencies, and customers; and

- Increasing customer expectations of responsiveness due to Internet facilitation of e-business interaction.

Intranet sites provide a universal interface to the organization's knowledge base, including access to relevant data and documents, where authorized. Enterprises also view interactive intranet sites as important to their operations, because they may offer a range of business benefits. For example:

- The capability to facilitate collaboration within workgroups and between workgroups (e.g., *eRoom*, *Quickplace* [Lotus], *Quickteam*, *Eproject*);
- The facility to reuse and share information, either knowingly or unconsciously supporting knowledge strategies within the organization;
- The opportunity for real-time updates of events occurring that may impact upon the organization's communication with shareholders, customers, or communities, as well as internal staff; and
- The capacity to reduce costs associated with the more traditional print and distribution methods.

There are different interpretations when trying to define content, with people often speaking in terms of data format published on Web servers, including HTML, images, graphics, PDF files, and similar formats. However, these data formats are essentially structured containers of information, and it is the information that is important when attempting to answer the question "what is content"? When put in abstract terms, the answers can be complex, as it is similar to asking the pervasive question "what is truth," yet two key kinds of content are facts and opinions (Chatelain & Yen, 2000).

There are a number of ways of creating and managing content for Internet and intranet Web sites. The ease with which organizations can publish information can conceal complexities associated with managing the content published on Web sites. Many sites appear to be managing documents and content using methods and systems that might expose them to risk. We shall now examine some of the ways that organizations might be managing Web content without the advantages of doing so within a controlled environment, which we propose as an integral part of the IDCM model.

Desktop Authoring Tools

There is a wide range of authoring tools used to create Web content. The tools used within enterprises may differ depending on the skills and experience of the authors assigned to prepare content and the sophistication functionality required. Tools used include:

- Text processors that produce basic markup, generally using HTML, the basic markup language for Internet browsers, or derivatives of HTML;
- General authoring applications, such as word processors, spreadsheets, or presentation tools (with content later converted to HTML/XML renditions);
- Specific Web authoring tools, such as MS *FrontPage*, Netobjects *Fusion*, Macromedia *Dreamweaver*, and *Fireworks;*
- Specific HTML or XML authoring applications (e.g., products offered by ArborText and Softquad); and

- Editing products incorporated within Web publishing and content management systems.

Content Assembly

There are a number of scenarios by which content for Web publishing is created within enterprises. For example:

- The shell or container is created using Web authoring software.
- Additional content may be derived from Web authoring or desktop productivity software.
- Additional content may also be generated from databases. This content is encapsulated within the shell or container that is created using Web authoring software.

Information for publication to Internet or intranet sites that has been developed using authoring tools is usually prepared by a limited number of end-users within an enterprise. However, as the development of Web sites becomes more complex, there is generally a requirement for more users to work on the content simultaneously. Given the frequency with which content can be updated on enterprise sites, the requirement for tools to manage the content becomes more pervasive.

The information that is to be published to Web sites may be subject to endorsement by various policy makers, such as product managers, or those in media and communications, corporate counsel, and governance. This may be reflected in authority or approval statements embedded in style sheets or individual pages. Pages must be delivered to Web sites within defined time frames (as well as be removed automatically on a specified expiry date or time).

When approved, depending on the extent to which the organization has delegated Web content preparation and publishing, the information is typically provided to a central Web administrator or group that is responsible for creating templates and content for publication that is consistent with corporate design standards.

Responsibility for information that is to be published on a business or government enterprise intranet site is often delegated to departments or workgroups authorized to publish content relevant to their own area or project's operations. The project may also contribute content for publishing at the enterprise level to facilitate information and knowledge-sharing and reduce unproductive activities.

The development of templates that may be used for Web content preparation is often managed by the Web administration function. Workgroups with a requirement for a Web site on an intranet may request a new template be created by a Web administrator, and the template will contain the style sheet. Once the new template is set up, the users within that workgroup who update the site may then use the template within a Web-authoring tool to create new pages for the site.

If the information has been created in a generic authoring application, it may then be pasted into specific Web-ready templates, additional graphics added, and the content posted to the Internet Web server. Links may also be maintained to document objects stored on file servers. As authorized users may create Web content using a variety of authoring applications, a formal standardization process is typically adopted. This process involves provision of markup for the intranet or the Internet, and may include procedures such as:

- Save or render the document as HTML or other viewable markup (e.g., XML using XLST or in cascading style sheet).
- Open the HTML/XML rendition from a Web-authoring tool (e.g., *Dreamweaver*).
- Run a markup cleanup on the markup code.
- Link markup to the relevant style sheet and template.
- Save the markup to the Web page.

Web content documents may contain the native authoring application document (e.g., MS Word), the rendition (HTML), and need to be associated with the resulting Web page created in the Web-authoring tool.

The Web administrator usually maintains the intranet Web site. Some workgroups may have Web sites on the intranet server to promote their services and provide links to relevant documents.

Dynamic HTML, Active Server Pages (ASP), and Java Server Pages (JSP) files are created with the likes of Programmers *File Editor* and Macromedia *Dreamweaver* and are used to provide extended functionality to HTML pages using scripts and ASP or JSP code. For example, interactivity with users may be provided to enable them to input to databases, which may be used to create pages dynamically.

Web pages can be created with a number of hyperlinks to other Web pages or to documents stored on network file shares.

The Web administrator may receive Web pages to be stored on the intranet from users in HTML format as email attachments or on removable media. ASP or JSP pages can be downloaded from the Internet as examples.

Content Registration and Validation

Although there are domain-naming protocols for Web sites, there are no standards for identifying Web pages. The pages are given file names by the authors when saved. There are no naming conventions specifically for such pages, though an enterprise may require Web administrators to follow any general naming conventions used by the organization. There is normally little rigor applied to the naming of documents. Sometimes, vital or important documents published to the intranet server may have their details registered in a database.

Metadata Provision

Even though metadata may not be employed with naming conventions or mnemonics, it may be embedded within Web pages to provide descriptive information about the pages in the same way as we mentioned for digital documents. In the following chapter, we give examples of metadata for content and agents (that is, characteristics of the medium) carrying the information.

There is great difficulty in providing controlled access to publicly available information on the Web, as seen with simple search engine retrieval of millions of documents. This has given rise to a number of schemes that have been applied to different document classes in order to provide greater control over description. Prominent among these are *Encoded Archival Description*, the *Text Encoding Initiative*, and *Dublin Core*, each of which has elements that are useful for document description. IFLANET maintains a site (International Federation of Library Associations and Institutions, 2002) that links to these and many other metadata schemes.[4]

Probably the most comprehensive approach to guidance for metadata description that is specifically related to document management is that being developed by the IEC (International Electrotechnical Commission, 2001b). Unfortunately, at the time of writing, agreement on the standard is yet to be reached, so we will not illustrate extracts from it here.

Save and Storage

Web pages are typically written in HTML or one of the more recent markup formats such as those within the XML framework and stored on magnetic disk. Files are saved onto the Web server into subfolders within the Web publishing structure.

Permissions may be applied on a folder level within this structure, to restrict access to Web pages from the Web browser. The server may be used to produce an index of all documents to provide fast searching facilities (provided that the Web Server supports indexing and search and retrieval capabilities).

Specific projects and workgroups may have their own folder structures. The Web administrator usually saves Web pages, but some folders have been set up as shares, and users save Web pages directly to the share.

Version Control

Assuming there is no Web content management system in place, simplistic version control measures may be applied using a variety of manual file naming standards, for example, saving an older version of a Web page with an extension of .OLD. Some authoring software automatically retains a prior copy of a file, perhaps using a file extension such as .BAK.

Renditions

Web pages may be HTML renditions of word-processor documents, spreadsheets, or other text files. Controlled documents, stored on the intranet server, may be stored as PDF renditions of the text documents stored on another file share. PDF renditions can be created that do not allow copying, only printing. They can be signed digitally and access protected in full or in part. Images of documents stored in TIF or BMP may be rendered to JPG for publication to the Web.

Compound Documents

The Web pages may include content directly taken from another file, so that when the file is updated, the contents of the Web page are updated. The Web pages may also include content directly taken from another file but that is combined at the time the Web page is requested.

Many Web pages contain embedded images, for example, through the <IMG> HTML tag, where the image referenced in the Web page is loaded into the page when the Web server requests the page.

Linked Web pages can also form compound documents, where a relationship exists between pages through the hyperlinks.

Hyperlinks

Hyperlink functionality is used within Web pages to navigate to other Web pages or documents or to another section within the same page by means of an anchor that is embedded within the markup script to provide the link. A hyperlink can be to a URL (Uniform Resource Locator or Web address) to a Web page on the same Web site or an external site, or to an image. The three types of hyperlinks are as follows:

- Relative link — The location of the file relevant to the current page, without the Web address; used for pages on the same Web site
- Absolute link — Uses the entire path to a file including the Web address and the file path; used for external Web sites
- Intra-page link — A link to an anchor (or bookmark) within the same page

Hyperlinks can be attached to text, images, or defined sections (hot spots) of images. Hyperlinks can be links to another Web page, a file, an image, or an email.

Following a hyperlink to another Web page will load the target Web page into the browser (or another browser window if defined). Following a hyperlink to a file will open the file in the Web browser, in the associated application, prompt the user for the application to open it in, or prompt the user to save or open the file. Following a hyperlink to an image will display that image in the Web browser. Following a hyperlink to email will open a new email message in the email client with the recipient email address already populated.

Hyperlinks to files from the intranet Web site are usually made to documents stored on logical file shares.

Viewing

Web pages are viewed in a browser. Web pages can be viewed by:

- Clicking on a hyperlink to a page;
- Performing a search on the intranet or Internet;
- Clicking on the hyperlink of one of the search results;
- Clicking on a hyperlink to a Web page from email or desktop office applications;
- Selecting a Web site from a list of favorites or from a browser history profile; and
- Viewing the page source directly through browsers or through linked viewers or editors.

Viewing is available to support standard office productivity tools (such as word-processing documents, spreadsheets, and presentations). Organizations may need to install special software to enable viewing of multiple types of formats, such as CAD files and TIF images.

Printing

Networked laser printers and color inkjet printers are generally available within enterprises for producing printed copies of Web pages that are accessed from intranet Web servers, the organization's own Internet site, or the global Internet community. Print formats may comprise simple copies of what is displayed on screen or the entire content of a Web page. Some Web sites provide for online reformatting of material to be printed, so the format is responsive to printout facilities such as page and paper size.

Security and Audit

Security over Web pages on the intranet server for authoring and viewing is managed via the network operating system security. Additional security can be placed on access to the Web pages by restricting access to users with valid username and password, which is applied to folder structures. Whether there are any audit procedures in place for accessing Web pages on intranet sites, will depend on rules embodied in the enterprise policy.

While organizations may provide all staff with access to either all or part of their intranet sites, they might restrict staff members from accessing the Internet. Some organizations adopt a *laissez-faire* style management approach and enable staff to access any Internet site, using logical constraints such as Internet usage policies to provide guidance on unacceptable practices.

Others may restrict access to specific sites (such as restricting the capability of staff in public agencies to only government sites for a specific jurisdiction). The opposite of the *laissez-faire* approach is distinguishable in those organizations that do not allow (all or most) staff members to access the Internet at all.

Access to Internet sites is generally audited. Reports can be derived to indicate such data as *user details*, *sites visited*, *dates*, *times*, and *access* location.

Archiving and Disposal

There are generally no archival or disposal procedures in place for Web pages unless the organization has implemented a Web content management system that supports the capability to maintain a records disposal functionality.

A number of countries have been concerned that much of the ephemeral material on the Internet may be of subsequent historical interest, and that attempts should be made to preserve it for public access. In some cases, there may even be a legislative requirement that requires a government agency to receive a copy of every document published, and this extends to digital documents.

The reality is that it is beyond the capabilities of even national organizations to undertake large-scale archiving of documents that have become obsolete or been superseded on the Web. Instead, there have been cases of policies that encourage organizations to maintain a history of their own material, with the national agency providing some recourse to material of readily identifiable historical interest.

An example is NLA's Pandora Archive (National Library of Australia, 2002). The selection policy for this archive recognizes that anything that is publicly available on the Internet is published, and that distinctions between categories of documents such as books, serials, manuscripts, working drafts, and organizational records are blurred in the digital environment.[5]

Limitations — Web Content

Table 6 provides an overview of limitations that may exist with the management of Web content within organizations.

Table 6: Web Content Management Limitations Checklist

• There is a lack of automated end-to-end business processes for managing the life-cycle of web content management from authoring through to staging, deployment, publication, updates, and archiving.
• There is a lack of version control over Web content, which carries the risk that outdated content may be published on Internet and intranet sites.
• There is a lack of synchronization between authored documents and rendered content, which exposes the organization to risk. Customers using the Internet or internal staff using the intranet may make a decision based on incorrect information.
• The system is restricted in terms of managing content preparation and publishing, while maintaining integrity.
• Web content may be static and managed through an information manager or Web administrator without association with dynamic databases because of limited server-side availability.
• The existing system is resource intensive for the Web administrator, who becomes a bottleneck in the process.
• Intranet content requires management and organization of multiple providers. (Business units that invest in Web sites and the people skills to manage sites may struggle to find relevant content and duplicate information published by other business units.)
• Web content may have to be multilingual to enable enterprises to provide interactive services to customers in different languages. The capability to deliver multilingual content may be severely hampered without tools to synchronize version updates.
• Web content may not be managed as a record, therefore creating an exposure to the organization.
• Publishing tools may not be developed with document management functionality.
• Diverse publishing tools are used across the site and are not coordinated.
• There are limited automated management tools for Web page management (expiry dates, bring-ups, etc.).
• Compound documents with many links may not have link availability monitored.
• Exponential growth of Web content rapidly overwhelms manual processes for maintaining the site.
• There are training and licensing costs for new tools for authors to be enabled to create Web content.
• Corporate visual standards are not maintained, due to the content being created by those with domain knowledge rather than graphical design professionals.

PHYSICAL DOCUMENTS

Document Creation

Physical documents may be created via a number of methods, many of which are digital in origin:

- Printed digital document;
- Printed template (form);
- Database application reports;
- Handwritten;
- Outgoing facsimile; and
- Outgoing correspondence.

In many cases, along with incoming documents, which are referred to later in the "Document Receipt" section below, the documents are aggregated on physical files for the benefit of organizational registry sections that maintain finding aids for the material. The form of the physical files can vary from generic folders to sophisticated containers bearing color-coding, labeling, and routing information.

Printed Digital Document

Enterprises provide authorized users with access to core operational systems and business support systems such as ERP Systems. They are also provided with document authoring applications at the desktop. The decision to print a document or report is generally at the discretion of the author, either for the purposes of review or to present a finalized version.

Similarly, users may print email with or without attachments. The same email may have been directed to one or more recipients. Consequently, the same document may be printed and kept by multiple users.

A user may also make annotations and notes directly on a printed document. The value of these notes and comments to the users may influence whether the document is registered and stored at the corporate, workgroup, or personal level.

Physical copies of a document may be utilized for a number of actions, such as edit, review, approval, distribution, or storage in personal, workgroup, or registry-managed filing cabinets.

With the exception of documents stored on corporate files, physical documents are generally not formally tracked or managed. Employees maintain their own information for their own specific purposes, e.g., personal folders and ring binders.

It is not uncommon in enterprises for large volumes of physical documents to be stored in workgroup or personal folders, or group filing cabinets, and the documents may never reach a corporate registry system. Documents that are referred for registration are often registered at the end of an activity.

Printed Template (Form)

In most enterprises, employees have the opportunity to utilize the digital version of form templates and complete the required details using the relevant desktop applications. However, employees may also print a blank template (as a form) and then complete the document by hand. Some scenarios are as follows:

- The physical document may be active in business processes, including manual review and approval processes. One or more employees may also record additional information against the form. For example, a *Workplace Injury* incident form contains the initial report by an employee, additional comments and recommendation by the line manager, and possibly additional comments or directives from safety personnel.
- The actual storage of physical documents created from a template may depend upon the nature of the form. Some templates created are utilized to record data and statistics that are then transcribed into a database application. Once the data is validated, the value of the document may diminish.
- The physical document may have either short- or long-term value or may be required for evidence of a transaction or to support a legal process.
- Physical documents may be produced from the incorrect version of a template, which means that incorrect information may be recorded on the printed form.
- Printed digital documents with signatures may be retained as evidence of approval.

An enterprise may have an RMS in place that pays specific attention to forms management, or has a specific forms management regime. This may apply particularly to forms that are used for capturing information from clients, for example, loan applications or insurance claims (Barnett, 1996). If this is the case, then forms should be subject to the following:

- Management of the forms, taking into account coordination of reproduction, supply, and distribution; procedural analysis for redundancy and usefulness; cost threshold; reproduction; and follow-up, such as regular checking of usefulness;
- Standards and guidelines relating to conventions like color and design consistency across forms; paper sizes; corporate identity; and data entry features such as box layout.

Database Application Reports

Reports may be generated from database applications, stored in digital form, then printed or simply printed directly from databases. Some scenarios are:

- Reports are utilized for various reasons — meetings, e.g., Workplace Health and Safety, performance indicators, monthly report attachments, and problem analysis (Helpdesk database).
- Printed copies of reports may only be stored if they are an attachment to minutes or something similar.
- Printed copies of database reports may be used for file management. For example, a printed copy of a database report may be maintained as a register for filed documents.

Handwritten

Some current scenarios for handwritten documents include:

- Enterprises may make available a template for "File Notes." This type of form is typically used for electronic file notes, but the template may be printed and used for handwritten notes.
- Handwritten notes may be retained in workgroup or personal filing systems and not recorded, although the value of and information contained on these notes may contribute to intellectual capital.
- Sketches of architectural forms may be made prior to or accompanying digitally produced drawings; it may be necessary to digitize such material for management in accompaniment with other drawing mentioned above.
- Handwritten notes are not normally registered, although they may be affixed to a document within an enterprise, workgroup, or personal file.
- "Stick-it notes" may be attached to one or more physical documents. These physical documents may be contained in a registered file.
- Handwritten forms or documents may be created to register a telephone inquiry.
- Metadata information (i.e., dates, author, and reason for creation) is not always recorded.

Outgoing Facsimile

Quite frequently in enterprises, each department or workgroup has its own facsimile machine or access to a machine in the near vicinity. Documents intended for outgoing facsimile transmission may be printed from digital documents or be handwritten. Some current scenarios include:

- A word-processor template for "Facsimile Transmission Cover Sheet" is available. The form may be used for generating facsimile documents, which are printed and then dispatched.
- An outgoing facsimile may be a handwritten note, using a printed version of the facsimile template, or simply ad hoc.
- Printed copies of facsimiles may be exchanged between departments or workgroups.
- Outgoing facsimiles may be (a) kept on a personal file, (b) kept on a workgroup file, (c) registered as a record, which would be the exception rather than the rule, or (d) discarded.
- There is generally no volume information available.

Outgoing Correspondence

Word-processing software (including letter templates) is normally used to generate outgoing correspondence items. If a user follows guidelines to determine that an item of correspondence is important and should be registered as a record, then the following mechanisms might apply:

- A printed copy of correspondence with a copy of all attachments (including facsimile or email transmission) is placed in out-trays, collected, and delivered to a Records Section (or Registry) for registration. The staff member signing the original document (e.g., correspondence) may initial these copies.
- This process varies if the authoring staff member has the physical file. The staff member may decide to retain the copy in the file folder and arrange for registration at a later date.
- An internal or outgoing item of email correspondence is printed and placed in out-trays for the Records Section or held on file for later registration into an RMS.
- Incoming mail items that are not previously registered may be referred to the Records Section for filing immediately or as time or activity permits.

Document Receipt

Physical documents may be received via:

- Inward correspondence, reports, forms, etc.;
- Incoming facsimile; and
- Documents handed over the counter.

Inward Correspondence

Enterprises may receive inward correspondence and physical reports in the following manner:

- Physical items are generally received each workday from the postal service. Items include a variety of formats — typed, handwritten, single page, multiple page, reports, drawings, maps, and compound sets of documents.

- Similar items may be received from a courier service.
- Time of daily delivery may vary from site to site.

Examples of processing that then occur include:
- There is an initial sort of the mail, where private and confidential items are out-sorted from the remainder.
- A second sort is done on the remainder, where documents are sorted into categories such as remittances, invoices, "official" correspondence, and non-core items (pamphlets, flyers).
- Items that are not official correspondence are date stamped and then sorted and distributed.
- In some cases, copies are made and filed before originals are distributed.
- Invoices are grouped together and forwarded to the Finance Department.
- All remittances are date stamped on the back of the document and registered in a database (computerized or manual register) before delivery to the Finance Department.
- Official items are readied for registration in an RMS, and then are sent for distribution.
- Items are distributed via an internal mail delivery at regular intervals during the day. Private and confidential items are distributed to the respective staff members. Some of these items may be returned to the Records Section for registration. Files and other items are also collected during this time and returned to the Records Section for filing or redistribution.

Most of these examples presume a unit that is carrying out the tasks at a corporate level. There may be repetition of this to an extent at a workgroup level, or there may be no corporate-level management of the process in smaller businesses that rely on individuals to undertake personal filing.

Incoming Facsimile

Documents may be received at one or many workgroup facsimile machines. Some scenarios may include:
- Facsimile gateways may not be installed so that all facsimiles are received in physical form.
- Facsimiles are referred directly to the addressee — no record of receipt is maintained at the facsimile machine other than the reports that can be randomly produced by the individual machine, if that machine has been installed with that option activated.
- Incoming facsimiles may be (a) kept in a personal file, (b) kept in a workgroup file, (c) registered as a corporate record, which would be the exception rather than the rule, or (d) discarded.
- Facsimiles may be received at the wrong facsimile machine and redirected to another facsimile machine, with no registration of receipt.
- There is typically no volume information available.

Documents Handed Over the Counter

Physical documents may be lodged at any location, for example, documents lodged as part of a tender process, or as part of a contract deliverable, at a customer service counter or reception area, or at a face-to-face meeting.

Registration

Overview

Enterprises typically use an RMS package for registering files, correspondence, and other hard-copy documents. The search capability is used to determine whether a file exists. Table 7 summarizes some of the processes that might apply.

However, the implementation of the RMS may not be universal within the enterprise. The following scenarios might apply:

- Some departments or sites do not use the system at all.

- Where an RMS is not used within departments or sites, there may be disparate registration and filing systems for hard-copy records. This may lead to duplication of effort involved in maintaining fragmented systems.

- Where departments or sites use the RMS, its use may not be universal among workgroups.

File Classification

Most RMS packages offer the functionality to support at least a three-tier File Classification Structure (FCS or File Plan). This represents the major aspect of metadata for physical documents, although it may be accompanied by a records finding aid that itemizes record series and provides descriptive information about each.

The RMS typically allows multiple parts for each file. Only one part may be open at any one time, but all parts are available for retrieval.

Documents are registered against the appropriate File Classification or number. The system might analyze the file open and close dates, compare the document to be registered, and allocate it to a particular part (if multiple parts exist).

The RMS generally allocates a unique File Number for each file automatically, based on the structure of FCS, and may produce a bar code representing the File Number. The bar code is typically affixed to the physical file cover. Alternatively, the number may be written on the file cover.

Table 8 provides an example of a numerical FCS using File Number = 11/4/22-02 as an instance. No physical file exists at the primary or secondary levels in this example.

The equivalent structure is shown in Figure 2.

Table 7: Registration of Corporate Documents

Condition	Record File # on Item	Request New File	Retrieve File	Create File	Dispatch File
File exists (in registry)	Y	N	Y	N	Y
File exists (not in registry)	Y	N	N	N	N
File does not exist	N	Y	N	Y	Y

Table 8: File Classification Structure Example

Classification	Description	Number Format	Example
Primary index	Main heading	11	Occupational Health and Safety
Secondary index	Subheading	4	Accidents
Tertiary index	Consecutive number	22	Motor Vehicle Accidents
Part files	Consecutive number	02	July 1997

Figure 2: File Classification Structure.

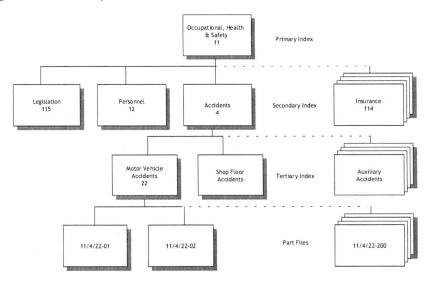

Document Registration

Core business documents are generally stamped using a rubber stamp impression, then registered in the RMS, which enables a document to be associated with a registered file, and assists in determination of the appropriate action officer to deal with the matter.

Documents are registered to the appropriate file classification or number. The system then analyzes the file open and close dates, compares that of the document registered, and allocates it to a particular part (if multiple parts exist).

The RMS generally automatically allocates a unique identifier to the document, i.e., a document number. It may also produce a bar code representing the document number, and this bar code is affixed to the physical document.

Storage of Files

Registered Files

Documents registered in the RMS are typically stored in chronological order on a physical file, which can be located in the following areas:

- In designated cabinets within centralized or decentralized Records repositories;
- On a staff member's desk or in a personal filing system;
- In an archive box location; and
- With a permanent loan officer.

Workgroup Cabinets and Folders

Documents may not be registered in the RMS and may be stored in workgroup cabinets or folders. There may be registers such as databases, spreadsheets, or word-processing documents that reference the location of documents.

If there are no workgroup registers, documents are located by browsing workgroup folders. There are no corporate controls, guidelines, etc., to assist in managing these types of storage facilities.

Personal Folders

Documents may be held in individual filing systems. Typically, there are no registers, and individuals can browse folders or rely on knowledge of document locations.

Search and Retrieval

The search and retrieval facilities for an RMS are based upon information recorded about the file or summary of a physical document. The database that records such material may be called a finding aid. A search result will return hits against files (or what in records management terms may be called a series) and physical documents, where stored metadata matches the search criteria.

Files

The search options relate to the fields or attributes contained at the file or series level, and these form the search matrix options through the use of the field codes, text, and Boolean search facilities. The most common search at the file level is on the File Title and Notes fields. The use of the wildcard option will return a greater list of results at the file level. From the results, a user may select a single entry and view the result list as well as have the ability to change or modify data held to that file.

Documents

The search options relate to the fields or attributes contained at the document level, and these form the search matrix options through the use of the field codes, text, and Boolean search facilities, similar to the file search. The most common search areas are the subject of the document, date received, and date of document.

Printing and Copying

Typical scenarios within enterprises are as follows:

- Unrestricted access to the majority of physical documents for copying
- No record of copies taken, with the exception of the Records Section, which maintains such a record
- Control advice placed on copy

Security and Audit

The security of the metadata for registered files and documents is managed by the RMS application. Physical files and documents are exposed to security risks, such as loss (involuntary or otherwise) and fire, although enterprises take every care to minimize the risk. Monthly audits of current file and document locations may be carried out using a hand-held bar-code scanner. Active records that are identified during each audit and current locations are transferred automatically from the scanning device to the RMS.

Archives

Physical records are more likely than digital records to have an established formal retention and disposal schedule in place. In some organizations, all registered files are kept. The current part, and one previous part (if applicable) of a file might be stored in the Records Section. All other files and file parts might be stored offsite in archive boxes.

The decisions about retention and disposal constitute the appraisal process that records managers and archivists undertake to:

- Establish the value of records.
- Identify the length of time for which records should be retained.
- Determine the form in which they should be retained.
- Assign the custodial and storage arrangements applying to long-term, offsite storage, or leading to destruction.
- Manage authorizations relating to destruction.

Enterprises normally establish their own schedules; however, in the case of government agencies, general schedules may be imposed upon departments by legislation that establishes the terms of reference of an archiving authority. For example, the National Archives of Canada administers a government records disposition program based upon enabling legislation.

We can make a distinction between two general types of schedule. The *functional* schedule is based upon functions such as human resources, sales, and accounting. These may typically be repeated in many divisions of large organizations or within separate government departments. The functional schedule will be applied across these for consistency of application by a corporation as a whole, or by a central organization such as a state archive. A *departmental* schedule is specific to a particular department or division and adopts the language specific to its own policy and administration.

The appraisal process leads to decisions about retention and disposal that usually take into account the following factors:

- Regulatory requirements: Legislation in areas such as evidence, taxation, financial institutions, corporations, and trade practices may require that certain types of documents be retained for stipulated periods; for public records, there are likely to be destruction requisites pertaining to privacy and security.
- Administrative: These requirements relate to planning and implementation of business processes.
- Financial: To provide accountability, these requirements are necessary.
- Historical: To show the social and political context.
- Scientific: To be able to refer to innovation and apply it to engineered environments.

Table 9: Appraisal Criteria Examples

Record Category	Appraisal Criterion	Examples
Administrative: Those records necessary for planning, organizing, and making decisions about the enterprise, and then carrying out its operations.	Evidential	• Strategic planning • Policy manual • Agenda and minutes of boards, committees, etc. • Project reports • Diaries
	Instructional	• Procedure manuals • Engineering drawings • Architectural plans • Software code
Legal: Records that demonstrate constitutions, obligations, and commitments of an enterprise and provide a foundation for decision making.	Evidential	• Contracts • Articles of association • Title certificates • Instruments of delegation of authority • Memoranda/heads of agreement
Financial: Records that provide evidence of pecuniary matters that have been conducted honestly and according to obligations.	Evidential	• Audit reports • Financial statements • Returns pursuant to legislation
Scientific: Documents that show how work leading to innovation has taken place, so that it may be repeated.	Evidential/Instructional	• Experimental results • Patent applications
Historical: Documents that show the social, political, and economic context in which the enterprise has developed.	Informational	• Promotional material • Company histories • Diaries • Still images and videos of promotions or events

A summary of such appraisal criteria is tabulated in Table 9. It should be noted that individual documents may well fall into several categories.

There may not be a computerized register for files that have been archived for a long period of time, but there is generally a physical index to the files. Individuals may also manage their own archiving and disposal for workgroup or personal documents, based upon value risk decision.

Limitations — Physical Documents

Table 10 provides some suggested limitations that may exist with the management of physical documents within organizations. However, the greatest challenge is to be integrative, in the sense that a system for managing physical documents can interact seamlessly with DMS for digital documents and provide effective records management for each and Web content management where required. Such an approach is necessary in order to minimize the fragmentation of documentary approaches that jeopardizes CRM. Perhaps Figure 3 will bring this home more forcefully.

Table 10: Physical Document Management Limitations Checklist

- Forms may be used that are based on superseded digital templates.
- Physical deterioration occurs through use and copying.
- There may be important documents stored and filed in workgroup or individual filing cabinets and not registered in an RMS or any other file or document registration system.
- Printed copies of documents may be annotated with important information that should be registered as part of the organization's intellectual capital.
- Printed reports from database applications may be used to support decision making, yet no physical or digital copies of the output may be registered and maintained. The data in the database may change subsequent to the report being produced, and the record of the output as it existed at the time of decision making is not available.
- Multiple methods and registration tools might be used for the registration and distribution of physical documents.

Figure 3: Integrated Management of Documents and their Content for Customer Service.

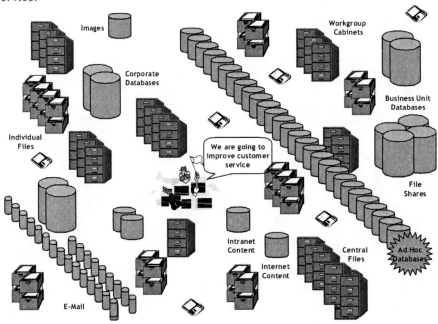

SUMMARY OF CURRENT DOCUMENT ENVIRONMENTS

In this chapter, we examined matters relating to different types of documents within organizations, so that we have been able to itemize issues relating to the handling of each type.

The major impediment to providing an efficient corporate document environment is the fragmented nature of critical business documents. For example, physical documents may be classified and stored in centralized or departmental records, or they may be held relatively unmanaged in workgroup filing systems or personal folders. Digital documents may be stored in the relatively secure network file systems under shared logical drives, or on personal computer hard disks, diskettes, or CD-ROMs.

These types of documents may contain crucial business information about an organization's assets, infrastructure, policies, practices, and operating procedures. This fragmentation represents a risk to an organization's capability to support configuration management, meet its regulatory compliance obligations, and retrieve information quickly to service its customers.

The fragmented documentation also poses risks to an organization's capability to implement new service delivery models for applications such as customer-relationship management and automated business processes that support e-commerce or e-business models.

It also provides a poor foundation for managing the development, publication, and management of Occupational Health & Safety (OH&S) documentation, impinges on the capability to delivery quality management and best practice systems, and will not support the development of knowledge-intensive management practices. In essence, instead of creating an environment in which corporate memory is available for sharing and reuse, the fragmentation inhibits shared learning within an organization.

ENDNOTES

[1]   We use "digital" and "electronic" documents interchangeably in this text: "electronic" in deference to common parlance arising from introduction of the electronic office; "digital" where we are specifically making a distinction from physical documents.

[2]   We are aware of an instance where a presentation was compiled using embedded images that resulted in a 20 Mb file. This same presentation was copied and reused at least twice, merely with text changes to the first slide to indicate the name of a different audience. The same file effectively was saved on the networked file system three times, each time consisting of 20 Mb. There may also be a tendency of users to pass such files around via email, further aggravating storage and processing problems.

In the case of presentations, it is usually more appropriate for images to be linked rather than embedded, provided that they are available via the server used to deliver a presentation for as long as the presentation is required.

For screen or Web compound documents, small images can effectively be presented at resolutions less than 100 dots per inch (dpi), and for documents to be printed, resolutions as low as 300 dpi may be acceptable.

[3]   For example, a black and white good-quality document consisting of 30 pages was scanned and output to PDF, resulting in a file size of 100 Mb.

[4]   Of particular interest are *GILS* in the United States and *AGLS* in Australia, which the respective federal governments have provided as guidance for description of government Web sites.

[5]   Examples of materials periodically stored include the Web sites for scientific conferences, sporting events of national significance, election campaigning, and government tribunal reports. It avoids organizational records and similar materials in the domain of archives and record management that are seen to be the National Archives of Australia, at least for national government materials.

Chapter 4

Characteristics of IDCM Systems

OVERVIEW

The last chapter reviewed the challenges of managing documents in business and government enterprises, where there is, as yet, no attempt to integrate different document and Web content systems. The IDCM planning model introduced in Chapter 1 proposes an integrative solution architecture to tackle an environment in which enterprises wish to manage different document systems and content distribution together. Here, we wish to elaborate on this model.

The IDCM model proposes a *management framework* and defines key *subsystems* relevant for organizations wishing to plan and implement an IDCM solution. Before we commence our discussion on the *management framework* in Part 2, we discuss the nature and characteristics of the *subsystems* relevant to IDCM solutions.

Consequently, this chapter describes the characteristics of the various subsystems available to help businesses plan integrative strategies for document and Web content management. It reviews the overall functionality offered by these subsystems and their applicability to the IDCM model. Later, in Part 3, we explore some of this functionality in more detail, and how it might be applied to managing documents and Web content.

Our objectives are to:

- Describe the subsystems available to support an enterprise's strategy for improving the management of documents and Web content.
- Show how the management of document and Web content environments is influenced by using the following IDCM subsystems:
    - Document management;
    - Email management;
    - Drawing management;
    - Document imaging and recognition technologies;
    - Workflow;

–   Web content management; and
–   Report output management (COLD).

•   Consider some aspects of the interfaces between IDCM subsystems and other business system applications.

First, however, we briefly review some essential differences between general information systems and a document repository management system, including DMS, drawing management, imaging, and Web content management systems. (For convenience, we will simply refer to these systems as an IDCM repository manager.)

An IDCM document repository manager is more than a database system, though it may include database software. A distinction between it and a general information system is that traditionally, information systems have been database-centric, whereas document and many Web content management applications are document-centric systems.

This distinction is best explained by saying that information systems have been typically implemented to capture and store data that are *derived* from source documents (usually physical documents). After data capture, the source documents might be filed in hard-copy form or microfilmed or perhaps converted to digital image. The link between the information system and the source document may be a document identifier attribute that defines the storage location of the document.

On the other hand, an IDCM repository manager is required to manage large quantities of digital documents of varying multiple formats, ranging in sizes depending on their structure and content, and the complex relationships between documents. (Such systems may also register details relating to physical documents, and may also have to synchronize versioning of physical documents with electronic renditions, and printed copies of the same documents.)

Table 1 provides a synopsis of the key distinctions between information systems, in general, and an IDCM repository manager.

Table 1: Information Systems and IDCM Repository Manager

Criterion	Typical IS	IDCM
Focus	Data	Document
Capture	Data is captured via: • Keyboard • Electronic data interchange (EDI) • Image captured using bar-code recognition, OCR, or Intelligent Character Recognition (ICR). • Smart cards	Documents and content are usually captured via several methods, including integration with: • MS Office tools • CAD tools • Email • Web-authoring and multimedia tools Digital images may be captured via: • Scanning • Fax capture • Digital cameras Metadata is captured to describe documents, including hard-copy documents that are stored in physical containers.

Table 1: Information Systems and IDCM Repository Manager (continued)

Criterion	Typical IS	IDCM
Retrieval	Search and retrieval scenarios are as follows: • Data may link to digital imaging repository or microfilm or point to a hard-copy document. • If a digital document is listed in the search result, the end user may be required to access the document separately. • There is no guarantee that a digital office document or digital drawing that is accessed from a nonmanaged repository is the current version.	Search and retrieval scenarios are as follows: • Data may be the search result (e.g., for reporting purposes). However, a search is typically invoked to retrieve a document or set of documents. • If a digital document is listed in the search result, the latest version of the digital document is accessible directly from the IDCM repository. • The end user has the assurance that the digital document and its content is the current version. • Integrated workflow may be used to route the document (or a link to the document) for purposes of collaboration or review and approval.
Devices	Typical devices include: • Client — personal computer [PC] • Servers — multiple types • Printers • Removable media (CD)	Same as typical IS +: • Scanners • Faxes • Optical disks • Display accelerators • Print accelerators
Software	Client and server operating systems Application development tools Database systems	Same as typical IS, but may also include: • Repository management software • Integrated workflow • Imaging software • Recognition technologies • Image enhancement tools • Viewing tools • Other features

DOCUMENT MANAGEMENT SYSTEMS

Terminology

In Chapter 1, we glanced at some historical considerations of what is meant by a document. Variation in understanding carries through to the present day, particularly when we link the terms document and management. Presently, *document management* may mean different things to different people, depending on their perspective. For example:

- Some people may see a *document management* system as a collection of hard-copy documents printed and stored in physical folders.
- Others may consider that a folder structure implemented with an operating system (e.g., Windows Explorer) is a system for *document management*.
- Some people use the term *document management* in the context of managing electronic documents, using the terms "Electronic Document Management Systems" or "Electronic Records Management Systems," or something similar.

- Sometimes, the term *document management* is used in the context of managing electronic documents as something distinct from systems that manage physical documents, referred to as "Records Management Systems." This is confused further by increasing recourse to "content management" to refer to management of Web-based documents and their associated architecture, versioning, and storage.

- Oftentimes, vendors who provide information systems such as ERP Systems or Maintenance Management Systems, indicate that they have *document management* capabilities. This is often not the case, as they are referring to a document register capability, not the implementation of inherent management controls over digital objects.

- Imaging systems, particularly those that make provision for version control, are regarded by some as being *document management* systems.

- Records managers, used to dealing with specific evidential document types, may have expanded their purview more widely to manage documents in general.

Therefore, the document management landscape is littered with confusing terminology, statements, and claims about functionality, and it is easy to see how enterprise executives and practitioners may get confused when trying to discern the nature and purpose of *document management*.

As is often the case in the implementation of information systems, the muddled expression in the area is a consequence of people converging on the same field from physical and digital perspectives, and mixing the terminology of management and computing. Along with the overstatement that accompanies the marketing of systems, this creates a good deal of perplexity. Wiggins (2000) has usefully elaborated on one area of differentiation by pointing out that the emphasis of document management is on its dynamic and transactional nature, whereas records management has an administrative emphasis grounded in organizing and safeguarding recorded information.

Therefore, the workflow emphasis of document management means that attention is focused upon operational needs and use, version control, individual items, and their indexing. In contrast, records management has a focus more on administrative control, particularly for regulatory requirements, retention, storage media, integrated series of items, and their classification. Nevertheless, we expect that in time, the different approaches will be harmonized.

MoReq (European Communities IDA Programme, 2001) makes a specific attempt to differentiate records and document systems. In this document, an "electronic document management system" and an "electronic records management system" are characterized in the way shown in Table 2.

We see that making the distinction between such systems is more a matter of emphasis within a particular application than of categorical distinction. Although we defined records as documents with particular characteristics, records management systems are not designed as specific types of document systems. Instead, they tend to share functionality.

Recordkeeping is always attentive to document content, so our integrative approach assumes that recordkeeping as depicted in Figure 1 of Chapter 1 is relevant to all

Table 2: Differentiating Document and Records Systems (Note: Adapted from Moreq © European Communities, 1995-2002. With permission.)

Document Management System	Records Management System
• Documents are to be modified or exist in several versions.	• Records may not be modified.
• Documents may be deleted by owners or those with assigned security levels.	• Records may not be deleted except in certain strictly controlled circumstances.
• Some retention controls may be included.	• Rigorous retention controls must be included.
• A document storage structure must be included, which may be under the control of users.	• A formal rigorous record categorization is maintained by an administrator, and it must be applied as a classification scheme.
• It is intended primarily to support day-to-day use of documents for ongoing business.	• It may support day-to-day working, but it is also intended to provide a secure repository for meaningful business records.

Table 3: Typical DMS Scenarios

Type	Typical Characteristics
Workgroup Usage scenario: Managing general office documents for a business development project within an enterprise.	• Horizontal focus • Low to medium volumes of documents • Multiple document types • Part of general office or workgroup productivity system • Images treated as another data type • Fax gateway capture and image edit capabilities • May integrate with ad hoc workflow or document routing • Costs depend on volume of documents, size of workgroups, and functionality requirements
Application Specific Usage scenario: Managing Quality Management System documentation in a pharmaceutical organization.	• Vertical focus • Medium to large volumes of documents • Specific document types (+ managing general documents) • Complex applications • May integrate with business operational and administration systems • May integrate with production workflow or ad hoc document routing • Costs depend on size of workgroup and complexity of requirement
Enterprise Usage scenario: Managing vital and important operational and administrative documents within a business or government enterprise.	• Horizontal focus • Large volumes of documents • Multiple document types • May integrate with ad hoc workflow or document routing • Specific applications may integrate with production workflow • Specific applications may be integrated with business operational and administration systems • Expensive – large capital investment

types of documents and their content, whether or not the material is digitized or available via Internet or intranet sites.

Categorization

There are so many different types of business usage scenarios and potential applications within an enterprise that to place document management systems into discrete categories is problematical. Typically, however, we find that the systems are implemented within enterprises for the following reasons:

- At a departmental or project level for managing all different types of relevant documents associated with the department or project — we shall classify this type of document management implementation as "workgroup".

- Across a number of functional boundaries for managing discrete classes of documents as part of a specific business process, or range of processes — we shall classify these implementations as being "application specific".

- At an enterprise level for managing all types of vital and important documents across multiple business processes — we shall classify these as "enterprise".

Table 3 provides an overview of the typical characteristics of these types of document management implementation.

Too much focus on trying to categorize document management systems can lead to confusion, because, for example, an "application-specific" implementation may be restricted to a "workgroup". A number of workgroups may make up an "enterprise," and so on. The actual application of document management within an enterprise relates specifically to the requirement of the organization.

Integration

As the name implies, the IDCM model aspires to combine in a seamless manner the many features of a document system. We believe an integrative framework best describes the type of solution that is required to manage designated documents throughout the continuum of their existence, and it should have the following properties:

- Enable document production, naming, and registration following enterprise standards for physical and digital documents.

- Implement repository (storage) management controls (versioning, access) over electronic documents, regardless of digital format (including images).

- Register and track physical documents, including film-based documents and similar objects (e.g., analogue videocassettes, audiotapes), as well as digital documents.

- Support a file plan and disposal schedule so that relevant documents (digital or physical) are managed as records of business transactions.

- Support integrated workflow and routing for automation of document review and approval processes.

A DMS must manage the complex relationships between documents, including version synchronization between electronic and hard-copy documents, and provide search capabilities that reduce the effort involved in trying to locate and apply institutional documents when they are promptly required according to routine or ad hoc demand.

A DMS, therefore, must manage the corporate memory in respect to document forms of business records. Making it work properly is an essential part of making effective use of the recorded part of an enterprise's intellectual capital. It is, therefore, a basic tool for handling knowledge in the sense that we described knowledge management in Chapter 1.

Functionality

The general features that we seek in document management systems include:

- Document production and capture;
- Version control;
- Metadata management;
- Classification;
- Check-in/check-out;
- Complex document relationships;
- Security of documents;
- Document review and approval;
- Search and information retrieval;
- Viewing;
- Archives and disposal;
- Digital signatures;
- Architecture; and
- Effective interfaces with other systems.

In the previous chapter, we looked at the characteristics of many of these features. Here we describe them in terms of advances that support integration.

Document Production and Capture

Most enterprises have a basic requirement for integration with their common office applications, specifically, office productivity software and email systems. The general aim should be to provide direct access to the DMS functionality from within the native desktop applications (word processor, spreadsheet, email, presentation graphics, and project management software).

The DMS might also be required to provide integration with template-based tools in authoring applications such as word processing, to enable business users to capture key information relating to a wide range of template-initiated documents, such as reports, memoranda, minutes, agendas, letters, faxes, and specifications. In the case of systems that are basically Web-oriented for content management, the documents may be produced almost entirely from templates.

Documents are represented using a Document Description Language (DDL). Typically, this may lie behind a word-processing program, and the program may provide the means of producing the document in a choice of renditions such as HTML or PDF.

Table 4: Considerations for Choice of DDL

- Script support — although roman characters may be represented readily, are there provisions for scripts such as Arabic or Thai or Korean, and can these scripts be integrated within a document?

- Structure — is explicit representation of the document structure possible? A DDL language that permits structural markup such as *title*, *chapter*, and *table* independently of form markup for margins, font sizes, etc., permits more flexible subsequent rendition and access possibilities.

- Style — are multiple styles available through facilities such as style sheets, and does the DDL make provision for application of these so that styles may be imposed concurrently?

- Complex documents — how effectively does the DDL provide for linkages to external objects that may be in other renditions or may require them, so that these can be used to contribute to a compound document (see below)?

- Metadata — if metadata are to be incorporated within documents or stored in an external database, does the DDL provide for default creation where possible and straightforward prompted creation where necessary?

Wilkinson et al. (1998) highlighted the need to select a DDL first and the software that supports it second. Because the data will probably have a longer life than the software, it may be used in several software environments, and the power of representation of the DDL may be more important than the functionality provided by the software. They describe a number of considerations for choosing a DDL. We summarized the expressive aspects of these in Table 4.

Other factors that may affect the choice of DDL relate to the environment in which it is to operate. For example, how easy is it to export, transforming documents to alternative renditions; or import, particularly when there may be a significant retrospective conversion from a legacy systems required. Other such factors include the facility with which documents may be updated and presented.

It is often necessary to capture documents produced externally to associate them with internal documents or to incorporate them within internal series. These may be introduced in a variety of ways, such as through local or wide area networks, via email, or on digital disks in a variety of formats. The bulk load of electronic documents, including drawings, from current file systems may be required. The metadata (see section under metadata, following) should be matched with the relevant electronic document objects during the data migration process.

Depending upon the business requirements, there may be a need for the DMS to capture electronic drawings by integration with CAD tools such as *AutoCAD* and *Microstation*.

Whatever the document source, the registration function should provide for a standard naming and classification scheme, and other metadata elements provided at the time of document creation.

Full-text indexing (which we illustrate in Chapter 12) is often incorporated in a DMS to establish search files for formatted or unformatted text. Third-party tools that are integrated with the DMS typically accomplish full-text indexing. The full-text indices are used to facilitate searches on the "content" of a document.

Version Control

Version control means that changes to an electronic document will not destroy the original, and that documents are effectively identified. At a minimum, this is by ensuring that a file management system maintains version numbers when successive versions of documents have the same name. However, the documents may also incorporate metadata (information about themselves) to describe the following:

- Creator: Who produced or contributed to the document.

- Content description: The subjects covered in the document.

- Origination date: When it was commenced.

- Completion date: When it was completed.

- Connected documents: Other documents associated with the one being created.

- Applications: Software used in association with the document.

- Processes: Business processes with which the document is associated (for example, inventory management, policy development, or legal cases).

The registration process that uniquely identifies the document should provide as much as possible for automatic creation of default metadata such as date, time, business process, and creator, and make the registration and naming information readily visible to the user.

Changes to documents will result in new versions of those documents. Some DMS support the capabilities for major and minor versioning.[1] This functionality may suit some business requirements.

Although there may be many versions of a document in the DMS, users will normally only see the current version. Older versions of documents are retained for audit and reference purposes. Older versions must be specifically requested, in which case, it is possible for an authorized user to locate and retrieve a previous version of a document or to "back up" to a previous version if the current version is found to be inappropriate.

A version should not be duplicated. If it is used in different applications, its use may be achieved by pointers from the files in those applications.

Each version of a document typically has its own security setting, enabling restrictions on user access, i.e., they are only able to see the current (or specific older) version of a document.

Although most document management systems make at least some provision for versioning, there has been a tendency with some Web-based systems emphasizing content to minimize provision for versioning or to permit such facilities to be deactivated. It is difficult to see how this could be accepted within a DMS because of the importance of identification for regulatory and audit purposes.

Metadata Management

The information about a document that assists in its management may take a number of forms. In general, these can be information about the content of the document or information about the document as an agent of content delivery. In summary, these metadata are:

- For *document as an agent*:
  - Description: For example, how many words are in it; when it was created?
  - Responsibility: For information relating to who created the material and who is accountable for it at individual and department levels; this may

also provide for provenance tracking if the document has passed through various areas.

– Administration: This may involve elements like access or appraisal based upon retention scheduling for retention or disposition.

– Configuration: To provide descriptions to assist with processing of data such as file format, type, or record size that are typically carried in header or label information of digital records.

– Connections: To point to any relationships between a document and other physical or digital documents referenced in the DMS; alternatively, the relationship can be to resources that control the content of information in a particular field, such as a thesaurus of descriptors or an authority file of organization names.

– Conditions of use: For elements that describe or link to availability statements, such as a *rights management* element if intellectual property is involved.

• For *document content:*

– Topic: This may be expressed as keywords or descriptors from controlled vocabularies that are used to describe subject matter, as well as by a classification scheme which may be developed by hierarchical categories.

– Coverage: This explains how the intellectual content encompassed spatially (for example, by geographical area or map coordinates) or temporally (time period that applies to the content).

– Role: As used, for example, to explain in which context the subject matter is applied, such as the business functions that it supports.

The individual metadata requirements of organizations are varied, and the DMS, while providing as much automatic metadata as possible at time of creation, must also provide for straightforward user modification of metadata at time of creation or subsequently.

The DMS should be able to bulk import metadata from current document registers (depending on the supported formats) and ensure effective and accurate population of the attribute data within the DMS. The DMS may also be integrated with a scanning hardware/software capability, so that scanned correspondence and reports are captured and managed as electronic objects within the DMS repository.

There may also be the requirement for the DMS to register metadata relating to physical documents and to track physical documents so that a metadatabase of descriptions of physical and electronic records is maintained.

Classification

Classification is an important activity for creating and managing metadata, so we deal with it separately here, particularly, because it is fundamental to the records management organization of the enterprise's documents.

The classification scheme requires an administrator who must be responsible for the development of the notation (the way the classification scheme is expressed) and the extension of hierarchies. A DMS should provide for inheritance of relevant metadata from upper levels of a hierarchy as new classes are opened at lower levels. Only the administrator should have privileges for file reclassification.

The *MoReq* specification (European Communities IDA Programme, 2001) that provides model requirements for the management of electronic records, emphasizes many provisions for classification, including the following:

- The need to support a minimum hierarchy of three levels;
- The need to provide a browsing capacity of the classification structure when a graphical user interface is employed;
- The need to enable the definition of multiple classification schemes for simultaneous application; and
- The ability to link a thesaurus to the classification scheme.

Therefore a taxonomy, whether or not it has been created within the enterprise, should have its notation (the codes that represent the classification scheme) expressible and expandable within a DMS.

Check-in/Check-out Documents

The DMS must feature facilities that avoid update conflict by the implementation of check-in/check-out services and management of editing changes to documents via version control.

When a user wants to change a document in the DMS, they must "check out" the document. The check-out feature locks the document (preventing other changes, but not preventing read-only access) and makes a working copy of the file for the user. The system also needs to identify that the document is being revised and maintain a distribution list of users who will be notified when a revision has occurred.

The original document in the DMS vault is never edited directly. Once the user has completed the changes to a document, the document is "checked in." Check in creates a new version of the document in the DMS and copies the changed working copy from the user to the DMS vault, and then releases the lock on the document. The original copy is not removed from the DMS vault, and it is not directly modified.

Complex Document Relationships

The internal structure of a single electronic document may consist of embedded objects (other documents) and multiple linked electronic office documents. This type of complex relationship between documents is frequently referred to as "compound documents."

The parent document provides organization and structure to the component documents that it contains. The document components can be updated independently or can be updated simultaneously; and they can be reused, in other words, forming part of more than one parent document.

The support for a compound document metaphor that enables integrity to be maintained of multiple bidirectional relationships between documents is likely to be a requirement for most enterprises. Management of this process can be expected to include:

- Reminders to modifiers of documents about other documents that may incorporate the modified one, so that a decision may be made about incorporating new versions;

- Routine linkage checking of anchors from within documents to external links so that a document administrator can be notified if compound documents are losing their component parts.

Furthermore, a DMS should provide the capability to maintain multiple renditions of the same document. For example, a version of a word-processing document may be saved in HTML or PDF format, for publishing, review, and approval processes. It is generally essential that the various renditions of a document be linked to the same version of the original document.

Security of Documents

Once a document is registered in the DMS, it is normally stored in its native format, protected, and controlled in a vault or repository. The vault provides the following integrity:

- The file that contains the content for the document is under control of the DMS and cannot be directly changed by any user, without system-imposed control procedures.
- The DMS will preserve a history of vaulted documents as they are modified over time.

The DMS must ensure that:

- Accessibility to folders and documents is restricted to only those personnel authorized to view or retrieve the documents.
- Individual users and groups will only be able to see those documents they are authorized to access.
- The types of actions that users and groups can perform against a given document are managed by access control.
- An administrator can modify user profiles so that access may be varied at file or record level according to individual or group user, function, document class, or date.
- Audit trails are maintained to the extent that compliance with regulatory requirements may be demonstrated, and the trails should be provided at different levels of aggregation (records, files, file groups); because of the extent of trail data that may be created, there may also be a need for periodic movement of older audit trail data to offline storage.
- Capture ad presentation of attempts by users to access denied records must be available.
- Varied reporting mechanisms should be available to enable presentation by user, classification group, or record.

It is beneficial if the DMS user or group access security, backup, and recovery processes are integrated with an enterprise's network operating system environment.

Document Review and Approval

The DMS should feature document-centric workflow functionality that enables controlled distribution of documents for review and approval. As the document proceeds through its continuum of use, it should be associated with appropriate people and project scheduling. Quite often, the workflow offered by vendors is not an inherent component of the core DMS but an additional module or third-party product, in which case, it is desirable that it integrates transparently with the DMS. The workflow should also integrate transparently with the enterprise's email system for notification of work packets and transmission of links to documents held in the DMS repository.

Review facilities should include the ability to post comments to a document without changing the document and the ability to schedule documents into appropriate publishing (or intranet/Internet availability) queues.

Search and Retrieval of Documents

One of the primary tenets for acquiring and implementing a DMS is to greatly reduce the time that users spend in locating and retrieving documents. The enterprise philosophy should be such that the DMS repository will be the only place users can be certain to find all documents of importance to business processes, including vital records.

The DMS should provide easy-to-use "intuitive" facilities for users to initiate searches that involve simple syntax and complex constructions, depending on their requirements.

Simplicity in searching may be achieved by the use of integrated menus within the authoring applications, hot buttons and shortcuts into application of choice, or DMS repository.

Users should be able to search the following:

- Attribute information (owner, document title, format, etc.), which may be drawn from metadata assigned when versioning the document;
- Combination of attributes (e.g., owner and date authored);
- Words in the text ("content") of the document; and
- Combination search covering attribute and content search.

The range of retrieval interfaces to facilitate this process varies greatly. For example, the search may be invoked by:

- Sets and logic that assume a complex search may be built using terms for which the intermediate results are stored in sets, and these sets may be referred to and recombined in different ways. The terms within sets and the sets may be combined using logical operators AND, OR, NOT — also known as Boolean operators or Boolean searching.
- Commands, assuming that the user is familiar with specific retrieval commands, can invoke searches. For example, it may be possible to expand hierarchies of file series or generically related terms by using an *expand* command. A search such as *Expand litigation* may be able to retrieve documents that include metadata such as "test case."
- QBE (query by example) assumes that the user fully or partially completes the detail of a formatted screen and that the software finds material that matches the attributes presented and displays them in the same format.

- Content search features can also be utilized, for example:
    - Truncation that permits the user to stem words that are being searched, generally using a wildcard symbol such as "*" or ":" — for example, "legislat*" will find occurrences of "legislation" or "legislators" or "legislating".
    - Proximity operators that permit the user to specify how close together words should be: "freedom (w2) information" may indicate that "freedom" must appear with two words of "information."
    - Field limitation, so that if the document content and metadata are separately identified, then searching can discriminate the context of a term's use; for example, Johnson/CRE would return documents created by Johnson, and Johnson/IDX might return documents about Johnson.

In some cases, a DMS enables regular searches undertaken by the users at their individual desktops to be saved, named, and stored until no longer required. Upon reactivating the stored search, the results are updated to ensure that any additional new information and new documents are displayed.

The search capability should provide the capability to include drawings and references to hard-copy documents in the search results list.

It should be possible to display accompanying search metadata with results lists as required, and to display or print summary results lists rather than entire documents when necessary. These lists should be presentable in various sorted forms based upon metadata elements chosen for sorting, such as creator, date of origin, etc.

Viewing

The system should enable enterprises to view documents in their native format, so that a word-processing document or spreadsheet is viewed by the associated word-processing or spreadsheet application. However, a viewing tool may be required where:

- The repository contains electronic document formats that are not supported by the available desktop applications.
- There is a specific requirement for enabling document contents to be displayed without loading the native authoring tool.

In many cases, a DMS utilizes a third-party viewing tool that enables a large number of office document formats to be viewed. Depending on the functionality, some tools provide markup and annotation tools that enable document reviewers to markup changes to documents.

Where drawings are maintained in the repository, it is common that vendors offer a separate viewer to enable drawing users to view, red line, markup, and annotate drawings.

Metadata held within a document, or referring to the document but held in an external database, should be able to be viewed concurrently with the document.

Archives and Disposal

If an enterprise maintains disposal metadata arising from appraisal information for documents, then this should be associated with document management procedures.

Examples of these metadata include the approval routing for particular documents and the scheduling information that may show how long they should remain online, when they should be moved to offline storage, copied to other media, or destroyed.

The scheduling information is likely to be based upon retention periods established from appraisal of document groups. This was summarized in Table 9 of Chapter 3. However, as has been pointed out by Kennedy and Schauder (1998), there are special problems in assessing the value of electronic records and managing their retention. These apply particularly when individuals regard the documents they produce as unofficial or private, rather than corporate, and they therefore exercise their own prerogative about how to retain or dispose of them. Other factors include:

- The easy loss of information from personal computers arising from inadequate backup regimes.
- The deletion of earlier generations of files by individuals from personal file spaces, because they do not appreciate the potential evidential or historical value.
- The difficulties of retrieving files that have been created by individuals without reference to standard corporate naming principles.
- The holding of information in a technologically dependent environment, which may lead to the information only being read with the associated hardware and software used to create it. It is important when archiving data to ensure that it may be read indefinitely, which is where structured scripting languages such as XML may prove more useful than, for example, proprietary word-processing formats.
- The need to determine the value of electronic records in the context of the system within which they are used, possibly making use of metadata, such as who authorized or created them or what transaction they took place within.

A DMS can link such people or dates within a schedule database to automatically produced reports that are actionable. In this respect, a retention or disposal schedule may function like a data dictionary, in that external metadata are used to control decisions applying within actual document files.

EMAIL MANAGEMENT SYSTEMS

We described the common characteristics of enterprise document environments in Chapter 3. We noted that there were limitations to the ways in which organizations manage their incoming and outgoing emails. In particular, we noted that emails may contain vital records of business transactions and decisions and that they are not generally well managed. They may be left in an end user's mailbox, deleted individually or in a group (including whole collections), or archived to a personal file. The transaction, unless printed and registered on a file, or otherwise recorded, is not known to corporate memory.

There are compelling requirements to store corporate, workgroup, and individual email messages or attachments where email is required as evidence of a business transaction, or where required by the user to be kept as a record. Given the volume of emails and the potential growth of this form of communication, users must have a simple means of saving emails (including email attachments) and capturing relevant metadata.

There is a range of options offered by IDCM systems for capturing email. For example, solution scenarios may include the following:

- Direct capture — This is the automatic capture of incoming and outgoing emails within a managed repository. These types of solutions are often referred to as an *email management system* or *email archiving solution.*
- End user capture — This is an integration of email client software with a repository that manages all types of digital documents (e.g., DMS).

When considering the types of solutions that best fit the organization, the most appropriate option is that application of the technology that best suits the business needs for managing email.

Direct Capture

An *email management system* or *email archiving solution* intercepts incoming and outgoing emails. They operate by taking a copy of incoming and outgoing messages that are managed by the email messaging system (e.g., MS Exchange, Lotus Notes Mail, and GroupWise).

They use customized business rules to "filter out" email that may not have a business context. These types of tools can filter out unwanted email such as spam and email received from news lists or information bulletins.

Products generally feature autocategorization, with tools ranging from simple to more complex applications. The systems have the capability to categorize based on metadata such as that contained in a header to an email message, such as the *to, from, subject,* and *date* fields in a message header. Some systems offer the capability to categorize based on information contained in the email message and attachments.

Other solutions categorize using the content and context of email by applying techniques, such as learning by example from previously processed email. These types of solutions might be valuable for capturing statistical information differentiated by the types of requests made by customers. For example, the statistics can aid call centers to monitor turnaround time frames for responding to email requests, or facilitate trend analysis (results of marketing campaigns).

These types of systems also have the capability to integrate personal mail archives that are often stored in personal shares on network file systems, local hard disks, or removable media. Some offer data compression techniques to help reduce the costs of storage.

Search options include the capabilities to search messages and text attachments. Depending on the capabilities of the system, searches might be invoked from an email client, desktop client application, or Web browser. The search results might be viewed, printed, forwarded using the email client, or perhaps faxed to a recipient.

Some systems are also able to apply rules defined in disposal authorities so that emails are purged from the system within a legal framework. In some cases, different retention schedules can be applied to specific categories of email.

End User Capture

This approach may best suit enterprises that do not wish to save all email sent and received into the email management repository, leaving it to the user to identify emails that need to be saved to a managed repository, typically a DMS. The organization should provide the user with defined policy and guidelines to clarify the types of emails that need to be captured as a record in the DMS repository. The end user would capture relevant business-related email into the DMS and might be prompted to make a decision, i.e., when sending an email.

The repository would need to tightly integrate with the existing enterprise email client software. There may be a number of desktop client interfaces to the repository, such as a separate client interface for managing technical and engineering drawings, and one for managing digital office documents. In those instances, it would be necessary for the email system to integrate with both interfaces to enable easy capture and search and retrieval of emails saved to the repository.

DRAWING MANAGEMENT
Business Models for Drawing Production

Many enterprises have a requirement to develop and maintain drawings as part of their engineering processes for planning, designing, constructing, and maintaining infrastructure and items of plant. There are many types of drawings, such as structural, electrical, plumbing, mechanical or civil, or piping and instrument diagrams. Enterprises have adopted a range of business models, based on their specific requirements for creating, editing, and publishing drawings. Some of these models are summarized in Table 5.

The Requirement to Manage Drawings

Irrespective of the business model adopted by enterprises, the production of drawings is a complex process that may be hindered by the pressures placed on it by reduced delivery cycles, regulatory demands, and the requirement for service providers

Table 5: Business Models for Authoring Drawings

Model	Description
Internal	The enterprise maintains its own drawing office(s), as part of an engineering department, or similar, for authoring, modifying, and publishing drawings. Authorized consumers release the drawings for viewing via defined engineering change processes.
Hybrid	The enterprise develops and maintains some drawings but may outsource other types of drawings (for example, new plant) to business partners or services providers, such as contracting companies. In these circumstances, the contractor develops drawings and provides them to the enterprise for review, approval, and viewing by authorized consumers. The contractor supplies an electronic drawing registry file (spreadsheet or database to assist bulk importing).
Project	The enterprise has a relationship with a business partner (engineering consultants, drawing contractors) to develop drawings for a specific project (such as a construction project). The business partner develops drawings and provides them to the enterprise for review, approval, and viewing by authorized consumers. The ownership of the drawings for long-term maintenance may vest with the enterprise or the enterprise's customer or business or alliance partner.
Outsource	The enterprise has an outsourcing arrangement (or external contract) for drawing development and maintenance functions to be managed by an organization, such as an engineering services company or an application service provider. The enterprise may make minor modifications to drawings or may develop new drawings for specific purposes.

to adhere to quality management systems. The production of drawings is an essential component of the engineering process, and there is a requirement to find drawings quickly, potentially for reuse, develop the drawings, and route them for review and approval to keep pace with project time lines.

In many production drawing environments, a single project may utilize a number of drafting officers to develop a set of drawings relevant to the project requirements. There may be division of labor principles so that specific drafting officers may be assigned to develop electrical drawings, while others are assigned to develop other types of drawings. For a large project, such as a major infrastructure construction, the division of labor may further apply to specific buildings or to specific floors.

In these types of drawing office situations (which may be physically located in different buildings or spread all over the world with 24-hour operations), there is a need to locate drawings quickly. There is a need to develop or modify complex technical materials, often in collaboration with project team members, business partners, or service providers. There is also a requirement to deliver drawings within stringent project time frames. The environment in which drawings are developed makes it compelling for drawing management policies, strategies, and systems that support quality management systems.

However, few enterprises are administering their drawings and technical documents in a well-managed environment. Most organizations that create or modify drawings make use of CAD tools for authoring and store digital drawing objects on networked file systems, local hard disk, or removable media. In this respect, we provided a list in Table 3 of typical limitations that apply when managing drawings. These are exemplified by behaviors such as the following:

- It is not unusual for authors to store digital drawings on local hard disk while editing, because a digital drawing may be a large file size, and end users may find it slow to download the drawing from a networked file server. This perceived delay might be due to file size or network traffic or both. [It may be claimed that these drawings are generally working drafts, but there may be concern from the perspective of logical (access) and physical (disk crash) security.]

- The digital objects may be quickly copied and distributed to multiple file systems and other storage media without the enterprise maintaining a record that multiple copies of the same digital object may exist uncontrolled in multiple repositories.

- Organizations tend to retain physical copies (paper and microform) of drawings as well as maintaining digital drawings. There may be multiple copies of the same drawing maintained at set locations within the enterprise, indeed within the same department, such as a project.

- Drawings may be created digitally but revised manually, for example, in the case of a minor revision or quick markup. Confusion can exist as to which is the primary copy of the drawing. Also, a drawing or sketch may be created or revised manually or by using an authorized CAD package, in which case, the drawing may not be published to or managed in a secure repository.

- The processes involved in managing the revision synchronization between digital and physical objects are labor intensive and time consuming. A revision change to a digital drawing may involve the extraction, removal, and replacement of physical drawings in multiple set locations.

- There is a tendency to utilize drawing registry systems of some type for registering drawings, but these tools do not implement management controls over digital drawing objects and may not offer facilities to manage revision synchronization between digital and physical objects.
- Manual workflow methods or messaging or collaboration tools are used for review and approval processes associated with drawings and technical documentation (such as specifications), and for collaborating with business partners and service providers.
- Access to digital drawings may be achieved via search or browse of folder structures, and in some cases, via intranet Web pages mapped to digital objects in the file system.
- There is a general move within enterprises to convert physical drawings (paper, microform) to digital image for accessibility (and potential reuse).

Use of a drawing management software package can provide the functionality for managing digital and physical drawings, and the synchronization between both types of formats. It is a strategy to address a number of the limitations.

There is often confusion within enterprises on the subtle differences between software systems that might meet the criteria for being categorized as either:

- A drawing registry system (or engineering file system) — primarily developed to register and track physical drawings; or
- A drawing management system[2] — primarily developed to register and manage digital drawings as well as register and track physical drawings.

We shall differentiate the two types of systems before we take the opportunity to review the capabilities of drawing management software.

Drawing Registry Systems

The term drawing registry system can be applied to an information system that enables users to register or index physical drawings in a database. Users can register data that describes a drawing. Generally, they also provide for generation of transmittals for issue of new documents, and management of the distribution of revisions to drawings and technical documents. They may also have the capacity to register a digital drawing in the database, but they do not implement automated controls over revisions of digital drawings.

The descriptive metadata includes drawing number, title, revision number, author, discipline checker/approver, approval date, and a range of other relevant elements. The systems typically provide a reference to the location of hard-copy drawings and may include a reference to the pathname(s) where the digital drawing objects are stored. They may or may not be able to provide a hyperlink to a digitally stored drawing.

Examples of software tools that are effectively "drawing registries" are:

- Specific drawing applications that store metadata relating to drawing objects but do not implement automated controls over digital drawing objects;
- Systems with broader application, such as ERP, Asset or Maintenance Management that store relevant metadata but do not implement automated controls over

digital drawings (These types of systems may interface with third-party document management systems that implement controls over digital drawing objects.); and

- Tables developed in productivity tools, such as desktop (PC) databases, spreadsheets, and word-processing documents, which enable end users to record details of drawing holdings.

Some vendors try to position these types of products as "drawing or document management systems." However, these types of systems do not implement automated features for check-in/check-out, version control, drawing revision numbering, or workflow for electronic authorization and management of the status of drawings in their transition through general drawing life-cycles. Consequently, vendor marketing rhetoric adds further confusion to the requirement for managing drawings.

Some organizations adopt a tactic of developing or acquiring software that provides a link between the drawing registry and the digital objects stored on a file system. This link can be achieved via a Web interface that hyperlinks metadata to the digital objects in the file system. The metadata might be an extract of the metadata stored in the drawing registry and can be refreshed at specified intervals. Elements of this approach are as follows:

- It enables a user to access the intranet browser, search drawing metadata, and obtain access to the required digital drawing object(s) quickly.

- There is no guarantee that the correct revision of a digital drawing is published to the Web because of the lack of adequate drawing management capabilities to assure automated revision control.

- It may be useful for an environment where drawings are fairly static, on the proviso that enterprises are prepared to accept the risks associated with lack of inclusive drawing management capabilities, but the risks would be increased in a dynamic drawing environment.

- The lack of comprehensive drawing management capabilities over digital objects may result in users having a lack of confidence in the interface and resorting to confirmation of the validity of documents by referencing physical controlled (or uncontrolled) copies of drawings.

- When users validate digital drawing objects by accessing physical controlled copies, then the interface does not support the information management principle of having timely access to accurate information.

Drawing Management Software

A drawing management system may be distinguished from a drawing registry system in that the software implements automated management controls over the digital drawing objects maintained within a vault-like repository and offers features such as check-in/check-out, automated revision numbering processes, and version control. The status of drawings is maintained as they pass through the engineering change life-cycle. Such systems also provide the capability to register and track physical copies of controlled drawings, and offer functionality to help synchronize digital and physical drawing objects.

The software evolved out of the opportunity to capture and manage drawings created by CAD productivity tools and usually provides as core functionality, automated features for check-in/check-out, version control, automation of drawing numbering, and drawing revision numbering. The software may also feature electronic document review and authorization, history logs, audit trails, and similar functionality.

The packages continue to evolve to meet changing business and technical requirements, and they may feature a diverse range of additional functionality (such as the capability to transition the status of drawings and combine workflow and life-cycle processes), as suppliers position their products for greater market share through richness of functionality.

Some products have evolved independently of DMS that implement controls over general office documents. Others have been developed to integrate with an existing "mainstream" DMS. Consequently, we now see drawing management capability offered as follows:

- Packaged software that is an application in its own right, i.e., implements its own client–server architecture, communications, and security module.
- Package software that integrates with one or more general DMS to provide those systems with the functionality to manage drawings.

The functionality offered by drawing management systems includes:

- Capability to manage electronic and hard-copy drawings, as well as technical specifications and manuals;
- Management of incoming and outgoing transmittals so that a record is maintained of such transactions involving drawings;
- Integration with CAD tools so that electronic drawings may be captured from within the authoring application (The CAD tools and versions supported depend on the drawing management software.);
- Capability for title block and metadata registration and updates to be synchronized, thereby maintaining metadata integrity between the information and minimizing data entry effort;
- Management of the referential integrity of parent–child relationships between multiple drawings; and
- Provision of viewing, red line, markup, and annotation functions for drawings and management of markups as separate objects to the source drawing.

Some drawing management software products have evolved to the extent that they now offer the functionality to manage digital office document collections, including complex document relationships and physical office documents. They may also offer records management functionality, either as a core component or an integrated product.

Drawing Management Solutions

The types of opportunities for improving drawing management within enterprises are a mix of business solution options and technical solution options. For example, enterprises may opt to do the following:

- Acquire a drawing management system.
- Acquire a DMS with drawing management capability.

- Outsource drawing management functions to an external application service provider and view (and perhaps markup) the current revisions of drawings via Web services.
- Maintain an existing environment.

We will examine these options in turn.

Acquire a Drawing Management System

This product has most likely evolved from a core focus of providing management controls for digital drawings generated by CAD productivity software. It should provide the functionality for managing digital and physical drawings, and the synchronization between both types of formats.

Enterprises may be interested in seeking a drawing management product that has the capability to implement controls over general office documents and provide workflow and records management capability, or be satisfied with acquiring a package that might be integrated with an enterprise document management solution at some later stage.

If the drawing management software is to be considered for all-purpose document management software, then each candidate software package must be evaluated against the requirements specification defined for digital and physical office documents, as well as the specification for drawing management.

Acquire a DMS with Drawing Management Capability

The enterprise focus may be on acquiring a DMS that offers functionality in all areas of digital document management, including drawings, and has the capability to track physical documents and manage documents that are records.

Most DMS solutions offer the ability to "manage drawings," but the actual functional capabilities of a DMS to manage drawings depends upon the business requirements. It is not simply a matter for an enterprise to state briefly that a DMS must be able to "manage drawings," because this type of statement is open to wide interpretation.

A DMS might provide (a) basic drawing management functionality, (b) rich drawing management functionality, or (c) something in between, and the actual solution required will depend on the enterprise's requirements for drawing production, distribution, and publication. Table 6 gives an example of the differences that DMS packages might offer for drawing management, using the two scenarios of core document management services and extended functionality.

Depending on the evolution in the development of candidate DMS solutions, suppliers may offer drawing management functionality that is a core element (i.e., inherent within the architecture) of the DMS, or an integrated drawing management package that provides the required drawing management functionality, potentially sourced from a third-party supplier. Irrespective of the chosen solution, the enterprise can expect to have to configure or customize (program) the functionality required to suit its own unique requirements.

Outsource

The business option of outsourcing drawing management to an external service

Table 6: DMS and Drawing Management Functionality

Scope of Requirement	Business Condition	DMS Services
The drawing management functionality required of the DMS is essentially core library services.	• The Drawing Office is not maintained. • The enterprise is primarily a viewer of drawings maintained by an external service provider. • A limited number of drawings are developed within the organization. • A business culture of manual workflow is associated with review and approval processes.	Core library services, such as: • Repository services to manage digital object • Tracking of physical objects • Check-in/check-out/search functionality not integrated at menu level with CAD tools • View complex relationships between drawings • View drawings via browser or DMS search or browse functions
The enterprise has extended functional requirements for managing drawings	• The Drawing Office is maintained. • A reasonable number of drawings are developed within the organization. • The culture of the organization is such that automated workflow is accepted as a key enabler to manage drawing review and approval processes. • The culture of the organization is such that automated workflow and Internet collaboration are key enablers for collaborating on the development of drawings and for review and approval processes.	Extended functionality, such as above, with the following types of additional functionality: • Check-in/check-out/search functionality integrated at menu level with CAD tools. • Automated workflow (with or without drawing life cycle support) for process improvement and management • Automated transition of drawings • Synchronization of DMS with title block attributes

provider, such as an engineering services company, contractor, consulting company, or application service provider, should be examined in terms of feasibility, cost–benefit analysis, and risks.

In those instances where drawing authoring functions are outsourced, it may be appropriate for the enterprise to:

• Resolve that its preference is to outsource or contract with organizations that, as well as providing compatible CAD productivity tools, also provide software for managing drawings.

• Negotiate a compatible DMS or drawing management software to facilitate collaborative exchange of drawings in a controlled manner during engineering drawing life-cycles.

Maintain Existing Status

The "do nothing" option implies that enterprises are comfortable with their existing situation. This may be because system functionality is already as desired, but it may be that an organization (having conducted feasibility and cost–benefit analyses) accepts the limitations of the current drawing environment, even if this means accepting the risks associated with fragmented information. It assumes that vital records will continue to be managed using the current tools.

While enterprises may implement improved practices to better manage information and make improvements to current tools (i.e., improved file structures), the level of risk needs to be analyzed in terms of the potential exposure to the organization.

There is increasing stringency of regulatory environment for electronic recordkeeping and audit trails, the potential for publishing drawing information to Web sites, which may impact on the organization to look at options other than the "do nothing" option. There is also the opportunity to integrate drawings with GIS, ERP, and Asset Management systems, and these types of opportunities place pressure on the "do nothing" option from the viewpoint of strategic or tactical business management.

Organization Readiness

A key aspect to consider during feasibility study or requirements analysis for drawing management is an organization's readiness to proceed with the implementation of either or both of core and extended drawing management functionality.

Many enterprises continue to rely extensively on physical drawings for planning, design, construction, and maintenance of infrastructure and plant. Given these conditions, there is a risk that, in the short term at least, drawing end users may be reluctant to rely on digital drawings for decision making, even with the implementation of a managed repository for drawings. The acceptance of digital drawings as the sources for decision making may be evolutionary, as users gain more confidence that they are accessing, retrieving, and marking up the correct versions of digital drawings.

Advocates of digital viewing, markup, and workflow may suggest that it is simply a matter of developing change management strategies designed to influence new behaviors in users that are accustomed to working with physical drawings and manual processes. While that view has merit, the following types of perspectives may challenge the change strategy and influence outcomes:

- Where the drawings are large or have complex details, engineers and maintenance staff may find it much easier to use physical drawings for viewing and annotation.
- They may continue to prefer paper copies of drawings from a usability perspective, because they can "flick" through multiple sets of drawings easily.
- Even when these drawings are held in digital form, users may find it much easier to print them out, view the drawings in physical form, and annotate manually.

The readiness of personnel to implement drawing management functionality is an influential factor that determines the type of DMS/drawing management software required. There are a range of options, including (a) core document management services, (b) extended functionality, or perhaps (c) a solution that provides core repository services with the capability to deploy extended functionality later, proportionate to an increase in user confidence.

DOCUMENT IMAGING SYSTEMS

Background

Enterprises that wish to adopt an integrative approach to managing documents may wish to consider the integration of imaging systems within the context of an IDCM project. When considering its requirements for imaging of documents, enterprises should take into account imaging capabilities that may be:

- Film-based imaging;
- Hybrid (film and digital); and
- Digital imaging.

Film-Based Imaging

This uses micrographics technology to capture images of documents on microfilm, and it enables people to view the images using a reader and print images if required using a microfilm reader and printer.

In a digital age, where document formats are constantly evolving, and virtual documents can be constructed in real-time mode from digital fragments, businesses often have concerns about the capability of systems to access document formats in the distant future. While there have been a range of standards developed for managing technology-dependent records, business and government agencies remain skeptical about the longevity of various digital media and the availability of systems that will enable them to access the data.

Microfilm has a longevity that is proven, provided the images are captured on a specific type of film and maintained in an environment that meets certain standards. These standards are available from AIIM International (refer to Appendix 3). Microfilm technology is mature and consistent. Images on a microfilm can be read without having to use hardware or software to transform digital data into readable form. It is a format that is acceptable as evidence in a courtroom (provided that the image capture process complies with any requirements prescribed by local jurisdictions).

The issues surrounding the longevity and accessibility of technology-dependent records remain for those documents that are generated digitally, such as email, word-processing documents, and CAD drawings. In some situations, it will be possible to produce COM directly from digital output for archival storage; in other cases, digitally generated documents may be printed (to be accompanied by authorized signatories) and then captured on film.

Organizations might benefit from converting relevant documents to digital image directly from microfilm. For example, a specific document collection might be converted to digital image direct from microfilm for publication to the Web. Records held on microfilm for prescribed periods might be converted to digital format for Internet access to the public.

We do not intend to provide further detailed coverage on film-based imaging systems, because there is already substantial published literature on the topic (see, for example, Saffady, 1978; Smith, 1978).

Hybrid Imaging

Hybrid imaging systems offer the benefits of using microfilm and digital imaging technology. These types of systems enable organizations to perform digital and analog capture of images during a single pass through a suitable scanner. The organization benefits from having a record of a business document in two formats. The dual formats might be useful for demonstrating best evidence in a courtroom environment. The organization also benefits from the long-term storage capabilities of microfilm as well as having the capability to access, display, and distribute digitized copies of images when required.

Digital Imaging in Context

Our focus is to analyze document imaging within the context of the IDCM model, and we view imaging as a constituent subsystem within the overall systems architecture.

While document imaging may be a requirement within the scope of an IDCM project, the characteristics of the imaging solution required may depend on the nature of the application, the types and formats of documents, the volumes of documents, search and retrieval, and performance requirements.

However, we make the following observations about typical business scenarios for document imaging:

- Document imaging may not be a requirement of an IDCM project. The scope of the project may relate only to the management of digital documents that are created using desktop authoring tools.
- Enterprises may wish to implement a self-contained document imaging system, particularly for scanning high-volume transactional documents to image format, without the requirement to implement version control over digital documents.

In the latter case, if the practitioner is specifying requirements for a production-level imaging system to manage high-volume transactional documents, then the requirements may need to be scoped and developed as a separate project, given the likely complexity of the requirement. However, the same type of methodology and approach that we have advocated in Chapter 6 can be applied.

Terminology

The term "imaging," when applied to documents, can embrace film-based or digital systems. In ANSI/AIIM terms:

- An "image" (in micrographics) is "the representation of information produced by radiation," and an "image" (in electronic imaging) is "a digital representation of a document" (American National Standards Institute & Association for Information and Image Management International, p. 53).
- "Imaging" is defined as a process of capturing, storing and retrieving documents regardless of original format, using micrographics and/or electronic imaging (p. 54).
- Electronic imaging is defined as a technique for capturing, recording, processing, storing, transferring and using images electronically (p. 34).

For our purposes, a "Document Imaging System" may be regarded as a system that captures hard-copy documents, converts the documents to digital image format, and provides electronic storage, search and retrieval, and security facilities.

Categorization

As was the case with DMS, it is difficult to put document imaging systems into discrete categories, due to the diverse nature of business opportunities, the types and volume of documents involved, the search and accessibility requirements, and the number of users involved.

However, it is not uncommon for document imaging systems to be implemented in the following scenarios:

- *Desktop imaging* is prevalent in small businesses to meet ad hoc scanning requirements, and in home environments for personal domestic use, such as scanning photographs and occasional business and personal documents. Desktop imaging systems may be used to capture a wide range of documents, but the imaging throughput is only low volume.
- *Workgroup imaging* is used where imaging tools such as scanning hardware and imaging conversion software are typically shared by integrating the hardware and software components into a workgroup's computing network.
- *Production imaging* is typically implemented for capturing, storing, and distributing high-volume documents, generally for a specific application, but it may include a diverse range of document types. These systems are often implemented for capturing and storing transactional documents and are generally incorporated within production workflow applications for managing end-to-end business processes.

Table 7: Typical Document Imaging Scenarios

Type	Characteristics
Desktop Usage Scenario: Ad hoc imaging – documents, photographs	• Small Office/Home Office (SOHO) • Low volumes of documents • Document images captured at the desktop workstation • Fax, OCR software, image edit capabilities • Retail commodity – component based • Cheap • Images may not be required for long-term document management but may be used as part of a process for producing output
Workgroup Usage Scenario: Incoming correspondence and reports for a small project team	• Horizontal application focus • Low to medium volumes of documents • Part of general office/workgroup productivity system • Images treated as another data type • Fax gateway capture and image edit capabilities • Recognition technologies may include barcode and OCR software • May be integrated with DMS repository • Costs depend on volume of documents, size of workgroup, and functionality requirements • Documents/images may form part of corporate information
Production Usage Scenario: Scanning of paper-based form applications, e.g., insurance claims processing, bank check processing, high-volume correspondence	• Vertical application focus • Large volumes of paper documents • Complex applications • Fax gateway capture and image edit capabilities • Recognition technologies may include barcode and OCR, ICR, and Optical Mark Recognition (OMR), via integrated toolkits • Integrated with business operational and administrative systems • Typically integrated with production workflow • May integrate with DMS repository but typically required imaging server and storage repository • Expensive – large capital investment (depending on requirement) • Documents and images are part of corporate information

Table 7 provides an overview of their typical characteristics.

These categorizations are indicative rather than prescriptive, because the boundaries that differentiate each classification (e.g., the volume of documents) are imprecise. Business needs for imaging are generally diverse, and there may exist, or be a requirement for, a number of different types of imaging applications within the enterprise.

- Desktop imaging

  Desktop imaging systems represent low investment and low risk, because the infrastructure is available "off the shelf," and it is virtually a commodity item for small business and home purchasers in Western societies. Purchasers can obtain desktop scanning, imaging, and image editing tools at a local computer store and integrate them with a personal computer.

  Desktop imaging systems represent low investment and low risk, and there is already a range of publications and magazines available on the market that provides information regarding the installation of desktop scanning devices, their configuration requirements, and their scanning techniques.

  They are typically not used for long-term archival storage of business documents. Consequently, the primary focus of this book is related to workgroup and production imaging system requirements within an enterprise.

- Workgroup imaging

  Workgroup document imaging may be required to meet a range of business needs, such as the inclusion of an image of a document or photograph into a report to management. Imaging may be required to capture items such as correspondence or technical documentation into digital format for reference purposes, or for publication to Internet or intranet sites. The requirement may also include long-term archival storage of business documents.

  Imaging tools that enterprises typically implement for workgroup-level imaging include capture devices such as scanning hardware and software that include a wide range of imaging conversion software, recognition software, such as bar-code technology, OCR, and ICR. Digital cameras are also used within workgroups to provide images of photographs taken.

  The imaging resources are typically shared in a workgroup environment by integrating the hardware and software components into the relevant workgroup's computing network. The networking of resources enables users to scan, register, validate, access, and retrieve digital images from desktop computers interconnected from networked file storage.

  The digital images for a workgroup may be stored on a networked file server or imaging server. Some organizations may have integrated imaging capture with a document repository. The images may be accessed using the imaging software provided with the desktop operating system, or a specific imaging application may be used.

- Production imaging

  The costs involved in the acquisition and implementation of production-level imaging systems are high, and the applications tend to be complex.

  Integration of document imaging systems and core business systems is typical of a production imaging implementation. Some production imaging systems may have certification to integrate with core business solutions (e.g., ERP systems). If not, suppliers of production imaging systems may have agreements in place with such vendors.

Irrespective, the imaging system needs to provide an Applications Programming Interface (API) that offers standard development tools and enables integration with core business applications. The system should also offer XML capability for developing custom modules for production imaging applications.

In the production environment, the image capture process may be integrated with workflow technology so that digital images of incoming physical documents, or links to such images, are distributed via workflow or may be published to the Internet or intranet using Web-publishing tools.

Production imaging systems might also be implemented for capturing paper forms and may be integrated with OCR/ICR technologies, which enable data to be automatically extracted from forms and registered in the imaging or core business databases. The recognition technologies may derive data from predefined zones on the form, from a range of fields (depending on the quality of the information on the source form).

Production imaging systems may support the capability to support distributed scanning, indexing, and validation of documents using a graphical user interface (GUI), such as a standard Web browser interconnected to a centralized (or distributed) imaging server.

Functional Overview

Imaging systems suitable to workgroup- or production-level imaging systems provide the following types of generic functionality:

- Capture of hard-copy documents into digital format;
- Capability to have (a) manual feed or (b) automatic feed capabilities, depending on the document types and the business requirements for throughput;
- Capability for scanning and conversion of different sizes of documents (the enterprise needs to specify sizes);
- Management of multipage images as a single entity (e.g., multipage TIF file);
- Scanning of double-sided pages (duplex scanning) if there is the necessary volume of double-sided documents and business requirement;
- Capture of clear images of pages within bound items (e.g., selected pages from technical manuals);
- Saving of images to specified file formats that suit the enterprise (For example, a document might be saved in PDF or JPG for publishing on a Web server, or as a multipage TIF for viewing or transmission.);
- Support of a range of resolution, contrast, threshold, and size settings to meet the diverse requirements of document capture within the enterprise;
- Support of capture of individual pages of a multipage document with an alternate default orientation (e.g., one or more landscape-oriented pages among multiple portrait-oriented pages);
- Capture of color or grayscale images to suit forms processing and other applications (e.g., colored contour maps);

- Ability to despeckle and deskew and remove borders;
- Capability to use blank-a-page dropout facility that eliminates imaging of blank pages in a document;
- Support of multilevel registration capabilities, including batch, folder, envelope, and document level indexing;
- Integration with character recognition technologies to enable text information to be extracted from scanned images;
- Integration with bar-code technologies to capture information from bar codes imprinted within documents or bar-code labels affixed to documents; and
- Capability to use optical mark recognition (OMR).

We extend our review of the functionality of document imaging systems in Chapter 15.

WORKFLOW MANAGEMENT SYSTEMS

Scope

Workflow management systems are designed to automate and implement controls over a diverse range of business processes, from the initiation of a process through to execution of all tasks and process closure. The subject of workflow and workflow management systems is quite extensive, and we attempt only limited coverage in this book. More detailed material has been published, for example, Schäl (1998), Leymann et al. (2000), Fischer (2002), and Sharp and McDermott (2001) discuss workflow in the context of business process modeling. The Workflow Management Coalition (WfMC) also publishes a range of literature, which can be accessed from the WfMC home page on the Internet (refer to Appendix 3).

Our primary focus is to discuss the role of workflow management systems within the context of an IDCM solution architecture, for implementing management controls over document review, approval and distribution, and Web content publishing processes. In this regard, we note that documents of some type typically form part of most business processes. The need for transparent interfaces between the workflow management system and the document and content repository management services is vital to ensure the integrity of information.

Enterprises that acquire workflow management systems and develop applications that help streamline administrative review and approval processes for important documents or Web content, can implement workflow processes without complex design, and potentially with minimal scripting (i.e., coding). The degree of simplicity or complexity will depend upon the user and system requirements for the workflow, combined with the skills and experience of the developer and the capabilities of the workflow management tools.

Enterprises may also require workflow management applications featuring processes that involve a large number of transactions, and usually entail the implementation of highly structured business rules. These types of workflow applications can be initiated by customers accessing an Internet site, or by telephony integration, or by being invoked after scanning large volumes of transactional documents (typically forms based). These types of workflow applications are generally serviced by production-level workflow systems, which may be integrated with production-level imaging systems. These applications are often complex and require skilled and experienced people to develop, implement, and maintain the applications.

Workflow Concepts and Evolution

Concepts

The term "workflow" can mean many things to different people. The business operations of an enterprise entail "work," and given that "work" is not performed in a vacuum, then it is not hard to imagine that "work" might "flow," though not always as well as desired. The liberal use of the term "workflow" by end users and information industry analysts, consultants, and suppliers can create confusion. For example:

- Some businesspeople may use the word "workflow" to describe a system that involves manual process steps, for example, "the workflow involves stamping incoming applications, registering them in the applications system, and then referring them to the correct action officer."

- Others may perceive workflow as an email system or other type of messaging or collaboration (GroupWare) tool, because these types of systems allow people to transfer work requests and documents to one or more recipients, enabling them to "route requests and documents."

- Some use the term "document routing." This may have had its origins in the manual document routing slips that records managers attached to hard-copy files or documents, or from the document routing functionality that enables end users to route digital documents directly from desktop office applications, using messaging and GroupWare infrastructure. The term is often used by an end user describing the application of workflow for document review and approval processes.

- In an effort to differentiate their product capabilities, particularly during the rapid development of workflow technology in the 1990s, suppliers often used labels and terms to describe functionality within their software, in order to differentiate products for marketing purposes. Similar functionality may have also existed in other workflow management systems but was described by a different label, leading to confusion in those coming to grips with the capabilities of such systems and workflow terminology.[3]

Definitions relating to workflow that try to provide scope and definition to the terminology include the following:

- "Workflow automation is the structure that is applied to the movement of information in order to improve the results of a business process. Workflow automation software actively manages the coordination of activities among people in general business processes" (Burns, 1994).

- "Workflow is a toolset for the proactive analysis, compression and automation of information based tools and activities" (Koulopoulos, 1995).

The general confusion over terminology was probably increased by an array of additional terms used by the workflow industry sector to try and position various types of workflow management solutions in the market. Potential consumers of workflow systems are confronted with "process-centric" workflow, "document-centric" workflow, "ad hoc" workflow, "collaborative" workflow, "administrative" workflow, and "production-level" workflow, and more recently, "embedded" workflow and "Web-enabled" workflow.

In 1995, as part of its strategy to develop workflow and workflow management system concepts, the WfMC[4] defined the terms as shown in Table 8 (Hollingsworth, 1995, p. 6).

The WfMC determined that workflow was concerned with "the automation of procedures where documents, information or tasks are passed between participants according to a defined set of rules to achieve, or contribute to, an overall business goal." It acknowledged that while workflow might be a manual system, "in practice most workflow is normally organized within the context of an IT system to provide computerized support for the procedural automation" (Hollingsworth, 1995, p. 6).

Consequently, a workflow management system consists of software (supported by hardware and communications) that enables organizations to develop applications for automatically routing and tracking work packets. Work packets might contain data, documents, references to physical documents, and links to Web sites, an example being a case file for processing in the insurance sector.

Work packets flow through a series of defined processes as a strategy to reduce the time required at each step of a business process. The concept of a workflow management system involves capturing a work item, using predefined rules to sequentially route information based on roles, and track packets as they progress through a business process.

Work packets can be routed one step after another or distributed to multiple action officers simultaneously, as a strategy to improve productivity. The step-by-step routing is referred to as "serial processing," while the simultaneous multiple distribution of packets is referred to as "parallel processing." The requirement for parallel processing needs to be defined by the business, and the capabilities to deliver parallel processing will depend on the capabilities of the workflow management software.

Work packets might also be routed using conditional logic, where a flow is determined by a predefined condition, such as:

Table 8: WfMC Definition of Workflow/Workflow Management

Term	WfMC Definition	Synopsis Derived from WfMC
Workflow	The computerized facilitation or automation of a business process, in whole or in part.	It relates to the automation of procedures, where documents, information, or tasks are passed between participants according to a defined set of rules to achieve, or contribute to, an overall business goal.
Workflow management	A system that completely defines, manages, and executes "workflows" through the execution of software with an order of execution that is driven by a computer representation of the workflow logic.	The management system was defined in the context of supporting procedural automation of business processes. The management system provides not only the automation of the business processes but also the invocation of appropriate human or IT resources for the various activity steps.

If claim <$5000, and if nil prior claim, then approve automatically.
If claim <$5000, but prior claim, then route to claims officer.
If claim range is $5000–$20,000, then route to claims officer.
If claim >$20,000, then route to claims supervisor.

Workflow Evolution

In Chapter 1, we made brief reference to the origins of workflow analysis with reference to Taylor's studies and the subsequent Hawthorne experiments that were seminal to the investigation of social context.

A lesson to be derived from social and managerial psychology research, is the need for adequate consideration of the milieu of inter- and intraworkgroup social interactions when introducing technology changes. These lessons apply not only to the implementation of workflow management systems, but to other subsystems defined within our overall IDCM systems architecture and for technology changes, generally. These aspects need to be identified and addressed as part of the overall change management strategy for the implementation of technology-based systems.

Although the early focus of the workflow management industry was on the high-volume transaction environments in the financial services and insurance sectors, during the 1990s, the industry turned to aligning workflow with document image processing technology. The alignment of the two technologies was viewed by suppliers as a key opportunity to improve market share, as it provided enterprises with an integrative approach that took advantage of the document capture and storage capability of imaging, combined with automated process management capabilities of workflow. The market opportunity saw some of the document imaging suppliers embed workflow capabilities into their systems or develop strategic alliances with workflow vendors.

The integration of workflow management systems with digital imaging systems offered a number of unique advantages that were, in fact, realized by organizations that had the requirement. For example:

*   Individual or batches of digital images could be routed automatically to action officers based on predefined rules, and the process life-cycle could be managed.
*   Digital images could be routed to more than one action officer, thereby enabling a number of simultaneous actions to be taken, potentially in diverse workgroups or locations, thus reducing life-cycle times for image- and workflow-enabled business transactions.
*   Workflow provided the capability to manage the distribution of images in a controlled way and also kept a record of the business transaction, while the imaging system provided a long-term, cost-effective storage option for large volumes of documents that were captured and converted to digital images.
*   Workflow had the capability to provide real-time (online) statistics relating to the processes.
*   Workloads could be balanced across workgroups.
*   Performance could be measured to assess workgroup productivity.

The advantages of using integrated document imaging and workflow were heightened by the Business Process Re-Engineering (BPR) movement[5] that had also emerged during the mid-1990s. Suppliers soon recognized that the capabilities of integrated workflow technology and document imaging provided enterprises with the types of technology tools that would enable them to implement strategies for BPR and achieve the types of sweeping outcomes that became associated with BPR as a technique. The BPR movement also provided the raison d'être for a range of analysis and modeling tools that enabled business processes to be mapped and (depending on the functionality offered) enabled modelers to analyze and review potential consequential changes to business processes ("what if" analysis).

However, early workflow and document imaging projects suffered implementation problems because of organizational, process, and technological factors. Industry projections for the take-up of workflow (and document imaging) technology were not realized. The difficulties in implementation (combined with cost factors) may have engendered a feeling of reticence in many enterprises to embark on workflow projects. Of course, document imaging and workflow management systems were maturing as technologies, and the cost of implementing production-level workflow and document imaging systems might have been prohibitive for many organizations, particularly those without a requirement for high-volume transaction processing.

The evolution of workflow systems saw the development of GUI tools that were marketed as an opportunity for business users to develop their own workflow modules once they had acquired a workflow management system. Typically, this involved having a vendor or system integrator undertake the development of an initial workflow application and also transfer skills to administrators within customer sites. It was anticipated that the trained administrator might then have the capability to develop and deploy workflow modules. The success of this skills transfer and application by the customer typically depended on the ease of use of the GUI, the flexibility of the workflow tool, the levels of training, skills, and experience of the administrator, and the complexity of the workflow solutions being developed.

Workflow tools developed to provide a more flexible development environment, multiplatform support, and support for heterogeneous computing environments. The evolution also witnessed the introduction of object-oriented development environments, which enabled objects to be developed and reused for a number of different processes requiring the same or similar functionality. However, many users continued to perceive workflow as applying only to mission-critical business applications, where there were predefined business rules and step processes that would benefit from the automation of repetitive tasks, support performance objectives, and deliver timely management reports on process cycles.

As workflow tools evolved, it became apparent that workflow systems were not only useful tools for automating structured processes within organizations but were also relevant for automating semistructured processes and for improving ad hoc business processes. The market became more sophisticated, and new tools emerged for business process automation. In order to differentiate the "types" of workflow, attempts were made to classify types of workflow (see the "Workflow Categories" section, following), and paradigms were assigned to various product types, describing workflow management systems as process-centric or document-centric workflow. To the business user, documents are involved in most business processes, so the distinction between process-centric and document-centric workflow management systems may have added an element of confusion during the rapidly evolving developments.

During the 1990s, there was widespread take-up of email systems within enterprises. These systems provided messaging capabilities supported by directory mechanisms for identifying users and assigning roles and attributes that described the user. Simultaneously, there was a take up of GroupWare software that enabled workgroups to collaborate and share information, using services such as bulletin boards, and also offered diary and scheduling services. These services evolved into messaging and collaboration tools (such as MS *Exchange*, Lotus *Notes*, and *GroupWise*, as examples) that now form a vital component of communications within enterprises.

The widespread adoption of GroupWare evoked debate about its capabilities for workflow functionality. Some conflicting views about differentiation between GroupWare and workflow management tools may have further confused potential consumers of workflow products, who found the workflow concept too nebulous.

Major suppliers of messaging and collaboration systems now offer specific workflow functionality for their respective products, as a built-in component of the core software or as a third-party module for integration. The integration of workflow functionality within messaging and collaboration systems enables users of those systems to invoke tracking for processes such as document review and approval, and semistructured workflow for administrative processes. However, the applicability of these tools for automating a process needs to be considered within the context of business functions and should be based on analysis and definition of requirements.

Other recent developments in the workflow sector include the following:

- The embedding of workflow in business operational systems for horizontal applications market segment, such as ERP systems for the automation of accounts payable, human resource management processes, and maintenance management (Some vertical market applications, such as land information systems targeted at the local government sector, are also known to be embedding workflow within their applications.);

- The embedding of workflow management functionality as a core component of DMS and CMS applications, rather than integration of third-party workflow products (The workflow automates business processes associated with document routing, approval, distribution, notification (typically via a messaging system), and managing the audit trail.);

- The integration of third-party workflow systems, including a product offered by the same developer as a DMS or CMS solution, which is not part of the inherent core functionality of the DMS or CMS (These workflow systems might be integrated with the DMS or CMS applications to enable controlled document or content review and approval processes.);

- The integration of workflow with drawing management tools to facilitate the automation of engineering change management processes and enable publication of latest drawing objects to intranet and extranet sites; and

- The development of Web-enabled workflow to enable information to be captured via Internet and intranet forms and be routed to action officers for decision making and timely response to customers.

These developments may have implications for business decision making, because the type of workflow choice will depend on the nature of the requirement. For example, a simple document review and approval might be achievable using workflow offered by GroupWare systems, but a DMS or CM application may also offer the same functionality. If the review and approval process involves a business application, such as processing invoices, the workflow capability might be offered by the ERP system.

Workflow Reference Model

We referred earlier to the role of WfMC in standardizing terminology, and in Chapter 7, we tabulate a list of their published standards. These include the Workflow Reference Model, which provides an architectural representation of a workflow management system and the levels where interoperability can occur. The Workflow Reference Model is depicted in Figure 1.

The WfMC adapted the model from a generic workflow application structure and then identified the interfaces within the structure that enabled workflow products to interoperate at various levels (Hollingsworth, 1995, p. 20).

The *workflow enactment service* that features in the central component of the model relates to a specific implementation or instance of a workflow management system. The enactment service interprets the process definitions, controls the processes, controls the sequence of activities, manages the user work lists, and invokes relevant application tools (Hollingsworth, 1995, p. 13). The enactment service may consist of one or more workflow "engines" (workflow software packages) or specialized engines. The specialized engines may support specific processes or have different characteristics, such as the support for production-level workflow, image handling, or greater flexibility for frequent changes, and may be supplied by one or multiple vendors (Leymann & Roller, 2000, p. 118).

Figure 1: Workflow Reference Model. (Note. From the Workflow Management Coalition. Reproduced with permission.)

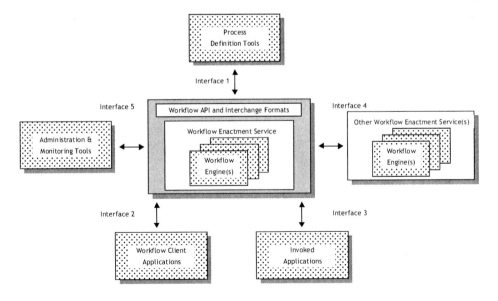

Table 9: Workflow Interoperability

Interface Number	Synopsis	Relevant Specification(s)
1	Defines interoperability between business modeling tools and the workflow management system	Process Definition Meta-Model and Workflow Process Definition Language (WPDL)
2	Defines available user functions for interoperating with the workflow management system	Workflow Client API Specifications (WAPI)
3	Defines the invocation of applications that can be included as a module within every workflow management system	Workflow Client API Specifications (WAPI)
4	Defines the mechanism for subprocesses between different workflow management systems	Workflow Interoperability Abstract Specifications; Workflow Interoperability — MIME Binding; Workflow Interoperability — Wf-XML Binding
5	Defines workflow audit data structure and requirements for compliance	Workflow Interoperability Abstract Specifications

The model demonstrates five different levels of interoperability, labeled interfaces 1 to 5, which are summarized in Table 9.

Standards are yet to be published for some of the interfaces, due to the complexity of the development work involved, particularly for interface 3, which involves multiple types of modules that could potentially be invoked by a workflow management system.

Applications

The current business environment places increasing demands on business enterprises to provide timely services within a quality management framework. There are increasing regulatory and legal compliance requirements relevant to recordkeeping, and the imperative to manage better while containing resource costs. This environment provides fertile ground for the development and implementation of workflow applications.

Workflow capabilities are now available in a range of applications, such as workflow modules within messaging and collaboration systems, and embedded functionality within ERP systems. Systems have been developed to offer a range of horizontal and vertical applications. Large enterprises may have the need for multiple workflow management systems to cover the diverse range of process automation opportunities. The requirement to have interoperability between diverse workflow engines may be vital in many organizations.

Business users need to be aware that the WfMC standards are not mandated but might be applicable for interoperability between workflow management systems, if there is such a requirement. Many vendors support the WfMC reference model at a *logical* level but do not provide off-the-shelf software modules that provide the *physical* capability to deliver the interoperability specifications produced by the WfMC.

Vendors might state that they "have the capability" to interoperate with other workflow systems, if required, but this would involve customization. There is little evidence to support the successful implementation of multiple diverse workflow solutions interoperating in a production environment to support multiple process instances.

Quite often, specifications within Request for Proposal (RFP) for IDCM solutions are developed by novices in the information industry and contain statements such as *"Conform to WfMC standards"* or *"Capability to conform to WfMC standards."* If there is no requirement for workflow interoperability, then these types of statements might be superfluous and treated as such by the suppliers responding to the RFP.

If there is a requirement, or it is foreseeable that there may be a requirement, the WfMC standards (which are quite technical in nature) should be reviewed in conjunction with a system architect before specifying requirements. For example, an enterprise might wish to specify support for the logical (metamodel) design and API definition provided as specifications by the WfMC, and might mandate these standards for the development of interfaces and management services. Otherwise, vague types of statements made in the context of an RFP may not make sense without the business specifying the standards that might be relevant to the business need.

Workflow Categories

Workflow Processes

During the period of rapid workflow evolution in the 1990s, industry analysts and consultants had a penchant for categorizing workflow into various domains based on the nature of supported processes, types of functionality, volume matrix, flexibility, and enterprise deployment capabilities. Quite a number of categorizations were published during that period, some of which helped to define the market.

One of the better-known schemes was promulgated by the Giga Group, which classified workflow management systems into four quadrants that classified categories of workflow based on:

- Overall value of the workflow to the business — the direct relationship of a workflow process to achieving the core outcomes of the business: range high to low.

- The degree of repetition with which a process is performed: range repetitive to unique.

Four processes could therefore be described:

- *Ad hoc* (low value; unique)
  This is generally used when describing the nonstructured routing of documents (or information messages) to one or more participants on a distribution list, including the cooperative review and production of documents typically involving individuals or workgroups. Ad hoc workflow systems typically leverage the collaboration systems infrastructure, which is based on messaging systems technology.

- *Administrative* (low value; repetitive)
  This type of workflow management system embraces simple structured electronic forms processing involving sequential steps with well-defined hierarchical paths such as leave applications. It generally features an electronic forms (e-forms) application that enables end users to capture data relevant to their specific business requirement and use integrated workflow to automate and manage the business processes based on predefined rules that apply to a particular application.

For example, an e-form might be used to apply for a leave of absence, and the workflow might route the request through the required endorsement and approval process and then notify the applicant of the subsequent approval. If the workflow management system has been integrated with an Employee Resource Information Management System, the details of the approved application could update the Leave database. Administrative workflow might also cover semistructured processes such as automated correspondence management, where, for example, correspondence for a specific function might be routed to a specific role within a department.

- *Collaborative* (high value; unique)

Collaborative workflow typically covers the semistructured processing associated with the development of technical documents, such as drawing manuals, where there are defined review and approval processes. Another example might be the development of meeting papers for Board and Executive meetings, the development of request for proposals and contract documentation, or the review and approval processes associated with software releases. It may involve instances where rules are applied to the collaborative development of products or where processes follow a familiar path based on object types.

- *Production* (high value; repetitive)

Production level workflow is evident in processing environments characterized by a high volume of transactions, large numbers of work packets or documents, well-defined structured (rigid, enforced) processes, and timing constraints. The aim of production workflow systems is to automate as many tasks as possible, until what is termed as Straight-Through-Processing has been realized, whereby the solution only requires manual intervention to exceptions that occur to the predetermined process (Fischer, 2002).

Production workflow emerged with production imaging systems but now offers a wider diversity of functionality and support for mission-critical lines of business systems, including CRM, Supply Chain Management, and Web-enabled application processes. Workflow management software has been integrated with telephonic systems, whereupon workflow processes might be initiated by voice or keypad recognition.

The production workflow processes may involve dispatching work packets across organizational functional boundaries. The finance and insurance sectors are a good example of production workflow systems for the automation of bank check processing, loan application processing, insurance underwriting, and claim processing.

Workflow processes have also been classified in terms of whether they exhibit "push" or "pull" traits as follows:

- *Push*

Push is generally related to tightly structured procedural workflow models. Like an assembly line process, the workflow management system might simply allocate a packet of work in a queue to the next available action officer. The action officer may not be able to reject the work packet or transfer it to another workflow user.

- *Pull*

  Pull is probably more evident in less-structured workflow models (perhaps ad hoc or collaborative workflow environments). The action officer may have the freedom to choose the next work packet from a queue and may have the authority to alter a workflow or transfer the packet to another workflow user.

Workflow Management Systems

Two categories have emerged, based on what "flowed" within a workflow, with the outcomes being characterized as document-centric and process-centric.

- Document-Centric

  If it is initiated by the flow of one or more documents, and the processes tend to follow a defined document life-cycle, it is termed "document-centric" workflow. Document-centric products are generally deemed to be those that are embedded within IDCM repository management systems or GroupWare systems. Documents follow step processes within the workflow based on a predefined structure, and a flow is typically initiated based on a change of status to the document. The information resource requirements in such a workflow can be fairly rigid; for example, the participant in the workflow might only need to access the document in the process in order to make a decision.

- Process-Centric

  Evidence of the characteristics of a "process-centric" workflow is shown when the flows between tasks are transferring control or responsibility and may or may not be initiated by the capture of a document. There may be less rigidity in the control of information needed to make a decision, with the participants having more flexibility to access the range of information resources needed to make decisions as part of each step process.

It is difficult to categorize types of software products because of the ever-changing level of functionality being developed, particularly when a diversity of software systems could claim to have workflow functionality. It is not straightforward to determine which workflow category suits a business requirement, until a Requirements Specification encompassing user and system requirements is developed, as described in Chapter 10.

For example, business users might be looking for a DMS or CMS package that offers "ad hoc" workflow functionality for document and content review and approval processes. However, a feature of an ad hoc type of workflow is that it has no predefined structure, which would be difficult to apply in the case of processes involving the distribution, review, markup, versioning, and approval processes associated with documents.

The processes associated with review and approval of content to be published to an Internet or intranet Web server can hardly be described as ad hoc. Most enterprises have mandated processes by which content must be submitted for review and approval before being published to Web sites.

A workflow management system should be implemented based upon its fitness for purpose derived from its capability to meet the Requirements Specification, rather than how it might be categorized.

Workflow Technology Options

Recent developments in workflow, including the availability of workflow modules for messaging and collaboration systems and the embedding of workflow functionality in business application systems, have produced a range of workflow management options. The most suitable workflow engine will depend on the nature and complexity of the requirement and the functionality supported by the potential workflow technology options. Options for workflow within the context of an IDCM solution are as follows:

- Messaging/collaboration systems/workflow

   There is generally a requirement for an IDCM solution to integrate with messaging and collaboration tools, so that email messages may contain links to document objects within the IDCM and allow attachment of documents from the IDCM. However, the IDCM solution should also support ad hoc and cooperative review and production of documents and reports, and it may be desirable for the IDCM to support integration with electronic forms for recordkeeping purposes in administrative workflow processes.

   If the requirement is for relatively simple document review and approval processes, then the feasibility of using workflow modules offered by messaging and collaborative systems should be considered. The workflow capabilities of messaging and collaboration systems generally include GUI designer modules for visually specifying information flows and business rules and for defining permissions associated with decision steps. They also support scripting languages to enable user customization of more detailed workflow processes. This type of workflow enablement of messaging systems has generated new developments, such as third-party workflow products that add functional value to leading messaging and collaboration products.

- Embedded workflow

   There is a tendency for suppliers of horizontal and vertical business software suites to embed workflow functionality within their system architecture to provide added value to clients that utilize their applications. This type of embedded workflow functionality is now being offered in ERP systems, possibly directly embedded in the ERP system architecture. (ERP providers that do not embed workflow may bundle third-party workflow product or products to support the automation of processes managed by the ERP system as noted under *Autonomous workflow*.

   The workflow software supports workflow modules that facilitate business process transactions managed by the ERP system. As it is embedded within the ERP application, the workflow management system may not support processes and functions outside the solution domain of the ERP architecture. If an enterprise has the requirement for workflow that is aligned with business processes enabled by the use of ERP systems, then it may be appropriate to consider the use of the workflow modules within the ERP system as a technology option.

   Workflow functionality can also be directly embedded in DMS or CMS products that provide the repository management of an IDCM solution. The use of workflow embedded within the core functionality of the IDCM repository management system is an option for organizations wishing to implement solutions for automating document review and approval processes, or publishing Web content to Internet or intranet sites.

One of the benefits of having workflow embedded within the IDCM repository management software is that there may not be a requirement for enterprises to purchase separate workflow server software licenses, as the licensing is typically bundled with the IDCM solution. Furthermore, as the workflow software is embedded within the IDCM, there is probably no requirement for separate server hardware, operating system, and DBMS to host the workflow server.

- Autonomous workflow

Autonomous workflow is defined by the WfMC as being functional without any additional application software, with the exception of DBMS and message queuing middleware (Fischer, 2000). Autonomous workflow is used in the context of IDCM, where the functionality required to automate document or Web content review and approval processes is not provided as an embedded component of the IDCM repository management system. An option may be to integrate a separate workflow product, which may be part of the vendor's own product range or be provided by a third-party supplier.

This option is often referred to as integrating the IDCM with "best of breed" workflow, which of course, depends on who defines the workflow tool. The benefits claimed for bundling autonomous workflow with the IDCM solution is that the workflow system may feature an open architecture, so that it is capable of being deployed with multiple IDCM packages and a range of DBMS and network platforms.

The acquisition of an independent workflow product can be useful for those organizations wishing to use the tool for workflow applications other than ad hoc document review and approval, where there is no requirement to integrate with the IDCM solution.

A requirement that needs to be explored when considering workflow-enabled processes within the context of an IDCM solution, is the need to maintain the integrity of documents or Web content files during their transition through a workflow process. It was a common oversight in early implementations of IDCM and integrated third-party workflow products for the integrity of the document to be exposed to risk during review and approval processes, due to the loose integration between the two systems.

While there has been a maturing of products and integration capabilities, there is still an extensive range of IDCM and workflow products on the market. Consequently, it is wise to specify the requirement that the versioning, status, and security of a document object stored in the IDCM repository are maintained during a workflow process. This requirement should be examined through validation tests during system evaluation in the procurement phase, and during system testing conducted as part of implementation.

The potential for multiple processors and server software to deploy workflow is another requirement that needs to be analyzed where third-party workflow products are to be integrated with the IDCM solution. This applies particularly to distributed computing environments, covering geographical locations, or campus-style computer networks. The server software costing structures for the workflow will depend on the licensing structures offered by the vendor and the deal that can be struck during the procurement phase of the IDCM project. However, an enterprise that may have, for example, ten interconnected sites, may require ten server licenses for the workflow, and these servers may also require that they be hosted on separate hardware processors.

DIGITAL SIGNATURES

There may be a requirement to utilize digital signatures for a range of opportunities within an enterprise. They are particularly relevant for e-commerce applications, document authorization, and workflow applications.

Digital signatures may be required for personal authentication of official documents, such as engineering drawings, quality documents, OH&S documents, work orders, email messages, electronic forms, and other workflow actions. The system used for authentication should be extensible to support authentication of external customers, service providers, and business partners.

It is noted that a range of collaborative tool or messaging systems already support Public Key Infrastructure (PKI) based authentication of email messages within the email client. Most office suites also support the use of digitized signatures.

Consequently, enterprises need to make a thorough examination of their business needs to determine whether there is a requirement for the DMS to offer support for digital signatures.

Metadata support for signatures is also being advanced. In the United States, the Signed Document Markup Language (SDML) has been proposed by the FSTC (Financial Services Technology Consortium, 1998). SDML is designed to:

- Tag the individual text items making up a document.
- Group the text items into document parts that can have business meaning and can be signed individually or together.
- Allow document parts to be added and deleted without invalidating previous signatures.
- Allow signing, co-signing, endorsing, co-endorsing, and witnessing operations on documents and document parts.

The signatures become part of the SDML document and can be verified by subsequent recipients as the document travels through the business process. SDML does not define encryption, because encryption is between each sender and receiver in the business process and can differ for each link, depending on the transport used.

WEB CONTENT MANAGEMENT

Since the Web has been part of the Internet, it has provided an avenue for publishing. At first, this amounted to simple display of textual material complemented by inline images. However, as the markup standards and software were developed, so too the authoring facilities for producing material have become more sophisticated.

Enterprises now have the choice of publishing material over the Internet, or making internal material widely available to personnel or business partners through intranets and extranets. We mentioned in Chapter 3 that many enterprises implemented Web sites and use a range of methods to publish content to these sites. We also noted that many of the existing methods for managing Web content have limitations, and that IDCM has the capability to overcome these limitations and provide a managed environment for the processes associated with publishing Web content.

Although CMS vary greatly in capability and intent, they have evolved to the point where the elements of functionality may usually be considered as content creation, presentation capacity, and management facility.

- Content creation

  This provides for authors to work in an environment that separates presentation and content. Functionality includes the ability to utilize elements of documents, for example, illustrations, paragraphs, or tables in different contexts; the ability to create associations between pages that survive restructuring; and the ability to produce metadata that describe the contents and purpose. These capabilities should now be available in such a manner that authors no longer need to be aware of the underlying markup.

- Presentation

  This may be for distribution of internal material such as manuals, training materials, reports, standards and specifications, and business forms over intranets, or for publishing, over the Internet, public information such as marketing information, company reports, and application forms.

  The generation of pages to be presented should be accompanied by template availability for layout, control of look and feel through style sheets, the ability to integrate multiple formats as compound documents, the provision of alternative renditions according to user needs, and individualization based upon user profiles (personalization).

- Content management

  Management of the content provision must enable version control, maintenance of integrity when multiple users are working on a single document, and security procedures for controlling access capability and producing audit trails.

  Dynamic provision of content to pages can be provided by managed interfaces to other subsystems, notably DBMS, so that structured data can be presented in current and validated form within compound documents.

  These can be undertaken within a workflow framework that is capable of accommodating distributed users, interfacing with other subsystems such as DMS, and administrative reporting of data, such as authoring and use of Web sites.

The limitations that we listed in Chapter 3 provide an overview of the types of constraints that apply within enterprise CMS. Although there is a consistent set of factors that applies to most enterprises, there are many aspects specific to particular enterprises. It has been said that CMS is a concept rather than a product (Browning & Lowndes, 2001). This adds weight to analysis of it within the umbrella of IDCM, where documents and their content may be considered more broadly than in terms of Web presentation. Document creation, management, and utilization, should be undertaken with reference to business requirements and workflow of business processes. Specific requirements, for example, management of multilingual content, can be provided for within an enterprise IDCM approach.

It can be seen that the capabilities reviewed above are shared at least in part with other IDCM subsystems. The IDCM environment has the capability to manage Web content within a continuum that includes initial creation processes, potentially in a distributed environment, through to managed archiving of content. The types of tools feature Web content repository management, integrated workflow management systems, and content publishing tools.

Some enterprises may only have a requirement for relatively low-volume content updates, while others are evolving their Web sites to enable greater interaction with customers (Internet) or internal decision makers (intranet). Other enterprises might have sites that feature a high degree of customer interaction, tailored content and personalization services, and high-volume updates to Web servers.

A range of options is available to manage an enterprise's Web content, irrespective of the size and complexity of the business processes and management requirements. The types of software solutions available to enterprises for life-cycle management of the processes associated with Web content can be tailored to meet specific business requirements.

Just as presentation principles have been developed over the years for traditional publishing, now there is increasing emphasis on the framework within which Web content is presented. One way of articulating this is through "information architecture," which goes beyond graphic design to provide for a combination of navigation and information organization to assist users with finding information more readily.

This presumes that an element of content management is an architecture that provides a model for information availability derived from analysis of organizational content, analysis of diversity of user needs, and structuring based upon the nature of the content, so that information users can readily identify the content they are seeking. Guidance in Web content presentation that aligns site organization and navigation to user needs and structure of content is provided by writers such as Rosenfeld and Morville (1998) and Hackos (2002).

ENTERPRISE REPORT MANAGEMENT (COLD)

In Chapter 1, we made reference to the use that enterprises have made of COM. It continues to be used as an archival storage medium for office documents. As optical digital media have been developed (see, for example, CD-R in Appendix 5), businesses have made increasing use of Computer Output Laser Disk (COLD). Often, this is described as Enterprise Report Management (ERM) technology. These systems store digital reports from core business databases and enable the data to be represented with graphical overlays to facilitate interactive communications, generally between suppliers and customers.

For example, a customer may make a telephone inquiry regarding an entry in a credit card statement. The financial provider is able to search the ERM system access and view the relevant database entry in a graphical mask that provides a digital representation of how the customer sees the credit card statement. If the customer requires supporting confirmation of the entry, the financial provider may have the capability to quickly retrieve an image of the signed credit slip that supports the transaction. ERM can, therefore, comprise another subsystem of IDCM.

The online retrieval capability provided by COLD is a great advance over that of COM, but it is only effective if descriptive indexes (metadata) are created along with images and are searchable via structured database software.

The amount of storage required for documents can escalate quickly, in terms of image storage[6] and in terms of the databases necessary for retrieval of metadata, so it remains important to make decisions about how and when material should be archived. Typical uses such as the financial transaction explained above or other low-use storage such as archived medical records still benefit from fast, effective retrieval when required. So too do records, which except for isolated examples, are not expected to be retrieved at all but which must be retained for regulatory purposes.

COLD systems that are to be used integratively as part of document and content management must provide functionality similar to that expected from these other systems. Particular capabilities that will ease the path to integration include:

- Support for inquiry and retrieval through Web interfaces;
- Ingestion (incorporation into repository utilizing compression and database index creation) of data in structured and unstructured forms;
- Use of standard compression formats that permit ease of extraction through other system interfaces;
- Provision for metadata elements that can be defined by users but are controlled through data administration;
- Management of large and rapidly growing index databases that can result from metadata elements (For example a database that records 10,000 billing transactions per day may be recording 100,000 data elements per day to be maintained in retrievable index files for elements such as data, name, amount, item, and so on.);
- Support for a repository that can include types of different data objects;
- Image enhancement facilities such as despeckling, contrast balancing, and cropping;
- Document integrity per medium of viewing and update controls;
- Ability to incorporate in the repository, COLD documents as well as others that may emanate from DMS or CMS;
- Control of processes through workflow routines;
- Provision for extraction and use of parts of documents;
- Facilities for high-volume printing; and
- Security management through group and user levels.

IDCM ARCHITECTURE

The IDCM systems environment should feature a scalable, flexible, and extensible architecture, which integrates with the enterprise computing environment to enable the system to grow with the organization and to enable knowledge to be shared with other business units.

The user interface must be nonintrusive and intuitive for all types of users, including casual and power users, as well as systems administrators. The document or Web content repository management subsystem may be required to support the capabilities to check-in and check-out and search or retrieve documents or Web content in a number of desktop operating and application environments.

Depending on the enterprise computing environment, the repository manager may be required to integrate with one or more operating systems (Windows, Macintosh, OS/2, Linux, etc.) or multiple versions of operating systems. The repository manager should also integrate with the enterprise's Web browser without the requirement to load proprietary software into the browser.

Depending on the enterprise requirements, the IDCM solution may also be required to support a three-tier client server architecture, where most of the business logic (i.e., complex document or Web content management functionality) is executed by a server hosting the IDCM repository services application. (Some enterprises may be adopting an "n" tier architecture, where applications are distributed on multiple computers in a distributed computing environment.)

The client server architecture for the system will be required to deliver a high level of performance during capture, search, and retrieval, and the special requirements for distributed computing environments need to be considered. For example, there may be a requirement to have distributed databases or document content servers, or there may be a requirement for replication of specific metadata or document or content objects.

Special considerations should be given to the needs of mobile workers (using laptops, hand-held devices) that spend some time processing documents away from the office environment. The IDCM solution should offer techniques that help mobile users to have the confidence that they are accessing and updating the correct version of a document or Web content component. For example, some users may wish to access the document repository via a standard Web browser, when in remote locations.

The system should feature integration with enterprise backup and recovery facilities to help assure the security of the information in the IDCM repository. Given the increasing reliance on digital documents and Web content for supporting business processes and maintaining records of business transactions, organizations may find it sensible to treat documents as *mission-critical* information. They may consider it prudent as a risk management strategy to invest in additional infrastructure (in addition to backup and recovery facilities) to ensure the availability of digital information in the event of a crisis.

SUMMARY

In this chapter, we explored how there are a range of key subsystems that may support an enterprise's integrative approach to deliver effective solutions for improving the management of documents and Web content.

We then described the nature and characteristics of the subsystems and reviewed the aspects of their characteristics and functionality. The analysis and definition of functional requirements for these systems are covered in more detail in Part 3.

However, we shall now take the opportunity in Chapter 5 to look at how IDCM subsystems may interface with other business systems and be associated with them to improve business processes. Chapter 5 also covers some typical applications of IDCM solutions.

ENDNOTES

[1]   For example, a document numbered 2.03 would be minor version 3 of major version 2.

[2]   Enterprises may find the use of the terminology "drawing management system" confusing, when considering the scope and requirements for packages to help with the implementation of management controls over drawing processes. This is not surprising, as suppliers often use the terminology to describe a range of software that provides varying degrees of functionality for implementing such controls.

[3]   People with restricted views or limited exposure to the current workflow market might consider workflow to mean only production-level systems that are designed to manage complex structured processes and high-volume transactions, or perceive them in terms of their well-publicized integration with production-level document imaging systems. There are now manifold opportunities for developing and implementing workflow systems.

[4]   A group of companies formed the WfMC, which was constituted as a not-for-profit organization comprising suppliers and business users to help the industry define the scope and framework of workflow and workflow management. The WfMC's tasks included the development of the concepts, terminology, and general structure of a workflow management system. It determined that it would define the major functional components and interfaces of workflow management systems and the interoperability between systems through the use of common standards for functions within the workflow management system.

[5]   Hammer and Champy (1994) saw reengineering as the fundamental rethinking and radical redesign of business processes to achieve dramatic improvements in critical contemporary measures of performance, such as cost, quality, services, and speed.

[6]   A typical page of text produces an image file of at least 30 kB. If the page includes images or graphics, the file size could easily be in excess of 50 kB, depending upon compression and resolution used. Filing cabinets of paper quickly translate into many megabytes.

Chapter 5

Business Systems Interfaces and IDCM Opportunities

OVERVIEW

In this chapter, we conclude the appraisal of the characteristics of IDCM systems that we commenced in Chapter 4. This chapter begins by reviewing IDCM opportunities in the context of their capability to interface with business operational and administrative systems. We relate these to document and Web content management in order to illustrate how IDCM can support other lines of business systems and their applications.

We then review some document management applications in business and government enterprises and associate these with Web publishing and content management in order to demonstrate the types of solutions that are feasible. There is a wide range of opportunities for deployment of IDCM within most business and government enterprises, and we will examine some examples of applications in different environments.

We emphasize throughout this chapter how IDCM can be deployed to support commercial and government planning initiatives, support regulatory and legal compliance, underpin continuous process improvement initiatives, and provide the foundation for exploiting enterprise knowledge.

Our objectives then are as follows:

*   Discuss how IDCM repository management systems (document and Web content) can interface with core business operational and administrative systems.
*   Discuss some specific document and content management solutions that may be applied in an integrated manner for managing important business documents and vital records.
*   Provide an overview of some opportunities for IDCM useful for specific document and content management applications in a range of vertical industry sectors.
*   Discuss the application of general document management functionality for workgroups and wider enterprise deployment.

Within the vertical market applications part of the chapter, we make reference to several case studies relating to different market sectors. These are cases for which there are references given in the general literature. Many more examples of specific case studies are provided by a number of the vendors listed in Appendix 4. The reader is referred to their Web sites for additional examples.

SYSTEM INTERFACES

In Chapter 4, we explained that IDCM solutions are unlikely to be implemented without giving consideration to interfacing with existing systems in associated areas. There are many areas of business activity that have an impact upon an IDCM system or are impacted by it. Depending upon the extent of integration, the functionality may be seen as part of an IDCM solution or as complementary to it. These other areas include:

- Knowledge management — where the recorded information in the IDCM system and the references to intellectual capacity of the organization, such as human resources expertise files or lessons learned and "Frequently Asked Questions" data may be effectively associated and retrieved. Thereby, they can be introduced to discussion threads or groupwork facilities for collaborative effort.

- Publishing — that implies that the viewing facilities are extended beyond the ability to provide different renditions. For example, if text is stored using a generic DDL, it is more likely to be able to be distributable to remote devices such as personal digital assistants (PDAs).

- Translation — particularly relevant to global corporations that may require content of the same versions in multiple languages, possible via fledgling online translation facilities, or more likely through manual production of alternate language versions of documents.

In this section, we review the applicability of IDCM when providing middle-ware services to support business systems. From the many possibilities, we consider:

- ERP systems;
- Plant control systems;
- Supply and maintenance;
- Geographical information systems;
- Financial management;
- Employee relations management;
- CRM systems; and
- Call center systems.

ERP Systems

Because ERP systems endeavor to provide for so many aspects of business processes, the benefits of integration with such systems cannot be underestimated. An enterprise system is typically modeled around a supply chain that looks to add value through stages such as planning of production, acquisition of materials, production, distribution, and marketing.

At each stage of the supply chain, knowledge is required and produced. A great deal of this knowledge is captured as information in documents. For example:

- Research and development leads to specifications or algorithms that may be applied in production planning.
- Engineering design may generate an SOE that is applied with acquisition and production.
- Sales reports may be fed back into marketing plans.

If such documentation can be associated with the functionality offered by IDCM systems, then enhancement to enterprise systems may include:

- Tracking regulatory or standards compliance for production processes;
- Using quality control and effective dissemination of standard operating procedure (SOP) material;
- Flexibly creating group reports, attribution and distribution and reduction of costs for general report management;
- Minimizing the use of printed reports;
- Sharing visualization of graphic materials, such as engineering drawings or assembly specifications or plant maintenance graphics; and
- Contextually linking retrieval capability to modules within enterprise software.

Plant Control Systems

Companies may have the requirement to implement and manage instrumentation and control systems to support the management of plant and control processes. These types of systems provide analytical measurement of process control data, such as pressures, temperatures, levels, flows, volume, water analysis, and conductivity.

Some companies also deploy a Supervisory Control and Data Acquisition (SCADA) system, which enables multiple items of equipment in many locations to be monitored and controlled from a central location. Duty operators are thus able to monitor the status of a particular process and to make the necessary adjustments.

The following types of functionality are achievable by integrating process control systems with an IDCM framework:

- Control and management of versions, revisions, and authorization processes for process control diagrams;
- Control and management for the generation of process control configuration objects;
- Control and management of download process control configuration objects to distributed control systems, and their return;
- Process control configuration object storage as configuration objects;
- Interface and management of monitory system reports and statistics; and
- Utilization of process control depiction as content in public documents or limited secure distribution to business associates.

Supply and Maintenance Systems

Enterprises may use a Supply and Maintenance (SAM) system or ERP system to support supply and maintenance management. There is generally a requirement for these systems to integrate with document management capabilities, so that documents and drawings relevant to the supply and maintenance processes of the plant, its equipment, and its facilities can be accessed quickly.

We make the following observations:

- Drawings and technical documentation (e.g., manuals) are often used as the source for registering information into a SAM system or module via keyboard data entry, with no direct integration between the business system and the source document objects.

- The lack of tight integration between the drawing register in the SAM system and module and its source documents (such as digital drawings) raises doubts in the minds of users as to the currency and validity of information. This may mean that users tend to confirm information held in the system by referencing original source documents.

When a user validates information in the SAM system or module against source documents, additional (manual) processes are required to be invoked, which means that the principle of having access to accurate information in a timely manner is not supported in the current environment.

The incorporation of the SAM system or module within an IDCM strategy (if cost effective), enables easy access and display of documents stored in the IDCM system from a variety of modules in the business system. It also enables users to store and manage reports and outgoing documents.

Designs, engineering drawings, specifications, SOPs data sheets, financial, production, and other reports and other documents can be immediately accessed by SAM system or module users as soon as the documents are released.

Batch reports and other related documents such as SOPs can be linked together to produce a complete digital record for final review and approval. This record can then be retrieved for future review and audit purposes.

Materials management should be enhanced as the union between a SAM system or module and IDCM enables engineers, technicians, planners, and operations personnel to share up-to-date information in a variety of formats, including text, graphics, CAD drawings, images, and multimedia.

Association of the proposed IDCM system with the SAM system or module may also provide the tool for managing the life-cycle of documents that describe plant assets, such as engineering drawings, specifications, and maintenance procedures.

Redlining and annotation capabilities enable users to review, mark up, and route documents to the outsourced drawing management provider, for revision, approval, and release of the documents.

A maintenance engineer using the SAM system or module could review scheduled maintenance activities for the next week. Where an item has to be replaced, the engineer would be able to list and view all of the relevant current documents, including maintenance procedures and relevant plant and equipment drawings.

Geographical Information Systems

Enterprises may have acquired a GIS that enables users to integrate geographical and metadata sources with the Internet or an intranet for display, query, and analysis using a Web browser. Typically, viewing capability via the Web has been achieved by a browser's native support for raster images, or via specialized plug-ins or applets to support (proprietary) vector images.

A GIS has potential multiple applications within most enterprises. Using environmental management as but one example, the GIS might be used to link geographic and laboratory and field data for predictive modeling to help organizations meet planning and compliance requirements.

The GIS can also be applied to facilitate asset management, by enabling asset and maintenance data to be displayed with visual indicators depicting specific items or events. Each item on the spatial display can be interrogated to determine attribute information relevant to the item, for example, a photograph of the asset, and details of planned inspections.

There are also applications that will make use of WAP technology to deliver real-time spatial information direct to handheld mobile devices, such as PDAs and mobile telephones, for example, the capability of travelers to access location information based on the positioning technology of the mobile telephone.

The limitation whereby Web browsers have only provided native support for raster images has been a restrictive factor in interactive use of GIS via Internet and intranet sites because of the need to refresh the image when a user pans or zooms. However, this type of limitation will be addressed by the development of new standards for geospatial data and interoperability. For example:

- The Scalable Vector Graphics (SVG) standard is an open standard language for describing two-dimensional vector graphics in XML. It provides a format for the display of vector images, supported natively within Web browsers. It offers the benefits experienced with XML, such as interoperability, extensive support, ease of utilization, and conversion.[1]
- The Geography Markup Language (GML) is a standard that represents geospatial objects or features incorporating real-world coordinates and associated real-world properties. The availability of GML's object properties makes it a suitable format for geospatial data interchange and is supported by the Open GIS Consortium.[2]

These types of display and interoperability standards might presage a much wider take-up of mobile mapping, where users are able to interact with GIS systems from mobile telephones or handheld devices, not only for displaying spatial views but also to create or update spatial data.

There may be a requirement for users to access the latest information held as content in documented form, while in a spatial view. It may be a specific object in a GIS view or related to a series of objects defined by views such as zones. The integrity of the data displayed in a GIS view might be assured when sourced from a GIS database, but the same level of integrity might not be assured when sourcing documents held on unmanaged file systems.

Consequently, there is a compelling case for associating the planning and implementation of GIS with the managed repository services offered as part of the IDCM solution architecture. The repository manager would maintain control over all versions of document content required to supplement the spatial views. To this end, suppliers of IDCM systems often have strategic partnering relationships with suppliers of GIS, so that there is cooperative development of the required integration services between the IDCM system and GIS.

This type of integration enables objects stored in an IDCM repository to be accessed from a GIS spatial view. The capability to integrate GIS and IDCM systems is extremely useful within a range of industry sectors, particularly where there is a requirement to view information spatially and then locate relevant supporting documents. The types of documents may include engineering drawings, plans, specifications, applications, manuals, or fact sheets, but the nature of these objects depends upon the business requirements for accessing documents from a GIS.

System integration between GIS into IDCM enables functionality such as:

- The retrieval of document objects from a search result based on spatial values;
- The filtering of document objects required for a spatial search based on values such as document type;
- The restricted selection of document objects based on a unique identifier and criteria, such as drawing number;
- Association of GIS-related documents with data and documents from other areas such as marketing to enhance decision making; and
- Ready identification of images and utilization of them for incorporation into public documents and promotional material.

Financial Management Systems

Many enterprises implement Financial Management Systems (FMS), sometimes as an integral module of an ERP system, for managing business or government financial information. An organization's FMS generally consists of modules for managing the chart of accounts, general ledger, accounts receivable, and accounts payable.

Most organizations are not yet sufficiently advanced with their ecommerce modules so that they are participating in electronic management of accounts receivable and accounts payable. For example, many organizations pay their accounts by Electronic Funds Transfer (EFT) but rely on manual submission of invoices from creditors.

There is generally a business interest in using imaging/workflow technology to facilitate the accounts payable process, which generally involves manual review and approval systems using hard-copy documents. The process of filing hard-copy documents such as invoices and supporting receipts is labor intensive. The data relating to the accounts payable transaction is stored in the FMS, but the retrieval of supporting documentation relies on manual processes.

The requirement to improve the business processes associated with accounts payable may be achievable via a number of options. For example:

- Develop e-commerce facilities that enable creditors to lodge invoice claims for payment via the Internet, and utilize Web-enabled workflow to automate review and approval processes and update the FMS.
- Implement imaging and workflow technology to assist with the capture, storage, search, and retrieval of accounts payable documentation. The use of imaging and

workflow technology facilitates quick capture and retrieval of supporting documentation.

The various options for workflow need to be considered to determine the capabilities of any workflow product offered by the FMS, or the capabilities of the system to integrate with imaging technology, and if necessary, third-party workflow software.

Employee Relations Management Systems

Most enterprises have implemented employee relations management systems that typically satisfy the processing of all or some of the following requirements: employee personal details, establishment and appointment details, payroll, leave, training and development, recruitment, occupational health and safety, performance, and workforce planning.

However, the current business processes associated with managing the human relations function within enterprises are generally manual-intensive processes. They are typically based on the creation of forms, which are managed manually through review and approval processes, to storage on hard-copy files.

These processes can involve handling delays and often create duplication of effort. There are also inadequate management controls over the manual processes. For example, there may be a lack of appropriate checks and balances relating to the submission of leave forms.

There can be an inadequate architecture for the receipt, processing, and management of electronic employee relations information. For example, the employee relations management system may lack the capacity to receive applications in electronic form with electronic update of employee relations data.

Business continuity may be compromised by the loss of employee relations files. For example, the loss of an employee file may mean that:

- Data stored on the employee relations management system could not be validated.
- There would be inadequate supporting information relating to old employee data, if it were not now stored on the system.

An IDCM environment offers the following opportunities for supporting the employee relations function within enterprises:

- The capability to register, manage, and retrieve important electronic documents (e.g., position descriptions, curriculum vitae), spreadsheets (e.g., calculations), email, and images (e.g., employee photographs, educational certificates, birth certificates, etc.);
- The use of electronic forms and integrated workflow, which support the electronic processing of applications for leave, nominations for training programs, and applications for positions;
- The ability to capture reports from the employee relations system and store them in a secure, managed repository;
- The ability to associate personnel training records with training materials content from courses attended, and updates to that content, for current awareness purposes; and

- The foundation to support any planned employee self-service initiatives by giving management and employees assurance that the correct documentation is being displayed on an interface (such as a portal), and then only to authorized users.

Customer Relationship Management Systems

Many DMS vendors have developed relationships with the suppliers of CRM systems, so that enterprises are able to provide an integrated information environment to their sales and customer service professionals.

The integrated information systems provide end users of a CRM system with quick access to electronically stored documents or location of physical documents that are relevant to a customer service matter. This type of integrated solution also has the potential to reduce turnaround times for managing customer requests and to reduce costs.

The integrated solution may assist enterprises in developing closer relationships with their customers and in learning to understand customers' needs, and then tailor products and services to their customers' unique requirements. Consequently, the integrated solution also has the capability not only to reduce costs but also to increase revenues.

We use the example of claims processing within the insurance sector to demonstrate the benefit of a solution that integrates the capabilities of CRM with an IDCM approach. If we look at the example of processing a motor vehicles accident claim, then:

- The CRM system might contain the details of the claimant, key attributes relating to the policy, and previous history of claims. (The CRM has the capacity to provide a universal view of customer information across lines of business and distribution channels.)
- The claimant's history of interaction with the insurance company evidenced in documents may be held in digital form in the IDCM system. The documents could have been digitally created or could be scanned copies of hard-copy documents.
- A customer service officer is able to access a customer's profile information stored in the CRM databases via an intuitive graphical interface, and also establish details of instances relating to previous claims.
- The customer service officer is able to access important documentation relevant to this claim instance directly from an IDCM system. These types of documents may include the customer claim form, accident report, and photographs of damage to the vehicle.
- Similarly, the customer service officer is able to view salient details of claims history and access documented records relating to previous claims quickly from within the CRM environment.

Call Center Systems

Call Centers are a vital link between an organization and its customers, can play a vital role in organizational customer retention strategies, and have significant impact on customer satisfaction levels.

Typically, call centers handle a wide diversity of requests from customers, who also expect call center personnel to have instantaneous answers to requests. Consequently, personnel are expected to absorb a great deal of knowledge regarding an enterprise's operations, products, and services.

The high staff turnover experienced in call centers can be an outcome of high workload and stress issues related to constant business demands for improving efficiencies (typically, reduced call handling measures) and operational performance monitoring.

Consequently, aside from addressing the organizational employee relations aspects of call center management, enterprises need to develop adequate strategies to ensure that information given to customers is accurate and consistent.

Knowledge strategies should ensure that information relating to an enterprise's operations, products, and services and call handling rules and logic are current and quickly accessible to call center operators. The solution to underpin the enterprise's knowledge strategies for call center operations needs to support the dynamics of business structural and process changes, and the latest information pertaining to the release or removal of products and services.

As an extension to or as an alternative to CRM and IDCM integration, IDCM vendors may have also developed relationships with the suppliers of customer interaction software used for automating call centers.

This type of strategic partnership enables businesses to introduce IDCM technology as a strategy to support business solutions, in this case, through the integration of telephony functionality within call centers. Personnel are able to access customer service information, IDCM, and integrated workflow technologies.

The IDCM repository manager gives call center personnel access to documentation at their desktop, which in this type of application has significant potential to improve productivity, and improve customer satisfaction. Staff members' satisfaction may also be increased if they are confident that they are always accessing the latest information relating to organizational processes, products, and services.

SPECIFIC IDCM APPLICATIONS

There are many different applications for IDCM when managing vital records and important business documentation. The following applications are a guide to the types of functionality that can be achieved:

- *Request for Proposal (RFP) documentation*: We review the management of RFP documentation, because the need to seek proposals for products or services is a widespread application within business and government. The example also covers a wide range of IDCM functionality, which can be applied to numerous document and content management applications.
- *Occupational Health and Safety system documentation*: This example is included because of the vital nature of documentation and the widespread requirement within business and government enterprises to manage OH&S documentation.
- *Quality (or Business) Management System documentation*: We include this example because of the implications of document control and document management when seeking accreditation to ISO 9001. The scenario and example are similarly applicable to ISO 14001 for environmental management systems.
- *Drawing management*: This example is included because the requirement to have access to the correct revision of a drawing is crucial in many disciplines, including

engineering services, plant maintenance, asset management, and construction engineering, across many industry sectors. Unfortunately, there have been a number of recorded fatalities due to workers taking action on plant and equipment items based on outdated drawing information, so the example is important in helping organizations to understand the risks involved.

- *Correspondence management*: This is included because of its generic nature to business and government enterprises. It is also a problematic area, because organizations find that relevant items of incoming and outgoing correspondence are not readily accessible due to breakdowns in the manual processes.

- *Forms processing*: Many documents in enterprises are forms-based and need to be captured and managed.

- *Agendas and minutes*: We included this example because enterprises normally publish agendas and minutes of meetings. A business organization should at least be keeping records of the general meetings of shareholders.

- *Records management*: This example is included primarily to show how an IDCM system may subsume the capabilities required of records systems covering digital and physical formats.

- *Online publishing*: This is included to show specific content management and its association with document management procedures.

- *General document management*: For workgroups and knowledge workers.

Similar techniques for managing vital records and important business documentation may be applied according to individual circumstances, albeit for different applications.

Requests for Proposals (or Tenders)

The high-level processes generally involved in the preparation, approval, and management of RFP (or request for tender) documentation, depending on the degree of business process automation, are as follows:

- The business unit that has the requirement for a product or service prepares a specification. The specification is developed using standard word-processing software, perhaps in a format based on a template. The document is saved to a logical drive on a file server during development of the specification.

- The specification may also consist of additional documentation in different types of formats, such as spreadsheet, project management, and CAD drawings. These documents are accrued as a "packet" in the logical drive on the file server and are associated by folder name.

- Once the specification has been prepared, it is referred for assembly of relevant contract documentation, such as general conditions of contract and special conditions of contract. The specification plus the contractual conditions, together with invitations to provide proposals, form the RFP documentation.

- The RFP, once edited and assembled, is printed for review and approval procedures. Once approved, the RFP is ready for release to potential suppliers.

- Many organizations print multiple copies of the RFP document for distribution, because (a) they do not have the facility to publish RFP via Internet Web services or (b) some or all suppliers do not make use of the Internet facility.

- The RFP can be converted to formats suitable for publication on the Internet, Web content pages are developed, and the content and tender documentation are migrated to a Web server for publication.

The following limitations are apparent with those types of methods for preparing an RFP:

- There is no centrally managed repository for templates that are used to create specifications and contract documentation. Consequently, the potential exists for end users to access and use superseded templates when developing specifications or RFP documentation.
- The existing method of document storage does not implement management controls over versions of documents. Consequently, there is the risk that a document (if not "read only") may be accidentally overwritten, particularly where existing documents are reused for the development of new specifications.
- There is the risk that multiple copies of a document may exist in multiple locations, without version control and synchronization. The risk is that an end user may access a specification or RFP that is not the correct version of the documentation.
- The method of publishing tender documentation to the Internet is manual intensive, and the reliance on "manual" Web publishing processes involves the risk that incorrect versions of objects may be published to the Internet.

The following examples of opportunities exist for improving the management of RFP documentation, using the scenario we have outlined, and using an IDCM approach, together with integrated workflow management software, and content management via Web publishing tools.

- Templates can be stored in an IDCM system, thus providing version control over templates and assuring a consistent structure and format for the individual document types that comprise the RFP packet, such as specifications, CAD files, conditions of contract, and proposal information.
- The templates can be associated with the relevant document types, so that metadata relevant to each key document type can be validated by the document database when a new document based on a template is saved to the DMS.
- The provision of a compound document construction within an IDCM approach enables the assembly of multiple documents of diverse formats to be associated with a particular RFP, thus providing management controls over the RFP packet as a single versioned entity.
- The multiple associated documents (specifications, conditions of contract) can inherit the formatting characteristics of a related parent document (RFP) and enable review and publishing with standard headers and footers, page numbers, and styles.
- The integration of the document management with workflow management software enables managed distribution of the content of documents for review and approval. Once the documentation is approved, it is ready for publication.

- An IDCM approach requires the capability to integrate with Web publishing tools so that the RFP packet (including related component documents) can be published to the Internet.
- The IDCM system can incorporate an interface with scanning and imaging devices and software to enable hard-copy documents, color brochures, and photographs to be captured and stored for publication as part of an RFP evaluation process.
- The IDCM system can be used to capture each proposal as a record of a business transaction, in a simple manner. It can also provide a managed repository for review of proposals and integrated workflow software for managing the proposal evaluation process.

Occupational Health and Safety (OH&S) Management System

An IDCM approach has the capability to reduce the risks associated with the lack of automated management controls over the publication of OH&S documentation on company Intranet sites.

Safety health and environment documentation may be developed using authoring tools such as word-processing software, and controlled copies of the documents are generally stored on a company's file server environment. Organizations generally maintain a database register of OH&S documents, and the documents may be published on an intranet site, via a manual transfer and publication process.

Incident reports involving OH&S may be submitted in hard-copy format and managed using manual processes, and a database register may be maintained for all incident reports and action items.

Issues that may have impact are as follows:

- There may be a risk that OH&S documents published on an intranet site may not be current, as there are no automated management controls over the editing or update and publication processes. The risk is that users may access and make decisions based on the incorrect version of an OH&S document.
- There may be no integration between the databases and the electronic objects. The risk is that there is not rigorous update or synchronization of database and document content.

IDCM reduces the risks by integration of database and document content files. Users accessing the documentation will have the confidence that they are accessing the correct versions of documents. IDCM will also integrate with workflow and Web publishing tools to manage publication of the correct OH&S documentation to the intranet or extranet (if the OH&S information is to be shared with business partners).

Quality (or Business) Management System

Enterprises regularly register Quality Management System (QMS) documentation in a Document Control Register. However, creation, update, and approval processes associated with the development and maintenance of QMS often involve the development of documents stored on file systems.

There is generally no direct integration between the database containing metadata for the documentation supporting the QMS, the document objects, and the intranet, where QMS information is often published. This fragmentation may pose a threat to the integrity of the QMS. Enterprises may require an integrated solution that will enable quality documentation to be published onto an intranet site and instill authorized users with the confidence that the very latest information is being published.

In these circumstances, the use of integrated document management, workflow, and Web publishing tools would provide the following:

- The opportunity to reduce the tasks involved in maintaining a manual system for managing QMS documents;
- The opportunity to reduce the time frame or requirements for the review, authorization, and distribution processes;
- The ability to produce reports listing documents not accessed within a given period, to assist in determining currency and validity;
- The chance to view background annotations regarding versions of documents; and
- The ability to reduce consumable costs involved in maintaining the manual system.

An IDCM system featuring managed repository services and workflow would support an enterprise's initiatives to achieve or maintain ISO quality accreditation and facilitate responsiveness in service delivery. The IDCM system may be utilized in the following manner for the management of QMS documents:

- Documents can be developed using desktop authoring tools based on standard document templates. The documents can be registered and stored in the IDCM system during development, thereby maintaining version control over the content of the documents.
- The DMS can be integrated with a flexible workflow management tool and email messaging system, enabling the automation of the review and approval process, with management controls over each document during the review and approval process for QMS documents.
- Workflow can be set to enable the progress of the review and approval cycle to be monitored and enable follow up action to be initiated, where required.
- IDCM can be used to automate the process for publishing approved QMS documents in PDF or HTML format to an intranet site, reducing the need for intervention by a Web manager and preventing users from modifying published documents.
- Integrated search and retrieval facilities may be provided using metadata describing QMS documents and the contents of the objects.
- The current databases (computerized or manual) used to register QMS documents can be decommissioned after migration of the data attributes to an IDCM solution.

Drawing Management

It is imperative for many enterprises to maintain drawings for operational and maintenance purposes. Management of drawings is vital in sectors including manufacturing, resources, construction, engineering services, and government.

Drawings are normally created using CAD software, but the output is often physical drawings that are managed using manual processes. The drawing function may be managed internally or contracted to a service provider, in which case, there is a need for version control and synchronization of drawings held by the company and the contractor.

Some companies have converted their hard-copy drawings to digital images, and some are contemplating doing so, particularly with the opportunities for quick transfer and collaboration with external parties using business-to-business (extranet) technology.

The integrity of drawings generally relies upon manual procedures, such as the transfer of digital drawings from a works in progress folder to an approved folder on a company's file server. There is risk involved, because there is no guarantee that the correct drawing has been transferred.

There is typically an inability to search one logical database to obtain all information relevant to engineering project documentation, quality documents, OH&S documentation, policy documents, and administrative files. Often, there is also an inability to provide for simple correlation of electronic versions of a document with its physical counterpart, in hard-copy or microform (such as aperture card) or both. Redline and markup of drawings is a manual process using physical drawings.

Transmittals within the organization, externally, or both, are mostly received from and sent to a distribution list or contracted service provider via hard-copy documentation.

Application of an IDCM approach is key to effective management of engineering drawings and associated documents. Essentially, IDCM will:

- Support the engineering project management processes and facilitate collaboration between an enterprise and its contracted service provider for drawing processes;
- Share one logical repository controlled by access permissions, which can be extended to all authorized members;
- Ensure that each member, authorized business partner, and service provider has access to the correct version of an engineering drawing, as well as a complete history of past efforts;
- Assist enterprises in delivering best practice in project management document control, and support the quality of its deliverables;
- Register project-based documentation as a record of a business transaction, in a simple manner;
- Provide the capacity to link images in as components of compound documents, and maintain current versions of the images; and
- Enable images to be passed to publishing components of the system in a controlled manner when required.

Correspondence Management

Many organizations receive large volumes of correspondence of many types, including letters from customers, deliverables from service providers, or shared information with business partners, reports letters, and advice relating to the regulatory environment. Some of these are general application and some industry specific. The typical processes are to sort the mail, possibly an initial sort to weed out mail items that are considered business correspondence, and then a second sort to differentiate types of relevant business items (e.g., applications, accounts payable, etc.).

Organizations usually have an information system for registering correspondence and other hard-copy documents. Some organizations continue to use manual index cards and methods for registering documents. However, access to the information system, which is generally called "the records management system" (RMS as introduced in Chapter 1), is not always universal within the enterprise, meaning that localized systems are used for recording correspondence away from the registry. Other types of records, such as employee relations files, may also be managed independently of the registry.

After registration, correspondence is then distributed by hand for action or information to designated officers. The correspondence might be distributed on a file, or it may be distributed as a loose-leaf item. It might be photocopied if it is to be distributed to more than one officer. The difficulty then arises of tracking the physical documents during the time that they are in an active life-cycle. Organizations may allow officers to update the status of a document using the RMS or require them to complete physical tracking slips for transmission to the registry for updating the document location status. This is a fragmented process, and there is a potential for duplication of effort in maintaining multiple registration and filing systems.

Outward correspondence is mostly generated using standard word-processing tools. The means of registering the document may involve printing a copy of the correspondence, with a copy of all attachments, and placing these documents in an out-tray for collection by registry personnel for registration in the RMS. However, if an action officer has possession of the file upon which the document is registered, the file might not be returned to the registry personnel for quite some time after a letter has been dispatched. We observe that in many organizations, there is no defined regime or no adherence to defined regimes for registering outgoing correspondence, so that a person doing an inquiry on the RMS might not find information that the correspondence has been sent.

Figure 1 provides an overview of fragmented registration of correspondence in an environment as described here.

An integrative approach can help deal with correspondence management in the following ways:

- Incoming items of business correspondence in physical format can be scanned and stored in an IDCM system.
- Documents can be sorted into batches prior to scanning to an IDCM system to enable common metadata relevant to a specific document type to be captured during the scanning process.
- Barcode technology and OCR/ICR capabilities can be utilized to capture key metadata from correspondence, particularly where it is forms-based (see section entitled "Forms Processing").
- Workflow packets can be initiated automatically based on the specific types of document in a batch. For example, all correspondence for a particular construction area on a major construction project could be routed to a role in that particular area.

- The integrated workflow management system could be used to coordinate all aspects of the distribution and tasks to be undertaken. Reference to this is made in Chapter 16.

- Action officers can use the ability to create, save, and manage letters of response, for example, to customers or business partners, perhaps using predefined templates for specific types of letters (e.g., response to customer, letter to business partner).

- The IDCM approach integrated with workflow can be used to manage the whole life-cycle of the process relevant to specific types or items of correspondence.

- IDCM and workflow management can provide quick search and retrieval for documents relevant to a particular work packet or for all documents a user is authorized to access.

- The need for users to register documentation in multiple information silos can be eliminated, because the metadata describing the document is captured once and is accessible to all. The additional metadata captured during the workflow is captured as part of the business process cycle.

- IDCM can provide the capability for an enterprise to register objects as a record and also retain the workflow as a full record of the life-cycle process for the particular work packet.

Although it is unlikely that there will be routine requirement to "publish" correspondence beyond the confines of a company, content management procedures can still be applied to making it available on internal intranets in association with workflow requirements.

Figure 1: Fragmented Correspondence Registration Scenario.

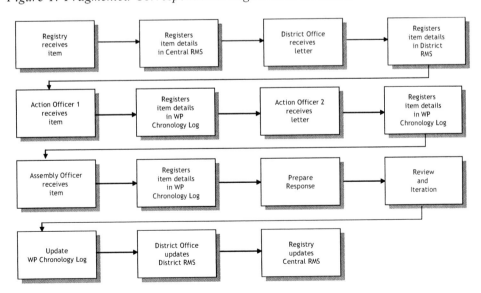

Forms Processing

Many situations occur when documents are forms-based, and the forms warrant special attention. Just as correspondence may be captured into an IDCM system, then distributed for processing, so too can forms be captured and distributed to relevant action officers.

Depending on the forms-processing application, there may be a requirement for enterprises to implement production imaging systems (refer to Chapter 15) and integrated production workflow systems (refer to Chapter 16) as part of its IDCM strategy. In addition to the capability to scan physical forms to digital image and route to relevant roles within the organization, recognition technologies (such as OCR and ICR; refer to Chapter 15) can be used for automating the data collection processes associated with forms processing.

It may be necessary to provide for a combination of digital and paper-based forms with synchronization between the two maintained so that the quality of data captured via either method is consistent.

Many business enterprises receive order forms from customers and need to maintain details as a record of a business transaction. The forms may be resident on the Internet as well as paper-based. Scanning the form will capture the image of the document, and recognition technologies can be used to extract relevant metadata for update of the FMS. Some examples of using recognition technologies for forms processing are as follows:

- Insurance and finance companies can make use of barcodes, OCR, and ICR to capture data from claims forms or to recognize marks made on questionnaires regarding customer requirements for insurance or finance.
- ICR has proven successful in processing medical claims processing, so that it is used to capture data from the high volume of claims forms being processed by medical insurers.
- Companies can utilize the technology for the digitization of payments received or for capturing credit applications that may contain handwritten information in designated areas of a form.
- Mark recognition systems can be used to score the answer to set test sheets in tertiary, secondary, and primary education systems.
- ICR can be used to recognize marks made on survey sheets when companies conduct market research, so that data is collected automatically from the source sheets and uploaded to a computer database.

Increasingly, enterprises are turning to digital forms. Particularly for internal work, they are using them to eliminate paper-based material with significant reductions in processing costs. Spencer (2001) reviewed the business benefits and provided many examples of applications and vendor software. In such situations, data transfer into business processing areas becomes much more straightforward. However, there remains the issue of forms management and maintaining normal document control functions, such as versioning for the form templates.

Content management for forms can be applied to design and production and "publication" of the forms, as opposed to the data they capture. A forms management program will need to ensure the compatibility of new forms with retired forms in order to maintain data quality by consistent capture mechanisms. For example, if a form requires a user to enter address information, and if the layout is changed, it must remain compatible with the corresponding fields in the database where the captured data ultimately reside.

Agendas and Minutes

The requirement to manage agendas and minutes for Board meetings, Management Committee meetings, and a diverse range of business meetings provides an opportunity for the application of an IDCM approach. IDCM can do the following:

- Provide an efficient method for creating, reviewing, and approving reports to Boards and Committees.
- Provide version control over the development of reports, agendas, minutes, and supplementary documents.
- Manage scanning of hard-copy documents to be attached to reports.
- Provide routing facilities for enabling electronic review and approval processes for reports, agendas, and minutes.
- Provide facilities for publishing agendas, minutes, and reports onto the intranet and integrate with Web publishing for approved versions to recipients on the Internet.
- Support the requirement to collate and print copies of agendas, reports, and minutes.
- Provide facilities to maintain a corporate record of Board and Committee decisions.
- Provide associations between established policies and the work areas and functions to which the policies apply.

Records Management

The emphasis on recordkeeping in many enterprises is changing from a focus on managing hard-copy documents to managing electronic objects. Elsewhere in this book (for example, in the previous chapter), we considered some of the perceived differences between records management and document management. Because we are taking the line that records, as defined for records management purposes, are subsumed by documents in general, then our emphasis is on finding functionality within an IDCM strategy that caters to the special features of records management.

For example, IDCM should encompass a repository that supports records management features such as those that provide for taxonomy of files or a classification scheme, and should associate with an organization's retention and disposal authorities. In this way, information objects involved in an electronic business transaction may be classified by information managers and be scheduled as records.

The following records features, which should be consistent with the ISO 15489 framework (International Organization for Standardization, 2001), are typical of records management features sought in an IDCM solution with minimal configuration customization:

- All relevant electronic objects should be captured in an IDCM, and where they are specifically identified as evidential records of business transaction, then records management classification and scheduling may be applied.

- All physical record items (e.g., hard-copy, microfilm, and videocassettes) should be able to be registered into the IDCM following the same principles as for digital documents.

- The IDCM should be able to encompass forms as described in the "Forms Processing" section above so that history of form development may be recorded through form versions, and so that formal retention procedures for form approval, design, and structure may be maintained.

- A classification structure using a taxonomy such as a "functional thesaurus" should be integrated with the DMS via the RM extension to classification of record items.

- This scheme should be integrated with retention and disposal scheduling metadata to enable automation of notification, scheduling, and disposal actions.

- RMS procedures used for internal files can be extended to information published by an enterprise, so that procedures for authorization, review, and withdrawal of published documents are maintained.

Online Publishing

Content management is regularly seen as management of an online publishing process for Web delivery of internal information to personnel. For example, an application may include business goals along the lines of the following:

- Deliver procedural manuals for technical staff.

- Provide sales information for marketing staff.

- Provide information in online form with formatted hard-copy versions printable on demand.

- Provide for authoring and authorization procedures so that information is relevant and accurate.

- Undertake procedures for regular updates and maintenance of links.

- Establish quality control procedures for verifying content.

Procedural requirements to make this possible may include:

- Provision of style sheets and templates to provide consistent formatting;

- Utilization of markup tools that enable production in multiple formats and fragmenting or compounding of documents according to requirements;

- Simultaneous online authoring by multiple authors using a tool that can associate database text and graphics and maintain versioning control;

- Production of different renditions of documents according to use requirements;

- Tagging of metadata so that documents being created may also be described; and

- Modification of content without breaking inbuilt links.

All of these approaches are familiar in IDCM systems, and within this text, we make repeated reference to them in different contexts and applications. However, the creation of content for Web distribution has meant that in some quarters, this form of document production process is seen as fundamentally new, when in practice, it is simply another delivery mechanism for digital documents — documents with a production process that must be managed.

Further, it is becoming increasingly problematic to differentiate between material that is published and material that is produced for limited distribution. The production processes and format of internal document production and external document publication were formerly very different. However, this is another of those fields in which formerly quite distinct procedures have become convergent through IT application. Facilities such as markup languages make the document production process uniform. Resulting digital objects may be extracted from internal documents and combined with other material in publicly available documents.

The definition of "publishing" has always included meaning relating to making personal things known to a wider audience, or humanity in general. When the publishing industry is taken into account, this meaning is overlaid with editorial involvement and approval processes and document presentation skills. It could be said that any enterprise that has a Web presence is now in the publishing industry. The extent of its involvement may depend upon how integrated is its approach to document and content management.

General Document Management

Most organizations require an IDCM that allows its employees to manage more effectively the wide range of documents prepared internally and obtained from external sources. IDCM should enable registration and storage of document types, such as formatted and unformatted text, images, faxes, drawings, pictures, presentations, photographs, sound files, videos, and Web content.

IDCM must also support a wide set of repository services to enable it to manage compound document relationships, engineering drawings, renditions, and Web content management. It is also required to integrate with existing desktop applications and have the extensibility, flexibility, and scalability to adapt to an enterprise's future information requirements.

The system must allow users to store electronic documents seamlessly into a repository from within document creation systems, paper document imaging applications, and electronic messaging systems. Documents must be stored in the application's native format or a common recognized standard format that faithfully preserves all formatting information and is printer independent.

The system must enable the registration of consistent metadata, customized to meet the varied requirements for classes of documents (e.g., drawing, email, correspondence, and presentation classes) to facilitate its retrieval. The impact on the end user needs to be minimized wherever possible by automatically collecting as much of this information as possible from the user's systems environment, and through the use of defaults associated with document templates, and the specific application being used to create the document.

The system should offer logical, nested folder structures to enable general workgroup electronic documents to be stored and accessed by browsing. The system should allow documents to be moved between folders, where appropriate.

The system should also feature check-in/check-out, version control, and management of renditions. In effect:

- When an author wants to change a document stored in the document repository, the system should provide a copy of the document and prevent further change access by others until the edited copy is saved back into the repository as a new version.

- The new version of a document should have appropriate time stamping, authoring metadata information, and standard naming to ensure that it is possible to uniquely identify this version and to trace the change history over the life of the document.
- IDCM must support version control where the most recent version is provided to users as the default, but users can view previous versions where authorized.
- It must provide a mechanism for ensuring that version control is maintained over different renditions of the same document. For example, an intranet user should be able to access the PDF version of a word document controlled by the IDCM solution.

Most enterprises will require IDCM to manage version control and referential relationships between compound documents, particularly in regard to engineering documents, strategic and planning documents, large reports containing compound documents, and Web content management.

There may also be a need to migrate document objects and any associated attribute data from the shared LAN server folders to the document management modules. Enterprises may require bulk conversion capabilities that reduce the overall cost of migration and minimize the risk of populating the IDCM system with corrupt or incorrect metadata.

Enterprises will also require the application of a rules-based approach to archiving and disposal of documents maintained within IDCM. This rules-based approach should ideally take into account disposal regulations that comply with relevant regulatory requirements and prevent the deletion of official records of business transactions prior to the period of time for which they must be kept. IDCM should also allow systems administrators to archive low-use documents to permanent or semipermanent storage.

BUSINESS STRATEGIES

The application of IDCM can support business strategies formed around the promotion of knowledge management or of e-business.

Knowledge Management

An organization's capability to support knowledge-intensive processes and encourage its members and business partners to create useful new knowledge is severely hampered by a fragmented document environment. IDCM can be a fundamental building block to the development of knowledge management strategies, as information is a key resource to assist with learning, sharing, and reusability principles. Information needs to be managed within an effective, integrated model (Hawryszkiewycz, 2000) upon which organizations can build to create a knowledge-sharing organization.

In Chapter 7, we examine organizational information policy that should be setting a context for document management policy. In knowledge terms, this may well have to take account of the matter of making tacit knowledge explicit — that is, identifying effective ways of making use of what people know, but which they may have problems in expressing.

This expression may be by way of doing something — work tasks employing knowledge in action that others may emulate; or by recording the knowledge — that is, getting it onto an information medium (a document) that others may subsequently use for learning. Trainers or technical writers may facilitate the technical communication that accompanies either of these approaches. The writers make the knowledge explicit using such devices as:

- Organizing knowledge into information representations that embody significance, sequence, and cause, using mechanisms such as categorization, workflow analysis, or expert systems;
- Making corporate knowledge available as Web content through sites managed to provide access to knowledge in lessons learned databases, training programs, and shared "soft" information, for example, from email;
- Analyzing and identifying user needs, where the users are those carrying out organizational procedures;
- Interviewing specialists and making their ideas explicit with words and graphics, particularly those aspects that may be generalized;
- Providing technical detail through research; and
- Expressing themselves using clearly understood terminology that is appropriate to the organizational context and its culture.

Knowledge strategy must therefore take into account how the knowledge may be documented and then effectively disseminated.

E-Business/E-Government

While the technology designed to underpin e-business is focused on information delivery, there is a compelling business requirement for information in documents to be managed as a strategy to support e-business initiatives. IDCM practices and technology need to be viewed as a core element of the information architecture that is required to support the new technologies for marketing, SCM, and service delivery via the "new economy" paradigm.

For example, some enterprises have a business imperative to make important paper-generated information digitally available as quickly as possible. A case in point is FedEx Corp., which established a scanning system to give international customers better access to information about shipments and faster customs clearance (Rosencrance, 2001). The technology provides image-enabled Web access to documentation on international shipments, reducing delays associated with customs clearance paperwork. Although customers previously had online access to shipment tracking, before the imaging systems were installed, it took several days for customers to gain access to shipment clearances for billing purposes. The customers can plan more efficiently based on anticipated delivery volumes, and company managers can plan staffing and routing, taking volume fluctuations into account.

VERTICAL MARKET APPLICATIONS
Banking and Financial Services

We mentioned in Chapter 2 that the financial services sector has traditionally invested in technologies such as document imaging and production workflow systems to help manage transactional documents, such as check processing, loan applications, and similar operational processes that involve large volumes of documents.

The application of IDCM within the financial services sector may provide the opportunity to manage transactional (typically forms-based) and nontransactional documents (general document management) within an integrated enterprise architecture that features:

- Production-level document imaging systems and workflow applications for high-volume transaction documents;
- OCR and ICR technologies to assist with capture, indexing, and retrieval of scanned documents;
- DMS that implement controls over administrative documents and email;
- Content management systems that manage information published to the Internet (customer facing) and intranet (business decision-making) sites;
- Personalization services to assist with the tailoring of content to customers and also to support the need to communicate with clients in diverse languages and interoperate within several cultures;
- Integrated secondary storage for managing structured data and reports, as well as documents not required for permanent storage, and archival management systems for long-term preservation of documents;
- Integration with ERM (COLD) and interfaces with data warehousing technologies;
- Implementation of mandated recordkeeping requirements in all document-related systems; and
- Integrated portal for enabling relevant staff to access transactional and administrative documents, where authorized.

An integrated solution for managing documents enables users to search and retrieve information across disparate data sources and enable the financial institution to implement more efficient and appropriate processes. The sharing of information will enable the financial institutions to produce more accurate results in an efficient manner and improve service levels to customers. It may also support the continuing use of records and archives for service-oriented initiatives, based on the specific requirements of the organization.

The deployment of an IDCM solution (including integrated workflow and Web publishing tools) provides the platform to support the management of Web content, providing "full life-cycle" management of content within the financial institution from document creation, through review and approval processes, to publication on intranet/Internet.

The implementation of IDCM solutions within the financial services sector may assist banks and other financial institutions to meet regulatory obligations and reduce the risk of brand damage and provide the foundation for knowledge management strategies. We note that the financial sector may not be in a position to effectively implement knowledge management strategies without adequate repository controls over administrative documents.

Pharmaceuticals

There are multiple potential applications for IDCM in the pharmaceuticals sector. The management of ISO quality management system documentation is but one example. There is a requirement in the manufacturing division, for example, for quality management system documentation to be quickly accessible to operational staff at work centers in the manufacturing process.

Where quality documents are prepared, amended, and authorized using manual-intensive processes, the management processes, including review and approval and distribution, are generally time consuming. One or more work centers in the manufacturing division may have a requirement to access the current versions of quality documents. Under manual systems, this entails maintaining a register of documents at each work center, and each newly created or revised document may have to be printed a number of times, depending on how many work centers require access to the quality document.

A Document Control Register might be used as the primary register for quality documents, but it generally does not implement management controls over the objects or the process. The Document Control System may produce a unique barcode label for each document that is to be stored, and associate each document uniquely to a work center via the format of the barcode. Each unique label is placed on each relevant copy of a controlled quality document prior to its distribution to a work center. The barcode details can be downloaded from a client workstation to a barcode reader to facilitate quality audit processes.

Generally, one hard-copy of each quality document is stored centrally under the supervision of the Quality Manager. Each hard-copy document contains the relevant authorizing signatures and is regarded as the primary controlled copy. Personnel in work centers might access hard-copy quality documents at their station by referencing a manual index, listed by document code maintained at the front of each document folder.

This type of environment has the following limitations:

- The distribution process involved in maintaining a hard-copy-based quality system is labor intensive and time consuming.
- Amendments to quality documents are processed manually without the types of controls available in integrated workflow management systems (refer to Chapter 16).
- Delays can occur during the authorization process for new quality documents and amendments, due to manual routing mechanisms.
- Changes may be made to documents without consultation with initial authors (if available).
- Operational users do not have the facilities to search on document attributes or on the content of documents, because of the hard-copy storage/retrieval/viewing paradigm.
- Redundancy might occur when new quality documents are created for processes that are already defined in existing documents.

- New or revised processes may make quality documents superseded or redundant, but the fact of obsolescence may not be reported.

The implementation of IDCM together with workflow management software may improve cycle times for production and distribution of quality documents to operators at work centers. An IDCM/workflow solution would enable the company to provide ISO quality documentation online to authorized users throughout the manufacturing division and reap the following types of benefits:

- Provide all authorized users with rapid access to the current versions of documents in a single logical document repository.
- Reduce the laborious tasks involved in maintaining a manual system for managing controlled documents, including manual production processes; copying and distribution; and maintenance.
- Reduce time lines for the review, authorization, and distribution processes.
- Produce reports listing documents not accessed within a given period to assist in determining currency and validity.
- Provide background annotations or notations regarding versions of documents.
- Reduce consumable costs involved in maintaining a manual system.

Professional Services — Legal

We mentioned in Chapter 2 that legal enterprises may have the requirement to allow lawyers to focus on billable work by quickly accessing documents relating to a matter that is being progressed on behalf of a client.

Case Example: Tarmac America Inc.
Study: How to save time and money in a less papered office
(Fink & Fisher, 2000).

Document management is Tarmac's combination of system hardware and software that allows a user to capture information from a range of sources, including paper, facsimile, email, Internet downloads, and handwritten notes. It is shared by the corporate law and property departments.

Users can file, store, copy, retrieve, and integrate captured documents into their business applications at the desktop. Images scanned using digital cameras are retained as images or converted to text documents via OCR. Records are indexed to a database, where information can be retrieved in customized word, phrase, or numeric queries.

A data compression system reduces the amount of computer data storage needed, and laser disks or hard drives are selected based upon user needs for speed, capacity, and cost control.

Tarmac America is confident the system has paid for itself through such benefits as:
- Increased productivity for paralegals, by improving the flow of information and ability to locate materials;
- Incorporation with email to maximize efficiency throughout the company, for example, by reducing delivery charges;
- General document retention and backup; and
- Physical space saving.

IDCM can help the legal industry by helping to reduce the drudgery out of locating documents such as matter (or case) files, precedents, minutes, correspondence, contracts, decisions, instructions, policies, regulations, operating procedures, and other types of documented information. IDCM assures that the latest version of a template or document is made available to authorized users.

The development of the matter file might comprise digital and physical documents, and the latter can be scanned to digital image and be processed using recognition technology to facilitate access and retrieval. Documents of all formats can be registered by recording metadata relevant to the object. The capture and registration of digitally created objects can be facilitated by integration with standard templates.

The law firm, or legal department within a corporation, may already be using templates — for example, templates might be established for legal precedents. However, the use of outdated templates and superseded precedent documents may present a security risk if left unmanaged, so again, there may be a requirement to make precedents accessible to authorized users in a managed environment that IDCM should provide. IDCM implementation should provide version control over the creation and update of templates and precedent documents.

IDCM can incorporate Web publishing tools that enable the latest versions of templates and documents to be published on the law firm's intranet, enabling easy access, search, and retrieval, yet retaining security over the objects. This type of application eliminates the requirement for templates and documents to be transferred "manually" from one server to another for publication to the intranet.

Utilities

The opportunities for the utilities sector are typical of those we discussed for specific IDCM applications earlier in this chapter. They are also similar to those for the manufacturing/engineering (see next) and engineering/construction sectors. Opportunities include:

- OH&S management system documentation;
- Quality or business management system documentation;
- Plant Control Systems documentation;
- Supply and maintenance management documentation;
- Integration with GIS; and
- Drawing management.

Case Example: Southern California Edison's San Onofre Nuclear Generating Station

Study: Document management for a SONGS (Keown, 2000).

Southern California Edison's San Onofre Nuclear Generating Station (SONGS) supplies power to the Los Angeles basin. It must demonstrate to regulatory agencies that plant activities are safely and effectively managed. Proposed changes must be reviewed for impact on plant configuration and design basis information. In 1994, SONGS began an initiative to develop an enterprise-wide electronic document management system that would replace an earlier DOS-based image-enabled application.

After a year-long product evaluation, SONGS decided to develop its own system using a phased approach. This effort included integration of a number of commercially available software components. Phase one, which began in 1995, took approximately 1 year and included the development of the application framework, the database, and electronic file storage subsystem. The Nuclear Document Management System NDMS release 1.0 entered site-wide use in 1996 and provided the architecture to bring the management of all of SONGS documents into a single application. The application can be run on any one of the more than 2000 Windows-based PCs attached to the LAN. Image print services are provided at more than 100 image-enabled print stations distributed throughout the site.

NDMS serves as the main repository for all records and revision control documents. The repository includes thousands of maintenance, operations, and administrative procedures, millions of legal, regulatory, and insurance records, hundreds of thousands of engineering design drawings, and thousands of business records.

For the health physics system, benefits included:

- Cost — Dollar savings for the radiation survey process were realized;
- Time lines —The time to deposit original surveys into the final record repository (NDMS) was reduced from months to hours;
- Completeness — Depositing radiation surveys into NDMS, rather than into file cabinets, reduced the chance of losing or using an outdated survey;
- Availability — Having images online greatly improved access to the current survey;
- Computer-generated indexing is enabled; and
- Ease of use for health physics personnel is realized.

There have also been general NDMS benefits such as:

- Safety decisions were improved by getting the right information to the right people when required.
- Productivity and efficiency (the time spent by employees locating and getting records and information) has been greatly reduced.
- Transferability, the product of the implementation team's efforts, includes concepts and a business process model that have been applied to other record types at SONGS.
- Regulatory compliance and flexibility are necessary, and records critical to plant safety or operations can be made available when and where they are needed, while retaining the benefits of a centralized records management program.
- Decommissioning four legacy systems is a benefit.

Manufacturing and Engineering

Among the many benefits of IDCM in the manufacturing/engineering sector is the capability of the system to implement repository controls over a diverse range of vital records and important documents, such as engineering drawings, quality documentation, marketing proposals, and contract documentation.

Using integrated publishing tools, users are able to access the current version of documentation, such as drawings, quality documents, and safety, health, and environment documentation on a company's intranet site. For example, maintenance engineers are able to have the assurance that the latest revisions of drawings, technical specifications, and equipment manuals are available on an intranet.

The system enables users to print uncontrolled reference copies of the current versions of drawings and technical documentation on demand, if required to facilitate construction, operational, and maintenance tasks. It also eliminates the need to file physical copies of controlled documents in repositories, potentially in multiple locations.

Engineering and Construction

The problems with fragmented document environments in the engineering services sector can be exacerbated when companies plan a period of significant growth, particularly the establishment of new business sites and offices. The volume of electronic documents can grow rapidly and increase exponentially as an increased number of users generates and stores more and more important documents in electronic form.

The business requirements for developing new markets, attracting new customers, and providing a wider range of engineering services to existing and new customers may also have a significant impact on the volumes of documents generated by and received by engineering companies. Furthermore, if an engineering services company chooses to continue with a fragmented document environment, it may be frustrated in its attempts to win new business.

First, competitors may be able to demonstrate to potential customers that they have already implemented a stable, well-managed document capability, thereby gaining competitive advantage. Second, potential customers may have already achieved the same capability and raise concerns as to why the engineering services company has not addressed the same types of problems. In this respect, it is noted that international engineering companies use sophisticated document management tools to support their key business processes.

IDCM has the capacity to facilitate the life-cycle aspects of a construction project from the initial steps of proposal development to completion of the project. We have already discussed the benefits of using IDCM for the development of proposals earlier in this chapter. It is applicable to the engineering and construction sector.

Case Example: Ove Arup & Partners
Study: Document management at Ove Arup & Partners (BRE Center for Construction IT & Construction Industry Computing Association, 1999).

This BRE/CICA study reports on the in-house *Columbus* implementation which provides for multiuser access to document data from all Arup offices, internationally, in "virtual project teams."
Benefits include:
- Keeping data closest to those who use it most;
- Reducing communications costs;
- License fee savings by avoiding commercial system;
- Improving user awareness of documents relating to a project;
- Effectively incorporating contract and temporary staff into procedures;
- Urgent update requests can be quickly handled in-house with deployment flexibility; and
- History, which is useful in job monitoring and costing and when billing for consumables.

An IDCM environment enables construction companies to harness all relevant documentation for commercial development, project, and administrative purposes. The system provides the support from proposal stage, through to engineering, construction, and commissioning of the infrastructure or plant.

It also supports the development of knowledge strategies by enabling information to be shared with key stakeholders, and reduce the risk of re-work being performed on a project-by-project basis.

Health Industry

The health industry is a document-intensive industry in a sensitive environment, involving records and reports about patients who are being treated by doctors and other clinicians. There is a requirement for a high degree of security and legal use of people's medical records and health information, which involves extensive procedures for handling and protecting information.

There are strong moves toward implementing electronic health records, which involve extensive document conversion, registration, and capture processes.

An IDCM approach in the health environment brings together the many aspects of medical records management so that information about patient care may be aggregated according to need. For instance, material concerning diagnosis, therapy, and medication regimes on a case basis may be associated with administrative material such as bed use

---

Case Example*: Washington D.C. Hospital Center*
Study: Washington D.C. Hospital Center. (Document management solution..., 2001).

> The Washington Hospital Center implemented a turnkey system with a modular design. It began with the admissions and patient financial services modules and plans to add the correspondence module to help it handle the thousands of letters and requests for information that come in daily.
>
> Patient information is organized by episode of care, allowing administrative and financial user to capture documents associated with the patient admissions process, including insurance cards, photo identification, admissions referrals, and insurance verifications. Other staff may subsequently retrieve documents according to date, name, social security number, or source of payment. Information keyed into the main patient information system is automatically placed into a patient's digital file rather than being printed out first and then scanned, so all documentation is kept together and readily accessible.
>
> Benefits include:
> - Accurate information about each episode of care and related patient and financial information is organized and stored within seconds and is immediately accessible. A dramatic improvement in ability to respond to requests from customers and insurance companies has been shown.
> - Callers no longer get busy signals, wait in long phone queues or stay on hold for long periods of time while representatives struggle to find information.
> - If a customer requests a bill, personnel are able to fax it or mail it that same day — as opposed to a week later.
> - Patient Financial Services has decreased the payment lag time between billing and payment from an average of 85 days to 69 days, substantially improving cash flow and, ultimately, overall patient care and service.

---

or accounting. All may be made available through a common interface to personnel with appropriate permissions.

There are many opportunities for IDCM, including workflow management. Integrated forms, XML interfaces, and workflow can be utilized to support management of clinical case notes. Information gathered during a workflow process can be added to a patient record using electronic forms.

Government — National/State

From the perspective of national government, much of the impetus for IDCM often relates to e-business initiatives. An example is the "Modernizing Government" program initiated by the United Kingdom Government, with the aim of positioning it at the forefront of e-business and e-commerce. The program includes initiatives that require, among other things, for all newly created public records to be stored and filed electronically by 2004, and all government services will be available online by 2005.

The Lord Chancellor has also committed to deliver the first tangible benefits of the *Freedom of Information Act* by November 2002, with a progressive staged implementation throughout the U.K. government until implementation is completed in January 2005. The Act is retrospective so that the benefits of a legally enforceable right of access will be available to members of the public seeking information held before the Act came into force.

Local Government

The local government sector is characterized by a wide diversity of business functions and processes, as it serves the local communities it represents. Local government authorities operate in a highly regulated environment, often being subject to scrutiny from Central or State government ministers, Central or State departments set up to administer local government authorities, FOI requests, and representations from the community that they represent.

Councilors or candidates vying for office often cite specific projects or plan specific programs to demonstrate the value of their remaining in office or being elected to office. Consequently, Council planning, strategies, and budget allocations can be influenced by political machinations. Office bearers and candidates may not view document and Web content management systems as a compelling case upon which to build their election prospects.

However, despite the multiplicity of tasks that local government authorities must perform, and the restrictions placed on authorities by regulation, legal compliance, best practice standards, and councilor and community expectations, there is quite a significant range of opportunities to use IDCM systems to develop innovative solutions to help deliver professional and timely services to local government.

Most of the information managed by local government authorities relates to property and customers. There is the requirement to manage development or building applications and permits and to satisfy searches against property information and restrictions impacting on land usage or property development. Although records are kept in property or customer databases, a large proportion of content is in objects such as applications, permits, specifications, drawings, and plans.

There is demand from the communities they represent for authorities to provide documented information available in a timely manner, to satisfy requests such as searches as to the status of rates outstanding against a property that is to be purchased. Searches may wish to determine matters such as whether a property is subject to vegetation orders, easements, or other conditions, or seek the supply of engineering or soil test reports.

There is innovative application in local government because of the requirement to manage many business functions and a multitude of processes with relatively limited budget allocations. For example, local government authorities are major users of GIS software, and are seeking the functionality to display spatial views on mobile devices, and input data to create and update maps.

The use of GIS as an interface enables users to develop spatial views of an authority's assets, such as properties, roads, swimming pools, and incorporation of overlays that represent sewerage and drainage information, planned commercial and residential developments, or planned roads. Other simple but effective usages include identifying zones that represent the bin collection area for specific garbage and waste contractors.

Many authorities have deployed GIS views of infrastructure onto the Internet, and some have embraced e-business strategies to enable authorized developers and planners, or private authorizers of building permits, to access information via the Web on a fee-for-service basis. In either case, there is a persuasive case for strategists within authorities to ensure that the correct information is being published to the consumer, due to the regulatory requirements for maintaining due diligence over the records of the authority. There may also be significant legal ramifications, involving payment of compensation and damages, if decisions are taken on incorrect information.

Local authorities may decide that a strategy to integrate GIS and IDCM systems is convincing. This strategy would enable consumers to access the corrected documents and content when in a spatial view, particularly where an authority exposes part of its infrastructure information to Internet consumers.

Management of customer requests irrespective of avenue of receipt is another area where IDCM is relevant. This type of strategy can involve tools that capture requests through multiple channels (such as intelligent voice recognition systems, portals, electronic forms, email, and imaging technology). Requests once captured can be routed via workflow management systems that support automation and management of processes. Integration with business operational and administrative systems (such as a land information system or customer database) may be required to validate property and customer information. DMS can be used to store digital images, email, and word-processing templates and documents, which can be used to formulate responses. The record of each customer tracking experience might be maintained by the workflow system.

Historical information relating to each customer can be maintained by an integrated system to ensure that the authority is able to obtain a view of all requests made by a specific customer, how it was resolved, and the performance of an authority in responding to the request. Overall performance figures can be produced from the workflow management system to enable the authority's management team to match performance against planned objectives and review strategies for redefining outcomes.

Many local government authorities are responsible for libraries, and there is increasing commonality between managing administrative and library documents, as we see below.

Libraries

In many enterprises that house their own special libraries, the increasing number of digital documents has made more obvious the convergence between library and RMSs. This has been given impetus by creation of internal content on intranets that may subsequently be published on the Internet. A demarcation between records systems handling internal documents and library systems managing the collection of external documents is not so marked, particularly when enterprises look for integrated approaches to all information and knowledge sources within knowledge management programs.

In the digital library environment, there has for some time been work carried out on so-called hybrid library systems that are capable of seamlessly managing physical and digital resources. Emphasis has turned away from collection of documents and is now focused on access to information. It seems reasonable to look forward to systems that are capable of managing internally produced documents and externally obtained documents or subscriptions.

For example, the same controlled vocabularies for metadata (thesauri, subject headings lists) can be used to provide access to content of library and records systems. Similarly, the digital documents in those systems may be structured using generic markup such as XML in such a way to facilitate relatively easy creation of compound documents from multiple internal and external sources.

The overall organizational process for handling these facilities is information management. However, management may choose to administer the process through an existing area such as a library that has information organization strengths or an "intrapreneurial" approach. Alternatively, it may be the publishing area, the records area, or the IT area, depending upon how much interest there is on overall provision of information architecture.

SUMMARY

We have now reviewed some applications of document and content management that are specific to a business process requirement along with the general applicability of IDCM for workgroup and enterprise deployment. We have also covered how IDCM has the capability to provide middle-ware services to support business operational and administrative systems. Some applications of IDCM in vertical industry sectors were provided.

These examples are intended to provide insights into usage scenarios for IDCM in business and government enterprises. There are many different types of potential opportunities that suit IDCM implementation, and we will leave it to readers to explore opportunities within their own environments.

This chapter concludes Part 1 of the book, which has been focused on understanding document and content management applications in the overall context of business planning at strategic, tactical, and operational levels. Part 2, which follows, is titled "Preliminaries," and it focuses on preparation through planning and initiating an IDCM project, developing a document policy, conducting feasibility studies, and developing a business case for IDCM.

ENDNOTES

[1]   Further SVG details can be located at http://www.w3.org/Graphics/SVG/.

[2]   Further GML details can be located at http://www.opengis.org/techno/specs.htm.

PART 2

Preliminaries

The aims of this Part are to:

- Assist business and project managers to apply information systems life-cycle planning techniques when initiating and progressing an IDCM project.

- Stress the importance of change management and the need to develop a change management strategy at project initiation and implement the strategy throughout the project life-cycle.

- Emphasize the importance of document management and Web publishing and content management policies as key subsets of an information policy.

- Recommend the rigor of the feasibility study approach to determine operational, technical, and financial feasibility of an IDCM opportunity, as a strategy to help clarify the project scope. The feasibility study is a logical precursor to a full requirements analysis study.

- Provide insights into strategies for building the business case for an IDCM solution, which is a vital component for securing resources (budget, people, and services) for an IDCM project.

Chapter 6

Project Life-Cycle Planning and Methodologies

OVERVIEW

This chapter deals with the planning aspects of an IDCM project, including scope, feasibility, and life-cycle development. It reviews the typical project deliverables that may be used during planning and subsequent phases.

The objectives are to consider and discuss:

- The importance of planning to the successful implementation of an IDCM solution, and the need to distinguish between *product development* and *project* life-cycles;
- A product development life-cycle that enterprises can use for an IDCM project;
- The steps involved in initiating and defining an IDCM project;
- An approach to aligning the development of a management framework with requirements for enabling an IDCM solution, including a review of key life-cycle stages;
- Development of a project organization structure that may be applicable for an enterprise IDCM project;
- Identification of a set of risks to form the basis of a Risk Management Plan; and
- Methodologies suitable for an IDCM project.

THE IMPORTANCE OF PLANNING

The most important key to the successful implementation of an IDCM solution is planning. If proper planning techniques are not applied during the conduct of an IDCM project, the project may fail or major difficulties may be encountered with the implementation of the system. These undesirable outcomes may have a major detrimental impact on the operations of the businesses or government enterprises involved, and typically involve extensive delays or significant levels of additional costs. Furthermore, major project failures may entail a large social and economic cost, and where project failures or major setbacks are experienced in government, they entail a direct cost to government and taxpayers.

Enterprises often manage the risks associated with complex document management projects by contracting out the work to professional services organizations. Consequently, much of the planning work associated with large IDCM projects has been accomplished or facilitated by consulting or systems integration companies. The specific methodologies used by these companies for the planning, specification, development, and implementation of an IDCM solution often remain their intellectual property, and do not appear in the public domain.

However, the project life-cycle planning techniques, methodologies, and tools required for planning and implementing IDCM systems are similar to the methods that might be applied to the package selection and implementation of any type of complex information system. DMS are distinctive in that, whereas most information systems involve the use of source documents for data creation, update, and search and retrieval, DMS capture and manage the source documents, as well.

Their complexity is brought home when one is reminded that documents are an intrinsic everyday part of business processes. The enterprise requirements typically involve integration with heterogeneous and evolving desktop operating systems and applications used to generate documents, the multiplicity of formats to be managed, and the implications for managing large file sizes on computer networks, which often feature low bandwidth for file transfer and communications.

Because of circumstances like these, there is a high degree of risk in planning and implementing IDCM systems. The requirement to capture and manage digital source documents invariably has a marked impact on how end users interact with documents in their day-to-day business environments. End users will be required to register documents using more rigor than is generally evident in managing office documents and will need to learn new techniques for accessing and sharing information. Consequently, appropriate communication and change management strategies are key requirements throughout the project life-cycle.

Structured methods for the development and implementation of information systems evolved from the need to address the divergent methods that were once evident in the development and implementation of computing systems. (We provide an overview of these types of methodologies later in this chapter.) Methodologies offer a structured series of steps and tasks that the practitioner can consider when commencing an information systems project, and also a set of techniques and tools that enable the project team to document user and system requirements in a structured way.

While structured methodologies may provide the type of life-cycle framework for planning, specifying, selecting, and implementing complex information systems packages, it is important to discuss how these types of planning techniques might be applied to an IDCM project. This chapter provides insights into the life-cycle planning of an IDCM strategy, commencing with project initiation through to the implementation of the solution.

PROJECT VERSUS
PRODUCT DEVELOPMENT LIFE-CYCLES

The life-cycle planning model will be facilitated by distinguishing between two planning life-cycle concepts that are interrelated when planning IDCM projects. These two terms are as follows:

- Project life-cycle; and
- Product development life-cycle.

Project Life-Cycle

The general life-cycle for all types of projects consists of a linear progression through the four phases shown in Table 1, as described by Verzuh (1999, pp. 22, 40).

Product Development Life-Cycle

Verzuh (1999, p. 23) points out that the development of a new product, including software products, adheres to the following series of steps that comprise a *product development life-cycle*:

- Requirements, which defines functionality and performance for the product;
- Design, which provides a detailed description of a product solution that will meet requirements;
- Construction, which includes building the product (in our case, software installation, configuration, and customization); and
- Operation, which is the product in operation during its life span.

Table 1: General Project Life-Cycles

Phase	Phase Overview	Typical Activity Inclusions
Define	• Project charter initiated • Project rules developed and approved • Project charter published	Definition of: • Aims and objectives • Scope • Constraints • Responsibilities • Change management process • Communication plan
Plan	• Project plan developed • Project rules modified (as required)	Planning of: • Risk analysis and management planning • Budget • Project schedule • Quality management
Execute	• Work performed as per project plan • Project goal achieved	~ As per project plan
Close Out	• Transition to next phase • Formal closure • Postimplementation review	Includes: • Next phase planning • Project completion activities • Project review and report

Normally, there would also be evaluation during the design and construction phases, and on the operational product.

It is significant for our purposes that a *product development life-cycle* may contain multiple *project life-cycles* (Verzuh, 1999, pp. 23–25). For example, a specific project life-cycle may be instituted for the requirements stage, and a separate life-cycle for the design stage, and so on.

Implications for IDCM Project Planning

Throughout the book, we make reference to projects arriving at an IDCM solution. However, in Verzuh's terms, each of these solutions can be thought of as a product which in many cases may comprise multiple projects. So although we will continue to refer to IDCM projects, we will now consider them within the framework of an IDCM product life-cycle. Consequently, the planning and implementation of an IDCM system should follow *a product development life-cycle methodology* that meets enterprise requirements.

The product development methodology may follow or be derived from a structured methodology used by the enterprise for information systems projects. Depending on the complexity of the IDCM project, the *product development life-cycle* could involve multiple "implementation" phases. Generally, on a large-scale project, such as an enterprise-wide deployment, it may be necessary to apply an evolutionary rollout strategy to help manage the implementation, and reduce risks associated with such a complex implementation.

Based on this differentiation between product development and project life-cycles, the *product development life-cycle* for an IDCM solution should contain multiple *project life-cycles*, which means that each stage of the product development would entail definition, planning, execution, and closeout.

IDCM PRODUCT DEVELOPMENT LIFE-CYCLE

Overview

Most enterprises are required to seek competitive proposals for information systems products, and it is typical for these commercial processes to apply to IDCM solutions.

Consequently, we have elected to separate the product development life-cycle of IDCM into two distinct phases:

- Phase 0 — "Planning," to cover all the planning aspects from the initiation of the project, policy and strategy development, the preliminaries (feasibility study and business case development), requirements analysis and specification, package acquisition, and selection.
- Phase 1 — "Implementation," to cover the planning related to the design, development, testing, and implementation of the IDCM solution.

These two phases consist of a number of *stages* that distinguish the product development life-cycle. These two phases are represented in Figures 1 and 2, respectively.

Conceptual Schema: Phase 0 — Planning

The product life-cycle depicted in Figure 1 provides a conceptual overview of generic stages that may apply to the planning phase of IDCM. The stages for Phase 0 include *planning*, *preliminaries*, *requirements analysis and definition*, and *package selection*. The project life-cycle of definition, planning, execution, and closeout should be applied at each stage. The closeout from Phase 0 would move the project to Phase 1.

The change strategy and communication components identified in Figure 1 and continued in Figure 2 should align and integrate with enterprise information policy (see Chapter 7) and with business strategy and other projects.

The planning and preliminary stages involve an understanding of the regulatory social and business context in which an enterprise functions, so that recordkeeping requirements may be derived from these. The extent to which existing enterprise strategies (such as the application of standards and IT) fulfill these requirements may then be reviewed. Then, any necessary redesign, implementation, and review can ensue.

Conceptual Schema: Phase 1 — Implementation

Figure 2 provides a conceptual overview of typical product development stages that may comprise the "Implementation" phase of an IDCM project. The Phase 1 stages include *implementation strategy and planning*, *design and development*, *implementation,* and *operation*. The project life-cycle also applies to each *stage*. We include postimplementation review as part of Phase 1, though it may be treated as a separate phase.

Figure 1: Typical Product Life-Cycle Stages: Phase 0 — Planning.

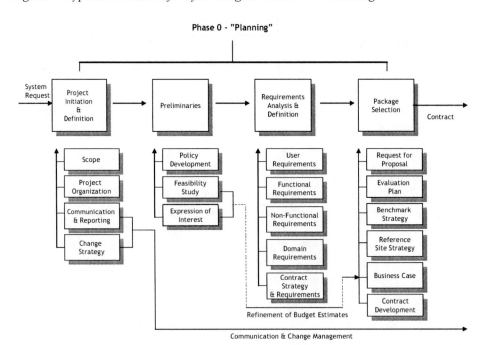

Figure 2: Typical Life-Cycle Step Processes: Phase 1 — Implementation.

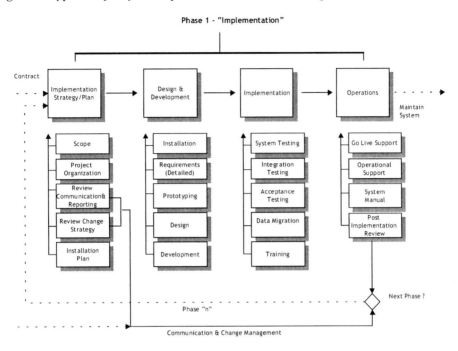

PHASE 0 — STAGE DEFINITIONS

The two key concepts embodied in the IDCM planning model that we discussed in Chapter 1, which incorporate a *management framework* and *systems* environment, should be aligned during the stages of product development. This alignment facilitates an integrative approach to the development of an IDCM product. We will examine this alignment for the *preliminaries*, *requirements analysis and definition*, and *package selection* phases, but first will examine the initial stage of the overall planning phase, and that is *project initiation and definition*.

Project Initiation and Definition

Project Initiation

An IDCM approach may be initiated for a number of reasons. For example:

- Executive management team initiative based on impact on business planning imperatives due to fragmented and unmanaged document environment, or frustration with complexities in delivering content to Web sites;
- Annual program of information systems projects;
- Business process owner identifies requirement for document management or compelling reason to manage Web content; perhaps other business process owners might show interest;
- Consistent pressure from information disciplines to improve practices associated with managing document and Web content management and applying recordkeeping standards.

An enterprise may use its own in-house methodology, techniques, and tools for initiating projects. Depending on the type of methodology adopted, the initiating document for an information systems project might be a Project Brief or Mandate (Bentley, 2000, p. 24). The project startup documentation typically consists of a set of terms of reference and details of the nominated project manager. A Project Board or a Project Sponsor, who is preferably a member of the executive management team, may approve the brief, mandate, or terms of reference.

The project management role is vital for projects comprising the IDCM product. Selection of a project manager includes the following considerations:

- Given the variety of disciplines and interests represented in such projects (refer to Chapter 1), the question of who should have responsibility for the project is important. Because hardware, software, and communications will all be involved, we consider that an implementation project should be coordinated as an information system project by a person qualified and experienced in managing complex information systems projects.

- The project manager should have specific financial and administrative delegations to provide adequate authority and decision making for the project. (The title may alternatively be "project coordinator" if the enterprise wishes to distinguish between internal project management role and the role offered by the contracted vendor, professional service, or system integration company contracted to implement the IDCM).

Verzuh (1999, p. 15) also makes the important observation that while project management as a discipline has the capability to transcend industry boundaries, the same cannot be said for project managers, who must be well acquainted with the focus of the project. He recommends that, aside from having skills in project management as a discipline, and business management (such as negotiating finance, organizational development, and communication skills), the project manager must have the technical subject matter competence.

Project Definition

The documentation issued to commence the project may be general rather than specific, so once the brief or mandate has been approved and issued, it is incumbent on the project manager to review it and clearly define the project. The project manager needs to articulate the aim and objectives of the project, its scope, the constraints, roles and responsibilities, planning for change management, and the definition of a communication plan.

If it has not already been done, a Project Board (or Project Steering Group) should be established representing executives. It will provide the overall direction for the project in terms of aim, objectives, scope, budget allocation, time frames, and a quality reference. The Project Board may then assign a Project Sponsor, a role that has the responsibility for providing executive guidance to the project.

The first step in the planning process for the IDCM project manager is to further define the project and commence the preparation of a Project Charter (or Project Initiation Document). This is a document that defines or confirms the aim, objectives, and scope of the project, reviews project constraints and the background to the requirement, and documents a list of key stakeholders.

During the development of the Project Charter, there is a requirement for a project manager to meet with executives and key stakeholders and communicate the nature of the functionality offered by IDCM systems, and set or reset expectations. Quite often, difficulty stems from perceptions by executive management that document management is relatively simple; after all, it is "just document management." Many executives, even in so-called technology savvy companies, seem to have the perception that a DMS involves placing pieces of paper inside cardboard folders.

If expectations are not properly set, management may continue to view the requirement in simple terms and have unrealistic expectations about the time frames for planning, defining, and implementing the system. Project coordinators should not carry unrealistic expectations through the project life-cycle, particularly if there is to be staged implementation to reduce risks, so it is best to manage expectations early in the project.

There may also be competition between numbers of workgroups, with each workgroup wanting to be listed as a high priority in the IDCM project. The diversity of workgroups and their unique requirements adds further complexity to the scope of decision making. In an enterprise where it has a high degree of autonomy, particularly financial autonomy, a disaffected workgroup may use its own budget to acquire a document management capability outside the enterprise initiative.

This type of internal competitiveness for resources, in this case IDCM capability, places the project coordinator under pressure and may result in compromises such as simultaneous multiple site deployment, that increase the overall risk of the project. Consequently, the assigned project manager needs an information systems background and excellent project management skills. In addition to leadership and communication, these include the capability to achieve a decisive and agreed scope and implementation strategy amid competing demands.

The preparation of a Project Charter requires the project manager and preferably the project team to meet with the project board, sponsor, and key stakeholders to obtain:

- A clear definition (or confirmation) of the aim of the project;
- An initial statement of objectives (which may embrace statements relating to operational, financial, and technical objectives);
- A clear definition (or confirmation) of the scope of the requirement;
- An identification of constraints on the project, such as budget provision for the project, time frames for the project, and quality standards to be adopted; and
- Confirmation of empowerment of project manager — financial and administrative delegations.

The project scope needs to be clearly defined, so that all stakeholders have a clear understanding of the boundaries. It is best that scope issues be resolved at the start of the project, not during its progress, to avoid a significant risk to success. Clear scope definition is vital for all document management projects, but it becomes multifaceted when the IDCM solution is to be deployed across the enterprise. The processes to achieve scope definition for enterprise projects are more difficult due to the overall size and complexity of the project.

A key consideration when planning the scope is that documents stored in the DMS during a staged implementation, for example, documents stored in a Supply Department's library, will not be available to unlicensed users. This type of issue needs to be considered by the project manager, and arrangements must be made to resolve the issue. The solution may involve providing read and view license only access to the repository, accessible using a native Web browser. An alternative may be to implement controlled publication of the documents to the enterprise's intranet site so that the content can be accessible.

The Project Charter needs to be quite clear on scope inclusions and exclusions and may need to address aspects such as (a) project phasing and sites, (b) proposed number of users of the system, (c) document classes, (d) functionality, and (e) migration and conversion requirements. An example of a scope statement is shown in Table 3.

During the development of the Project Charter, it helps to define critical success factors, for example:

- Cost justification of the IDCM system;
- Management team commitment;
- Active line management support;
- Adequate funding;
- Realistic expectations (cost/time frames);
- Management of change; and
- IT infrastructure capacity.

Project Planning

Once the Project Charter has been prepared, reviewed by key stakeholders (including project sponsor), and approved by the Project Board, the IDCM project manager then develops the Project Plan. The development of the project plan consists of analyzing key activities and tasks, identifying milestones, and developing a project schedule. It also includes the development of assumptions and dependencies that underpin the key planning dates in the project schedule.

The plan may also consist of an impact statement that generally covers the impact of the IDCM project on other projects and the potential impact of the IDCM solution on business planning and operations. There is a requirement for risks to be identified and mitigation strategies developed, and the development of a detailed budget and cash flow for this phase of the project.

Change Strategy

Management of change is an important component of any implementation strategy. Transformation cannot be pursued effectively unless those who are affected can contribute to the change process. Account must be taken of organizational culture and behavioral aspects of personnel that are relevant to the environment in which the IDCM solution is to be deployed. Team meetings are likely to be required in order to communicate and seek input to proposals, evaluate reasons for change, and introduce processes. All personnel who will be affected by change should be:

- Introduced to the IDCM project;
- Made aware of their anticipated role in project implementation and ongoing management;
- Given the opportunity to express and resolve their concerns;

- Provided with regular communication concerning scheduling of project execution, and subsequent operational changes, including introduction of hardware and software; and
- Given training that is appropriate for their new or revised work functions.

There are several roles that may be differentiated within change management. They can be described as follows:

- *Sponsor*, who justifies a change and therefore makes it legitimate in the eyes of those affected. In the case of an IDCM strategy, this could be top management promotion of document and content management within a framework of support for strategic plans, such as information support for business processes. The sponsor gives the project credibility and authority, and needs to be able to communicate a vision (Kotter, 1996).
- *Change agents* are members of the team led by the project manager who must get the new or revised system functioning. They must obtain and retain commitment from the management team and from end users. The project manager provides direction and support in order to invigorate the process.
- *End users*, who are the objects of the change, are likely to appraise the sponsor's commitment and the change agents' communication and technical skills as they form their support or resistance. Their attitude will be molded by perceived threat to their control over their work environment, while having their workplace frame of reference changed.

Models of change management usually owe something to understanding of organizational dynamics building on Lewin's theories of change. For example, Kotter (1996) sees change in terms of a stepwise approach beginning with "defrosting the status quo" (developing a sense of urgency for doing things differently), then taking the change actions, and then anchoring those changes in corporate culture. Like Lewin[1] who similarly used freezing as a metaphor for the change process, he sees a need to shake free of an existing level of operation in order to move to a new level, and then stabilize at that.

Preliminaries

A schema representing alignment of the management framework and the systems environment during the stage we have labeled *preliminaries* is conceptualized in Figure 3.

The stage requires a diagnostic review of an enterprise's document and content environment, and a more comprehensive review that can utilize SWOT (Strengths, Weaknesses, Opportunities, Threats) analysis. The enterprise will also be able to produce a better risk assessment of its current information management procedures relating to documents, records, and content. Outcomes of this phase will include:

- Policies that cover the diversity of information management requirements within the enterprise and provide the context for the development of procedures and definition of requirements for document and content management;
- A feasibility study report as to the operational, technical, and financial appropriateness of business and technology solution options; and

Figure 3: Phase 0: Preliminaries Stage.

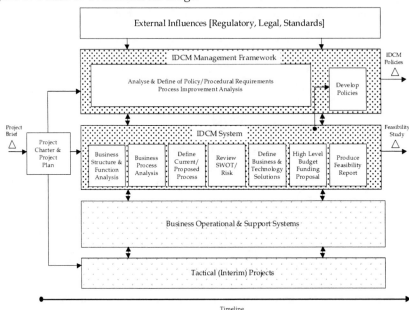

• Analysis of the scope and intersections between IDCM strategy and the enterprise's core business systems.

The preliminaries stage will deliver an overall strategic framework, consisting of policies, scope definition, business and technology solution options analysis, and forward recommendations for implementing an IDCM solution. Within this framework, there may also be opportunities to make tactical improvements to the current systems. Examples may include cost-effective changes to an existing system that is able to incorporate a forms management program, or Web-based content delivery that is able to make use of a streamlining of existing authoring practices and systems to eliminate redundancy.

Requirements Analysis and Definition

These planning outcomes from the preliminaries stage should frame the policy development and feasibility study stages that are necessary precursors of the *requirements analysis and definition* stage, which is depicted in Figure 4.

The requirements phase covers the analysis and definition of the enterprise's requirements within an integrative framework. In the example, these requirements would take into account any standards that must be applied (for example, from government policy) or which may be applied, and may include:

• Metadata conditions, classification and thesaurus application, and disposal authorities;

• Records that are technology-dependent;

• Recordkeeping within the enterprise's core business and administrative systems and that supports operations and administrative business processes; and

Figure 4: Phase 0: Requirements Analysis and Definition Stage.

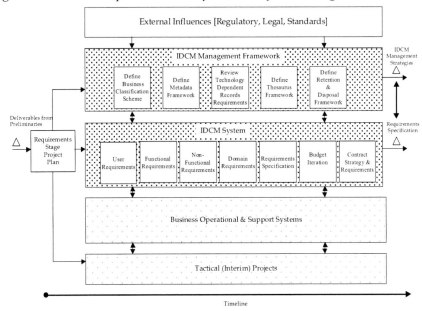

- Management of content for publishing based upon integrating material from documents systems and dynamic databases.

 The key outputs will be:
- Information management strategies that extend policy to the detailed analysis of tools for document and content management; and
- A requirements specification for an IDCM system that takes into account the range of the enterprise's requirements with respect to physical and electronic documents, multimedia, technical documentation, and Web content (for Internet and intranet applications).

Package Selection

 The following stage is *package selection*, depicted in Figure 5.
 This stage can include:
- Logical design of the metadata, classification scheme, thesaurus, and disposal authorities;
- Development of procurement plan, selection criteria, development of the commercial aspects of the specifications for an IDCM solution, preparation and release of an RFP;
- Desktop evaluation of proposals from suppliers or systems integrators and benchmark testing of shortlisted solutions;
- Selection of packaged software to support the enterprise's requirements for IDCM; and
- Refinement of the business case for implementation.

Figure 5: Phase 0: Package Selection Stage.

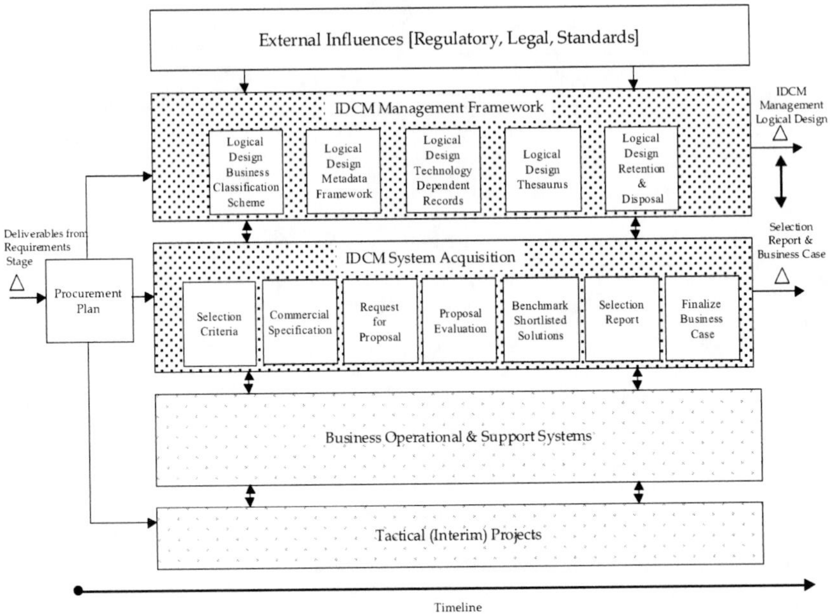

If resources (budget and people) are made available, the product may then proceed to implementation.

PHASE 1 — STAGE DEFINITIONS

Figure 2 provided an overview of Phase 1 implementation. As was the case with Phase 0, detailed depiction of application is possible for each stage. We shall confine ourselves the *design and development* and *implementation* stages.

Design and Development

Following the Package Selection phase, and assuming that the Selection Report and Business Case are approved, the enterprise might embark on the *design and development* stage, which is depicted in Figure 6.

This stage can encompass:

- Development of the metadata, classification scheme, thesaurus, and disposal authorities within the policy framework;
- Integration of authorities and records within the design of the IDCM system;
- Configuration and customization of document, records, and content software to meet enterprise requirements;
- Preparation of Change Management Plans, and Data Migration Plans (metadata and objects from existing systems);
- System testing.

Figure 6: Phase 1: Design and Development Stage.

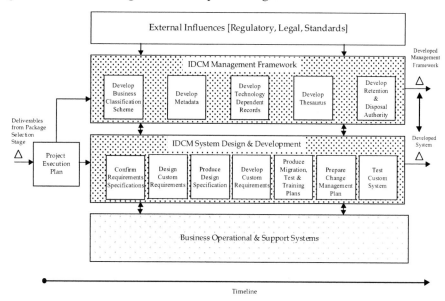

Notice that provision for tactical projects has not been made at this stage, due to the stage of the development of the IDCM solution.

The key outputs are a developed IDCM solution leading to the implementation stage as shown in Figure 7.

This stage covers the implementation of the solution into appropriate pathfinder sites (for proof of concept) and business functions. The solution will embrace policies,

Figure 7: Phase 1: Implementation Stage.

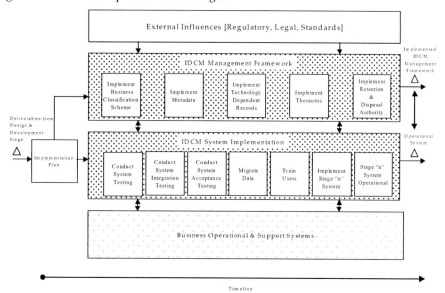

procedures, tools, and packaged software to provide a holistic approach to implementation.

Once an enterprise is satisfied that the solution meets requirements validated during this phase, the IDCM solution (policy framework and systems) will be deployed progressively within business units based on enterprise priorities.

The progressive implementation of the solution will be defined in an implementation plan that may need to be iterated for progressive deployment of the solution. The priorities for implementation may be based on imperatives such as level of risk, the need for IDCM to support emerging initiatives, or a logical extension of the pathfinder implementation.

Table 2: Project Charter Structure and Content

Structure	Content
Document history	Provide the history of the author, review approval, and revision processes.
Glossary	The glossary should define the terms and describe their use within the document.
Executive summary	This should be relatively brief, though sufficient to convey the overall message relating to the project planning; topic list should include business benefits, success criteria and factors, project approach, synopsis of key responsibilities, and cost strategy.
Introduction	This provides a definition of the purpose of the document, background information relating to the project, a list of stakeholders and of reference documents.
Project definition	It is important that enterprises clearly define the aims, objectives, scope, and outcomes of an IDCM project and make them relevant to the business requirements. • Aim: The definition of the aim of the project needs to present a clear message to stakeholders and needs to be specific about the required project outcomes. Statements such as "the aim is to implement a document management system" are tenuous and open to wide interpretation. • Objectives: The objectives of the project need to be addressed in terms of operational, technical, and financial requirements, which need to be subjected to rigorous examination during the feasibility study.
Project approach	A definition of the general delivery strategy, i.e., the formal stages during which the project will progress, the information systems methodology to be used, as well as reporting requirements, project hand-over responsibilities, and the requirements for a postimplementation review.
Deliverables plan	Key deliverables may include deliverable name, authors, reviewers, approvers, and target dates.
Communication strategy	This consists of an analysis of key stakeholders, and the development of strategy and mechanism to meet specific needs of individuals and groups.
Change management strategy	The change management strategy needs to capture the outcomes of a Change Requirements Analysis or initiate that type of analysis. Change management embraces many cultural and behavioral aspects relevant to the environment in which the IDCM system is to be deployed, and not just a brief analysis of training requirements.
Project organization	Examples are provided in this chapter cover: • Structure • Roles and responsibilities • Resource strategy • Resource training
Evaluation	The project outcomes need to be evaluated; the charter should include a statement of: • Critical success factors • Performance indicators • Performance assumptions
Conclusion	A brief synopsis of the salient features of the project charter, effectively reflecting the professional advice and recommendations contained in the Executive Summary.

KEY PROJECT DOCUMENTS — PHASE 0

We now provide an overview of the typical structure and contents of a Project Charter (or Project Initiation Document) and Project Plan for Phase 0 of the IDCM project.

Project Charter

Table 2 provides an overview of the characteristic structure and contents that can be used for developing a Project Charter for an IDCM project.

We now provide examples of starting points for:

- Scope statement;
- Statement of constraints;
- Project approach definition;
- Deliverables plan; and
- Project organization.

Scope Statement

Table 3 provides a simple example of a scope statement to illustrate the requirement.

Table 3: Scope Statement — Example

Scope Statement – IDCM Project
Preamble:
Due to the risks associated with implementing complex information systems at simultaneous sites within the enterprise, the IDCM system will be implemented in phases; scope defined for Phase 1 is:
Inclusions:
• Phase 1 will be to deploy the system to the Supply Department.
• It will be restricted to 50 users in the Purchasing and Contracts Group, and will exclude the Warehouse.
• It will include electronic documents, including email that supports business transactions.
• It will also include the capability to scan office documents sizes A (or A4) to B (or A3), but not large-size formats.
• Documents stored in the Tenders and Contacts folders on the current network drives will be migrated to the system and matched with data extracted from the document register in the office database.
• It will implement document repository services functionality, plus two workflow modules for document review and approval of (a) release of request for proposals and (b) contract approval.
• The workflow will be used in conjunction with web publishing tools to deliver content in the form of a released request for proposal to the Supply Department's Internet site at (*define*).
• Versions of authoring documents and rendered content published to the Supply Department's Internet site will be synchronized via the document/content repository.
Exclusions:
• Phase 1 will not include drawings, or their publication to the Supply Department's intranet site. It is proposed that drawings will be included in Phase 2, as will publication of content to the Supply Department's intranet site.
• Backfile conversion of large-size formats is subjected to a separate Feasibility Study to determine cost and benefit, but that is outside of the scope of this project.

Table 4: Typical IDCM Project Constraints

Constraint	Example
Financial	Project cost, capital costs, materials, revenue, and resource costs
Personnel	Lack of people with appropriate experience or qualifications
Time	Time to deliver the results, the critical date when results are needed
Quality	The scope, specifications, and standards to be achieved

Table 5: IDCM Project Approach Definitions

Step Process	Key Activities	Date
Planning	Planning covers: • The development of the Project Charter • The development of a Project Schedule (annexed to Charter)	~
Preliminaries	Preliminaries step will cover: • The development of a document management policy that supports the enterprises information policy, as a strategy to provide a policy framework for the implementation of the IDCM system • The conduct of a Feasibility Study to determine (and confirm) the operational, technical, and financial viability of the project • The development of a Business Case to provide (or confirm) the cost justification and benefits strategies for the IDCM project.	~
Requirements Analysis	During the Requirements Analysis phase, the focus will be on requirements determination (fact-finding, current functions, potential improvements) and requirements analysis, with the key deliverable being a set of requirements specifications. The deliverables will cover: • Requirements Specifications for the business units involved in Phase 1 implementation of the IDCM solution • Requirements Specification for the packaged software to support the Phase 1 and enterprise implementation of the IDCM solution • Requirements Specification to define the architecture, performance, and administration requirements of the IDCM solution • ~	~
Package Selection	Package Selection step will cover: • The development of a Contract Strategy to seek suitable IDCM solutions using enterprise commercial processes; the contract strategy may involve the selection of qualified potential suppliers and system integrators based on a prequalification report • The development of RFP, including selection criteria; the enterprise's Requirements Specifications for the IDCM solution are typically annexed to the RFP • The preparation of an Evaluation Plan by which the IDCM project team will conduct the evaluation of proposals received from potential suppliers and system integrators • The definition of a benchmark strategy by which products (short-listed following project team evaluation) will be subjected to functional benchmark assessment, and performance benchmark assessment (for specific aspects of the nonfunctional specifications). • The documentation of a Reference Site strategy by which to check and visit reference sites for short-listed potential suppliers and system integrators, which is a key part of the overall evaluation process • ~	~

Statement of Constraints

The Project Board typically imposes constraints on an IDCM project, and these constraints may impact on the conduct of the project activities and the methodology used to meet the required outcomes. Young (1998, p. 51) identifies the constraints in Table 4 as being typical of the constraints that may apply to projects.

There may be other constraints, and the project team needs to closely analyze the terms of reference, seek clarification on any potential constraints, and articulate all constraints within the project definition statement.

Project Approach Definition

There is a need to identify and document the step processes involved in achieving the project outcomes, and Figure 1 is useful as a reference point. Typically, the project approach might embrace the types of descriptions defined in Table 5.

Deliverables Plan

An example of a Deliverables Plan that can be used for *Phase 0* of the project is shown in Table 6. The Deliverables Plan will be reviewed later, during the development of the Project Execution Plan for *Phase 1* of the IDCM solution implementation.

The deliverable review needs to be in accordance with the Deliverables Plan, and there needs to be a project completion "sign-off" for *Phase 0*. The Project Sponsor typically authorizes this plan.

Table 6: Typical Deliverables Plan

Deliverable (Examples)	Author	Reviewer	Approver	Date
Project Charter	~	Key stakeholders	Project Sponsor	~
Document Management Policy	~	Key stakeholders Project sponsor	Project Board	~
Web Publishing and Content Management Policy		Key stakeholders Project sponsor	Project Board	~
Feasibility Study Report	~	Key stakeholders	Project Sponsor	~
Business Case	~	Key stakeholders Project sponsor	Project Board	~
Requirements Specifications	~	Key stakeholders	Project Sponsor	~
Contract Strategy	~	Key stakeholders Project sponsor	Project Board	~
Request for Proposal	~	Key stakeholders Project Sponsor	Project Board	~
Evaluation Plan	~	Key stakeholders	Project Sponsor	~
Benchmark Strategy	~	Key stakeholders	Project Sponsor	~
Reference Site Strategy	~	Key stakeholders	Project Sponsor	~
Contract	~	Key stakeholders Project Sponsor	Project Board	~

Table 7: Project Roles and Responsibilities

Role	Designate	Responsibility Synopsis
Project Board	~	Responsibilities include: • Determine the objectives and scope of the project. • Receive reports on the progress of the project. • Provide collective executive guidance as required. • Accept project deliverables where specified as "approver" in the Deliverables Plan.
Project Sponsor	~	Responsibilities include: • Monitor the conduct of the project. • Provide guidance to the project team. • Facilitate resolution of any problems or issues. • Review and endorse (specified) project deliverables for approval by Board. • Accept project deliverables where specified as "approver" in the Deliverables Plan.
Technical Director	~	Responsibilities include: • Provide specialist advice and guidance regarding integration of IDCM within enterprise technical environment. • Facilitate the information technology aspects of the project.
Project Manager	~	Responsibilities include: • Assure timely and satisfactory completion of the project • Manage the project to budget, time, and quality requirements • Secure assistance of internal or external expertise to resource the project, as required. • Manage the project team as a united group.
Project Team	~	Information and Business Analyst(s): Assist with the analysis of business requirements for IDCM systems; contribute to definition of IDCM software functionality, planning, requirements, and deployment strategies. Records Manager(s)/Archivist(s): Provide knowledge-domain expertise pertaining to records management and archival principles, practices and requirements for managing physical and digital documents. Consultant(s): Provide specialist advice regarding IDCM software functionality, planning, requirements, and evaluation and deployment strategies; provide external perspective to IDCM solution implementation and insights into problem solving.

Project Organization

The roles and responsibilities assigned to the IDCM project will depend on the enterprise business environment and the scope and nature of the IDCM implementation. The roles and responsibilities defined in Table 7 may prove useful as a baseline for further development.

Project Plan

Table 8 provides an overview of the typical structure and contents that can be applied to a Project Plan. For those organizations wanting a single document, the plan may be incorporated with the Project Charter

Table 8: Project Plan Structure/Content

Structure	Content
Document history	Provide the history of the author, review approval, and revision processes.
Glossary	The glossary should define the terms and describe their use within the document.
Introduction	Recapitulation — details from Project Charter
Project definition	Recapitulation — details from Project Charter
Key planning dates and project schedule	The charter should define key planning dates, including milestones and events, critical dates; it should also be accompanied by a Gantt Chart as a "Project Schedule," that provides a detailed definition of planning activities.
Assumptions and dependencies	The charter should contain a list of all assumptions and dependencies that are known at project initiation.
Impact statement	The types of impacts that need to be considered include: • Project impact — the impact of this project on other projects underway within the organization and any interrelationships that may need to exist and be managed • System impact — the impact of the system on the organization, including impact on customers, business partners and service providers, internal end users, other information systems, and documentation
Risk assessment/ management strategy	The risk management strategy should include an assessment of risks known at the time of project initiation, and each risk might be identified in terms of the following: • Risk • Likelihood • Consequence • Severity • Mitigation Examples of an indicative set of risks are included with this material.
Budget	The budget should provide details for this phase of the project. Detailed analysis of the costs and benefits of the entire product development life cycle will need to be developed as part of the Business Case and ratified once proposals have been evaluated from prospective vendors, suppliers, or systems integrators.

For example, impact and risk assessment determination may be undertaken, making use of a SWOT analysis, in order to structure the expression of impacts for better understanding.

Project Assumptions and Dependencies

It is important that the Project Plan contain a list of all assumptions and dependencies that have been identified. An example to use as a starting point for a statement of assumption and dependencies is shown in Table 9.

Table 9: Project Assumptions and Dependencies — An Example

Assumptions/Dependencies — IDCM Project
Assumptions: • The manager of the Supply Department will manage the cleanup of documents and metadata as a separate (but interrelated) project. • ~
Dependencies: • The implementation of the IDCM is dependent on the manager of the Supply Department completing data cleanup in accordance with the Project Schedule. • ~

Table 10: Phase 0 Risk Assessment/Mitigation Strategy — Example Extract

Risk	Likelihood	Consequence	Severity	Mitigation
Scope creep	Low	Delays or need for additional resources that may not be readily available	Medium	Highlight and discuss all instances of scope creep, and raise formal change requests where applicable; all requests to change of scope shall be authorized by the Project Sponsor and managed as a change to the project plan by agreed Change Control processes; effective communication plan
Loss of key project resources	Medium	Loss of knowledge pertaining to the project; serious project delays may occur	High	Secure current resources for remaining phases of the project; identify, source, and secure additional resources early; succession planning for nominated resources
Users dislike concepts, philosophy, and rigor of managing documents	Medium	System will not be successful	High	Develop an agreed Change Management Plan; market and communicate the benefits of the system

Risk Assessment and Management Strategy

Table 10 provides an example of a Risk Assessment/Mitigation Plan for *Phase 0*, which lists some of the known risks at project initiation. The Risk Assessment/Mitigation Plan should be complemented by a Risk Register, which can be used to record new risks and mitigation strategies. Risk Assessment/Mitigation Plan and Risk Register will be updated during the development of the Project Execution Plan for *Phase 1* implementation.

KEY DOCUMENTS — PHASE 1: IMPLEMENTATION

We shall look at planning aspects for Phase 1: Implementation in more detail in Chapter 21, which is devoted to implementation planning. That chapter provides an analysis of the planning framework and action strategies that are suitable for Phase 1: Implementation and considers some of the key documents relevant to implementation.

METHODOLOGIES

We will now briefly examine some of the structured information systems methodologies that are available to assist with the planning required for an IDCM system implementation. Essentially, there are two interrelated types of methodologies to consider when planning an IDCM project:

- Structured methodologies for information systems projects, which (depending on the methodology) provide an overall framework for projects from project initiation through to implementation;

- Project management methodologies, which are complementary to the structured analysis and design methodologies, and focus more specifically on the project management techniques associated with information systems projects.

Structured Methodologies

Information systems are implemented in enterprises in many ways. Systems may be installed using generic commercial software to avoid the need for internal development. They may be outsourced so that a contractor undertakes analysis and design specific to the enterprise. They may be a group of relatively independent and uncoordinated systems developed by end users or adaptations of particular modules of enterprise systems. They may be developed internally by prototyping and iterative development with end users; or they may be applied in a structured formal manner that may embody prototyping.

We will examine the formalized approach to systems analysis, because it has elements of interest to each of the other approaches, and because it may have particular application to IDCM systems. The formalized approach has been initiated to work in accord with the subsequent design process that is necessary for the implementation of information systems. It was developed in association with process-centered techniques appropriate to the mainframe processing applications introduced in the 1960s and 1970s. In this environment, it was customary to work within the framework of a System Development Life-Cycle (SDLC). The SDLC has been described in many ways, but usually in terms of steps like the following:

- Project initiation;
- Feasibility study and preliminary investigation;
- Requirements analysis and definition that may include prototyping;
- Preliminary design that may include prototyping;
- Detailed design;
- Development;
- Implementation; and
- Operations and maintenance.

It is important to appreciate that this sequencing, while being useful to assist in project management terms, does not necessarily mean that each step concludes completely before the next commences. In IDCM terms, as we saw in Figure 1, package selection is a key step that may be required after the "analysis" step (unless the IDCM software package has already been identified or is in situ), with the view to utilization of a commercial package. Prototyping may be required depending on the complexity of the configurations and customization required for the usability of the package and the implementation strategy agreed upon between the client and provider.

There is a range of structured methodologies available commercially, such as:

- DAFNE in Italy;
- iAPT Methodology, which offers a quality management system for information systems projects;
- Information Engineering (IE) in the United States;

- MEIN in Spain;
- MERISE in France;
- Object Modeling Techniques;
- SDM in the Netherlands;
- Soft Systems/Multiview;
- Structured Systems Analysis and Design Method (SSADM), which is the standard development method for government agencies in the United Kingdom, and which has also been widely adopted there by the business sector;
- Vorgehensmodell in Germany; and
- Yourdon Structured Analysis and Design.

Some of the commercially available models offer full life-cycle support, and others offer support for specific phases of the information systems life-cycle. It is not within the scope of this book to discuss the scope of particular methodologies, but Tudor and Tudor (1997) provide a comparison of the following methods: Soft Systems Method/ Multiview, SSADM, IE, Yourdon Structured Method, and MERISE, as well as a review of Object Modeling Technique.

There have also been several approaches toward method standardization for information systems projects. These include development of *Euromethod*, a project that was initiated by the European Commission to facilitate information systems planning between European Economic Community member states (European Software Institute, 2002), and *DSDM* (Dynamic Systems Development Method) established by a consortium of UK software suppliers and purchasers (Flynn, 1998).

ISO has promulgated a life-cycle standard (International Standards Organization & International Electrotechnical Commission, 1995), as well as a series of standards under the name of *SPICE* (Software Process Improvement and Capability dEtermination) program. SPICE takes a broad view of the software process, including managing and acquiring software comprising process assessment, process capability determination, and process improvement (International Standards Organization & International Electrotechnical Commission, 1998).

If guidelines similar to these are followed, then documentation arising from different project stages (International Standards Organization & International Electrotechnical Commission, 2000) could be as follows:

- Feasibility study request;
- Feasibility study report;
- System design study request;
- System design study report;
- System design study;
- Acceptance report; and
- Evaluation reports.

Structured design methodologies have proven important in environments where there are significant numbers of IT professionals, and where it has been necessary to make a transition from entrenched manual approaches to computer-based equivalents.

However, many of these systems have already been designed, and it is seen as a greater imperative to establish strategic value from existing data collections or from enterprise systems. Designers of IDCM may well find that the design must be undertaken with respect to an existing enterprise system that already embodies some document management functionality.

Recordkeeping professionals have also developed methodologies for implementing records management systems. For example, in Chapter 2, we made reference to DIRKS (National Archives of Australia, 2000) as an example of an approach to planning and implementation of electronic recordkeeping. DIRKS is based on records management practice that is documented in ISO 15489 (International Organization for Standardization, 2001). The eight-step approach listed in Chapter 2 may be regarded as an example of how such conceptual schemas can be utilized in order to promote business effectiveness (doing the right things), through its preliminary analysis steps, and efficiency (doing things the right way), through its design and implementation steps.

Given the complexity of specifying, selecting, developing, and implementing an IDCM solution that meets enterprise requirements, it is important that structured methods be applied throughout the product development life-cycle. The rigor and discipline of a structured development method will facilitate the development and implementation effort within an IS planning framework and reduce the risks to the projects involved within the enterprise IDCM system deployment.

While these types of structured methodologies are general rather than specific, and extended information is required to address the unique requirements for an IDCM project, these types of methodologies provide generic step processes and techniques that may be useful for the IDCM project team. This book attempts to provide some insights into those unique requirements for an IDCM solution, so that an enterprise may use its methodology of choice for the project and supplement it with specific information relevant to an IDCM project.

Project Management Methodologies

A structured methodology for an information systems project may provide the product development methodology for phases of an IDCM project but may need to be supplemented by a project management methodology that focuses on the project life-cycles relevant to the product development and implementation. SSADM, for example, provides structured methods and techniques for the Feasibility Study and Requirements Analysis steps of an IS project life-cycle. The project team may supplement SSADM with a Project Management Methodology such as PRINCE2™(United Kingdom Office of Government Commerce, 2002) for planning the design, development, and implementation aspects.

The analysis of project management tools and analysis of project management best practice are not within the scope of this book. However, there are a number of industry organizations that provide professional advice in this respect.[2]

Templates for a Project Brief and Project Initiation Document can be located at the official PRINCE2™Web site (United Kingdom Office of Government Commerce, 2002). The templates can be customized for enterprise preferences.

SUMMARY

In this chapter, we covered the importance of planning in the successful delivery of an IDCM project. We reviewed the differentiation between a product development life-cycle and project life-cycle planning, and indicated that an IDCM solution is effectively a product and should be subject to product development life-cycles.

We also stated that a product development life-cycle can consist of a number of project life-cycles and suggested how an IDCM project can be conceptually split into at least two phases, called Phase 0 — Planning and Phase 1 — Implementation. We discussed some key aspects of project life-cycle planning that can apply to the Phase 0 — Planning phase, and shall look further at project life-cycle planning for Phase 1 — Implementation during Chapter 21.

ENDNOTES

[1]   Lewin is often quoted as having said that something can be truly understood if you try to change it. His force field theory of change management assumes that driving and restraining forces apply in any situation in which change may occur. Examples of driving forces are supervisory pressure, competition for advancement, or bonuses as incentives; the restraining influences may be personnel apathy or resentment, underresourcing, or inadequate technology.

[2]   The Project Management Institute provides education, research, standards, and publications relevant to project management, from initiation through to project execution. Details of the Project Management Body of Knowledge are at: http://www.pmi.org.

The Association for Project Management developed standards in project management that reflect current practice in broad commercial and industrial sectors. Details are at: http://www.apm.org.uk.

The International Project Management Association exists as a promotional organization for project management internationally and offers baseline competency standards. Details are at: http://www.ipma.ch/.

Chapter 7

Policy Framework for IDCM

OVERVIEW

This chapter deals with the development of a policy framework that enables an enterprise to articulate its policy for managing documents and content, the general principles that support the policy, and the strategies for effective implementation of the policy.

The development of a policy framework is not dependent on an investment in IDCM. The policy framework can be developed to apply improved practices for managing documents using existing tools (e.g., network file systems and physical filing systems), although the benefits offered by a managed repository would not be forthcoming.

However, the development of an information management policy is a recommended prerequisite to the specification of requirements for an IDCM because of the following:

- The policy document typically articulates principles that provide a contextual foundation for the process of requirements analysis and determination and the preparation of a Requirements Specification for an IDCM system.

- The policy generally defines strategies that require action plans to be developed and implemented by roles with assigned responsibilities. The requirements analysis and determination tasks associated with IDCM may depend upon the successful conclusion of some strategies and actions.

- The policy may reduce the risk of slippage in the project schedule during requirements analysis and determination and during the preparation of the Requirements Specification.

We believe that the IDCM policy framework should be developed, communicated, and accepted within the enterprise prior to commencing the Requirements Specification(s), which we will discuss in Chapter 10. We also believe that IDCM policy must be positioned within the overall context of an enterprise's information policy framework, which we shall discuss later in this chapter.

Our objectives in this chapter, therefore, are to express contributing factors to a document policy, and to do this within the broader framework of an enterprise information policy which we see as a desirable authority that frames document policy.

CONTEXT

Documents are not created and processed in a vacuum. As Sutton (1996, p. 96) explained, the objective of a document management policy is to ensure that the use of document resources supports the mission of the enterprise in a cost-effective manner. Furthermore, the effective implementation of the policy will improve the official use of knowledge, documents, and management practices.

If we are to align document resource usage with the mission of the enterprise, we can apply an IDCM policy framework similar to the information planning principles suggested by Synnott (1987). From this viewpoint, the policy may then be developed within the context of management planning at strategic, tactical, and operational levels, so that we can understand document resource utilization and requirements within the context of these three management tiers.

These three tiers of management planning typically involve managing the challenges of the following:

- External influences, such as the legislative and standards environment, customer and business partner expectations, and evolving document formats; and

Table 1: Examples of Strategic, Tactical, and Operational Factors Influencing Document Management Policy

Factor	External	Internal
Strategic	• Statutory and regulatory environment • Quality standards • Environment standards	• Enterprise's corporate plans and strategies • Commitment to quality management system • Commitment to environment management system • Commitment to information sharing and knowledge transfer • Information policy
Tactical	• Customer expectations on service delivery • Business partner expectations on digital collaboration and exploiting business-to-business models	• Business operational plans (e.g., project-based workgroups) • Information management • Information sharing • Business continuity planning
Operational	• Document management standards • Records management standards • Document formats	• Information capture • Quality assurance • Business continuity support

- Internal imperatives articulated in institutional objectives that may address issues ranging from knowledge management to planning business continuity (disaster preparedness).

The matrix in Table 1 provides some examples of strategic, tactical, and operational factors that can be considered when developing document management policy. The examples are differentiated into external and internal influences.

AIM OF IDCM POLICY

Policy is normally framed with reference to the overall mission and objectives of an enterprise. Among these overall objectives, there should typically be some that relate to information policy. These may lead to objectives relating to document management, content management, information resource management, and knowledge management. There will be overlapping concerns arising from information issues in areas such as authority, access, privacy, and preservation.

Our concern here is specifically with documents. The aim of a policy might be defined as "support the enterprise mission and objectives by providing a clear definition of rules, principles and associated strategies for effectively managing documents and their content as an information resource, and meeting recordkeeping obligations."

OBJECTIVES OF IDCM POLICY

The objectives of an IDCM policy may include:

- To provide a clear policy framework that applies to managing documents and content within the enterprise to support the enterprise mission and objectives;
- To define the principles that must be embraced to give effect to the policy, addressing the strategic, tactical, and operational requirements for managing documents and content within the context of external influences and internal business imperatives;
- To define strategies for the effective implementation of the policy and assign roles and responsibilities for strategy implementation; and
- To provide the criteria against which the effectiveness of the policy and associated strategies are to be evaluated.

SCOPE OF IDCM POLICY

The scope of the IDCM policy depends upon each individual enterprise's requirements for improving the management of documents and content. For example, the organization may be considering document or publishing systems at a number of levels, including:

- Enterprise-wide application;
- Specific "fit for purpose" vertical application (e.g., managing quality management system documentation, or providing Web content to external contractors); and

Figure 1: Document and Content Management Policy within Information Policy Framework.

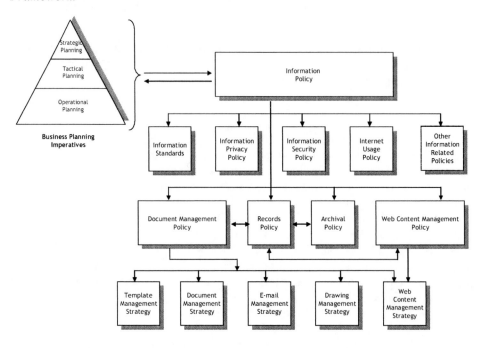

- General (horizontal) application of documents and content (e.g., managing all types of documents within a specific department or workgroup).

Depending on the nature of the requirement, the IDCM policy framework may need to embrace a range of subpolicies and strategies to meet the complexities of diverse document types. The operational environment (government, financial, education, manufacturing, etc.) will influence the subpolicy requirements. Figure 1 provides a framework for specific policy within the context of information policy in general. It includes separate interrelated components for templates and forms, general (office) documents, drawings, email and Web content.

Regardless of the circumstances, the enterprise needs to take into account the management requirements for documents and Web content in the context of their life-cycle and record continuum. There is also a requirement to consider the interchange of documents with business partners, service providers, customers and community groups, where appropriate.

INFORMATION POLICY

An enterprise's information policy should be the primary instrument for planning the utilization and development of information and knowledge. The information policy should provide the overarching policy, principles, standards, and guidelines for the effective management of information to support the enterprise's mission and objectives.

Table 2: Information Policy Components

Policy Component	Example
Definition	• Define the enterprise mission and objectives and the requirements for managing documents within the organization to promote knowledge and information sharing
Acquisition	• Ensure that documentation acquired from external sources or generated from within the enterprise is fit for purpose and managed
Utilization	• Exploit information fully, to meet all current needs, and to help meet changes in goals and in the operational environment • Use knowledge and information ethically in all internal and external dealings, including appropriate privacy • Provide appropriate human and financial resources for managing and developing the use of information and knowledge • Ensure that it reaches, on time, and in the right format, all the people who need to use it • Provide appropriate intellectual control using metainformation
Evaluation	• Audit the use of information regularly to ensure that what is needed is available and that it is used appropriately and to good effect • Provide for a coordinated overview of total resources of knowledge and information • Develop and apply reliable means of assessing the costs and value of information and the contribution it makes to achieving objectives • Establish conditions for pricing information
Disposal	• Identify conditions under which information media may be eliminated
Authority	• Identify the people responsible for managing specific resources of information, and those who are "stakeholders" in them, and ensure that the authority and delegation of the managers of information resources match the responsibility they carry
Communication	• Promote information interchange between managers of information resources and between them and stakeholders
Infrastructure	• Develop and maintain an infrastructure of systems and ICT to support the management of information resources and information interactions within the organization and externally
Access	• Pursue maximum openness of access to information inside the organization and externally • Provide appropriate security levels • Safeguard current and historical information resources so that they remain accessible for use at all times
Preservation	• Ensure preservation of the organization's "memory" in the form of its knowledge base • Provide for business continuity with backup and re-establishment procedures for records supporting critical business processes
Familiarization	• Provide appropriate education and training to enable members of staff to meet their responsibilities in using knowledge and information
Evolution	• Align the definitions as goals evolve and change • Seek to use information to support the management of change initiatives to benefit the organization and to create new knowledge • Use this policy as the basis for information strategies that will support business strategy

The enterprise information policy may contain a subset of policies, principles, standards, and guidelines covering important information policy areas such as:

- Information security policy;
- Internet usage policy and guidelines;
- Web content policy and guidelines;
- Online service delivery resource management;
- Document management policy framework; and
- Electronic recordkeeping standards.

This type of information policy approach offers a coherent framework for enterprises to use to develop, implement, and review appropriate policies and practices for information resource management. The policy framework also assures that information, both Web-based and non-Web-based (e.g., printed publications) is more readily located and retrieved and that published information is current, correct, and accessible.

From Figure 1, we can see that the information policy provides the overall strategy and principles concerning how information is to be managed within the enterprise. There are also a number of supporting policies. We included three as examples: the information privacy policy, the information security policy and the Internet usage policy. We have also itemized groups of information standards that are likely to contribute to the exercise of policy.

Although enterprises may have separate policies for standard documents, drawings, email, and Web content, an integrative approach suggests a single consolidated policy covering all documents.

The diagram highlights that there is an interrelationship between document management policy and records policy. We take the view that not all documents created, captured, and managed within an enterprise are "evidence and information" that is required to be kept as a record "in pursuance of legal obligations or in the transaction of business," as records are defined in the international recordkeeping standard ISO 15489-1:2001 (International Organization for Standardization, 2001, p. 3).

Similarly, not all records are in the form of physical or electronic documentation but may be represented by information held in transaction processing systems or management information systems, such as asset management systems.

Given that the document management policy fits within the overall information policy framework, then the policy elements that directly relate to information planning can be utilized as the basis for defining relevant policy components at the operational management level. In Table 2, we adapted a range of policy elements from Middleton (2002) to suggest components that are appropriate for information planning.

POLICY LEVELS

Sutton (1996, p. 95) noted that policy development typically moves from the general to the specific, and this statement is directly relevant to the requirement to analyze IDCM policy in terms of strategic, operational, and tactical management. We will now examine the types of strategic, operational, and tactical factors that may impact upon document management policy and strategy formulation, taking into account external influences and business imperatives.

Strategic Factors

Examples of strategic factors to be considered include external influences and internal business imperatives, such as:

- Statutory and regulatory environment(s) (external influence);
- Enterprise corporate planning;
- Commitment to quality management system; and
- Commitment to environmental management system (EMS).

Statutory/Regulatory Environment(s)

Statutory and regulatory requirements govern the activities of enterprises and much of the governance imposed by legislating authorities' impacts on the management of documents and records within the context of the business environment.

Statutes and administrative regulations may influence the enterprise document environment in a number of ways. For example, governments may:

- Regulate the overall corporate environment at a macro level using such legislative or regulatory powers as:
  - Corporation laws, which typically cover the financial and administration management requirements of commercial enterprises;
  - Taxation laws, which may prescribe the requirements for lodgment of taxation documentation; and
  - Occupational health and safety regulations, for example, the extent to which industrial accidents must be documented, or the extent to which documentary preventive measures are applied.
- Regulate enterprise policy, strategies, and behaviors within the context of the industry in which the enterprise operates, such as:
  - Mining;
  - Pharmaceuticals;
  - Financial services; and
  - Government sector, for example, through statutory reporting requirements.
- Regulate specific aspects of information management, including statutes or regulations covering specific areas, such as:
  - Intellectual property — through such mechanisms as copyright and patents, to protect intellectual property produced by the enterprise, as well as to enable use by the enterprise of property produced by others;
  - Evidence — cover the requirements for the admissibility of evidence and the particular implications for recordkeeping (A court may need to examine records as evidence of an organization's decisions and actions.);
  - Freedom of Information (FOI) — public sector agencies are required to provide public access to information, including electronic records, unless the requested information falls within one or more of the exemption categories generally prescribed under relevant legislation;

-   Privacy — use of information about individuals for lawful purposes, which must relate directly to the functions or role of the agency (The information must be secure, accurate, relevant, complete, and not be misleading.); and
-   Archives — for public sector records, mandate the arrangements under which they must be retained and released to the public.

In many instances, the legislation may impact the document environment within organizations by prescribing or otherwise regulating the templates for forms that are used for making applications and providing approvals or otherwise specifying the format of reports to government.

The document management policy will need to embrace the requirement for the enterprise to comply with those statutory and regulatory requirements for managing business documents and recordkeeping that apply within their respective area or areas (in those cases where enterprise operations are covered by multiple jurisdictions).

Enterprise Corporate Planning

We looked at the types of challenges facing business and government enterprises in Chapter 3. Given the diverse challenges and business planning imperatives to be addressed by executive management, there is often not much time available for them to consider the beneficial implications of effective IDCM on enterprise planning, particularly in the areas of information sharing and developing intellectual capital.

One vital factor in the development and implementation of successful information policy and realization of IDCM is to align policy formulation with key business strategies defined in the enterprise's corporate plan. An enterprise corporate plan typically covers a 3-year period and provides the organization's mission, long-term vision statements, corporate objectives, strategies, and performance evaluation measures.

Consequently, it is imperative that practitioners responsible for developing the IDCM policy framework determine the key strategies identified in the enterprise corporate plan, which may involve a range of business planning imperatives, with specific implications for document and content management. For example:

•   New service delivery models (e.g., involving use of Internet technologies and Web content);
•   Supply chain management strategies;
•   Customer relationship strategies;
•   Business partner, and service organization's accessibility, availability, and reliability of documents;
•   Commitment to safety and occupational health;
•   Commitment to quality management system; and
•   Commitment to environment management system.

We will now draw on two of these examples, i.e., an enterprise's commitment to (a) quality management system and (b) environmental management as examples of strategic planning imperatives that may be aligned with the IDCM policy framework and IDCM planning.

Commitment to Quality Management System

A strategic requirement for an enterprise may be to implement quality management systems that govern the development and deployment of its products and services. The quality objectives for many enterprises are to seek accreditation under ISO's quality management framework embodied in the ISO 9000 series with requirements in ISO 9001 (International Organization for Standardization, 2000).

Those enterprises seeking accreditation under ISO 9001 recognize that document and data controls are important components of the quality management system, and documentation may be viewed as the foundation of the ISO quality system (Hoyle, 1994, p. 34). The standard specifies the requirement to have documented procedures to define the controls required, with criteria as follows (International Organization for Standardization, 2000, clause 4.2.3):

- Documents are approved for adequacy prior to issue. The approval process is typically a two-step process including a review by a subject matter expert followed by standard compliance review.
- Documents are reviewed and updated as necessary and reapproved. This requirement places emphasis on an enterprise's internal review processes for identifying updates to documents, making the updates, and obtaining reapproval.
- Changes to documents and current revision status of documents are identified. This requirement may mean that all changes to quality system documentation must be tracked to identify the nature of the changes made between revisions of a document.
- Relevant versions of applicable documents are available at their points of use. This requirement has implications for the distribution of documents, regardless of document format (e.g., electronic or physical document).
- Documents must remain legible and identified.
- Documents of external origin are identified, and distribution processes are controlled.
- The unintended use of obsolete copies of documents must be prevented, and documents need to be suitably identified if they are to be retained for any purpose.

The standard also requires that records be established and maintained, "to provide evidence of conformity to requirements and of the effective operation of the quality management system." Furthermore, the standard specifies that "records shall remain legible, readily identifiable and retrievable" and that procedures be established for the "identification, storage, protection, retrieval, retention time and disposition of records" (clause 4.2.4).

The implementation of document control systems to satisfy the ISO 9000 standards is an intricate process that involves interpretation of the standard's requirements and the development of an extensive range of policy, system, and procedural documentation.

Irrespective of whether enterprises seek accreditation under these standards, any organization wishing to implement a quality management system will need to address the vital role that effective management of controlled documents will play in implementing and maintaining the quality system.

The authority, review, update, and distribution processes referred to above may all be facilitated through Web content management.

Commitment to Environmental Management System

A number of EMS models have been developed in the last decade in response to the requirement to meet the environmental challenges facing manufacturing and industrial enterprises. For example, the British Standards Institute (BSI) developed BS 7750 in 1992 and revised it in 1994. The European Union established its Eco-Management and Audit Scheme in 1993 as a voluntary regulatory model that was to be adopted by member states.

However, while there have been a number of alternative environmental standards, at an international level, it is the ISO 14000 series that provides the framework. For example, ISO 14001 standard (International Organization for Standardization, 1996) has requirements for document control and records management that are similar to ISO 9001.

For instance, enterprises must maintain procedures to enable location of documents, conduct periodical reviews of their adequacy, ensure that current versions are available at locations where the functions that they describe are to be performed, and carry out procedures for removal and retention of obsolete documents, if necessary.

Procedures for the identification, maintenance, and disposition of environmental records must be undertaken. These include linkage to associated activities, establishment of retention periods, and storage for preservation purposes and to facilitate retrieval.

The EMS documentation and document controls are a major challenge at every phase for those organizations wishing to achieve EMS. As with ISO 9000 series, effective management of controlled documents will play a vital role in implementing and maintaining the environmental management system.

Tactical Factors

Examples of tactical factors that may need to be considered include external influences and internal business imperatives, such as:

- Customer expectations;
- Business partner expectations on digital collaboration and exploiting business-to-business models;
- Business operational plans and the role of documents in the context of the processes that support business operations; and
- Continuous business improvement.

External Influences

Development of IDCM policy may have to account for external factors, such as the following:

- Customer expectations on responsiveness and accountability are increasing in the business and government sectors.
- Customer expectations are also increasing in relation to access via the Internet/WWW.

- E-business initiatives for interacting between business and customers are emerging, as are e-government initiatives for interacting between government agencies and the communities they represent.
- Business partner expectations are increasing on document interchange using WWW technology, such as extranets and application of open systems approaches to exploiting documents through use of markup languages such as XML to facilitate development of projects, products, and services.

Internal Imperatives

Business obligations that are likely to have an impact upon the development of the IDCM policy include:

- Mergers or acquisitions of organizations, services, products, or projects;
- Provision of internal information to contractors and service providers;
- Divisional initiatives for continuous business improvement;
- Establishment of projects, for example, a construction project to develop new infrastructure;
- Divisional proposals for new services or products;
- Product development;
- Infrastructure or asset management strategies that involve document-intensive processes;
- Integration of an ERP system with document technologies for a specific purpose (e.g., accounts payable application); and
- Implementation of knowledge management strategies that associate informal and formal communication processes.

Operational Factors

The types of operational factors that may impact on IDCM within an enterprise include the implementation of information policy and tactical approaches making use of the following:

- Document management standards;
- Recordkeeping standards;
- Metadata standards;
- Workflow standards; and
- Internal conventions and formalisms, for example, Web site look and feel.

Document Management Standards

Document management standards have typically been developed at the operational level, specifically the technical level, primarily to address interoperability between information systems offering document capture or management capabilities, workflow, and integration with desktop and business applications.

Details of many of these standards and emerging industry standards in the area of document and content management are generally accessible from AIIM International (see Appendix 3), which has also published a recommended practice report (Association for Information and Image Management International, 2001) for the implementation of Web-based document management technologies.

Also of relevance in this area are the standards of the IEC (International Electrotechnical Commission, 2001a,b). Their document management principles and methods have recently been released. The second part, on metadata and reference models, is under review prior to release at the time of writing.

The AIIM report includes details of AIIM published standards that may be used when developing the document management policy. Some of these are published in association with the American National Standards Institute (ANSI). Examples of standards and specifications are listed in Tables 3 to 5.

Document services technologies provide for management of digital documents, including maintenance of access restrictions. For example, this may mean check-in/check-out control to those in a department working on a document update, and read-only access to those outside this department.

They also provide for conversion of documents into formats for network availability, such as HTML or XML, and for automated publishing to structured Web sites for general access.

The AIIM report also lists a range of document management industry guidelines that may be useful for practitioners developing policy. These are shown in Table 6.

Table 3: Document Services Standards

AIIM Document Services Standards
The following standards are offered by AIIM for document services: • Document Management Alliance (DMA) specification, which defines the interfaces that enable uniform search and access to objects in multivendor document repositories. For example, to enable the document management application from vendor "A" to access documents held in the repository of vendor "B." • Open Document Management API (ODMA), which specifies interfaces that document applications can use at the desktop client level to enable integration with other applications. For example, the capability to integrate a desktop application (such as a word-processing system) with a document management client application.

Table 4: Digital Imaging Standards

AIIM Digital Imaging Standards
The following standards are offered by AIIM for electronic image management (EIM): • ANSI/AIIM MS44 – 1993, Recommended Practice for Quality Control of Image Scanners • ANSI/AIIM MS52 – 1991, Recommended Practice for the Requirements and Characteristics of Original Documents Intended for Optical Scanning • ANSI/AIIM MS53 – 1993, Recommended Practice: File Format for Storage and Exchange of Image: Bi-Level Image File Format: Part 1 • ANSI/AIIM MS44 – 1993, Recommended Practice for Quality Control of Image Scanners • ANSI/AIIM MS52 – 1991, Recommended Practice for the Requirements and Characteristics of Original Documents Intended for Optical Scanning • ANSI/AIIM MS53 – 1993, Recommended Practice: File Format for Storage and Exchange of Image: Bi-Level Image File Format: Part 1 • ANSI/AIIM MS55 – 1994, Recommended Practice for the Identification and Indexing of Page Components (Zones) for Automated Process in an EIM (electronic image management) Environment

Table 5: Storage Standards

AIIM Storage Standards

The following standards are advanced by AIIM for storage management:

- ANSI X3.212-1992 (R1997) – 130-mm Rewritable Optical Disk Cartridge for Information Interchange
- ANSI X3.220-1992 (R1997) – Digital Information Interchange 130-mm Optical Disk Cartridges of the Write-Once, Read Multiple (WORM) Type, Using the Magnetic-Optical Effect (reaffirmation)
- ANSI/ X.3.234-1993 (R1998) – Test Methods for Media Characteristics – 130-mm Re-writable Optical Disk Data Storage Cartridges with Continuous Composite Servo (CCS)
- ANSI/ISO/IEC 13549-1993 – Data Interchange on 130-mm Optical Disk Cartridges – Capacity: 1,3 Gigabytes per Cartridge.
- ISO/IEC 11560:1992 – Information interchange on 130 mm optical disk cartridges using the magneto-optical effect, for write once, read multiple functionality
- ISO/IEC 14517:1996 – 130 mm optical disk cartridges for information interchange – Capacity: 2,6 Gbytes per cartridge
- ISO/IEC 15286:1999 – 130 mm optical disk cartridges for information interchange – Capacity: 5,2 Gbytes per cartridge

---

Table 6: List of AIIM Guidelines

AIIM Guidelines

The following guidelines are offered by AIIM in its recommended practice report:

- ANSI/AIIM TR2-1998 – Glossary of Document Technologies
- ANSI/AIIM TR15-1997 – Planning Considerations, Addressing Preparation of Documents for Image Capture
- ANSI/AIIM TR21-1991 – Recommendations for the Identifying Information to be Placed on Write-Once-Read-Many (WORM) and Rewritable Optical Disk (OD) Cartridge Label(s) and Optical Disk Cartridge Packaging (Shipping Containers)
- ANSI/AIIM TR25-1995 – The Use of Optical Disks for Public Records
- ANSI/AIIM TR27-1996 – Electronic Imaging Request for Proposal (RFP) Guidelines
- ANSI/AIIM TR28-1991 – The Expungement of Information Recorded on Optical Write-Once-Read-Many (WORM) Systems
- ANSI/AIIM TR31:1-1992 (reaffirmed 1998) – Performance Guideline for the Legal Acceptance of Records Produced by Information Technology Systems Part 1: Evidence
- ANSI/AIIM TR31:2-1993 (reaffirmed 1998) – Performance Guideline for the Legal Acceptance of Records Produced by Information Technology Systems Part 2: Acceptance by Government Agencies
- ANSI/AIIM TR31:3-1994 (reaffirmed 1998) – Performance Guideline for the Legal Acceptance of Records Produced by Information Technology Systems Part 3: Implementation
- ANSI/AIIM TR31:4-1994 (reaffirmed 1998) – Performance Guideline for the Legal Acceptance of Records Produced by Information Technology Systems Part 4: Model Act and Rule
- ANSI/AIIM TR32-1994 – Paper Forms Design Optimization for Electronic Image Management (EIM)
- ANSI/AIIM TR33-1998 – Selecting an Appropriate Image Compression Method to Match User Requirements
- ANSI/AIIM TR34-1996 – Sampling Procedures for Inspection by Attributes of Images in Electronic Image Management (EIM) and Micrographics Systems
- ANSI/AIIM TR35-1995 – Human and Organizational Issues for Successful EIM System Implementation
- ANSI/AIIM TR40-1995 – Suggested Index Fields for Documents in Electronic Image Management (EIM) Environments

---

Table 7: Technical Standards

Examples of Technical Standards

The following de facto standards are frequently encountered when considering IDCM technologies:

- Common Object Request Broker Architecture (CORBA) is a vendor-independent architecture and specification for creating, distributing, and managing distributed objects in a computer network. It was developed by the Object Management Group (OMG) and provides a standard protocol that enables interoperability between CORBA-based programs developed by the same or another vendor, and operates on most computers, operating systems, programming languages, and networks. Further details can be found at: http://www.omg.org.
- Dynamic Data Exchange (DDE) is an MS Windows mechanism that permits the two-way passing of instructions and data between applications. There are many ways of using DDE, including linking, remote control, and embedding. Further details can be found at: http://support.microsoft.com/default.aspx?scid=kb;EN-US;q122263.
- Java™ 2 Platform, Enterprise Edition (J2EE™) manages infrastructure and supports the Web services to enable development of secure and interoperable business applications. Further details can be found at: http://java.sun.com/j2ee/index.html.
- Enterprise JavaBeans (EJB), developed under the Java Community Process 2, streamlines the development and deployment of J2EE applications to simply integration. Further details can be found at http://java.sun.com/products/ejb/2.0.html.
- Image and Scanner Interface Specification (ISIS), which is a de facto document imaging standard, was developed by Pixel Translations. The ISIS tool feature scanner and printer controls assist in the viewing of images, compress and convert the format of image data, and read or write files containing image data. Further details can be found at: http://www.pixtran.com/products/isis/isis.shtml.
- Object Linking and Embedding (OLE) is Microsoft's structure for creating compound documents. Further details can be found at: http://support.microsoft.com/default.aspx?scid=kb;EN-US;q86008.
- Component Object Model (COM) is an architecture that allows applications to be built from binary software components. COM provides the foundation architecture for higher-level software services, including OLE. Further details can be found at: http://www.microsoft.com/com/tech/com.asp.
- Distributed Component Object Model (DCOM) is Microsoft's architecture for distributing object components and comes as part of the Windows operating systems (Windows 95 and later). It is distinct from CORBA, although a gateway between DCOM and CORBA may be developed to enable client object interoperability. Further details can be found at: http://www.microsoft.com/com/tech/DCOM.asp.
- Simple Object Access Protocol (SOAP) is an XML protocol for exchange of information in a decentralized, distributed environment. Further details can be found at http://www.w3.org/TR/SOAP/.
- TWAIN defines a standard software protocol and API that regulates communication between software applications and imaging devices. It enables scanned images to be directly available to the software application that is used to access and manipulate the images. Despite popular belief, TWAIN is not an acronym. Further details can be found at: http://www.twain.org/.
- Web-based Distributed Authoring and Versioning (WebDAV) is a set of extensions to the HTTP protocol that allows users to collaboratively edit and manage files on remote Web servers. Further details can be found at: http://www.webdav.org/.
- eXtensible Markup Language (XML) is the universal format for structured Web data and documents. Further details can be found at http://www.w3.org/XML/.

At the operational level, there are some de facto standards technologies that are directly relevant to the document management industry. Examples are in Table 7.

Consideration of applicable technical standards may be outside the scope of the document management policy development and more related to a technology policy.

However, practitioners need to be aware of the terminology used within the industry to communicate about the technological aspects of document policy.

It may also be appropriate to consider the document formats to be adopted within the enterprise, aside from the formats supported by standard desktop authoring tools (such as word-processing, spreadsheet, and presentation tools). For example, it may be appropriate to have an agreed set of document protocols for imaging file formats (e.g., documents = TIFF version 6.0, or PDF, pictures = JPG, video = MPEG, etc.).

Recordkeeping Standards

ISO 15489 *Information and Documentation — Records management* (International Organization for Standardization, 2001) is the international standard that provides guidance on the management of records.[1]

The ISO standard is provided in two parts: Part 1: General ISO (15489-1) and Part 2: Guidelines (15489-2). Part 1 of the standard covers the following scope, *inter alia*:

- Management of records in all formats or media, created or received by any public or private organization in the conduct of its activities, or any individual with a duty to create and maintain records;
- Guidance on determining the responsibilities of organizations for records and records policies, procedures, systems, and processes;
- Guidance on records management in support of a quality process framework to comply with ISO 9001 and ISO 14001; and
- Guidance on the design and implementation of a records system.

The scope does not include the management of archival records within archival institutions.

The scope of Part 2 of the standard is an implementation guide to Part 1, for use by records management professionals and those with responsibility for managing records in organizations. It offers one methodology to help organizations implement records management and also provides an overview of the processes and factors to be considered.

The intention of the standard is that the "standardization of records management policies and procedures ensures that appropriate attention and protection is given to all records, and that the evidence and information they contain can be retrieved more efficiently and effectively, using standard practices and procedures" (International Organization for Standardization, 2001, part 1, p. vi.).

The standard further states that "Records contain information that is a valuable resource and an important business asset. A systematic approach to the management of records is essential for organizations and society to protect and preserve records as evidence of actions. A records management system results in a source of information about business activities that can support subsequent activities and business decisions, as well as ensuring accountability to present and future stakeholders" (p. 4).

Given that documents are essential components of business practices, and that the standard has a strong focus on systematic approaches for protecting and preserving records as evidence, then enterprises should consider the implications of the ISO 15489 standard when developing a document management policy framework.

Furthermore, ISO 15489 is a relatively high-level document, and enterprises developing a document management policy framework may need to determine whether countries in which they operate have developed (or plan to develop) supporting standards or guidelines that address specific national requirements.

The standard purports to provide guidance on records management in support of a quality process framework to comply with ISO 9001 and ISO 14001, which we discussed earlier. Both ISO 9001 and ISO 14001 made reference to the control of records but lacked guidelines on effective recordkeeping practices that ISO 15489 provides.

Metadata Standards

In its broad sense, metadata (or metainformation) can be any data or information descriptive of other information. They may include filing schemes, classification schemes, mnemonics used in file structures, thesauri for describing subject content, records disposal schedules, and the like.

Since the advent of the Web, *metadata* has been more particularly used to represent schemes for describing digital documents, and metadata standards have been primarily designed to assist with the online publication of information via the Internet and also to facilitate recordkeeping by providing a systematic and consistent means of describing electronic records. These metadata are therefore applicable to Web content management.

There have been central government initiatives to require standard metadata at government Web sites and attempts to have these applied at national and regional levels. However the full adoption of these is yet to be seen. A well-known example is the U.S. *Global Information Locator Service* (GILS, 2002).

GILS standardizes a number of elements used for describing material on Web sites. There are 22 of these so-called core elements, a number of which incorporate subelements. Federal agencies may supplement these with elements of their own. We show a number of these elements in Table 8.

The "repeatable" column indicates whether an element may be used more than once in a document description. In Chapter 4, we made a distinction between *agent* metadata and *content* metadata. In this example, the controlled subject index terms would be content metadata, and the rest would be agent metadata.

Similar approaches to this have been pursued at the national government level in other countries. At the local government level, some agencies have plans to negotiate adoption of the metadata standards with their respective community businesses and special interest groups to foster improved Internet access to services and information.

Major work in the development of metadata standards for online resource discovery has been based on the Dublin Core initiative, which is aimed at the development of interoperable online metadata standards that support a broad range of purposes and business models. A summary of basic Dublin Core elements is shown in Table 9. Links to development of this and many other metadata standards are at the *IFLANET* and *Metadata.Net* sites (International Federation of Library Associations and Institutions, 2002; Distributed Systems Technology Centre — Resource Discovery Unit, 2002)

In the Dublin Core table, **element** refers to the data element from a Web site that is to be described; **refinement** refers to subelements of which there may be instances within an element, for example "date" has five different possible instances with different meaning; and **encoding scheme** refers to the authority against which the metadata are validated, for example, "language" should be validated against the ISO or RFC lists.

Table 8: Extract from GILS Core Elements

Core Element	Repeatable	Description
Title	No	This element conveys the most significant aspects of the referenced resource and is intended for initial presentation to users independently of other elements. It should provide sufficient information to allow users to make an initial decision on likely relevance. It should convey the most significant information available, including the general topic area, as well as a specific reference to the subject.
Originator	Yes	This element identifies the information resource originator.
Date of Publication	No	This is the discrete creation date in which the described resource was published or updated, though not for use on resources that are published continuously such as dynamic databases. Date of Publication Textual may also provide additional information such as when the resource was originally published. This element may be as: • **Date of Publication Structured:** Date described using the ISO 8601 prescribed structure (fixed eight characters, YYYYMMDD) • **Date of Publication Textual:** Date described textually
Controlled Subject Index	Yes	This element is a grouping of subelements that together provide any controlled vocabulary used to describe the resource and the source of that controlled vocabulary comprising: • **Subject Thesaurus** (Not Repeatable): This subelement provides the reference to a formally registered thesaurus or similar authoritative source of the controlled index terms. • **Subject Terms Controlled** (Not Repeatable): This subelement is a grouping of descriptive terms drawn from a controlled vocabulary source to aid users in locating entries of potential interest. Each term is provided in the subordinate repeating field: **Controlled Term.**
Sources of Data	No	This element identifies the primary sources or providers of data to the system, whether within or outside the agency.
Methodology	No	This element identifies any specialized tools, techniques, or methodology used to produce this information resource. The validity, degree of reliability, and any known possibility of errors should also be described.
Purpose	No	Provides why the information resource is offered and identifies other programs, projects, and legislative actions wholly or partially responsible for the establishment or continued delivery of this information resource.
Schedule Number	No	This element is used to record the identifier associated with the information resource for records management purposes.
Record Review Date	No	This element identifies a date assigned by the Record Source for review of this GILS Record.

Table 9: Dublin Core Elements and Qualifiers — For Current Versions Refer to http:/ /dublincore.org/

Element	Refinement(s)	Encoding Scheme(s)
Title	Alternative	—
Creator	—	—
Subject	—	LCSH MeSH DDC LCC UDC
Description	Table of Contents Abstract	—
Publisher	—	—
Contributor	—	—
Date	Created Valid Available Issued Modified	DCMI Period W3C-DTF
Type	—	DCMI Type Vocabulary
Format	Extent	—
	Medium	IMT
Identifier	—	URI
Source	—	URI
Language	—	ISO 639-2 RFC 1766
Relation	Is Version of Has Version Is Replaced by Replaces Is Required by Requires Is Part of Has Part Is Referenced by References Is Format of Has Format	URI
Coverage	Spatial	DCMI Point ISO 3166 DCMI Box TGN
	Temporal	DCMI Period W3C-DTF
Rights	—	—

Although schemes such as Dublin Core and GILS are useful in giving guidance, particularly for description of Web-based documents, they do not have the focus on document management of the document management standard of IEC (International Electrotechnical Commission, 2001a,b). At the time of writing, the second part of this standard which explicates document management metadata elements remains under review, so we refrain from reproducing examples from it here.

However, there are extant detailed recordkeeping metadata standards that may be applied to documents. For example, these include the Australian Federal government guide (National Archives of Australia, 1999), and a derivative, VERS (Public Record Office of Victoria, 2000) which extends the Federal guide to deal with records requiring long-term preservation.

Workflow Standards

Workflow management systems are influenced by the following:

- De facto standards within the information industry that impact on information systems development environments generally; and
- Interoperability standards specified by the WfMC [These standards are not mandated or de facto standards, but are specifications recommended by the WfMC (as a not-for-profit organization) to facilitate interoperability between workflow management systems.].

De facto industry standards are important for an enterprise wishing to align workflow management tools with its IT architecture and enterprise mandated or recommended development standards. The current range of de facto standards includes XML, EJB, J2EE, MIME, and TCP/IP.

In Chapter 4, we described how workflow vendors in conjunction with other interested parties, including business users, have worked within the framework of the WfMC to address interoperability of workflow management systems.

Table 10: WfMC Published Standards

Standard	Year Published	Synopsis
Workflow Reference Model	1995	Describes architecture of a generic workflow system
Workflow API (WAPI) Naming Conventions	1995	Relates to naming conventions for WAPI APIs
Workflow Client API Specifications (WAPI)	1998	Defines APIs for process operations relating to workflow client software
Workflow Audit Data Specification	1998	Provides standards for logging operational audit data
Terminology and Glossary	1999	Definition of technical terms and common synonyms used within the workflow industry
Process Definition Meta-Model and Workflow Process Definition Language (WPDL)	1999	Provides a process definition model and interchange language
Workflow Interoperability Abstract Specifications	1999	Defines sequence of logical messages and contents
Workflow Interoperability — MIME Binding	2000	Defines interoperability for MIME-encoded messages
Workflow Interoperability — Wf-XML Binding	2000	Defines XML-based encoding of interoperability messages

WfMC has promoted collaboration and education to achieve a shared understanding of workflow in a rapidly evolving and maturing technological environment. It has published a range of workflow standards that are summarized in Table 10. Further information relating to these standards is available for review at the WfMC home page on the Internet (refer to Appendix 3).

POLICY CONSTRUCTION

Policy Structure

A definition of the types of elements that should be included in an enterprise document management policy was provided by Sutton (1996, p. 95):

- Purpose: the reason the policy exists.
- Objective: a description of how the enterprise will pursue the policy.
- Definitions: the words used and what they mean.
- Scope Statement: the boundary of the policy.
- Rules of Conduct: a framework for thinking about how document management should be done.
- Authority: the span of control for implementing the policy.
- Review and Update: description of the rights to change the policy and the circumstances under which it should be changed.

These can also be applied to IDCM policy, and to them, we can add Outcomes, so that the benefit to the enterprise is articulated, and Performance Indicators to indicate how the impact of the policy is felt.

Sutton (1996, p. 95) acknowledged that an enterprise may have its own preference for labeling the policy elements, but stressed that the elements must be considered in development of the enterprise document management policy.

There is also a requirement for the policy to be actually implemented, as it would seem pointless for an enterprise to spend time and effort analyzing and formulating policy if it is simply acknowledged and largely ignored. There is a need to define the policy and adopt an approach that gives effect to the policy in a meaningful way that can be communicated to stakeholders, both internal to the organization, and external (as required, for example, contractors).

The development of a document management policy is not an isolated event that occurs at a single point in time. The policy needs to evolve to take into account new external influences, internal imperatives at the strategic, tactical, and operational levels, also taking into account new technological innovations, new document formats, or content delivery.

Given that an IDCM policy has to be developed and implemented, we believe that there are two types of deliverables associated with it:

- IDCM policy, which contains a succinct statement of the policy, scope, and the principles and guidelines that support the policy; and
- IDCM strategy plan, a document designed to give effect to the policy by defining specific strategies to give effect to the implementation of the policy.

Table 11: Suggested Template for IDCM Policy

IDCM Policy Template		
Enterprise Policy No. _____ **IDCM Policy**	Version no. Approval Review date	_____ _____ _____
Policy statement:	Succinct statement of the policy.	
Objectives:	The objectives of pursuing the policy.	
Definitions:	Terms used and their description.	
Scope:	The scope of the policy.	
Principles:	List of key principles that support the policy statement.	
Guidelines:	Guidelines that will assist readers understand the intent, scope, and objectives of the policy.	
Owner/Responsibilities:	Responsibilities allocated to roles within the enterprise for specific actions.	
Outcomes/Benefits:	Value to the enterprise.	
Performance indicators:	Measures of effectiveness.	
Dates:	Implementation date. Review date. Cancellation date.	

Some organizations prefer that policy and strategies be embraced within one document. However, it is useful to have two separate documents, so that the succinct policy can be published to an intranet site for internal consumption, and an Internet site for the information of business partners.

The strategy plan is an in-depth document that includes more comprehensive details of the policy, and a decomposition of the principles into action strategies. It may include aspects such as specific tasks with allocated roles and responsibilities, key milestones, critical success factors, and evaluation criteria. The strategy plan may be published for external consumption outside the organization, or it may be restricted for internal enterprise usage.

We propose that the structure provided in Table 11, which builds upon Sutton's suggestions, is a usable template for a document management policy.

The policy statement will characteristically be expressed with respect to the information policy of the enterprise as a whole. The principles that underlie it are likely to be along the lines of the following:

- Provide appropriate identification of documents and Web content;
- Make sure that appropriate security and access procedures are provided for them;
- Provide for quality information in documents and Web content;
- Ensure appropriate procedures for preservation, retention, and disposal; and
- Provide for flexible information retrieval approaches.

Strategy for dealing with each of these principles may then be expressed within a framework along the lines of that shown in Table 12. It suggests a range of different sections (or chapters) within the document, but the final structure depends on individual

Table 12: Suggested Template for IDCM Strategy Plan

IDCM Strategy Template		
Enterprise Strategy No. _____ **IDCM Strategy**	Version no.	_____
	Approval	_____
	Review date	_____
Section 1: Introduction		
Purpose	Purpose of the document.	
Strategy overview	Information that provides background to the development of the strategy.	
Strategy imperatives	Summary of external influences and internal imperatives that leads to the formation of IDCM strategy.	
Aim and objectives	Aim and objectives of the strategy.	
Scope	Scope of the strategy.	
Critical success factors	Specific factors that are critical to the success of the IDCM strategy.	
Evaluation criteria	Criteria against which the performance of the enterprise in achieving the strategy aim and objectives will be evaluated.	
Strategy owner	Ownership of the strategy and overall responsibilities as owner of the strategy.	
Section 2: Definitions		
Definitions	List of definitions of terms used that are relevant to the IDCM policy, principles, and strategies.	
Section 3: Statement of Policy and Principles		
Policy statement	Succinct statement of the policy — reused from IDCM policy.	
Principles	List of key principles that support the policy statement — reused from IDCM policy.	
Section 4: Principle 1 and Strategies		
Principle statement	Statement of first key principle that supports policy.	
Principle outline	Defines aspects such as the scope of the principle, the imperatives for the principle, or an overview of circumstances leading to the development of the principle.	
Strategies	Statement of specific strategies that have been developed to give effect to the implementation of the principles (that underpin the enterprise policy statement).	
Responsibilities	Roles that are assigned to the development and implementation of the strategies.	
Time line	Relevant time lines and milestones relevant to the development and implementation of the strategies.	
Section 5: Principle 2 and Strategies		
Principle statement	Statement of second key principle that supports policy.	
Principle outline	Requirements are the same as for the first key principle.	
Strategies		
Responsibilities		
Timeline		
Section 6 to "n": Principle 3 — "n" and Strategies		
A section for each principle that supports policy and the definition of the strategies that support the principle, roles and responsibilities, and time line.		

organizational preferences. Each of the principles identified above may then be elaborated within this framework.

For example, if we took the principle concerning document identification, the strategy may make reference to prevailing metadata guidelines and say that data elements for documents must include:

- Unique identifier;
- Document type (for example drawing, memorandum, etc., as defined in enterprise Document Type Definitions for XML);
- Title;
- Creator(s);
- Dates such as creation and distribution;
- Descriptive keywords (according to the organization's functional thesaurus);
- Retention guidelines;
- Review period;
- Reference documents;
- Version; and
- Status.

Similarly, with respect to appropriate security and access procedures, the accompanying strategies may be along the lines of:

- Establish automatic backup procedures;
- Arrange remote storage of backup data;
- Document procedures for recovery, including backup and restart, and ensure that procedures are in place for informing all relevant staff who must implement them;
- Train end users in backup procedures used by the enterprise;
- Prepare a disaster recovery plan that conveys authorities for access, hardware, and procedural alternatives; and
- Carry out an annual test of the procedures.

POLICY IMPLEMENTATION

It is not unusual for the formulation of enterprise policies to be developed and managed by individuals or workgroups without the discipline required of an approved enterprise project. In these circumstances, there may be delays to the development of policy or the policy (once formulated) may not be promulgated throughout the organization.

Our view is that for the policy and associated strategy documents to be formulated in a responsive, efficient, and effective manner, the development of the IDCM policy needs to be managed as a project within the organization. When this is the case, executive management should assign the project resource(s) and provide a project brief (or terms of reference) that includes a statement of objectives, scope, deliverables, exclusions, constraints, and time frames.

In regard to the promulgation and communication aspects of policy implementation, Sutton (1996, p. 95) observed that policy promulgation involves the policy having to be "taught in a manner that will instill understanding and trust." The specific approaches for promulgating and communicating the policy need to be developed as part of the document management strategy.

Once the IDCM policy is developed, approved, and published (as required), the IDCM strategy is the baseline planning document for the implementation of the policy. There will be a range of strategies contained within the IDCM strategy, each requiring specific resource allocation, action plans, and time frames for completion.

Consequently, the implementation of the strategy should also be managed as a project within the organization, to provide the necessary resources, communication, and reporting structures to facilitate a successful policy promulgation and strategy implementation. It is likely that procedures will need to be developed to support the IDCM policy and strategy, and resources will need to be allocated to define new procedures or confirm or modify existing procedures to meet the requirements of policy and strategy initiatives.

One of the proposals that may emerge from the development of the strategy may be a recommendation to utilize an IDCM system. The strategy may propose use of the IDCM for managing vital and important business documents on an enterprise basis, or scoped to a specific application or department or workgroup within the enterprise. The ensuing recommendation may be to do as follows:

1.   Conduct a feasibility study to determine the applicability of IDCM.
2.   Determine budget estimates and commence the initiation of a business case.
3.   Prepare a system requirements specification as a prerequisite to the acquisition of an IDCM solution.

A decision whether to progress directly with the system requirements specification may well depend on the level of effort that the enterprise has already put into evaluating the feasibility of IDCM.

In Chapter 8, we will examine the role of the feasibility study in determining the operational, technical, and financial feasibility of implementing IDCM.

SUMMARY

IDCM policy should be developed within the framework of an enterprise information policy. The information policy can be articulated at strategic, tactical, and operational levels, and we provide some examples of policy components that are likely to be considered by managers. These range from the regulatory environment at the strategic level through customer expectations at the tactical level to technical standards at the operational level.

We itemized many of the standards and introduced some of the recent developments with recordkeeping and metadata standardization.

We then introduced a framework that we consider can be used for structuring the formation of policy.

ENDNOTE

[1]   The Australian Standard AS4390, *Records Management* was the starting point for the development of the ISO standard.

Chapter 8

Feasibility Study

OVERVIEW

In this chapter, we examine the relevance of using a feasibility study as a key component of life cycle management that may be used when embarking on an IDCM project. The feasibility study may be used to conduct a preliminary investigation of requirements and to determine the operational, technical, and financial feasibility of an IDCM project.

As noted in the preface, we observed that many DMS projects, promoted and initiated by proponents of document management, are not developed to reach desired outcomes. Instead, there are results, such as the cancellation of a project midway through its life cycle, or project delays and misadventure due to nonalignment with business objectives, lack of project ownership and executive management resolve, or inability to implement effective change management.

Therefore, enterprises should consider the feasibility study as an essential component of the IS life cycle for an IDCM project. If an enterprise adopts the "rule of thumb" philosophy that a project is 80% planning and 20% implementation, then the feasibility study is a core component of that planning. If an enterprise does not get the preliminary planning and definition correct during the feasibility study, then it is unlikely to get it right at all.

Consequently, the objectives of this chapter are to do as follows:

- Discuss the role of the feasibility study in the overall context of investigating requirements for IDCM.
- Consider the type of methodology that can be applied to conducting a feasibility study for an IDCM project.
- Raise awareness of some of the issues that should be explored when defining the problem and selecting feasibility options.
- Provide a template that may be used for preparation of the feasibility study report.

We provide provisional checklists that may be useful as "starting points" to assist practitioners when investigating the feasibility of an IDCM application.

ROLE OF THE FEASIBILITY STUDY

Purpose

The purpose of a feasibility study is to determine whether the implementation of an IDCM system supports the mission and objectives of the enterprise. It is an initial assessment of requirements conducted prior to commencing a more detailed requirements analysis investigation (refer to Part 3).

Objectives

The objectives of the feasibility study for IDCM are as follows:

- To define the problem for which a document and content management solution is being sought;
- To examine available business and technology options for solutions to the problem;
- To identify and analyze potential costs, and to list potential benefits of solution options;
- To determine a preferred option for recommendation to the Project Board;
- To establish priorities for implementation of an IDCM solution (if that solution is the preferred option);
- To identify an initial set of risks and issues that needs to be managed if the preferred option is adopted; and
- To gather adequate financial estimates to underpin the development of a Business Case (which is explored in Chapter 9).

Scope

The feasibility study must have a clearly defined scope. Time and other resources are generally not available to conduct a feasibility study that covers all types of business processes where document and content management opportunities exist. Effectively, documents are the core elements in virtually every business process, and many of these are amenable to "publishing" or making available to a limited extent, so there is a need to scope the feasibility study. As we mentioned in Chapter 6, planning strategies for an

IDCM project may involve establishing an initial set of priority business operations that feature a diverse range of processes and wide representation of document formats. For example, if we select five key business operations that have priority for IDCM, then it is these five areas that should be subject to feasibility study.

Rationale

While the feasibility study is an initial assessment of the viability of IDCM and the practicability of achieving a successful implementation, its importance should not be understated. The study is not a superficial review that only requires scant attention. Early identification and resolution of issues will support the later phases of the IDCM project.

In many organizations, the number of desired projects exceeds the capacity of the organization to undertake them. It is necessary to rank proposals and to ensure that there is not initiation of projects to "fix" systems that are already working. A project committee or review board can be expected to determine feasibility with respect to:

- Senior executive knowledge and support for anticipated outcomes;
- Whether it is accommodated within the framework of the organization's policies;
- Its practicality in terms of organizational resources; and
- Whether it is happening at an appropriate time in relation to other activities.

Flynn (1998) asserted that projects may be undertaken to improve efficiency or effectiveness. We see efficiency in terms of improving:

- *Capabilities*, which in the case of an IDCM, might involve faster retrieval of documents, or markup formatting of internal documents for publication; and
- *Communication*, which in the case of an IDCM, may mean better routing of documents or utilization of parts of records for Web content.

Effectiveness is seen in terms of business process improvement through:

- *Control*, which for IDCM involves providing a quality system that improves accuracy and provides more consistent description of contents, perhaps through consolidated metadata for Web content, digital records, and descriptions of physical records;
- *Competitive advantage*, which for an IDCM system may mean better customer relationships through easier location of, and recourse to, relevant material; and
- *Cost*, where repetitive labor cost of organization, filing, and finding may be reduced, or redundant processes can be rationalized to enable cost reduction.

Assuming that it passes through these hoops, any information systems project is typically assessed in terms of three decisive factors: operational, technical, and economic feasibility (Shelly, Cashman, & Rosenblatt, 2001; Kendall & Kendall, 2002). These factors apply when reviewing the viability of IDCM. We will examine them within the context of the strategic, tactical, and operational levels of the organization, which is the tiered structure for management information planning that we discussed in Chapter 7.

The review of the feasibility will assist enterprises to prepare the business case for budget allocation to establish projects for the specification, acquisition, development, and implementation of an IDCM system.

CONTEXT

We discussed in Chapter 2 the diverse and complex challenges facing today's business enterprises, and the types of business planning imperatives that may influence a system request for IDCM. However, such system requests do not always provide sufficient information on which to proceed with specification, acquisition, and implementation.

Too often, busy business executives or well-intentioned information management professionals simply state a general requirement such as "We need a document management system that can be linked to Web content" as the basis for the system request. This observation may be quite strategic, perceptive, and inspirational, but an independent observer might ask, "What for?" In other words, there is no specific business requirement that supports the contention that IDCM is required.

Some organizations purchased a DMS with potential for content management, but the implementation languishes because of circumstances such as:

- There is no clear definition of the business problem that the organization is trying to solve.
- Ideology or technology (or both) drive the acquisition of the DMS, based on the efforts of well-meaning devotees or technologists, but there is no commitment from business owners to support the system.
- There is a lack of business readiness to implement a DMS associated with content management due to competing organizational pressures or organizational behavior or cultural issues; there may also be lack of commitment to the discipline that IDCM brings to document processes.

In terms of understanding business readiness to implement IDCM, there should be no misconceptions about its potential impact at strategic, tactical, and operational management levels within the business environment. The importance of recognizing this impact can be attributed to:

- Every person in every enterprise uses documents in some form in the day-to-day administration of their specific tasks, some to a higher degree than others.
- Intranets with Web interfaces provide the capability of distributed access to the content of the documents, internally, with business partners, or with the general public, to the extent that the content is made available or appropriately structured.
- There is a substantial emphasis on utilizing digital documents (including email, messaging systems, and word-processing documents) for management decision making.
- There are compelling legal and duty of care requirements for digital and physical documents to be managed as records of an enterprise's business transactions.
- Once IDCM is implemented, it will impact on how an end user interacts with documents, and the degree of impact depends on the functional and operational capabilities of the selected system, but particularly on the degree of consultation that has taken place with the end users during testing and prior to implementation.
- There will be a requirement for end users to register metadata for new documents saved to the IDCM system, with specific fields validated by database rules, instead of the (quite often) unfathomable file names given to documents in file systems.

- There may be a requirement for end users to capture and register important business emails that were not managed effectively prior to IDCM. (For example, emails may have been lost or deleted. Even if not, they may have been printed and filed in physical filing systems, or left in the email messaging system, or copied in bulk to removable media such as a CD (possibly without a search or retrieval tool).

While IDCM offers important benefits to an organization that is having difficulty managing important documents, the following complexities may arise if the system is not subjected to feasibility study analysis:

- The specific problem that is to be solved may not be adequately defined, which may result in vagaries during implementation planning and lack of business acceptance.
- All of the stakeholders may not have been identified at the outset, which can mean that not all requirements are taken into consideration during the requirements analysis phase. Consequently, software chosen during package selection may not meet the overall requirements of the business unit(s) or organization.
- Competing business priorities may mean that the business may not be ready for dedicating time, money, and resources to the implementation of the system.
- An inadequate understanding of the scope and requirements for document management and use of content within the enterprise may result in the acquisition or development of a system that fails to meet the diversity and complexity of requirements for enterprise deployment.
- The wrong type of solution may be acquired.

Quite often, organizations adopt the approach of implementing a pilot system without the rigor of conducting a thorough feasibility study. However, this type of strategy can be unworkable for a number of reasons, including the cost of IDCM infrastructure, professional services fees, and change management requirements to deploy a pilot system. Pilots can also be awkward, because workarounds are required to enable end users not involved in the pilot to access relevant documents stored in a DMS repository.

The feasibility study provides the opportunity for enterprises to obtain a clear definition and understanding of the problem in the context of other enterprise document applications, as well as the various options that are available to provide a solution to the problem, and a preferred option.

Later in this chapter, we will look at some fundamental questions to be considered during the investigation of feasibility, but first let us look at a methodology for conducting the feasibility study.

METHODOLOGY

In Chapter 6, we referred to the wide range of structured methodologies for the life cycle processes associated with the specification, development, and implementation of information systems. The following methodology for a feasibility study draws on the Stage 0 — Feasibility module of SSADM for its approach. The feasibility study is a project

Figure 1: Feasibility Study.

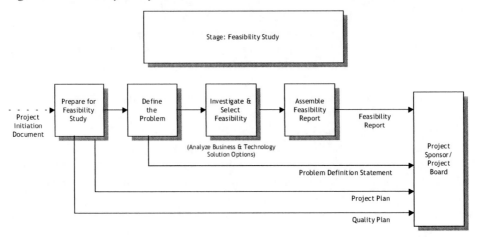

(albeit potentially a subproject of a larger project), and organizations may find it useful to draw on project management methods, such as PRINCE2, for guidelines and templates.

Schema

Figure 1 provides a schematic of the feasibility study step processes, drawing on the step processes defined in SSADM.

Entry Criteria

The typical inputs to the feasibility study stage are:

- System request for an information system that involves improved management of documents;
- Project initiation document (PID) for a feasibility study; and
- Terms of reference for a feasibility study.

Depending on the type of input used by the enterprise, the input document should contain a definition of:

- Project objectives;
- Scope of the feasibility study;
- List of relevant stakeholders;
- Project organization (roles and responsibilities);
- Constraints on the study (such as budget, time frames, and resource availability);
- Clear statement of deliverables; and
- Reporting requirements and milestones.

The following examples of supporting project documentation are desirable prerequisites:

- Information policy;
- Document management policy;
- Records management policy;
- Content management and Web publishing policy; and
- Information management and technology strategic plan (or information systems strategic plan).

Exit Criteria

The key deliverables prepared during the feasibility study phase include:

- Project plan;
- Quality plan;
- Problem definition statement; and
- Feasibility study report.

In addition, depending on the specific methodology and the modeling and analysis tools adopted by the practitioner(s) conducting the feasibility study, there may be other outputs, including:

- Context diagrams;
- Data flow diagrams (Level 1);
- Logical data structure definition;
- Requirements catalog;
- Document catalog; and
- User catalog.

Approach

It is not within our scope to define a specific approach to conducting a feasibility study, because processes and techniques are well documented in IS methodologies and other published literature. For example, the approach in Table 1 draws on SSADM step processes for conducting a feasibility study, and these steps may be useful for enterprises embarking on such an approach for examining the operational, technical, and financial feasibility of an IDCM implementation. Alternatively, enterprises may have their own methodologies and templates for conducting a feasibility study or similar process that involves preliminary investigation of an IS.

Techniques

Techniques that can be used during the conduct of the Feasibility Study include:

- Data flow diagrams (or similar process mapping techniques);
- Logical data modeling;
- Requirements analysis;
- Requirements definition;

Table 1: Feasibility Approach

Process/Activities
Prepare
• Review Project Brief/System Request.
• Review supporting project documentation.
• Map the current business and document management environment (refer to Techniques).
• Identify initial requirements and register in the Requirements Catalog.
• Assess scope and complexity.
• Identify and confirm stage constraints and time lines.
• Identify stakeholders and the nature of their interest.
• Establish and confirm reporting requirements.
• Review and agree on scope with the Project Board.
• Produce project plan for the study.
Define
• Identify key business unit managers and end users.
• Determine and assign methods and techniques to the study team.
• Define the business and document management environment (refer to Techniques).
• Define the Web content and publishing environment.
• Identify relationships between records management, documents, and content provision.
• Extend mapping of current operational processes (as required).
• Register end user profiles in the User Catalog.
• Register document object types in the Document Catalog.
• Develop requirements, and register in the Requirements Catalog.
• Define the current technical environment, and register in the IT Systems Catalog.
• Produce Problem Definition Statement that encapsulates:
(a) Current environment
(b) Required environment
(c) Gap analysis demonstrating difference between current and required environments.
(d) Prioritization of requirements
• Agree on Problem Definition Statement with the Project Board.
Select
• Review the Problem Definition Statement.
• Review corporate strategic objectives and policies relevant to the scope.
• Review business tactical objectives, policies, and requirements relevant to the scope.
• Identify and confirm the initial set of mandatory requirements for IDCM.
• Review the business system options, which define the functional scope of the option.
• Review the technical system options, which define a potential technology environment for the implementation of the option.
• Develop realistic feasibility options — minimum three options plus the "do nothing" option. (Feasibility options are typically a combination of business and technical feasibility options.)
• Select preferred option and develop action plan for that option.
• Recommend selected option to the Project Board.
Assemble
• Produce the Feasibility Study Report (a template is provided later in this chapter).
• Sign off Feasibility Study Report by the Project Board.

- Options analysis; and
- Gap analysis.

Project Team

The feasibility study should be established and managed at an executive level by the Project Board (or Project Steering Group), which has the overall project responsibilities that we discussed in Chapter 6. The project team might consist of a mix of functionaries from the organization, including representatives from operational business units and also from the information disciplines, such as IM and IT. Consultants or relevant specialists might complement the project team to help define the problem and to provide an external perspective on the various business and technology solutions available.

It is important that each and every member of the project team has an open approach to problem solving and solution opportunities and not have a preference for any specific business or technology solution. In this respect, if the organization intends to use product vendors or systems integration companies (that may be aligned with products) during the feasibility study, there is the risk that there may be a loss of independent thinking in resolving the business or technology solution outcomes.

INVESTIGATING FEASIBILITY

Earlier in this chapter, we indicated that the feasibility of information systems can be assessed in terms of three key factors: operational, technical, and economic feasibility. We also discussed in Chapter 7 that information planning should occur at three levels within enterprises: strategic, tactical, and operational levels of planning. Consequently, when conducting a feasibility study, we may need to examine operational feasibility within the context of these three levels of management planning. The relationship between investigating feasibility at the three levels of management planning and selecting feasibility in terms of operational, technical, and financial feasibility is depicted in Figure 2.

We now consider issues relevant to IDCM that can be investigated during feasibility examination of this application of an information system. We acknowledge that strategic, tactical, and operational management issues cannot always be easily

Figure 2: Management Planning and Feasibility.

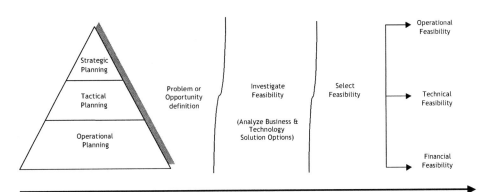

Feasibility Analysis

Table 2: Feasibility — Business Planning Imperatives

Condition	Observations
Is the requirement for an IDCM system aligned with the enterprise's strategic objectives as defined in its Corporate Plan?	It is useful if the organization actually has a Corporate Plan. If IDCM is not aligned with strategic objectives, then the chances of a successful outcome are low.
Will the IDCM system directly support strategies, projects, or products aligned with achievement of enterprise business planning initiatives?	Practitioners may find it feasible to build a compelling business case for IDCM, where it can be demonstrated that the requirement for the system is directly aligned with the enterprise mission, objectives, and strategic business planning initiatives.
Are there legislative and regulatory imperatives for managing documentation?	The legislative and regulatory framework that applies to the jurisdiction in which the enterprise operates may offer the basis for a compelling case to be developed for IDCM. The current mismanaged document environments may pose a high risk to an enterprise's capability to satisfy legislative and regulatory requirements.
Is there a high likelihood of class actions, discovery, and litigation?	Fragmentation and redundancy of documents in multiple file systems may impact an enterprise's capability to provide evidentiary support for business decisions, and involve delays in providing documents that are sought during legal discovery. The delays can prove expensive because of the need to engage professionals to try and find relevant documentation without the benefits of a managed document repository.
Is there potential for brand damage to occur due to lack of IDCM policy and systems to support the implementation of the policy?	One of the consequences of poor policy or the failure to implement it using adequate processes and tools is the potential for damage to the organization's brand. Given the high degree of reliance on electronic documentation to support business decision making, the strategy to protect brand name may be a compelling requirement for organizations to develop and implement systems for managing business documentation.
Is there a compelling requirement to implement IDCM to underpin quality management or environmental management systems?	The requirement to implement management controls over quality documents is a key aspect for organizations that seek accreditation under the ISO 9000 standards or the ISO 14000 environmental standards. The feasibility of using DMS and integrated workflow to implement management controls over document creation, review, approval, and publication as part of these ISO standards may provide the basis for a specific application of IDCM. The solution may be progressively deployed later for managing other types of documents and publishing content within the organization.
Is IDCM required to support a specific business application designed to improve customer service, better manage supply chains, or support operational information systems?	Most business enterprises are moving toward greater use of e-commerce and e-business solutions as Internet-enabled channels for such initiatives as delivering product to market, improving services, supply chain management, and interchanging document-based information with business partners and customers. There is a need to implement management controls over digital documents that may form a key part of these strategies through availability of content.
Is the IDCM system being implemented to reduce the risks associated with security threats and support business continuity operations?	A consequence of the availability of desktop authoring tools, such as word processing and email systems, is the proliferation of digital documents within organizations. Many business decisions are made on digital documents (e.g., email and attachments), and there is a requirement to manage the security of these documents from a wide variety of vulnerabilities and threats, including physical security threats. The requirement for IDCM might be an appropriate strategy that provides a managed environment to help counteract security threats or to support the enterprise's Business Continuity Planning.
Does the organization have an information policy?	If so, then work within its framework; if not, then establish with senior executives a rationale for proceeding in line with corporate objectives.
Do policies exist for document, records, or content management?	If so, they should be consolidated to provide a framework of rules that govern IDCM within the organization. If not, the project team is advised to develop policy before progressing with requirements specifications.

Table 3: Feasibility — Executive Commitment

Condition	Observations
Is there a high level of commitment for IDCM by all or most members of the Executive Management Team?	If there are mixed feelings about the applicability of document technologies on the Executive Management Team, then the project may be at a higher risk than if there was group consensus at strategic management.
Has a Project Board been established for the IDCM project, and if so, is it representative of the strategic business interests?	The Project Board has an important role in providing strategic direction to the project at the executive level. It may help to promote the project at strategic, tactical, and operational management levels. The Board should not be drawn mainly from the information disciplines, but preferably represent strategic business interests. If the Board has not been established or there are plans to establish such a board but nothing much has happened, then the project may be at high risk.
Is the Project Board "committed" as a group to the project?	If the Board has been established but the members have many priorities elsewhere or have a blasé attitude, then the feasibility of a successful project is low. If all members of the Board do not embrace the project, or support is only lukewarm, it should act as an early warning indicator. Failures of a project can be due to inability of executive management to maintain its resolve in supporting IDCM, particularly during periods of conflicting business priorities.
Is the Project Sponsor a member of the Executive Management Team?	The opportunity for IDCM requires commitment at an executive management level to provide the necessary level of strategic support for the establishment of a project and the resolve to maintain the commitment. If the sponsor is a member of the Executive Management Team, feasibility may be rated higher.
Does the Project Sponsor represent business operations, rather than corporate (administrative) support?	The application of IDCM to support business operational planning may represent less risk with a project sponsor that represents business operations, than a sponsor that represents administrative support. Preferably, a sponsor from IT should not champion IDCM.

classified into domains of operational, technical, and financial feasibility, as much can depend on the political, structural, and cultural behaviors within organizations.

Operational Feasibility

A series of tables is provided, beginning with Table 2, in which we successively look at operational feasibility from different management levels. For each tabulation, several pertinent questions concerning planning conditions are accompanied by commentary about impacts upon those conditions.

Strategic Planning

Remaining at the strategic level, it is then useful to consider the extent to which the orientation of senior management, and the culture within which the enterprise's business operates, are amenable to an IDCM implementation. The commitment at an individual level and cooperation at a corporate level must be evaluated. Refer to Tables 2 through 4.

Table 4: Feasibility — Organizational Culture

Condition	Observations
Is there an information sharing culture within the organization?	Many organizations *talk* and *strategize* about developing information sharing as part of their knowledge management initiatives, or as part of a learning organization process. However, these strategic notions need to be examined at the tactical and operational planning levels to determine the extent to which end users are able to *demonstrate* that they are committed to information sharing.

A complication with proceeding with the acquisition or development of an IDCM solution where there is not a demonstrable commitment to information sharing, is that end users may use unauthorized methods for storing business documents outside the DMS repository, thus, in many ways, defeating the purpose of implementing the system. |
| Is the organization culture such that users will readily adapt to the change, whereby documents will be registered at the desktop? | The implementation of IDCM may have significant ramifications for end users that have been accustomed to applying minimal information to describe a document. Often, a document has been given a short file name, quite frequently meaningless to anyone, including (as time goes by) the author.

IDCM may require users to complete a registration profile to capture metadata that defines the properties of the document and its content. There are techniques (as we discuss in Chapter 12) for minimizing data entry, but the fact remains that users are typically required to put more effort into document capture and content creation processes than has been their custom. There may be high risks to the project unless this aspect is adequately discussed with and supported by the end users. |
| Is the culture of the organization such that there may be political motives for withholding information? | There is a need to determine whether there are any political implications to documents being withheld from a repository. Some members of the management executive may wish to withhold the sharing of document-based information that would otherwise be stored in an IDCM system. |

Tactical Planning

Planning at this level is concerned with putting strategies into action, and is therefore concerned with shorter range aspects of dealing with workplace operations. Here, we provide three tabulations of consideration of questions that arise.

Workgroup understanding has particular significance for the concept of the learning organization fostered by knowledge sharing. Some enterprises have sought to institutionalize the processes of personnel "stretching themselves" so that they are constantly investigating the margins of their domain — by learning more. In such enterprises, it is anticipated that staff would be motivated to pursue the initiatives mentioned in Table 5 to foster their own learning.

The instances described in Table 6 emphasize the integrative aspects of document management as it is implemented with respect to other systems that support business processes. It is detrimental to business process support to treat documents and their content in isolation. Similar examples relating to project management follow in Table 7.

Table 5: Feasibility — Workgroups

Condition	Observations
What is the potential impact of other organizational projects on the implementation of IDCM technology? Does the organization have the capacity to absorb multiple technology streams?	Whether there are other projects within the organization that may impact an IDCM project must be determined. For example, if the organization is implementing an ERP system, it may have limited project resources to allocate toward other projects, or the impact on the end users may be such that the organization does not want to manage simultaneous large complex projects. Competing large system projects may influence the timing of project initiation, depending on resource availability, the implications for the target end user environment, and the ability of the organization to manage change effectively.
Are operational and administrative workgroups supportive of document technologies?	IDCM projects that are mandated by the corporation without little cognizance given to the needs of workgroups can meet with difficulties. People may be influenced by formal and informal interactions within workgroups, and administrators must recognize this. While it is important to have management support at the "corporate" level, it is imperative to have the support of operational and administrative workgroups.
Do workgroups enjoy learning new skills? Do they actively support change and training programs?	Workgroups that support new initiatives and the opportunities to learn new skills are likely to be more adept at accepting the changes involved in the implementation of an IDCM. Some observers seem to take the view that there are "age" or "generation" factors involved in determining whether workgroups are likely to embrace change and new skills. Many of these claims are unfounded, and among the most important criteria in determining change and skill development are the formal and informal decision-making interactions that occur between people in the workgroup environment.

Technical Feasibility

Technical procedures influence operational feasibility. The day-to-day level of management already has had to come to terms with how any existing system functions within standard operating procedures or is associated with other systems within an enterprise. The group of tables (Tables 8 through 12) provides examples of conditions that should be taken into account when examining operational feasibility related to infrastructure, documents, document imaging, workflow, and migration.

Financial Feasibility

Preliminary investigation of financial resourcing and project estimate considerations are addressed in Table 13.

SELECTING THE FEASIBILITY OPTIONS

The emphasis on examining the feasibility options is to determine the preferred option from a range of alternatives, based on best fit to operational, technical, and financial feasibility. The preferred option should be the solution that best satisfies

Table 6: Feasibility — Business Process Improvement

Condition	Observations
Is there a requirement to implement continuous business improvement using document management?	Workflow combined with an IDCM may provide the basis for improving a specific end-to-end business process. The capabilities of workflow may provide a wide range of opportunities for improving processes associated with documents and their content. The requirements may include the use of workflow for managing transactional documents (captured via the Web or integrated with document imaging or facsimile systems), and automated review and approval processes for administrative documents and Web content.
Are collaborative and messaging (e.g., email) tools increasingly being used as the basis for business decision making?	Many business decisions are today being made using email and attachments, and there is a risk in many enterprises that these decisions are not being recorded, or if they are recorded, it involves printing out email and placing copies on physical files. Where this practice is not adopted, there is high risk that the record of decisions using email is not being maintained at all, or if so, then not properly.
Is there an opportunity to improve asset information by integrating GIS?	There may be a requirement to have an integrative approach to managing infrastructure or property assets by combining the spatial search and view functionality of a GIS and the management controls over documents stored in a repository. For example, GIS users could access current documents relating to infrastructure, property, applications, and permits, relating to objects displayed in a spatial view. The integration of GIS and DMS technologies may support asset management strategies within the organization.
Is there a requirement for rapid access to documents from an ERP system? Is there a requirement to access documentation relating to materials management or maintenance systems?	IDCM enables users of an ERP system to access documentation relating to supporting financial transactions, and to correlate employee data with information stored in documents supporting employee relations matters. Examples are terms and conditions of employment, job descriptions, occupational health and safety policy and procedures, and employees' resumes._ Integration with materials management and maintenance systems may provide quick access to current versions of documentation, such as drawings, material data safety sheets, technical specifications, manuals, and work orders.
Is there a requirement for document management to manage the risks associated with business transactions conducted using email or other collaborative and messaging systems?	Many organizations are having difficulty managing the large volume of email messages that are received as normal part of operations. Chapter 3 covered some of the key issues, and appropriate requirements analysis is discussed in Chapter 13. Enterprises may consider it appropriate to acquire and implement IDCM to improve the management of email and attachments. If an IDCM system is to be deployed specifically for managing email, the organization should consider change implications for managing other types of digital documents created at the desktop, but not associated with email.
Is there a requirement for IDCM to manage the capture and processing of correspondence?	The integration of document scanning, recognition technologies, document repository management, and workflow may assist with managing the capture and dissemination of correspondence received by the organization. The system would also manage the authoring and review and approval processes with outgoing correspondence. The organization then has evidence linking transaction instances with particular customers.

Table 7: Feasibility — Project Management

Condition	Observations
Does the organization have internal project management and technical resources that are experienced in complex client/server information systems implementations?	There is a range of service delivery models that can support IDCM implementation, including the delivery of the system by a vendor, or by a system integration company, or the engagement of an Application Service Provider .
	Regardless of the delivery model that is finally adopted, the organization requires project management and technical resources to support the project. For example, there is a need to prepare (or validate if a third party is used) specifications for the system. There may be a need to prepare RFP and contractual documentation and negotiate the contract. There may also be a requirement to make decisions about preferred DBMS, order hardware and install or configure operating systems, and resolve issues with the existing systems.
Does it look like the project will be resourced on a part-time or ad hoc basis? Do IDCM project team members have to fulfill other duties?	It may be preferable to establish a project team that is fully dedicated to the task of specifying, acquiring, and implementing an IDCM system. The decision on resourcing arrangements may depend on the scope and nature of the application. However, there should be a dedicated internal core team allocated to work with the system from concept through to implementation.
Does the organization have experience in developing, negotiating, and managing systems integration contracts?	The implementation of IDCM solution typically requires professional services and system integration effort to deliver integrated product sets, such as repository management, records management, imaging, workflow, and content publishing. The system has to integrate with desktop/server computing environments and network operating systems and deploy on DBMS. There may be requirements to integrate with a line of business systems. The enterprise may need to have experience with systems integration contracts to be assured of having a legal framework for effective implementation.
Does the organization have experience in identifying and managing risks in an IS environment?	The level of project risk will depend on the complexity of the potential IDCM requirement, particularly the level of systems integration requirements, the culture of the organization, and change management imperatives. These risks will need to be identified, contingency strategies developed, and the risks managed during the project life cycle.
What is the organization's experience in developing and implementing change management strategies?	Effective change strategies and management of change may be a vital component of the project, depending on the nature of the requirement. The organization needs to consider its own capabilities in respect to change management and consider its strategy for the project.
Does the organization have an effective model for engagement of suppliers and third-party contractors?	The engagement of a supplier, system integrator, or other third party is typically defined within the boundaries of a legal contract. However, there has to be a working relationship between the organization and the supplier, essentially in terms of methodology, process, tools, and templates. While the contracted supplier may offer its own approach and tools, the organization should be in a position to define its own model for engagement with third parties.

operational requirements and is the most technically and financially feasible option to resolve the defined management problem.

One approach, depending on the nature of the organization (i.e., more or less emphasis might be placed on operational, technical, or financial aspects of the options) may be to review feasibility in the following sequence:

Table 8: Feasibility — Infrastructure

Condition	Observations
Is there already a DMS or content management software in place? What are its future directions?	An enterprise may have already implemented DMS, records management, or content management systems and consider moving to a "next" generation development of such systems, or be considering replacement of products from different vendors. The organization should take into consideration the practicalities of continuing to use the existing systems and determine whether the new features and enhancements offered by moving to other products permit interfacing and represent value for money.
Has the organization implemented or does it plan to implement adequate IT infrastructure to support an IDCM project?	Undertaking an IDCM project may have significant impact on the IT infrastructure within the enterprise. When considering feasibility, organizations need to consider whether the existing infrastructure has the capacity to support the implementation of an IDCM system. Issues to consider include the desktop hardware, operating systems, availability of servers to provide a development and production environment for the IDCM, capacity of LAN bandwidth, and the nature and capacity of WAN links.
What is the capacity of the WAN links within the enterprise?	The relevance of items such as WAN links will depend on the nature of the IDCM implementation. For example, if the implementation is restricted to a central system with no requirement to access documents from the system from WAN-connected remote sites, or no foreseeable plans to deploy the system in such sites, then the implications may not be that important. However, if it is planned to provide remote access to documents via WAN links or to implement a distributed system, perhaps with potential document replication requirements, then the WAN infrastructure is a significant factor.
Has the organization implemented a SOE for its desktop computers?	The implementation of an SOE, and standard application software, templates, and configuration files is a condition that may assist with IDCM implementation. If there is no consistent operating environment on desktop computers, the diverse range of computers may not all have the capacity for installed IDCM client software.
	During the feasibility study, determination of technical feasibility is assisted by obtaining a definitive list of all desktop computers, hardware configurations, operating systems, applications software, and configuration files. This assists with the preparation of the domain specifications (refer to Chapter 19). Organizations that maintain an Asset Register of IT infrastructure and equipment should be able to provide reports that define capacity of desktop and server computers.

- Review operational feasibility, because if there is no business requirements for IDCM, there is little point in reviewing technical and economic feasibility.
- Review technical feasibility next, as there is a requirement to have an understanding of the systems architecture(s), tool(s), and resource requirements to support the feasibility options, and in particular, the preferred option.
- Review economic feasibility last, based on the outcomes of operational and technical feasibility.

Table 9: Feasibility — Documents

Condition	Observations
What document formats are to be included in the IDCM system?	The enterprise should not presume that, without investigation, it knows or can anticipate all the types of document formats that are used within its business units. While the organization may have deployed a standard desktop operating system and applications environment (with consistency in tools such as email, word-processing, spreadsheet, and presentation graphics), quite often there are special tools needed for specific document authoring, development, and publication.
What are the integration expectations for document formats?	Quite often, organizations specify in RFP documentation that DMS products are to integrate with the document authoring applications used within the organization. However, these products may not offer tight integration with applications other than the most prevalent applications on desktops, and perhaps only with popular office suites and drawing packages. The organization should define the key applications where integration may be required; taking into account that integration may not be achieved for all applications without customizing the system.
How does the organization manage its drawings and technical documentation?	Drawings are vital documents in many organizations, because they provide essential information to develop new assets, maintain existing assets, and various revisions of drawings may represent a record of the business activities associated with a specific enterprise or project. Regularly, organizations embarking on document or content management projects fail to take into account requirements for managing drawings. Drawing and technical documentation need to be examined in a similar way to transaction and administrative documents.
Are disposal schedules well defined?	The development of disposal schedules is a recommended prerequisite to the development and implementation of an IDCM project to provide the rules by which documents may be retained and disposed.
Are long-term archival requirements defined?	Archiving of documents may be viewed as relating to those documents that are not required to be kept permanently but which have to be located in secondary storage as well as documents that are required to be kept permanently. Different rules may apply to archival requirements. An Archival Policy and associated strategy, including such matters as retention of outdated Web site content is recommended as a prerequisite to the implementation of IDCM.

The end result of the feasibility analysis may be a business system option, a technology system option, or most likely, a mix of both.

An enterprise should identify a range of business system options that might be applied to help resolve the problem associated with managing business documents. For example, *some* options might be:

1. Do nothing, accepting the risks of a fragmented and redundant document environment on organizational effectiveness. This option, while an anathema to information disciples, may be a business solution outcome based on a number of organizational factors. For example, the organization may perceive that the cost of implementing IDCM does not represent value for money. Alternatively, there may be other higher project priorities, or the culture of the organization and behavioral change implications may be too complex.

Table 10: Feasibility — Document Imaging

Condition	Observations
Is document imaging a potential requirement, and if so, has the imaging opportunity been qualified?	As with all information systems, use of document imaging costs and benefits should be subjected to feasibility analysis. It may be pointless claiming that documents can be retrieved "quickly" if there is little requirement to access documents frequently. It may not be prudent to position a case for imaging to "save space" if the organization plans to use the space to install a pot plant. Again, there is not much benefit in claiming the need to "OCR good quality documents" if a copy of the documents already exists in text format on unmanaged file servers.
If so, has there been examination of the feasibility of digital versus microform imaging versus hybrid (film/digital) systems?	When considering its requirements for converting physical documents to image format, an enterprise needs to examine the capabilities offered by digital imaging systems, film-based imaging systems, and hybrid solutions that combine the rapid access features of digital imaging with the long-term archival features of film technologies.
Is the imaging requirement specific to high-volume forms processing or low-volume ad hoc scanning?	The nature of the imaging requirement dictates the complexity of the application and the level of investment that may be required. For example, the scope and nature of the requirement may range from ad hoc occasional scanning of documents to complex high-volume production imaging systems. We cover the types of document imaging applications more fully in Chapter 15.
Is the backfile conversion of hard-copy documents considered a requirement?	Organizations should carefully examine the business requirements for converting a backfile of hard-copy documents to image format. There are many issues involved in backfile conversion, particularly of large and diverse document collections. It is often not simply a matter of passing documents through a scanner. There are issues relating to the characteristics of the documents, capture requirements, image quality requirements, registration requirements, magnetic storage and accessibility requirements, as well as longer-term secondary storage, and perhaps archival requirements.
Has the organization any previous experience in implementing imaging technology?	Depending on the nature of the imaging requirement, particularly if there is a high-volume production-level imaging requirement, the lack of experience in implementing imaging technology may impact on the enterprise's capability to adequately define (among other things) image processing requirements, quality requirements, and performance requirements.

2.   Continue using existing tools (e.g., networked file systems, nested folder structures), but improve the way that the enterprise manages documents and their content by developing a document management policy and using the current tools available to the organization, including networked file systems, to provide better facilities. For example:

- Develop an agreed FCS to implement for current folders and documents contained in logical network drives.
- Develop and implement naming conventions for classes of core business documents, to invoke rigor over document saving regimes and help with data migration.

Table 11: Feasibility — Integrated Workflow

Condition	Observations
Has the organization any previous experience with implementing automated workflow?	Workflow functionality may range from simple ad hoc workflow modules, where a workflow may be used to route a document for review and approval, and it may extend to an advanced production workflow environment, depending on the nature of the requirement. Organizations that have not had experience in implementing automated workflow systems may not have an understanding of the processes required to deliver automated workflow solutions, particularly where more advanced workflow solutions are required. An enterprise needs to consider the feasibility of its requirements, because the level of investment in the technology may depend on the simplicity or complexity of the requirement.
Are the workflow process requirements identified and documented?	Automated workflow processes, as with all information systems, need to be subject to feasibility and definition. An organization may have the view that it will automate many processes using workflow, but it may be necessary to restrict the workflow to a specific processing requirement or standard module, so that the scope of the requirement can be managed. For example, if an organization plans to integrate workflow with IDCM for a wide range of processes, and plans to produce an RFP for a fixed price implementation, then it may be necessary to examine the feasibility of an initial set of workflow modules first. Once feasibility is validated, the organization may then specify the workflow requirements in detail during the Requirements Analysis phase.
Are users who are expected to receive workflow notifications via email or workflow in-tray, readily accessible to a desktop computer, and do they understand email technology?	Some organizations decide to adopt workflow and route messages to an end user's in-tray or notify messages via email. However, the enterprise needs to be assured that end users (particularly field staff) regularly use their desktop computers to check email (and would potentially check workflow in-trays) for notification. This aspect of feasibility may have implications for change management.

- Review all document templates, and develop standard templates where required.
- Train staff to send links to documents rather than the documents themselves (wherever possible). Train staff not to save documents that are already saved elsewhere.

3. Pilot an IDCM system in a specific site, or for a specific business function or process, to demonstrate proof of concept. This option may be combined with improvements elsewhere within the organization using current tools. This might be suitable for an organization that does not wish to invest in IDCM at an enterprise level, but wishes to use the project as a test to determine or confirm the advantages of the system and identify any shortcomings for resolution.

4. Mandate the implementation of an IDCM package or combination of software for progressive deployment within the enterprise. This outcome may derive from approved document and Web content management policy. The enterprise may consider applying a planned evolutionary rollout strategy to minimize the risks associated with the organizational change.

Table 12: Feasibility — Data Migration

Condition	Observations
Have data migration requirements been considered?	Organizations will need to consider the feasibility of migrating data from existing document registers (e.g., registry systems) and documents (e.g., stored on file systems) to the IDCM system. It is pointless making statements in specifications or later in an RFP such as "the ability to migrate data or documents." It begs the question, "which data/documents"? There is a need to consider the feasibility of a range of data migration strategies based on evaluation of current systems.
How clean is the current data that may need to be migrated to the IDCM system?	The old adage "garbage in, garbage out" for IS projects continues to apply. The enterprise needs to examine the quality of metadata in applications, such as existing registry systems, and the file names used to describe existing documents in file share systems. The enterprise may need to define strategies to clean data in existing systems as a prerequisite to migration of the data to an IDCM system.
What is the status of the document collection, and is there potential for duplicated versions of the same document to be migrated to the IDCM system, having an impact on system integrity?	It may be appropriate for the enterprise to develop scripts and analyze the extent of duplication of the same documents on existing file systems. An attachment to an email from a Chief Executive Officer, for example, may be saved in hundreds of file share locations, including workgroup and personal shares. The organization may wish to consider clean-up strategies as a prerequisite to the implementation of IDCM.

Table 13: Financial Feasibility

Condition	Observations
Where is the source of funding for the IDCM project?	If there is no budget funding for the project, it may be necessary to submit a proposal for funding, supplemented by a business case (refer to Chapter 9). Organizations will need to determine the extent of funding that will need to be sourced from Capital Expenditure funds, and the funding required from Operational Expenditure funds.
Have preliminary estimates for the project been developed and qualified?	Consideration will need to be given at a conceptual level during the feasibility study to the following types of costs: • Hardware and networking costs, including potential upgrades to client/server architectures • Licensed application software components, including document management, records management, imaging, and workflow components, with potentially fax integration, digital signatures, and other types of interrelated applications • DBMS: is their leverage from existing enterprise licensing structures for DBMS? • Planning and requirements development • System development (including custom application development or configuration) • Data migration and backfile conversion • Implementation, including testing, training, and support • Change management • Maintenance and support • What costs would be required for air travel, transfers, and accommodation for remote sites? • Costs estimates will need to be validated during the development of the Business Case (see Chapter 9)

This option may involve the deployment of the solution to one or more initial ("pathfinder") sites to assist the organization in gaining further knowledge about the capabilities of the technology, in obtaining project implementation experience, and in developing a working relationship with the solution provider. The initial implementation may include logical (and physical) system architecture, data model, and reusable object libraries to assist with progressive deployment in relevant sites across the enterprise.

DELIVERABLES

The primary deliverables from the feasibility study, drawing on SSADM, are as follows:

- Project Plan, which provides the planning document for the conduct of the feasibility study;
- Quality Plan, which defines the quality processes relevant to the feasibility study approach and deliverables;
- Problem Definition Statement, which is output from the "Define the Problem" step process, and consists of a summary of requirements that, once endorsed by end users, is submitted for the approval of the Project Board; and
- Feasibility Study Report, which is the final deliverable from the feasibility study stage (There should be a separate feasibility study report for each business function within the defined scope. Similar to the problem definition statement, the report, once endorsed by end users, is submitted for Project Board approval. The report becomes an input document to the requirements analysis stage.).

FEASIBILITY STUDY REPORT

Table 14 can be used as a guide for the structure of the feasibility study by those who are not obliged to follow one determined by their own organization.

SUMMARY

The value of the feasibility study stage should not be underestimated. It is an important aid in helping enterprises define the scope of the problem or opportunity of managing documents and their content and determine, at an early stage in the project life cycle, how the implementation of an IDCM system can support the corporate mission and objectives.

It is a useful process for determination of a range of business and technology solution options, and it provides information that will be useful as inputs to the *Requirements Analysis* phase, which we will discuss in Part 3.

It is the logical precursor to the development of the Business Case, which we will examine in the next chapter.

Table 14: Feasibility Study Report Template

Feasibility Study Report — Example Template

Document History
- Document Location/Revision History/Approvals/Distribution

Glossary
- Terms/Description

Executive Summary
- Recommendation
- Problem or Opportunity Definition Summary
- Target Environment Summary
- Options Analysis Summary
- Preferred Option
- Way Forward

Introduction
- Purpose
- Background
- Project Definition (aim, objectives, and scope)
- References
- Acknowledgements

Problem Definition
- Business environment
- User environment (User Catalog)
- Document environment (Document Catalog)
- Technical environment (IT Systems Catalog)
- Benefits of current environment
- Limitations of current environment
- Summary

Factors Influencing Future Directions

Strategic
- Enterprise mission and objectives
- Strategic business planning imperatives
- Legislative and regulatory requirements
- Long-term budget strategy

Tactical
- Tactical business planning imperatives
- Management reporting requirements
- Information system interfaces

Operational
- Accessibility and usability requirements
- Operational reporting requirements

Target Environment
- Outline target environment description
- Gap analysis

Table 14: Feasibility Study Report Template (continued)

Feasibility Study Report — Example Template

Solution Option Analysis

Option 1
- • Operational feasibility
- • Technical feasibility
- • Economic feasibility

Option 2, 3 , 4, and "n" options
- • Operational feasibility
- • Technical feasibility
- • Economic feasibility

Preferred Options
- • Justification
- • Recommendation

Impact Statement
- • Impact on business
- • Impact on other projects
- • Legislative/policy issues to be resolved
- • Technology issues to be resolved

Summary and Conclusion
- • Feasibility study outcomes
- • Way forward statement
- • Conclusion

Appendices
- • Context Diagrams, Data Flow Diagrams, Logical Data Structures, and supporting documentation

---

Chapter 9

Building the
Business Case

OVERVIEW

This chapter covers the development of a business case for the acquisition and implementation of an IDCM strategy. It provides insights to assist managers faced with the perplexity of acquiring executive management commitment and resources (budget funding, people, and services) for an IDCM solution.

The objectives are to:

- Discuss the role of the business case.
- Position the business case within the context of the IDCM project life-cycle.
- Consider the type of methodology that support business case analysis and preparation of the Business Case Report.
- Review the challenges faced by practitioners in championing IDCM projects.
- Discuss real-world strategies for aligning IDCM strategies with business planning imperatives.
- Discuss the role of pathfinder systems.
- Review typical considerations for cost–benefit analysis of IDCM solution options.
- Provide a structure for the Business Case Report.

ROLE OF THE BUSINESS CASE

Purpose

The business case and its underpinning financial model are an integral part of planning for the acquisition and implementation of an IDCM solution. Its primary purpose is to demonstrate the value proposition of the proposed solution by quantifying tangible benefits, qualifying intangible benefits, and defining project impacts.

The term "business case" is not universal. Some organizations may use terms such as "Business Plan" or "Justification Study," but the purpose is essentially the same, and that is to demonstrate the value proposition of IDCM.

Objectives

The business case, within the context of the information systems environment, is a formal proposal to executive management to secure budget approval and obtain resource allocation for projects comprising IDCM.

The objectives of the business case process include:

- Articulate the IDCM strategy, with a concise definition of the problem that is to be solved, review solution options, and determine a preferred option.
- Demonstrate that the preferred solution option is based on the best available information and vigorous financial analysis.
- Provide a comprehensive definition of the strengths, weaknesses, opportunities and threats, and risk analysis relevant to the project.
- Justify the appropriation of funds and resources for a project.
- Define a high-level implementation strategy to demonstrate that the approach to implementing the solution has been well thought out.

Scope

The business case is aimed at addressing the business and economic viability of an IDCM solution that satisfies the requirements defined in the Project Charter (refer to Chapter 6). The specific scope of the business case generally includes the statement of benefits, tangible and intangible, and financial models that qualify the value of the investment. Financial models include methods such as Return on Investment Analysis (ROI), Payback Period, and Net Present Value (NPV) analysis. We will look at these types of modeling techniques shortly.

Rationale

In Chapter 8, we proposed that preliminary investigation should be initiated early in the project life-cycle to determine whether an IDCM solution was feasible in terms of three interrelated domains: operational, technical, and financial feasibility. During that investigation of feasibility, various business and technology solution options should have been examined objectively in order to establish feasibility across all three domains.

During the feasibility study, it may have been necessary to seek Requests for Information (RFIs) from suppliers in order to determine indicative costs for the system, based on the requirements captured during the feasibility analysis. The costs determined during a feasibility study are only indicative, because the total costs for the solution will not be known until commercial proposals have been sought from suppliers.

The feasibility study costs are likely to be subject to caveats based on the requirement to continue with the development of detailed requirements specifications (refer to Part 3) and seek proposals from suppliers for the development and implementation of the solution. It is not until the final costs of a solution are known that a business case can be finalized, where the level of risk associated with the financial estimates is acceptable to the enterprise.

The business case should draw on the business and technology solution options developed during the feasibility study and provide new insights into the solution options based on new information derived from the commercial process involved with selection of the preferred solution provider (or a short list of providers).

It is unlikely that enterprises will invest in IDCM solutions without having a business case that demonstrates that the investment represents a value proposition. This proposition may include tangible benefits, such as increased revenues or reduced operational costs, and intangible benefits that, although they may not easily be quantifiable, deliver value to the business. The business case provides the opportunity to define the project outcomes and impacts, quantify tangible benefits, qualify intangible benefits, and use financial modeling to support the value proposition.

CONTEXT

The business case is typically prepared once the costs of the proposed IDCM solution are known, and these cannot be firmly established without seeking a proposal from suppliers for the installation, configuration, development, and implementation of the system. Enterprises typically receive proposals from suppliers during the Package Selection process (refer to Chapter 20), and these proposals should be based on a detailed Requirements Specification (refer to Chapter 10).

However, there may be a requirement for enterprises to provide indicative figures for the implementation of an IDCM solution, in order to initiate or develop the project. Figures may be required at the time of project initiation planning to help communicate and sell the concept of the project during the development of the Project Charter (Chapter 6), or during the Feasibility Study analysis (Chapter 8).

Consequently, the development of the business case may be predicated by a series of provisional business investment scenarios that provide forecasts of indicative costs and benefits before firm proposals are received from suppliers. The accuracy of the project forecasts in the business investment scenarios should improve as the project matures and more information is known about the requirements for the IDCM solution. Figure 1 illustrates the iterative nature of budget estimate scenarios, showing refinement of estimates as the project matures through its project life-cycle, with each refinement providing increasing levels of confidence in the accuracy of the estimates.

In this example, we demonstrate that initial market research conducted by the project team provides early indications of the cost estimates involved in the implementation of an IDCM solution. The market research may involve discussions with sites where there have been similar size implementations of IDCM solutions, perhaps in kindred industries, discussions with suppliers, consultants, or industry analysts. The project team should judge indicative cost estimates and develop some benefits statements based on market analysis, and determine confidence levels based on risk.

During or after the conduct of the feasibility study, the project team may decide to develop a RFI and seek expressions of interest (for budget purposes) from suppliers or system integrators. The RFI may be based on the scope defined in the Project Charter and preliminary statement of requirements captured during the feasibility study. The cost estimates may be iterated with greater levels of confidence, once the expressions of

Figure 1: Business Investment Scenarios.

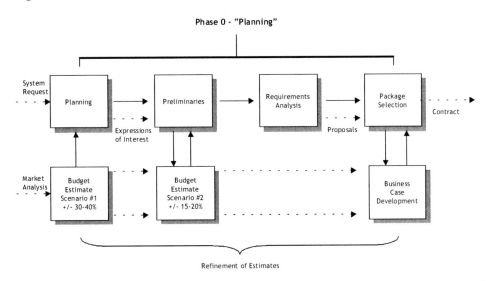

interest are received, but enterprises should be aware of risks associated with cost estimates provided in expressions of interest. The types of risks are as follows:

- The project scope might be too wide, restricted, or vague for suppliers to be able to provide reasonable cost estimates. (How definitively scope is defined will depend upon the experience of the project team.)
- The requirements obtained during the feasibility study are probably too high level to be able to provide firm cost estimates. [The system requirements, including functional, nonfunctional, and domain requirements (refer to Chapter 10), are typically defined at a detailed level during the requirements analysis and definition stage.]

The project team needs to consider these risks when developing and iterating cost estimates, and reflecting the extent of risk in the confidence levels (e.g., ±15% or ±20%) that they apply to the costs they have derived from the expressions of interest provided by suppliers and system integrators.

METHODOLOGY

The methodology adopted for developing the business case for an IDCM solution will be similar to the methodology used within enterprises for general information systems projects.

Entry Criteria

The typical inputs to the business case are as follows:

- Feasibility study report (refer to Chapter 8);

- Interim proposals (i.e., expressions of interest) from suppliers in response to RFI, which may be useful to develop an *initial* business case model;
- Requirements specification (refer to Part 3); and
- Formal proposals from suppliers (refer to Chapter 20).

The following examples of supporting project documentation are desirable prerequisites to the development of the Business Case:

- Information policy;
- Document management policy;
- Web publishing and content management policy (Internet and intranet Web sites);
- Records management policy; and
- Information management and technology strategic plan (or information systems strategic plan).

Exit Criteria

The key deliverables prepared during the business case include the following:

- Business case report, which covers the analysis of business and technology solution options, confirms options reviewed in the feasibility study, and defines the preferred solution;
- Financial model, which includes a Financial Strategy and Cost–Benefit Analysis Report and Risk/Sensitivity Analysis; and
- Project management plan, which defines the implementation strategy, describes the project organization and resource requirements, and produces statements of assumptions, dependencies, and risk.

Approach

A typical approach to developing a business case begins with recapitulation of the background to the project, problem definition statement, the aim and objectives, scope of the requirement, and the required business outcomes. The outcomes from the project need to be quantifiable and projected over the investment period (say five years), in terms of any incremental income and expenditure, incorporating capital and operational expenditures.

The range of business and technology solution options to resolve the problem and achieve the business outcomes needs to be analyzed objectively and presented with risk analyses to support the advantages and disadvantages of each option. The case for the preferred option needs to be objective and detailed in such a way that it provides a compelling case for the appropriation of funds and resources for the project.

One of the key features of the business case is the SWOT analysis, which helps enterprises to determine the viability of the IDCM solution. The SWOT analysis helps to align the opportunity with strategic business planning imperatives and enables the project team to review the external and internal influences that impact on business planning. It also helps the project team to consider the relative strengths and weaknesses of the current document and content management environment, and assesses threats and opportunities relating to the application of IDCM solutions.

The business case incorporates a Cost–Benefit Analysis (CBA), which consists of the financial modeling designed to support the value proposition. The analysis reviews the benefits that can be quantified, though often excludes those benefits that are difficult to quantify without making assumptions that might enfeeble the veracity of the benefit analysis. However, the unquantifiable benefits can be used to support the business case.

The evaluation of business and technology solution options should be subjected to risk assessment to determine the risk factors associated with relevant options. The risks should be considered in terms of the operational, technical, and financial risks posed by each business and technology solution option. Usually, the outcome of most information systems projects that include IDCM strategies is a combination of business and technology solution options.

When considering the risk of the project, enterprises can set generic indicators that help to qualify risks. These are useful for developing a risk and mitigation strategy for projects involving IDCM systems. For example, enterprises can qualify risks based on indicators such as:

- Risk may be high if the project exceeds certain value or involves multiple departments, branches, or workgroups.
- The time to implement a project is greater than a specified period. The risk may be that the business process requirements change, and the technology solution may be impacted by rapidly evolving technology.
- The change impact on management and end users, and impacts on other projects, services and product development, may be substantial.
- Potential impact on brand image, through an impact such as decreased customer service or the business credit rating, may be seen.
- The nature of the financial model (i.e., large capital investment) or delivery models (i.e., involving long-term outsourcing or partnering arrangements) may change.

In recent times, SWOT analysis has been linked with the balanced scorecard approach proposed by Kaplan and Norton as a way of maintaining a balance between financial and nonfinancial measures of business performance. The nonfinancial categories may be associated with factors such as customers, internal processes, and innovation outcomes (R&D), but may be chosen by an organization to reflect its own mission. In each case, the goals for a particular factor, its relationship to other factors, and measures to see if the goals have been attained, are considered together. The approach addresses intangibles and endeavors to value the skills and competencies of personnel. It may, for example, include dimensions relating to professionalism (collaboration, current awareness) or people orientation (team functioning, personnel competency acquisition). It is applicable to evaluation of IDCM readiness. Kaplan and Norton broadened their approach to propound a support mechanism for moving from use of scorecards to strategy implementation in general (Kaplan & Norton, 2001).

The many different elements of an enterprise's competitive situation can be brought together in a consolidated evaluation. Factors can include the emphasis to be placed upon teamwork, the extent of customer orientation, how quality may be improved, and how quickly an organization can react to market conditions. The emphasis is on strategic planning rather than operations. If it is to be applied to IDCM, it might embody the following elements:

- Innovation capacity:
    - Existing software platforms
    - Research capacity within the enterprise
    - Ability to present material for publishing
    - Open systems approach
- Customer relationships, evaluated in terms of the following:
    - Customer satisfaction through perception of adequacy of responses to information requests
    - Cooperative programs with contractors and document support for these
    - Flexibility of design that permits customization of products and services
- People and learning, with respect to the following:
    - Staff skills and extent of training in new applications software
    - Extent of ICT implementation compared with similar enterprises
    - Information services introduced or planned
    - Communications audit
- Governance and strategy:
    - Extent of employees' awareness of information, publishing, and content objectives
    - Extent of budget committed to IDCM development
    - Project management performance (such as on-time delivery, cost overrun) for specific projects
    - Extent of information service utilization
    - Document and content management match with enterprise objectives
    - Proportion of information management plans put into effect
    - Extent of support for business processes
    - Financial performance, such as ability to meet budgets

Techniques

The business case involves a detailed analysis of the costs of the system and the benefits of an IDCM solution and a common economic technique for helping to justify the appropriation of funds and resources for a project is the CBA.

The CBA compares the projected costs with the expected benefits. Whereas the business case involves analysis of tangible and intangible benefits of information systems projects, the cost-benefit analysis may not include an analysis of intangible benefits, unless values that can be realized are assigned to these benefits.

There are a number of methods used within the CBA process to help determine economic justification of the system, and these are summarized in Table 1.

Detailed examples of such CBA methods in relation to information systems are provided by writers such as Mcleod Jr. (2000) and Shelly, Cashman, and Rosenblatt (2001). Enterprises are likely to have their own policy and procedures that define the financial modeling processes for information systems projects. Later in this chapter, we will examine some of the cost factors that need to be considered when developing the financial model to support the business case for an IDCM project.

Table 1: Cost–Benefit Analysis Methods

Method	Description
Payback analysis	This compares estimates of the value of accumulated benefits of a project with the accumulated costs. The payback point is reached when the two are equal. Payback analysis requires determination of the length of time it takes for an investment to pay for itself. The economically useful life of the system is the period between the commencement of systems operation and when the operational costs of a system begin to rise significantly.
Break-even analysis	This compares the cost of a current system with that of a new one in order to identify a break-even point. Operational costs of the present system are likely to increase as operations expand. The investment period is that period up to the break-even point. Assuming that a new system has been implemented, then the return period follows.
Return on investment analysis (ROI)	ROI provides an accounting-based indication of profitability with respect to net investment or project implementation cost. A ratio is derived between estimated total benefits (return) received from a project and estimated total costs (investment). The higher the ratio, the stronger the indication of the expected returns per amount spent. A decision may be made to set a predetermined ROI for a project to meet before it is considered profitable.
Present value analysis	This is the discounted current value of income that will be received in the future. The present value of a future dollar is the amount of money that, when invested today at some specified interest rate, would grow to exactly one dollar at that point in the future. The specified interest rate is called the discount rate, or opportunity cost.

Tools

Enterprises are likely to have their own tools for the development of business cases for information systems projects. The tools might include templates for the Business Case Report and templates (such as spreadsheets) that embed predefined formulas incorporating the rules (for example, rate of depreciation) and guidelines for the project team to build financial models that suit organizational requirements. For example, organizations may require a specific rate of depreciation, or there may be a requirement to include a component for shareholder added value for projects exceeding a specified amount. The level of effort involved in analyzing and preparing the business case, and the level of detail required, should be commensurate with the complexity, cost, and risk of the project.

CHALLENGES

In those organizations where document management is viewed as just good management practice, its champions may be in the fortunate position to secure executive management support and funding for enterprise or application-specific IDCM projects. However, that does not seem to be the case for what would seem to be the embattled majority. Many information aficionados argue a case for managing an enterprise's so-called *unstructured* information based on the well-intentioned concept that an organization "needs a document and Web content management system." But, this is akin to saying that an organization needs a DBMS for managing its so-called *structured* information.

When enterprises wish to manage so-called structured data, they generally do not position their case by saying, "we need a DBMS." They are more likely to say that they need a new financial management system, or a laboratory information system, or a land information system, or claims management system, or whatever. Each of these is supported by a database, but this does not warrant a business case being based on having a "database management system." So, why do information champions try to position requirements for managing unstructured data by saying that they "need a document (or Web content) management system"?

Organizations probably have a requirement for such a system, but many have difficulty trying to build a business case on that observation alone. Furthermore, document and Web content repository management may only be a part of the overall software solution. Do the enterprises also need workflow, or do they also need digital signatures, or imaging, or recognition technologies, or to apply recordkeeping or other enabling software? We would end up with a proposal for "an (integrated) document management, content management, workflow, drawings, imaging, recognition technologies, digital signatures, COLD and recordkeeping system," which sounds ridiculous when trying to mount a business case.

Many well-intentioned project champions try to argue a business case for an enterprise IDCM based on just "good business practice." While this approach may appear logical and sensible from the perspective of information management disciples, it is not necessarily a winning strategy. Executives perhaps pay lip service to the good business practice but give credence and a higher priority to document management when conditions such as the following exist or emerge:

- Document or content management generates revenue.
- Document or content management saves operational costs.
- Document or content management eliminates high risks (particularly, if there are risks associated with aspects such as duty of care relevant to the executive).
- The regulatory environment mandates adequate controls over document and content management.

It would be difficult to convince a mining executive that an IDCM is going to help increase revenues by 2% due to improved document or content management practices, unless there is an opportunity to align the IDCM project with an e-business strategy that generates revenue. Otherwise, the capability to increase revenues by improving mining production is best left within the domain of industrial engineers. If enterprises plan to align IDCM with revenue generation, the benefits must be quantifiable, and may be subject to performance review during the postimplementation review of the IDCM project.

Similarly, it may be difficult to argue the case that an IDCM saves operational costs argued on the premise that the system will better allow the enterprise to "manage and find documents or content." The costs associated with implementing and maintaining an IDCM solution, particularly at an enterprise level, are relatively high when compared with the benefits, as perceived by executives. For example "wow, we get version control over our documents, and might be able to find them quicker...how much did you say the investment was again? Well, we can look at IDCM once our immediate priority projects are completed. We don't really have the budget this year.... Maybe we can find some money for a small project next year, or the year after...." Does this sound familiar? Airline takeover bids are not going to be won or lost based on whether an IDCM solution is in place or not, so project champions need to consider how executive management sees the relative importance of their project within overall business planning imperatives and priorities.

Where would a document management project fit within the priority list of a Chief Executive Officer (CEO) within a major corporation or government agency? Would the requirement for document and Web content management be listed among the top 10 priorities for your organization's CEO, or for that matter within the top 50? In major enterprises, where CEOs are determining strategies to meet shareholder demands for increased and sustained profitability, organizing acquisitions, takeovers, and mergers, and surviving in the jungle of competition, it may not immediately suggest itself.

CEOs are occupied developing organizational planning strategies aimed at meeting the types of business challenges that we discussed in Chapter 2. They may not consider document management a high priority, at least until document policy is connected with the legal discovery process associated with litigation, and there is potential for payout of multimillion dollar damages in claims actions.

For example, a State Supreme Court in Australia[1] recently found that the country's biggest tobacco company destroyed thousands of internal documents to subvert court processes to deny a lung cancer patient a fair trial. When handing down a damages judgment to the patient, the Judge said that the company's solicitors had advised a new document retention policy that was, in effect, get rid of the documents but claim an innocent intention (Birnbauer, 2002).

Some executives have no appreciation whatsoever of what might be meant by a "document management project," because practitioners may not have adequately socialized the concepts with executives in their organizations. One CEO expressed his concept of document management to us as being "you put a letter in a folder and give it to the secretary." Statements such as this indicate how important it is to achieve consciousness of documents policy within information policy related to an organization's mission and objectives. It is this that we emphasize in Chapter 7.

While executives may be impressed by a requirement for document and content management within the respective business and government enterprises, they may balk at the costs involved in providing the hardware, software, and professional services, to deliver a fit-for-purpose solution for their organization. The nature of the requirement may involve an integrated solution comprising document repository management, records management, document imaging, workflow for document review and approval processes, digital signatures, data migration, and perhaps, backfile conversion.

It is difficult to substantiate ROI and payback models based on concepts such as good business practice of "improving the integration management of our documents." It is easy for executives to shy away from making a substantial strategic investment in such systems technologies, when there are many competing projects requiring budget investment.

In an attempt to help organizations establish a compelling business case for IDCM, industry analysts published information about the extent of time that an average user spends on saving, accessing, and retrieving documents under current document models, without the implementation of IDCM. There are also statistical analyses related to the inefficiencies of current Web content management practices. While these guidelines are useful, using them should be tempered by the realization that:

- The statistics tend to be generic observations based on sampling, either for a specific industry sector or multiple sectors.
- The technique used to conduct the observations and to derive data may not follow a recognized research methodology for data collection and analysis.
- The statistics are particular to organizations and unlikely to be transferable.
- The benefits typically focus on the speed of search and retrieval of documents or content but tend not to show the offsets (for example, the amount of time that might be spent by users in registering metadata that describes the content of documents and Web objects).

Even if the statistics were directly applicable, and the benefits can be shown, how does a champion obtain approval for the initiation of an IDCM project given the types of circumstances we discussed? The subject of document management may not sound stimulating, but it becomes more compelling if executives appreciate a company's exposure to risk, as this is the case, with so much internal content of documents being potentially publicly available or available as Web content to service providers and contractors.

The "prophet without honor" syndrome applies when someone has a good concept but does not have influence with the executive in order to bring it to fruition. What we have here is the "prophet without budget" syndrome. Champions of document management from the information disciplines must find a way of securing business case approval for an IDCM project despite the difficulty of producing economic quantification.

The choices for information managers or IDCM project champions may include:

- Do nothing.
  If the "do nothing" option is selected, then it might be conceived as all too hard, and enterprises might decide to wait for another day.
- Implement minor improvements.
  Minor improvements can be made by such initiatives as improving naming conventions, better structuring folder hierarchies, and eliminating poor document and content management behaviors.
- Try for "seed" funding for proof of concept for a specific application, or at a specific site, and try to secure funding for a wider implementation later.
  One of the expectations that will need to be managed when establishing a project to demonstrate proof of concept is that the cost of the infrastructure, software licenses, and development costs may be significant, depending on the arrangements with the supplier. For example, there may be limited scope to secure licensing cost reductions based on bulk purchase. We examine the opportunity for "pathfinder" projects later in this chapter.
- Establish the importance of information in planning and policy forums.
  This is not a short-term solution to substantiating business cases. However, if information policy and its components such as documents, records, and content policy are articulated at every opportunity, and embodied in enterprise planning

documents, then business cases are at least supported by less quantifiable benefits derived from policy.

The concept of doing nothing or making minor improvements is probably an anathema to the information disciple. In our first chapter, we mentioned the range of media that have carried information content since antiquity. The more recent varieties of digital media still represent information that is recorded using the available technology. The problems associated with managing information as "content" in containers that we call "documents" are not going to magically disappear. The problems will be exacerbated with the rapid use of documents in digital form for decision making, and the increasing volume of content published on Web sites.

ALIGNMENT WITH BUSINESS PLANNING

Perhaps the best way to overcome the "prophet without budget" syndrome and develop a business case for an IDCM project is not to call it a "document management" project at all. Let us consider a range of IDCM scenarios:

- Alignment with management concepts that are in vogue and have the right flavor (like "knowledge management") or process improvement supported by technology that evokes management interest (like SCM or CRM).
- Positioning as component infrastructure for resolving real-world business problems.
- Positioning as part of horizontal business management applications.
- Promoting to reduce risk and satisfy regulatory compliance.

Contemporary Management Theory and Technologies
Knowledge Management

We observed in Chapter 5 that an organization's capability to support knowledge-intensive processes and information sharing to create useful knowledge is likely to be severely hampered if organizations have a document environment with the types of characteristics we described in Chapter 3.

Consequently, any organization developing a strategy for information sharing and knowledge management needs to address how knowledge may be documented effectively, made available for reuse, and disseminated as part of knowledge processes.

The champion of document management may be able to grasp the nettle and align document management as an integral (prerequisite or corequisite) foundation for the development of knowledge strategies, thus contributing an effective, integrated model (Hawryszkiewycz, 2000) to support a knowledge-sharing organization.

The IDCM project could be assigned a suitable brand, to demonstrate its alignment with knowledge management, and possibly provide a more appealing orientation. To establish this, innovative project teams could consult with the corporate communications or marketing department in order to create "branding" for a project. Catchphrases such as "knowledge will power," which is directly relevant to the energy sector, is a typical example of how projects can be aligned with brands.

SCM/CRM

In Chapter 5, we considered how IDCM could be aligned with SCM and CRM strategies or another type of strategy that involves improved processes and underpinning technology to achieve business outcomes.

When developing the business case for an IDCM solution, the project champion can consider whether there is benefit in aligning the IDCM project with other strategic projects. This approach enables IDCM to be promoted as an integral part of a larger strategic business project.

The stratagem may secure the funding to enable an initial implementation of an IDCM solution to support the larger business project. It may also provide the IDCM project team with the opportunity to deploy the IDCM solution as an integral component of other projects within the enterprise, and for general document and content management requirements.

Solving Real-World Problems

This approach requires advancing cases that are pertinent to an organization and show the relevance of document and content management. For example, we can illustrate with some actual issues:

- ***What has an IDCM strategy got to do with five schoolchildren each month being left stranded on bus stops before and after school?***

  Due to one organization's fragmented information environment, five children each month were left stranded at bus stops awaiting transportation to and from after-school care. The only reason the organization became aware that the children were at bus stops is when a concerned parent rang to apprise the customer service center of the facts and to express major concerns about the organization's failure to demonstrate its duty of care to the children.

  The problem lay in the way that information was being managed from the time a customer request for school transportation arrangements was made, until the information was actually received by the bus driver. Five requests per month were being mislaid or lost, resulting in children being exposed to risk, with the specific problem being the fragmentation of information processes.

  Once the problem was identified, the organization also recognized other potential risks with managing customer requests, and initiated a project for a customer request tracking system. This project had high visible attention from management due to the risk to the organization and the executives based on duty of care responsibilities. The overall architecture for the system involved the development of a customer service application, workflow management, scanning, and an IDCM to manage all documents associated with receiving and responding to customer service requests.

  Once the IDCM solution was acquired and installed as part of the customer request tracking initiative, it was then feasible to plan the deployment of document management functionality for other specific applications, and for general document management throughout the organization.

- ***What has an IDCM strategy got to do with exploration and development of oil wells?***

  The exploration and development of oil wells is an extremely resource-intensive and costly exercise. The functions of exploration and discovery, as well as the development (and later construction, commissioning and operational) processes involve highly qualified and specialized resource staff. The problem becomes exacerbated and costs rise if an organization finds that different exploration teams cannot quickly locate documents relevant to the process. It becomes further exacerbated if two exploration teams working in isolation start to explore the same well. Subsequently, an oil well exploratory documentation system was implemented, with backbone architecture consisting of a DMS together with a workflow management system.

- *What has an IDCM system got to do with steel production?*

  A project consisting of 20 professionals, including engineers from different disciplines, had been assembled to resolve a problem with the production of steel that was costing an organization a significant amount of lost revenue. The project had been established and operating for 26 months before a request was initiated for a DMS. The requirement was to integrate with system management tools for capturing outputs of tests being conducted to help determine the cause of the problem, and to better manage project documentation. Although the document management requirements were not particularly complex, the irony is that the problem with the steel production had already been resolved some years before, but the company had lost the knowledge of how to solve the problem. Aside from staff losses due to retrenchments and natural attrition, vital documentation had been kept on local computer drives that had been thrown out when the company upgraded its computing networks.

- *What has an IDCM solution got to do with management and rehabilitation of criminal or community offenders?*

  The processes associated with the management of criminals and community offenders are extremely document intensive, and the implications of lost or mislaid information may contribute to a fragmented information management environment. It is not unusual, on occasion, for correctional institutions to inadvertently release offenders before their due sentence, not through lack of staff dedication, but purely through the application of poor information management. Prisoners are unaware that there has been a problem with them being released early, and may be interrupted while returning to routine, to be returned to the correctional institution. On a more serious note, instances have occurred where a serious offender has been inadvertently released from the justice system, in place of a minor offender, due to poor information management. Given the specific importance of reliable, accurate, and timely documentation within the justice sector, covering police, courts, correctional, and community institutions, organizations may gain leverage for an IDCM based on the requirements for an integrated offender management system or integrated justice administration system.

- *What has an IDCM got to do with managing infrastructure?*

  Many organizations have the requirement to manage existing assets or to deploy new infrastructure. The management of assets or infrastructure development typically involves the requirement to create or access drawings, develop technical specifications, define and manage proposals, enter into contracts and agreements, and manage leases and property files. It involves providing diverse types of reports in multiple formats to regulating authorities, and interacting with community groups and special interest organizations. Asset management and infrastructure development may also involve the requirement to have spatial views of information using the facilities of a GIS.

The case for an IDCM solution is compelling to support asset management and planning, development, and deployment of infrastructure and plant. However, the overall business case for the IDCM solution is perhaps best aligned as part of an overall business strategy to mitigate the many risks associated with asset management and infrastructure deployment. In effect, the IDCM solution can be considered as part of an information systems project to deliver "asset management" functionality or as part of a project's requirements to provide an integrated information management solution for managing development and deployment of infrastructure (plant and equipment).

Underpinning Horizontal Business Management Applications

In Chapter 5, we reviewed a number of applications that might be supported by IDCM systems. Another example is where an IDCM solution can be incorporated within a Contract Management System to support the processes associated with managing procurement and contract processes.

Most enterprises have a requirement to manage procurement and contract processes, from the development of initial technical and commercial specifications for the development of an asset, or provision of a service, through to contract execution and ongoing management. The procurement and contract processes are typically complex, time-consuming, and document intensive, and may involve the management of "head" contracts, and multiple subcontracts, involve scheduled payments, part payments for work performed, and revision of rates and conditions. Many organizations implement contract management systems to support the business processes associated with procurement and contract management, but often continue to store vital documentation in nested folders on unmanaged file systems.

An opportunity exists for organizations refining a contract management system, to seek a solution that embeds document management functionality. There are solutions on the market, where a supplier has incorporated (potentially through an OEM arrangement) document management functionality as an integral component of a contract management system. The implementation of this type of system would enable vital documents associated with procurement and contracts to be managed, and may provide the foundation for wider adoption of document technologies within the enterprise.

An IDCM solution can be viewed as essentially middle-ware, so it is difficult to establish a business case for generating revenue and reducing operational costs without aligning the capability to a business planning imperative, such as contract management or developing customer relationships. Other drivers might include improving customer services, better managing assets, or improving infrastructure deployment. Each of these types of initiatives is typically supported by vertical applications, such as CRM, call center management systems, and asset management systems. Alternatively, or in addition, the IDCM system might be positioned as part of a proposed integrated workflow management implementation to provide a managed document repository that supports the automation of an end-to-end business process.

Risk Management and Regulatory Compliance

There is a strong case for implementing DMS to manage risks or where the regulatory environment demands it, but in many instances, the implementation is typically associated with a vertical application. For example, the application of IDCM for the management of regulatory documents in the pharmaceuticals sector is a compelling application associated with risk. If the documentation submitted as part of the regulatory process is flawed, there is the potential for significant revenue losses due to delays in delivery of product to market. The use of an IDCM for managing quality documentation for companies seeking to achieve or maintain certification to ISO 9001 is another type of instance that is related to risk management.

In many enterprises, the page content published to intranet or Internet sites is relatively unmanaged. Furthermore, the processes associated with the development of content are typically cumbersome, time consuming, and lack the controls necessary to ensure that the correct pages are being displayed on the Internet or intranet sites.

Organizations may also be exposed to risk, because there is a legal requirement for them to reproduce a "record" of a transaction involving an Internet Web site or information published on an intranet site (e.g., health and safety information). Given the capabilities to dynamically represent content on the Web, it is imperative that organizations implement control systems for managing the content to meet recordkeeping requirements.

We return to IDCM systems and their capacity to manage digital objects that comprise Web content in Chapter 18. However, we emphasize here that the requirements for managing Web content may provide the IDCM project champion with the wherewithal to secure budget funding for an IDCM solution, particularly given the regulatory implications. The content management process encompasses a life-cycle from document creation (generally using standard desktop tools) through to Web publishing.

If management approval is forthcoming for an IDCM solution to manage Web content, the project team can consider the applicability of deploying the tool for other document management applications within the enterprise. If this is the case, then the project team will need to ensure that the selected package has the capability to meet a wider range of functionality, applicable to the enterprise's relevant document management requirements that we discuss in Part 3.

PATHFINDER SYSTEMS

If an organization wishes to invest in document management, then it may fund a project to implement IDCM for a specific site, consider the outcomes in terms of real business benefits, and determine whether funding will be provided for a wider implementation. Many organizations refer to these as "pilot" projects, a term that has the connotation that the system may be discarded if the implementation is not successful.

While this approach has the benefit of a contained implementation, thus making risks more manageable, there may be disadvantages. The investment required in terms of planning, defining, selecting, and implementing an IDCM solution is quite significant, even for a pilot project, and this type of project generally warrants a more strategic commitment from executive management and planned budget allocations for longer-term deployment of the IDCM systems within the enterprise. The risk is that the pilot project may not be successful. This may be for a number of reasons, such as:

- The enterprise is not experienced with defining the scope and requirements for an IDCM solution that is potentially to be deployed enterprise wide.

- Suppliers may not have experience in delivering IDCM functionality within the specific industry sector.

- Suppliers may not be able to offer highly skilled and experienced resources, due to competing demands or their inability to attract the required types of resources to the organization.

- Change management and communication are not managed well. There is user resistance to the implementation.

If the pilot approach is adopted as a tactic to demonstrate the benefits of IDCM, project champions need to manage the many risks associated with the project. Otherwise, a necessary project may be perceived as unsuccessful from the pilot and have a dramatic negative impact on the potential for implementing an IDCM solution across multiple business units.

The alternative may be to position an initial IDCM systems implementation as part of a specific business application that embraces a range of business and technology solutions, brought together as a holistic solution to a particular requirement. In this case, the pathfinder IDCM solution is implemented as middle-ware for a specific application, such as CRM or asset management, and the technology is tried and tested in an environment where there is a compelling business requirement. It is, in effect, a part of the solution, not the entire solution, and its presence may well be "hidden" to the user, with documents captured into and retrieved from the repository transparently with the host application.

Although the project champion may define the scope and requirements for an IDCM solution that meets the specific application requirements, the requirements specifications can include a selected set of user requirements that embrace wider requirements within the organization. Furthermore, the requirements specification can define the types of functionality expected from an enterprise IDCM solution, as well as the nonfunctional (sizing, architecture, and performance) and domain requirements for a potential enterprise deployment. Consequently, using this type of approach, an organization is then able to choose an IDCM solution that not only meets a specific application requirement but also provides the strategic architecture and functional capabilities for later deployment of IDCM systems. The later deployment may be for one or more additional specific (vertical) applications or for general (horizontal) deployment across the enterprise.

If this type of approach is adopted, then the organization needs to consider its overall strategy for IDCM. An organization may plan not to acquire an "enterprise"-capable IDCM but to acquire and implement a number of "fit-for-purpose" DMS repositories over time. This fit-for-purpose strategy may deliver real benefits from the nature of the application and implementation, but it may have downsides in terms of repository cross-integration, support for multiple products, and training issues.

If an organization wishes to acquire an enterprise IDCM solution for deployment for vertical and horizontal applications, then the project champion needs to define requirements, not only for the specific initial application (aligned to real business planning imperatives) but also to define the additional strategic opportunities. For example, planned developments may include a diverse range of potential applications and general document management requirements.

The organization needs to consider the diversity of its long-term requirement for managing documents of different formats. If the organization does not look at the diversity of requirements and formats, they may end up with a solution that is relevant for the specific initial application domain but that has constraints in other domains. For example, an IDCM system used to support quality documents may not have the capability to integrate at the menu level with CAD tools, and thus, may have restricted drawing management functionality.

A properly considered strategy should provide an IDCM solution that has the architectural and functional capability to be deployed for the specific business application, which can, in effect, become a forerunner for an evolutionary enterprise-wide deployment of the system. Project champions should find it an easier course to travel if they can align planning for an IDCM system with a compelling business driver, such as those examples we discussed earlier in this chapter. The more difficult approach may be to try and argue the case for an IDCM solution in isolation of a real business imperative.

COST–BENEFIT ANALYSIS

We will now examine some of the costs associated with an IDCM project, in order to develop an informed view of hardware, software, communications, and professional services requirements relevant for implementing an IDCM solution. This leads to a restatement of some of the generic benefits to be realized with implementation.

Costs

The costs associated with an IDCM systems implementation include:

- Capital expenditure — acquisition of hardware, software, networking, and infrastructure; and
- Operational expenditure — costs associated with the maintenance of hardware, software, networking, professional services, and support.

These types of costs may not always be applicable. For example, an enterprise may have outsourced its technology support to a technology services company, which provides the required hardware, software, and services to support business applications under a prime contractor style arrangement. In these circumstances, the costs for IDCM are operational costs, as the outsourced technology services company may absorb the investment of capital expenditure and the service charged to the business as operational costs.

The same applies to the delivery of document and Web content management services to an enterprise using application service provider (ASP) arrangements, whereby the ASP provides the hardware, software, networking, and services to deliver and maintain a managed document environment for a business enterprise. The costs involved are primarily operational costs, because as is the case where an enterprise has outsourced its technology support, the capital costs are absorbed by the ASP.

Nevertheless, irrespective of the financial model to be adopted for funding an IDCM solution implementation and its ongoing support and maintenance, enterprises need to have an understanding of the types of capital expenditure involved. This will assist them in developing the budget for their own capital expenditure programs or in validating or better understanding the types of capital costs to be absorbed by an external provider, either an outsourcing partner or ASP.

The infrastructure requirements for the IDCM systems depend on the nature of the system architecture (refer to Chapter 19) and the scope of the system and subsystems involved in the IDCM application (e.g., document repository management, records management, document imaging, recognition technologies, and workflow subsystems). Typical expenditure items for consideration include:

- Infrastructure costs;
- Software costs; and
- Professional services costs.

Infrastructure Costs

Indications of the typical items that need to be considered when considering infrastructure costs are shown in Table 2.

Software Costs

It is necessary to take into account that suppliers offering proposals for IDCM solutions offer a range of different pricing structures. For example, suppliers may construct pricing that involves:

- Cost matrix covering each server instance of the IDCM software and each desktop client, or a matrix that licenses desktop clients, but not servers;
- Cost matrix that offers a price for each server instance of the IDCM software but free (or low-cost) desktop client applications, particularly where a Web browser is utilized as the interface with the end user;
- Price may exclude DBMS license with the expectation that the enterprise will provide the DBMS licenses, or it may include costs for runtime database license or full DBMS licenses offered as part of the software solution infrastructure; and
- Price may include incentives, such as a quoted price for a specific number of licenses, but a more attractive price for a larger number of licenses, including what might be attractive offers based on "enterprise" licensing scenarios.

Many variations on these options may apply. When considering the pricing for software, consideration must be given to the supplier's licensing strategy for the software. Some suppliers offer the price based on "named user" licensing, whereas others may offer "concurrent user" licensing, and others may offer "enterprise" licensing.

"Named user" licensing may avoid the system administration overhead of managing concurrent licensing arrangements but may be more expensive. "Concurrent user" licensing might be attractive to an enterprise because of potential cost savings, but some administrative overheads may occur if an enterprise exceeds its concurrency levels. For example, provision should be made for timed log out of users who forget to log out explicitly from the IDCM system, thus releasing the license.

Table 2: Infrastructure Items

Item	Considerations

Production IDCM server(s)	• What are the requirements for production servers to implement the IDCM in order to meet performance requirements (refer to Chapter 19). Consider whether separate servers are required for the following:
	  - Document/content management server
	  - Web publishing server
	  - Records management server
	  - Document imaging
	  - Workflow
	  - DBMS
	  - Other server components
	
	• Is the IDCM to be implemented in a distributed computing environment (i.e., multiple sites)? Then, what system architecture is recommended for the production servers, and is it necessary for production servers to be located at multiple sites?

Web server(s)	• Has the enterprise implemented Web server(s) for Internet and intranet sites? Will there be a requirement to acquire new Web servers, upgrade the existing Web servers, or deploy additional Web servers to distributed sites as a result of the project? If so, will funding for new Web servers, Web server upgrades, or extensions of existing facilities be funded by the IDCM project, or funded separately, perhaps as part of IT infrastructure upgrade?
Development server(s)	• What are the requirements for a development server? Where is the development server to be located, and what other infrastructure requirements may be needed, e.g., communication devices, racks? • Would an existing server have the capacity, or would it be made available, to act as the development server? Can all the licensed software be accommodated on the development server?
Test server	• Is there a requirement for a dedicated test server? Will the development server be used for testing?
Desktop computer	• What types of hardware upgrades are required for all or any desktop computer devices to enable the IDCM implementation? • Are hardware upgrades to computing desktops funded by the IDCM project or other source (therefore, outside the scope)? If another source, what is the dependency on the funding being made available to upgrade the desktop infrastructure? • Are desktop computers adequate for displaying large-size documents such as drawings and images? Is there a requirement to upgrade monitors or provide acceleration boards for display?
Communication networks	• Are the existing LAN facilities capable of supporting the IDCM implementation? What network upgrades or additional devices might be required, and are they to be funded from the IDCM project budget? • Is the existing WAN infrastructure adequate for accessing documents from the IDCM — consider the IDCM architecture (e.g., centralized, distributed, or replication services)? Are upgrades to the WAN funded by the IDCM project or as part of infrastructure upgrade generally?
Scanners	• Are the existing scanners within the organization capable of meeting the scanning and imaging requirements? • How many scanners will be required for document imaging (decisions based on overall business requirement, volume of documents, and size of documents)? There may be a requirement to have different scanners to handle image conversion based on the different sizes of documents. • Is a dedicated desktop (workstation) computer required for each scanner? If so, provision shall be required for scanning workstations.
Recognition server	• Are the recognition services (OCR, ICR) such that a separate server is required to manage the recognition processes?

Table 3: Server Software Licenses

Item	Considerations
Document (and Content) Repository Manager Server Software	• Determine the number of services that will be required based on the proposed system architecture. The number of content servers will depend on the architecture strategy, including centralized or decentralized content servers. If decentralized, then the number of copies of the server software licenses required needs to be determined.
Web Publishing Server Software	• Determine the requirements for the Web publishing component of the solution. Is the Web publishing component bundled with the document and content repository server, or is it a separate integral module that needs to be priced separately? How is licensing determined? How many licenses will be required to meet the requirement?
Workflow Management System Server Software	• Is the workflow management server software a core component of the document and content repository server architecture (i.e., it cannot be unbundled from the IDCM repository management software)? If so, are there any specific software elements that are required that may have to be included in the pricing? If not, and the workflow is a separate integral module, or a third-party software, what pricing scenarios apply to the workflow server software? Is the workflow server software required to be installed on a separate physical server for each networked site in a distributed computing network, or does one workflow server license cover all sites?
Document Imaging Server Software	• What are the costs of the document imaging server licenses? How many servers are required? What is the price structure for the document-imaging server licensing?
OCR/ICR Server Software	• Is the OCR/ICR server bundled with the document imaging server component or is it a separate server component that needs to be priced? How many OCR/ICR engines are required?
Records Management Extension Server Software	• IDCM solutions may not offer records management capabilities as part of the core system. The records management component may have to be costed separately, so how many server licenses are required, and what is the basis for the pricing (e.g., named user, concurrent user)?
Database Management System	• IDCM packages require a DBMS for storing metadata about document objects and their relationships. Some packages store documents as objects within the DBMS. Consequently, when developing costs for a target IDCM solution, the practitioner will need to consider the costs of the DBMS and the funding strategy.
	• What are the requirements for DBMS licenses? Does each module that might be required to provide an IDCM solution require separate DBMS licenses, for example, does the Workflow Management module (or Document Imaging Server) require a separate DBMS instance to the Document and Content Repository Manager module? If so, what are the licensing cost implications?
	• Does the enterprise have a corporate license for the required DBMS? Is the project able to have leverage off corporate licensing structure for DBMS?
	• Does the IDCM supplier offer the DBMS as a runtime license? If so, does the license cover all relevant modules of the integrated software suite?
	• What additional costs are involved in securing and training DBMS resources to support IDCM implementation and ongoing operations, if the enterprise does not have its own skills?

Some indications of the items to be considered when analyzing software costs are shown in Table 3, which deals with server-based licensing, and Table 4, which looks at desktop (client) licensing.

Table 4: Desktop Software Licenses

Item	Considerations
Client operating system	• Does the IDCM system run on the existing operating system platform for desktop PCs, or will it be necessary to upgrade the operating system as a prerequisite to implementation? If an upgrade is necessary, then what is the funding strategy, and does it need to be met from the IDCM project budget?
Client applications	• Is there a requirement to upgrade the desktop applications (such as word processing, spreadsheet, presentation graphics, project, or CAD software) as a prerequisite to the IDCM solution implementation? If so, are the costs to be met from the IDCM project budget or met as part of a separate funding strategy?
Document management client	• Suppliers of IDCM solutions may package the cost structures for the system in different ways. Some may combine the costs of the desktop IDCM client with the costs of the Document and Content Repository Server (or where relevant, other server products, such as workflow or document imaging).
Web content client	• What tools are required at the desktop level for managing Web content? How are these tools priced?
Records management client	• Is the records management component of an IDCM solution already bundled within the core software? If not, what is the cost for the client software for those end users who may require to apply recordkeeping regimes to digital and physical documents or capture Web content as a record?
Workflow client	• Is there a need for a separate workflow client, or is the workflow functionality embedded within the client software offered for functionality such as document management or records management? What is the pricing structure for the workflow client component, if required?
Document imaging	• What special requirements exist for viewing images? If ad hoc or workgroup imaging, there might only be a requirement to access images in the repository using the same tools that might be provided for viewing other digital documents where the native application is not available. Or, perhaps the solution might use an imaging viewer that is provided with the desktop operating system. If production imaging, the imaging system might offer its own viewing tool integrated with the production imaging server to enable rapid access to images where high-volume retrieval is required.

Professional Services Costs

Professional services are required to install infrastructure, install and configure software, and design, develop, and implement the IDCM solution. The enterprise may elect to do all or part of these tasks, but where there are resource shortages or lack of skills and experience, much of the work for at least the initial implementation of an IDCM solution is likely to be contracted to a service provider.

Consequently, consideration needs to be given to the professional services costs involved, and the following table provides an indication of what needs to be considered. This list of services can be used by enterprises to determine whether their RFP and supplier proposals cover the required professional service requirements.

Table 5: Indicative Service Costs

Item	Considerations
Install server hardware and configure operating system	• Services will be required to install and test the hardware for each of the required servers, and install, configure, and test the operating system, if these are not being handled internally.
Install DBMS	• Services will be required to install, configure, and test the DBMS. Enterprises may have their own internal DBMS management resources, but input will also be required from the supplier or systems integrator to assist with configuration suited to IDCM solution.
Install and configure server software	• The supplier or systems integrator might best manage the installation and configuration of the relevant server software components due to the particular skills and experience required to install, configure, and test the packaged server software components.
Install and configure desktop software	• The supplier or systems integrator might best manage the installation and configuration of the desktop components required. However, if the enterprise is seeking knowledge exchange as part of the IDCM project, then the supplier or systems integrator can install and configure an initial number of desktop systems sharing the knowledge with the enterprise's internal resources, before handing over for subsequent internal installation.
Develop requirements specifications	• There may need to be provision for the development of more detailed requirements specifications than those compiled by the enterprise. The definition of detailed specification can be complex and time consuming, so enterprises may have to make provision for iteration of existing specifications and refinement for design, development, and implementation. The supplier or systems integrator will have the use of packaged software to prototype requirements into more detailed models. • Enterprises should be conscious of "excessive" cost provision for development or iteration of detailed requirements, and assure that the time and resource effort is "fit for purpose" to the overall scope and complexity of the requirement. The scope of the project in terms of functionality may need review in order to achieve a timely implementation. There might be provision for more complex functionality to be incorporated later or perhaps not at all.
Design specification	• The transition of an approved requirements specification to the overall design of the IDCM solution must be provided.
Development	• The IDCM solution will be constructed based on an approved design specification. The construction (or "build") may consist of configurations made to the packaged software, integration and configuration of components of the packaged software, and customizations (scripts, programming) to provide enhanced functionality not met by the core packaged software.
Implementation	• Implementation services might include change management, training, migration of the system from development to production environments, system changeover management, data migration, implementation of policy and procedures, and on-site support during go-live operations.
Postimplementation	• Provision should be made for a postimplementation review, but third-party analysts should conduct the review, for independent consideration of whether the project achieved its planned objectives and outcomes.
Travel and accommodation	• Enterprises may need to make provision for accommodation and travel costs in their cost estimates. For example, the supplier or systems integrator may not be located in the same city as the enterprise. Furthermore, the enterprise may require deployment of the IDCM solution in a range of geographically diverse business sites, which may require the project team to travel.
Logistics	• What office accommodation is required? What desktop hardware and software and internetworking are required for the project team? What equipment, such as desks, chairs, furniture, telephones, faxes, printers, and photocopiers are required, and for what estimated duration? Where will these items be sourced? Does provision need to be made in the project budget? What consumables are required?

Benefits

An IDCM repository management solution that is functionally fit for purpose and well implemented, should deliver the following generic benefits to the enterprise (depending on the specific business requirement):

- Provide an integrated document and Web content management environment by which an enterprise is able to harness all relevant documentation for commercial, governance, project, and administrative purposes.
- Secure an enterprise's information assets in documentary form, while increasing the information sharing potential of the organization.
- Enable the enterprise to develop as a knowledge organization, whereby information is shared with key stakeholders, and the risk of rework being performed on a project-by-project basis is significantly reduced.
- Provide the foundation for integration with other business systems to reduce data capture processes and support automation of specific tasks, thereby supporting continuous business improvement activities.
- Provide the means by which vital and important documentation is published or otherwise made available to internal and external stakeholders in a controlled manner, using an interface that is simple to use.
- Reduce the risk of decision making based on incorrect information by assuring that staff members, external business partners, and customers have the confidence that they are accessing the current version of documents or making decisions on published Web content that is correct.
- Reduce the risk of losing vital information captured in information sharing technologies such as email, by capturing relevant email documents as a record.
- Provide the capability to manage all types of document objects, electronic (in multiple formats) and hard-copy documents from document generation or capture to secondary storage or archival.
- Manage and synchronize the archiving of documents, electronic and physical, in accordance with an approved disposal authority.
- Provide a search and retrieval facility that enables authorized users to access document and Web content assets via a simple interface that makes it easy for users to browse, initiate simple searches, and initiate complex searches, covering metadata, content, or both.
- Implement security regimes that are flexible so that users and groups are authorized to access documents and Web content files that are required to support their business processes.
- Support regulatory and corporate governance requirements, and provide a means of quickly accessing and retrieving information through discovery processes.
- Provide more efficient storage, retrieval, and circulation of documents.
- Minimize the amount of time spent on locating and retrieving documents, allowing employees to have more time to focus on core business activities.
- Enable simultaneous viewing of documents, where authorized.

- Circulate, store, and manage less paper copies of documents, making processes more efficient and supporting environmental policy.
- Enable flexible adaptation and responsiveness to changing business requirements.
- Provide tools for management reporting on document- and Web-content-related activities, aligned to performance goals.
- Implement backup and disaster recovery procedures that ensure business continuity for critical business documents.
- Support quality control through validation and approval procedures.
- Improve decision making and strategic planning based on quick retrieval of relevant information.
- Enable automated document and Web content review and approval processes.
- Enable image capture by scanning physical documents or using digital cameras.
- Interface with distribution mechanisms including email and fax.
- Provide a foundation for continuous business improvement activities.
- Provide a full history of any document, including all revisions and mark-ups made and who has changed, viewed, and printed the document.

Document imaging has the potential to offer the following types of benefits, depending upon the business requirements and the operational, technical, and financial feasibility of the application:

- Convert paper documents to digital, film-based, or hybrid image environments in an efficient manner.
- Provide rapid access (search and retrieval) of imaged documents from a managed repository.
- Enable data capture processes to be optimized using batch management techniques, barcode, or character recognition technologies.
- Minimize the problems with the management of paper documents (e.g., misfiling, loss, inadvertent or willful destruction, defacement, and alteration).
- Make available copies of images to other relevant parties, including business partners, interagency transfer, and to customers, where applicable.
- Reduce time and effort involved in photocopying documents. Distribute digital images using collaborative tools (e.g., email), or Web technologies.

Workflow has the type of functionality that can help enterprises transform from function-centric organizations to customer-centric process organizations. Workflow implemented in conjunction with IDCM repository management provides a cohesive environment for managing changes to documents and Web content in a structured way. The following types of capabilities may be achieved via integration of workflow with an IDCM solution:

- Users can create, launch, and participate in workflow, and can electronically route links to documents, folders, and other objects (such as Web content) for review and approval.

- The workflow manages the life-cycle processes associated with a document review and approval process.
- The use of workflow, integrated with IDCM, makes it easy for the management of collaboration within project teams, and supports the controlled management and publication of deliverables, such as proposals, specifications, and reports.
- Workflow helps to identify where delays and bottlenecks occur in a business process, and produces statistical reports for performance and evaluation purposes.
- The workflow associated with a document and Web content review and approval process can be saved as a record of the business transaction, thus supporting the enterprise's recordkeeping policy and strategies.

If it all works well, then the benefits include the following:
- Information-driven, rather than technology-driven processes;
- Improved access to and security of documents;
- Increases in productivity and profitability;
- Easier compliance with standards and legislation;
- Better relationships with customers;
- Training improvements for employees; and
- Foundation for knowledge management.

However, while it is not difficult to define the generic benefits of IDCM, it is not straightforward to assign a value to the benefits. If organizations are trying to justify systems based on the strategy that it is just "good business practice," there needs to be a compelling case based on operational document management requirements. We mentioned that industry analysts developed models that might be useful, but these models should be treated with caution, as they may not be applicable to the business environment in question.

Consequently, it may be difficult to support a business case for implementing IDCM based on generic productivity claims. It is necessary for the project champion to develop a case that meets the specific requirements of the organization, on the assumption that organizations wish to determine savings specific to their own document environment. The savings offered in the business case may have to be tested, because they may be held to account at performance evaluation during a review of the outcomes of the system implementation.

The benefits may need to be looked at in terms of the overall business application, which is why preliminary implementation for a specific application can be of assistance. Benefits analysis should include tangible benefits, increased revenues and reduced operating costs expressed in real money terms, and intangible benefits, including peripheral savings.

BUSINESS CASE REPORT

The Business Case Report contains a detailed description of the project, including background information, aim and objectives, scope, stakeholder analysis, financial

Table 6: Business Case Report Template

Business Case Report — Example Template

Document History
- Document location/revision history/approvals/distribution

Glossary
- Terms/descriptions

Executive Summary
- Problem definition
- Business drivers
- Comparison of options
- Preferred option
- SWOT analysis (summary)
- Outcomes and benefits, identified cost–benefit (summary)
- Funding strategy (summary)
- Project management (summary)
- Risk assessment (summary)
- Recommendation

Introduction
- Purpose
- Background
- Project definition (aim, objectives, and scope)
- Project methodology
- References
- Acknowledgements
- ~~~~

Outcomes and Benefits
- Solution definition (key strategies, products)
- Statement of outcomes and benefits
- Alignment to business planning (strategic, tactical, and operational levels)
- Schedule for delivery of quantitative benefits
- Schedule for delivery of qualitative benefits
- Analysis of priorities

Project Management and Implementation Strategy
- Project management strategy
  - Project organization
  - Roles and responsibilities (including provision for managing the delivery of outcomes)
  - Project schedule (high level)
- Implementation strategy
  - Implementation strategy options analysis
  - Comparative analysis (prior experience, other sites)
  - Preferred implementation strategy

Impact Statement
- Solution impact (e.g., impact on customers, regulators, enterprise, business units, organization and culture, other systems, requirements for change management, training)
- Project impact (e.g., impact on other projects, resources)

Funding Strategy
- Capital expenditure requirements
- Operational expenditure requirements
- Cash flow analysis

Table 6: Business Case Report Template (continued)

Business Case Report — Example Template
Economic Viability (Cost–Benefit Analysis)
• Return on investment analysis
• Payback analysis
• Present value analysis
• Comparison of options — economic viability
Risk Assessment
• Operational risks
• Technical risks
• Financial risks
• Risk and sensitivity analysis
• Risk management strategy
Conclusion

strategy, costs and benefits, major assumptions, and risk and sensitivity analysis. Enterprises are likely to have their own templates for these reports, but we include Table 6 as an example structure that includes business case analysis and provision for a high-level project management plan.

SUMMARY

While it is arguable that good document management supports good business practice, practitioners may find that it is hard to build a business case for IDCM based merely on the premise of "better managing documents" or "improving Web content management." Innovative presentation of a business case for an IDCM may be required, and we offered suggestions for that purpose.

The development of the business case is an iterative process that commences at project initiation with indicative estimates for investment of capital and operational expenditure, and is refined during key stages of the project, e.g., feasibility study and package selection. The final Business Case Report should provide well-defined cost structures that represent low risk to the enterprise.

This chapter concludes our analysis of the preliminary processes associated with an IDCM project. In Part 3 following, we focus on the analysis and definition of requirements for the integral components of an IDCM solution.

ENDNOTE

[1]   The court's discovery rules provide for parties to litigation to exchange relevant information before formal trial hearings begin.

PART 3

Requirements Analysis and Definition

This Part of the book aims to:

- Review the necessity to analyze and define the requirements for IDCM.

- Provide insights into the types of analysis and definition required.

- Provide a specification framework to help enterprises focus their analytical efforts and resources.

The suggested specification framework in this Part aspires to:

- Assist organizations to produce specification deliverables within a structured context.

- Incorporate both user and system requirements.

- Examine the functional requirements for an IDCM solution in terms of the standard range of document authoring tools within organizations.

The functional analysis also features a range of indicative checklists that act as primers (i.e. basic coverage to assist organizations develop and frame their own sets of functionality statements for incorporation within Requirements Specifications.

Chapter 10

Requirements Analysis
and
Definition
Framework

OVERVIEW

This chapter discusses a framework that enterprises can use for structuring the requirements analysis and definition stage of an IDCM. The framework provides guidance on analytical processes and specifications necessary to capture the overall requirements for an IDCM solution.

The need for objective analysis and articulation of requirements is a relevant strategy that enterprises can adopt to reduce the risks of acquiring an IDCM solution that does not meet requirements.

Our objectives in this chapter are to do the following:

* Review the requirements analysis and definition stage within the context of the IDCM planning life-cycle.

* Discuss the importance of requirements analysis and definition.

* Review the requirements analysis and definition process.

* Review the techniques and tools that support requirements analysis and definition.

* Consider the types of specifications necessary for adequate definition of an enterprise's requirements for an IDCM solution.

ROLE OF REQUIREMENTS ANALYSIS AND DEFINITION

Purpose

Requirements analysis and definition is the next stage in the Phase 0 conceptual planning and development life-cycle that we discussed in Chapter 6. It includes the determination, analysis, documentation, and validation of requirements for IDCM. The primary deliverable from this stage is a requirements specification that encapsulates the diverse business and technical requirements of the target environment. The requirements effort includes user, functional, and technical requirements for IDCM.

Objectives

We consider that the requirements analysis and definition stage for an IDCM project should be preceded by a feasibility study (refer to Chapter 8), in which case, the objectives for requirements analysis and definition can be declared as follows:

- To *confirm* the problem for which a document management solution is being sought;
- To document the current logical environment at a detailed level, involving steps such as analysis and documentation of information flows, analysis of existing document repositories, and metadata requirements;
- To document the current physical environment that supports the logical environment, including a definition of the IT infrastructure, such as client and server hardware, software, databases, and network and communication systems;
- To analyze and determine the target logical environment (including user and system requirements for the IDCM system, and revised information flows), and to define system and data migration and change management requirements, and relevant standards;
- To define the target physical environment in respect to IT application integration requirements, information standards, networking and communications interoperability, and overall enterprise information architecture; and
- To *reexamine* available business and technology options for solutions to the problem, and to *confirm* the preferred solution option recommended in the feasibility study report.

Where an enterprise has elected not to conduct a feasibility study preparatory to proceeding with the requirements analysis and definition stage, it should consider examining requirements in terms of operational, technical, and financial feasibility or applying feasibility analysis techniques throughout the requirements analysis and definition stage.

Scope

The scope of the IDCM requirement should have been defined in the Project Charter (refer to Chapter 6), and the width, breadth, and depth of the requirements analysis and definition effort is largely governed by the scope and nature of the project. For example:

- If the IDCM solution is targeted for enterprise deployment with an initial set of priorities, then the scope might be restricted to specific business processes within nominated priority areas.
- If the project is constrained by site, business functions, or processes, then the requirements analysis and definition effort needs to address those specific areas.

In either case, if it is proposed later to extend IDCM to an enterprise-wide application for relevant business units, then the requirements analysis and definition effort may need to be extended. This extension can include a diverse range of processes, at least at a conceptual and high-level logical schema, to help identify the types of potential business applications for IDCM and priorities for deployment of the solution. This strategy may also help to discover a wider range of document authoring tools and document formats within enterprises.

Rationale

We stated in Chapter 6 that the most important key to the successful implementation of an IDCM system is *planning*, and we indicated that the planning life-cycle included the requirements analysis and definition stage. This stage forms an essential element of *product development life-cycle* planning for information systems projects (regardless of whether a solution is to be a new application system, or packaged software, which is generally the case with IDCM).

It is often difficult to convince executive management that adequate provision needs to be made in IDCM product planning for the tasks associated with analyzing requirements and producing a detailed specification of requirements for projects leading to the product. Therefore a "requirements" definition may remain at a conceptual level. This may be suitable for a feasibility study but not for a specification that will be used as the basis for package selection, contract negotiation, and development and implementation of an IDCM solution.

It may be felt that because the IDCM is packaged software, or because it is perceived as consisting of middle-ware services, there is no need to allocate time and qualified resources to the requirements analysis and definition effort. Otherwise, they may perceive the need, but based on issues such as inadequate management experience with such projects, business priorities, or resource constraints, the requirements analysis and definition effort may be constrained by time and resources (including the provision of inadequate or unqualified human resources).

While different IDCM solutions may offer comparable functionality in a core range of services, each has variations in usability, architecture, and performance. Regardless of which solution may be chosen, the IDCM core software must be configured or customized to meet business requirements. The only structured way of stating those requirements and validating whether a package has the capability to meet an organization's business and technology models is through requirements determination and analysis, and *production of a requirements specification*.

Sometimes, enterprises take the view that they will select an IDCM product because "XYZ Organization is using it." "XYZ" might be an organization that is in a similar industry sector, perhaps a competitor. However, this type of "rule-of-thumb" assessment does not mean that the requirements analysis and definition stage should be bypassed, because the specific configuration and customization requirements of the IDCM system are likely to be different from that of "XYZ."

The XYZ organization might have different business processes (particularly at the detailed level), different attitudes to information management, different styles of leadership and management, and different organizational culture and behaviors. An IDCM installation at XYZ might also be constrained in terms of functionality, architecture, and performance. The project team and perhaps the solution provider at XYZ might herald an IDCM project as a success, but an independent observer reviewing the project might determine that the solution does not satisfy all operational, technical, and financial objectives. This type of information may remain confidential to XYZ, and the supplier might not draw attention to any difficulties with the XYZ implementation.

The time and resource effort for the requirements analysis and definition stage should not be underestimated. Enterprises often have difficulty providing documentation that defines existing business processes, and often, have difficulty articulating their *current* business processes at a detailed level, let alone identifying new and emerging requirements. They may be unable to describe their document collections with the level of meticulous detail that is required for configuring an IDCM system.

This inability of many organizations to understand their own business processes and their lack of *knowledge* about the contents of key information resource collections is paradoxical, given the importance of documents in the context of business transactions and administration. This continuing ignorance remains an enigma.

A further challenge that a project champion might face is the inconsistent use of the term *requirement* within the information systems industry sector. Sommerville (2001, p. 98) pointed out that requirements might be seen as a "high-level, abstract statement of a service that the system should provide or a constraint on the system," and at the other extreme, "a detailed, mathematically formal definition of a system function." Sommerville distinguished these two types of requirements, by referring to the first type as *user requirements*, and to the second type as *system requirements*. We will come back to these concepts shortly.

The importance of having thorough analysis and detailed definition of requirements cannot be understated, as the specifications output from this stage provide the crucial foundation upon which the IDCM solution will be developed and delivered. The risks that may arise, when an enterprise puts an inadequate level of effort into detailed requirements analysis and definition, are illustrated by risks such as the following:

- The business requirements could be inadequately articulated so that the stakeholders may be unable to follow clearly any revised processes that emanate from the requirements analysis. They may be unable to distinguish a compelling advantage in the new processes or to recognize the role and benefits of an IDCM solution.

- The lack of detailed requirements may hinder the commercial processes associated with package selection, e.g., RFP. Where requirements are unclear in an RFP, potential solution providers will have a need for consistent requisition of information from the enterprise in order to submit an informed solution proposal.

- The documentation of vague requirements may lead to blurred responses from suppliers, which can result in delays in commercial processes for package selection, and delays in contract development and finalization, due to the need for the enterprise to requisition further information from suppliers.

- Vague requirements definition may also lead to conflict between the organization and its selected supplier during the (postcontract) Phase 1 implementation, and legal disputes may result. The following example presents a scenario that demonstrates the potential for postcontract disputes.

Case Scenario: *Vague Specifications*

Let us assume a scenario in which an enterprise specifies a vague logical requirement that IDCM "must include the ability to integrate with email systems" and the supplier responds "Complies." A contract is awarded to the supplier, but later, it is determined that the supplier is unable to provide a software product (component module) that provides integration between the DMS and the enterprise's email system. The enterprise takes issue with the supplier and cites the requirement in the specification (which should form part of the contract). The supplier contests the enterprise's position by confirming that its product complies with the requirement as specified, because the solution integrates with email systems but not the specific email system used by the enterprise.

In this instance, the enterprise should have stated its requirement in a more definitive way, nominating the email client/server environment (logical and physical), versions of software, and patch releases. The supplier should have better researched its potential customer's IT environment.

- The supplier of the IDCM solution, or systems integrator, may be unable to design the configuration or any customization required to the core software unless requirements are adequately defined.
- Ambiguity, omissions, and errors in a requirements specification may result in problems being experienced during the development (configuration and potentially customization) of the IDCM system, and delay the implementation.
- The IDCM product selected may not have the required levels of usability, functionality, and performance, thereby adding constraints to the implementation of the solution, and potential restrictions on its wider deployment within the enterprise.
- A product selected as a single point solution (specific application) may not offer an architecture that enables enterprise deployment. This may mean that an enterprise has multiple document management applications, each of which requires separate licensing and maintenance arrangements. Each will also require separate system administration effort, requiring the organization to support (or source) multiple skilled and experienced system administration resources.

In summary, the overall impact of poor requirements analysis and definition may be that there are significant delays experienced during the Phase 1 — Implementation (Chapter 6) life-cycle, and the project may not achieve its aims and objectives. The enterprise might find that the IDCM implementation is not extensible across the enterprise (or other business units). A worst-case scenario is that the project or system extension plans are abandoned.

As a strategy to reduce these risks, and also to help enterprises better understand their own business environment and document management requirements, we believe that requirements analysis and definition is an important aspect of the product development life-cycle planning for IDCM. The degree to which an organization articulates its requirements is a key factor that underpins a successful project.

CONTEXT

Chapter 6 emphasized that document management projects need to be managed within an overall *product development life-cycle* and demonstrated the applicability of using structured methods that are germane to information systems projects, for guidance. The applicability of using a *project life-cycle* approach to support the IDCM product development life-cycle was also covered in Chapter 6, where in Figure 1, we depicted a conceptual schema for planning Phase 0 of an IDCM. The conceptual schema depicted four stages, covering planning; preliminaries, including feasibility study; requirements analysis and definition; and package selection.

The feasibility study, as we saw in Chapter 8, is a preliminary assessment of a proposed IDCM application in terms of operational, technical, and financial feasibility. It should provide information with which organizations may build a compelling business case (refer to Chapter 9) to secure budget funding and resource allocation for the implementation of an IDCM solution.

During the feasibility study, there will also have been an initial analysis and definition of requirements for the system. Upon completion of the feasibility study, enterprises should have captured a high-level definition of requirements from management and end users (and potentially business partners and customers) and documented these in a feasibility study report. This report should be an input document to the requirements analysis and definition stage.

The requirements analysis and definition stage should extend the work already documented in a feasibility study report. If there has been no feasibility study, then an enterprise needs to analyze and capture the high-level requirements as well as the detailed requirements for its proposed IDCM solution. It may also review business and technology solution options and examine the overall requirement in terms of operational, technical, and financial feasibility.

METHODOLOGY
Schema

The schematic depicted in Figure 1 of the step processes for the requirements analysis design stage is based upon Shelly, Cashman, and Rosenblatt's (2001) approach to the systems analysis phase of an information systems project.

The schematic provides an overview of the stages that are likely to follow a feasibility study and lead to requirements specification.

Figure 1: Requirements Analysis and Definition.

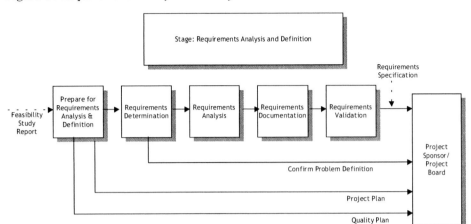

Entry Criteria

The typical inputs to the requirements analysis and definition stage may depend on whether it was preceded by feasibility study, in which case, the input is:

- Feasibility study report.

Alternatively, if there has been no feasibility study, then the inputs might be:

- System request for an information system that involves improved management of documents;
- PID (refer to Chapter 8);
- Terms of reference for conducting requirements analysis and definition.

Additional inputs might include supporting project documentation, such as that defined for the feasibility study phase in Chapter 8, and may include a provisional business case that has been developed based on the findings of the feasibility study.

Exit Criteria

The key deliverables prepared during the requirements analysis and definition phase include:

- Project plan for the requirements analysis and definition stage;
- Quality plan, which may have been prepared for the feasibility study, but potentially, now iterated with new information;
- Problem definition statement, which may be a reconfirmation of the statement developed during the feasibility study stage; and
- Requirements specification.

Depending on the methodology and the modeling and analysis tools adopted by the practitioner(s)' determining requirements, other outputs can include:

- Context diagrams;
- Level 0 diagram;
- Data flow diagrams or process models;
- Process descriptions; and
- Logical data structure definition/data dictionary.

Approach

Where an enterprise has its preferred methodology for information systems projects, then this structured systems methodology will be applied to IDCM development.

Supporting information can also be obtained from many published texts that focus on systems analysis and design or software engineering, and which may provide suitable background information on requirements determination, analysis, and specification of information systems. Works by Kendall and Kendall (2002), Sommerville (2001), and Shelly, Cashman, and Rosenblatt (2001) are typical of the texts that provide background information to requirements analysis and definition.

In the case of the last mentioned, the steps shown in Figure 1 are summarized in Table 1.

Table 1: Systems Analysis Approach

Process/Activities
Requirements Determination
This is primarily concerned with eliciting the facts about the current business model, (i.e., planning imperatives, business processes, document objects, collections, and registers) and the current systems model (IT applications and infrastructure environment), as well as capturing new and emerging (e.g., impending legislation) requirements.
Requirements Analysis
This is the process of analyzing the facts that have been gathered and reviewing the options for addressing existing constraints within the document management environment, as well as meeting new and emerging requirements. As we saw in Chapter 8, when reviewing the feasibility study stage, the options need to be considered in terms of operational, technical, and financial feasibility.
Requirements Documentation
This covers the preparation of a requirements specification that encapsulates the current business model and the existing system model and defines requirements to overcome the constraints with the existing system and meet the new and emerging requirements. (As we will see, there may be a necessity for a set of requirements specifications in order to adequately define specific aspects of requirements for an IDCM project.)
Requirements Validation
This covers the processes involved in authenticating the outcomes of the work performed during determination, analysis, and definition. It involves, among other things, confirming functionality with diverse groups that have a vested interest in the system, ensuring that there is no duplication of requirements, and reviewing the relative importance of the requirements in real-world terms of budget and project time lines.

Techniques

The requirements analysis and definition process usually involves the preparation of logical and physical descriptions of the current system, and the logical description of the required system.

We do not describe specific techniques in this book. Suffice to say that the techniques applied in the analysis and definition stages are generally addressed in commercially available structured information systems methodologies, some of which we listed in Chapter 6. These methodologies provide the framework for defining the relevant processes, functional requirements, and data elements for the acquisition of packaged software, or the development of an information system, to meet specific business requirements.

Analysts may choose to use a range of traditional analytical tools such as data flow diagrams, process maps, entity relationship diagrams, flowcharts, decision tables and decision trees, as well as structured English descriptions to support the requirements determination, analysis, and documentation effort. These general information systems tools may, of course, be applied for IDCM.

Alternatively, perhaps in conjunction with these tools, the enterprise may utilize business process modeling techniques and tools such as workflow process modeling using IDEF diagrams or swimlane diagrams (Sharp & McDermott, p. 137).

REQUIREMENTS SPECIFICATION

Structure

The requirements specification for an IDCM system is the primary deliverable from the requirements analysis and definition phase. However, depending on the extent and complexity of the requirements, the project team may need to deliver a discrete number of specifications that, when combined as a set, comprise a requirements specification document.

We will follow Sommerville's (2001, p. 98) characterization of *user requirements* that define the high-level abstract requirements, and *system requirements* that set out the requirements in detail. The next level of detail is the *software design specification*, which is used for the detailed design and implementation of software and is not within the scope of our present discussion.

User requirements should specify the external system behavior and avoid the characteristics associated with system design. They should be written in natural language so that a nontechnical user can understand the statements of requirements. The use of natural language for documenting requirements has its limitations (primarily due to ambiguity, confusion, and blending of requirements) and, hence, the need for the *system requirements* documentation, which provides a more detailed catalog of requirements (p. 106).

System requirements documentation is often termed a *functional specification*, and this type of specification may serve as a contract between the purchaser and supplier. Too often, enterprises release a RFP for an IDCM system based on *user requirements* (high-level abstract requirements), which does not contain adequate detail at the *system requirements* level. The organization may later experience implementation problems as a result.

Furthermore, the *system requirements* documentation is classified into three sub-sets (2001, p. 100):

- *Functional requirements*, which describe the functionality or services to be provided by the system at a detailed level, for example, in the case of an IDCM system, detailed definition of how the system is expected to function during document life-cycle processes;

- *Nonfunctional requirements*, which describe the requirements that are not specifically related to functionality, for example, aspects such as the reliability, interoperability, and performance requirements of the IDCM system; and

- *Domain requirements*, which are derived from the environment domain of the system, rather than user functionality, for example, constraints such as the IT operating and applications infrastructure, technology standards, or requirements of legislation impacting the IDCM system.

We regard this classification of requirements types and documentation as useful when preparing a requirements specification for an IDCM system that will accompany an RFP that seeks competitive proposals from vendors, suppliers, or system integrators. These specifications are relevant regardless of whether an IDCM system is required to support a specific business application, support the processing of specific types of transactional documents, or be deployed across the enterprise for either transactional or nontransactional documents.

However, this degree of specification may not always be required. Instead, prevailing circumstances may be that an enterprise has implemented a DMS for Business Unit "A" and plans to implement the system in Business Unit "B." Hopefully the enterprise has already determined that the existing DMS capability meets the *functional* and *nonfunctional* system requirements for Business Unit "B." In such circumstances, the analysis and definition effort can be targeted at specific *user* and *domain* requirements for Business Unit "B," on the understanding that the existing package would be utilized for IDCM.

Discrete Specifications

The applicability of the requirements framework proposed by Sommerville to IDCM projects, and the types of analysis and definition activity required for each component in the framework, are reviewed in the remaining chapters of Part 3. The relationship between Sommerville's suggested requirements framework and subsequent coverage in Part 3 chapters is summarized in Table 2.

SUMMARY

We emphasize the importance of conducting a thorough analysis of requirements for an IDCM application and the documentation of detailed requirements encapsulated in a specification.

Depending on the nature of the complexity of the requirements for IDCM, a set of specifications that fulfill different purposes may be needed when describing these requirements.

Table 2: Functional Requirements Overview

Specification	Chapters
User requirements	Chapter 11: User Requirements
System requirements	Incorporated in the following chapters:
Functional requirements	Chapter 12: Functional Requirements — Digital Office Documents
	Chapter 13: Functional Requirements — Email Management
	Chapter 14: Functional Requirements — Physical Office Documents
	Chapter 15: Functional Requirements — Document Imaging and Recognition Technology
	Chapter 16: Functional Requirements — Workflow Management
	Chapter 17: Functional Requirements — Drawing Management
	Chapter 18: Functional Requirements — Web Content Management
Nonfunctional requirements and domain requirements	Chapter 19: Nonfunctional and Domain Requirements

When we adopt Sommerville's framework of user and systems requirements documentation, the following types of component specifications are relevant:

- User requirements specification;
- Functional requirements specification;
- Nonfunctional requirements specification; and
- Domain requirements specification.

This type of requirements analysis and definition framework appears particularly relevant when an organization wishes to acquire and implement an IDCM system for a diverse range of functionality throughout the enterprise.

In the next chapter, we will look at the structure of a *user requirements* specification, before going on in Part 3 chapters to provide an overview of functional, nonfunctional, and domain requirements to be considered during the analysis and specification of requirements.

Chapter 11

User Requirements

OVERVIEW

In the last chapter, we discussed an integrative approach to developing requirements for information systems, applying Sommerville's framework of *user* and *systems* requirements documentation. We now extend that discussion to consider an approach that might be useful when planning activities for analyzing *user requirements* for an IDCM endeavor. The information derived from the analysis of user requirements will be a key component of the requirements specification.

Our objectives are as follows:

*   Discuss the role of the user requirements analysis in the context of IDCM;
*   Discuss the analysis and definition of strategic requirements for IDCM systems within the context of enterprise business planning;
*   Discuss the specification of tactical requirements for an IDCM solution at the site, workgroup, or business process level of an enterprise;
*   Consider the requirements for specifying interfaces to business systems;
*   Discuss the documentation of operational requirements with some specific reference to archiving and preservation concerns; and
*   Discuss extended requirements for IDCM solutions.

ROLE OF USER REQUIREMENTS ANALYSIS

We noted in Chapter 10 that the user requirements component of the requirements specification is primarily a high-level abstract statement of requirements written in a natural language that a nontechnical user can understand (Sommerville, 2001, p. 106).

The analysis and definition of user requirements is an important component of an IDCM initiative, because it:

- Enables the project team to draw on the work that may have already been done during project planning or business case development, to align IDCM requirements with strategic business planning imperatives;

- Provides the project team with an opportunity to analyze and define requirements for business process improvement using IDCM systems as a key component of the supporting information systems architecture;

- Gives the project team the opportunity to take a step back from an immediate requirement (such as focusing on operational planning) and review the end-to-end requirements of a business process;

- Provides an opportunity to consider the process improvement opportunities that might be realized using integration of document repository services with workflow and document imaging and fax capture tools;

- Provides an opportunity to consider integration with business applications such as ERP, maintenance, plant control, land information, patient management systems, and GIS;

- Facilitates the development of new thinking regarding life-cycle opportunities for managing documents in various stages of specified business processes, covering creation through to rendered content on Web servers, and management as a business record;

- Helps analyze and define the current processes at an operational level (This analysis includes processes associated with capturing, storing, and retrieving documents. It can be used to define the current logical file structures, review document naming conventions, and review behavioral aspects related to managing documents.);

- Assists the project team in determining the types of search criteria that users may require from the system and also with the definition of reports that users may require;

- Helps the project team to determine the nature of the current document environment, including analysis of document registers and collections, and to determine the quality of the data and documents;

- Assists in and helps identify the types of authoring tools being used and the types of document formats that may need to be supported by the IDCM solution;

- Provides the opportunity to document database models and application logic supporting existing document systems, and to determine requirements for data migration;

- Provides the opportunity to identify system changeover requirements (where applicable), migration requirements for data and documents stored in existing files and repositories, and any requirements for backfile conversion of hard-copy documents;

- Helps to identify and develop requirements for change management; and

- Enables policy, development, and implementation issues to be identified and documented.

The approach to be adopted for analyzing and defining user requirements will depend on an enterprise's preferred methodology for information systems projects. The emphasis in this book has been to align IDCM planning with an enterprise's strategic, tactical, and operational levels of information planning. We consider it practical for enterprises to begin analyzing and defining user requirements at a strategic level, and then progress into more detailed analysis at the tactical and operational levels.

User Needs Analysis

Requirements analysis may be regarded as just one aspect of user needs analysis. User needs analysis is more broadly interested in the information-seeking influences that apply to different groups of people. For example, such analysis may endeavor to take into account:

- *Cognitive factors*: For example, how confident are users of a document system that the information in the documents that they are seeing is accurate, reliable, and pertinent? Can they make confident decisions or judgments using it?

- *Affective factors*: For example, are users of a document system so swamped with retrieved information that they have apprehension or anxiety about retrieving material? There may be so little ability to discriminate when retrieving, that they are alienated by vast amounts of unique material, all of which seems to be pertinent to what they are seeking.

- *Situational factors*: For example, is there any apparent reward for the time spent in learning to use a retrieval system? Does the time and effort spent accessing documents justify what is ultimately obtained?

On one hand, the methodologies that deal with processes for addressing these areas tend to concentrate upon the content of the information sources that the users seek. Therefore, appropriate sources are identified to service the user's requirement. On the other hand, there is a concentration upon the process that the user embarks upon to seek information, and therefore, upon the product or system that services the requirement.

The latter approach leads to requirements analysis and is what we are concentrating upon in this chapter. However, the former approach, which may be termed resource assessment,[1] may also be brought to bear for IDCM. What it does, is determine a big picture of group use that identifies the limits within which a user community is likely to work. For example, checklists have been suggested that ask the following questions (Middleton, 2002) of the user group:

- What is the subject matter?

- To what use will the information be put?
    - Fact-finding: Answering specific questions
    - Current awareness: Keeping up to date in a known area
    - Research: Investigating a new field
    - Background understanding: The briefing function
    - Idea provision: Providing stimulus, unstructured when the users do not know what they are seeking

- What is the nature of the information?
    - Methodological, theoretical, statistical, historical, etc.

- What is the intellectual level required?
- What viewpoint is taken?
    - Schools of thought, political orientation, for and against views, etc.
- How much is required?
- Is quality an important factor?
    - Refereed research, authoritative sources, corporate Web sites, etc.
- How current must the information be?
- How quickly is it required?
- Are there geographic limitations?
- In what form is it to be presented?
    - Digital, executive summary, tabulation, etc.

If for users of an IDCM solution, some of these questions provoke meaningful answers, then it is incumbent upon the repository and associated retrieval system to provide for them. This resource analysis stage should lead to a more specific analysis of requirements, where the processes for achieving the answers are identified.

The same range of methodologies: interviewing, observation, utilization of existing functional documents, surveys, self-reporting, workshops, prototyping, and the like, may be used for resource assessment and requirements analysis in determining user needs.

Requirements Analysis and Planning Levels

It is difficult to neatly structure requirements analysis and definition effort into the three categories of planning, because requirements analysis tends to be an iterative process. Information obtained during analysis at any level of planning may influence requirements that have already been documented.

Figure 1 demonstrates that the level of detail involved in requirements analysis and definition increases exponentially as the analyst progresses from the strategic level of planning to operational planning, and demonstrates iteration.

Figure 1: User Requirements Analysis.

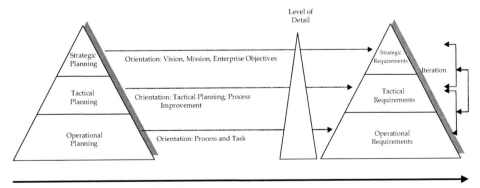

User Requirements Analysis

During the analysis and definition of user requirements, process flows may be mapped, system interface requirements defined, document environments examined, and business improvement opportunities identified and reviewed. The techniques and tools that may be used have been identified in Chapter 6.

The information and documentation derived during the user requirements analysis process will provide the basis for the development of a user requirements specification, as a component item of the set of documents that make up the overall requirements specification.

Where there has been a preliminary investigation of the IDCM opportunity, then the feasibility study report (refer to Chapter 8) may contain a provisional listing of requirements, potentially aligned with the three levels of planning, that will assist the analysis and definition of requirements at a detailed level.

STRATEGIC REQUIREMENTS

The analysis at a strategic level needs to determine (or confirm) the user requirements relevant to crucial business planning initiatives and organizational change imperatives, so that the relationship of IDCM requirements to strategic planning is clearly defined. The user requirements specification can be structured so that it provides "top-down" information about the business or government enterprise, commencing with information relating to the organization's mission, key business strategies, and other relevant business planning information that places the document management requirement within an overall business context. An example of what may be included at an enterprise overview level is included in Table 1.

The alignment of user requirements for document management with business planning may be useful for the enterprise, as it can give the enterprise a better

Table 1: User Requirements — Strategic

Structure	Content
Business vision	Statement of enterprise vision
Mission statement	Statement of enterprise mission
Objectives	Statement of corporate objectives
Values	Statement of organizational values
Business functions	An overview description of key business functions
Planning imperatives	Business planning initiatives and organizational change imperatives that are relevant to document management (refer to Chapter 2 and Chapter 5 for contextual information)
Emerging issues	Indications of new or emerging business issues that might be relevant to the requirement (for example, new legislative requirements)
Document environment	Brief high-level synopsis of current document environment, sufficient to understand potential impact on business planning imperatives
Imperatives for IDCM	Brief description of why the IDCM endeavor has been initiated — relate to business planning imperatives and current document and Web content environment
Summary	~

understanding of its *own* requirements for document management within the context of its vision, mission, objectives, and key business planning priorities. The alignment may also be of assistance to potential suppliers of the IDCM software, as it enables them to gain an appreciation of the nature of the organization and the key business drivers for better managing documents.

TACTICAL REQUIREMENTS

The requirements for an IDCM solution that are applicable to the tactical level of business planning can relate to functions and processes within a designated site or workgroup within the organization, or for a specific business application.

Table 2: User Requirements — Tactical

Structure	Content
Tactical planning imperatives	Tactical plans that are relevant to document management — for example, the purchasing and contracts group may be planning to implement e-business initiatives for managing contract development.
Structure and functions	Organization structure of the supply department and purchasing and contracts group, and a description of the key business functions.
Current business model	Description of the (relevant) end-to-end business processes within the purchasing and contracts group — for example, it may be a description of the life cycle business processes involved in awarding contracts for services; the description might also include a definition of existing interfaces to other processes and systems, and identify the strengths and limitations of the existing business model.
Proposed business model	Description of revised processes, taking into account the opportunities offered by solutions such as IDCM software; the model should also include a definition of the required interfaces to other processes and systems.
Supported information systems	Information systems that are used by the purchasing and contracts group, including legacy systems, if any, used to manage physical and electronic documents.
Search and reporting requirements	Search and reporting requirements at a *tactical* level, i.e., composed in natural language by the user; the requirements should include specific search and retrieval criteria, and reporting requirements of the system, insofar as it impacts the purchasing and contracts group [Note that the detailed definition of document collections (file systems, foldering systems), object types, and formats should be included under *operational* information planning.].
System interfaces	Requirements of the IDCM solution to interface with other business systems, such as an ERP system, CRM system, or GIS (as examples).
System changeover	System changeover may include the business requirements for migrating from an existing document registry system to the IDCM.
Change management requirements	Change management requirements relevant to the purchasing and contracts group — issues identified during requirements analysis that might be relevant to the implementation, for example, there might be a need for specific users who are not within the scope of a Phase 1 implementation to share documents that are secured within the IDCM repository.
Training requirements	Training requirements that are relevant to IDCM end users, key users, help desk, and system administrators.
Policy issues	Policy issues identified during analysis of requirements — these issues will need to be resolved during the development and implementation of the IDCM.
Summary	~

When considering tactical requirements, readers should note that:

- If there is more than one site, workgroup, or business application that is within the scope of the IDCM initiative, then separate specifications might be required for each application.

- If it is planned that the IDCM solution is to be deployed progressively throughout remaining (relevant) business units across the enterprise as multiple phases of the IDCM implementation, separate specifications might also be required. (Refer to our comments later in this chapter on "Extended Requirements Analysis.")

We will use the implementation of document management capabilities for the purchasing and contracts group of the supply department (refer to the scope statement in Chapter 6) to *illustrate* the tactical requirements for an IDCM solution. The structure of the tactical component of the requirements specification can include information as indicated in Table 2.

Elements of this information may be derived from the feasibility study phase of the requirement, with new knowledge acquired during the analysis of requirements in this stage of the project. Let us look at some specific aspects of the tactical user requirements definition.

System Interfaces

It is difficult for solution providers to offer fixed-price or firm-priced proposals for projects, when the level of requirements definition for interfacing an IDCM system (document repository manager or workflow, for example) with business application software is abstract. For example, a stated requirement such as "ability to integrate IDCM with GIS" is quite vague, as there are no logical process details to support the statement of requirement.

Most IDCM suppliers would claim the "ability to integrate" their products with a GIS, but the enterprise and the supplier may need to understand more details: what are intersecting interface points, what are the requirements, and is there a specific GIS product?

Consequently, enterprises may find that proposals are easier to evaluate and project execution and planning effort and costs better understood, if requirements definition is cultivated during the requirements analysis and definition phase.

In this case, it might be appropriate to provide process flows that define the logical requirements for interfacing with a GIS, and also include a definition of the physical GIS environment in the domain requirements specification (refer to Chapter 19).

The same type of comments would apply to the business process requirements for integrating with other horizontal business applications, such as ERP and CRM systems, or vertical applications such as contract management, plant control, land information, and patient management systems, to name but a few examples.

The definition of processes for the interface requirements should also include a logical data model and data dictionary for the target business systems, where this type of information is available. However, this may be unavailable if it is the intellectual property of the owner of the relevant business system.

System Changeover

It is important that an enterprise, where the requirement exists, defines its system changeover and data migration requirements. This may be relevant where an existing document or drawing registry system is to be decommissioned as part of the implementation of the IDCM solution. This section of the book should be read in conjunction with data migration, which we discuss in this chapter under "Operational Requirements."

There are a number of scenarios that might apply:

- There is no system changeover or data migration, which is the simplest scenario.
- An existing document or drawing registry system is to be decommissioned concurrent with or subsequent to the implementation of an IDCM solution.
- Document or drawing data is maintained as part of a system that provides a wider range of functionality, e.g., document registry information in an ERP or maintenance management system, which is not to be decommissioned. We will deal with this aspect shortly, when discussing data migration.

If an existing document or drawing registry system is to be decommissioned, then it is incumbent on the enterprise to consider its system changeover strategies and requirements. There are a number of strategy options:

- Direct cutover;
- Parallel operations; and
- Phased changeover.

Direct Cutover

The direct cutover option occurs when the change from an existing system to the IDCM solution is effected upon a particular predefined date. This option has the advantage that operational costs are minimized and, assuming data is migrated from the existing system to the IDCM solution, users would only be required to access one repository for capture, update, and inquiry. In addition, statistical and other reports would only be obtained from one repository. This option has the disadvantage of no easy fall-back position should, for example, the IDCM solution fail due to a critical error that cannot easily be detected and rectified. Furthermore, there might be a wide staff impact, which would need to be managed under a change management plan.

Parallel Operations

Another option is the parallel operations of the existing system and the IDCM solution until the new system is proven to be sustainable. There would be a wider staff impact than experienced under the direct cutover method, as users might be required to record data in both systems, thus increasing the time taken to effect business processes. Using this option, the risk factor is low, but the operational costs in running two systems might be high (unless the existing system is used for purposes other than those being taken over by the IDCM solution).

Phased Changeover

The phased changeover option enables a particular group of users or defined scope of functionality to be processed using the IDCM solution, while the remainder is processed using an existing system. For example, the purchasing and contracts group of the supply department might save all documents into the IDCM solution, while the engineering department maintains an existing drawing register until the IDCM solution is deployed to manage engineering drawings. This option minimizes the risk of the direct cutover approach and might be less costly than the parallel processing option. It may also support the progressive deployment initiatives identified as part of the IDCM implementation strategy.

However, one of the disadvantages of this option might be that, given the inability to access the IDCM solution by nonlicensed users, users might be required to access multiple data and document repositories to satisfy a specific search. It may also mean that necessary information for statistical and other reports needs to be obtained from multiple data repositories. Given that these scenarios probably apply in the existing document environment, disadvantages might not be a major concern in the short term.

System Changeover Analysis

The decision on which of the system changeover models best suits organizational requirements can only be answered when taking into account the specific circumstances of the overall IDCM requirement. The following *types* of questions might be considered during preliminary investigation (feasibility study) to help determine the most appropriate system changeover option. The outcomes will impact the enterprise finalizing its implementation strategy.

- Is the IDCM implementation to be phased?
- Will other users require access to the existing system during the progressive deployment of the IDCM solution?
- Are there any financial imperatives to decommission the existing system earlier rather than later? If so, does the scope of the IDCM implementation support early decommission of the system?
- Does the existing system support users who are not within the scope of the initial IDCM implementation?
- What are the impacts on accessibility, collaboration, and reporting?

Changeover Requirements Definition

The enterprise will need to provide the following information relating to the existing systems environment when defining its requirements for system changeover:

- General description of the system and subsystems that comprise the information system to be decommissioned;
- Applications and operations environment for the system;
- Logical database design of the database schema and physical design, if available;
- Data dictionary for the system, which provides detailed definitions that support the logical database design;
- Database sizing information — the total amount of data held in the database (noting provision made for associations such as database pointers and space for expansion);

- Document object repository definition (if a DMS being decommissioned) — covering the definition of objects (types, volumes, formats, compound interrelationships);
- Transactional usage analysis, preferably including a breakdown of update and search and retrieval functions; and
- Definition of the physical data model.

Change Management Requirements

The implementation of an IDCM solution often provides a catalyst for continuous process improvement strategies, by using the latest technology innovations to manage and deliver services. However, there are change management implications that need to be considered when reviewing user requirements. For example:

- Authors of documents may be required to enter registration information (metadata) that captures the properties of a document, which may not be an integral part of an end user's day-to-day business operations. The implications of applying metadata capture need to be considered in the light of enterprise culture and workgroup behavior.
- Target end users may already have existing systems for document registration (e.g., word-processing, spreadsheet, or local database) that meet their requirements for locating and retrieving documents and may be unconvinced of the overall benefits of the system (potentially an isolationist view).
- Management might be seeking a shift in the way an enterprise conducts its business administration, with a transformation from a hard-copy-centric business culture to the capture, dissemination, exchange, collaboration, and storage of electronic information at the desktop.

The requirement may exist for the purchasing and contracts group (using our example) to collaborate with other workgroups in the supply department or other business units, such as the engineering department. This may involve collaboration on the development of specifications that may form part of a contractual documentation. If we make an assumption that the purchasing and contracts group is an initial site within a wider enterprise deployment of IDCM, the engineering department may not be included within the scope of the project.

The project team thus needs to give consideration to how collaboration will be enabled with the engineering department during the initial IDCM implementation, which is restricted to the purchasing and contracts group. The documents stored in the IDCM repository might not be accessible to the engineering department unless the initial phase includes licensing relevant users within that department to access the IDCM software. If it is not possible because of budget and functionality restrictions to include relevant users of the engineering department, then transitional arrangements may need to be developed.

A nonlicensed user may require access to documents in the IDCM repository and may obtain an electronic document from a licensed user (e.g., by email). The non-IDCM user might update the document without referring it to the IDCM repository. For example, the purchasing and contracts group could collaborate with the engineering department by sending documents as attachments using email, but there is a risk that a document versioned by the engineering department would not be captured as the latest version in the IDCM repository.

As another example requiring change management effort, an IDCM user might access a document from a shared file system and save the document to the IDCM repository. Non-IDCM users will not be able to access the repository, and there is a risk that a copy of the same document (or earlier version) may be maintained on a file system. This scenario creates a high risk, because a non-IDCM user may access and update the copy of the document on the file system without recognizing that another copy is under the control of the IDCM repository.

Another example relates to the requirements of end users who are highly mobile. Let us consider an end user from the purchasing and contracts group who visits another site office (without a laptop that could contain licensed software) and requires access to documents in the IDCM. The user might be able to gain access to the purchasing and contracts group's library of documents using a browser, but there may need to be special provision made for relevant plug-ins that enable access from the remote browser.

The project team should consider the nature of the resources from within the enterprise and the level of effort that will be required to implement and maintain the IDCM solution in the purchasing and contracts group. There may be requirements for technical and key-user system administration support during the implementation and ongoing system operations.

These are but a few aspects of change management issues that need to be analyzed and requirements defined. The requirements for change management may be varied, and much depends on the nature of the enterprise, its philosophy toward information management, and the extent to which it gives (or plans to give) effect to managing information as an asset. If there is no demonstrated commitment from management at the strategic and tactical levels of the organization, then that aspect is a change management issue that needs to be addressed.

The change management requirements need to be identified as part of the user requirements specification and may be used as the basis for formulating and executing a change management plan.

Training Requirements

Adequate training will be essential for the acceptance and smooth operation of the IDCM solution. When using the system, it must be integrated within an end user's operational environment to the extent that it is not seen as an impediment, but as an enhancement, to effective performance.

It is incumbent upon the organization to define its training requirements. Depending on the business requirements and the nature of the solution, training might need to cover the following types of user:

- General user — Adequate training to ensure that the end user is able to satisfactorily meet individual work requirements;
- Key user — A higher level of training might be required for a number of nominated end users, which will provide them with the skills required to act as a local systems administrator;
- IT helpdesk — Helpdesk staff will require training in the IDCM management and helpdesk-related activities; and

- System administrator — There may be a requirement for technical staff to be fully trained in the complete operation, maintenance, and management of the IDCM solution.

The definition of training requirements may also include details of training accommodation available within an organization, size of training rooms, availability of networked computers in the training room, and the configuration of the desktop and server systems installed for training. The definition may also include details of training equipment and aids, such as overhead projectors, whiteboards, and other similar logistical tools. These types of details will help suppliers determine their training strategy and costs for training when submitting proposals.

Policy Issues

The requirement for policy formulation and development might be identified during the definition of user requirements, particularly if the enterprise has not formulated a document management policy prior to the commencement of user requirements analysis. Issues may also emerge after the development of a document management policy, which may require iteration of the policy, depending on whether the issue relates to that policy or to a specific aspect of tactical business process. For example, the applicability of consistent metadata standards might not have been adequately considered and developed.

OPERATIONAL REQUIREMENTS

At the operational planning level, if we progress with our example of the purchasing and contracts group, definitions can include those aspects listed in Table 3.

Archival Management

In some organizations, the management of archives will be an assigned distinctive operation and will warrant specific requirements analysis. The preservation and storage of documents in archives is increasingly catered for as part of a continuum that proceeds from records management processes. The terms "records management" and "documents management" are sometimes used as if they mean the same thing. Refer to Table 2 in Chapter 4 for commentary on this.

Certainly, for either terminology, the processes view documents in terms of creation, distribution, storage, and effective retrieval. However, to professionals working in the area, records are those documents retained for evidentiary value. This should mean that records management systems are a subset of DMS. The reality is that there is confusion of terminology, particularly since the advent of computer systems applications. This is because some document management applications have been implemented with a particular emphasis, for example, imaging, with little regard to records management principles. Conversely, some records management practices have paid scant regard to digital versions of documents, and how they may be dealt with in a manner integrated with print documents.

Table 3: User Requirements — Operational

Structure	Content
Document management environment	Definition of the current document environment for transactional and nontransactional documents for the purchasing and contracts group — the description should include an analysis of capture, storage, search, retrieval, and archival of documents (The content in Chapter 3 might be useful for understanding the way documents might be managed within the current environment and the issues involved.).
Definition of user profiles	Description of the roles that will be using the IDCM within the purchasing and contracts group and any roles external to that workgroup that will be included within scope.
Document types and formats	Document object definitions for sites, workgroups participating in the relevant business process, or site-specific requirements.
Document registers	Description of the manual or digital registers that are used to record documents — these registers may include client- and server-based information systems and desktop applications (word processing, spreadsheet, and local databases).
Document collections	Definition of document collections, including analysis of (physical) file and (electronic) folder structures, document types, document formats, volumes of documents, and review of strengths and limitations of the management of the collections — the description covers document stores [electronic and physical file systems and local storage (local hard disk, removable media, physical trays)].
Document management requirements	Document management requirements at an operational level should include a logical definition of current and required logical cabinet structures, foldering and metadata requirements, and specific report output forms.
Archival requirements	Specific requirements for archiving documents and Web content.
Migration requirements	Requirements to migrate documents from existing document stores to IDCM — define what cleanup actions are proposed (if any) prior to migration of documents with poor metadata (Also includes requirements to migrate metadata from localized document registers such as databases, spreadsheets, word-processing tables, or capture metadata from manual systems.).
Backfile conversion	The conversion of physical documents to digital (or film) image or the conversion of film-based document image collections to digital image.
Summary	~

Records management systems have paid particular attention to legal obligations inherent in the documents, the physical storage of them, their administrative control as manifest in provenance and in sequence of custody,[2] and appraisal and retention principles. Their orientation is evidential and historical.

On the other hand, documents management systems are closer to the actual transactions that are taking place with documents as they pass from person to person as a consequence of workflow. Of prime concern are operational requirements identified in system analysis, version control, and levels of access.

Both approaches are concerned with metainformation in the form of description of the documents being handled. However, in records management, the metainformation is often provided in stand-alone finding aids based upon the way the records are classified, whereas in document systems, the metainformation may well be encoded with the documents using file naming and document naming and indexing strategies.

With increasing use of digital documents, it is reasonable to expect the convergence of the two alternatives to continue. We have seen this happening, for example, within government bureaucracies. One example of determining the importance of retaining electronic documents is to characterize them as personal, group, or corporate, and then

Table 4: IESC "Benefits of the Application of Electronic Office Technologies"

Task	Technology	Benefits	Levels
Authoring	Word processing	• Sender prepares document, may be enhanced by later editing	Individual
		• Spelling and proofreading software enhances quality	Individual
Writing	Word processing	• Editing ability enhanced creating process	Individual
	Groupware	• Collaborative production of complex documents	Workgroup
Phoning	Voicemail	• Receipt acknowledgment	Individual
	Email	• Accurate messages	
		• Message can be sent to a distribution list at one time	
	Facsimile	• Conversion is documented on paper	Individual
Document generation	Word processing	• Enhanced editability	Individual
	Drawing/charting	• Graphics can be used to supplement text	Individual
	Analysis Processing	• Graphs and tables can be used to support context	Individual
	Image	• Photographic quality pictures can be "attached"	Individual
	Groupware/ workflow	• Collaborative production of complex documents	Workgroup
	Desktop Publishing	• Compound document can be created and printed assimilating varying input described above	Corporate
Meeting	Joint diaries	• Enables faster scheduling of people and resources	Workgroup
	Groupware	• Collaborative effort in meeting supported	Workgroup
	Email	• Faster notification, invitations, and minutes distribution	Workgroup
Scheduling	Diary	• Easily modified: no "ink" versus "pencil"	Individual
		• Automatic scheduling of regular items and reminders	
	Workflow, email	• Automates overt scheduling	Individual
Travel	Diary/calendar	• Availability of people is known throughout the organization	Corporate
	Email	• Message can be sent and received at the most convenient time	Individual
Analysis	Analysis processing	• A wide range of cooperating software can be used for data analysis	All

itemize the benefits for electronic processing of types of information tasks. This was done by IESC (Australia. Information Exchange Steering Committee. Electronic Data Management Sub-Committee, 1993), and we summarize their approach in Table 4.

This was then used to establish what are considered to be the essential elements of a corporate electronic document profile or "context." We illustrate these in Table 5.

This type of metainformation can be included in an information repository or data dictionary for an organization. Information concerning the provenance and the required retention period for a document is therefore stored within a document. This means that the DMS may then include procedures for automatic listing of documents that are to be discarded, so that final decisions may be made concerning them.

The International Standards Organization is proceeding toward the development of a standard for what is called an open archival information system (OAIS), based upon the *Red Book* (Consultative Committee for Space Data Systems, 1999), in order to establish the principles for an archive to provide permanent or indefinite long-term preservation of digital information. This is expected to provide a framework for the development of subsequent standards on matters such as interfaces between archives, submission of source and metadata material to archives (ingest), access and retrieval, and migration across media and formats.

It anticipates explanation of functional entities for such a system as shown in the *Red Book* illustrated here as Figure 2.

These may be explained as follows:

- *Ingest*

  Provision of the services and functions to accept submission information packages (SIPs) from producers (or from internal elements under administration control) and prepare the contents for storage and management within the archive. Functions include:

Table 5: IESC "Essential Features of a Corporate Electronic Document"

Feature	Computer Assigned	Default Possible?	Mandatory?
Unique identifier	Yes	Yes	Yes
Author/originator	Yes	Yes	Yes
Owner/manager	No	Yes	Yes
Classification	No	Yes	Yes
Controller	No	Yes	Optional
Date/time of creation	Yes	Yes	Yes
Date/time of registration	Yes	Yes	Yes
Title	No	Yes	Yes
Sentence/retention period	No	No	Yes
Keywords	No	No	Optional

Figure 2: Red Book Illustration of OAIS Functional Aspects of Archival Management.

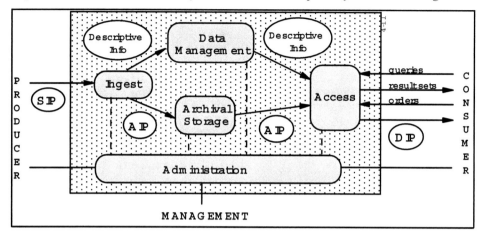

- Receiving SIPs;
- Performing quality assurance on SIPs;
- Generating an archival information package (AIP) that complies with the archive's data formatting and documentation standards;
- Extracting descriptive information from the AIPs for inclusion in the archive database; and
- Coordinating updates to archival storage and data management.

- *Archival storage*

  Provision of the services and functions for the storage, maintenance, and retrieval of AIPs. These functions include:
  - Receiving AIPs from ingest and adding them to permanent storage;
  - Managing the storage hierarchy;
  - Refreshing the media on which archive holdings are stored;
  - Performing routine and special error checking;
  - Providing disaster recovery capabilities; and
  - Providing AIPs to access to fulfill orders.

- *Data management*

  Provision of the services and functions for populating, maintaining, and accessing descriptive information, which identifies and documents archive holdings, and administrative data used to manage the archive. Functions include:
  - Administering the archive database functions (maintaining schema and viewing definitions, and referential integrity);
  - Performing database updates (loading new descriptive information or archive administrative data);
  - Performing queries on the data management data to generate result sets; and
  - Producing reports from result sets.

- *Administration*

  Management of the overall operation of the archive system. Administration functions include:
  - Soliciting and negotiating submission agreements with producers;

- Auditing submissions to ensure that they meet archive standards;
- Maintaining configuration management of system hardware and software;
- Evaluating the contents of the archive, and periodically requesting archival information updates;
- Providing system engineering functions to monitor and improve archive operations;
- Developing and maintaining archive standards and policies;
- Providing customer support; and
- Monitoring changes in the communities that the archive is designated to service.

- *Access*

  This supports consumers in determining the existence, description, location, and availability of information stored in the OAIS and allowing them to request and receive information products. Access functions include:
  - Communicating with consumers to receive requests;
  - Applying controls to limit access to specially protected information;
  - Coordinating the execution of requests to successful completion;
  - Generating responses (information dissemination packages, result sets, reports); and
  - Delivering the responses to consumers.

These entities are in addition to what are termed "common services," such as operating systems, networking, and security.

Preservation

Another operational area that may require distinctive requirements analysis of operational requirements is the general area of preservation. We come to digital preservation via two avenues. In either case, the aim is to have available for long-term storage and access, data in digital form. However, these data may have originated in print form, in which case, substantial effort may be necessary to convert the data to digital media and to describe them so that they may be readily accessible. Alternatively, if they have been originated digitally, there will be conversion issues arising from getting the data into a viable accessible format.

Users are primarily concerned with identifying relevant content or resources. However, user needs analysis should also make clear the digital forms in which they exist and software associated with their capture and retrieval, along the lines illustrated in Table 6.

Drive for organized approaches to archival access to digitized material comes from a variety of sources, including:

- Businesses utilizing office systems that produce corporate documents that have been judged worthy of long-term retention;
- Architectural and engineering firms that need to refer back to historical graphical and design material;
- Scientific organizations with large collections of data such as that collected by radiotelescopes or environmental monitoring devices, which need to be stored for continuing experimentation; and

Table 6: Preservation Resources

Type of Data	Resource Content	Associated Software
Alphanumeric	Data sets:	Text editors
	Databases	Markup authoring
	• Transaction files	• HTML
	Software	• SGML
	Office documents	• XML
	• Word processing	Word processor
	• Spreadsheets	DBMS
	Print conversions via OCR	Report writers
	Desktop publishing	Presentation
Audio	Oral histories	Analog–digital recording
	Music	Speech recognition
	Speeches	Speech synthesis
		Synthesizers
Video	Motion pictures	Analog–digital recording
	Animations	Digital cameras
Graphics	Maps	Geographic information systems
• Raster	Photographs	CAD/CAM
• Vector	Computer-aided design	Business graphics and design
	Clip art	Image editors
	Image processing	Publishing
	Presentation graphics	Computer generation
	Courseware	
	Simulation and modeling	
Multimedia	Potential for each of the above	Potential for each of the above
Compound documents	Potential for each of the above	Potential for each of the above

- Government instrumentalities required to preserve documents for legislative purposes or any organizations requiring evidential records.

Within these groupings, many parties have an interest in digital preservation, and the means by which it is undertaken. Naturally, the originators of documents are interested. Others that are concerned include repositories, publishers and distributors, educational institutions, legal depositories, information service providers, and funding agencies. They must face a number of challenges when considering the archiving process (Task Force on Archiving of Digital Information, 1996). These include the following:

- *Outmoded technology*
  Despite the fact that digital media may be fragile and have relatively limited shelf lives, even when storage conditions are optimal, they are still likely to outlive the associated technology for reading them.
  Refreshing of data, using regular copying to a new medium, is used to preserve information but presents problems unless the data are encoded in a format independent of the hardware and software used to access the information. It may be employed, providing there is software able to process the data for current use. Often, current software and hardware are not backwardly compatible. There is not the financial imperative for the developers to build such facility into software development deadlines. This leads to interoperability problems and the need for additional software to be written to enable information processing.

- *Migration*

  This requires regulated periodic transfer to successive hardware and software configurations. There are cases where refreshing may not be possible because of format incompatibilities. Migration is then employed, in which case, stringent quality control must take place to maintain authenticity and minimize loss of data. The tenets of open systems interconnection and standardized data exchange formats may alleviate authentication problems in time. However, data that have been created on earlier systems may have to be stored together with their retrieval software to permit use.

- *Rights management*

  The management of intellectual property represented in digital information, and the balancing of reasonable rights of access for users, with the legislative and moral obligations to creators, may involve a significant number of stakeholders.

- *Infrastructure*

  The societal and business structures that we developed over half a century of dealing with information technology have still to mature to the stage where there is effective systematic approach to dealing with information issues — that is, a more profound infrastructure.

  The multiple, interrelated factors required for effective preservation programs are still being developed for documents that record the corporate memory.

- *Institutional framework*

  This is a framework that provides for commonly held understanding of what is required for a regime of capturing corporate information.

  As the requirements of the digital environment become clearer, existing institutions may need to make structurally significant changes. New structures may emerge to achieve archival capture for digital information.

- *Disaster preparedness*

  As with physical materials, preparation for recovery in the event of catastrophic circumstances is an essential aspect of a preservation strategy. This means that strategies must be in place to protect facilities against the effect of physical damage and of subversive access. It also means that routines should be in place utilizing backup onto storage media or mirroring at other remote sites, to enable data recovery in the event of loss or corruption of the working data.

  Recovery planning must involve identifying and prioritizing information assets, which may be carried out as part of an information mapping or audit process. Toigo (2000) emphasized that recovery planning must concern itself with identifying business-critical information stored on paper, and with the interdependencies that may exist among paper-based and digital data, source documents, and worker knowledge that makes data usable.

A variety of factors must be taken into account when making preservation decisions. For each resource type itemized in the figure, these involve considering:

- How were the data created? Data that are digital original, while not requiring the conversion procedures necessary for print or photographs, nevertheless, may require reformatting or software development and management for continued use.

- How available and organized for access are the data? They may be organized in a file structure that provides mnemonics for access or may be accompanied by metadata embedded or in separate files that assist retrieval. However, it may be necessary to create access aids at the time of conversion.

- In what form were the contents received for preservation? They may be on different physical media, which must be integrated in a usable fashion though scanning procedures, which entails workflow decisions for conversion.

- What usage restrictions may apply? A regimen for obtaining clearances may have to be instituted for copyright material.

- How much documentation is there that describes the resource? Authenticity, extent, and completeness need to be ascertained for confidence in validity.

Workflow must therefore take place in a managed project environment that includes:

- Image conversion through high-quality scanners capable of dealing with high resolution and producing archival images;

- Production of derived images (thumbnail, monochrome, service, archival, and in different compression formats), that are appropriate for the retrieval, transfer, and viewing milieu;

- Integrated image description through indexing and other metadata that are linked with images;

- Avoidance of data loss by provision and maintenance of hardware and software compatible with files, or a program for reformatting files into standard formats; and

- Online and backup offline storage, created using appropriate magnetic and optical media.

Data Migration

The requirement for data migration can comprise a number of different scenarios, viz:

- The requirement to migrate data from an existing information system that provides registry or document management functionality prior to system changeover;

- The requirement to migrate data from local databases (such as document or drawing metadata stored in spreadsheets, word-processing document tables, or workgroup databases); and

- The requirement to migrate document objects from an existing file system.

Migration from Existing Information System

The alternative options for data migration (including document objects) from an existing registry or DMS will depend upon the approved strategy for system changeover. Some of the options might include:

- *No migration* — Under this option, there would be no migration of data (including documents) stored in the existing system. This option might be considered appropriate, if the data in the existing system is considered irrelevant to future requirements or the integrity of the data is such that it is not worth investing in a cleanup operation prior to migration. This option may have the benefit in that it is the least costly option in terms of migration effort. If the data is unclean, it also means that poor data is not migrated to the new IDCM system. However, its disadvantage is that it may be necessary to keep multiple systems working, which is unlikely to be cost-effective. If the existing data is not considered worthy of cleaning up, the enterprise might consider decommissioning the whole system, data and all, which will have implications for recordkeeping.

- *Partial migration* — The organization may decide upon migration of part of the data in the existing system. The implications for recordkeeping may need to be investigated, as it may be necessary to maintain the integrity of transaction logs and audit trails as evidence of business transactions and activities. Also, there needs to be a determination as to whether the existing system is still to be maintained, but with no update access to database records (and associated document objects) that are to be migrated to the new system.

- *Full migration* — This option would entail the migration of all data to the new IDCM solution. The organization may wish to consider its requirements for transferring transactional logs and audit trail information to maintain a history for recordkeeping purposes. There may also be requirements to conduct a data cleanup prior to migration, which, if this approach is adopted, will need to be taken into account as part of the implementation strategy.

Situations can also arise where an existing system stores metadata relating to documents, and there might be no plans for it to be decommissioned. For example, a maintenance system might reference documents and rely upon the availability of that metadata for other operational modules. In these cases, the enterprise will need to consider how it plans to implement an integrative approach such that the materials management system has access to the document-related metadata that it requires for other operations, meanwhile storing metadata (and potentially versioning metadata) in an IDCM repository management solution.

Migration from Local Registers

Many business units and workgroups use spreadsheets, word-processing documents, or locally developed databases to register metadata relating to their documents. These registers enable them to search for documents based on defined keywords, and the system provides a reference as to the location of the document in the file system. These registers provide valuable metadata that could be imported into the IDCM repository manager, in association with the document objects on the file system.

Consequently, enterprises should examine whether these types of metadata repositories exist and whether they contain metadata that better describes documents than the file name extensions given to objects in the file system. Depending on the quality of the data, it may be feasible to perform migration of the data from these local database registers once a cleanup operation has been effected.

Migration of Document Objects

Most suppliers are able to offer (or source) tools that will assist the bulk load of documents from existing repositories, if this is a requirement. These tools should be able to offer validation of objects and metadata derived from local registers that are used to describe documents, to ensure that data and objects are correctly associated in the IDCM solution.

However, enterprises need to examine their requirement for the migration of document objects from an existing file system. When we consider the limitations of managing digital documents in current environments (Chapter 3), we can understand that the metadata associated with documents may be nothing more than file names, many of which are not useful in describing the contents of the document.

Requirements for object migration may need to be examined in terms of the nature of the documents, the existing metadata applying to the documents, accessibility, search and retrieval, recordkeeping, and security implications. The requirements need to take into account the overall value of the documents to the organization.

Migration Implications

Aside from reviewing the cleanliness of data in existing registers and repositories, organizations may need to give consideration to mapping classification systems that are implemented in current registry systems or DMS to the IDCM solution. For example, it is not uncommon in organizations for multiple classification systems to be used for file and document management, and for managing drawing and Web content.

If the organization intends to standardize on a classification scheme that supports its business operations, there may be a requirement to reclassify data and objects that are migrated from current systems. If that is the case appertaining, then there will need to be a user requirements specification prepared to map data and objects registered under the current scheme to the new classification model.

Backfile Conversion

The enterprise might consider the conversion of inactive physical documents to digital image, which is often called "backfile conversion." Careful consideration needs to be given to the scope and requirements for backfile conversion, because there can be a tendency to underestimate the effort. Research published in Australia in 1993 (Deloitte Touche Tohmatsu, 1993) indicated that 65% of organizations surveyed had underestimated the document conversion effort. Results of a similar survey published in 1997 (Deloitte Touche Tohmatsu, 1997) reported similar results, with between 60 and 65% of organizations surveyed underestimating the document conversion effort.

Backfile conversion from a novice's perspective might appear to be a simple exercise, but the analyst must consider the feasibility of the overall requirement in terms of meeting the organization's corporate and information management objectives. The requirement for backfile conversion needs to be rigorously examined during the feasibility study (refer to Chapter 8), in terms of the operational, technical, and financial feasibility of converting collections of existing physical documents to digital image format. Indeed, the backfile conversion process may need to be reviewed as a separate project or subproject to the overall IDCM requirement.

When considering backfile conversion, the analyst needs to closely examine the document collection and the value of converting the collection (or components of the collection) to image format. As with the analytical processes that we described for scanning active documents, it is necessary for the analyst to consider the type, characteristics, and quality of the documents and potential implications for scanning. The analyst also needs to consider the level of preassembly required (such as removal of staples) and batching requirements (e.g., annualized files), prior to imaging, as well as the current methods of registering the documents. Also, the analyst needs to consider the types of documents, volumes, sizes, formats, and the implications for throughput and image capture.

The organization needs to consider the type of service delivery model that might be most relevant for performing the backfile conversion. If an organization considers that it will perform the backfile conversion in-house, then it may need to undertake a risk assessment that takes into account:

- The size and complexity of the work;
- The number of scanners required to throughput the volume of documents within the time frames required (There may be a requirement to have different types of scanners to meet the requirements of different sizes of documents.);
- The skills and experience of internal resources in terms of capabilities (project management, assembly, batching and indexing techniques, digital scanning, inspection and registration effort) to undertake large-scale conversions; and
- Whether managing backfile conversion is an essential core business activity for the enterprise, and if not, whether the organization should perform the service in-house.

Based on the outcomes of the risk assessment, the enterprise might wish to continue with a strategy to manage the conversion in-house, or it may wish to consider letting a contract for the backfile conversion to a service bureau. If the business solution option is to contract to a service bureau, then a service specification (Fruscione, 1995) should be developed and form part of the contract executed between the enterprise and bureau service.

The specification for a backfile conversion project should include (as a minimum) the following types of requirements:

- Definition on the background of the requirement;
- Definition of the document collection to be converted to image format [document types, volumes, characteristics (e.g., sizes, single/duplex, colors, legibility, fragility, etc.);
- Scope of the requirement, including a description of the end-to-end processes required (from document collection to return) and security requirements;
- Conversion strategy, including options for scanning onsite or offsite, collection and return operations, the storage and disposal of physical copies of documents;
- Specifications for quality reference standard(s) against which the quality of scanned images and captured metadata can be tested;
- Definition of specific conversion requirements, including:
  - Tracking documents requiring conversion
  - Preparing documents for scanning (including special assembly requirements)
  - Scanning drawings to meet the standard(s) defined in the quality reference
  - Inspecting images to assure quality scanning

- Capturing and validating metadata to assure the quality of index data captured during the scanning process
- Using media and methodology for return of scanned objects and metadata
- Uploading images to repository and metadata to enterprise systems, and validating association links between metadata and objects;
- Definition of project management requirements and the application of quality standards for all phases of the conversion process; and
- Definition of risk and associated mitigation strategies.

Given the research outcomes (that we have mentioned in this section) relating to backfile conversion projects, it is recommended that enterprises clearly validate the business need by determining operational, technical, and financial feasibility. If the business need satisfies these three aspects of feasibility, then organizations should clearly articulate their requirements for backfile conversion in a specification. This specification will be the basis for seeking proposals and can form part of the contract with the service bureau that is awarded the conversion work.

EXTENDED REQUIREMENTS ANALYSIS

We discussed in Chapter 6 how the implementation of an IDCM solution within an enterprise might require a phased implementation strategy. There may be an initial site, workgroup, or business application that will be the pathfinder implementation for the remaining sites and applications within an enterprise. We have been using the purchasing and contracts group of a supply department as an example site. However, the following circumstances may apply:

- The purchasing and contracts group does not manage documents that support the asset maintenance management processes of the enterprise. These types of documents might have unique characteristics that distinctly differentiate them from contract documents. For example, there may be a requirement to access asset maintenance documents from a GIS or asset management system, or both.
- The purchasing and contracts group does not have a requirement to access drawings during the design and construction phases of an engineering project or during operational and maintenance phases. There may be such a requirement for the engineering department.

If we did not take these circumstances into account, then risks such as the following may apply:

- The selected IDCM software might suit purchasing and contracts but may not be suited to maintaining asset maintenance documents, or may not have proven interfaces to GIS.
- The enterprise might end up with an IDCM that manages contract documents but may not feature rich drawing management functionality (refer to Chapter 17).

Consequently, it may well be prudent to extend the requirements analysis of the business environment beyond the purchasing and contracts group to include a diverse group of other business units, or for other specific document processing applications. There might not be a need to understand detailed requirements for end-to-end business processes. It may be sufficient to understand the diverse range of processes, the different types of documents and formats, and the complex relationships between documents that exist within the enterprise.

SUMMARY

While there is a tendency in the information systems industry for participants to promote the concept of a solution that meets "user requirements," quite frequently, inadequate attention is given to the actual user requirements analysis. For example:

- Too often, practitioners lack knowledge about the extent of effort required to scope, define, and develop *user requirements*.
- Frequently, analysts confuse *user requirements* with the *system requirements* (i.e., functionality) of an IDCM.
- Often, management allows too little time and allocates too few skilled and experienced resources to conduct thorough requirements analysis.

The failure to identify, understand, analyze, and define user requirements adequately may represent a significant risk to the project, because the users are those who will have to work with the system and will judge it from its usability and functional, operational, and performance effectiveness. The final arbiter of the success of an IDCM implementation system is not the project team or the supplier, but the end users who have to utilize the system as part of their day-to-day work environment.

In the next chapter, we will look at the types of analysis that can apply to the development of functional specifications for digital office documents. This is the first of a number of chapters devoted to functional components of the *system requirements* for an IDCM solution.

ENDNOTES

[1] When carried out in libraries, it may be called reference service.
[2] Embodied in principles such as *respect des fonds*, which requires that record series remain in original order and not be intermingled with material emanating from other agencies.

Chapter 12

Functional Requirements – Digital Office Documents

OVERVIEW

This chapter is the first in a series that reviews the requirements analysis and definition for IDCM functional requirements. We noted in Chapter 10 that functional statements are an integral part of the development of system requirements specifications for IDCM systems, as distinct from the user requirements that we covered in Chapter 11.

In this chapter, we focus on the functional requirements analysis of digital documents within the office environment of business and government enterprises. We consider requirements that are applicable to most types of these documents. Some characteristics that are specific to email, digital drawings, imaging, workflow, and Web content, are discussed in separate chapters. We also provide a series of functionality checklists that practitioners should find useful when defining the functional requirements for IDCM.

Our objectives are to explain the attributes and how these may be expressed in requirements analysis for:

- Document authoring;
- User profiles;
- Document volumes;
- Document capture;
- Metadata utilization;
- Storage handling;
- Version control;
- Renditions;
- Compound documents;
- Association through hyperlinks;

- Full-text indexing and retrieval;
- Document viewing;
- Printing;
- Security and audit; and
- Scheduling for archives or disposal.

DOCUMENT AUTHORING TOOLS

Many enterprises have implemented computer networks consisting of client and server architecture, which enable users to create and save documents at their desktop, then store, share, and print these documents using the facilities of the computer network.

The types of desktop authoring tools that are generally provided consist of word-processing, spreadsheet, presentation graphics, and email facilities, and may include more specialized tools such as project management software, drawing tools, and Web authoring tools, along with specific types of desktop publishing tools.

Many of the authoring packages that are available save files in their own file formats particular to the application. Consequently, enterprises are faced with a document management paradigm that includes formatted and unformatted text, as well as a variety of formats for images, video, sound, drawings, graphics, Web content, and physical documents.

Enterprises may also have provided some users with particular types of desktop authoring tools designated for specific purposes. These can include mathematical calculation tools and other types of scientific analysis tools that may not be widely distributed.

There is a requirement to determine the authoring software used on desktop computers (PCs) to create, update, and view electronic documents within the enterprise. Practitioners need to conduct a full review of personal productivity tools within an enterprise, taking into account not only the typical office suite of software tools, but also engineering drawing tools, project management software, and similar types of applications.

It may not be possible to determine all desktop software within an enterprise, because some workgroups have the autonomy to acquire particular applications designed to help them meet the contingencies of business. However, there should be an attempt to define all of the applications and file formats that will be managed by IDCM.

The definition of desktop authoring software can be represented in the requirements specification as a checklist along the lines that we show in Table 1 to indicate the minimal information to be defined in the specification.

Table 1: Checklist for Desktop Authoring Tools

Requirements specification — Minimum information about desktop authoring software:
▪ The name of the desktop authoring application.
▪ The filename extension that denotes the file format.
▪ Usage scenarios — Define whether the application is used enterprise wide or is confined to specific workgroups. If the latter, identify the relevant workgroups.

USER PROFILES

Users of document management have varying requirements. Some require the functionality to create and save documents, view and print documents, and participate in a document workflow. Other users simply have the requirement to view documents, or a particular set or types of documents. For example, in a pharmaceuticals environment, personnel in the manufacturing division may only have the requirement to access and view standard procedures and operating instructions.

It is important to have a clear analysis of user profiles so that required functionality is determined. This information is quite difficult to assemble in large enterprises, because there is a high degree of mobility of the workforce, and there is also the need to consider what contracted resources will require access to the IDCM system. However, as the costs of IDCM are often structured based on the types of functionality required by users throughout the enterprise, best efforts should be made to determine the user profiles.

Consideration should be given to whether the functionality required by the users is best met by providing document management functionality within a desktop operating environment (such as MS Windows), or whether their specific requirements can be met through a Web browser environment.

A basic checklist for a requirements specification is provided in Table 2. Note that it may be necessary to differentiate this profile information by geographical location within large enterprises.

Table 2: Checklist for User Profiles

Requirements specification — Basic user profile information:
• The scope of the user base. • The functionality required of IDCM for each group of user. • The profile type (operating system or Web browser). • The anticipated concurrent number of system users.

DOCUMENT VOLUMES

Enterprises typically have little knowledge of the number of digital office documents created or received. There is a need to have a clear understanding of present and future likely volumes (if this type of information can be projected) of digital documents. This helps to determine the information architecture for the deployment of an IDCM system.

Analysis of current holdings of digital documents is typically conducted by examination of the logical file shares on an enterprise's networked file servers. This can be a complex and time-consuming task, and enterprises may make use of a script to help practitioners obtain detailed information about the types of information required. It would be useful to also ascertain the volume of each type of document format in each logical share.

It is difficult to obtain information about documents stored on individual desktop hard drives or removable media (e.g., diskettes), and quite often, the decision is taken to disregard these documents. However, the practitioner needs to be fully apprised of the types of documents that may be stored on local hard drives or removable media, as there

Table 3: Checklist for Document Volumes

Requirements specification — Document volume basics:
▪ Location of the file server(s).
▪ Logical share name.
▪ Used storage capacity.
▪ Projected storage requirements.
▪ Conversion requirements.
For each logical storage device, a linked tabulation of:
▪ Logical share name (and hard drive names and removable media).
▪ Document formats (specify).
▪ Volume of documents for each specified format.

may be substantial implications if core business documents are not migrated to the DMS from these types of file stores.

In some circumstances, legacy file formats may require conversion, or a proportion of physical documents may require digitization, and volume estimates will be necessary for the migration program and for subsequent storage requirements.

A basic requirements specification for document volumes would include the checklist in Table 3.

DOCUMENT CAPTURE

Digital documents are typically created using desktop authoring tools in the following manner:

- **Create a new document from a template.**

  Many desktop applications, such as word-processing systems, provide the facility to create templates. These are files that contain formatting to allow a document to be created for a specific purpose (such as reports, specifications, and correspondence items such as memos, minutes, agendas, facsimiles, and letters). Typically, standard templates are stored in a template folder on a networked drive. The author keys the required data into the template document, using predetermined captions within the relevant template as a guide. Some templates are configured to help standardize presentation of documents, for example, by generating header and footer information, including objects such as logos, and providing page numbers and copyright notifications.

  An enterprise that has a managed forms program will also have templates for these, so that versions of forms used for capturing data via paper-based forms or screen input are generated and controlled. Although the same data may be required of either version, there can be variation in design to accommodate direct screen entry as opposed to scanned or keyed entry from paper forms.

  There may be variations in templates for Web content that correspond to documents originally produced through templates in word-processing software. Although the content is the same, and even if the word-processing software purports to provide renditions in markup form suitable for Web presentation, formatting variations may require alternative templates. This can happen, for example, when information architecture for Web display includes use of frames or banners as part of the screen assembly.

- **Create a new blank document.**

  Most desktop authoring applications provide the facility to create a new blank document. In reality, the blank document is usually based on the application's native blank-document template. In the case of Web content, new documents created newly for a publishing program, rather than being introduced from a DMS, are likely to be produced within the constraints of style sheets.

- **Reuse an electronic document.**

  The author opens an existing document and saves the document as a new document, or version, and then edits the document; or edits the document, then saves it as a new document or version.

- **Generate database reports.**

  Digital documents may also be generated as reports from database applications. These reports are typically saved as part of the application system storage module, or are exported to desktop tools, such as a spreadsheet or a word-processing document, and are then saved in a nested folder on a local file server.

  When databases are used to help with dynamic creation of Web content, the data will obviously have already been created and controlled through a DBMS, possibly through Web-based forms. The extracted data will typically be presented within the confines of static material (also subject to forms control) that may include banners, logos, and links to support navigation, such as breadcrumb trails that show a hierarchical or linked pathway leading to the present screen.

- **Scan documents to image format.**

  Imaging technology may be used to capture electronic documents. For further details, see Chapter 15 on document imaging and recognition technologies.

Electronic documents may be received as email messages, or attachments to emails, or by copying files from removable media. Some particular characteristics of these are considered in Chapter 13.

Documents received on diskette, CD-ROM, and other media may be captured by simple transfer of the files to a file system, personal drive, or removable media. Users typically achieve this by using standard operating system file management tools (such as MS Windows Explorer).

Where organizations have adopted template-based creation processes, a key limitation may be that an electronic document is generated from a superseded template. This can occur when:

- Document templates have been updated but not versioned correctly or not distributed to all users (including laptop users).

- A user creates a new document from an existing document that was created using an earlier (now out of date) template.

- Hard copies of templates used as forms may be in use, even though the template may have been superseded.

- There may be no synchronization mechanism (either manually, electronically, or written procedure) to update templates stored on certain laptop computers.

A user can create a document with a current template and save it. If it is modified later, the template upon which it was based may have changed. If the user realizes that an old template has been used, the user may attempt to put the contents of the document into the new template.

However, if this is accomplished by opening a new document based on the new template, then copying the entire contents of the old document into the new document and saving it, the outcome may not work as expected. For example, if the new template had any formatting changes such as font, sizing, etc., the new template format changes may be lost when the old document is transferred into the new template.

When a user needs to create a document based on a template, the user may have difficulty identifying the template required. This may be due to a combination of the current naming and classification conventions, lack of retrieval tools, and the large number of corporate and site-specific templates maintained by enterprises. This may result in the user creating a new blank document, cloning an old document, or using an incorrect template. Therefore, part of the analysis may involve consideration of whether an organization's existing template collection should be rationalized.

Often, there are no management controls over save regimes, which is a particular problem when authors reuse existing material to create new documents or versions and save the new contents with the same file name and version.

When considering the functionality required of IDCM, users must be able to create and receive digital documents using desktop applications in a nonintrusive manner. In other words, the IDCM system should not be perceived as an additional burden during document creation. Users should be able to create and receive documents using the same desktop tools with which they are familiar and should not be required to activate procedures that place additional burdens on their document processes.

The IDCM system should provide the capability to integrate with templates created by authoring applications, to enable business users to capture key information relating to fax, email, and a wide range of template-initiated documents, such as reports, memoranda, minutes, agendas, letters, and specifications.

Where a template is available, the desktop application should invoke the template from the IDCM system. The storage of templates in the repository will provide a managed environment for templates, so that the correct version of the template will be presented when invoked at the desktop.

The IDCM system must allow users to save electronic documents into its repository from within office desktop applications. The integration of a DMS with office productivity suites and email clients must be transparent to the user during the capture process, for example, when the user saves a document, it is achieved in the normal manner for that application.

The system might also be required to provide the capability to capture types of electronic document formats other than those from office applications, including images from workgroup level document imaging applications. This may be extended to include reports from business information systems and possibly output from plant control systems.

Depending on the requirements of the enterprise, the save regime within the IDCM system should also enable users to save documents to external stores such as a network file systems, local hard drive, diskette, or CD-RW.

Table 4: Checklist for Digital Document Capture

Consider whether the following functions are applicable to the requirement, and determine the level of relevance (mandatory or optional):

- Users able to save and register ("check-in") digital document objects to the IDCM system from defined desktop authoring tools; the required applications should be defined in a list of document authoring tools in the user requirements specification.
- Check-in/check-out (and search functions) integrates at a menu (or icon) level within common desktop authoring tools (e.g., office productivity suites and email clients).
- IDCM system integrates with office productivity suites so that data captured in a document registration profile is automatically populated into an associated template, or vice versa.
- Multiple "save" regimes are supported, with the default being the IDCM system, i.e., save to the IDCM repository, save to a file system (server or workstation, or removable media).
- Check-in/check-out functions integrate at an icon (or similar) level with the Web browser.
- Predefined save "protocols" are supported, based on document class and application type.
- Registration profile invoked when a document on a file system is checked in to the IDCM repository.
- New documents may be assembled from existing documents and document fragments, without recreating the information.
- Save to IDCM repository, capability restricted on document types not preauthorized.

IDCM can also provide an environment that allows a high degree of reuse of existing document assets by enabling users to assemble new documents from existing documents and document fragments, without recreating the information.

In many organizations, there are document types that may be saved by a user that are not approved by the enterprise, such as particular types of Internet content downloads, e.g., MP3 files. Therefore, an organization may wish to provide controls over file types that may be saved within the repository.

The requirements specification should include a definition of how organizations create and receive digital documents. It may also include a definition of the ways in which enterprises typically generate and receive electronic documents.

It may also include a list of the templates currently used, indicating the template name and its purpose and usage scenarios, such as its availability enterprise wide or restricted to specific workgroups. Table 4 is a checklist to guide the compilation of functionality required of IDCM for creation and receipt of digital office documents.

METADATA REGISTRATION AND VALIDATION

Many enterprises have no standards for identifying and recording electronic document metadata. Some have a standard whereby document names, which may include path names, are inserted into document footers at least in the case of word-processed files. Metadata are essentially application dependent and can be largely captured automatically by the desktop authoring application. Most enterprises have not developed and implemented document naming conventions. The usual situation is that authors give file names to electronic documents when saved, but typically, there is little rigor applied to naming of documents. Many authors do not make full use of the long filename capability offered by the desktop operating system and frequently describe documents with file names that are almost meaningless.

Table 5: Checklist for Metadata Registration and Validation

Consider the applicability and relevance of the following functionality: <ul><li>Intuitive interface for registration.</li><li>Sets of attributes may be associated with classes of document.</li><li>Unique item identifier generated for each object stored in the system.</li><li>Values (date, author, and other attributes common to a particular class of document) may be prepopulated based on user profile and document and application class.</li><li>Value designation may be assigned (such as, "Controlled," "Vital," "Important," "Workgroup," and "Personal").</li><li>Personalized default settings enabled in user profiles.</li><li>Data entered in document template fields to be validated and stored as metadata.</li><li>User registration minimized based on document class (e.g., personal documents).</li><li>Existing metadata profile may be updated to change document class and to correct errors.</li><li>Dynamic desktop may be configured to user's most frequent registration choices (e.g., ability to register some documents with consistent metadata other than the document title).</li><li>Data validation using mandatory fields.</li><li>Data validation by invoking unique values.</li><li>Data validation using controlled lists for specific fields where values are restricted.</li><li>Data validation during registration of free-text fields (e.g., use of spell checker).</li><li>Data validation using integrated keyword thesaurus.</li></ul>

There is generally a requirement for enterprises to review the current methods for applying metadata and document naming conventions. Often, organization-naming conventions for documents are not applied, because they are too difficult to implement and maintain. Document authors are renowned for using nondescriptive filenames, and they fail to include document property information (with the exception where document file names may be included in document footers). Consequently, it is frequently difficult for users to rapidly access and retrieve documents in a simple manner.

We made reference in Chapter 3 to the usefulness of naming conventions, and in Chapter 7, we referred to developments in metadata standardization. These should be taken into account when considering the ways in which metadata will be applied.

The IDCM system must be able to record consistent metadata about a document to facilitate its retrieval. The impact on the end user should be minimized wherever possible by automatically collecting as much metadata as possible from the user's system environment, from default values associated with document templates, and from the specific application being used to create the document. Essential data would be validated before being stored in an IDCM database, using techniques such as mandatory fields, controlled lists, and default settings based on document or user profiles. Once the data have been validated, the document may then be saved into the repository.

A checklist for defining metadata registration and validation requirements is shown in Table 5.

LOGICAL STORAGE REGIMES

When a document is created or updated, the author adds content, and the document may be saved to the local file server, hard disk, or removable media, or be printed or discarded without saving. Typically, within enterprises, users are encouraged to save documents to the appropriate logical network drive. However, documents may not

Table 6: Checklist for Logical Storage

Logical storage – Functionality considerations:

- Documents stored in the native format of the authoring application.
- Documents may also be stored in recognized standard formats (e.g., XML, HTML, or PDF).
- Nested graphical folders represent logical views of documents.
- File classification scheme (or similar option).
- IDCM administrator may create or modify folders within the FCS.
- Documents may be represented in a folder and in multiple (virtual) folders.
- Documents may be moved between folders and maintain referential integrity of links to metadata.
- Documents may be promoted easily within FCS structure with minimal add and modify metadata.
- Related documents may be associated (e.g., documents relating to a project).
- Folder may be deleted – Function cannot delete a physically stored document.
- Folder schema integrated with desktop operating system and Web browser.

always be saved to a managed drive. Instead, they may be resident on a hard drive, diskette, or other type of removable media, or printed then discarded without saving.

Digital documents are generally stored in their native format, regardless of data representation, including formatted and unformatted text, email, templates, images, technical drawings, plans, photographs, sound, and video clips. Detailed examination of data types and their relationship with document types is outside our scope, but Duyshart (1997) provides a useful overview. The documents are usually stored in nested folders contained on shared logical network file server drives, personal network drives, local hard drives, or removable media.

In addition to the authoring application's native format, the IDCM system may also store documents in a recognized standard format (e.g., PDF, HTML, or XML) that is printer independent. In such cases, it may be necessary to decide whether faithful preservation of formatting information is required or forsaken in favor of the ability to retain content and represent it differently.

The IDCM system should enable storage of documents in a manner that allows them to be retrieved easily — a combination of registration details and save location may provide this capability. Potential save scenarios could be hierarchical folder structures, an FCS, or a combination of these options.

The system should support logical, nested cabinet and folder storage hierarchies, preferably as a direct integration with the operating system exploration functions and Web browser environment. It should allow documents to be promoted from one hierarchical level to another. For example, documents that have been managed at a workgroup level might be promoted to an enterprise structure, where appropriate.

The system should allow an IDCM administrator to create the folders within each structure for storing electronic documents within an approved FCS. This capability of folder creation within the FCS should be disabled for other IDCM users within workgroups.

Table 6 gives guidance for determining and defining the types of logical storage functionality required of an IDCM system.

VERSION CONTROL

A number of scenarios may apply to version control in organizations that have not implemented a managed document environment. The following examples are for guidance:

- Version controls may be applied to certain controlled documents (such as drawings or contract documents).
- There is usually only limited or no version control applied to standard templates, which are the guides used to create important business documents.
- There are generally no business rules for identification and control of document versions on the majority of documents.
- Individuals or workgroups may apply simplistic version control measures to their own documents that are at odds with supposed institutional controls.

The following types of methods might be used (singularly or mixed) when version control is applied without the benefits of a DMS.

- Allocate a filename and then a numeric or alphanumeric code (e.g., 0.1) to a filename, then increment the code when a new version of a document is saved.
- Manage physical copies of the documents as the primary version of the document.
- Use a computer or manual register to store version details.

Where enterprises apply version controls without the benefits of a DMS, the controls are usually managed manually by a designated user (or users) within the enterprise, and therefore, are prone to human error.

It is important to determine the types of version control processes that exist within the enterprise. Version control implemented using the limited measures and techniques described above, may cause the following problems:

- The controls are usually managed manually by a designated user (or users) within the enterprise, and therefore, they are prone to human error. The manual version control of electronic documents applied on an ad hoc basis provides ineffective versioning control and may be easily breached (for example, forgetting to increment the manual version number, multiple files in nested folders).
- Standard templates may be stored on desktop computers, rather than on servers, which means that the latest version of a template has to be distributed to each desktop, using distribution software or manually.
- These same templates generally have to be distributed to laptop computers, which represents a challenge in an environment where workers are becoming increasingly mobile in their business operations.
- Sharing of documents becomes difficult due to the diverse range of individual versioning techniques, and because users may not understand another staff member's technique. Users may not feel comfortable with existing methods and may not have the confidence that they are accessing the latest version of a document.
- A user might store copies of the electronic document in their own user space so that they know it is the "right version," or print and store a hard-copy of the latest version. These methods exacerbate the problem, because a locally saved electronic document (or printed version) may be superseded, and therefore, the user would be accessing the wrong document.

- Users on a computer network may be required to access documents from a centralized logical file share. Instances can occur, particularly to improve speed of access and retrieval, where remote sites copy documents to local shares. This uncontrolled copying represents a potential data integrity issue, because users may continue to access a local copy of a document that has been superseded.

Version control is paramount for effective management of an enterprise's business documents. The IDCM system must ensure that business documents are saved into the repository and cannot be subsequently altered or tampered with, i.e., the original is not removed from the IDCM repository and is not directly modified. The system must feature facilities that avoid update conflict by the implementation of check-out/check-in services.

It should be a requirement that the original document in the IDCM repository is never to be edited directly, but a working copy of the file can be checked out for the user. The IDCM system must lock a checked-out document, preventing other changes, but permitting read-only access. The system may also be required to signify clearly that a

Table 7: Checklist for Version Control

Version control – functionality considerations:
<ul><li>Version control is supported for all types of electronic documents deposited in the IDCM system.</li><li>Document checkout is from the IDCM system to a file system (server/workstation) for editing.</li><li>Checkout feature locks the document within the IDCM system (preventing changes, but permitting read-only access) and makes a working copy of the file for the user.</li><li>Visible lock serves to identify that the document is being revised.</li><li>Check-in creates a new version of the document and copies the changed working copy from the user to the IDCM system, and then releases the lock on the document.</li><li>A new document begins a new version chain.</li><li>Multiple versions of a document are supported. How many versions are required to be kept online?</li><li>Latest version is default version for update and display.</li><li>Previous versions may be accessed as read only, and with a warning that it is not the current version.</li><li>Authorized user(s) may have the capability to create new copies of documents that discontinues application of version control.</li><li>Document may be copied from the IDCM system to a file system (server/workstation).</li><li>Document may be checked out or copied to a laptop or handheld palm device. (Need to confirm synchronization of device and repository on check-in.)</li><li>Document may be checked out or copied from the IDCM system to a diskette or other removable media.</li><li>Version control for new documents can be optionally selected by the user and is the default for specific classes of document types or templates, e.g., reports and memoranda.</li><li>Assign default (but editor overridable) security profiles to each version of a document, enabling restrictions on user access, i.e., they are only able to see the current (or specified earlier) version.</li><li>Recent versions of documents are retained on-line – previous versions are available near-line or off-line for audit or reference purposes. (State the number of versions required on-line.)</li><li>Metadata is versioned and synchronized with the document version.</li><li>Capture and display of current document editor and date and time last saved are part of the version control metadata.</li><li>Configurable metadata are associated with versions to identify status and purpose (e.g., permanent, draft, final, etc.).</li><li>Audit reports are provided on versions.</li><li>Predefined user or group with an interest in a particular type of document is notified when a revision has occurred.</li><li>Document comparison function may be invoked for selected versions of a document.</li></ul>

document is being revised and also maintain a distribution list of users who shall be notified when a revision has occurred. In the case of published Web content there is likely to be an authorization structure so that a document is not released until it carries the imprimatur of the designated authority.

Once the user has completed the changes to a document, the document is "checked in." Check-in creates a new version of the document in the IDCM system and copies the changed working copy from the user to the IDCM vault, and then releases the lock on the document.

Suggestions for version control functionality are provided in Table 7.

RENDITIONS

We use rendition to mean the production of an alternative digital data representation of the same document. Therefore, there may be multiple digital objects that manifest the same document. Documents may be created as a rendition of the native format, such as a PDF or HTML object rendered from a word-processing document, particularly where it is planned to publish content to the intranet (or Internet). Another example are word-processed content rendered to RTF format for exchange with an external party, or a JPG image rendered from BMP or TIF file formats. Alternatively, there may be situations where documents authored in markup formats native to the Web are rendered in print publishing formats for physical documents.

It is necessary to obtain a clear picture of the requirements for rendition management within their respective enterprises, and the extent to which alternative renditioning is provided for Internet/intranet display, print publishing, or exchange with other systems. There may also be significant requirement for word-processing documents to be rendered to PDF format for distribution by email or diskette to business partners or service providers.

Version changes to an original word-processing document may be managed "manually," which may present a risk if the original document is updated, and the rendered HTML or PDF version is not updated. Consequently, the IDCM needs to maintain the interrelationship between rendered documents during versioning processes. In this way, users of the rendered versions can be assured that they are accessing the most current version of the original document, regardless of its format.

Table 8 lists the types of functionality that might be expected from the IDCM system for managing renditions.

Table 8: Checklist for Rendition Management

Rendition management – basic functionality:
• Multiple renditions of the same document may be generated and managed by the IDCM system. • Integrity of the various renditions is assured during the process of versioning a document. • New renditions may be generated when the original source document version is checked in and saved. • Document owner may be notified when a new rendition of a versioned document is available for print publishing.

COMPOUND DOCUMENTS

We use compound document to mean a document created at the time of viewing that comprises components from several digital sources in different formats brought together for display so that they manifest themselves as a coherent document.

Compound documents within the office document environment are, in many cases, produced and managed through the use of technology such as CORBA and DCOM. While this technology allows the development of complex compound documents, it has limitations with regard to access and version control of embedded or linked documents.

Increased use of intranet and Internet sites for document publishing and distribution is likely to increase the need for managing compound documents (e.g., one Web page object containing a mix of HTML/XML with associations to JPG, PDF, TIF documents) and maintaining explicit linkages created between parent–child documents. Compound documents also exist when a virtual document is created based on multiple fragments that are obtained from source SGML formatted documents.

There is a high risk of integrity problems in maintaining relationships between linked documents without the implementation of IDCM. Close examination of compound document requirements is necessary.

For example, linked spreadsheets may be used in a finance department for managing budgets and accounts. If the spreadsheets are migrated to an IDCM system, it needs to be able to identify and manage the links between these documents, so that relationship integrity is maintained, particularly during document check-out and update processes.

Consideration of Web site management is important to understand what, if any versioning procedures have been employed and the extent to which these account for compound documents that represent the enterprise's business activities. It may be necessary to extend analysis where SGML formatted documents are used extensively in the organization, and review the requirements for compound document management with print publishing.

Table 9 lists the types of functionality that might be expected from the IDCM system for managing compound documents.

Table 9: Checklist for Compound Documents

Compound documents – functionality considerations:
▪ Referential integrity is maintained of multiple bidirectional relationships between documents.
▪ Components of a compound document can be checked and updated independently, or simultaneously, while maintaining integrity of compound relationship.
▪ Components of compound document may be reused (e.g., forming part of multiple parent documents).
▪ Users are enabled to view multiple bidirectional relationships between documents.
▪ Single, unique document entity is maintained regardless of the number of times it is a component or is the initiator or target of a link.
▪ User is prompted on checkout to confirm maintenance of multiple bidirectional relationships.

HYPERLINKS

Enterprises use hyperlink "anchors" within documents to enhance navigation to specific content references and to steer to other documents (including multimedia) stored on networked file systems or local hard drives. Hyperlinks are also used in much

Table 10: Checklist for Hyperlink Navigation

Hyperlink navigation — functionality considerations:

- Hyperlinks may be inserted into a document stored in the IDCM system.
- Hyperlinks may be inserted into specific content within a document stored in the IDCM system.
- IDCM browse and search functionality facilitates creation of hyperlinks.
- Navigation by hyperlinks that reference another filename and invoke viewing of the document or retrieval of a relevant document is possible.
- Navigation by hyperlinks that reference content within another file and invoke retrieval of relevant file, and position cursor at anchor link, is possible.
- Latest version of a document is displayed when navigating to hyperlink.
- Notification is displayed when the anchor link is not contained in the latest version of the document.
- User selects relevant previous version, where anchor link is not contained in the latest version.
- Consider requirements/interfacing/security issues for any documents stored outside IDCM repository that hyperlink to documents stored in repository.

the same way with marked-up pages developed by enterprises for deployment of content on their Internet or intranet Web sites. Hyperlinks are typically displayed in formatted text (such as word-processing documents, HTML pages, and similar formatted text) in a default color, or with distinctive representation, such as underlining.

Many organizations use the hyperlink functionality within word-processing systems to create links to content within policy documents or to navigate to other documents for important business documents, such as policy and procedural documentation. For example, each procedure document within workplace health and safety documentation could include references to multiple procedural documents and contain hyperlinks to those documents. The hyperlinks between procedural documents give end users quick access to referenced documents.

Given the widespread use of hyperlinks within digital office documents, end users will have an expectation that the IDCM system supports hyperlink navigation capabilities. The analyst needs to analyze and specify requirements and consider the change management implications if a candidate IDCM solution does not offer hyperlink management functionality, but offers to manage references to documents by alternative means, such as using metadata to link referenced documents.

Where an IDCM solution supports hyperlink navigation for documents within its repository, the situation might occur where documents stored external to the system (e.g., on networked file systems) contain hyperlinks to documents within the repository. In these circumstances, there are potential interfacing requirements and also security factors to be considered.

Even when full functionality is available for published Web content, organizations will probably wish to follow standards relating to provision of content for users who are hearing- or sight-impaired. This means mainly that text alternatives to embedded images or audio should be provided, but it may extend to a management system to ensure that there are text alternatives to hyperlinked audio or image files, on the assumption that such users have text-interpretation equipment.

Table 10 lists the types of functionality that might be expected from the IDCM for enabling hyperlink navigation.

FULL-TEXT INDEXING

Records stored in databases are usually structured so that individual data elements are stored in searchable files or tables. The advent of generic markup languages led to increasing structure of formerly unstructured textual documents, such as memoranda and correspondence. This makes documents more amenable to database structuring.

However, even when the documents are not structured, indexes to them can be created that enable searching. This is achieved by parsing the full text of the document and producing files that include data such as the relative position of words, omission of words kept in a stoplist (high-use words such as the article "the" that are unlikely to be required for retrieval). If there is markup in the document, an indication of such elements as paragraph positions might also be included.

The illustration Figure 1 shows how the indexes for the first three lines from a promotional brochure might be created in indexes with a stoplist. By storing the word positions in an index, free-text software may subsequently be used to achieve phrase searching or searching of terms in a certain proximity to each other.

If documents do not contain standard markup, then a text parser should be able to examine individual terms in documents and store the terms in searchable files. By also storing relative positions for terms, the parsing software will make provision for phrase or proximity searching.

If documents contain standard markup, for example, from a document-type definition defined within XML, then index files may also be used to store the tags (data element labels). These files enable searching to be subsequently refined to specific document elements, such as "Title," or parts of metadata as mentioned in the following section. Desirable indexing functionality is listed in the following checklist.

Figure 1: Inverted File for Full-Text Indexing.

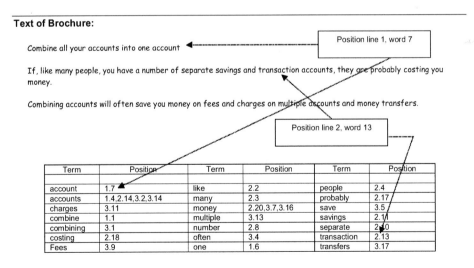

Text of Brochure:

Combine all your accounts into one account   Position line 1, word 7

If, like many people, you have a number of separate savings and transaction accounts, they are probably costing you money.

Combining accounts will often save you money on fees and charges on multiple accounts and money transfers.

Position line 2, word 13

Term	Position	Term	Position	Term	Position
account	1.7	like	2.2	people	2.4
accounts	1.4,2.14,3.2,3.14	many	2.3	probably	2.17
charges	3.11	money	2.20,3.7,3.16	save	3.5
combine	1.1	multiple	3.13	savings	2.1
combining	3.1	number	2.8	separate	2.10
costing	2.18	often	3.4	transaction	2.13
Fees	3.9	one	1.6	transfers	3.17

Assuming the stopword list: is a, all, and, are, if, have, into, of, on, they, will, you, your

Table 11: Checklist for Indexing Functions

Indexing functionality considerations:
• Ability to derive index files based upon parses of word strings.
• Ability to record relative word positions to enable subsequent phrase or proximity searching.
• Ability to derive distinct index files based upon tags from data elements identified in markup.
• Ability to stipulate stopword lists so that commonly used terms with no retrieval value are omitted from indexes.
• Consider the requirements for format filters that need to be supported by the indexing component of the solution. Specify the file formats that are required.

When full-text indexing is available, it is likely to be used also on structured data elements, such as those used to capture metadata. A data element like *title of document* may be treated in the same way as the full text, as illustrated above. However structured fields such as those containing keywords may use a combination of full-text index and an additional index that retains precoordinated keywords (known as descriptors) to assist searchers.

For example, in Figure 1, "savings accounts" does not appear as a text string, but it could be assigned as a descriptor from a thesaurus, then it would appear in that form in a browsable index file for searching.

The indexing capabilities of an IDCM solution needs to support all the file formats required for facilitating searching. Therefore, an enterprise needs to review its requirements for text indexing and stipulate the range of file formats to be supported. Consider applications such as word-processing, spreadsheet, presentation graphics, email, project management, and drawing tools, as examples, and specify the file formats.

The extent to which index files can be structured for use or are associated with controlled vocabularies such as thesauri, will have a profound effect on information retrieval, which we consider under our next heading.

SEARCHING DOCUMENTS

Most network operating systems and desktop operating systems found within enterprises provide "find" facilities that enable users to search for digital documents based on a filename or document content or both.

These tools enable users to seek content that can be restricted to a specific drive, folders, and subfolders. They may restrict the search parameters by providing filters (such as date and file type).

While these tools offer basic search and retrieval functionality, they are not always widely used within an enterprise, because general users are unaware of or are not trained to use the functionality available. They may simply prefer to browse folders or return to favorite documents.

Furthermore, there are likely to be performance restrictions on the "find" tools provided specifically where large document collections are involved, and particularly when content searches are initiated, because there is no preindexing of document contents.

A range of search tools is available that increases the performance of filename and document content searches on network systems (and desktop computers), but these tools typically do not provide a managed repository that offers version control, rendition, and compound document management.

Comprehensive search facilities of the document storage domains are a primary requirement for the implementation of an IDCM, which should be the central repository for all types of electronic documents used within the enterprise. The IDCM should give users confidence that all documents can be found there by filename or by content.

The IDCM should, therefore, provide comprehensive search and retrieval capabilities, which will greatly reduce the time required for locating and retrieving documents. The content aspects should be searchable on attribute information (owner, document title, format, description, etc.) and words in the actual content (full-text searching).

A single search tool is desirable to allow search and retrieval of documents, regardless of location and format, using content and metadata. The IDCM should provide users with levels of search mechanisms ranging from the simple to the complex. The search tool should also attempt to maximize the relevance of retrieved documents without adversely impacting performance. This may be achieved by algorithms such as frequency counts of search terms within documents.

The system should feature simplicity in searching, which may be achieved by the use of integrated menus within the authoring applications, hot buttons and shortcuts into the application of choice, or repository. Some IDCM applications integrate with Web portal technologies to provide an intuitive interface and search tools that enable searches to be activated using metadata or document contents or both. A typical approach to simple query formulation is Query By Example (QBE). With this interface, the user constructs a query by completing or partially completing a table or formatted screen. The results are usually presented in the same format as the query.

Simple searching is usually all that is necessary for searching for known documents, however, advanced searching features are necessary when the user is endeavoring to research a subject area, which may initially be poorly defined. Even if the concepts are well-defined, it may be difficult to estimate the extent of documentation available, and search flexibility is required to tailor results.

Examples of functionality that can be provided for advanced searching include the following:

- **Logical connectivity**

  This is often referred to as use of Boolean operators (after the Boolean algebra that underlies it), and essentially means that the repository is treated as a universe of documents from which subsets can be extracted using concepts associated by the logical operators, AND, OR, or NOT.

  This facility is widely used by experienced or professional online searchers. However, it is often criticized as an approach that is counterintuitive for occasional users of databases. Occasional users may confuse conversational and written use of AND, OR, and NOT with logical use of these operators.

  Explicit use of logical operators can be avoided, however, as is seen on many Internet search engines. The searcher simply enters a string of search terms as descriptors or natural language. The retrieval software searches for all of them, then produce ranked output based upon those with the highest frequency of occurrence and association.

- **Set retention**

  This feature provides for intermediate results being held in sets. Therefore, a user can associate and reassociate different components of a search in order to modify the results. The retrieved sets may be combined in different ways, to broaden or narrow the search according to requirements. This means that the software must maintain an interim history of what the searcher is doing.

- **Field limitation**

  This means that while there are default searchable fields, it is possible to confine a search to a specific field (data element type) in order to improve material. A simple example may be that it is necessary to distinguish documents produced by a person from documents produced about that person. If there are metadata that provide a data element such as *personal name descriptor*, then a search could be limited in this respect.

- **Proximity searching**

  This means that strings of terms may be searched with an operator inserted to state how far the words may appear from each other in the document content. This requires that the files storing the searchable terms must also store information about the relative positions of terms, as shown in Figure 1.

  For example, a search of a repository that contains the document shown in Figure 1 using "Find 'savings' within 3 words of 'accounts'" would retrieve this document because of the positioning information recorded in the index file.

- **Truncation**

  The wildcard facility familiar when searching filenames may also be employed for searching content. In this context, it is often known as a truncation feature and may be applied implicitly or explicitly. Explicit application may provide the ability to stipulate the extent of word stems. For example, "Find *account****" may be a way of finding content that mentions words such as "account" "accounts" "account-ing" but not "accountancy" because a three-position stem is specified using the asterisks.

  This facility is particularly useful when there is no controlled vocabulary and searching needs to be carried out on large amounts of full text with variation in expression of content, or if a database has poor quality control over data entry. It may also be useful to employ an internal truncation facility that provides for spelling variations such as in international organizations, providing a search to look for alternative spellings such as in "Find *organi*ation*** and *behavio*r**" within terms.

- **Hierarchical expansion**

  When a database is associated with a controlled vocabulary or thesaurus, it is possible to implement the retrieval software in such a way that expanded groups of terms may be searched, by reference to the controlled vocabulary.

  For example, the thesaurus of the Seattle City Clerk (2002) includes the descriptor *SOCIAL-INSURANCE*, and incorporates term relationships as follows:

  > bt SOCIAL-WELFARE
  > nt DISABILITY-INSURANCE
  > nt SOCIAL-SECURITY
  > nt UNEMPLOYMENT-COMPENSATION
  > rt SOCIAL-SERVICES

  The *nt* indicates narrower terms. In an IDCM, if a vocabulary such as this was employed, it would be possible to generate an automatic search of the *nt* terms: *DISABILITY-INSURANCE*, *SOCIAL-SECURITY*, and *UNEMPLOY-MENT-COMPENSATION* simply by entering *SOCIAL-WELFARE* as a search term.

- **Statistical association**

  This feature provides for automatic retrieval of records when the terms that are used in the content of documents (but which have NOT suggested themselves to the searcher), have a high degree of association with the terms that ARE used by the searcher.

  Degree of association is normally determined by an algorithm that compares the total number of occurrences of a word in the repository documents, with the number of times it appears jointly with other words. If the value of this exceeds a certain coefficient, then documents that contain those terms that are greater than this value, but which were not used by the searcher, are added to the retrieval result. This can lead to retrieval of a great deal of irrelevant information but may be necessary in circumstances where a wide view of documents or published Web content is sought.

- **Relevance feedback**

  With this feature, useful documents that have been retrieved following an initial search are marked, and their metadata description or content are used by retrieval software to find further documents that match the description.

  At a simple level, this may mean once the author of a useful item has been identified, the software may be sent off in search for other material by the same author. At a more developed level, the subject content metadata or indexing from the database is used for feedback, and the user is prompted to utilize this for extended searching. Where a controlled vocabulary or thesaurus is employed, then thesaurus feedback

Table 12: Checklist for Search Capabilities

Information retrieval – search functionality consideration:
■ Search on metadata (e.g., action officer, subject, etc.) and words in the actual content of the document from a single entry point.
■ Search on metadata relevant to a specific document class, e.g., memo, report, etc.
■ "Boolean operators" (and, or, not) are provided for combining metadata fields in complex searching.
■ "Boolean" to be used to formulate searches against full-text indices. (State the type of operators required.)
■ Phrase (explicit or implied) and proximity searching is based upon locations in index files.
■ Ability to retain interim search sets during a search is available, so that they may be recombined in different ways.
■ Statistical and word frequency search techniques use semantic and fuzzy logic techniques to improve search performance and reduce complexity of search constructs.
■ Search of multiple folders or restricted to specific folders, document types, or other groupings based on document location or owner is possible.
■ Browse multiple folders or a specific folder.
■ Search results may be filtered in order to increase precision.
■ Search results may be ranked in order of perceived relevance.
■ Search queries are saved for reuse.
■ Search queries are saved at enterprise and workgroup hierarchical levels.
■ Document or set of documents may be selected as being representative of relevant documents and then search and retrieve can be invoked for "like" documents.
■ Integrated thesaurus capability for searches is available.
■ Spell checking is enabled on search field.

would involve referring to the vocabulary and having the software present to the searcher terms such as those marked as *rt* (related terms as in the Seattle example above).

In addition to search formulation functionality, it may be useful for the retrieval software to provide operational support facilities additional to the searching facility. These may involve features such as in-context help for searchers. This means that the software tracks search strategy and, on request, provides suggestions for different search terminology, variation in logical operators, etc.

Another capability is for regular searches undertaken by the user at their individual desktop, to be saved, named, and stored at the desktop or user profile level until no longer required. Upon reactivating the stored search, the results are to be updated to ensure the latest documents and any additional new documents are displayed. More search features along with examples and explanation in more detail are provided by Middleton (2002).

The checklist of search capabilities in Table 12 provides a basis for functionality that might be expected from search facilities to be integrated with the IDCM.

VIEWING DOCUMENTS

Enterprise users may view documents by launching the native authoring application for the relevant document. (For example, MS *QuickView* is generally available for viewing certain types of file formats, and Adobe *Acrobat Reader* is available for viewing PDF files. A variety of tools (e.g., Kodak *Imaging* for Windows, MS *Photo Editor*) are available for viewing images.

Enterprises may continue with a strategy to launch the native authoring application as the viewing tool for a specific document. However, there may be a requirement to view documents where the native authoring tool is not available, and requirements analysis will need to determine if available viewers can accommodate this.

Examples of functionality provided by a viewing tool integrated with the IDCM are listed in Table 13. A different type of viewer may be required for viewing drawings, plans, and other types of large-size documents, and this aspect is dealt with in Chapter 17 on Drawing Management.

Table 13: Checklist for Viewing Tools

Consider the applicability and relevance of the following functionality:
• Viewer enables (relevant) documents to be displayed without loading the native authoring tool.
• Viewer supports multiple formats.
• Launch Reader for viewing PDF files.
• Viewer supports annotation tools to enable document reviewers to mark-up changes to documents.
• Annotations are managed as a separate object to the associated document.
• Checkout the native document from the viewing tool.

PRINTING DOCUMENTS

Networked laser printers and color or black and white inkjet printers are available for producing printed copies of electronic documents.

Table 14: Checklist of Printing Capabilities

Consider the applicability and relevance of the following functionality:
▪ Digital documents of standard size (e.g., letter 8.50 × 11.00 inches or A4, depending on local requirements) printed from IDCM to networked laser printers.
▪ Digital documents of larger size (e.g., size B or A3) on existing networked laser printers that support such types of trays.
▪ Provide the full range of capabilities offered by the desktop operating system environment, relevant to the functionality supported by the networked printing devices; e.g., print a selected portion of a document.

It is necessary to ascertain and define the typical procedures that apply to printing documents within the organization. A complete physical description of networked or stand-alone printers (color laser or inkjet, black and white laser or inkjet) should be provided in the physical description of the current IT environment.

Users will require the capability to print digital documents to an enterprise's networked printers directly from the IDCM system. Users may also require the same capabilities for printing provided in the desktop operating environment, such as printing a selected portion of a document.

Basic printing functionality to be supported by the IDCM system is summarized in Table 14. Different types of printing devices, such as plotters, may be required for drawings, plans, and other types of large-size documents as indicated in Chapter 17, which discusses engineering and technical drawings.

SECURITY AND AUDIT

Security over documents on networked file systems is managed via the networked operating system. Limited security is generally applied over documents stored on local hard disk drives (including laptops), and virtually no security is implemented for removable diskettes and other media, unless locked in a safe. Many organizations and users do not realize the security implications of storing documents on hard disk drives or removable media. This type of activity represents a security vulnerability to enterprises, particularly when critical business documents are stored in these environments.

Network operating system security and audit facilities are the primary means of managing user authentication and access controls to documents stored on shared file systems. The practitioner needs to determine the extent to which organizations have implemented logical and physical security over networked file systems, local hard drives, and removable media.

One or more logical drives on the network file systems may be secured according to workgroups or functional areas within the enterprise, and also secured at a lower hierarchical level, to individual users and groups. A logical drive may also be secured on an individual user basis. The requirements for the IDCM system should include a definition of the user and group security profiles that apply to folders and to specific classes of documents.

Documents can also be stored on local hard drives to restrict access to only those logging on to the machine, or if stored in the user's profile (e.g., desktop), to the specific user. The storage and securing of documents on local hard drives and use of password systems for restricting access at a document level are risks. There is no corporate knowledge of the existence of the documents secured on local hard drives, and there is typically no managed backup of hard disk resources. The physical disk may become unusable.

Some enterprises have also used desktop application security features such as password control to control document access and update. However, the use of passwords to restrict access at a document level is also a risk, because the password(s) may be lost, the people knowing the password may leave the organization, and the files may not have been backed up and become corrupted.

The requirements for security and audit capabilities of the IDCM system apply also to email, drawings, physical documents, Web content, imaging, and workflow, which have not been discussed in this chapter. Consequently, the overall functionality capabilities for security and audit within IDCM are discussed in Chapter 19.

ARCHIVES AND DISPOSAL

We need to make clear that the connotation of "archives" varies in the information professions. The term "archive" is often used in the IT industry in the context of the removal of digital documents from online direct access storage. Contrast this with how archive is used in our Glossary to describe a body of records, often with a perspective of more *permanent* storage of vital business documents.

We prefer to use the term "secondary storage" for removal of documents from online direct access storage and use the term "archive" in its traditional sense of retention of evidential records.

Enterprises may not have implemented retention and disposal regimes for the secondary storage or archival of electronic documents. Many organizations tend to solve the management issue of storing the burgeoning number of electronic documents merely by providing more magnetic, optical, CD, or DVD storage to store the documents. However, provision of more storage capacity is not really managing the document environment, but merely provides a temporary convenience.

Generally, archival and disposal practices for digital documents are jointly handled by users and IT staff, but there is typically no overall operational approach to the management of electronic documents that takes into account legal and operational business requirements.

Frequently, so-called "archival" activities are ad hoc to the extent that users may delete documents, copy documents to removable media, or may use compression tools (for example, *Winzip*) for archival purposes.

Earlier, in Chapter 2, we gave some details of how guidance is available for implementation of electronic recordkeeping strategies using the DIRKS approach (National Archives of Australia, 2000). This stepwise approach for applying the tenets of recordkeeping to digital records may usefully be considered for IDCM.

A consequence is that an IDCM system should make provision for metadata concerning retention or disposal scheduling decisions about documents, so that administrative, legal, evidentiary, historical, or scientific status may be indicated and used to precipitate actions concerning a document's retention.

When determining and analyzing the retention and disposal requirements for electronic documents, consideration should be given to whether:

• Retention scheduling has been implemented over electronic documents.

- Scheduling that has been implemented for physical documents can apply to electronic documents.
- Secondary storage strategies are defined and in place for nonpermanent documents, so that documents that have a retention life (for example, 7 years) are managed in offline storage repositories that can be accessed by the IDCM system.
- Archival strategies are in place for managing permanent technology-dependent documents, and this type of requirement might best be addressed in an enterprise's Archival Policy.

As with security and audit requirements, the archival and disposal capabilities of IDCM apply to email, drawings, physical documents, Web content, imaging, and workflow, which are examined more specifically in following chapters.

REQUIREMENTS DEFINITION

In Table 15, we give a number of examples of requirements that may be defined for utilization of digital office documents in general within IDCM.

Table 15: Functionality Examples — Digital Office Documents

Functional Statement	Comments
Desktop authoring	
Output file format utilization	State the range of file formats produced by different types of authoring software within the organization.
Record specific-purpose application integration	Identify the situations in which special purpose authoring software, such as tools for graphics support or mathematical symbols, are employed.
	These applications may be recorded in a data dictionary that supplements the document repository. It may be necessary to produce different renditions of documents for repository management.
User profiles	
Cater for usage loads	Establish the likely number of simultaneous users and system loads at different time periods.
Enable task differentiation	Establish the functionality required by different categories of user, so that access levels can be established. Minimally, this would be for viewing, input, and administration, but within these, distinction may be made at the level of providing or viewing data for data elements or naming the data elements.
Document volumes	
Provide for appropriate storage and a pathway for expansion	Establish the number of documents presently in existence by combining data from file shares and from material stored on local drives that is likely to become shared.
	This is problematic, because it means that duplication, redundancy, and multiple renditions should be estimated, along with identification of "personal" material at specific locations that should be copied to share servers, at least for backup.

Table 15: Functionality Examples — Digital Office Documents (continued)

Functional Statement	Comments
Document capture	
• Template provision	Determine if there is systematic production of templates for documents that are aligned with workflow.
	There may also be forms management that systematizes the way documents for data capture are derived and controlled.
• Creation	Itemization of responsibilities for creation and modification according to workgroup areas, along with software employed.
• Registration	A registration profile is to be maintained for repository documents with "check-in" process.
	Documents saved into a repository may have to conform to authorized form and metadata.
• Reports	Production of management reports that provide statistics on document production and
Metadata	
• Interface with authoring	Document authors should be able to add metadata additional to that which is automatically created and presented. For example, where an authored document is associated with a hard-copy document, metadata describing the physical document may be required.
	Certain metadata such as authorship and dates, or assigned defaults, should be used for prepopulation of metadata elements.
• Validation	Instances of metadata elements can be validated against a variety of possibilities ranging from numerical range limits through to thesauri, which may be used to prompt for additional terminology at creation and retrieval phases.
Logical storage	
• Formats	Identify range of native formats and renditions, and extent to which compression is employed.
• Organization	A File Classification System should conform to regulated naming, and hierarchical folders that employ the naming.
• Association	As documents are moved between folders, the integrity of links to and from them should be maintained.
Version control	
• Document types	Is there support for all document types in the repository?
• Versioning	"Check-out" provides for working copy to workstation and locks registered copy; "check-in" produces a new registered copy.
	Metadata are synchronized with document versions.
Compound documents	
• Presentation	Documents created at time of viewing require integrity to be maintained in links in both directions between documents.
• Fragments	Parts of documents may be utilized in multiple parent documents.
• Maintenance	Routine checking of links is carried out to monitor and maintain links.

Table 15: Functionality Examples — Digital Office Documents (continued)

Functional Statement	Comments
Navigation	
• Hyperlinks	Most recent versions of documents must be referenced from hyperlinks.
Indexing	
• Parsing	Index files produced from parses of word strings can record relative word positions to support subsequent contextual searching.
• Index files	Distinct index files are derived from different metadata elements to permit subsequent differentiation in searching.
Information retrieval	
• Search capability	Formulation of searches permits logical connection of concepts and ability to save set results for subsequent recombination and maintenance of search histories.
• Output display	Displays may be ranked according to algorithms that endeavor to determine relevance, for example, word frequency counts.
Presentation	
• Viewing	Facilitate document display without having to load authoring tools.
• Annotation	Provide support for notes that may be attached to documents and subsequently be managed in association with documents.
• Highlighting	Enable indication on screen displays (possibly using reverse video) or printout (using bold type) of what has led to retrieval.

SUMMARY

This chapter reviewed key aspects of managing digital office documents and considered the types of functionality that may be required of IDCM as a strategy to improve the management of digital office documents.

We included a range of checklists that practitioners may find useful as a primer for developing specifications for using an IDCM system that meets their enterprise's requirements, and concluded with a basic requirements functionality guide.

We now look at the functionality that may be required of an IDCM solution for managing a special kind of digital office document, and that is business email.

Chapter 13

Functional Requirements – Email Management

OVERVIEW

In Chapter 4, we indicated that there were various technology options available to organizations for capturing email as a record of a business transaction. We briefly examined the characteristics of two options for capturing email:

- Direct capture of email using an email management system; and
- End-user-invoked capture of email by saving an email to a DMS.

In this chapter, we examine the functional requirements that may be appropriate when compiling a specification for managing email using either the direct capture method or save to DMS.

The objectives are as follows:

- Consider requirements for managing email that evidences a business transaction or activity.
- Consider some technology solution options.
- Review the functionality that might apply when defining requirements for capturing email as a record of a business transaction or activity.

REQUIREMENTS ANALYSIS

Given the growth in use of email as a messaging tool for business transactions, it is important for enterprises to analyze business and user requirements for managing email. There should be a strategy to determine the most feasible business and technology solution options. These options should be examined during the feasibility study (Chapter 6).

During the analysis of user requirements, enterprises may wish to examine the volume of email generated and received by the organization. They may also wish to examine the types of emails received, as these may impact the business and technology solution option outcomes. The compelling requirement is to capture emails received or generated within organizations that represent a record of a business transaction or document the business activities.

Consequently, when examining its options, an enterprise might wish to make a distinction between different email types. These are sometimes differentiated as follows:

- *Personal email*: These emails are of a private nature and do not constitute a record of business transactions or activity. The use of the enterprise email system for personal email may be discouraged by the organization, depending on the style of organizational leadership, security issues (e.g., viruses), and risk management.
- *Transient email*: These may assist an enterprise in conducting its business but do not need to be retained for recordkeeping purposes. Transient emails may include such things as agendas for meetings, staff bulletins, or marketing material.
- *Business email*: These types of emails record a business transaction or document a business activity. The disposal of these types of emails should be subject to disposal authorities that meet jurisdictional and business requirements.

It is possible to come up with other categories, such as the discursive email that discusses the content of reports, research, or policy, and the email that seeks input to content development. If these or any personal or transient email contains any record of a business transaction or activity, then they need to be classified as a business email and managed accordingly.

Email technology and formats are evolving, and there may be implications for retrieval of email. This may not be a problem for emails that are subject to relatively short disposal periods, say 3 to 5 years, but may have implications for longer-term, indeed, permanent archiving of email. Consequently, organizations should closely consider their requirements for managing email within the context of recordkeeping, and review long-term retrieval implications of these technology-based records.

The organization should also consider the implications of any emerging use of email communication within the context of supporting revised business functions or processes, including notification mechanisms for workflow, interaction with customers using the Internet including the Web, or supporting processes associated with publishing content to Web sites.

TECHNOLOGY OPTIONS

When considering technology solution options, there is a diverse range of opportunities for capturing email and filtering unwanted email, and collaborating using email. However, the requirement to manage email as a *record* of a business transaction or activity may come down to a discrete range of options:

- Print the email and store it in physical format (paper or microfilm). The printed email may need to be associated with a physical file for the application of disposal authorities. This option is time-consuming and may not be sustainable with the exponential growth in the use of email for business communications.

- Implement a FCS using the existing messaging infrastructure based on folders. This option might be a piecemeal solution (depending on the size of organization and volume of email). There are still implications associated with managing personal email files and also for search and retrieval and the application of corporate-wide metadata and disposal regimes.
- Use the *direct capture* tools for managing business email.
- Implement *end user capture* of email by saving to a DMS.

We will briefly review the direct capture and end user capture options for email management.

Direct Capture

This technology incorporates systems that integrate with enterprise messaging systems to capture emails into a managed repository. Some email management systems that are used to manage email as records are integrated within the infrastructure of the relevant messaging system. Other systems act as external repositories, capturing copies of email messages that are received or generated. Either type of system may have the capability to filter out messages using predefined business logic.

The issues that may need to be addressed include the architecture of the solution and its scalability to support large and distributed organizations. There may be compatibility issues relating to the integration of the software with the specific product(s), versions, and patch releases of products used within an enterprise's messaging systems infrastructure. Other considerations include storage aspects, as systems may store emails in both the messaging system and managed repository, while others may store tags or links in the messaging system that reference emails stored in the managed repository.

When considering the solution strategy, there may be legal issues to resolve. For example, where solutions move emails from a messaging system to a managed repository, there may need to be a supportive audit trail.

End User Capture

This approach would require the implementation of a DMS that integrates with the email client software so that a user is able to save a message in the email system directly to the DMS repository. The enterprise must take care to specify the email client software and integration requirements, and validate the functionality during product assessment.

While DMS products have the capability to help organizations capture and manage emails, there are varying degrees of product maturity. High-level abstract statements that might appear in user requirements, such as "ability to capture incoming and outgoing email" may not be sufficient to select a product with sufficient maturity to meet organizational expectations.

Therefore, the functional statements defined by the enterprise will be important in determining whether the solution can meet its complete requirements. The relevance and importance of the statements of functionality for email management will depend on the enterprise, its culture toward email as a means of communication, its email policy, as well as corporate and individual behavior.

REQUIREMENTS DEFINITION

Direct Capture

The types of functionality to be considered when reviewing requirements for direct capture of email into an email management system include capabilities such as:

- Integrate with the messaging and email system infrastructure (the organization will need to define its messaging systems infrastructure, including client and server software, hardware, and communication systems).
- Filter out messages using predefined business rules (organizations should define the business rules at least at an abstract level).
- Autocategorize email messages based on metadata and content.
- Represent email in business-definable virtual hierarchical classification system (represent by folders).
- Quarantine email based on configurable business rules (e.g., confidential emails, spam, and offensive content).
- Apply rules for recordkeeping life-cycle management and disposal authorities.
- Support information classification security as well as security mechanisms inherent within the messaging system infrastructure.
- Support secondary storage of email on diverse media types, and the archival of email as a permanent record, while providing search and retrieval capability.
- Enable search and retrieval on email message metadata/content and content in text-based attachments.
- Enable Web-based and messaging client access for browse (hierarchical classification folders) and search and retrieval on metadata and content.
- Provide an integrated reporting tool (preferably with a library of customizable templates).
- Feature architectural scalability to support high-volume email transactions and to support management of email in organizations featuring distributed messaging infrastructure (where relevant).
- Feature integration with heterogeneous messaging infrastructure (for those environments supporting multiple messaging systems).
- Satisfy legal requirements to demonstrate the authenticity of capturing the email to the managed repository and the inviolate condition of the messages.

End User Capture

Table 1 provides statements of requirements that provide a provisional basis for specifying integration of a DMS with email client software.

The DMS repository will require the same type of repository management and system administration, including archival processes as digital office documents, which we covered in Chapter 12. The notable exception to managing email as digital documents is the inability to check out for editing an email message (or attachment) that has been saved as a record. If an attachment has to be updated, then the DMS should provide a copy of the document which when checked-in to the DMS, should be saved as a separate object.

Table 1: Catalog of Email Management Functionality

Functional Statement	Comments
Integration – messaging and email services	
• Enable users to continue creating electronic mail messages using enterprise email client without the requirement to use another form of email messaging system.	The enterprise needs to declare its preference for email messaging software, because some DMS offer their own inherent email messaging functionality.
• Save mail message and attachment(s) from within the email client in a simple manner.	The ideal functionality might be that the DMS features transparent integration with the enterprise email client during the capture process. Organizations need to confirm the simplicity with which users are able to capture emails into the DMS.
• Save mail message only.	This functionality is required where a mail message has no attachment, or contains an attachment that the user does not want to save (e.g., a company logo appended to the email).
• Save attachment(s) only. • Save selected attachments only.	Enables users to simply save the attachment without saving the email message. Enterprises may wish to review how simple it is for the DMS to capture and register multiple attachments. How difficult is it to save selected attachments only?
• Save mail messages and attachments as one object.	Enables the end user to capture the message and attachment(s) as one object. This may be required for managing a message or attachment as a *record* of a business transaction or activity.
• Save mail messages and attachments as separate objects, and provide linkages. • Save mail message and link to an existing document(s).	Enterprises should validate how this functionality is achieved. Frequently, DMS software implements this relationship between message and attachment object(s) as links in a compound document relationship. Linkages might otherwise be achieved via metadata links, but, unlike compound document functionality, this technique might not offer automatic notification of relationships.
• Initiate "save to DMS?" notification at send function.	This functionality might be required as a prompt to alert users to make a decision on whether the email or attachments need to be saved to the DMS. While it does not guarantee that all relevant business emails will be captured, the prompt does at least require a decision from the end user.
• Save "sent" email to DMS via mouse operation.	Enables the end user to capture the message and attachment(s) once the email has already been sent.
• Invoke DMS search to detect if email is already saved. If so, prompt re-save as separate document.	The DMS might be able to offer the functionality to automatically detect if an email message has already been saved. However, this might not be easily achievable, because different people might save the same message, each with the same metadata (e.g., subject title). If this functionality is offered, how is the save notification managed in a distributed messaging environment?
• Provide multiple "save as" regimes within the email messaging client, with the default being the DMS.	Enables end users to save electronic messages to external stores such as a server file system, hard disk, or diskette. Enterprises need to consider whether they wish to provide this functionality to end users. If so, determine if it is preferable for the relevant object(s) to be saved to the DMS first, which might then allow an uncontrolled copy stored on the file system.
• Provide a classification scheme to assist end users with cataloging of messages and attachments.	Supports the requirement to save business emails within the structure of a three-tier FCS or apply a keyword classification hierarchy.
• Provide "save as" icon within the email messaging client. • Disable "save as" icon if email has been saved to DMS.	Provides simplicity of invoking the functionality to save email to DMS. Enterprises might consider if a number of icons might be applicable: save message, save attachment, or save message and attachment. The icon should be disabled if the message has been saved.

Table 1: Catalog of Email Management Functionality (continued)

Functional Statement	Comments
Registration	
• Prepopulate DMS registration profile with attributes derived from the message.	This functionality is to automatically populate the DMS system and custom metadata registration module with the attributes contained in the email message. For example, date, time, sender and receiver, subject title, and so on. Enterprises should examine the extent to which the transfer of metadata from the email client to the DMS registration module is achieved.
• Provide facilities for automatic categorization of email.	This type of functionality is identified as an emerging requirement. It involves the capability of the DMS (or other email management software) to automatically categorize email by identifying types of email by their content. This is an immature technology at this stage, and the area needs to be watched. There are potential variances between business imperatives and regulatory requirements.
• Capture email as a permanent record of a business transaction.	The DMS will be required to comply with specific requirements for maintaining permanent records. The enterprise might be affected by government jurisdiction on the formats required for maintaining email records. State the formats required to be supported.
• Check-out of email message saved as a record not permitted. • Check-out of attachment saved as record not permitted.	An email message is stored in the DMS as a record of a business transaction. Unlike other digital documents, it should not be checked out for editing but be available for view only to authorized users. Preparation and editing of draft email messages should be managed within the email application. If the email record has an attachment, then the attachment cannot be checked out for editing, but a copy might be made for further collaborative work.
• Support email threads based on subject.	Emails relating to particular threads can be linked and viewed within the DMS.
• Integrate with email software templates and forms.	Templates and forms created in email software applications can be integrated with the DMS, primarily for object capture and automatic transfer of metadata from the template or form to the DMS. How is this achieved — through core functionality, or will the solution require scripts to be developed using API?

SUMMARY

The management of digital email documents is a complex requirement, primarily due to the high volume of messages received and the difficulty in quickly differentiating personal and transient emails from those that represent a record of a business transaction or activity. Filters apply to assist organizations in differentiating email based on predefined business logic, but it may not be possible to easily cater to every type of contingency.

Regardless of the technology solution option that is adopted, the organization needs to address email management as part of its overall information policy, and specifically, in a policy that is devoted to email management. Quite often, email policies discuss aspects such as email etiquette, which is important, but they fail to address the compelling issues relating to managing emails and attachments as a record of a business transaction or activity.

We will now consider the requirements for managing physical office documents, which we discuss in Chapter 14.

Chapter 14

Functional Requirements –
Physical Office
Documents

OVERVIEW

This chapter addresses the functionality for managing physical office documents using IDCM technology, so that the organization has a solution that enables them to manage digital and physical documents.

Our objectives are as follows:

- Consider the context of the requirement to manage specific types of physical documents as a business record.
- Analyze some key aspects of the functional requirements that are relevant when registering and managing physical documents.
- Provide a checklist to guide enterprises that might act as a primer for defining their requirements for managing physical files and documents.

CONTEXT

Many organizations associate the management of physical documents with centralized or decentralized registries under the province of "registry" or "records" staff who are the custodians of records. However, this may not always be the case, because in many enterprises, physical documents are handled by most business units, as part of an "official" or "corporate" file, or as part of a business unit's own filing management.

The terminology "records management" is frequently associated with "physical documents," yet the term "records" applies to a wider variety of information assets other than simply physical documents. Therefore, there may need to be a paradigm shift in thinking in some organizations about what type of information constitutes a record. For example:

- Transactions involving electronic objects (such as email and attachments) may represent a record of a business transaction.
- Database transactions in an ERP system may represent a record of a business transaction.
- Content published to an Internet or intranet Web site upon which a business transaction or decision is made may represent a record.
- A business transaction managed as part of an automated forms processing or workflow application may represent a record.

Some organizations maintain "records management systems" that do not manage all the records of an organization. Furthermore, these systems primarily reference physical documents at a corporate level and might not be used to manage important physical documents at the workgroup level. Workgroups might maintain word-processing or local database registers of important physical documents, such as policies and rules that apply within the workgroup.

Issues that must be considered include the following:

- Although physical documents may be required as evidence of business transactions, there are many to which this does not apply — they may simply be printed copies of electronic documents used by an end user for local reference purposes.
- Some physical documents that are records might be registered in a system other than the corporate registry system. For example, invoices might be registered in an ERP system.
- Other types of physical documents might be workgroup collaborative documents or personal documents held by individuals to facilitate their day-to-day work activities. These physical documents might be escalated from a level of workgroup ownership to become corporate documents.
- Some physical documents might represent records of business transactions but do not end up being registered in the corporate registry system.

It is important that the requirement to manage physical documents be adequately addressed in the enterprise's document management policy, which we discussed in Chapter 7. The policy should adequately identify those types of physical documents that need to be managed as records and provide examples of those that do not.

Elements of information policy (Chapter 7) should also address the privacy, copyright, and intellectual property issues associated with documents, and the archival policy should address the requirements for retention and disposal of documents that are records.

It is expected that there will be requirement for evidential physical documents that support business transactions to be maintained for the foreseeable future to meet legislative, evidential, and enterprise policy requirements. Consequently, the IDCM solution must support effective management of physical documents and enable relevant physical documents to be captured and retained as a record of a business transaction for the period required by disposal authorities developed under archival policy.

There may also be a requirement to maintain physical copies of workgroup documents, printed from electronic documents, produced from database systems, or received in physical format. Workgroups might access and maintain a combination of corporate physical files and workgroup-specific files in the short term. The interrelationships between corporate and workgroup level documents and how these should be managed need to be examined and addressed as a strategy emanating from document management policy.

IDCM FUNCTIONAL MODELS

The functionality for managing physical documents within the IDCM architecture is achievable in a number of ways, which are illustrated in the following examples of how DMS can be used to manage physical documents:

- An inherent core component of IDCM architecture model features a balanced richness of functionality between management of physical and digital office documents (as well as drawings and Web content files).
- An inherent core component of IDCM architecture, but the DMS component is richer in functionality for managing physical documents than for managing digital office documents. This type of scenario occurs where traditional RMS (i.e., systems for managing physical document as "records") have been developed to incorporate digital document management capabilities.
- An inherent core component of IDCM architecture model, but DMS is richer in functionality for managing digital office documents than managing physical documents.
- The module for managing physical documents is a third-party tool integrated with the DMS. The extent of the transparency of the integration will be dependent on the richness of the integration between the DMS and the third-party product. The nature of the capabilities supported by integrated solution will again depend on the functionality provided by both modules, and how available they are integrated.
- A Drawing Management System might manage the physical (controlled or uncontrolled) copies of drawings and technical documentation. The system might also offer the capabilities to manage physical documents used in the general office environment (as well as digital office documents).

REQUIREMENTS ANALYSIS

The functionality required for managing physical documents covers a range of business requirements:

- Registering physical documents;
- Classifying physical documents;
- Registering physical files;
- Managing physical files and documents;
- Tracking physical files and documents;
- Searching and retrieving physical documents;
- Disposing of physical documents;

- Supporting census of physical documents; and
- Providing system administration, security, and audit.

Document Registration

The system must support the capability to register a physical document. There are many methods to achieve this, using various products, so it is important for enterprises to produce a clear specification of the current situation for physical documents. For example, some organizations may always create an "official" or "corporate" physical file first, and then assign documents to the physical file. Other organizations may not have a physical file but associate each document with a "logical" file by assigning a classification structure to the document.

Where a physical document is to be registered, and it is a published copy of an digital document, the IDCM system must link the physical document to the digital document during the registration process. Rules must be applied to ensure that version integrity of both documents is maintained. A version of a physical document (e.g., v0.1) should not be linked to another version (e.g., v0.2) of the digital document. However, enterprises should be careful when considering this type of requirement, because a printed document may represent a physical "view" of multiple linked digital documents (such as a "parent" spreadsheet that derives information from other "child" spread-sheets).

The system should also support enterprise metadata standards, which should be defined in the *User Requirements* component of the specification. The metadata might feature contextual data (date, author, etc.) and structural data (letter, report, etc.), to assist in the identification of the physical document as an agent. The system must validate the metadata prior to creation of a new document record and output a unique reference number to distinguish each physical document registered in the DMS as an item.

It is important for the context in which the document is used to be maintained for evidentiary and legal purposes. For example, a physical form that defines *standard conditions of procurement* might be used many times for procurement of goods and services, but its use in each procurement instance is unique. Any subsequent updates to the form should not impact on its usage in specific prior instances of procurement.

Document Classification

The system should enable end users to associate a physical document with a FCS. It may be insufficient merely to describe the functionality required in simple terms, such as "support classification scheme," because that does not convey much information about the organization's particular requirements.

Many organizations have not embraced a consolidated FCS for managing docu-ments. They may support multiple classification schemes, particularly if there have been amalgamations or takeover of businesses. Different schema might exist based on geographical locations, business sites, workgroups, or be distinguishable by the types of documents involved, e.g., physical documents in corporate registries, electronic documents in file systems, drawings, and Web content.

A common FCS should be considered throughout the organization for all document formats. There may be a requirement for sites or workgroups to extend the common scheme to meet specific requirements, but this type of activity should be defined during policy and strategy development.

Consequently, it is incumbent on the organization to define its specific requirements for associating physical documents with a FCS, and define the nature of the FCS that the system is required to support. Disposal authorities can also be linked to the FCS, so that there is categorized association between schedules and documents. This definition should be included as part of the development of the business management framework for document and content management. The classification and disposal schema should be referenced in the *User Requirements* component of the Requirements Specification and referenced within the context of the *Functional Requirements* component of the specification.

When preparing the functional requirements for the methods of classification maintenance, the organization should consider what alternatives might suit its particular exigencies. For example, the system might enable end users to enter a classification, if they are likely to be familiar with it. The system should enable browsing of a classification hierarchy to assist selection of appropriate classification. As an aid to support change management, the system might offer the functionality to provide a short list of classifications used by a particular workgroup, i.e., a favorites list configured for the workgroup, or even provide default classification according to user account.

File Registration

Mostly physical documents are stored as part of a collection of like documents on physical files, which may be represented by folders, binders, or something similar. Metadata for file registration needs to be associated with enterprise metadata standards, and enterprises should also define, as part of its *User Requirements*, the metadata types that will be required at the physical file level, e.g., File Number, File Title, File Description, Current Status, Location, disposal, and similar types of attributes.

The system should generate a unique number that identifies the file, i.e., the "file number", which can be derived from the enterprise FCS. If we draw on the example provided at Figure 2 in Chapter 3 (p. 83), then the "Motor Vehicle Accident" file number first part would be represented as 11/4/22-01 as expanded in Table 1.

The IDCM system may have to support a range of file numbering schemas, depending on the requirements of the enterprises, and how files are presently cataloged within organizational sites and workgroups. In these instances, it may be appropriate for the enterprise to develop a consistent file numbering scheme, but if this is not practicable, then the enterprise will need to state its specific requirements for file numbering in its statement of *User Requirements*.

If the enterprise supports the creation of part files, then the *User Requirements* specification needs to identify how part files are created within the organization, and how

Table 1: File Number Example

Component Number	Classification Term
11	Occupational Health and Safety
4	Accidents
22	Motor Vehicle Accidents
-01	First part (first accident)

they are numbered within the file numbering schema that apply within the organization, such as how the file parts are represented in the example above.

Barcode Production

The enterprise might have the requirement to print barcode labels for affixing to files or documents. The barcodes could be generated during the file and document registration process. A state of requirements for how the system will be required to support the production of barcode labels may include incorporation of purchased preprinted labels.

The requirements should include the usage scenarios that would require the generation and production of barcodes, the volume of barcodes (based on file and document registration analysis), and the format of the barcodes. It is important that an organization clearly define the barcode requirements, so that the enterprise can assess (during functional benchmarks of products) that the IDCM system is able to provide the functionality required.

The organization should define any existing barcode recognition facilities that it uses, such as wands that it might use for file and document census activities. An IDCM system may be required to produce barcodes that are capable of being read by the existing equipment and, if this is a requirement, then it should be stated, and the barcode recognition systems should be defined.

Managing Physical File and Document Collections

The system will be required to manage physical document collections, which may consist of files or individual documents filed in a logical series, e.g., by file number, contract name, or matter number. The end user needs to be able to assign physical files and documents to storage locations, move items between storage locations, and also migrate files and documents to secondary (or inactive) storage when they are not being accessed frequently. The system might prompt a user to move files or documents to inactive storage based on an event trigger, such as a specified period after a file has been closed. The system should also allow the return of a physical file or document from inactive storage to an active status, if the need arises.

Tracking Physical Files and Documents

The system must enable physical files and documents to be tracked as they move from location to location. Some systems may only offer tracking at the file level, on the assumption that the traditional recordkeeping practice is for documents that are "records" of an organization's activities to be kept in files. However, it might be the case that not all of the physical documents that are "records" are kept on registered physical files. Some physical documents might be contractual terms and conditions, which might be filed at the document level using a unique contract number. If these documents are registered in the IDCM system, there may not be a requirement to create a physical file.

Consequently, the tracking features of the IDCM system may need to cover the requirement to track physical files (containing physical documents) and physical documents that exist independently of files. Some organizations may have a requirement to use the barcodes affixed to files and documents to assist in automating processes associated with tracking movements. This practice is often referred to as conducting a file census, which we will discuss.

The effective utilization of an IDCM solution may mean that information relating to the current status and location of a file or document needs to be accessible from desktop computers within each workgroup. Decentralized access to file and document movements enables end users to rapidly retrieve information, and also allows them to update movements from their own workstations, if authorized.

Search and Retrieval of Physical Files and Documents

The IDCM model proposes a universal interface and integrative search and retrieval capability that enable users to search and retrieve metadata, documents, and content using functionality of the type that we examined in Chapter 12 in the "Searching Documents" section.

The same facilities for search and retrieval of digital documents may be sought from a database that provides brief (surrogate) descriptions of files. For those enterprises that may only be interested in implementing a solution for managing physical documents, then the requirements defined in Chapter 12 still provide a primer for developing the functionality required in a finding aid database.

Disposal of Physical Files and Documents

The disposal of physical files and documents should be in accordance with an approved disposal authority. The disposal authority should be associated with the FCS, and the same authority should apply to physical and digital documents within an enterprise.

It is recommended that the disposal authority be approved prior to the design and development of the IDCM solution for the enterprise. The disposal authority should be implemented before or in conjunction with the IDCM solution, such that specific types of files and physical documents referenced by the system are disposed of in accordance with an approved authority.

The IDCM solution might be required to record information that provides evidence that a document was destroyed *legally*. Details might include details of the documents destroyed, when, how, and by whom.

Support Barcode Tracking or Census

Enterprises may wish to utilize barcode technology to assist with managing file and document tracking or to conduct a scheduled census of existing physical file and document holdings. When defining its requirements for barcode supported tracking or census, the enterprise should include a definition of its current barcode tracking or census devices and software, if these are already used.

If these items are intended to be used as part of the IDCM solution, it is imperative that:

- Existing barcode systems have the capacity to read the barcode produced by (or for) the proposed IDCM system.
- The system can be demonstrated to have the capability to upload data read from existing barcode systems.

These requirements, if they are applicable, should be clearly defined in the *User Requirements* specifications.

System Administration, Security, and Audit

The conceptual view of the IDCM model is that system administration (metadata maintenance, FCS maintenance, management of the thesaurus, etc.) as well as security and audit trails will be managed by a single logical system. We envisage that the single logical system would cover digital office documents, email, drawings, images, and physical documents. We review the requirements for system administration, security, and audit in Chapter 19.

REQUIREMENTS DEFINITION

Table 2 provides basic examples of statements of requirements as a starting guideline for managing physical documents using an IDCM solution.

SUMMARY

A DMS, depending on the state of development of the product, should offer the capability to register and manage physical documents and digital office documents as part of its core architecture.

However, not all DMS applications are able to adequately address the requirements for managing physical documents, because they may have evolved from an environment that focused mainly on digital document management.

At the same time, there are DMS applications that are good at managing physical documents, because they have evolved from RMS applications that had their origins inthe management of physical files and documents.

Table 2: Functionality Primer — Physical Documents

Functional Statement	Comments
Integration – Desktop/Network Operating/Database Management Environment	
• Integrate with desktop operating system environment.	State the product(s), version(s) and service releases of the desktop operating system(s) that will be used by the enterprise.
• Integrate with enterprise Web browser and server environment.	State the product(s), version(s) and service releases of the Web browser(s) that will be used by the enterprise.
• Integrate with network operating system environment.	State the product(s), version(s) and service releases of the network operating system(s) that will be used by the enterprise.
• Comply with enterprise standards for the database management system environment.	State the enterprise's standard database management system environment, including product(s), version(s), service release(s), and patches supported.
Determine whether there is a requirement by the enterprise for the physical document management component to be certified to the (relevant) operating system or database management system by an independent authority, and if so, state the requirement.	

Table 2: Functionality Primer — Physical Documents (continued)

Functional Statement	Comments
Document Registration	
• Provide a consistent interface and approach for registering physical documents and digital office documents.	The user should have the same "look and feel" and similar registration steps, when an end user is required to register a physical document or a digital office document.
• Enable a user to register a physical document effectively.	The enterprise should define its current methods for registering physical documents, and state any specific requirements that might be relevant for registration. For example, what specific metadata needs to be captured for a physical office document?
• Support the enterprise metadata standard as defined in *User Requirements*.	The organization should define its standard metadata schema as part of the *User Requirements* component of the requirements specification.
• Populate registration template with selected items of metadata derived automatically from the user's systems environment.	This type of functionality should be a feature of registration, as it eliminates the need for a user to select (from lists) or key in information that should already be known to the computing environment.
• Validate metadata prior to committal of document registration record.	The validation requirements are similar to those that would be applied for registration of digital office documents. Features might include controlled lists or buttons, or other performance-enhancing data capture techniques.
• Enable physical document to be registered with specific status of Controlled Copy or Uncontrolled Copy.	This type of capability might be useful when there is a need to distribute physical copies of documents to multiple sources, and where each copy has to be *managed*.
• Produce unique identifier for each physical document registered into the system.	Each document should be registered uniquely within the system.
• Support capabilities to link physical documents.	The system might be required to provide links that associate physical documents. For example, an item of outgoing correspondence might be linked to an item of incoming correspondence.
• Associate physical document with registered electronic document.	There may be a requirement to link a physical document to an existing registered digital document. Each document (physical and digital) would be uniquely identified to the system, but the user might want to create a relationship between the two instances.
Document Classification	
• Support the enterprise FCS as defined in *User Requirements*.	The organization should define its business classification framework as part of the *User Requirements* component of the requirements specification.
• Support an enterprise FCS across all document and content types.	The FCS offered for physical documents should be common across all document types. In other words, the same scheme should apply for physical documents as applies to digital office documents, email, drawings, and Web content.
• Enable a disposal authority to be linked to the FCS.	The process of document disposal might be simplified if the disposal rule for a document is inherited from the classification that is applied to it.
• Provide mechanisms for timely and effective classification of documents.	Types of performance-enhancing mechanisms might include, e.g., manual entry of classification, favorites list, and easy navigation of hierarchical classifications.

Table 2: Functionality Primer — Physical Documents (continued)

Functional Statement	Comments
• Support thesaurus of common terms to meet the requirements defined in the *User Requirements*.	It is probably not adequate to simply make the statement "Capability to support thesauri?" What would this statement mean? Any system has the "capability" to support a thesaurus. The enterprise needs to define its specific requirements for application of a thesaurus. Is there a specific thesaurus in mind? What are the requirements for the thesaurus?
• Provide thesaurus to support an unlimited number of terms and (specified) numbers of levels, and to support relationships between thesaurus terms.	Define how terms should be managed in the thesaurus, e.g., a single term is defined once but may be used in many contexts. What are the required relationships between thesaurus terms, e.g., hierarchical, associative, and equivalence relationships?
File Registration	
• Create a physical file as a container for physical documents.	The system must enable an authorized end user to create a physical file and index the file.
• Support the enterprise metadata standard as defined in *User Requirements*.	The organization should define its standard metadata schema as part of the *User Requirements* component of the requirements specification. The enterprise should define the metadata types that will be required at the physical file level, e.g., File Number, File Title, Document Description, Current Status, etc.
• Validate metadata prior to committal of document registration record.	The validation requirements are similar to those that would be applied for physical documents.
• Create a new file volume (or part file).	It is important for organizations to define how part files are created, and what numbering scheme applies.
• Create new file volume (or file part) based on predefined rules within the system.	Enterprises need to define the rules that would apply.
• Provide a unique identifier for a physical file that is derived from the enterprise FCS.	The unique identifier for a file may be derived from the FCS, but the enterprise needs to define its specific requirements.
Produce Barcode	
• Print unique barcode labels that can be preconfigured, depending on enterprise *User Requirements*, for use at the following levels: (a) File level (b) Document level (c) Box level	The barcode labels must meet the enterprise's requirements for files, documents, and boxes. It should define usage scenarios, volume of barcodes, and formats of barcodes in its *User Requirements* specification. During the evaluation process, enterprises should ensure that the barcode production facilities support required usage scenarios and formats.
Storage Management	
• Support management of storage locations that identify collections of (controlled) physical files and documents.	The enterprise should detail (in *User Requirements*) the storage locations that are relevant. There might be multiple storage locations, and they might be distributed across a number of sites or workgroups.
• Provide capability to manage inactive storage locations.	The enterprise needs to define (in *User Requirements*) the (relevant) inactive storage locations and also any event triggers that could be used to initiate transfer of files and documents to inactive locations.

Table 2: Functionality Primer — Physical Documents (continued)

Functional Statement	Comments
Tracking Physical Files and Documents	
• Assign an action officer to a physical file.	There may be a requirement to assign one or more action officers to track a file or document. If so, the enterprise should clearly state its requirements.
• Assign an action officer to a physical file or document.	Similarly, if there is a requirement to assign documents that are not maintained on files to an action officer, then the enterprise needs to specify its requirements.
• Track physical file movements.	The *User Requirements* specification should contain a description of how files are tracked now, and draw on that information to derive requirements for file tracking using the IDCM system.
• Track movements of physical documents.	The *User Requirements* specification should identify those specific requirements where document types, which are not supported on registered files, need to be tracked.
• List physical files and documents that are to be transferred.	The system might be required to generate a report that shows files or documents that are queued for transfer to another location.
• Support the capability for file reconstruction.	The system might be required to register the transfer of a physical document(s) from one physical file to another and maintain a history of the associations between files and documents.
• Support the management of requests for a file movement.	The system might enable an end user to register a request for a file or document, which means moving the item from its existing location to another. The enterprise might wish to inform the parties that the request has been initiated. Once the request has been satisfied, the system might initial an email to both parties advising of this status.
• Support resubmit functionality (bring ups) and other file and document event triggers, and support the capability to record a reason for the event.	There may be a requirement for files or documents to be placed in storage until a date specifically nominated by an action officer. The system should generate a list of files or documents that need to be removed from storage by a predefined data, to return to the action officer. This type of activity might be related to other events as well; for example, a file that is required one month before the end of the financial year. Enterprises need to clearly define their requirements for resubmit functionality and other event triggers that might be required in the *User Requirements* specification.
• Manage locations for archived physical files and documents.	Enterprises should define the locations where files are archived. The system should have the provision to register new locations.
• Provide capabilities to number and register archives boxes.	Define how numbering and registration of archives boxes occurs, and add any suggestions for modifications to the processes in the *User Requirements* specification.
• Maintain movement history.	The system should be required to maintain a history of all movements (including unique identifier, physical file and file part number, date of movement, and movement location or user).

Table 2: Functionality Primer — Physical Documents (continued)

Functional Statement	Comments
Disposal	
• Provide the capability to apply disposal actions and rules associated with specific types of physical files and documents.	This is a need for the enterprise to define the characteristics of the disposal actions (e.g., transfer to, destroy, archive) based on disposal authority schema. Enterprises should also state the types of rules that might be applied, including actions based on series (such as time, event, or both).
• Provide the capability for the disposal authority to cover (or transparently integrate) physical and electronic documents.	This type of functionality needs to be specified and tested during product evaluation.
• Generate a report when physical files or documents are due for disposal, highlighting relevant dates (e.g., last modified, disposal date) and disposal actions.	Enterprise should state any specific requirements that might apply to the generation of the report, including format requirements, timeliness, etc.
• Enable authorized users to modify a disposal action.	The enterprise should indicate whether this type of requirement will apply, and under what circumstances.
• Enable an inactive file or document to be reactivated.	Where an inactive file or document has been reactivated, it will be necessary to review the retention period.
Census Management	
• Enable bar-code reading devices and software to accurately read labels produced by the IDCM system.	The existing devices and software should be stated as part of the *User Requirements* specification. Is it absolutely essential for these devices and software to be an integral part of the system, or are they dated and might potentially be decommissioned in favor of later technology? If so, then this aspect should be made clear in the specification. During evaluation processes, confirm and test which bar-code devices and software are supported by the offered IDCM solutions.
Reports	
• Provide reports that are defined in the *User Requirements* specification.	The enterprise should define the reports that are required from the system in its *User Requirements* specification.
• Provide a reporting tool that provides generic reporting capabilities.	There may be a requirement for ad hoc reports from the system, in which case, it will be necessary for the IDCM system to feature a reporting tool that enables system administrators to extract and publish relevant data from the system.
System Administration	See Chapter 19.
Maintaining Security and Audit	See Chapter 19.

Neither of these types of systems may have yet evolved sufficiently to offer an IDCM solution for managing physical and digital documents that wrests the best functionality from both evolutionary paths. However, business demands for software that manages all types of documents is likely to drive integrated solutions.

Depending on the organization's requirements, the management of physical documents as a module using a DMS may require a high degree of sophistication to achieve synchronization of aspects such as versioning between digital and physical documents.

Irrespective of any technology option that might be utilized to support improved management of physical documents, there is the requirement to consider the strategic, operational, and tactical requirements of the enterprise. Furthermore, the management of physical documents needs to be addressed within the context of a management framework that embraces policy, procedures, standards, change management, and effective change management.

In the next chapter, we look at the functional requirements for document imaging systems, which may offer enterprises solutions for converting relevant physical documents to image format.

Chapter 15

Functional Requirements – Document Imaging and Recognition Technologies

OVERVIEW

In this chapter, we review the requirements for document imaging systems that enable the scanning and conversion of physical documents to image format. We also review the functionality offered by recognition technologies (such as barcode and character recognition tools).

Our objectives are to do the following:

- Discuss the requirement to identify existing document imaging systems when considering IDCM solutions.
- Provide a framework for determining requirements for imaging and scanning in workgroup and production applications.
- Review the application of recognition technologies for facilitating data capture during scanning.

The project planning, feasibility study, and user requirements strategies that we discussed in Chapters 6, 8, and 11 apply to this context.

REQUIREMENTS ANALYSIS

Context

The importance of requirements analysis for document imaging projects was confirmed over a decade ago (Hall, 1991, p. 33) with the publication of a set of applied factors relating to imaging projects. These applied factors could be integrated into a logical statement of requirements, similar to following a road map. Hall also expressed concerns about the lack of business knowledge and understanding relating to imaging technology, when he indicated (1991, p. 11) that many potential customers lacked the insight and experience with digital imaging systems, which at that point was an emerging technology.

While consumer knowledge may have increased with general digital imaging capabilities, particularly with the wide availability of cheap desktop imaging tools, there still appeared to be a knowledge gap in regard to requirements analysis for workgroup- and production-level imaging systems as late as 1998. The observation was then made (Wasner, 1998, p. 2) that so much information in organizations remained in paper format because of the uncertainty surrounding the design and implementation of a document imaging system. He stated that while users generally believed that converting paper to digital information was desirable, they did not know how or where to get started. (Costs and other factors might also have had implications for document imaging startup projects.)

It is not as though published literature was not available. Wiggins (1994, p. 155) acknowledged that "requirements" are a key feature of the information life-cycle and devoted considerable attention to the functionality associated with the two most common types of imaging, i.e., digital imaging and film-based imaging. The coverage included many functional aspects of document imaging technology and its environment.

The importance of understanding the specific project management and require- ments analysis aspects of document imaging projects was investigated by Asprey (2000), whose research substantiated the value of feasibility study and requirements analysis for document imaging projects. It also recommended the development and publication of extensions to existing information systems methodology to cover the specific requirements of document imaging systems.

The recommended prerequisites to the functional analysis for a document imaging requirement are *project planning* (Chapter 6), *feasibility study* (Chapter 8), and *user requirements* (Chapter 11). We will consider the feasibility and user requirements analysis within the context of document imaging.

Feasibility Study

The feasibility study determines the operational, technical, and financial feasibility of the business application and the role of imaging in supporting an end-to-end business process. It should also identify the potential capabilities for integrating imaging capture, storage, and retrieval with an IDCM repository. Having established a business case based on the feasibility study that a document imaging application and integration with an IDCM system adds value to a business process, then it is necessary to analyze and determine requirements for the system.

User Requirements

The *user requirements* analysis for a document imaging requirement should follow the guidelines provided in Chapter 11, i.e., definition of user requirements at strategic, tactical, and operational levels. The analysis of strategic and tactical requirements for document imaging will be virtually within the same context as described in Chapter 11, but there may be some subtle differences at the level of operational requirements analysis. For example, when defining the current document environment, the analyst will need to determine whether an enterprise has already implemented technology for capturing digital images.

The practitioner needs to determine and specify any and all existing document imaging capabilities within the organization. The information will help to maintain an asset inventory of this type of information systems infrastructure and may also be useful for apprising potential suppliers of the capabilities of current imaging systems. Let us now consider some suggestions for reviewing and defining any current imaging applications and infrastructure within the context of document scanning; scanning to OCR, ICR; facsimile capture; digital cameras, and microform digitization.

Existing Imaging Applications

It is important for the practitioner to describe the existing imaging applications in terms of business usage scenarios, installed software, hardware, and internetworking components. The information will help determine whether:

- The existing imaging systems can meet the functional requirements of the intended application.
- There are any additional hardware or software components (such as automatic document feeders, accelerator cards, etc.) that might be applicable for increasing the capability of the existing imaging systems.
- The existing systems are capable of integration with the repository services of the IDCM system, so that the DMS is able to import (individually or in bulk) images and metadata derived (or created) during the capture process.
- There may be a requirement to bulk load images from an existing image repository to a new IDCM environment. (There may be a requirement to convert existing images to a new format before bulk load).
- There are requirements for capturing computer output (invoices and statements, reports) and integrating imaging and COLD solutions.

The items listed in Table 1 help to define existing workgroup-level scanning devices and software (for example, image capture, barcode technology, OCR, ICR) within an enterprise.

Table 1: Checklist for Existing Document Imaging Installations

- Purpose (e.g., scanning size A (or A4) and B (or A3) contract documents).
- User profiles.
- Hardware (e.g., workstation and server; scanning devices, including brands and models).
- Special imaging devices (e.g., cards for accelerating viewing and printing).
- Features (e.g., paper size, document feeder, bar-code recognition).
- Imaging software (e.g., including imaging software name and version).
- Recognition software (e.g., bar code and OCR software name and version).
- Operating system (client or server operating system used to host all imaging and recognition software components).
- Configuration (e.g., universal serial bus ([USB] connection to a networked computer).
- Resolution and format (e.g., supports 200 dpi, 300 dpi, or 400 dpi, and is saved as TIF, PDF, etc.).
- Volume (20 documents per day, consisting of an average of 15 pages each).
- Special requirements (e.g., supports duplex scanning).
- Secure storage capacities.
- Backup and archiving.

Existing Recognition Technologies

OCR scanning might be used within the enterprise to convert a hard-copy document into an electronically editable (text) document. The capability is generally required when electronic text versions of documents are not available, and there is a requirement to reuse the text of a document to create a new document or to convert the contents of the document for search and retrieval purposes. The types of documents that might be converted to text using OCR are good-quality typewritten documents, such as specifications, legal documents, forms, and facsimiles. The existing OCR software systems used within the organization should be part of the definition of existing document imaging tools. The organization may also use ICR technology to capture text from physical forms, and perhaps invoke e-forms processing. The current environment for ICR and forms processing needs to be defined.

Incoming Faxes

The types of information listed in Table 2 might be useful for defining existing facsimile or gateway installations.

Table 2: Checklist for Existing Fax Capture Installations

- Purpose (e.g., capture of claims applications).
- User profiles.
- Hardware (e.g., fax gateway for client or server — include brands and models).
- Capture software (e.g., including software name and version).
- Recognition software (e.g., OCR software name and version).
- Operating system (client or server operating system used to host all fax capture software components).
- Configuration (e.g., client or server network integration).
- Standards (e.g., compression standards).
- Volume (50 documents per day, consisting of average two pages each).
- Support for email via fax or email gateway.
- Special requirements.

Existing Digital Cameras

Digital cameras may also be part of the workgroup environment for business activities such as marketing and communications, operational purposes (e.g., plant maintenance), safety and environmental support, investigations, and equipment registers.

Digital cameras may store images on a diskette, which can be removed from the camera and inserted into a desktop computer. The images can then be copied (or transferred) from the diskette to the desktop or file server. Alternatively, the images may be stored on a card and later downloaded to a desktop computer or file server using a cable.

Digital cameras may also be used for capturing video, storing fragments as data on a tape, which is later downloaded to digital storage devices or transferred to analog video format.

Table 3: Checklist for Existing Digital Camera Capabilities

- Purpose (e.g., business usage scenarios).
- User profiles.
- Hardware (e.g., brand and model).
- Features (e.g., saves to diskette or tape).
- Resolution and format (e.g., resolution mostly 1024 × 768; saved in JPG or MPG format).
- Volume (e.g., five single images per day).
- Special requirements.

Like the requirement to define existing document scanning tools, it is necessary to specify the digital camera capabilities that already exist within the organization. Table 3 provides an example of how enterprises might describe existing digital cameras and software.

Digitization of Microforms

Enterprises may be using microform digitization techniques to convert existing analog images into digital images. The digitization may occur as the result of a dedicated project that is managed internally or outsourced to an imaging bureau service. For example, copies of drawings may be maintained on microform aperture cards and converted to digital format.

Alternatively, digital images may be a by-product of a microfilm-based capture process, where an organization has determined to retain microfilm for archival and recordkeeping purposes and wishes to use digital images to provide users with quick access and retrieval from desktop computers.

The nature of any project or application where microform images are being converted to digital images should be defined. Table 4 provides a checklist for this purpose.

Once the imaging environment within the enterprise (or imaging installation specifically relevant to the IDCM application) has been researched and documented, it is necessary to analyze and determine the requirements for the imaging functionality required for integration with the IDCM system. We shall consider these requirements in respect to document scanning, including the use of recognition technologies such as OCR, and then other document imaging techniques, such as facsimile capture and digital cameras.

Table 4: Checklist for Microform to Digital Conversion Projects

- Purpose (e.g., business usage scenarios).
- Type of microfilm (e.g., aperture cards, film).
- Size (16 mm , 32 mm).
- Registration (index) database structures and data definition.
- User profiles (where required).
- Hardware (e.g., brand and model of digitization tools — if used internally).
- Features.
- Resolution and format (e.g., saved as TIF, JPG, or PDF).
- Volume (e.g., 3000 images per day from bureau service, until conversion completed).
- Special requirements.

REQUIREMENTS DETERMINATION — DOCUMENT SCANNING

During the feasibility study, the enterprise should have considered the option of outsourcing all or part of the document scanning requirements to an external imaging service bureau. When an organization determines that all or part of its imaging is to be outsourced, then it is wise to develop a Service Specification, as advocated by Fruscione (1995). This type of specification encapsulates the scope of work to be performed, detailed scanning requirements, logistical arrangements (such as document collection and return), and project management requirements within an overall quality management approach for outsourcing document conversion and indexing. The detailed scanning requirements for the service specification may be drawn from the information provided in the remainder of this chapter relating to document scanning, but it is up to the practitioner to define the particular scope of work, logistics, and project management requirements.

User Profiles

User profiles for imaging within the enterprise may consist of a range of requirements. Some users may have responsibility for capturing, quality inspection, and registration of images in the IDCM system, while other users may have the requirement to search for document images, view, and print them.

It is necessary for the information relating to users to be profiled as part of the requirements specification. It will help the enterprise and the IDCM solution provider to understand the requirement for imaging within workgroups. It will also help to resolve the proposed IDCM architecture, including accessibility to images for users on remote networks. Table 5 provides a brief synopsis of user profiles for a workgroup imaging system.

Table 5: User Profile Scenarios

Workgroup Name Role	Engineering Services Number	Comments
Scanning/Inspection/ Registration	2	Scanning of office-size documents;.inspection performed by alternate operators; registration of metadata.
Search/View	40	Search of metadata to retrieve images; view images; approximately 200 image retrievals per day.
View (remote sites)	20	Twelve users at Remote Site 1 and nine users at Remote Site 2 need to search and view images; approximately 100 image retrievals are obtained per day.

Document Profiles

There is a range of functionality offered by document imaging hardware and software systems that may meet the diverse range of document capture requirements of an enterprise. Much of the functionality depends on the nature of the physical documents to be scanned, and it is important that an organization clearly defines the characteristics of the documents that are to be scanned.

The imaging environment within an enterprise is generally characterized by the potential requirement to scan and digitize a wide diversity of physical documents of varying sizes, text and graphic legibility, colors, and paper quality. These documents may arrive randomly or as part of a structured (claims) or semistructured (e.g., correspondence management) business process.

Given the wide scope of potential imaging requirements within an enterprise, the analysis of the types of documents to be converted to digital image is an important part of requirements determination. The definition of the types of documents that are to be scanned to image and their characteristics and volumes will help the enterprise and the potential IDCM solution supplier to gain a more detailed appreciation of the business requirements. It will also assist with a determination of the architecture of the solution. The first step is to determine the document types involved in the imaging requirement.

Document Types — ad hoc Imaging

The digitization requirement for an ad hoc imaging requirement may include physical documents such as incoming correspondence, signed outgoing correspondence, project documentation, photographs, brochures, manuals, articles or excerpts from media sources, and deliverables from contractors, to name but a few. Table 6 provides an indicative list of document types to be considered for ad hoc imaging requirements.

Document Types — Application Specific

The types of documents involved for a specific application of document digitization within the workgroup or production imaging environment depend on the nature of the business processes involved. Table 7 provides an indicative list of some document types that may need to be considered for "application-specific" imaging requirements.

Table 6: Examples of Ad Hoc Document Types

Determine document type — for example (items that are typically outside structured business processes):
• Incoming correspondence.
• Original items of outgoing correspondence that have been signed.
• Copies of outgoing correspondence that may be initialed.
• Photocopies and printed facsimiles.
• Handwritten or typed text.
• Items on colored paper.
• Front covers of thick reports.
• Photographs and glossy items, such as postcards, brochures, etc.
• Items that have been highlighted using colored highlighters.
• Items that have a combination of photographs and text.
• Selected pages of manuals or reference books.

Table 7: Examples of Specific Application Document Types

Determine document type — for example:
• Invoices.
• Checks.
• Claims.
• Applications.
• Drawings and transmittal notes.
• Forms-based applications.
• Requires OCR/ICR for forms capture or for invoking e-forms processing.

Table 8: Document Characteristic Definitions

For each document type, describe the following:

- Size (e.g., range is A (or A4) to B (or A3)).
- Single or duplex (double sided).
- Color.
- Typical number of pages.
- Format (e.g., preprinted form, handwritten, typed).
- Quality.
- Volumes (e.g., single versus duplex, daily, weekly, or monthly volumes, seasonal variations, peaks, troughs, and comparative types of statistical analyses).

Document Characteristics and Volumes

It is necessary to have a thorough understanding of the characteristics that apply to each document type and the volumes of documents involved. Table 8 defines the characteristics that apply to documents for scanning within a workgroup. The volume analysis needs to include an examination of the daily, weekly, or monthly volumes, seasonal variations, peaks, troughs, and comparative types of statistical analyses. It also needs to clear differentiation of the volume of documents received as single-sided versus double-sided (duplex), as there may be a requirement to acquire a scanning system that features duplex scanning capabilities or is able to scan color documents.

Document Preparation

Document preparation is a major project and requires a planned quality process to ensure that all documents are captured and processed. The quality processes need to incorporate review mechanisms to handle missing documents. There also need to be defined processes to ensure the integrity of the relationship between documents captured and registration (index) information that is to be stored in the databases.

It cannot be assumed that the physical documents are of sufficient quality to provide a legible digital image for viewing once they have been scanned. Some existing documents may have been crinkled, folded double, or torn. Documents may be fragile or falling part, particularly older ones. They may have had fluids or sticky food particles spilled on them, or have been otherwise impacted by similar destructive forces in today's office environments.

The legibility of all or some of the documents may be poor due to age or handling conditions. A document may be typed or handwritten on colored paper (e.g., blue ink on blue background). Typed text may be faint, and handwriting may be faint and a scrawl or not otherwise distinct. A document may be fastened with a staple or paper clip, and these types of normal office fasteners will need to be removed prior to scanning. Special attention also needs to be given to documents that have been prepunched with holes (to store in ring binders). Documents with prepunched holes might need to be fed through a scanner's auto feeder in such a way that the punched holes do not cause a paper jam or otherwise impact throughput.

The practitioner also needs to consider the requirements for scanning documents in batches, which might assist preparation, scanning, registration, and distribution processes. Documents of a particular type can be assigned into a batch environment, where the same preparation and scanning processes occur. Metadata that are common to the batch of documents (e.g., scan date, scan operator, date received, document type), can then be associated with each document at an item level during image registration and search and retrieval. Batch scanning of documents may also assist the process of document distribution, once the documents have been scanned and committed to the IDCM system using integrated workflow technology.

The processes for preparing documents for scanning, capture processes, inspection, and registration prior to permanent image storage need to be examined by the enterprise in order to determine an efficient and effective life-cycle. This strategy is particularly relevant for high-volume ad hoc and application-specific document imaging applications. Considerations might include the following:

- Does the application require separate workstations for capture, inspection, and registration? If so, then this requirement needs to be clearly stated, along with the cost for factoring into the project budget.

- Is it appropriate to resource the inspection (and registration) functions with different operator(s) than the operator(s) that did the preparation or scanning?

Document Scanning

Business scenarios within enterprises for document scanning are far too diverse for this book to offer a blueprint template for specifying scanning requirements. Typically, however, organizations have a requirement to scan a wide range of documents (ad hoc) or specific types of documents, usually forms-based (application-specific), or both.

Administrative requirements for imaging within the office environment may only involve capturing documents of standard sizes. However, there may be a specific business application for scanning larger-size documents or roll plans, and this application will typically require large-format scanning devices and software, different than the devices normally used for general administrative documents within the office environment.

Given the cost of hardware and software infrastructure, and the specialist skills and experience that may be involved in scanning documents, particularly large-format documents, organizations might consider whether the inspection, scanning, and registration processes might be best outsourced to an imaging service bureau. If it is decided to perform the scanning in-house, then it will be necessary to specify the capabilities required of the scanning subsystem, including those required for handling larger-size documents.

The following capture aspects of an imaging project may need to be considered by the practitioner when defining requirements:

- Bi-tonal, grayscale, or color imaging;
- Resolution;
- Scanner throughput capacity or redundancy; and
- Microfilm and digital image output.

There are so many options for document imaging, that here we provide purely a summary of key points.

Bi-tonal, Grayscale, or Color Imaging

The scanning requirement may involve a determination as to whether images are to be captured in the following digital representations:

- Bi-tonal is where the scanning subsystem converts source documents into pure black and white digital images.
- Grayscale occurs where the scanning subsystem recognizes colors and different shades of black on source documents and captures the images in shades of gray.
- Color imaging is where the scanning subsystem is capable of recognizing color on source documents and is able to represent the colors in the converted image.

There is a wide range of imaging applications within enterprises, where the consideration of bi-tonal, grayscale, and color scanning may be relevant. Due consideration should be given to the various opportunities offered by the different representations, because:

- The different representations may offer real business benefits in capture, readability, analysis, and accessibility of digital images.
- Once the source document is digitized, the representation may be set. For example, it is not possible to use manipulation tools to render a black and white image into color, and it would require a re-scan using color imaging technology.
- The representation may impact upon the display subsystem (e.g., display monitor, graphic device drivers) and on the printing subsystem (e.g., capability to print large-size images, color images).

Table 9: Bi-tonal Imaging

Characteristics of Bi-tonal Imaging
Usage Scenario: Normally used for scanning black and white documents, such as incoming correspondence and typed reports. *Advantages:* • Requirements for most black and white office documents are covered. • Scanning throughput is typically higher than grayscale or color scanning. • File size is smaller than grayscale or color (depending on format and compression techniques). • Grayscale effect might be achievable for bi-tonal images using a grayscale enabled display subsystem. • Bi-tonal imaging may be cost-effective, provided that it meets business requirements. *Limitations:* • Bi-tonal imaging is not best where it is important to capture shades of gray. • Forms applications may utilize color, and there may be processing benefits in capturing hard-copy forms in color. • A bi-tonal image cannot be converted to grayscale or color. The source document needs to be re-scanned. • Contrast needs to be adjusted during scanning to ensure that all information is readable (e.g., where documents are of poor quality, colored highlighters are used, or multiple colors are featured). • Scanning might be at a higher resolution than color. • Thumbnail images may not be of adequate quality for business use. • OCR/ICR tools may not deliver optimal results from scanned bi-tonal images.

Table 10: Grayscale Imaging

Characteristics of Grayscale Imaging

Usage Scenario:
Used for scanning documents that contain graphics or photographs, or line drawings that may be shaded with colors.

Advantages:
- Photographs or applications that require more detail and shades of gray are better represented.
- Images may be easier to read than bi-tonal due to smoothing effect created "depth" dimension (i.e., more information describing the image).
- Grayscale file may be embedded inside a bi-tonal file, thus keeping a manageable file size (e.g., grayscale photograph embedded inside a black and white application).
- Image clarity may assist image inspection and registration processes.
- The background of old or damaged documents may be easier to discern during scanning.
- Image capture during OMR applications may be improved. For example, the correctly marked choice on a form designed for an OMR application may be more easily detected using grayscale (provided the latest marking is the darkest notation in a designated box or circle on the form).
- Image capture during an OCR application, particularly for old or damaged documents, may be improved, provided the OCR software supports the capability.
- Resolution may not be as important for grayscale images as for bi-tonal, depending on the quality of the image required.
- Grayscale imaging may be beneficial for digitization of archival microfilm that contains grayscale information.

Disadvantages:
- Images may be slower to scan than bi-tonal. Video cards may be preferable to Small Computer System Interface (SCSI) devices for throughput. Check developments in grayscale scanners and processing boards. If considering grayscale, need to evaluate performance of scanners when images are output in grayscale, not while producing bi-tonal images.
- File size may be significantly larger than bi-tonal and may have an adverse impact on computer networks, intranet and Internet, and storage space, depending on compression capabilities of imaging system.
- The display and printing subsystem may be impacted due to image size, depending on compression capabilities of imaging system.
- Compression techniques may be lossy, which means that if there is sufficient loss on an image, then the relevance of grayscale may be negated.
- Cost may be a factor, depending on the business requirement. The costs of scanning, display, and printing subsystems are generally more expensive than bi-tonal scanning, display, and printing devices.

Table 11: Color Imaging

Color Imaging

Usage Scenario:
Color imaging is normally used with documents with color, such as forms, maps, plans, and photographs, or documents of poor quality, with use of colored highlighter pens, notes in margins, or feature multiple colors.

Advantages:
- The color schema of a form may be used to an advantage during data capture.
- Images, when viewed, may better delineate different colored zones of a map or plans, for example, contours.
- The scanning subsystem may offer the capability to scan color forms in duplex.
- Color images may make it easier to identify a particular document within a set during viewing, provided that multiple colors are used to distinguish relevant documents.
- Thumbnails, when used, allow for easy recognition of colored documents.
- Lower resolution scanning can be used, as color provides depth and clarity.
- Contrast adjustments are not needed during the scanning process.

Table 11: Color Imaging (continued)

Color Imaging

Disadvantages:
- Images may be slower to scan than bi-tonal and grayscale, but throughput speed comparisons depend on a range of factors including hardware, software, and formats.
- File size may be significantly larger than bi-tonal and larger than grayscale and may have an adverse impact on computer networks, intranet and Internet, and storage space, depending on the compression capabilities of the imaging system. (File size might not be an issue, depending on format and compression and resolution.)
- Display and printing subsystem may be impacted due to image size, depending on the compression capabilities of the imaging system.
- A color monitor is required to display images in color.
- A color printer is required for color output.
- Scanning, display, and printing subsystems costs may be a factor.

There are some key aspects to consider when reviewing requirements for bi-tonal, grayscale, and color imaging, and we provide synopses of characteristics from Table 9 to Table 11.

Resolution

It will be necessary for a supplier to size the storage requirements for an imaging system, and the types of resolution required for various documents will have an impact on image sizes and therefore storage capacity. The practitioner should consider the types of resolutions that might be applicable to the various types of documents involved in the imaging project.

This is not a simple task, because the requirements for resolution will vary, depending on the nature of the documents and the quality of the documents. For example, correspondence might be scanned at 200 dpi, but a letter received with feint typing or almost illegible handwriting, may need to be scanned at a higher resolution.

Table 12: Resolution Examples

Type of Document	Example Resolution	Constraints/Issues
Standard-size typed correspondence	100 dpi	Good quality documents, particularly those featuring multiple colors, margin notes, highlighted colors, may be captured at lower resolution than bi-tonal when scanned in color.
Standard-size typed correspondence	200 dpi	Must be good quality, legible, typed original document; file size is "relatively" small, facilitating exchange and collaboration.
Engineering drawing	300 dpi	Depends on quality, legibility of the drawing; drawings that are not good quality or not legible may require higher resolution, potentially 400 or 600 dpi (The drawing, depending on the nature of the requirement, may also be scanned in grayscale or color.)
Corporate brochure	600 dpi	Higher resolution may be required to capture the fine detail of a corporate brochure (The brochure might be scanned in color or grayscale.)

Table 12 provides indicative resolutions on the caveat that practitioners must examine whether these examples are valid for their particular requirements. It may be appropriate for the practitioner to scan a random set of (relevant) documents and evaluate the outcomes of the scanning.

The potential implications of scanning at a higher resolution are as follows:

- The speed of the scanning process may be impacted. However, modifications to the scanning process may prove useful. (For example, scanning a 300 dpi document in landscape orientation and using automatic rotation techniques may produce a scanning performance that is similar to portrait-oriented documents scanned at 200 dpi.) These types of opportunities need to be examined and specified, if required.
- The larger file size will typically impact storage and transmission requirements. (There may be a need to re-scan at a lower resolution and save to a different format for publication of a document, such as publishing a corporate brochure to the intranet or Internet.)

Once a source document has been converted to a digital image, the resolution may not be improved without re-scanning the source document using a higher resolution.

Scanner Throughput Capacity

Throughput speeds marketed for scanning devices are typically achieved under controlled "laboratory style" conditions and are probably not achievable within the enterprise environment. The speed with which documents are scanned will depend on a range of factors, including the capability of the scanning processing software and the nature of the documents to be scanned. The scanning operator may have a requirement to adjust resolution and contrast during bi-tonal scanning for a poor quality document, or a document may have to be fed into the scanner manually. The scanning process might be interrupted due to poor document preparation. It would be appropriate for enterprises to bench test scanning throughput speeds based on a mixed set of the organization's documents, as a strategy to help determine realistic throughput speeds.

Microfilm and Digital Image Output

There may be a requirement for enterprises to capture microfilm images as output from the same scanning process when documents scanned are scanned to digital image. This process may be applied in the case of enterprises located in jurisdictions where the legal admissibility of digital images has not been ratified by legislation, or where the legislation is unclear, or where there is uncertainty about the admissibility of digital images.

The process can also be appropriate where enterprises have a concern about the preservation aspects of digital images, including the evolution of data formats and capability of technology to access and view permanently archived digital images. The capture of a microfilm copy of a document may also help against the risks of accidental erasure of images on media, such as magnetic storage devices (disks and tapes), hence, the benefit of storing digital images on WORM devices.

Digital images can be preserved over time by planned periodical conversion of digital archive collections to new formats, but this practice requires discipline on the part

Table 13: Document Scanning

Consider the relevance of the following capabilities:

- Capture covers the defined range of defined document types (consider ad hoc and "application-specific" scenarios).
- Provide manual feed or automatic feed capabilities.
- Enable scan and conversion of different sizes of documents (specify sizes).
- Support random entry of various sizes (specify sizes).
- Enable multipage images to be stored and managed as a single entity (e.g., multipage TIF file).
- Enable duplex scanning for double-sided documents, while maintaining correct page sequence.
- Capture clear images of pages within bound items (e.g., selected pages from technical manuals).
- Save images to specified file formats (that suit the enterprise) — consider the relevance of TIF, GIF, JPG, PNG, and PDF formats.
- Support a range of scanning resolutions to meet the requirements of the defined document types.
- Enable user selection of resolution, contrast, and size settings, preferably selected from a table or similar display that enables end users to configure settings for specific document types.
- Pre-set default resolution settings for different types of documents (e.g., say 200 dpi for typed size A (or A4) correspondence, 600 dpi for a corporate brochure).
- Feature threshold settings at the scanner.
- Support capture of individual pages of a multipage document with an alternate default orientation (e.g., one or more landscape-oriented pages among multiple portrait-oriented pages).
- Feature blank page drop-out facilities to eliminate scanning of blank pages in documents.
- Split or merge documents and batches.
- Display an error message when a paper jam occurs during scanning.
- Provide a simple jam clearance and recovery operation.

Capability relevant to grayscale imaging:

- Identify which of the foregoing capabilities are relevant to the scanning requirement.

Capability relevant to production-level imaging environments:

- Allow new images to be added to existing stored documents prior to images being committed to permanent storage (e.g., optical disk, CD-writable media, etc.).

Capability relevant to archival and records management:

- Consider whether microfilm images are required as output in addition to digital images from the scanning process.

of organizations, and not all enterprises apply appropriate preservation techniques. Microfilm may provide an alternative record for risk mitigation.

Table 13 provides a list of document capture scenarios that enterprises may find useful when considering the definition of requirements for their specific imaging applications.

Document Inspection

The analyst also needs to document the nature of the inspection processes to be adopted to assure that the quality of each captured image meets the business requirements. The quality of scanned images can be impacted by influences such as:

- Poor quality original documents;
- Paper being skewed during the scanning process;

- Poor operator training;
- Inappropriate scanning settings (such as resolution and contrast settings) [Various types of documents, such as black and white, color, and half tones may impact settings.];
- Double feeds during scanning; and
- Missed pages for indexing.

Except for low-level ad hoc imaging applications, scanned images are not generally inspected during the scanning process. Consequently, images of scanned documents will need to be stored by the IDCM system and queued for inspection and registration. In a high-volume document environment, the inspection and registration functions take place before the committal of images to write-only devices, such as optical laser and CD-writable disks.

Furthermore, it is important to determine the level of quality inspection required, based on the level of risk that a business is prepared to accept. The following scenarios might be considered:

- The inspection of scanned images against source documents might require a validation of 100% of all pages scanned.
- The level of validation might only be, for example, 10%. Consider whether the system should support random selection of images for inspection or preconfigured settings, e.g., every tenth form or page of a document, depending on the business requirements.

Obviously, the higher requirement for quality inspection equates with a higher level of effort, and therefore, higher costs are involved.

Some requirements to consider for validating image quality are provided in Table 14.

Table 14: Quality Inspection of Images

Consider the relevance of the following types of inspection capabilities:
• Provide inspection methods that support the business requirements (state the level of validation required).
• Enable a re-scanned image (or images) to be correctly positioned in a multipage document.
• Split or merge documents and batches.
Support clean-up functions:
• Deskew is for adjusting images from pages skewed in the scanning process.
• Rotate is for adjusting images of pages that were inadvertently inverted during scanning.
• Despeckle is for removing small specks on images (i.e., from dust or dirt on scanned pages).
• Crop is for trimming an image.
• Support software (or knowledge base) helps resolve common problems with scanning.
For production-level imaging systems, in particular:
• Queue images for quality inspection and registration prior to their committal to permanent storage (e.g., optical disk). This is relevant for high-volume document image processing.
• Enable inspection of images at or before registration (indexing) and prior to the permanent storage of the image in the IDCM repository.

In high-volume imaging environments, the practitioner may need to specify the conditions required for holding scanned images in magnetic storage prior to committal to permanent storage, such as on an optical disk. For example, the requirement may be for the magnetic storage subsystem to provide the capacity to queue three working days of captured images for inspection and registration.

Document Registration and Validation

It is essential that digital images are registered (or indexed) to assist with search and retrieval. There are some considerations:

- The precise nature of the business requirement dictates the level of registration required.
- Metadata should be acquired at its source, wherever possible, and validated.
- The same types of registration and validation regimes as specified in Chapter 12 for digital office documents may be relevant.
- Registration profiles may be required to support indexing of different classes of documents.
- There may be a requirement to add or modify registration profiles for emerging requirements.
- Recognition technologies provide tools for extracting metadata as a by-product of the scanning process.
- Metadata may be captured once for a batch of scanned images, and be associated with each image in the batch.
- Metadata relevant to the document image might exist in business operational or administrative systems, which can be associated with captured images.

Production-level imaging systems may be required to integrate with a diverse range of core business applications, such as ERP systems, claims processing systems, law enforcement, or operational maintenance systems. In these circumstances, the interoperability requirements for document registration must be clearly specified.

For example, if data is stored in existing business systems, it might be possible to integrate metadata in the business system database with scanned images, perhaps by using barcode recognition technology during scanning, and then establishing links between the database and the image repository.

It is essential that the practitioner closely examine the opportunities offered for simplifying metadata capture and registration to reduce the effort required in having to

Table 15: Document Image Registration

Consider whether the following types of capabilities may be relevant:

- Metadata obtained via a document scanning subsystem should be transparently imported into the IDCM database and associated with relevant stored images.
- Provide facilities for scanning documents in batches to reduce data capture requirements.
- Feature the same types of manual registration functionality that were supported for digital office documents (refer to Chapter 12).
- Enable indexing and validation of images (and OCR text) to be performed at remote sites using a standard Web browser, thick client application, or terminal server emulation.

capture registration information using manual data entry. The statements in Table 15 may provide some insights into registration of images into the IDCM repository.

Search

The search capabilities relevant for document images might include the following types. (These capabilities should be read in conjunction with the search capabilities defined in Chapter 12 for digital office documents).

- Search using metadata captured during registration may be relevant to retrieve images based on index information.
- Facilities for content searching will not be available for raster images (unless a separate text document has been produced using OCR technology).
- Browse folder or search folder capabilities may be required.

Display and Viewing

The requirements for viewing an image depend upon the type of imaging application and the business processes involved. The following scenarios are indicative of those that might apply to diverse imaging opportunities with enterprises:

- The image viewer provided with the operating system (e.g., the Kodak Image Viewer in the MS Windows environment) might be applicable for viewing low volumes of TIFF or multi-TIFF images.
- Other desktop imaging tools might be suitable for viewing low volumes of JPG, GIF, or PNG images.
- The viewing tool provided with an IDCM system for office documents might be applicable for viewing images of office documents that are stored in, or proposed to be stored in, an IDCM repository.
- The viewing tool provided with an IDCM system for drawings might be applicable for viewing images of drawings.
- A production imaging system may offer a viewing tool that is an integral part of the overall imaging capability.
- Annotation tools might be required to mark up images.

Table 16 provides some suggestions about display and viewing for the practitioner.

Table 16: Display and View Capabilities

Consider the following items that might need to be resolved during requirements analysis:
• Consider the size and resolution of monitors available to all users of the system. Images may need to be displayed at, or near, full size, on any PC connected to the imaging system.
For production-level requirements, in particular:
• Provide high-resolution workstations to be used for quality inspection of images, or registration should display an entire page (size A or A4) unimpeded by any other applications.

Printing

There may be a requirement to support color printing. For low-volume ad hoc imaging, low-volume color laser or inkjet printers can meet this requirement at a workgroup level. High-volume color printing may involve a more substantial investment in printer hardware. There might be a requirement (depending on the capacity of existing printers) for enterprises to provide printers that output in standards (such as PostScript Level II). Consequently, it is essential that printing capabilities be analyzed and that anticipated throughput requirements be specified. For high-volume environments, the enterprise may wish to consider whether printer redundancy (black and white and color, if relevant) is required to assure business continuity in the event of a single printer failure.

Architecture

In Chapter 19, as part of the nonfunctional and domain requirements, we consider some of the architectural aspects for an IDCM solution and take into account matters such as system sizing and performance and system administration. There is material there that may provide insight into the nonfunctional requirements of a document imaging system.

However, there are specific considerations relevant to document imaging technology that include techniques to improve the capture, search, and retrieval performance of document imaging systems. When considering the performance aspects, techniques that may be useful for the analyst to consider when defining requirements include prefetching, disk setting, or disk clustering.

Prefetching

Production imaging systems may offer the capability to "prefetch" pages or images as a means of accelerating retrieval speeds. This means that when a document is retrieved from the magnetic or optical storage subsystem, the system will anticipate that the user will call for the second and subsequent pages of the document. The system begins to queue these pages in magnetic storage for quick retrieval. It may be preferable for the system to support page-level access in a prefetching environment to prevent whole documents from being retrieved before an end user can commence viewing the content.

Furthermore, there may be a business need that requires images to be processed at a remote site on a WAN, with the potential problem that the communications network would not offer the performance required for quick retrieval of images. Depending on the business requirement, it may be feasible to retrieve required images from the central system and download the images to a storage medium at the remote site during off-peak periods. Using this type of prefetching method, users at remote sites may be able to use images that were downloaded during the night (for example) for processing the next working day.

Disk Setting or Disk Clustering

Another optimization technique is disk setting (or clustering), whereby the analyst reviews the requirements for a logical arrangement of documents on the optical storage subsystem, as a strategy to reduce the number of optical disk load and unload actions. For example, an organization may scan documents relating to its employees and store them as images randomly on an optical storage system.

Delays might occur where the retrieval of a high volume of images for one employee is required, and they are distributed over multiple optical disk platters, some loaded or unloaded (perhaps all might be unloaded). The problem may be exacerbated if a separate inquiry is made for a large number of images for another employee, and the same storage conditions exist.

A potential solution is to facilitate speed of access and retrieval by designating specific optical disks for storage of images relating to employees with surnames in the A–C category, another disk for D–F, and so on, with sufficient space to allow for expansion within each allocated disk. This type of disk-setting, or clustering, would then allow all images for an employee with the surname A to be retrieved from the platter (or platters) designated to store the A–C categories.

Standards

Some of the standards relevant to document imaging include:

*   Support for industry standards such as TWAIN/ISIS;
*   Support standard API protocols for integration with core business applications and desktop software;
*   Support XML, J2EE capability for developing custom modules for production imaging applications; and
*   Standards published by AIIM International (refer to site listed in Appendix 3).

REQUIREMENTS DETERMINATION — RECOGNITION TECHNOLOGIES

Barcodes

Barcodes offer a range of functionality for capturing information from documents during the scanning and OCR processes. Table 17 identifies typical barcode usage scenarios for document scanning.

Table 17: Barcode Usage Scenarios

Barcode Scenarios	Description	Examples
Identify document	Barcode uniquely identifies a document	A barcode is used to preface a document or is attached to the leading page of each document, e.g., incoming correspondence.
	Barcodes can be preprinted	A student re-enrollment form might be preprinted with a barcode that uniquely identifies the student.
Identify new document	Barcode is used to identify a new document in a batch	The start of each new document in a batch is uniquely identified by a barcode.
Metadata capture	Barcode is used to provide reliable metadata for a document identifier	Data captured from the barcode can be used to assign an identifier in the IDCM system.
	Barcodes can also be used to capture additional metadata	A barcode can be constructed to capture additional metadata relevant to a specific requirement, for example, a particular scanning location, as well as the document identifier; barcode identification on color document using color scanners.

The practitioner will need to consider the barcode structure and definition, and whether barcodes are to be batch printed within the enterprise or by a third-party organization. It is essential that the barcodes produced and affixed to documents be in a format that will be compatible with the scanning software that is to be installed. Most workgroup and production-level scanning systems support barcode recognition software that recognizes the standard Code 39 barcode format.

Optical Character Recognition

Background

OCR may be defined as software that is used to convert digital images that have been captured from hard-copy documents into editable text documents. OCR may be used to capture metadata from machine-printed forms and may also be used to convert good quality print documents to text ("document processing").

OCR is often used when electronic versions of documents are unavailable, and OCR might avert the necessity to retype large documents. Furthermore, OCR might also be used to output text from facsimile transmissions and capture text from newspapers and journal articles.

There are a number of devices that support image capture for OCR, but the desktop scanner is the one device generally used to perform the capture functionality. The imaging system converts the hard-copy document to a noneditable image, which contains multiple pixels, and which cannot be edited. The OCR system uses algorithms to try and determine the characters and produces a text file output.

It is important, particularly in high-volume document environments, that the quality of an image is optimized, using tools such as orientation adjustment, removal of speckles, and desk wing, before OCR processing is invoked. The OCR output may be saved as a text (TXT) file or in formatted text, such as a word-processing or spreadsheet file, PDF format, or HTML.

The output may be stored on a network file system or imaging server (depending on the nature of the requirement) or in a DMS, where implemented. The OCR file can be accessed using typical office viewing and editing tools that correlate with the output format of the text.

Categorization

OCR exists as package "out of the box" software or a toolkit. A toolkit is essentially a set of programs and utilities that enables software developers to customize OCR software to meet the requirements of a specific application. The decision whether to use OCR software or an OCR toolkit is generally related to the nature of the document imaging system. Table 18 provides an overview.

Functional Overview

The key functionalities offered by OCR technology (although it may not be available in all available software products) includes the following:

- Conversion of digital images to text (This enables the printed information from hard-copy documents to be obtained in editable text.);
- Use of tools that enable images to be optimized for conversion to text (It is noted

Table 18: Typical OCR Scenarios

Imaging Environment	OCR
Desktop	Packaged software – OCR may be bundled as a part of other software, e.g., facsimile transmission software. OCR may be bundled with the software supplied with a scanner. When bundled with other software, OCR software may be a reduced set of the functionality otherwise available in the full version of the packaged software.
Workgroup	Packaged software – OCR may be packaged, but the decision depends on the volume of documents to be imaged, the imaging application installed, and the OCR requirements. The package may consist of a single user license installed on a PC within a workgroup network segment, with the capability to store output to a networked file system for sharing and security. Alternatively, the installation may consist of multiuser licensed software, with the same storage and sharing and security facilities.
Production	OCR toolkit – The decision depends on the volume of documents to be imaged, the imaging application installed, and the OCR requirements. OCR capability in production imaging environments needs to be fast and accurate, otherwise, too much time is spent on validation of the text output. OCR output may be stored on a networked file system, imaging repository, or within a DMS library, depending on the specific requirement. Production environments may involve forms-processing applications.

that where OCR software is used in addition to existing imaging software, then the imaging software might also offer these or similar tools.);

- Functionality of Lexicon (or dictionary) (Text that is not recognized by the lexicon may be highlighted and presented to the user for validation. An alternative is to edit the text in a word-processing system that supports a dictionary.);

- Output of text in a variety of formats [For example, depending on the package, the text might be output into MS Word (or another word processor), MS Excel (or another spreadsheet), HTML, and PDF formats.];

- Ability to send text to email packages such that a user is then able to dispatch the output to a specific distribution list;

- Integration of voice, so that text can be read back to a user for validation;

- Recognition of table and spreadsheet formats and maintenance of layout; and

- Provision of intuitive wizards to guide users with no or minimal training through the OCR process.

The following functionalities are more likely to apply to production imaging systems, but may also be evident in high-volume workgroup imaging as well:

- OCR integration with workflow may be offered, which may be relevant to a workgroup or production imaging environment.

- Scheduling functionality may be available. Images might be captured in batch and then scheduled for OCR processing during a period of low activity. This may be important for production imaging systems, particularly where large volumes of documents may have to be converted using OCR.

- Automatic zoning tools may be provided, which are designed to decompose pages and identify text from graphics, so that the OCR engine processes text, not graphics. Automatic zoning might be relevant where there are high volumes of diverse document types.

Table 19: OCR Functional Capabilities

Consider whether there is a requirement to use OCR for recognition of text in quality, printed documents, and the following initial set of capabilities might be checked as to their relevance to your requirements. (It may be important to specify the existing scanner or imaging software capabilities within the enterprise so that a determination can be made as to whether the investment can be protected).

- Operate within the desktop operating system(s) that will be used by the enterprise. State the operating system(s) required.
- Determine if the product is certified to the operating system by an independent authority.
- Check the capability of scanning multipage documents simply and effectively. The simplicity and effectiveness of the system should be checked.
- Provide intuitive wizards to guide users with no or minimal training through the OCR process.
- Support preprocessing tools that enable images to be optimized for conversion to text.
- Support for conversion of text to the following types of formats may be required, for example:

  Word processing, spreadsheet, plain text (TXT), and rich text (RTF), for editing and review

  Hypertext Markup Language (HTML) and Extensible Markup Language (XML) for publication to Internet or intranet

  Portable Document Format (PDF), relevant for legal applications and regulatory requirements (Specify whether the requirement is to support PDF "Normal," PDF "Image Only," or PDF "Image + Text.")

- Launch the relevant desktop authoring software (e.g., MS Word) directly after OCR processing, if this is a requirement.
- Support OCR of bi-tonal, grayscale, or color images (define specific requirements).
- Support integrated lexicon or dictionary for error detection and correction (compare with potential capability to use dictionary within word-processing package). Highlight exceptions in the text for validation.
- Prompt user to perform quality inspection of OCR text prior to registration of the document into the IDCM repository, i.e., use spell-check facilities.
- Support mix of viewing capabilities. Specify if there is a need to view images and text simultaneously. If so, specify whether horizontal or vertical viewing of images and text is required. (Note: viewing capability may be impacted by the capabilities of the display monitors within the organization.)
- Integrate with messaging technology, e.g., send to e-mail — seek confirmation of the mail applications supported (e.g., MAPI compliant).
- Integrate with workflow management software (state specific requirements).
- Enable voice integration, such that text can be read back to a user for validation.
- Recognize table and spreadsheet formats, and maintain layouts.
- Enhance images to increase accuracy of output (relevant for hard-to-read documents such as some facsimile documents, poor quality text).
- Integrate with Web publishing technology to convert documents to output and publish multipage Web documents with hyperlinks.
- Scan, OCR, and edit simultaneously. This may be difficult in high-volume (production imaging) environments, where OCR operations may need to be separate from the scanning operations.
- Recognize multiple languages within the document (if this is a requirement).
- Support output in multiple languages. This may or may not be important to an organization, but make sure the OCR system can output to your own language.
- Assure that there is support for industry standards such as TWAIN.

Production-level requirements, in particular:

- Operate within the server operating systems that will be used. State the operating systems required (e.g., Windows, Macintosh, OS/2, Solaris, Unix/Linux).
- Schedule OCR conversion activities. Specify whether OCR is to be activated at scheduled periods, and state the requirements.
- Extract metadata from specific zones on high-volume document and forms processing. Consider the applicability of automatic zoning (diverse range of documents) or manual zoning (standard documents such as forms), because OCR systems may offer different functionality.
- Assure that there is support for industry standards such as ISIS.

- Manual zoning tools, or page templates, may be offered, that operate in a similar fashion to automatic zoning tools, with the exception that they typically apply to high volumes of the same document types, as evidenced in forms-processing applications.

The enterprise may wish to consider the requirements for OCR technology as an aid in converting scanned images to text or extracting metadata from predefined zones in a form to assist with registration.

When converting a physical document to text using OCR, the quality of the output achieved from the OCR process will depend upon the nature of the physical documents being scanned and the experience of the operator doing the scanning. For example, if characters on a document cannot easily be read or easily distinguished by the human eye, then the OCR application will probably have difficulty as well. Experienced operators may use techniques such as scanning at a higher resolution or making contrast adjustments to assist with OCR processes.

Furthermore, preparation of images using tools such as orientation adjustment, despeckle, and deskew utilities before OCR may enhance the quality of the text output. One needs to take into account that existing (or specified) imaging software may also offer this type of functionality.

OCR suppliers may make claims about the accuracy and performance capabilities of their products, but these results are normally achieved under laboratory conditions. The best way for an enterprise to gain confidence about the level of accuracy of OCR packages may be to:

- Specify requirements for OCR;
- Conduct product tests using batches of typical documents from within the organization; and
- Evaluate the results.

Table 19 provides some suggestions for determining functionality for OCR systems.

Some further observations are that a wide range of factors may impact the speed of the OCR engine. These factors include the volume of documents involved, the resolution at which documents are scanned, the layout of the documents, and whether multiple languages may exist in the document.

Advanced Character Recognition

Background

Advanced character recognition technology such as ICR software extends OCR functionality by offering a wider variety of tools for recognizing hand print, OMR by means of sensing checked, circled, crossed boxes, mixed printed and handwritten fields, barcodes, and signatures.

The primary focus of ICR is in the domain of "forms processing." ICR provides the opportunity to reduce manual data entry effort by quickly capturing and validating as much data as possible.

While ICR can also be used to capture unstructured information using intelligent document processing, it is probably best used for semistructured processing, such as forms containing definable read areas on the document.

The output from ICR is metadata that is passed to the next stage of processing, which typically involves integrated workflow to enable the next step of the business process, postdata capture, to be invoked.

Categorization

Like OCR, ICR systems can be acquired as a packed solution or delivered as a toolkit for enabling ICR functionality to be embedded within an enterprise's own systems, or third-party products.

Functional Overview

The following types of functionality may be relevant to an enterprise's requirements:

- Capturing metadata from machine and printed semistructured documents, such as forms, i.e., "forms processing";
- Capturing metadata from images regardless of whether bi-tonal, grayscale, or color images;
- Detecting different types of forms or documents to facilitate the process of capturing metadata;
- Removing background and cleaning up images prior to data extraction;
- Configuring field types to improve recognition, i.e., defining fields such as dates, currency, post codes, character types, numeric parameters, and so on;
- Supporting multiple languages;
- Configuring read areas for specific document types;
- Supporting dual mode operations to enable data comparison between two data entry operators;
- Providing facility for simple operator confirmation or correction of characters that ICR recognizes with a low confidence level;
- Supporting easily-configurable user-defined validation routines such that changing business rules can be applied to ICR processing;
- Assuring capability to validate captured metadata against business databases (potentially via ODBC), such as look up for post code, city, etc.;
- Supporting fuzzy matching to facilitate validation;
- Enabling flag validation failures for operator intervention; and
- Supporting multiple import and export formats.

REQUIREMENTS DETERMINATION – FACSIMILE AND DIGITAL CAMERAS

Facsimile Management

In Chapter 3, we discussed the typical methods for managing inwards and outgoing facsimile transmissions within enterprises. Furthermore, earlier in this chapter, we stipulated the requirement to define existing facsimile systems to understand the business and technology aspects of these systems. Registration of incoming and outgoing facsimile transmissions is important for vital business documents, and enterprises may wish to have incoming/outgoing facsimiles managed electronically, with items captured and stored in the IDCM repository.

Users may have the requirement to dispatch facsimiles from their desktop computers, with the option to capture facsimiles that represent business records as a registered item in the IDCM repository. The end user should have the option to signify that the facsimile is a formal record and be enabled to register the item into the IDCM repository in a simple manner.

The system should also have the capability to receive, capture and manage digital images of incoming facsimiles. The system should enable end users to signify that specific facsimile images are a record of a business transaction. The system might feature integrated workflow for managing the processes associated with the distribution of images to end users. The system may also be required to integrate with the enterprise's messaging infrastructure to provide a central point for users to access notifications, with links to facsimile images stored in the IDCM repository.

If an organization plans to integrate incoming and outgoing facsimile capture and management within an IDCM solution, the following types of functionality might act as a primer for development of functional specifications:

- Providing the facility for outward facsimiles to be captured into the IDCM repository;
- Enabling digital copies of both inward and outward facsimiles to be registered as a record of a business transaction;
- Providing automated facilities for inward facsimiles to be captured into the IDCM accessible by links routed (by workflow/email) to action officers;
- Enabling integration with facsimile gateways for inward facsimiles to be captured in image format for registration into the IDCM repository;
- Integrating with the enterprises' electronic messaging system(s) to provide a single point of access for users to send and retrieve correspondence (Specify the messaging systems.); and
- Integrating with the address directory so that electronic correspondence with external personnel can be transmitted automatically by email or facsimile, whichever is available or most appropriate.

Digital Cameras

Earlier in this chapter, we indicated that enterprises should define the existing digital camera capabilities that exist within the organization. Enterprises should explore, within the context of the IDCM solution, their requirements for managing still and video images that are captured using digital cameras.

Typically, images are downloaded from digital cameras, using (a) diskette, (b) tape, or (c) direct download from camera via cable interface. The objects are stored on a networked file system. The technology may not yet have evolved to enable direct capture from digital camera to the IDCM repository, and it may be necessary for enterprises to load the objects into the repository from the file system.

In such circumstances, the objects are treated much the same as for digital office documents when loaded into an IDCM repository. In other words, once transferred into the repository, the end user will be required to register the item using metadata, and associate it within a user/group security regime.

SUMMARY

In this chapter, we provided background information about the nature of document imaging systems and discussed formulating requirements for workgroup and production-level imaging systems.

The analysis and specification of requirements for document imaging can be a complex task, depending on the specific business application and required technology. The imaging requirement should be examined within the planning context that we proposed in Chapter 6, and the requirements analysis framework we discussed in Chapter 10.

There may be a requirement for the document imaging system to integrate with another business system, e.g., claims processing system, in which case, that aspect of the requirement needs to be analyzed and defined as part of the user requirements documentation.

Quite often, imaging systems, particularly production imaging systems, are integrated with a workflow management system that enables captured images to be routed in a controlled manner to specified roles. The analyst needs to define the nature of the integration with the document and the flows involved in the workflow.

We will discuss the requirements for workflow management systems in the next chapter.

Chapter 16

Functional Requirements – Workflow

OVERVIEW

In Chapter 4, we reviewed how workflow management systems might be considered an integral component of IDCM architecture. We discussed the high-level functionality of workflow management systems and considered some of their capabilities.

We noted that workflow management systems extend the functionality of core document and Web content repository services by enabling the controlled distribution of documents for review and approval. Furthermore, they also support controlled processes for publishing new or updated content to Internet and intranet Web sites.

Our primary objective in this chapter is to extend our discussion on the role of workflow within the context of IDCM by reviewing the types of functional requirements to be specified when analyzing and determining business and technology options for integrating workflow with document and content repositories.

REQUIREMENTS ANALYSIS

The analysis of requirements and development of specifications for the use of workflow for business process automation, including document/Web content review and approval processes, should follow a similar approach to the framework proposed by Sommerville (2001, p. 98), which we discussed in Chapter 10. This approach encompasses user and system requirements, with the latter being divided into three subsets: functional, nonfunctional, and domain (Sommerville, 2001, p. 100).

User Requirements

Approach

We discussed an approach to analyzing and determining user requirements for IDCM solutions in Chapter 11. The principles of defining user requirements at the strategic, operational, and tactical levels applies to workflow management applications, with the general exception of ad hoc workflow processes. The outcome of this analysis is a specification that contains the business models and the specific application requirements for the workflow management system.

Process Modeling

It is important to model and define the workflow routines required, or at best, a sample of workflow modules required when seeking proposals from suppliers, so that there is a clear understanding of the types of workflow processes envisaged for document or Web content review and approval. This will give an enterprise better understanding of its own requirements for workflow and will assist suppliers in giving a firm price when submitting proposals for the development of initial workflow modules.

Organizations may find business process modeling tools useful when analyzing and modeling workflow requirements. The techniques and tools that might be useful during the development of a requirements specification were discussed in Chapter 6. The acquisition of business process modeling tools (which might be available as part of a workflow product) provides enterprises with a tool for the definition of existing and required workflow processes. The complexity of the workflow requirements may dictate the type of functionality required from the process modeling toolkit, ranging from an uncomplicated drawing tool to more sophisticated business process modeling tools that provide simulation and analytical functionality.

Change Management

There are potential cultural and political implications that may need to be managed during consideration of workflow. Workflow systems have the capability to enable owners of the workflow to stipulate time constraints and also provide the tools by which to monitor the progress of workflow during the entire business process and obtain performance reports. Individual employees, workgroups, or staff associations may view planned implementation of workflow as a means of imposing management controls over the users of the system, i.e., the employees.

Enterprises also need to consider the interactions of individuals within social groups and interactions between groups, and there is a need for clear and open communication from project initiation to project completion. Enterprises need to closely examine the cultural and political implications of introducing workflow, and this is best carried out during a feasibility study, when business and technology solution options are considered.

Functional Requirements

The functional requirements of the workflow management system are defined in a specification that sets out expected functionalities, how they meet user requirements, and how they support the business process model. We discuss some key points that are relevant to functional requirements analysis for workflow systems in the remainder of this chapter, within the context of document and Web content review and approval processes. We also included an initial catalog of functional requirements that might be a useful starting point for enterprises considering using workflow to support document and Web content review and approval processes.

Nonfunctional and Domain Requirements

The nonfunctional requirements for workflow management systems are typical of most information systems and relate to architecture and system performance. The domain requirements relate to definition of the enterprise's IT infrastructure into which the workflow management system must integrate. The technical requirements should be developed and included as part of the nonfunctional and domain requirements for the IDCM solution, which are covered in Chapter 19.

FUNCTIONAL REQUIREMENTS ANALYSIS

Workflow Client

Enterprises need to give consideration to the type of workflow client that might best suit their organization's needs. Workflow client interfaces have been generally developed to integrate with one or more of the common GUIs to desktop operating systems (e.g., MS Windows, OS/2, and Macintosh). Desktop operating systems evolved rapidly during the 1990s, and the trend continues into the new millennium. Frequent product releases meant that the client software for workflow management systems had to be redeveloped or absorb new functionality to keep pace with the new operating system developments.

Since the mid-1990s, consequent upon developments in Web browser technology, many enterprises adopted strategic directions that position the Web browser as the preferred client interface for accessing organizational information in the form of documents, multimedia, and database systems. The workflow management industry responded to these strategic directions within business and government by investing in the development of workflow technology that incorporates the standard Web browser as the user interface. The benefits claimed for using a Web browser as the client interface to a workflow management system are as follows:

- The direction is consistent with the adoption of the Web browser as the interface of choice in enterprises.
- Dedicated desktop client application software is not necessary for participants in the workflow.
- The requirement for software upgrades to be distributed to the desktop is reduced, although there may be a requirement to make configuration or plug-in changes to the browser.
- The ubiquity of the Web browser interface may make it easier for collaborative development of projects to extend to participants outside the organization, such as business partners and service providers.
- New participants in the workflow process can be engaged quickly (noting that there will be change management and training requirements).

However, enterprises are in different stages of the transition to a Web browser client for accessing information assets. Similarly, developments in workflow management software are such that some vendors are better positioned strategically to deliver Web browser enabled workflow functionality. For example, some vendors developed browser-enabled process definition software but did not develop a Web browser interface to the system monitoring or system administration functions.

If enterprises are defining workflow requirements for ad hoc document review and approval workflow, or collaborative workflow within projects, or external workflow with business partners, they will need to consider system interfaces. For example, there will need to be consistency between the workflow client, the IDCM repository client, and the email client (for event notification).

Consequently, during the feasibility study or requirements analysis and definition stage (refer to Chapters 8 and 10), enterprises need to develop a clear understanding of their specific requirements for the workflow interface. When defining requirements for the workflow management software, they must consider the following:

- The product, version, and service release of the Web browser software package to be used as the proposed interface to the workflow management system;
- The status of the uptake of Web browser functionality within the enterprise;
- The status of the email or messaging client (e.g., Web browser based or client application);
- The functionality required by IDCM software in desktop client or Web browser client, and the current state of functionality offered by IDCM repository management products, identifying the gaps; and
- The functionality offered by workflow management systems in a desktop client or Web browser client, and the current state of functionality offered by IDCM repository management products, identifying any gaps.

Enterprises wishing to use workflow to collaborate with external participants in the development of projects, documents, and reports will need to consider the requirements of each business partner and service provider. For example, it would not be prudent to acquire the workflow package that interacts with the enterprise Web browser environment but does not support the Web browser deployed by a business partner or service provider.

Process Definition

The workflow management system should provide process definition, design, and configuration tools that enable end users to construct simple document review and approval templates quickly. These tools should enable end users to define the life-cycle of the document review and approval workflow, from the creation of the workflow through to its termination. These tools should feature a GUI and definition aids, such as wizards and drag and drop functionality to assist end users.

It is expected at this stage of workflow evolution that simple to advanced document review and approval workflow processes should be defined and configured without the need to resort to customization (development of scripts). However, the workflow management system should also offer standard industry tools for customization, such that more complex workflow processes can be defined by trained technical staff within the organization or by qualified systems integrators.

Workflow Management

The same type of GUI should be provided to enable authorized users to view or modify a workflow during its life-cycle process. An authorized user should be able to invoke the following types of capabilities during the workflow process:

- Allocate priority to workflow tasks;
- Change priority to tasks during processing;
- Redirect a specific task or groups of tasks, e.g., for absentees;
- Escalate workflow based on conditional logic;
- Allocate pending status to a workflow; and
- Recall a workflow.

Note that these are just some of the wide range of functions available.

The workflow may have the capability to activate automatically a workflow process based on an event trigger, such as routing documents to a specific role based on a defined date. For example, trigger a workflow to initiate reporting for an end-of-month board meeting.

Workflow System Administration

The nature of the relationship between the IDCM repository services and workflow will have a bearing on the administration of the workflow system. If workflow is embedded as a core item of functionality inherent within the IDCM repository manager, it is likely that the workflow will be administered using the same tools available for the IDCM repository. If the relationship is one of integration between an IDCM repository manager and a workflow product, then the workflow system may need to be administered separately from the IDCM repository. The latter instance would mean that technical end users might then have to be trained and gain experience in using two types of system administration tools, and potentially a third, if the integration of a document imaging system is also involved.

Enterprises may need to examine the extent of the administration commitments required for the workflow system, because technical systems administrators in enterprises generally work under extreme time constraints. In short, the workflow should offer an intuitive interface that enables system administration functions to be performed as simply as possible, without having to rely on complex syntax commands. Regardless of the architecture of the IDCM repository manager and workflow, the workflow should provide flexible tools (graphical interface, drag and drop) for management of user security, permissions, and access, potentially with electronic authorization.

Workflow as a Record

Workflow management systems can have an important role to play in providing a record of evidence or a business transaction. We noted in Chapter 7 that a record was defined (ISO 15489-1:2001, p. 3) as "information created, received, and maintained as evidence and information by an organization or person, in pursuance of legal obligations evidence and information or in the transaction of business." Essentially, a workflow process may represent all or a component of a business transaction, as well as the context in which a document (or set of documents) is created, received, and maintained, including transition states.

Different workflow management products may offer different types of physical implementation with regard to how the record is captured and managed. For example, it may be stored and saved as a workflow object that captures the totality of the transaction, including the document with the correct version. Consequently, it is important for organizations to document their logical requirements for the capture and management of a workflow as a record of the transaction. Business users should review the capabilities offered by the solutions during the package selection stage.

Production Workflow and Web Enablement

If the requirement is for high-volume structured workflow processes involving images, documents, or Web-enabled business processes, it may be appropriate to consider production-level workflow systems. These systems provide the architecture to capture work packets, distribute them in accordance with preset rules, manage the distribution of work packets throughout the business process life-cycle, and update core business systems.

Integration with Email

Most end users in business today are generally comfortable with the concepts and use of email and have grasped at least the rudimentary essentials of a Web browser. Most users will check their email daily, and perhaps log onto favorite Web sites using a Web browser. The email system (email client or Web based) has become the central notification point for business users. Whereas earlier workflow technology tended to feature separate in-trays for incoming tasks, there is strong end user support for the email client to be the single notification system for messages, and this aspect should be considered during the requirements analysis. If integration with an email client is a requirement, then practitioners will need to specify the products, versions, and service releases the enterprise is using for its collaboration and messaging infrastructure.

Document Access

It should be simple for users to access documents and other objects (e.g., folders) in the IDCM repository from the workflow system. The workflow system should support the capability to route links and shortcuts to single or multiple documents in the IDCM repository within the workflow. Users should have the capability to access these documents directly from the message using the links and shortcuts.

Document routing workflow systems that do not yet support this capability may require users to initiate a search of the repository based on the document identification, which is a two-step process. Alternatively, the workflow may copy and insert single or multiple documents from the IDCM repository as attachments within the workflow message. This practice may introduce version and security complications if the integrity of the object in the workflow is not synchronized with the original object in the IDCM repository.

The link or shortcut method is quicker and simpler for end users and may help gain user acceptance of the technology. It also offers a mechanism for maintaining the integrity of documents during a workflow process. The requirements might also include the capability for users to browse folders or search for other objects in the repository at specific points in a workflow process.

Drawing Management and Workflow

There are implications when a process managed by an embedded workflow within a component of an IDCM solution is not available to end users who do not have access to the component software. For example, a drawing management system might be an integral part of the overall IDCM solution, but it might embed its own workflow for managing the processes associated with changes to engineering drawings. Engineers and draftspersons may have access to the workflow and processes and (where authorized) be able to review the progress of the workflow and make adjustments. However, end users who are not licensed to use the drawing management module might not have access to information (such as workflow statistics, reports, and the like).

FUNCTIONAL REQUIREMENTS DEFINITION

Defining the functionality of a workflow management system that manages document and Web content review and approval processes is a complex task, which is relative to the business processes involved. Therefore, we cannot provide a "blueprint" that enterprises can simply adopt as a template because of all the complexities and variables involved, some of which are outlined as follows:

- Enterprise requirements for workflow are extremely varied. Some organizations have not implemented simple workflow systems. Others are considering document review and approval workflow systems. Still others are looking at integrating

Table 1: Primer of Workflow Functionality

Functional Statement	Comments
Integration – Desktop/Network Operating/Database Management Environment	
• Integrate with desktop operating system environment.	State the products, versions, and service releases of the desktop operating systems that will be used by the enterprise.*
• Integrate with enterprise Web browser and server environment.	State the products, versions, and service releases of the Web browsers that will be used by the enterprise.*
• Integrate with network operating system environment.	State the products, versions, and service releases of the network operating systems that will be used by the enterprise.*
• Comply with enterprise standards for the database management system environment.	State the enterprise's standard database management system environment, including products, versions, service releases, and patches supported.*
* Determine whether there is a requirement by the enterprise for the workflow management client to be certified to the (relevant) operating system or DBMS by an independent authority, and if so, state the requirement.	

Table 1: Primer of Workflow Functionality (continued)

Functional Statement	Comments
Integration – Messaging/Email Services	
• Integrate with enterprise collaboration and messaging systems for automatic delivery notification of a workflow controlled task via email.	Specify the products, versions, and service releases that the enterprise uses for its collaboration and messaging infrastructure.
• Route a link or shortcut to a document in the IDCM repository rather than an attachment to participants that have access to IDCM repository services within the enterprise domain.	Make sure that enterprises confirm that the "enterprise domain" covers all IDCM repositories within the organization. Confirm that the link access to a document via workflow is not restricted to a specific library.
• Discern whether a workflow recipient is outside the IDCM enterprise repository domain, and route an attachment rather than a link to a document in the IDCM repository.	Use for sharing documents with end users who do not have access to the IDCM repository or for collaboration with external business partners via extranet.
Integration – Document Library Services	
• Define a specific life cycle for a particular class of document, and initiate workflow based on the life cycle definition.	Note that the same class of document (e.g., a request for proposal for a specific project) may have a specific life cycle from the time it is created until the time it is archived. It may be appropriate for the workflow management system to initiate a workflow based on the life cycle definition of the specific class of document (e.g., request for proposal).
• Provide a transparent link from the workflow to document objects stored in the IDCM repository during the workflow life cycle.	Note that this transparent access might be achieved via links or shortcuts to single or multiple documents from the IDCM repository when initiating a workflow process.
• Enable end users to insert additional links or shortcuts to documents during the progress of the workflow packet.	Enable users to create a response document (such as a letter to customer) during the workflow, and (for management control) the next participant in the workflow will receive a link or shortcut, rather than the document.
• View a document involved in a workflow, at any stage, by an authorized user.	Define access rights in the IDCM repository. Depending on how the IDCM repository and workflow products are bundled by the supplier, the authorized user may need to be authorized in the IDCM repository and the workflow.
• View annotations in a workflow, at any stage, by an authorized user.	Make sure that annotations can be viewed after a workflow has been terminated. Make sure that the annotations can be viewed when the workflow exists as a record.
• Provide the capability for end users to browse or search objects (documents, folders) in the IDCM repository at steps in the workflow process.	Define where this functionality is required in the workflow process, and ascertain whether the functionality is supported at each step.
• Integrate with the IDCM repository to enable the current version of drawings, electronic images of plans, and technical documents to be retrieved and managed within a workflow.	Assure that workflow supports the retrieval and display of documents, such as drawings and images, in native application or viewing tool. Also assure that version control is maintained during all stages of a workflow.

Table 1: Primer of Workflow Functionality (continued)

Functional Statement	Comments
• Integrate with the IDCM repository so that users access the current version of templates developed in desktop office applications for production of form letters, checklists, and work instructions.	Provide security to the user to complete templates that may be required to be as complete forms or as data entry. The workflow system may be required to allow different users with different security permissions complete sections of the template. The system would be required to differentiate the components of the template and enable insertion of data based on the security permissions. Stipulate the current versions of the desktop office applications being used.

• Maintain integrity of objects in the IDCM repository during every stage of a workflow process. Rules might be as follows:
  – The current "released" version of a document must be the document that is accessible for viewing by nonauthors.
  – Authors within the workflow process are able to view the latest version of the document (as edited).
	Note that this functionality is the essence of using workflow for document review and approval.
	
	Instruct enterprises to stipulate their specific processing requirements in terms of the transition of document objects (including versions, status, and security) throughout the workflow process.
	
	Advise enterprises to validate the correct versioning and security of objects during the entire life cycle of the workflow process during the package selection process (refer to Chapter 20).

• Modify (automatically) the status and security of a document in a workflow process once it has been approved. Rules should be as follows:
  – The status of the latest version of the document is changed so that it is the "released" document for viewing by end users.
  – The previous released version of the document is superseded and not available for viewing, except by designated authorized users.
	Instruct enterprises to stipulate their specific processing requirements in terms of the transition of document objects (including versions, status, and security) throughout the workflow process. There needs to be a definition of the requirement to maintain the workflow as a record, as the process of releasing the document and superseding the previous version is a record.

Process Definition Tools	
• Provide process definition, design, and configuration tools that enable end users to construct simple document review and approval of templates quickly.	Develop the workflow system so that it features process definition tools such as a GUI, wizards, and drag and drop functionality to assist end users.
• Provide standard industry development tools to enable customization of more complex workflow processes.	Note that suppliers might be required to provide development tools that enable integration with business systems such as ERP, GIS. Advise enterprises that they should state their preferred development tools (e.g., Java, ActiveX), based on their strategic software development directions and the skills and experiences of technical staff.
• Provide an object-oriented environment that features reusability of objects.	Note that enterprises may require an object-oriented process definition environment, so that defined objects inherit functionality from other objects for reusability.
• Provide flexible definition and management of template (form)-based processes.	Determine whether enterprises require a workflow system to support templates and forms, including creation and modification.

Table 1: Primer of Workflow Functionality (continued)

Functional Statement	Comments
• Provide a library of customizable templates that support rapid development of standard (horizontal) workflow processes.	Determine whether enterprises are able to acquire a workflow system that will provide a library of templates for various types of forms, thus enabling the templates to be customized with relative ease and facilitating development of general workflow modules.

Workflow Management

• Support a wide variety of items, such as digital objects and data, within a work packet.	Design the workflow system to enable users to access work-item-related data, as well as objects within the workflow module.
• Specify length of time a work packet is to spend in a queue before alert notification.	Enable administrators to arrange the workflow system to notify a specified role in the event that a work package has been too long in a queue awaiting the next process. The system might be configured to send the alert via email to the nominated role.
• Identify resource constraints, such as time constraints and staff availability.	Allow the workflow system to be configurable to enable constraints such as resources, public holidays, and scheduled holidays, to be defined as part of the management logic.
• Support serial routing of work packets to defined roles.	Note that this is the basic requirement of any workflow system.
• Support parallel routing that enables a work packet or item to be distributed to more than one role or action officer.	Provide parallel routing, which enables a workflow packet to be distributed to two or more action officers simultaneously.
• Support "rendezvous" functionality for work packets that are split for parallel routing, enabling rejoin and reconciliation.	Explain rendezvous, which is the stage where the inputs are the action work packets from parallel processes. The rendezvous specifies the next action and invokes the transaction.
• Support cyclical style workflow, such that the completion of one workflow process may automatically trigger another process.	Determine whether there is a requirement for the completion of one workflow to invoke another workflow process. If so, define the workflow requirements, and indicate the intersection between the processes.
• Redistribute work packet where the queue is overloaded, or where action officer is absent (planned or otherwise).	Enable an authorized person to have the capability to reassign a workflow.
• Enable workflow to be captured and stored as an electronic record.	State the enterprises' logical requirements for how a workflow is to be captured and managed as a record.

Workflow Monitoring

• Provide simple (graphical interface) access to monitor and modify workflow during its life cycle process.	See comments following under *Process Definition Tools*.
• Feature the following types of monitoring capabilities:	

• Feature the following types of monitoring capabilities:
  - Allocate priority to workflow tasks.
  - Change priority to tasks during processing.
  - Redirect a specific task or groups of tasks, e.g., for absentees.
  - Alert delays in a workflow process.
  - Escalate workflow based on conditional logic.
  - Allocate pending status to a workflow.
  - Support suspension and reactivation of work package when all required work items are reconciled.
	Read the list of functional statements that provides some examples of monitoring workflow. Enterprises should review and develop these to their own requirements.

Table 1: Primer of Workflow Functionality (continued)

Functional Statement	Comments
Performance and Monitoring	
• Produce workflow metrics to facilitate performance reporting.	Identify inefficiencies or blockages in the workflow with the help of metrics.
• Provide easy-to-use and fit-for-purpose end user report generation capabilities.	Instruct the enterprise to define specific reporting requirements that are "fit for purpose."
• Support the scalability required for deployment across the enterprise.	Instruct the enterprise to define the specific scalability requirements. For example, the initial workflow requirement may be constrained to a specific project. It may be proposed to deploy a set of workflow processes across the enterprise progressively.
Systems Architecture/Performance	
• Enable distribution of objects over networks from a central server.	Determine if workflow objects can be distributed from a central server. If not, then there may be implications for environments that support distributed computer networks. It may mean that separate hardware, operating system, database management system, and workflow server licenses are required to host the workflow system, with cost, maintenance, and support implications.
• Support optimization techniques that minimize impact on infrastructure systems and maintain security.	Enable optimization techniques that might include support for workload balancing to assist with the equitable distribution of work packets.
System Administration	
• Provide flexible tools for system administration, such as configuration of user security, permissions, and access. • Provide electronic authorization mechanisms.	Determine whether the administration of a document review and approval workflow management system, using the same utilities that might be provided for the IDCM repository system administration (covered in Chapter 19), may be a preferred option for organizations. If this is the case, then it should be so specified. See comments in this catalog for the *Process Definition* tool.
• Assign security levels at each stage of a workflow and for specific tasks.	Advise enterprises to define the security required based on business usage scenarios.
• Provide flexible management of user security, permissions, and access, with electronic authorization.	Assure that the workflow system will provide administration capabilities that meet the requirements of the enterprise. The enterprise should specify the nature of the administration functionality required.
• Feature tools for simulating functionality and performance of a workflow.	Enable this type of capability for its importance in simulating the functional and performance capabilities of complex and high-volume workflow processes.

workflow as part of their Web-enabled business operations. Consequently, in addition to document-centric routing, there may be a requirement for a workflow management system that embraces wider functional and nonfunctional requirements for administrative workflow or production workflow.

- Workflow tools are now embedded in key business planning systems, such as ERP systems, Employee Resource Management Systems, and Land Information Systems.
- Workflow management systems are constantly evolving in terms of capabilities of product functionality.
- Development tools and capabilities fluctuate with the volatility of technologies associated with the Internet and intranet Web environments.
- Categories assigned to workflow are fluid. For example, ad hoc systems are providing increased functionality, while production workflow systems are offering greater flexibility to make them attractive to wider markets.

As a starting point, however, enterprises can make use of the condition statements in the catalog shown in Table 1 when determining the functional requirements for a workflow management system that is integrated with or embedded within an IDCM. We have deliberately not tried to differentiate functionality between the workflow "types," particularly because we cannot anticipate an enterprise's specific requirements, and the workflow market is too volatile to sustain defined categorization of functionality.

Enterprises should develop, add to, or modify these condition statements according to their particular needs and circumstances. In developing their requirements specifications, they can differentiate between those conditions that are mandatory, those that are highly desirable, and those that are desirable. These factors may well have an impact on the selection of a workflow management solution that is "fit for purpose."

SUMMARY

In this chapter, we discussed workflow, primarily within its relationship to IDCM and requirements for document and Web content review and approval. It is apparent that workflow had its origins in the study of better ways of processing work and the development of assembly line processing techniques. With the advent of automated workflow management systems, there have been rapid advances in the capabilities of the technology, to a point that there is now maturation of the technology.

Innovative workflow applications can assist businesses in transforming from functional-centric organizations to customer-focused organizations by automating processes that cross the boundaries of organizational structural hierarchies. Its integration with IDCM repository services provides a cohesive environment for managing changes to documents and Web content in a structured way. The workflow industry and professional services companies are tasked with helping enterprises to better understand how they might exploit the capabilities of the technology. The types of initiatives that will help meet that challenge are delivery of innovative and workable solutions that are sustainable and represent value for money.

The requirements for workflow at a business or government enterprise level are exceedingly varied, ranging from ad hoc document review and approval to complex production-level systems, supporting Web content management strategies for CRM, SCM, and application processing opportunities.

Table 2: Workflow Decision Choices

Workflow Type	Possible Decision Choices
Ad Hoc/collaborative	Workflow module embedded or integrated with enterprise's preferred collaboration and messaging environment
	Workflow functionality embedded within the IDCM repository that also integrates with collaboration and messaging environment
	Third-party tool that is integrated with the IDCM repository, that also integrates with collaboration and messaging environment
Administrative/production (ERP embedded)	If much of an enterprise's structured or semistructured business processes are being managed by an ERP system that embeds workflow or certifies particular third-party products, then production or administrative level workflow management requirements might be met by the ERP system or solution partner.
	However, embedded workflow capabilities might be constrained to only those processes managed by the ERP system. Where there are a wide range of requirements, it may be appropriate to consider autonomous workflow systems with a scalable, flexible and extensible architecture, and proven capacity to integrate with diverse enterprise business systems.
Administrative/production (no ERP, requirement is separate from ERP process, or strategic autonomous workflow system for multiple deployments)	Some organizations may require a highly functional workflow management system. For example: • Those that have not adopted an ERP system. • Those that adopted an ERP system but still require a production or administrative level workflow management system, particularly in support of e-business initiatives
	These organizations may have a requirement for a highly functional autonomous workflow management system.

In this volatile environment, it is difficult to maintain clear definitions of workflow types and boundaries, and it is too complex to codify a simple set of functional requirements for a workflow management system that will meet the workflow requirements of an enterprise.

However, the information presented in Table 2 might be useful for enterprises when considering their workflow requirements.

Enterprises need to consider these types of decision choices during the analysis of business and technology solution options during the feasibility study stage, and again review their choices in the requirements analysis stage. This analysis will enable an enterprise to better understand the scope of its workflow requirements and the types of choices for which it may have to find a solution.

In the next chapter, we discuss the analysis and definition of requirements for management of engineering and technical drawings.

Chapter 17

Functional Requirements – Engineering and Technical Drawings

OVERVIEW

In Chapter 3, we discussed a range of subsystem options for managing engineering and technical drawings. The most suitable system solution is the one that meets the business requirements.

This chapter extends the discussion on engineering and technical drawing management systems that we had in Chapter 3. Our objective now is to examine the functional requirements for a system to help enterprises to better manage engineering and technical drawings.

REQUIREMENTS ANALYSIS

If the enterprise is determined to proceed with the acquisition of a drawing management package, there is a diversity of scope and business needs within organizations, ranging from sites that need basic functionality to sites that need rich drawing management functionality.

Consequently, it is imperative that enterprises clearly analyze and define their requirements for drawing management, so that the organization has the best chance of acquiring a software package that meets their defined requirements. One of the first points of analysis is to determine user profiles.

When we discuss the requirements analysis phase for drawings, we will refer to "drawing management software" or express the requirement as part of an "IDCM system." A stand-alone drawing management system or module integrated with a DMS might provide the functionality. The best technology fit will depend upon the enterprise's business requirements.

User Profiles

When determining requirements for drawing management software, the organization needs to determine the user profiles. We need to define the number of people within the organization that create drawings, review or approve drawings, and view drawings. The definition of the user profile will help to:

- Determine the client software that might be suitable for the profile.
- Determine the costs for the licensed software.

A user profile might be prepared using the template provided in Table 1.

Table 1: Drawing Management — Example of User Profile

Location	User Class	Required Functionality	Total Users	Concurrent Users
Drawing office	Author	- Use drawing templates - Create drawings - Create renditions - Register drawings - Make revisions - Check-in/check-out - Initiate a drawing workflow, router, or distribution - Search for drawing - View drawing - Print drawing	20	8
Engineering design	Review/approve	- View drawing - Review drawing - Markup drawing - Initiate/participate in a drawing workflow - Approve drawing - Print drawing - Search for drawing	10	4
Plant maintenance	View/markup	- View drawing - Markup drawing - Initiate/participate in a drawing review workflow - Print drawing - Search for drawing	48	10
Drawings administrator	Key user administration	- Maintain and manage configuration - Maintain security profiles - Maintain templates - Create/maintain workflows	1	1
IT administrator	System administration	- Backup and recovery - First line of technical support - System enhancements and development	1	1
			80	24

Desktop Integration Requirements

When an organization requires extended drawing management functionality, enterprises need to establish whether it is the same desktop client that is offered for managing digital office documents or whether a separate desktop client is required.

Quite often, particularly where an integrated drawing management product is offered, specific desktop client software is used for authors that create drawings or technical manuals, or participants in review and approval, and automated workflow processes associated with engineering change management.

If there is a requirement for a separate desktop client for drawing management functionality, enterprises should assure themselves of the following:

- The drawing client software satisfies the same type of desktop integration requirements that were discussed for managing digital office documents (Chapter 12).
- The drawing client software integrates with the email messaging system, so that the drawing package and email client are integrated to the same extent as discussed in Chapter 13.

CAD Software Integration

The organization may have a requirement for direct integration of the drawing management module with CAD tools, so that key document management services (such as check-in, check-out, search and retrieval) are accessible from within the CAD package used within the enterprise.

The enterprise may need to consider whether the following types of functional requirements are applicable:

- Enable check-in, check-out, browse, and search and retrieve functions while in an active session of the enterprise's standard CAD packages. It is necessary for the organization to specify the CAD products and versions, and it is preferable to specify applicable software patches and service releases.
- Integrate the requirements with the specific versions of the CAD tools being used within the organization. Enterprises should clearly identify the CAD tools (state the correct versions) that need to be integrated with the drawing management software.

CAD Templates

The IDCM has the capability to manage CAD templates that are used as the basis for developing new drawings. Templates are treated as objects in the IDCM in much the same way as other types of digital documents, in that the system implements version control over the templates, so that drafting officers are assured that they are accessing the current version of a template when initiating a drawing. This capability may apply to drawing offices (or similar) or where drawings are developed in collaboration with external business partners.

Drawing Number Schema

It is necessary for the enterprise to have a clear understanding of the types of numbering schemes that are used for numbering drawings. Some organizations have a standard drawing numbering scheme throughout the enterprise, while others, particularly where there have been business mergers, take-overs, or laissez-faire style management approaches, may support multiple numbering schema.

Practitioners need to clearly define the numbering schema used in all relevant locations, because it is important for the organization to acquire drawing management software that supports the numbering schema. Alternatively, as part of its change management process, the organization may decide to rationalize multiple drawing numbering schema and implement a standard numbering scheme throughout the enterprise.

If the drawing management module does not support the enterprise numbering schema, there is a potential for significant ramifications, such as:

- The vendor may offer to develop the functionality to meet the drawing numbering schema. However, the cost of the development may be prohibitive, and then there is a need to maintain the customized module through subsequent version releases of the IDCM system.

- The organization may have to alter its drawing numbering schema to suit the dictates of the software, which may be a major change management issue that does not fit with expectations. There may be a requirement to renumber hundreds of thousands of existing drawings, although this might be overcome by an attribute in the IDCM system that captures the old drawing number.

The enterprise should also consider, where relevant, the requirement for creating drawing numbering schema for new drawing offices, sites, and collaborative ventures with business partners. If this is a requirement for the enterprise, one of the issues to review during evaluation of products is the simplicity with which new drawing numbering schema can be configured within the drawing management module.

One requirement that may be important for organizations is for the drawing management module to automatically allocate the next serial number during the process of registering a new drawing. Consideration should be given to whether this requirement needs to be extended to cater for multiple drawing number schemas.

Special consideration may need to be given to drawings where the same drawing number has been allocated, but they are differentiated by a sheet number. In these circumstances, the drawing number plus the sheet number comprise the primary key that is the unique identifier for the drawing number.

Another requirement that organizations may wish to consider is the capability of the drawing management module to preallocate drawing numbers, which may be applicable where external contractors seek a list of numbers for allocation to drawings that they are developing. Other options might be considered during the feasibility study analysis, such as enabling contractors to access the drawing module of the IDCM system using a secure extranet interface and workflow.

If there is such a requirement, then it is important for the enterprise to define current methods for preallocation of drawing numbers, and determine what modified or additional functionality might be required, and give consideration about the requirements to synchronize incoming drawings from contractors, which have had preallocated drawing numbers, with metadata or objects within the system.

Revision Number Schema

As with the issues with the drawing number schema, enterprises need to define the types of revision numbering schema used for numbering revisions of drawings. The same types of important ramifications we discussed with drawing numbering schema may also apply to revision numbering, i.e., as follows:

- There may need to be costly customization of the IDCM system if the revision numbering schema cannot be configured as part of the "out of the box" packaged software, and then there is a need to maintain the customized module through subsequent version releases of the IDCM system.

- The organization may have to alter its revision numbering schema to suit the dictates of the software, or determine some type of workaround processing to suit specific requirements.

Enterprises might also consider if they have a requirement for the drawing module to support major (revision) and minor (version) numbering. If this is the case, then it is important to define the specific format required for the numbering.

Again, similar to preallocated drawing numbers, enterprises may need to define the logical requirements for synchronizing revision numbers in drawings from contractors, with metadata in the drawing management application.

Title Block Integration

Enterprises may wish to consider if they have a requirement for synchronizing the metadata that identifies a drawing with attributes (metadata) in the drawing title block. This type of functionality allows the metadata in both registers (i.e., IDCM database and drawing title block) to be synchronized during registration and update of drawings. However, consideration may need to be given as to which register is considered the primary source for synchronization, to avoid data integrity conflict.

View and Markup Tools

The use of CAD tools is typically the domain of drafting personnel, who utilize the software as part of their normal routine. Engineering staff may also have access to CAD tools for review and markup, but not always. Furthermore, there may be other staff within the enterprise that have a requirement to view drawings, and potentially redline, annotate, or mark up drawings, though access by them to the CAD software may be neither cost-justifiable nor required.

Consequently, drawing management packages normally provide integrated viewing tools with the capability to view drawings at a desktop workstation, using a browser-enabled viewer or via a desktop viewer. The view typically offers redline and mark-up facilities as well, so that an engineer may mark changes required to a drawing, or maintenance personnel may point out modifications required based on maintenance work.

However, as we discussed earlier, the enterprise needs to examine the acceptability of viewing and markup of digital drawings. There may be logistical issues as well. The viewing tool might support redlining capability that is cumbersome. For example, there may be difficulties with freehand drawing — some end users may be more dexterous with a computer mouse than other users.

The size of display monitors might increase the level of acceptance for end users — the minimum requirement may be 19" monitors for users regularly accessing drawings. However, the provision of large-size monitors may not be acceptable if the end user has to access a number of drawings simultaneously, or if there is complex detail within the drawings, in which case, users may find it more acceptable to continue to use hard-copy drawings and mark them up manually.

It is necessary for enterprises to determine the formats of the drawings that are to be supported by viewing tools that will enable end users to view drawings. They must also decide whether viewing is required via Web browser or operating system desktop, or both. It is important for enterprises to clearly define all of the drawing formats required to be supported and any other formats (for example, technical journals, images, and specifications) that the drawing viewing tool will need to support.

Enterprises need to take into account not only the formats required from CAD tools within the organization, but also formats that might have been generated using superseded or previous versions of CAD packages. They also need to consider formats of CAD drawings received from external service providers or business partners (which might use more up-to-date versions of a CAD package than the enterprise uses).

One of the key functional aspects that may need to be considered when reviewing drawing management software as part of an IDCM suite is that, generally, two different types of viewers may be offered by IDCM vendors. One integrated viewer may be offered for viewing and markup of digital office documents, and a second integrated viewer may be offered to view digital drawings and provide redline and mark-up capabilities for drawings.

Advanced drawing packages will save redline and mark-up details as separate objects to the referent drawing object, so that the integrity of the drawing object is maintained. However, redline and mark-up objects may only be accessible via the viewing tool that was used to create the objects. If there are two independently integrated viewers, potentially from different suppliers, it may not be possible for a user with the digital office viewer to view redline and markups created using the drawing viewer, and vice versa.

Consequently, the requirements for viewing digital office documents and digital drawings need to be analyzed and clearly defined in a requirements specification. Enterprises should determine whether a functional dichotomy exists within the solutions being evaluated, determine the potential impact on the organization if it exists, and discuss strategies with the supplier as to how to resolve a dichotomy.

If there is requirement for redline and markups for drawings to be viewed via the office viewer, the obvious answer would be for the IDCM to open a viewer that supports both types of environments. However, it may not be practical to provide the same tool for viewing office documents and drawings, because the viewers for drawings are normally more expensive than viewers for digital office documents, or they may not support all of the office formats required.

Classification Structures

Enterprises may have a requirement to provide a project-centric structure for managing drawings and associated technical and project documentation. This type of arrangement would enable all types of relevant objects to be accessed using browse, search, and retrieval functions.

It may also be the case that the classification structure provided in existing legacy systems (such as drawing registry systems) is no longer relevant. The drawing registry and drawings might have been inherited by the enterprise during a merger, take-over, or company or government restructure. The enterprise needs to examine the classification schemas applied to current drawing environments, and determine its requirements.

The classification structure being considered for drawings should be analyzed and defined in terms of a hierarchical classification system that is consistent with the system implemented in the IDCM as part of the enterprise file classification.

Compound Document Relationships

There is a need for synergy and collaboration between drafting officers working on these complex projects. The information synergy is often achieved by attaching copies of other drawings relevant to the particular project or subproject as background overlays to the drawing being produced. The drafting officer that develops an electrical drawing will effectively be overlaying the drawing over other design files, so that the drawing set appears as a single entity, whereas the files are, in fact, quite separate. The background overlays are called "reference files."

CAD software packages typically store all reference files as part of each associated master design file. When a design file is accessed by a drawing user, the CAD system automatically displays the master file and associated reference files to the user. This type of compound document relationship functionality is proprietary to each type of CAD software package, and was generally developed before the introduction of Microsoft's OLE technology, and later developments.

It is important for enterprises to understand this concept when analyzing and defining requirements for a packaged solution. Many software packages may claim to support "compound document management functionality," but this claim may relate to support for management of OLE links. The packages may not support the management of parent and child relationships between drawings, such as evidenced in reference files.

Given that drawings will be migrated and stored to a host drawing management environment that is, in effect, "foreign" to the CAD software, the drawing management software must manage the relationships between drawings so that the user is advised that reference files exist, or the software may open the reference files automatically, together with the design file.

The management of these compound document relationships is likely to be a key requirement in drawing offices and similar environments, where there is a lot of drawing development. Where enterprises are recipients of drawings, rather than creators, there may still be a requirement to know that the linkage relationship exists between the drawings. Enterprises may also need to take into account that end users who are not provided with drawing management client software may not be able to view the linkages between drawings, but simply view them as independent objects in the IDCM repository.

Transmittals

Many enterprises continue to use hard-copy forms for transmittal of drawings (and technical documentation) within the organization and to and from external business partners or service providers. The minimum functionality required is to enable end users to tag documents, or provide similar functionality for transmittal, and enable the users to record details of manual transmissions.

A transmittal note typically needs to include attributes such as the drawing number, current revision number, and drawing title, and generally includes transmittal number, data sent, whether an acknowledgement is required, the number of copies of a drawing sent, the media in which the objects are sent, an indication as to whether there is a requirement to resend the next revisions, and a place to include a general message to the recipient.

It is not uncommon for drawing management modules to offer automated transmittal processes as an alternative to manual transmission. For example, the drawing management system might be able to output a copy of the relevant drawing metadata to templates, which can be set up in the IDCM system using word-processing or spreadsheet packages.

The automated transmittal based on the template, and the associated drawings, can then be dispatched electronically to business partners or service providers via email or integrated workflow. Alternatively, the metadata (and associated objects) might be published directly to a secure Internet site (extranet) that is accessible by the partners and providers. However, the organization needs to consider its state of readiness in terms of culture and behavior when reviewing requirements for automation of transmittals.

If transmittal automation is required, the enterprise needs to define its specific requirements. For example, a list of transmittal recipients (such as external drawing contractors) will be required. There needs to be a means of tagging drawings for transmittal, or there may be filters applied to automatically tag drawings based on a specific business rule. The tagging method overcomes the potential for errors in manually typing or writing drawing numbers on transmittal advice notes. Instead, the user is able to tag relevant documents in the drawing management system.

If a tag system is to be used to identify drawings for transmittal, then there may be a requirement to clear tags (or similar) once the transmittal has been sent, and there may also be a requirement to update the drawing status during the process covering issue of transmittal to receipt of a revised drawing. During this period, the drawing status might be required to show that the drawings are subject to revision under transmittal. End users that are so authorized may need to be able to check the drawing management system to determine which drawings are subject to revision.

It may also be necessary to have a means of flagging that an acknowledgement is required from the recipient. From an information management perspective, the system may be required to generate a report of acknowledgements pending, to show those transmittals sent where no acknowledgements have been received.

Consideration also needs to be given as to the processes required for generating a transmittal when there have been revisions to documents that are already subject to a current transmittal. The system may be required to support a status of transmittals pending and to produce a register of documents that have already been transmitted to recipients, which have been later revised. This status should be cleared upon generation of the transmittal for the revised documents.

There may also be the requirement to register updates in the drawing management system for drawings (and other types of relevant documents) that are received from contractors. These drawings are usually in a batch accompanied by a transmittal note, which we might reference as a transmittal received object. Again, there may be the requirement to define the attribute data that are to be captured relating to the transmittal received object and define business process requirements for updating the drawing management system with the revision number and status for each drawing in the batch.

Distribution List

During the design and construction phases of an infrastructure project, there is a requirement for construction to be based on the latest drawings and technical specifications. In the absence of well-managed procedures or automated distribution facilities, updated drawings and specifications may not be provided to contractors in a timely manner. There is the risk that the requirement to issue the updated documentation may be overlooked.

Similarly, a drawing that has been included as part of a scope of work during a current tender process may be revised. There needs to be a notification mechanism to warn affected parties that a drawing, which is involved in a tender process, has been revised. The risk otherwise is that tenders may be lodged with pricing and contractual obligations based on outdated information.

There needs to be a simple way to automatically notify all interested parties when a drawing has been revised or reissued as a different drawing number. This may involve the IDCM system supporting an automated distribution list of parties that have a specific interest in a drawing or set of drawings. When a revision occurs, the system should automatically generate a transmittal advice to the relevant parties, such as a subcontractor.

The enterprise might consider whether there is a requirement for the drawing management module to support virtual distribution lists, associated with a particular contract or project, subproject, or type of drawing (e.g., electrical drawings). In other words, drawings for a subproject would be routed to a distribution list of members that have an interest in drawings for that subproject. All electrical drawings, regardless of project, might have to be routed to a specific role or group that has a specific interest in electrical drawings.

Printing

The organization needs to consider its printing requirements for drawings. It may be quite feasible to use existing installed laser printers to print drawings up to B size (A3 ISO metric standard). Suppliers of drawing management modules will typically support printers that are compatible with the operating system, but this aspect needs to be checked. Organizations should define the printer types and validate that the drawing package supports printing by testing the functionality.

In many cases, drawings may be much larger-format documents than B size (or A3). In these instances, there will be a requirement to print drawings to a plotter. Organizations need to define the plot devices that are already installed, because they may desire to retain old plotters that continue to provide reliable service. It is important to state the requirements for printing to the existing plotting devices, and state whether there is any intention to upgrade plotters. The enterprise needs to be assured that the drawing management module will support the plotting devices specified in their requirements and types of files that need to be printed.

Workflow

The enterprise may have a requirement for using integrated workflow or business process automation tools (refer to Chapter 16) to manage the transition of the status of drawings during the drawing management life-cycle. These types of tools may be integrated with the drawing management module, or the IDCM might utilize the inherent or integrated workflow module offered as part of a DMS packaged software.

The use of automation tools for managing the drawing life-cycle processes may suit the enterprise, where there is extensive development of new drawings or frequent modifications to drawings. There may also be a requirement to collaborate between sites, including the potential to automate the life-cycle during collaboration with business partners or service providers.

When reviewing the options for automation of drawing processes, the enterprise may need to consider the facilities offered in enterprise systems, such as maintenance management systems. They also need to consider the capability to manage the entire process from creation to review, authorization, and importing into a system based on functional location and other properties in the drawing title block. When evaluating potential products, the enterprise may also need to consider whether the business process automation is achieved via the workflow tool that will form an integral core component of the IDCM system or whether the drawing management solutions offer their own workflow tool.

Where an IDCM solution offers an integrated drawing management module that features its own workflow tool for managing life-cycle changes with drawings, the enterprise might find that end users who do not have the drawing management client software, may not be able to view the workflow process. This may or may not be an issue, but it needs to be considered, particularly if there are any implications from a recordkeeping perspective, as records managers may have a requirement to access workflow from a regulatory or organizational perspective.

Digital Signatures

Enterprises may wish to consider the relevance of using digital signatures for review and approval signatures on drawings. Many engineers and maintenance personnel prefer to "see the signature" on a hard-copy drawing before making decisions. The use of digital signature technology for visualization of signatures on a digital drawing may be helpful in facilitating change management.

Synchronization of Drawings

We mentioned earlier that many enterprises continue to rely on having access to physical drawings for planning, design, construction, and maintenance of infrastructure and plant equipment. Given the cultural factors and potential functionality restrictions of electronic markup of complex drawings, the drawing management module will probably have to cater to the management of multiple formats of the same drawing object. For example, drawings might be held in digital CAD form, TIF, DGN, or PDF formats for publication, as well as in physical form (paper or microfilm).

The drawing management module may need to be able to place management controls over revision processes and manage access to digital objects, as well as track copies of physical drawings held in set locations, as well as record the existence of microfilm versions. Aside from this type of functionality, there will be a requirement for the drawing management module to synchronize the management of updates to all formats, when a new revision of a drawing is released. If this synchronization is not achieved, then the enterprise will end up having incorrect drawing revisions stored physically in set locations, such as on microfilm.

Drawing Register

One of the key requirements for many engineering environments (construction projects being but one example) is the capability of the drawing management system to generate a primary register of drawings, called a Drawing Register. This register is a list showing the latest information about drawings, which can be displayed and printed, for example, for field site work.

The register typically lists the primary information relating to the drawing, for example, a unique identifier such as drawing number, revision number, or document title. It may also provide tag identification for drawings that have been tagged for transmittal.

If a register of drawings is a report that is required from the IDCM system, then the enterprise needs to specify the template format for the register of drawings, and the frequency of the output required. If an IDCM system does not offer this type of functionality as standard, it may be feasible to initiate a search and produce a report based on predefined criteria, and then export the data into a flexible, simple desktop productivity tool, such as a spreadsheet.

A typical template for a drawing register, sorted by drawing number, which might apply in a construction environment, is as provided in Table 2.

Drawing History

It is imperative for the drawing management module to manage the history of drawings, so that there is a clear record of all markups, revisions, reviewers, and approvers. This requirement may be needed to provide an historical record of the changes to infrastructure and plant equipment over time, and may be required to support legal discovery purposes.

For example, the enterprise may need to provide the specific revision of a drawing that was released at a specific point in time, perhaps as an exhibit in litigation regarding an industrial accident, or to support a dispute over a contracted construction requirement. The drawing history needs to be accessible for viewing but not for edit.

An example of a template for a drawing history report is provided in Table 3.

Table 2: Sample Drawing Register

Drawing Number	Revision	Drawing Title	Status	Date Received	Date to Client	Date Approved	Comments
BG-123	5	Main Engine Room – Effluent Mechanical Flow	A	30-6-2002	30-6-2002	1-7-2002	Amended pump

Table 3: Sample Drawing History Report

Drawing Number	Current Revision	Drawing Title	Status	Archive Date	Origin	Revision Archived	Date Received
BG-123	5	Main Engine Room – Effluent Mechanical Flow	A	30-6-2002	Design Office	4	01-01-2002

Audit History

An audit history report might have to be produced. The report may follow the same format as that shown in Table 5, with the addition of a column that would be used to include details of *who* made the new revision or changed the status.

Project Structure

The drawing management software may be required to provide a project-centric structure for managing project documents, where all document object types (including drawings) can be grouped by projects for browse, search, and retrieval functions. Users may require the capacity to create a new project, assign groups within the project, and specify user and group security profiles, as well as folder and document level security.

Search Facilities

The same type of search facilities that we discussed in Chapter 12 generally apply to searches for drawings. However, drawing management software also typically offers the capability to search text within CAD files (the system needs the capability to index words in drawings and manuals) to assist with search and retrieval operations. Enterprises should specify the types of searches required, and define sort criteria that might apply to drawings. For example, sort on drawing number, project, subproject, category, origin, status, type, and similar types of attributes relevant to the specific organizational requirement. The system should also have the facility to include saved (or predefined) searches and to assist with identification and retrieval of drawings based on attributes such as functional location or equipment name.

ERP Integration

Enterprises may use an ERP system (or similar) to support supply and maintenance management. There may be a requirement for the IDCM system to integrate with the ERP system, so that documents and drawings relevant to the supply and maintenance processes of the plant, its equipment, and its facilities can be accessed quickly.

The integration between the ERP system and the IDCM system would enable authorized users to easily access and display drawings and technical documentation stored in the IDCM system from a variety of ERP modules, the functionality of which needs to be specified. (It would also enable the ERP users to store and manage reports in the IDCM system.)

For example, depending on the functionality required and level of integration between specified ERP modules and the IDCM system, designs; engineering drawings; specifications; standard operating procedures; data sheets; financial, production, and other reports and other documents would be immediately accessed by ERP users upon release.

Materials management would be enhanced, as the integration between ERP and the IDCM system would enable engineers, technicians, planners, and operations personnel to effectively share up-to-date information in a variety of formats, including text, graphics, CAD drawings, images, and multimedia.

For example, a maintenance engineer using the ERP system could review scheduled maintenance activities for the next week. Where an item has to be replaced, the engineer would be able to list and view all relevant current documents, including maintenance procedures and relevant plant and equipment drawings of the equipment.

Most ERP systems offer a "drawing registry system" that stores relevant metadata pertaining to a drawing (Drawing Number, Title, Revision, Status, Date Last Revised, Reference Drawing Number, Site Code, and other attributes), but the products are unlikely to offer a secure IDCM repository.

If there is a requirement to integrate the ERP system with the drawing management module of the IDCM system, it is essential that a requirements specification be prepared to define the integration requirements. It would also be valuable to determine from the ERP provider, information relating to the IDCM packages certified as integrated modules, or IDCM partners with whom the ERP provider has a relationship.

When defining the requirement for the ERP and IDCM implementation, the analysis will need to consider the ownership of the metadata, because (for example) the materials management module of the ERP will require key metadata relating to drawings to enable materials management processes to be invoked, and the drawing management module of the IDCM system will also need to maintain specific metadata relating to each drawing object, for revision processes, search and retrieval (for users outside the ERP domain), and perhaps for automated business process management routines.

Object Load Capabilities

There may be a requirement in the enterprise to load drawing objects and other types of technical documentation from existing file systems and other types of storage media into the IDCM repository. The following options might be applicable:

- Low-volume object load — This might be achievable using drag and drop functionality from existing storage systems into the IDCM system. In this type of circumstance, the attribute data from existing drawing registry systems would not be automatically synchronized with the loaded objects.
- Medium-volume object load — This might be achievable using scripting to enable the objects to be loaded into the IDCM repository and metadata derived from existing drawing registry systems to be loaded into the IDCM tables. Depending on the scripting, metadata might not be automatically synchronized with the loaded objects.
- High-volume object load — This might be achievable using a bulk loading utility provided by the vendor. In this type of situation, it is quite common for bulk loading tools to enable metadata extracted from existing drawing registry systems to be captured into the IDCM repository and synchronized with loaded objects.

Table 4: Bulk Load Issues

Issue	Comment
Cost	The cost of the bulk loader software utility is typically relatively high.
Restrictions	There may be restrictions on the use of the bulk loader utility. For example, it may be licensed for use on only one desktop computer and may have a device that physically restricts usage. This type of restriction may mean that, where multiple file servers are involved, there is a requirement to progressively move the loader from one location to another. The enterprise needs to consider whether a laptop might be useful as the host device, because the laptop can be moved from one network segment to another relatively easily.
Value	There may be an issue regarding the long-term value of the bulk loader. Once the organization has completed its migration of (relevant) objects from existing file systems, the requirement for the bulk loading tool may diminish.

Enterprises may also wish to consider the types of issues raised in Table 4, as these issues may arise when considering the acquisition of a bulk loader utility.

Drawing Conversion

Many enterprises are developing initiatives to scan and convert physical drawings (e.g., paper, film) to digital images, as a strategy to enable authorized end users quickly to access, retrieve, and display drawings using facilities such as intranet sites and Web browsers. We examined some of the requirements for conversion of physical documents to digital images in Chapter 11, which reviewed user requirements for system changeover and data migration.

During the scanning of physical drawings to digital image, the enterprise may wish to consider inherent or third-party software that enables metadata (such as drawing number, title, revision number, checked or authorized by) to be captured during the scanning process. This process assists with upload of metadata and digital images to the IDCM repository management system.

Quality of Digital Drawings

Some organizations converted all or part of their drawing holdings to digital image format (typically TIF) or to microfilm (such as an aperture card). This type of initiative enables authorized users to retrieve, display, and print drawings using the facilities of the desktop computer, and perhaps an intranet Web site, or an extranet site for collaboration with business partners or service providers.

The enterprise may have a requirement to migrate these digital images of drawings to the IDCM repository, which will implement management controls over all digital drawings and associated documents to assure that the correct revisions of drawings are published to the intranet or extranet site, as required.

When considering its requirement for data migration of digital images of drawings to the IDCM, an enterprise may wish to review the following:

- **Do the digital image formats represent the current revision of the drawing?**
  Problems can occur when an organization scans its drawings to digital image and then continues to use hard-copy drawings for markup and revisions, without ensuring that the digital image copies of the drawing are updated. Consequently, the digital images are no longer current. The problem is exacerbated when the digital

copies of the images have been distributed to various set locations within the enterprise, meaning that multiple copies of outdated images of drawings are being maintained (and potentially acted upon).

- **Is the quality of the digital images adequate?** Enterprises may carry out conversion internally or outsource the conversion process to an external provider. Frequently, they ignore the need for a requirements specification that stipulates specific service requirements, and they fail to spell out the need for an end-to-end quality assured process for the conversion. The result is poor quality images. Those carrying out an internal conversion may not have adequate experience in scanning large-format technical documents. An amateurish bureau service may utilize inexperienced staff, with inadequate quality controls, to perform the conversion. Enterprises trying to cut costs may find that drawings are scanned at inadequate resolution to increase throughput. There may also be inadequate controls over the metadata capture, so that primary key information (e.g., drawing number) is keyed without validation, resulting in difficulties with reconciling digital images with any existing drawing registry systems.

If these types of issues are identified within the organization, the requirement may be to redo all or part of the imaging process based on a requirements specification that defines the specific details required of the conversion process, and the end-to-end quality assurance of the process.

REQUIREMENTS DEFINITION

The requirements catalog provided in Table 5 may provide some starting points useful for enterprises wishing to consider the types of functionality that they seek in drawing management software. The enterprise should determine which of the functional items are "mandatory," "highly desirable," or "desirable" to their requirements, and specify additional detail as required.

SUMMARY

In this chapter, we tried to cover some of the salient issues that enterprises may need to consider when reviewing requirements for drawing management tools. The requirements for drawing management need to take into account the business models that enterprises utilize (or plan to utilize) for production of drawings, the volume of drawing production activity, the status of the drawing collection in terms of digitization and business process automation, and the culture and behaviors of the organization.

There are a variety of tools that support drawing management, and organizations need to have a specific statement of requirements, embodied in a requirements specification for drawing management, to assist with the selection of a strategic tool. The tool needs to integrate with current client, network, and database operating environments and CAD productivity tools and potentially have the capabilities to integrate with other business systems including ERP systems, asset management systems, maintenance management systems, and GIS. In the next chapter, we review the functional requirements for managing Web content.

Table 5: Initial Catalog of Drawing Management Functionality

Functional Statement	Comments
Integration – Desktop/Network Operating Environment • Integrate with desktop operating system environment. • Integrate with enterprise Web browser and server environment. • Integrate with network operating system environment. • Comply with enterprise standards for the database management system environment.	Specify the products, versions, and service releases that the enterprise uses as its: (a) Desktop operating systems (b) Web browsers/servers (c) Network operating systems (d) Database management systems
Integration – Messaging/Email Services • Integrate with enterprise collaboration and messaging systems for automatic delivery notification of a workflow controlled task via email.	Specify the products, versions, and service releases that the enterprise uses for its collaboration and messaging infrastructure.
Drawing Management Environment • Manage general digital and physical office documents.	Note that where there is a requirement for the users of drawing management software to also manage digital and physical office documents, the drawing management software must be evaluated against the requirements specification defined for those document domains.
Add New Drawing • Add a new drawing to the repository in a way that minimizes data registration. • Allocate the next unique drawing serial number automatically, during the Add New Drawing process.	See also, integration with CAD tools. However, if integration with CAD tools is not a requirement, the enterprise may wish to drag and drop CAD objects into the repository, which would invoke a registration screen that enables users to associate the drawing with a project folder and input metadata relevant to the drawing class. Refer to information under "Drawing Number Schema."
Integration with CAD Tools • Integrate with CAD productivity tools to enable check-in/check-out of documents while in an active CAD session. • Enable browse and search of documents while in an active CAD session. • Store CAD templates and manage version control so that drafting officers are accessing the current version of drawing templates. • Synchronize metadata and title block attributes during drawing registration and revision processes.	Nominate the specific CAD products (including versions, patches, and service releases) used within the enterprise. Specify browse and search requirements from the CAD productivity tool, including the capability (if required) to browse the folder structure of the file system. Be aware that enterprises may wish to review the templates currently in use, and develop or revise existing templates before including a draft template as part of the requirements specification.
Drawing Number Schema • Support the drawing number schema used within the enterprise – typically in multiple sites/locations.	Define the current drawing number schema.

Table 5: Initial Catalog of Drawing Management Functionality (continued)

Functional Statement	Comments
• Support capability to define a drawing number scheme for a new location.	Specify the types of emerging requirements for new locations.
• Preallocate drawing reference numbers. • Synchronize incoming drawings with preallocated numbers.	Specify the requirement for exchange of drawing numbers with external contractors (or internal CAD operators, where required) in advance of drawing production. Determine requirements for synchronizing drawings that have been preallocated drawing numbers.
Revision Number Schema • Feature a revision numbering process that meets enterprise requirements.	Document the current revision numbering schema and define future requirements.
• Support configurable major or minor revision numbering.	Specify the major or minor revision numbering schema if this functionality is required.
Compound Documents • Support the management of complex and compound document relationships, such as multilayered relationships between CAD files.	Assist the organization in considering its requirements for managing compound drawing layers and also complex relationships with other documents, e.g., referenced manuals or specifications.
• Manage relationships where one drawing number may be associated with multiple sheet numbers, in the formula (e.g., Drawing # + Sheet 999).	This may only be a requirement where enterprises use sheet numbers to distinguish drawings that relate to the same set.
• Support compound document relationships.	Support compound document management where the drawing software is required to manage compound document relationships between general documents.
Printing • Utilize existing laser printer services to print drawings to size B (or A3).	Be aware that the existing laser printer services may be suitable for drawings to size B (or A3), but for larger drawings, definitive detail that is useable, might require plotters (see next).
• Utilize plotting capabilities to print large-format drawings, e.g., E size (metric A0). D size (metric A1). C size (metric A2).	Specify the existing plotting facilities within the enterprise, planned replacement of plotting facilities, and any new requirements for plotting devices. (During package selection, ensure that the drawing management system has the capability to support the drivers for existing or planned plotting devices).
• Support plotting for individual items or batch plotting. • Initiate plotting services via drag/drop.	Specify and determine whether plotting can be initiated from various interfaces, such as: (a) Drawing management client (b) Viewer (c) Desktop operating system client or Web browser Determine what additional tools might be required to support plotting requirements at the required interfaces.
• Print a transmittal • Print a transmittal that has been closed	Specify that existing laser printer services will be used to print transmittals, if that is the requirement.
Classification • Support a tiered hierarchical classification scheme for drawings.	Keep the classification scheme for drawings consistent with the file classification scheme adopted for information management within the enterprise. The tiered structure might support three levels, based on key business functions.

Table 5: Initial Catalog of Drawing Management Functionality (continued)

Functional Statement	Comments
Project Structure • Provide a structure for managing project documents.	Define requirements for creating, modifying, and archiving projects. Determine workgroups, user and group security, and folder- and document-level security.
Distribution Lists • Maintain distribution lists for notification of drawing revisions. • Establish virtual lists associated with drawings for a particular project, contract, or type of drawing.	Specify the business process requirements. The distribution lists should enable drawing revisions to be notified automatically to enterprise and project resources, with a specific interest in a drawing or a set of drawings.
View/Redline/Mark up • Integrate with desktop operating system environment. • Integrate with enterprise Web browser environment. • Integrate with drawing management software	Specify the products, versions, and service releases that the enterprise uses as its: (a) Desktop operating system (b) Web browser/server Specify and validate that the viewing tool integrates with the drawing management software. Ensure that the versions of drawing management software and viewing tools are synchronized.
• Invoke viewing tool for viewing drawings and other types of technical documentation.	Specify when viewer is to be invoked, i.e., (a) User does not have access to CAD tool. (b) CAD productivity tool does not support drawing format. (c) CAD user invoked for viewing and redline and markup.
• Integrate with viewing tool that enables browse and search of documents.	Determine if it is useful to invoke browse and search from the viewing tool.
• Provide a viewing or redline and markup tool that supports multiple file formats.	Specify the file formats that apply to the CAD productivity tools within the organization and those that may have to be viewed (e.g., file formats from superseded drawing systems, drawings supplied from external contractors).
• Enable red lined/marked up drawings to be managed as separate objects within the drawing management system.	Redlines and markups/annotations created using the viewing tool, should be saved as separate objects in the document management repository, but linked to the parent drawing object.
• Trigger advice to drawing user that redline and markup files exist.	Note that where a redline or markup file exists for a specific CAD object, the drawing management software may trigger advice to the end user when retrieving the object, or provide some simple means of establishing that redline and markup files exist. Novices may otherwise overlook redline and markup files. Organizations should specify their requirements.
Transmittals • Maintain register of transmittal recipients.	Enable the system to provide a list of the recipients of transmittals. Specify the functional requirements for the recipients list, including capability to create a recipient and update the recipient's details.
• Tag a single document or group of documents (or provide similar functionality) for transmittal.	Specify the current methods for identifying documents for transmittal.
• Generate transmittal for single recipient or multiple recipients.	Document the requirement (if any) for generating transmittals to single or multiple recipients. Define the circumstances when this type of functionality is required.

Table 5: Initial Catalog of Drawing Management Functionality (continued)

Functional Statement	Comments
• Automate tag process for single or group of documents using a filter based on specific business rules.	Define requirements for tagging multiple groups of documents.
• Automate transmittal process (system might integrate with word-processing or spreadsheet templates, or publish transmittal to Web site).	Specify attributes to be include in transmittals. Specify the requirement to clear tags (or similar) once transmittal has been sent. Specify the requirements for updating drawing status during the process, e.g., transmittal pending.
• Search and view status for drawings, e.g., Pending Revision.	Specify search and view requirements and filters.
• Register updates to drawings received from Transmittal Received.	Specify the information that needs to be captured when a transmittal is received together with a batch of drawings. Ensure that the capability to capture a batch of documents is specified where relevant. Specify the requirement for updating drawing status during the process, e.g., need to clear (e.g., Pending Revision status).
• Manage transmittals for drawings later revised.	Define requirements for transmittals where a document that has been issued to a recipient is later revised. Nominate whether there is a requirement for printed Pending Transmittal report to be produced and printed.
• Cancel a transmittal.	Define requirements for canceling a transmittal. Define security access privileges to cancel a transmittal. Define recordkeeping requirements for canceling a transmittal process. Is there a requirement for the cancelled transmittal to be maintained as a record, maintaining referential links to the drawing objects involved in the cancelled transmittal?
• Delete a transmittal.	Allow the drawing management system to default to not enabling a transmittal to be deleted, because the transmittal is a record of a business transaction. Specify under what circumstances, if any, a transmittal can be deleted. Determine security access privileges to delete a transmittal.
Email/Workflow	
• Route transmittal and attached documents via email. • Enable transmittal received and attached documents via email.	Define requirements. Note that if the recipient of the email (including an external contractor) is a user of the drawing management system, then the transmittal should route only a link to the documents.
• Route transmittal and attached documents via workflow. • Enable transmittal received and attached documents via workflow.	Define scope and requirement for workflow. Clarify whether workflow participants are internal end users or external recipients, or both. Determine whether the recipient of the workflow (including an external contractor) is a user of the drawing management system. If so, then the transmittal should route only a link to the documents.
Digital /Physical Office Documents	
• Synchronize revision management for electronic drawing objects; renditions, such as TIF images; physical controlled documents; as well as microfilm.	Support of information management within the drawing environment is a requirement. In organizations where there is a strong reliance on physical documents, the system must not only manage revision of digital drawing objects but also support synchronized revision updates to physical objects.
Drawing Register	
• Provide register of drawings for use by management and field staff.	Define the template required for the drawings register report.

Table 5: Initial Catalog of Drawing Management Functionality (continued)

Functional Statement	Comments
• Complete a Filter Drawing Register report for specific business needs.	Define filtering requirement of the drawing register so that the report might be filtered on attributes such as "discipline" (electrical, structural, etc.).
• Customize drawing register for flexible reporting.	Define requirements for the types of custom drawing register reports that may be required. Define if there is a requirement to customize the drawing register title for specific purposes.
Drawing History	
• Enable view of drawing history.	Drawing history is a record of all revisions. View or browse drawing history, but security must restrict edit.
• Capture drawings as a permanent record at assigned points in the life-cycle.	This requirement covers the situation where enterprises want to capture drawings that might be part of a design set at a particular point in a project, as a permanent record. For example, at a particular point where construction is completed.
Rendering	
• Render a CAD object to another format (e.g., for viewing or publication).	Consider that the system may be required to render CAD objects (or other technical digital documentation) to other formats. For example, there may be a requirement to render a CAD drawing to PDF, and TIFF for viewing, OCR for text indexes and retrieval, or a thumbnail for quick viewing. Organizations should specifically state their requirements for rendering, including required formats, frequency, and usability factors.
Data Migration	
• Provide tools that enable bulk upload of drawings.	Review this aspect further later in this chapter.
• Enable bulk upload of metadata from drawing registry system(s).	Stipulate the drawing registries involved (e.g., engineering file management systems, word-processing tables and spreadsheets, and desktop databases).
• Map metadata to uploaded drawing objects.	
Business Process Management	
• Manage the full change life-cycle associated with revision of drawings.	Note that some systems offer life-cycle management of drawing processes, including state transition of drawings in a revision life-cycle. This may involve workflow or a module for life-cycle management.
• Feature automated processes for drawing change management, including red line and markup and revision.	Consider this requirement in the light of the organization's overall requirements for drawing change management. The culture of some organizations is that they are not ready for business process automation of drawing revision and approval processes. Other organizations may require this type of process to be managed within the constraints of an existing system.
Archiving	
• Support archiving requirements for drawings.	Define requirements in terms of the organization's retention and treatment schedule for projects, drawings, and associated documentation.
• Archive documents by project.	Define requirements for archiving documents by project. Define requirements for restoring archived projects.
• System Administration	
• Simplified administration for drawings and documents — one system interface for system administration of all types of document management.	Assure that if a drawing management software only option is selected, then the administration of the system needs to be so that it is intuitive for the system administrator. If the drawing management software is to be integrated with a DMS, then there needs to be a single interface for system administration covering drawings and general documents.

Table 5: Initial Catalog of Drawing Management Functionality (continued)

Functional Statement	Comments
Search	
• Feature core search capabilities for drawings similar to those recognized for office documents.	Define required search criteria in conjunction with those described for office documents. Add any criteria (e.g., text in CAD) that apply to specific requirements.
• Search text within CAD files to assist find and retrieve operations.	The drawing management software might have the capability to search text in CAD files, or renditions of CAD file objects, and may include the capabilities to index text such as title block, reference file names, and tag attributes within drawings.
• Sort on drawing attributes.	Specify the specific drawing attributes relevant to organizational requirements, e.g., drawing number, project, subproject, category, origin, status, type, or similar characteristic.
Audit	
• Provide audit trail for all revisions and issues of drawings and documentation managed by the system.	

Chapter 18

Functional Requirements – Web Content Management

OVERVIEW

When we looked at the characteristics of document and Web content management in Chapter 3, we noted that there could be many limitations with how enterprises manage content published to Web sites. In Chapter 4, we demonstrated that subsystems exist within the IDCM framework to address these types of limitations.

The importance of relevant and timely content cannot be understated. Its presence has a significant impact on the quality, effectiveness, and popularity of a Web site, with some observers (Chatelain & Yen, 2000) jesting that "content is the next frontier" on the Internet. If visitors to a site are not satisfied with its content, the "one click" factor applies — these visitors are one click away from moving from one Web site to another site.

Depending on the nature of the Web site, the effectiveness of content might be measurable using a range of performance criteria. For example, transactional logs stored on Web servers may provide an indication of how much navigation is carried out within a site. There has also been a great deal of analysis of how the content may best be structured in an information architecture (Rosenfeld & Morville, 1998), and development of evaluation schemes that establish qualitative criteria for evaluation of various factors, such as how the functionality, design, authority, and validity of a site influence the substance of the content (Auer, 2002).

In this chapter, we extend our discussion on the capabilities of IDCM systems to manage Web content, irrespective of whether the content is targeted for Internet or intranet sites. We review the functional requirements for a managed IDCM environment that provides cohesive end-to-end management of processes associated with the development and management of Web content.

Our objectives are as follows:

- Review the types of functionality offered by IDCM solutions for implementing management services over the Web content life-cycle.

- Provide a checklist of functionality that provides a primer for organizations when considering their specific requirements for managing Web content.

REQUIREMENTS ANALYSIS

Scope

In Chapter 4, we noted that while CMS differ in purpose and capacity and intent, they have evolved to the extent that we can summarize their capabilities within the context of:

- Content creation, relating to the development of content using a wide range of authoring tools, including text editors, word processors, spreadsheets (and other office tools), tools such as HTML/XML editors, and specific Web authoring tools. This includes the application of effective tools to convert content from paper-based and other physical media into the digital environment.
- Content management, relating to managing the life-cycle of content from content creation through to publication of content to Web servers.
- Content presentation, which relates to the publication of content as static, dynamic, or transactional content. They allow flexibility in reusing information effectively.

The essence of our approach has been to develop an integrative model for managing document and Web content, and take the view that our frame of reference is confined to the first two items of CMS capabilities, covering the creation and management of Web content.

We leave aside the presentation of content by application servers (such as ATG *Dynamo*, BEA *Weblogic*, and IBM *WebSphere*, to name a few). These applications assimilate content from multiple sources (including business databases, HTML pages, rendered documents, such as PDF, or fragments) and publish the content to the Web in real time. The functionality of how Web servers assimilate and present content to Web sites is covered in a wide variety of books and journals, and it is beyond our frame of reference.

Approach

The selection and implementation of appropriate software is but one component of the organization's requirement to manage Web content and should not be viewed in isolation from other business requirements. These requirements include the need to develop policies and procedures, analyze and redesign business processes, review standards, and develop guidelines, within a project approach that epitomizes quality and risk management. This type of approach will enable businesses to develop and implement successful Web content management solutions, regardless of size and complexity.

The structured approach offered by the IDCM management framework provides enterprises with a model by which to address the business and technology solution options for the deployment of enterprise content management functionality. This approach includes planning (Chapter 6), policy development (Chapter 7), and requirements analysis and definition (Chapter 10), with specific emphasis on defining user requirements (Chapter 11), functional requirements (this chapter), and the nontechnical and domain requirements for the system (Chapter 19).

The processes for requirements analysis and development of specification of Web content management solutions should align with a framework similar to that proposed by Sommerville (2001, p. 98). This approach defines a model for the development of specifications that embrace user and system requirements. The system requirements component is divided into three subsets: functional, nonfunctional, and domain requirements. Information about the scope and structure of the requirements analysis and definition for user, nonfunctional, and domain requirements is covered in Chapters 10 and 19.

FUNCTIONAL REQUIREMENTS ANALYSIS
Content Creation

The capture capabilities should enable users to create content with the authoring tools mandated by the organization, or perhaps those with which they are familiar. These tools may include text editors, applications such as word processors, spreadsheets, text editors, presentation and project tools or specific Web authoring tools, or HTML/XML editors. Content formats may also include image formats, sound files, and digital video segments. An IDCM solution should enable users to capture developed or acquired content into a managed repository.

As with the functionality we defined for capturing digital office documents, the repository should support the editing process by providing check-in, check-out, and version control functionality. Again, like the functionality for managing digital office documents, the integration between the authoring tools and the repository manager should be such that it is transparent to the user. If it is too meddling for a user to capture the content to the repository, the system may not be acceptable from a usability perspective, which may have an impact on successful implementation.

Depending on the enterprise requirements, the system should also enable users to capture existing Web pages direct to the repository. Similar to the capture of content from authoring tools, the integration should be relatively simple for the user, so as not to be intrusive.

Likewise, where images are captured as part of content, then the document scanning, digital cameras, and fax capture functionality should be well integrated with the repository. The same comments could also apply to sound files and digital video segments that might be produced by professionals using ancillary devices.

Content Management

The IDCM model might feature a range of content management capabilities. These features are virtually the same as we described in Chapter 12 for digital office documents, because developed or acquired content, with the exception of data that is derived from databases, is effectively that of digital documents. We acknowledge, of course, that the digital documents might also include images, email, and formats that support technical and engineering drawings, and these can be published as content.

The project champion should not be overly concerned with whether they are looking for a "content management" solution or a "document management" solution.

Effectively, "document" files and "content" files (including HTML, images, and multi-media) are digital objects that act as a container for information. The name that might apply to a technology does not really matter, except for leverage of marketing advantage, so the project champion may be best to focus on finding a solution that *meets the business requirements*.

As an aside, in the Preface, we noted that some of our ancestors were known to have written information on tortoise shells. So perhaps in those days, industry pundits coined the term "t-enablement" or "shell" management (which probably confused those ancestors who used tree bark as a means to record information).

However, we might review some of the essential components of the requirements for managing content by recapitulating some of the key features that support business requirements for managing content. The requirements include repository management services and automated workflow (potentially with incorporation of digital signatures for authorization processes).

The system should feature versioning capabilities that ensure that an author (or a team of authors working in collaboration) can be assured of updating the correct versions of documents. The versioning facilities should exhibit check-in, check-out, and object locking capabilities that we reviewed in Chapter 12, and may need to capture emails using the capacities defined in Chapter 13. They might also need to include revision management capabilities for digital drawings, because CAD files may be rendered to a suitable format for publication to a Web site.

The versioning of Web content has also been an aspect of the work of the WEBDAV group in developing an interoperability specification. The frame of reference for the group (IETF WEBDAV Working Group, 2002) included the storage of revisions of a document for later retrieval, and for supporting collaboration on development of documents. The group's work also included metadata for interlinking related Web pages, the capability to achieve name space management using hierarchical structures such as provided by digital filing systems. The framework also includes the capability to prevent overwrites on documents during editing processes. As can be seen, much of the work has an association with the management of documents to be published as Web content.

Taking into account the similar capabilities for managing Web content that are applicable to those that we have already described in other chapters for various formats of digital documents, we can summarize those areas where businesses analyze requirements as follows:

- The IDCM should enable content to be created using desktop office applications or special Web authoring tools.
- The managed content may include a wide range of content types, including HTML, XML, image formats, sound files, and video scripts.
- Integrated workflow (refer to Chapter 16) can provide a managed environment for automated review and approval of Web content.
- The system might also use workflow for automating the life-cycle processes associated with managing the content from creation through to publication, as well as postpublication processes, such as replacement and archiving.
- Integrated digital signatures might support the workflow process by providing controlled signatures for review and approval processes.

- An integrated Web publishing system may feature automatic generation of tables of contents, figures, and indexes as required, and store the completed publication back in the IDCM repository.
- Integrated Web publishing tools may then enable documents to be published to a Web server from the IDCM, which would maintain control over the presentation of content objects.
- Published content would be accessible from standard Web browsers, with access security to the original content managed by the IDCM repository manager.

REQUIREMENTS DEFINITION

The following statements of functionality provide a primer for organizations wishing to develop specifications for using an IDCM in the context of Web content management.

SUMMARY

The integration of IDCM repository management tools with Web application servers may provide organizations with a cohesive environment for managing documents from initial authoring using predefined templates to publication on intranet and Internet Web sites, and subsequent archival of the content. It also provides a managed repository that enables content in the form of documents in any format published to a Web site to be maintained as the historical record of published material. We now conclude Part 3 by reviewing the nonfunctional and domain requirements for an IDCM solution.

Table 1: Indicative Catalog of Functionality for Web Content Management

Functional Statement	Comments
• Content creation/receipt	Allow users to create Web pages in nominated authoring tool using the relevant template set up by the Web Administrator or Web content from an authoring application such as a word processor.
	Provide a simple and fast process to add or modify a hyperlink in word processor or nominated authoring tool to a document within the IDCM repository.
	Support classification scheme and metadata standards defined by the enterprise.
	Support XML pages and XML content development.
	Capture hard-copy formats and scan; convert to digital image formats.
• Content registration and validation	The registration and validation requirements for Web content and Web pages are essentially the same as the requirements for electronic documents, defined in Chapter 12.
• Content save/store	Permit users to save their Web pages into the repository from nominated authoring tools, and Web content generated from word processor, spreadsheet, text editor, or presentation or project tools.
	Provide transparent integration of the IDCM system with nominated authoring applications during the capture process.
	Save downloaded Web pages or received Web pages into the IDCM in a nonintrusive manner.
• Version control	The version control requirements for Web content and Web pages are essentially the same as the requirements for digital office documents, defined in Chapter 12.

Table 1: Indicative Catalog of Functionality for Web Content Management (continued)

Functional Statement	Comments
• Renditions/ publishing	Publish Web pages that have been through the enterprise's standardization process (if used) to a user-specified location.
	Provide a mechanism for documents within the IDCM to be published in PDF format to be hyperlinked from intranet or Internet Web pages.
	Transform content types generally, including HTML on the fly.
	Assess capability to deliver high- and low-bandwidth HTML renditions as well as the native format, as opposed to "static" rendering processes.
	Provide document review and approval processes for documents with a high level of security before publication to a Web server.
	Maintain location of the published or rendered document within the IDCM.
	Associate Web content documents, their HTML rendition, and the resulting (nominated) authoring application HTML Web page document.
	Maintain integrity of updates to documents in the IDCM system with any renditions of the document (such as published to PDF for the Web).
• Compound documents	Note that the compound document requirements for Web content and Web pages are essentially the same as the requirements for electronic documents, defined in Chapter 12.
• Hyperlinks	Note that the hyperlink requirements for Web content and Web pages are essentially the same as the requirements for electronic documents, defined in Chapter 12.
	Enable content authoring tools such as word processor (nominate authoring tool) and create hyperlinks directly to documents within the IDCM system, for the purposes of inserting hyperlinks into Web content.
	Link hyperlinks to the current version of the document, and maintain links during version changes.
	Apply relevant security to documents stored in the IDCM system that are hyperlinked from an intranet Web page.
	Give the user an option to make a document viewable as read-only when creating a hyperlink directly to a document in the IDCM repository.
• View Web pages	View hyperlinks in Web pages to documents in the IDCM system with the same requirements as indicated for electronic documents, as defined in Chapter 12.
	View Web pages stored in the IDCM from the Internet Explorer Web browser.
	Support a process that enables documents within the IDCM hyperlinked directly from the intranet to be escalated in classification (e.g., from a "workgroup" to a "corporate" document).
	Retrieve Web content quickly and in a consistent time from all sites, meeting the performance requirements, similar to those defined in Chapter 19.
• Workflow	Support ad hoc review and approve workflow for development of Web pages.
	Provide automated review and approval for publishing of documents.
• Security	Provide integrated security for managing Web content in the IDCM repository.
• Audit	Provide audit functionality with the same requirements as indicated for electronic documents, defined in Chapter 12.
• Search	Provide search functionality with the same requirements as indicated for electronic documents, defined in Chapter 12. In addition, there may be a requirement to browse a designated area of the IDCM from a search facility on the intranet (or perhaps extranet).
• Publishing	Support automation of components, including indexes, tables of contents, lists of figures, table lists, and reference documents.
	Support on-demand publication and the capability to publish documents based on predefined schedules.
	Support style sheets for layout control, page wizards, and similar techniques.
• Usability	Allow personalization of the users' desktops.
	Support multiple formats for diverse display devices, such as workstations, kiosks, and touch screens.
• Data migration	Migrate metadata, content, and templates from existing content repositories.
• System integration capability	Integrate with nominated enterprise applications, such as email, ERP system (e.g., SAP or Peoplesoft), enterprise workflow systems for interchange with or direct integration into the CMS, and nominated Web servers (e.g., IIS, Apache, Netscape, Lotus Domino).
	Integrate with nominated application servers (e.g., ATG *Dynamo*, BEA *Weblogic*, and IBM *WebSphere*).

Chapter 19

Nonfunctional and Domain Requirements

OVERVIEW

In this chapter, we will examine requirements determination and analysis that may be useful for defining the nonfunctional and domain requirements for an IDCM solution, including system sizing, architecture, and performance requirements. We also include a discussion on domain requirements, such as those for information technology and system administration.

Our objectives are to do the following:

- Document the requirements for system sizing and mass storage.

- Consider the types of requirements analysis that enterprises apply to help suppliers of IDCM solutions offer an architecture solution that may meet enterprise requirements.

- Define system performance requirements with known caveats and assumptions.

- Define the requirements for the IDCM system to integrate with enterprise desktop, server, and network operating environments.

- Define the requirements for the system development environment.

- Document the system administration requirements for the system.

NONFUNCTIONAL REQUIREMENTS
System Sizing and Mass Storage

Enterprises will require the IDCM system to provide a secure repository for the management of documents and Web content and provide storage for digital documents in secondary or archived storage. Consequently, enterprises will need to have suppliers provide an IDCM system sizing profile (including magnetic storage and mass storage capacities) to support the deployment of the IDCM for the specific application site (for example, Phase 1) and for subsequent implementations, potentially enterprise wide.

This type of sizing cannot be developed in a vacuum, and the enterprises will need to define the current mass storage capacities and provide an analysis of trends that may impact upon capacity planning. Factors that should be taken into account include the following:

- Enterprises are making greater use of digital documentation — trends might be apparent from statistics on the growth of digital document holdings on file systems over a 3-year period.

- There may be a requirement to have the IDCM system capture email messages and attachments that reference a business transaction.

- The IDCM solution will support the retention of multiple versions of documents. Enterprises may need to consider the specific types of documents that are likely to be subjected to multiple versions, and how many versions of specific document types are to be maintained online.

- There may be a requirement for renditions of documents to be kept in the IDCM repository. For example, word-processing documents rendered to HTML or PDF for publication on Web sites might both be managed within the IDCM repository.

Enterprises should also give consideration to the potential impact on capacity planning that is to be achieved by improving inappropriate document management practices. For example:

- Clean multiple copies of the same files held on the same or different file systems.

- Reduce file sizes by appropriate training directed at overcoming some of the limitations we raised when discussing digital documents in Chapter 12.

Capacity planning helps to define the recommended hardware configuration for the IDCM solution and should provide growth capability, for example, for 3 years. Suppliers will probably have their own capacity planning methodology, but it would be useful for the enterprise to understand the formula for determining capacity planning for its initial and planned deployment of IDCM functionality.

Suppliers should be requested to provide a recommended hardware configuration that has sufficient storage capacity and scalability to meet the IDCM implementation requirements, and capacity for 3-year growth. Planning information might need to include online storage, offline (secondary) storage, archival storage, etc.

Suppliers might also be requested to provide recommended mass storage configuration for the entire digital document collection (for the target IDCM environment), with allowance for growth over 3 years. Details might include the following:

- How each type of mass storage is expected to be used;

- The reliability, capacity, expandability, and redundancy offered and administrative tools available; and

- The interface, architecture, hardware configuration, required options, etc.

System Architecture

Many enterprises have centralized operations, others have a distributed computing environment, and they may have a highly mobile workforce. There is a need for the system to provide a scalable, flexible, and extensible architecture to meet current usage demands and future growth demands identified in business planning.

There are probably a number of different architectural scenarios, particularly in a distributed computing environment, and suppliers might be requested to provide options with an analysis of the various types of applicable topology, including (but not restricted to):

- Centralized database and document object stores;
- Centralized database with distributed document object stores;
- Distributed database with distributed document object stores; and
- Replication services.

The IDCM architecture, system configuration, and sizing must cover initial deployment requirements and planned installations for the progressive deployment of the IDCM within the enterprise as required. The architecture needs to achieve and sustain a level of performance, particularly during its evolutionary deployment within an enterprise that satisfies the users of the system, and enables documents to be shared easily.

Suppliers should be required to provide sizing of the system server and desktop configuration, RAM, cache, storage capacity, and other configuration requirements. However, this information can only be gleaned from suppliers with a reasonable degree of confidence if the enterprise has accurately defined its document collections, growth trends, usage patterns, and IT infrastructure.

In order to have suppliers provide a strategic IDCM architecture that will meet these requirements, it is necessary to define the current system factors that may impact the system architecture, particularly in a distributed computing environment.

These factors include the following:

- Document sizes and compositions — The document sizes and compositions for the current environment should be defined in the User Requirements Specification (Chapter 11).
- Infrastructure definition — Desktop client or server hardware or software configurations and network systems, the current IT environment, should be defined as part of the Domain Requirements Specification, which we discuss later in this chapter.
- LAN/WAN architecture, topology, and usage patterns — The LAN/WAN infrastructure and LAN/WAN usage patterns should be specified in a definition of the current IT environment that should be defined as part of the Domain Requirements Specification.

Depending on the requirement, the proposed architecture analysis should address issues like those itemized in Table 1.

Table 1: Primer for Architecture Issues

Consider the following types of issues relating to system architecture:
- The capacity to support the document collections in the current environment, new requirements (versioning) with allowance for growth over, for example, 3 years.
- The capabilities to meet the performance objectives specified in the Nonfunctional Requirements Specification.
- The profile type (operating system or Web browser).
- The anticipated concurrent number of IDCM users.
- The capacity to support the document collections in the current environment, new requirements (versioning) with allowance for growth over, for example, 3 years.
- The capabilities to meet the performance objectives specified in the Nonfunctional Requirements Specification.
- The capability for an authorized user to search multiple libraries transparently (if that is a requirement).
- The capability, where the architecture proposes multiple servers, for an authorized user to search across multiple servers transparently.
- The implications of additional bandwidth, if any, for the implementation of the proposed architecture.
- The relevance of optimization services such as replication services or terminal emulation software within the proposed architecture (The options analysis should include the relevance and appropriateness of technologies such as distributed repositories, replication, and terminal server emulation technologies.).
- The capability to replicate metadata and document and Web content stores.
- The provision of a development server for development, testing, and training libraries.
- The minimum and recommended configuration requirements for workstations for general document management and drawings and technical documents.
- The minimum and recommended standards for configuration requirements of servers, databases, and operating systems, including service releases and patches for all items.
- The pricing options for the system architecture options.
- The status of certification of the supplier's products to the network operating environment (including client, server, and interoperability) (Suppliers should be required to provide certification from an independent source that their products are certified. It may not be adequate to have a supplier certify its own product to the domain.).

System Performance

In the current business environment, users may be unaware of the physical location of file shares to which they have access rights. In a highly mobile environment, for example, a user from London may travel to New York, but the user drives may still be mapped to a London server, as the user's home location. The user will probably notice a significant reduction in speed of retrieval when accessing documents away from a home location. Furthermore, users may also have trouble sharing documents with colleagues if they are unaware that the drive they have mapped as, e.g., "J: Drive," is different from the "J: Drive" of a user from elsewhere.

Users may be able to search and retrieve documents located on remote servers provided they have permissions and know (or are reminded) how to map the relevant drive. Given that the user may be highly mobile and may have the requirement to search multiple servers and libraries, users will expect the IDCM to provide a high level of system performance. Consequently, the IDCM solution must meet satisfactory performance levels so that the system achieves and sustains the support of the user base within the enterprise.

Enterprises need to define their specific performance criteria for the system, and this performance should form part of the contractual arrangements with the supplier. It is difficult to gain supplier commitment to meeting and maintaining system performance, as there are a number of variables and constraints that are external to the IDCM that may impact the performance capabilities of the system. However, the enterprises should recognize these variables and constraints and state the assumptions they made in defining performance criteria.

Table 2 is a partial list of assumptions from some recent cases that can be used as a starting reference when considering requirements for system performance of the IDCM. The enterprises' assumptions must be developed and clearly stated in the Nonfunctional Requirements Specification.

The mandatory requirements might then be developed for inclusion as part of the Nonfunctional Requirements Specification. Table 3 provides an initial list of performance criteria from a recent case that might be considered as a basis for further review and consideration by enterprises when defining performance requirements.

When looking at the performance requirements of digital document imaging systems, the enterprise will need to take into account the nature of its throughput and

Table 2: Performance Assumptions

- Supplier will stipulate configuration of desktop PC.
- Supplier will stipulate number, range of sizes, and average size of documents in the repository; range of numbers and average number of metadata attributes per document; number of documents that are text-based and have been indexed; and the specific configuration applied to indexing of text documents.
- Desktop PC is LAN/WAN connected, with LAN/WAN bandwidths reflecting the enterprise's environment. The performance criteria do not apply over a modem connection.
- The relevant native application (e.g., MS Word) and viewing tool will be open due to the performance evaluation.
- Two additional active Windows sessions are open on the desktop (e.g., MS Outlook and MS Excel).
- Ten users are simultaneously accessing the IDCM (and the same library if appropriate), doing the same activity as is being tested.
- Performance will be measured in the Windows and browser operating environments.
- Retrieve and view functionality will be tested using the native application and viewing tool provided by the IDCM.
- Performance will be measured under the enterprise's normal daily LAN and WAN load conditions, as per the usage scenarios defined in LAN Usage Patterns and WAN Usage Patterns.
- Response times are measured from when the user strikes the transmission key until the full data-set or document is displayed on the workstation screen, whichever is relevant for the test.

Table 3: Performance Requirements

- Launch the IDCM client within 5 seconds of invoking application.
- Save a 40 Kb Word document within 3 seconds after completion of profile at check-in.
- Retrieve and view 40 Kb Word document within 3 seconds of object request.
- Retrieve and view a 2 Mb Word document, containing an embedded object (e.g., image), within 8 seconds of object request.
- Save a 2 Mb drawing (e.g., DWG) within 8 seconds after completion of profile at check-in.
- Retrieve and view a 2 Mb drawing within 8 seconds of object request.
- Retrieve and view three (separate) linked Excel spreadsheet files, size 30 Kb each, that form part of a compound relationship, within 10 seconds of object request.
- Return a single candidate result list based on a primary key search of the metadata within 5 seconds.
- Return a multiple candidates result list based on an index term search of the metadata within 10 seconds.
- Return a ranked result list based on a single term search of content within 15 seconds.
- Achieve and maintain performance levels at 95% continuity.
- Instruct suppliers to stipulate what other assumptions they made in recommending an IDCM architecture that meets the performance criteria.

retrieval requirements. The performance criteria need to be relevant to the imaging requirement. It may be pointless to insist on a scanner delivering 10,000 images per hour, if there is only a requirement to process 40 pages per day in an ad hoc imaging environment. However, there should be a definition of the throughput requirements for the scanning and retrieval subsystems, particularly for production-level imaging requirements.

We mentioned in Chapter 15 that scanning devices do not deliver the throughput speed performance claimed in marketing brochures, and this needs to be considered when taking developing requirements for performance. The analyst needs to be specific about the definition of throughput and the performance conditions, so that potential suppliers have a clear understanding of the requirement. For example, the throughput requirements for an imaging application may define characteristics, such as "the throughput speed for the scanning subsystem will be a minimum 1200 letter (or A4) size pages per hour, with barcode recognition, at 200 dpi scan resolution."

In regard to image retrieval, there may be a need, particularly with production-level imaging systems, to specify performance requirements for retrieval of images from magnetic storage and optical storage. For example, the enterprise may require a retrieval speed of 2 to 3 seconds for a letter or A4 size image, scanned at 200 dpi, held in magnetic storage. The performance requirements might make allowances for retrieval of images from, for example, loaded optical disk, on a local area network segment, which might be in the vicinity of 5 to 8 seconds.

The analyst needs to be careful when specifying performance requirements, because retrieval speeds are impacted by a variety of conditions, such as whether the image is being retrieved from magnetic or optical storage. Furthermore, the paper size of the image (e.g., letter, legal, or A4) and the scanning resolution, both of which impact the physical size of the image, need to be considered when specifying retrieval speeds. Finally, if an image is retrieved from optical, the retrieval speeds can be impacted by conditions such as whether or not the relevant disk is loaded or unloaded. If a disk is unloaded, retrieval performance for a letter or A4 size image scanned at 200 dpi might be 15 seconds, allowing time for the disk to be loaded (automechanical process).

The number of users accessing the magnetic and optical disk storage subsystems can also impact retrieval speeds, and the performance tests should simulate multiple users (for example, 10) simultaneously accessing the system.

The foregoing discussion on system performance includes some performance criteria for IDCM solutions. However, these criteria are provided as *examples only* to demonstrate what be simulated under benchmark assessment (refer to Chapter 20). It is important for organizations to develop their own performance criteria, and it is also important that performance requirements be tested under operational conditions, taking into account the constraints and assumptions stipulated by the enterprise and supplier.

DOMAIN REQUIREMENTS
Information Technology Environment

The enterprise should provide a detailed description of the current IT environment in a structured schedule (or as output from an asset management system), and include the definition (potentially as an appendix) in the Domain Requirements Specification. The description should include the following types of details:

- Communications infrastructure, services and protocols, including physical, data link, network and transport layers of the computing network environment. It should also include a definition of the types of switches, routers and hubs deployed in the computing network.
- Application/database servers deployed that are relevant, particularly if there are requirements for the IDCM solution to integrate with existing business applications. The following details might be defined (as a minimum) for each separate application: the server hardware, operating system, application software, and database management system.
- File/print servers that are deployed on the network, including the server hardware, operating system, and a specific statement of purpose of server usage (preferably including a definition of the file shares managed on specific file servers).
- Mail servers used on the network, including server hardware, operating system, and the mail applications supported. Include details of any collaboration tools that are used, either as an integrated suite (mail, calendar, scheduling, contacts, etc) or individual products.
- Fax gateways/servers that are installed on the network, which is important if there is a requirement to integrate the IDCM solution for capturing incoming and managing outgoing facsimile transmissions.
- Web and proxy servers used on the network, including server hardware, operating system, the software applications supported, and their functionality.
- Profile of desktop computers (or workstations) used on the network. Is there a standard operating environment (SOE) for desktop computers? If yes, stipulate the SOE and any known departures from the standard. If not, then specify the typical configurations of desktop computers. Include definitions of client hardware, operating system, and a profile of the applications software used on the computers.
- Printers available for network printing services. Include type of printer (laser, dot matrix etc), hardware definitions, connectivity methods, and protocols supported. Make sure that any printers that have been configured for high volume image printing are clearly identified and defined, particularly if there is a requirement to print high volume images. Include any plotters that are installed, particularly if there is a requirement to print large formatted drawings.
- Remote communication tools that enable users to connect to the enterprise LAN, including typical brands of modems used and performance capabilities and the software used to access the LAN remotely.
- Backup and recovery tools available, including a description of the media used, including details of brand/model of media (include all types used). Also stipulate the software used for backup and recovery processes.

The definitions should include details of software versions, service releases and patches for operating (client and server), application (client and server) and database systems, wherever possible for all software deployed on the enterprise's computing network that is relevant to the IDCM requirement.

The IT environment definition should also include specific strategies that may impact the IDCM architecture and its implementation within the enterprise domain, such as plans to replace or upgrade the desktop operating environments, or to replace or upgrade the network environment. There may be plans for standardization of database management systems, or the replacement or upgrades to browsers, and other similar types of foreseeable planned changes to the IT environment.

Desktop Operating System Integration

The IDCM will most likely be required to integrate with and operate on the enterprise desktop environment, and the typical operating environment for the desktop should be included in the description of the current IT environment. We made the assumption (for the purposes of example) that MS Windows is the operating system at the desktop.

The enterprise should have suppliers specify the minimum and recommended desktop configurations for each of the software solutions offered, i.e., the IDCM (electronic and physical documents) document imaging, workflow, and records management capabilities.

When describing the domain requirements for integration with the desktop environment, the statements in the following table can act as a baseline for development of the Domain Requirements Specification.

Table 4: Desktop Environment

- Integrate with desktop operating environment (specify the system environment precisely, e.g., MS Windows, MS Office, MS Outlook, and detail the product versions and service releases).
- State minimum and recommended desktop configurations for each of the software solutions offered.
- Install and configure IDCM desktop component easily. Suppliers should be required to state typical installation and configuration time frames for each desktop, and these time frames should be subject to benchmark assessment.
- Supply IDCM product-sets independently certified to the desktop operating and applications environment.

Web Browser Integration

Many enterprise personnel use the desktop operating system interface (e.g., Windows) to access desktop authoring systems and documents stored in file systems, local disks, and removable media. However, many enterprises adopted the strategic direction to make as much information and functionality as possible available through its intranet.

Users may wish to access the intranet browser to search and retrieve documents, or may wish access to the document repository via the Web browser, where viewing documents through a viewing tool is quicker than loading the proprietary software, when in remote locations with slow access. Consequently, the IDCM should at least fully support searching and document retrieval using Web browser software that does not require proprietary software.

Enterprise users are expected to progressively demand richer functionality for integration with authoring applications and documents via the Web browser. Consequently, there may be a requirement to check-in and check-out documents via the browser as well as enable search and retrieval functionality. The statements in Table 5 can be used

Table 5: Web Browser Environment

- Integrate with Web browser environment (specify the system environment precisely, e.g., MS Internet Explorer, and detail the product versions and service releases).
- State minimum and recommended desktop configurations for each of the software solutions offered.
- Provide integration with IDCM via native browser — suppliers should be required to state what plug-ins are required to achieve integration with the browser, and state whether there are any potential configuration issues with the plug-ins in the event of browser upgrades.
- Install and configure Web browser component easily. Suppliers should be required to state typical installation and configuration time frames, and these time frames might be subject to benchmark assessment.
- Supply IDCM product-sets independently certified to the Web browser environment.
---

to consider the browser environment, taking into account advances in browser and IDCM technologies.

Network and Database Integration

Networked database servers and file systems for print sharing and file storage are generally deployed across enterprises. The definition of the server or network should be included in the definition of the current IT environment. The IDCM must be capable of integrating with the network operating system, and provide the capability to integrate with database applications via standard protocols (refer to Table 6).

Table 6: Network Integration

- Provide synchronization of user account details with the (specified) network operating system. Suppliers should be required to provide details on how user login and authentication are achieved. Suppliers should also provide status on independent certification of IDCM product-sets to the (specified) network operating system.
- Integrate with (specified) messaging and collaboration server, e.g., MS Exchange, Lotus Notes, or GroupWise, for messaging and collaboration. Provide status on independent certification of IDCM product-sets to (nominated) messaging and collaboration server.
- Support standard protocols applicable to (nominated) messaging and collaboration server (e.g., MAPI, POP3, HTTP, etc.). Suppliers should state which protocols are relevant to the enterprise messaging domain and where each are used in the IDCM.
- Integrate with (specified) database management system. Suppliers should provide details on recommended DBMS, with particular consideration given to preferred database relevant to the enterprise (e.g., potentially taking into account distributed requirements).
- Integrate with other (specified) database applications using standard protocols. Suppliers should be required to state which protocols are supported.

System Development Environment

Domain requirements for the IDCM development environment need to be stated. They might feature an IDCM development environment that:

- Includes server and desktop machines (Enterprises might establish if there are existing server and desktop machines that might be available for the development environment, and provide the specifications to suppliers.);

- Features an object management approach to deliver functionality; and

Table 7: Development Environment

- Provide development tools with a graphical user interface development environment. State the development tools that will be provided, and detail what they will allow the system administrator to configure or develop. The supplier might be requested to provide examples or screenshots where necessary.
- Provide recommendation on number of server and desktop machines required and minimum hardware specifications for these machines.
- Provide an integrated suite of applications development tools that addresses the need for rapid applications development using high-level languages and macros and the need for low-level tools for solving relatively rare but important technical interface and performance requirements.
- Support key industry standards including SQL and ODBC/JDBC compliant.
- Provide an Open API that exposes all the functionality of the IDCM.
- Support object-oriented reusability paradigms that provide the ability to define objects, provide the ability to define object properties, and allow object hierarchies and inheritance.
- Support integration and interoperability standards. Enterprises to define relevant standards and suppliers must state which standards are supported.
- Request that supplier advise if (any) available client and server devices can be used in the IDCM development environment and, if so, for what role.

- Is consistent with evolving IT standards (industry and International standards organizations), particularly with those relevant to applications development and middle-ware.

Some domain requirements that have been useful in recent cases include the types of descriptions in Table 7.

System Administration

Given that the IDCM solution must integrate with the existing IT environment, it is imperative that the system administration for the system be integrated transparently into the computing environment of the enterprise. We will consider the following types of capabilities:

- Virus protection;
- Backup and recovery and redundancy;
- Security and audit;
- Data migration utilities;
- Monitoring and management tools;
- System installation and configuration; and
- Management of upgrades.

Virus Protection

Most enterprises have deployed virus protection software at the server and at the desktop level to help detect and disinfect computer viruses. Virus software might be deployed on desktop computer, on the messaging servers, and on Web servers. This type of environment covers protection from virus infection at the desktop level, with additional protection provided for incoming email and Internet content.

Given the potential vulnerabilities to enterprise data, documents, and Web content due to virus infection, it is an important requirement to maintain the integrity of metadata and documents stored in the IDCM solution. Tools, patches, and settings on the desktop may afford this protection. However, it might be appropriate to seek advice from suppliers of the IDCM systems to determine the methodology and tools applied for maintaining integrity of data stored in an IDCM repository.

Backup and Recovery and Redundancy

It is imperative to implement backup and recovery procedures and tools for existing databases and file systems. These support mechanisms should be implemented across distributed computing networks. When defining its requirements for integrating IDCM backup and recovery with the existing systems, the enterprise should clearly specify any factors that impact backup and recovery operations. For example:

- The operating hours of the organization's premises, where backup services might be required;
- Existing rules and implications for backup in the current computing environment that may impact implementation of backup and recovery procedures;
- LAN/WAN environment and performance in a distributed computing environment;
- Methods for changing backup tapes (or other media), and the size and capacity of storage media used; and
- Constraints on the current backup and recovery processes.

The enterprise might also define its strategies to implement redundancy in network and server infrastructure to reduce single points of failure. These strategies might include initiatives, such as keeping spare configured routers, purchasing servers with dual power supplies, and maintaining storage units with two controllers. It may also include the provision for mirroring of file systems and replication of databases.

The implementation of an IDCM system, particularly at an enterprise level, will be critical to the day-to-day operations of an organization. The IDCM will be required to manage metadata about documents and Web content, and as such, there should be an expectation of high system availability and performance. Some of the issues to consider are as follows:

- The metadata component will be stored in a DBMS, and documents and Web content cannot be accessed if the database is corrupted or otherwise not operational.
- There may be a requirement to back up IDCM configuration files as well as repository contents to facilitate recovery.
- In the event of a complete failure and full IDCM recovery, the synchronization between the database and document content files is critical.

The existing backup and recovery systems of the organization should be defined as part of the domain requirements, and suppliers should be required to state whether the existing backup infrastructure can be utilized for the IDCM implementation. Otherwise, they might provide a recommendation on the backup infrastructure required, including definition of architecture, expandability, maintenance, capacity, etc.

Table 8: Backup/Recovery/Redundancy

- Provide the recommended backup architecture and expandability for the digital document collection, with allowance for growth over 3 years.
- Utilize existing backup software tools, if applicable, for IDCM backups. State all backup software tools that the IDCM supports for backup, and recommended backup software tools including all add-on components required, and dependencies, etc.
- Configure system for backups to occur between chosen times (nominate schedules required). Provide estimates of time required for backups. State alternate backup strategies.
- Perform backup while IDCM is functioning. Users may continue to use IDCM during backup process.
- Back up documents and metadata currently open by users.
- Enable users to retrieve and view replicated (or redundant) resources in the event of a host system failure. Provide details of how this is achieved.
- Rebuild database and content stores from redundant resources in the event of system failure. Provide details of how this is achieved.
- Maintain integrity of versions during restoration of documents.
- Identify the components of the IDCM system that are critical, such that failure of any single component will prevent operation of the system.
- Identify the requirements for redundancy of the IDCM and the critical components of the system, including metadata and content files, to optimize system reliability.
- Restore entire metadata and document content stores to assure one-to-one integrity between metadata and document content stores.
- Enable selective restoration of a single and a group of documents during recovery.
- Make sure that selective restoration has no visible effect on IDCM functionality to users.
- Restore documents and metadata direct to IDCM, and maintain original permissions of document. State method used to restore documents and metadata.
- Restore entire IDCM to a state of full functionality, onto new hardware with minimal configuration and taking minimal time. State method used to prepare hardware, configure, perform the restore, and estimated time for each step.
- Backup software produces notification of status (minimum: successful, unsuccessful and what the problem was) of backup and restore jobs.
- Report on integrity of versions after restoration of documents.
- Provide scenarios and pricing of different levels of redundancy that can be applied to the solution. (Include details of hardware, software, licenses, management, and configuration required for each level of redundancy.)

The existing or recommended backup infrastructure should provide growth capability, and the enterprise should provide detailed analysis of the likely backup capability requirements for a specified number of years. Suppliers should be requested to provide details of how existing backup architecture would be utilized, expandability, assumptions, limitations, and dependencies.

Furthermore, it is also imperative that suppliers be requested to identify the components of a proposed IDCM solution that are critical, such that a failure of any single component will prevent operation of the proposed system. Also, suppliers should be required to identify the components for redundancy of the IDCM and its critical components, as well as metadata and content files, to optimize system reliability.

A provisional list of requirements to be considered is provided in Table 8. Some of these requirements may not be applicable to the enterprise environment, and the list is only provided as a means of provoking ideas, not as a definitive statement of requirements.

Security and Audit

The network operating system security and audit facilities are the primary means of managing user authentication and access controls to documents or Web content

Table 9: Security/Audit

- Prevent users from having direct access to the metadata and content files by any means other than the IDCM.
- Use the network operating system to authenticate users. (Suppliers should be asked to provide details on level of integration with network operating system for authenticating users, details and examples of how this is performed, and expected limitations.)
- Provide an immutable audit trail for actions performed on a document or Web content (enterprises should state minimum requirements).
- Provide the ability to customize the recorded audit trail actions (e.g., check-in, move) for specific classes of documents or Web content.
- Use the network operating system to manage access control privileges.
- Provide security alerts to an object owner and IDCM administrator in regard to repeated attempts to access secure documents or Web content by an individual.
- Provide access permissions based on user and group security definitions.
- Provide a range of security rights (enterprises to state minimum requirements).
- Provide folder level security and document level security for specific (sensitive) documents or Web content.
- Produce security management reports to identify usage patterns, security classification practices of users, audit reports, and integrity checks.
- Provide the system administrator with sufficient security rights to retrieve and view all documents or Web content within the IDCM repository.

stored on shared file systems. Application security features such as password control can also be used to control document and Web content updating. These security regimes are applied at the folder level and document level, and on Web servers. Security may also be invoked at the application level for specific business systems that may not integrate with the network operating system security regimes.

Enterprises should be seeking to apply comprehensive, uniform, and operationally manageable security and audit practices to documents and Web content managed by an IDCM solution, and the preferable requirement may be to integrate transparently with and use the security features of the network operating system. Table 9 gives an overview of some of the features that might be sought in an IDCM security model.

Data Migration Utilities

As discussed in Chapter 11, there may be a requirement to migrate documents and associated metadata from existing information systems, logical file shares, or local storage systems, to the IDCM solution.

The enterprise may need the capability to import pre-existing documents, in single and batch modes, and to enable registration of imported documents. The use of batch import tools might reduce the cost of document migration and minimize the risk of populating the IDCM with corrupt or incorrect metadata.

Tools might be available that enable metadata to be "abstracted" from specific types of documents (e.g., documents based on templates). In such a way, the metadata (without manual validation) may be registered into the IDCM for searching, with reference links to the source documents. When checked out of the IDCM for editing, the metadata can then be user validated upon check-in.

Table 10: Bulk Import Tools

- Provide capability to bulk load digital office documents, drawings, images, and Web content formats from network file systems (and perhaps CD-ROM). Enterprises should provide a definitive list of the formats and volumes to be loaded.
- Provide capability to bulk load attribute data relating to documents from document registers (nominate relevant word-processing, spreadsheet, and database formats).
- Enable bulk loaded objects to be linked to attributes migrated from document registers.
- Support validation of metadata during import process.
- Maintain functional hyperlinks between documents and to content within documents during data migration.
- Provide capability to abstract metadata from digital document collections using abstracting techniques.
- Support the capability for import of multiple versions of a document with user configurable filename and version increments and latest version notification. For example, report1.doc, report2.doc, report3.doc, etc.
- Provide the ability to bulk load user-specified emails stored on the file system. Enterprises should state formats required.

It may be important that hyperlinks between documents and within document contents be retained, and this aspect should be examined closely when reviewing the capabilities of bulk import tools.

Table 10 gives an overview of some of the features to be considered when analyzing requirements for bulk import tools.

Monitoring and Management Tools

There may be a need for monitoring tools in the IDCM systems environment to monitor trends in usage and space used, etc., to aid in management of capacity planning, database optimization, etc. Such tools could be used to proactively manage the IDCM from an IT perspective and provide important statistics to the systems administrator. Tools to allow training administrators to easily sample document naming and other registration details might provide an insight into usage of the system and allow ongoing

Table 11: Monitoring and Management Tools

- Provide intuitive graphical user interface for database and monitoring tools, management tools and system administration tools. (Enterprises should state specific requirements for monitoring and management tools).
- Report statistics and trends of usage by users of the IDCM solution, disk usage, number of documents and Web content files stored, versioning applied to documents and content, size of database/s, number of documents/Web content of different types etc.
- Enable alert notifications sent to system administrator for key events. Enterprises should state specific requirements, clearly differentiating any reporting notifications from those already provided by database systems or network operating systems.
- Enable system administrators to manage user and group levels of security, assign access permissions and other similar types of administrative functionality. Enterprises should clearly state administration requirements in this regard.
- Enable system administrator to manage all facets of IDCM solution from single instance of administration.
- Enable system administrator to manage multiple document and Web content servers from single instance of administration.
- Enable optimization of full text index functionality of the system.
- Enable development of workflow modules constrained to specific roles, e.g. system administrator.
- Maintain transaction logs that support the requirements for system audit (see comments below).
- ~

training to be tailored to common problems experienced with document registration. Some options are listed in Table 11 for consideration.

When defining its requirements for maintenance of transaction logs, an enterprise should be specific as to its requirements. For example, for document and Web content management, organizations may wish to capture date, time, and user-id for actions such as (where relevant): user login, attempted/failed system login (transactions that may be managed by the network operating system). They may also wish to capture events such as object creation/revision/deletion, annotation creation/ revision/deletion, document check-in, checkout, printing, and relocation of objects to secondary or archival storage. The specific transaction logs for workflow and other modules within the IDCM architecture will depend on the nature of the application and specific event logging requirements, and these also need to be defined by the enterprise.

System Installation and Configuration

The enterprise may require a simple and effective means of installing the IDCM client software for the desktop operating system and Web browser client plug-ins (where necessary). The installation of the IDCM server software, particularly in a distributed computing environment, should be a relatively uncomplicated process. The means of integrating the IDCM with enterprise desktop authoring applications should also be uncomplicated. There must also be a simple, effective process for invoking startup of the document or Web content services and database subsystems. Similarly, there should be tools available to validate the integrity of system linkages and control files. There may also be a requirement to uninstall the IDCM client and server components, and tools should be available to assist in this process. The items listed in Table 12 provide starting points for consideration.

Table 12: Installation and Configuration

▪ Provide simple, effective means of installing IDCM client for desktop operating system and Web browser client. (Suppliers might be requested to demonstrate installation processes during benchmark assessment — see Chapter 20.)
▪ Provide uncomplicated means of installing IDCM server in the network operating and database environment effectively. (Suppliers might be requested to demonstrate installation processes, depending on organizational requirements.)
▪ Feature simplicity in integrating the IDCM client with desktop applications (taking into account document, drawing, and email management integration requirements). These capabilities might also be reviewed during assessment of products, if required. Particular attention should be given to desktop applications with which integration is not supported "out of the box."
▪ Provide straightforward process for invoking startup of document and Web content services and database subsystems.
▪ Provide capability to uninstall IDCM client and server components. Suppliers might be requested to describe the processes and identify the tools available for support of uninstalling client and server components.

Upgrades and Modifications

The primary requirement is to maintain metadata, documents, Web content, and integrity of relationships between metadata and documents and Web content after any modifications to the IDCM system. It is important that any modifications (upgrades, new versions, service packs, hot fixes, bug fixes, etc.) to an IDCM solution be managed to ensure the integrity of the documents and Web content, ensure that metadata is maintained, and ensure that the functionality of the system is sustained.

The enterprise should insist on formal sign off of any upgrade requirements and plans for installation and configuration of upgrades. All modifications must be performed on the development environment and tested thoroughly before being rolled out into the production environment.

Suppliers might also be requested, as part of any contractual agreement, to provide statements in advance of expected future upgrades to the software systems. This may help enterprises determine whether they would benefit from upgrading to newer versions of software, and consider the ramifications of choosing not to upgrade to the newer versions.

SUMMARY

An overview of some of the nonfunctional and domain requirements that may need to be considered when developing Requirements Specifications that cover nonfunctional requirements and domain requirements for an IDCM solution was provided. Enterprises should note that domain requirements are not restricted to information technology constraints but may also include other types of fundamentals, such as legislative restrictions (e.g., copyright issues), enterprise data standards, and similar constraints on the application domain (Sommerville, 2001, p. 105). In Chapter 7, in particular, we itemize a number of the documents that may detail such constraints.

This chapter concludes our discussion on requirements analysis and definition on IDCM solutions. We now move into Part 4, which deals with package selection and implementation planning.

PART 4

Package Selection and Implementation Strategies

In this Part, it is intended that the following information be presented:

- Review the processes involved in acquiring an IDCM solution, and methodologies for conducting evaluations of various solutions.

- Provide tips for reviewers of IDCM solutions that might be useful during the evaluation process.

- Discuss the importance of having a contract as the basis for an engagement model with the supplier of the IDCM solution.

- Discuss the importance of the implementation strategy within the context of implementation of IDCM solutions.

- Discuss the types of mechanisms used to facilitate implementation, including project execution planning, the importance of well-defined design, development, and testing regimes, and system changeover and migration strategies.

- Discuss the importance of risk identification and management.

- Reemphasize the importance of change management, which is an important key to the successful implementation of an IDCM solution.

Chapter 20

Package Selection

OVERVIEW

This chapter covers the typical procurement processes for selecting an IDCM solution and contains useful techniques for validating various solutions against requirements and negotiating a contract with a supplier.

Our objectives for this chapter are as follows:

- Discuss the requirements for developing a procurement (or contract) strategy and review the various procurement options that enterprises might use to select an IDCM solution.

- Discuss the requirement for an Evaluation Strategy as a methodology for reviewing proposals from suppliers, and provide an example Evaluation Plan template.

- Discuss the benefits of conducting a Benchmark Assessment as a method of helping to discern the most appropriate IDCM solution for the enterprise, and provide an example Benchmark Specification template.

- Consider the types of functional gaps that might be identified between requirements and offered solutions.

- Discuss the importance of reference site checks and the added benefits of reference site visits.

- Consider the types of issues that may need to be considered when determining final selection, and the submission of a Selection Report.

- Discuss the requirement for the development and execution of a comprehensive contract as a strategy to facilitate successful implementation.

PROCUREMENT (OR "CONTRACT") STRATEGY

Background

Once an organization has developed its requirements specifications (Part 3) and set aside adequate funding to cover the likely costs of the installation, configuration, design, development, and implementation of an IDCM solution, then it needs to determine its procurement strategy. The procurement strategy is defined in a Procurement Plan, together with a definition of resource requirements, risk management, time frames, and project schedule.

Purpose

The Procurement Plan provides the methodology and approach by which an organization will secure an IDCM solution. Most enterprises will already have in place a policy and guidelines covering formal procurement processes for the acquisition of information systems, and these will provide a framework in which to develop a Procurement Plan for an IDCM solution.

Objectives

The objectives of a Procurement Plan are as follows:

- Reconfirm the scope of the requirement.
- Reconfirm budget estimates (indicating degrees of confidence).
- Define the procurement strategy, i.e., the methodology and approach for managing the procurement of an IDCM solution.
- Provide a plan that defines the deliverables from the procurement process.
- Define the privacy and confidentiality requirements that will apply during the commercial processes.
- Define or cite the requirements for transparency at all steps in the commercial processes.
- Identify risks associated with the procurement process, and provide mitigation strategies.
- Define the project resources for managing the commercial processes associated with the procurement.
- Define the time frames for the procurement process.
- Provide a project schedule for delivery of the procurement strategy.

Scope

The scope of the Procurement Plan should cover all aspects relating to the procurement of the IDCM solution from the development of the procurement strategy, until a contract is executed with the supplier of the system involved.

Entry Criteria

The inputs to the development of a Procurement Plan are as follows:

- Project charter (iterated as required based on new knowledge during the project life-cycle, with changes and subsequent versions of the charter approved by the project sponsor);
- Feasibility study;
- Requirements specification;
- Budget (based on provisional business case development); and
- Implementation strategy.

The implementation strategy should have been defined as part of the project planning process that was discussed in Chapter 6. However, the implementation strategy may need to be iterated based on new knowledge acquired during the feasibility study and the requirements analysis and definition processes.

The following types of inputs are desirable prerequisites:

- An enterprise's procurement policy, guidelines, and templates; and
- Change management strategy (perhaps a provisional strategy that may need to be reviewed with the supplier of the system).

Exit Criteria

The key deliverables included in the Procurement Plan are as follows:

- Procurement strategy for IDCM;
- Procurement methodology and approach, for example, links to the following:
    - Evaluation Plan
    - Benchmark Specification
    - Selection Report;
- Statement of confidentiality, privacy, and transparency of approach;
- Procurement resources and resource management; and
- Procurement project schedule.

Context

It is important for an enterprise to pursue commercial procedures that are beyond reproach, while being compatible with organizational tendering and contract requirements. Therefore, tenderers should be able to assume the integrity of processes and be assured that all parties are dealt with uniformly. This need for transparency is important, because quite often, enterprises have already worked with or been approached by suppliers prior to the letting of an RFP and may have developed some preconceived ideas on the potential outcome of a procurement process. Also, champions of IDCM projects may have views that are shaded by prior experience with products, perhaps in another organization.

Consequently, the first step in a procurement process is for the enterprise to confirm that its policy for the procurement of information systems provides adequate guidelines that will assure that its commercial processes are transparent to all parties. Many private sector companies and government agencies will have developed procurement policies and guidelines that cover the exigencies for transparency in procurement processes. Guidance in these areas is normally very detailed for public sector procurement. For example, the Australian federal government provides best practice guidance (Australia. Department of Finance and Administration, 2001). These include:

- Accountability

  Public officials, answerable for spending public money, must include provisions in tender documentation and contracts that alert prospective providers to the public accountability requirements of the government, including disclosure to legislature. This accountability is enforced by legislation that should be cited in documents.

  There is also the need to specify that the National Audit Office may have access to contractors' records and premises to carry out appropriate audits, and to establish what is to be regarded as commercial-in-confidence (for example, fee structures or intellectual property) when designing any contract.

  Further, the government department must ascertain those details of a contract that may be exempt under *FOI* or *Privacy* legislation or not subject to standard disclosure mechanisms such as *gazette* reporting.

- Ethics

  Public expectation of government officials is that they will deal with buyers and suppliers on a basis of mutual trust and respect, and conduct business fairly, reasonably, and with integrity. Therefore, there is anticipation that is enforced by Privacy, Public Service, and Crimes legislation that their code of conduct will:
  - Recognize and deal with conflict of interest;
  - Deal with suppliers even-handedly;
  - Consider seeking appropriate probity advice;
  - Not compromise their standing by accepting gifts or hospitality; and
  - Be scrupulous in use of public property.

Vendors will have confidence that such principles are employed if they are reinforced by conditions that are explicated when they are invited to present proposals. An RFP can be expected to incorporate general conditions relating to the procurement process, and these conditions should explicitly state how the enterprise proposes to assure transparency of the process.

It is important that the project sponsor be kept fully briefed on the methodology and approach to package selection and be provided with reports at the conclusion of each key phase. The project sponsor will be responsible for sign-off of deliverables during the package selection (with specific key deliverables, such as the selection report, being approved by the Project Board).

Procurement Options

There is a range of processes that may be relevant to an organization's requirements for procurement of IDCM solutions. For example, an organization may release:

- An RFI that seeks expressions of interest from suppliers and systems integrators. (The organization may seek to shortlist solution providers and then release a restricted RFP to those on the shortlist.);

- An open RFP;
- A restricted RFP, based on a strategy that prequalifies suppliers; and
- A published (open) RFP based on specific prequalification criteria.

Request for Information

Some advantages and disadvantages of using an RFI are summarized in Table 1.

The strategy to use an RFI to confirm budget requirements is only feasible if the organization provides adequate definition of scope and implementation strategy, a detailed Requirements Specification, and defensible selection criteria. Similarly, using an RFI to shortlist solution providers is feasible if the organization stipulates detailed requirements, not only for the required system but also for supplier capabilities, reference sites, and other types of evaluation criteria. However, if the organization is going to seek expressions of interest based on this level of detail, it may be more appropriate to have a one-step process using an RFP.

Table 1: Synopsis of RFI Usage

Advantages	Disadvantages
Enables enterprise to determine extent of available solutions.	Entails two-step process for organization that is time-consuming and resource intensive.
Enables interested suppliers to present their company and product credentials.	Entails two-step process for organizations that are shortlisted to participate in RFP.
Provides a less painful exit for those suppliers not shortlisted, rather than dedicating time and resources to participate in RFP and not be selected.	
May enable enterprises to obtain views on whether budget is adequate.	Assumes that scope, implementation strategy, and requirements specifications are adequately defined.
	Suppliers may be unable to provide definitive pricing for solution if requirements are too vague.
	Suppliers may underestimate or overestimate budget depending on commercial acumen and risks.
May enable organizations to determine a shortlist of potentially suitable suppliers.	Assumes that scope, implementation strategy, and requirements specifications are adequately defined.

Open Request for Proposal

Some advantages and disadvantages of using an open RFP are summarized in Table 2.

The option to use an open RFP has advantages in that it is a one-step process, and the organization still enjoys the benefit of getting proposals that may embrace a wide range of solutions. It may also be less time-consuming and resource intensive than a two-step process. If the RFP demonstrates that the budget allocated for the project is inadequate, an organization may elect to contract a solution based on fit to budget rather than fit to requirements, which is potentially high risk. A solution provider with best fit to requirements may therefore be disadvantaged.

Table 2: Synopsis of Open RFP Usage

Advantages	Disadvantages
Enables enterprise to determine extent of available solutions. Enables interested suppliers to present their company and product credentials.	Involves receiving proposals from extensive range of solution options, but potentially from companies that do not have the products, service and support capabilities, or reference sites to reach a shortlist of preferred suppliers.
Offers one-step process for organization and suppliers that can potentially be less time-consuming and resource intensive for both.	Wastes supplier resources (time and money) to submit proposals in cases where suppliers do not have a chance of making the shortlist. Suppliers may have put less time and effort into an expression of interest using RFI approach and been assured of knowing whether shortlisted or not.
Confirms whether budget is adequate.	Wastes supplier time if budget is not adequate to meet the solution option that best fits the requirements. May lead an organization to select based on budget rather than solution, which may be high risk.

Restricted Request for Proposal

A synopsis of advantages and disadvantages of a restricted RFP appear in Table 3.

The strategy to use a restricted RFP, when used in conjunction with an RFI process, is still a two-step process. If the restricted RFP strategy is used in isolation of the RFI process, then there needs to have been a prequalification process and an approved strategy to differentiate why one solution option is participating, while another is not.

This type of prequalification is often found at the government level, where central agencies mandate or recommend specific types of solutions based on evaluations of products and suppliers by the central agency. However, while these types of initiatives may have a positive impact by removing time-consuming prequalification processes, they can be based on a restrictive view of requirements. We envisage that the types of

Table 3: Synopsis of Restricted RFP Usage

Advantages	Disadvantages
Enables enterprise to restrict RFP to those solutions in which they are interested.	Requires strategy to prequalify suppliers (where these are not shortlisted from RFI process).
Enables a restricted set of suppliers to present their company and product credentials.	Disqualifies other suppliers without the opportunity to present product and company credentials (unless the restricted set is derived from the RFI process).
Enables the organization to focus its interests on a restricted set of solutions.	Disqualifies the organization from seeing a wider range of solution options (unless this aspect has been addressed as part of the prequalification strategy or is the outcome of an RFI process).
Offers less time-consuming and resource-intensive process than using an open RFI.	Efforts may still be time consuming and resource intensive if restricted RFP follows from an RFI process.

document and Web content management solutions likely to be satisfactorily implemented are those that integrate transparently with enterprises' business processes, and overall solutions may embrace requirements that cover more than initially prescribed.

However, where there is no formal prequalification process, the decision to eliminate suppliers or products from a candidate list of solution options can often be fraught with danger, because assumptions (for example) that a product does not feature a key aspect of functionality may not be sustainable. Products are evolving rapidly, and new functionality is built into products, or integrated with products, particularly when there is a compelling requirement to do so to maintain commercial viability. Furthermore, the prequalification process may ignore that a particular product or solution offering might be proposed by more than one supplier, and there might be commercial advantage by reviewing a complete range of options.

Published RFP

The advantages offered by the Internet and Web might be used to support a process that combines some of the aspects of an RFI with those of an open RFP. For example, the enterprise might advertise the availability of an open RFP to those organizations that meet specified prequalification criteria. These can be published to an Internet site, and access to the downloadable RFP might be restricted to those suppliers that satisfied the prequalification criteria.

One organization adopted this type of strategy to publish an open RFP, which could be accessed only if a supplier agreed that the company and product requirements satisfied published prequalification criteria. It also incorporated the payment of a registration fee, which was refundable only if a compliant proposal was submitted. The process adopted is briefly described in Table 4.

Table 4: Example of Published RFP

RFP Process via Publication on Web
• Enterprise prepares advertisement and sends for news media publication. Advertisement contains link to host Web site containing published details relating to the scope of the requirement, implementation plan, and prequalification criteria. (Access to the RFP is not available at this point.)
• Prospective supplier reviews the prequalification criteria published on the Internet host Web site and determines whether company and product have capability to meet the mandated requirements in the prequalification criteria.
• Prospective supplier confirms having read the prequalification criteria and completes and submits a registration page, at which point, the enterprise database is updated with registration details.
• Enterprise database generates an email to procurement project team to notify of new registration.
• Procurement officer acknowledges prospective supplier by email and notifies electronic funds transfer bank account details for deposit of registration fee.
• Finance officer advises that payment of registration fee has been received and provides receipt number and date, which are updated in registration database.
• Commercial Officer, once fee is paid, dispatches email to notify potential supplier with the link to access the RFP documentation. The email contains a user name and password to access the RFP documentation on the Web site.
• Potential supplier accesses Web site to download relevant RFP documentation.
• Registration deposits are refunded to suppliers that submit proposals compliant with the conditions of proposal.

REQUEST FOR PROPOSAL

Overview

The RFP is the key deliverable that enterprises will produce in order to seek licensed software, hardware, communications devices, and services with which to implement an integrative solution for improving business processes, effecting document management best practice, and satisfying recordkeeping requirements.

The material for the RFP is compiled from the following:

- The inputs to the procurement planning process, including project charter, feasibility, and the procurement strategy, will provide source material for the introduction component of the RFP.
- The general conditions relating to the submission of proposals by suppliers may include specific and general conditions, such as:
  - Definition of "conformance" for proposals (the form and contents that the proposal must incorporate);
  - Conditions of submitting prices;
  - Lodgment of proposals; and
  - Other conditions relating to submission of a proposal.
- The conditions that underpin the contract may be entered into with the selected supplier.
- The requirements specification is also an input to the procurement planning process, and it forms the essence of the RFP in that it describes the requirement being sought.
- Forms and ancillary documentation facilitate the submission of a proposal.

Enterprises may prefer to have a single supplier take full responsibility for the supply and implementation of the IDCM solution, particularly where there is likely to be a consortium of suppliers offering different products that make up the overall solution. It is the role of the *prime contractor* to take full responsibility for the proposal and, if awarded the contract, all aspects of the work, including "ownership" of the products provided by third parties and the management of subcontractors. If this is required, then the RFP needs to define the role of the *prime contractor* and seek a response from suppliers that they clearly understand and acknowledge the role of the prime contractor.

Template

Enterprises may have their own template for a RFP, but the one provided in Table 5 might assist those organizations yet to embark upon complex information systems projects.

Conditional Statements

When preparing an RFP, enterprises might wish to develop a response format for defining the relative importance of the functional items defined in the Requirements Specification and for assessing the level of supplier's capabilities against each requirement. An example response template is provided in Table 6.

Table 5: Example RFP Template

Request for Proposal — Example Template

Document History
- Document Location/Revision History/Approvals/Distribution.

Glossary
- Terms/Description.

Part A: Introduction
- Introduction.
- Project aim and objectives.
- Scope of the requirement.
- Implementation strategy.
- Procurement strategy.
- Selection criteria.
- Evaluation methodology.
- Forward planning (opportunities for next phase implementation).
- Conditions relating to submission of proposal.
- Conditions of contract.
- Summary.

Part B: Requirements Specification
- Background.
- Business environment.
- Document environment.
- User requirements specification.
- Functional requirements specification.
- Nonfunctional/domain requirements specification.
- Appendices — supporting documentation (data flows, etc.).

Part C: Proposal Submission Documents
- Proposal form.
- Product schedules.
- Licensed software schedules.
- Supplier schedules.
- Service schedules.
- Pricing schedule.
- Response formats — Requirements Specification.

Part D: Draft Contract
- A draft of the contract that the organization proposes to execute with the successful supplier.

Table 6: Example Response Template

Reference	Requirement	Relevance	Response Code	Comments
2.11.4.3	Integrate check-in/check-out and search functions at a menu (or icon) level within desktop authoring tools defined in Requirements Specification clause	M	C	*The product supports this requirement by integrating with each of the tools specified at clause x.*
2.11.4.4	~			

The enterprise completes the first three columns, and the supplier submitting the proposal completes the last two columns.

The *relevance* column enables the enterprise to codify whether a requirement is considered *mandatory* or *desirable*, and some enterprises may prefer to differentiate between *mandatory*, *highly desirable*, and *desirable* requirements. The "M" in the example is coded as a *mandatory* condition.

The *response code* column enables the supplier to codify how its solution meets the requirements based on predefined codes specified by the enterprise. The enterprise might specify the following codes, as an example:

- C — Core: Functionality is inherent or is a core component ("out of the box") of the current release of the product.
- D — Development: Functionality is not inherent in the core product offered but may be provided by using the product's toolkit or API.
- T — Third party: Functionality is provided via integration with the offered third-party product.
- P — Planned: Functionality is planned for a new release of the product within 6 months. (Suppliers will provide supporting documentation.)
- N — Not comply: Functionality is not offered by the solution.

EVALUATION PROCESS

Evaluation Strategy

It is incumbent upon an enterprise to ensure that it has an approved evaluation strategy that provides the policy and guidelines for conducting evaluation of proposals. The strategy should be incorporated into an Evaluation Plan, and it may be appropriate from a probity perspective for a signed copy of the evaluation strategy and plan to be approved by the project sponsor and lodged with the company secretary or legal representative before the commencement of proposal evaluation.

The evaluation strategy is required to continue the organization's commitment to a transparent procurement process and to ensure that each member of the evaluation team adopts a consistent, transparent, and well-documented approach to the evaluation of proposals. For example, when considering proposals for IDCM solutions, evaluators may encounter many issues with which the situation makes it difficult to assess the capabilities of the potential software. From a technical viewpoint, these might include the following:

- Server capacity — If data are maintained in one place within an IDCM system, and documents are copied to users on request, then production of copies of large documents, particular drawings, and graphics may cause network capacity problems.
- Association with other applications — When data must be collected from other files, such as linked compound documents or AutoCAD cross references, then check-in/check-out procedures may have difficulty in associating these files at the source.

Table 7: Project Evaluation Stages

Evaluation Step	Processes
Step 1	• Tender registration.
	• Compliance assessment.
	• Prequalification compliance assessment (may exclude some tenders).
	• Evaluation report (stage 1) to project sponsor detailing outcome of evaluation at stage 1 and a recommended course of action to proceed to evaluation stage 2.
Step 2	• Requirements specifications assessment.
	• Tenderer capability assessment.
	• Overall assessment (without price and value for money taken into account).
	• Price and value for money assessment.
	• Overall assessment, considering results of price and value for money assessment.
	• Shortlist proposals for benchmark assessment.
	• Evaluation report (stage 2) to project sponsor detailing outcome of evaluation stage 2 and a recommended course of action to proceed to evaluation stage 3.
Step 3	• Benchmark assessment.
	• Reference site visits.
	• Evaluation report (stage 3) to project sponsor detailing outcome of evaluation stage 3 and a recommended course of action to proceed to evaluation stage 4.
Step 4	• Overall assessment reviewed based on knowledge of benchmarks and reference sites.
	• Selection of preferred proposal.
	• Selection report to management with recommendation for award of contract.
	• Presentation of selection report.

- Association with other documents — Check-in and check-out systems may prevent users from linking to source documents if they were stored in secure areas.
- Auditing — This is the extent to which there needs to be a record of changes.
- Availability versus security — Users may be unable to work locally with files during IDCM system downtime.
- Workflow functionality — While allowing message transfer, the system may lack the functionality to notify of messages via a dedicated email system.

The evaluation strategy should provide details of the assessment process that enable enterprises to document and resolve these types of functional issues, along with criteria relating to project management capacity, commercial compliance, supplier capability, and price and value for money in order to provide for overall assessment. The way in which this evaluation is carried out must be made available to vendors. For example, a staged assessment may take a form such as that provided in Table 7.

Evaluation Plan

The components of such a strategy may then be expressed as steps within a plan, perhaps with requirements such as shown in Table 8.

Table 8: Evaluation Planning Step Processes

Evaluation Step/ Component	Assessment Objectives	Requirements/Examples
Step 1 *Compliance*	This will be the first assessment. Its aim is to put aside submissions that do not comply with the conditions of submitting a proposal that were defined in the RFP. Those proposals that do not pass the compliance assessment may not be further considered.	• Complies with the stated conditions for submitting a proposal and conformity with the general requirements of the RFP. • Agrees with conditions of contract. • Agrees with any other additional clauses defined in the RFP. • Supplier understands the role of the *prime contractor* and acknowledges that the role is accepted. • Observes other compliance conditions.
Prequalification	This assessment is designed to put aside those proposals that do not comply with the prequalification requirements. They may not be further considered.	• Supports a thin client- or Web-based functionality for search and retrieval without the requirement to have the browser act as a "thick client" by incorporating proprietary software. • Supports an "n"-tier client server architecture, where most of the IDCM functionality is executed at the server. • Follows other prequalification conditions.
Step 2 *Requirements specification(s) assessment*	The aim of this step is to assess the proposed solutions from a requirements perspective and to identify the solutions with the greatest potential to satisfy the Requirements Specification.	Displays capability of the offered solutions to meet user, functional, nonfunctional, and domain requirements defined in the Requirements Specification.
Supplier capability	This step is to determine the structural, management, and client profiles for each supplier. Also, it is used to determine whether suppliers have the financial capability, experience and reliability, and the qualified resources to implement and support the project. (Reference site assessments might only be conducted for shortlisted suppliers.)	• Delivers an effective and reliable solution that delivers high performance in a distributed computing environment. • Provides track record of delivering solutions in a distributed computing environment on time and within budget. • Has size and competence of technical workforce to configure, develop, and implement the system. • Supplier has financial stability of the supplier. • Demonstrates ability to understand the culture of the organization and to effectively manage change. • Has the ability to facilitate business process reforms and effectively deliver work redesign initiatives. • Shows capability to support and maintain solution according to SLA. • Demonstrates other supplier capability conditions.

Table 8: Evaluation Planning Step Processes (continued)

Evaluation Step/ Component	Assessment Objectives	Requirements/Examples
Price and value for money	This step is to determine the overall total costs for each solution and alternative solution offered by the supplier. (Some organizations may elect not to review the prices offered by suppliers until the functional evaluation has been completed, so as not to be predisposed toward a potential solution based on pricing factors.)	• Demonstrates capability to implement a solution that is within the budget allocation for the project. • Offers a solution with value for money based on an overall total cost of ownership for the project over a certain time period (for example, 5 years). • Provides other price and value conditions.
Overall assessment	The overall assessment is used to select the preferred solution based on the outcomes of the previous assessments, and it takes into account any additional criteria defined for the overall assessment.	• Displays manageability, integration, and usability of the overall solution proposed. • Shows ability of supplier to demonstrate understanding of the scope of work to be performed, conditions of contract, and the Requirements Specification. • Provides technical, managerial, and financial capacity to execute the proposed contract. • Outlines the level of overall risk to the project. • Highlights other conditions.
Step 3		
Benchmark assessment	The benchmark assessment is to evaluate the shortlisted solutions from step 2 to assure that the offered solution satisfies the user, functional, nonfunctional, and domain requirements defined in the Requirements Specification. The assessment may also include a performance assessment of specific components of the system.	• (Benchmark assessments are discussed later in this chapter.)
Reference sites	The reference site assessment is to determine the operational, technical, and financial capabilities of the solution based on previous implementation sites.	• (Reference site assessments are discussed later in this chapter.)
Step 4		
Selection	This step is the culmination of all evaluation activity and concludes with the submission of a Selection Report with recommendation for award of contract.	• Reassesses solutions offered based on outcomes of benchmark assessments of shortlisted suppliers and outcomes of reference site strategy. • Displays gap analysis between final shortlisted solution offerings. • Reviews overall assessment. • Prepares Selection Report and presents to management.

EVALUATION TOOLS — WEIGHTED SCORING

Approach

Within the framework of an evaluation plan, an enterprise may elect to use a weighting approach to scoring specific requirements during the assessment process. This type of approach supports the assessment strategy once the commercial compliance and prequalification assessments are completed, i.e., *after* step 1 in Table 8.

A Weighted Scoring Plan may be developed to the point of having a hierarchical scoring technique that provides a quantitative benchmark against which the responses from suppliers can be evaluated. The objective of using a weighted scoring methodology for this evaluation is to provide a quantitative measure against which the key criteria can be evaluated.

Table 9: Extract from a Weighted Scoring Plan — Levels 1 and 2

	Key Criteria	Score	Links
Level 1	Requirements specification capability	50	Level 2-1
	Tenderer capability	20	Level 2-2
	Price and value for money	20	Subjective — Checklist is in the IDCM workbook
	Overall assessment	10	Level 2-3
TOTAL		100	
Level 2			
1. Requirements capability			
	Electronic documents	40	Level 3-1
	Electronic mail	10	Level 3-2
	Drawings	10	Level 3-3
	Physical documents	10	Level 3-4
	System administration	15	Level 3-5
	System architecture	15	Level 3-6
TOTAL		100	
2. Tenderer capability			
	Deliver an effective and reliable solution that delivers high performance in a distributed computing environment.	15	Defined in the IDCM project workbook
	Prove a track record of delivering solutions in a distributed computing environment on time and within budget	20	Defined in the IDCM project workbook
	Determine capability and availability of suppliers' technical staff to deliver IDCM solutions in a distributed computing environment	12.5	Defined in the IDCM project workbook
	Determine size and competence of technical workforce to configure, develop, and implement the system	12.5	Defined in the IDCM project workbook
	Assess capability of the tenderer to support the implementation in the longer term with guaranteed performance levels	20	Defined in the IDCM project workbook
	Assess the financial stability of the supplier's company	20	Defined in the IDCM project workbook
TOTAL		100	

Table 10: Extract from a Weighted Scoring Plan — Levels 3 and 4

	Key Criteria	Score	Links
Level 3			
1. Functional and technical capability — electronic documents			
	Creation/receipt	10	Level 4-1
	Registration	15	Level 4-2
	Storage	10	Level 4-3
	Version control	10	Level 4-4
	Renditions	5	Level 4-5
	Compound documents	13	Level 4-6
	Hyperlinks	5	Level 4-7
	Viewing	5	Level 4-8
	Imaging	5	Level 4-9
	Routing/workflow	5	Level 4-10
	Printing	2	Level 4-11
	Search capability	15	Level 4-12
TOTAL		100	
Level 4			
1. Creation/receipt			
	Support multiple "save" regimes, with the default being the DMS, i.e., save to the DMS repository, save to a file system	1	
Mandatory requirements are scored out of 1, Highly desirable .7, and Desirable .2	Enable users to register ("check-in") any electronic document object, as defined in the list of desktop authoring applications defined in clause x	1	
	Integrate check-in/check-out and search functions at a menu (or icon) level within authoring tools	1	
	Integrate with office document templates such that data captured in the template is automatically populated into the document registration profile	1	
	Integrate check-in/check-out functions at an icon level with browser specified in ~.	.7	
	Support predefined save "protocols" based on document class	.7	
	Initiate a registration profile when a document on a file system is checked into the DMS repository	.7	
	Assemble new documents from existing documents and document fragments, without recreating the information	.7	
	Restrict save to DMS on document types not authorized by the system administrator	.2	

If we were to follow the example plan provided in Table 8, the result may be a scoring plan along the lines that will be illustrated in the two tabulations shown in Table 9 and Table 10, respectively. The first tabulation establishes level one criterion, and then at a second level, shows the elaboration of these criteria at level 2 for the requirements and tenderer capabilities.

Issues

Enterprises should consider the overall advantages and disadvantages of using weighted scoring before adopting such a strategy. The results of weighted scoring invariably contain some extreme comparative values when individual functions at the lowest level are compared within the overall weights (20% of 20% becomes 4% and 20% of 30% becomes 6%). It is difficult to establish whether the 6% property is 50% more important than the 4% property.

A major issue with weighted scores is that once a scale is adopted, scores are, in effect, "ordinal" scores, meaning that they identify the order of preference and not the magnitude of the difference. However, weighted scoring systems multiply scores by weights and then calculate a "weighted" score for two items and then express results as if they convey a magnitude. A score of six is not necessarily 1.5 times the worth of a score of four. The scores imply a comparison not a value.

Consequently, an enterprise should give due consideration to whether it plans to use weighted scoring as a tool and consider the implications of the scores derived from the methodology. Regardless, weighted scoring should not be the final arbiter of the recommended solution. Rather, it might be considered an analysis tool that contributes to the overall assessment.

The results of scoring need to be considered in the light of a range of other factors that need to be considered during the evaluation process, such as the overall risk of each proposed solution, information provided in support of the proposal, and reference site checks.

REFERENCE SITES

An invaluable part of the selection process is the ability to examine operational versions of the software functioning at reference sites, assuming that they cooperate with enterprises to facilitate checks. Criteria that may be taken into account are as follows:

- Accessibility — Whether the information provided is adequate to contact the reference site without further reference to the vendor.
- Applicability — Whether the reference site put forward is of similar nature to the proposed installation and whether the implementation put forward relates to the proposed IDCM implementation.

Interview scripts should be prepared for on-site administration, though it may be necessary to conduct interviews by telephone to remote sites. The scripts can be forwarded to the reference site before an interview to enable site representatives to understand the types of information required and be better prepared to respond and perhaps provoke comment on other related issues during the interview process. Some points that may be included in the scripts are as follows:

- The enterprise should provide an introduction, the nature of the tendered IDCM project, and the role of its interviewees in that project. It would also be useful to provide information on the nature of its own business.
- Scripts should include provision to enter the company's name, contact, and type and size of business.

- The interview may gather some general information on the nature of the business of the reference site and the role of the person or people participating in the organization.
- How long has the organization been using the IDCM?
- What modules have been implemented?
- What aspects of the implementation caused problems or concerns?
- What aspects of the implementation have had a significant impact on the organization?
- What response times, in general, have been experienced in accessing and checking in documents to the IDCM.
- What has been the degree of acceptance by users within the organization?
- How much reorientation of workflow has occurred?
- Have follow-up evaluations and use assessments taken place?
- What experience has the organization had with the supplier in regard to provision of services, project management skills, and consultancy?
- How effectively has the supplier handled the culture of the organization and effectively managed change?
- What selection process did the organization undertake to select a solution?
- How long did the implementation take to complete? Was this on time as per project planning?

These may, of course, be varied according to the nature of the reference site and its implementation and its capacity to cooperate in providing information. The organization should establish the relevance of potential reference sites based upon the similarities of the implementation (e.g., same or similar industry sector, scope and size, and functionality).

We believe it is vital that, wherever possible, reference site information be validated by actual visits to reference sites, rather than by telephone or written communications. On-site visits will help the reviewers gain an environmental perspective to the implementation and gain insights from visual observation and informal discussions, which are not likely to eventuate during telephone or written communications. Interviews at reference sites should include discussions with end users and not just project champions (who may have a biased view on the success of the project).

BENCHMARK ASSESSMENT

Purpose

Benchmarking is often used as a management term to indicate that "we are not altogether happy with the way that we are doing things ourselves, so we are going to look elsewhere for best practice."

Our meaning, focused as it is in the systems area, is more confined. In a procurement situation, it is about trying to compare a shortlisted group of application possibilities to see which will perform most effectively according to the criteria that emulate the environment within which they are expected to function.

Objectives

Benchmark assessment may be undertaken for shortlisted applications in order to:

- Enable the shortlisted suppliers to demonstrate the functionality, capability, and features of the proposed system configuration.
- Obtain an objective assessment of the properties of the offered systems and the overall capability of the solutions.
- Clarify and validate compliance of the offered systems against the Requirements Specification.
- Determine the performance of measurable items offered as part of the proposed configuration.
- Assess the supplier's capability to implement and maintain the proposed configuration.

The benchmark affords the enterprise an opportunity to meet with the supplier and assess the relative strengths not only of the solution but also its understanding of the requirements. The enterprise can also fathom the supplier's ability to understand the culture of the enterprise, its likely capabilities in interacting with people with diverse skills and experiences, and its ability to manage change.

These objectives may be pursued within a framework of the following:

- Business usage scenarios that cover typical and atypical day-to-day usage requirements of the offered solution;
- Functional assessment, which covers validation of mandatory requirements as offered by the core products tendered (This assessment will include the technical architecture and software development tools offered.); and
- Performance assessment that covers the performance of specific modules of the proposed solution and the strategic architecture, stability, and usability of the offered solution.

Methodology

The methodology that is applied is likely to include:

- Determination and confirmation of benchmark dates and a structure that addresses business usage and performance testing with the shortlisted suppliers;
- Development of a Benchmark Plan that defines the benchmark aim, objectives, and methodology, as well as the system configuration requirements for conducting the benchmarks (The plan will also define the roles and responsibilities, during the benchmark, particularly focusing on the interests of the benchmark participants from the enterprise.);
- Preparation of a Benchmark Specification that will provide the business usage scenarios, a checklist for confirming requirements defined in the Requirements Specification, and a schedule of performance requirements;

- Provision of the Benchmark Plan and Benchmark Specification to the suppliers approximately 10 days in advance of the benchmarks (based on negotiated dates);
- Demonstration of the benchmark conducted on the version of software offered as part of the solution proposal (It is imperative that the benchmark be conducted as stated. Each shortlisted supplier must provide a configuration environment at its own installation that is equivalent to the operating environment of the requesting organization, as defined in the Benchmark Specification.);
- Request that the supplier demonstrate the offered solution's capability to satisfy the business usage scenarios, meet the functionality defined in the Benchmark Specification, and otherwise demonstrate the performance, capability, and features of the offered system (The enterprise will need to understand any assumptions that the supplier has made when formulating its solution response to the benchmark specifications.);
- Provision of the opportunity for the enterprise to obtain a view of the overall architecture, stability, and usability of the offered solution; and
- Documentation by the enterprise of the instances where the tendered system does not meet specified functionality or performance levels (where tested).

Logistics

The enterprise should assemble a sample range of mixed documents (digital and physical) that support the business usage scenarios and tests that will be conducted during the benchmark assessment. These should be compiled and provided to the supplier in advance of the benchmark assessment.

It is important to have balance during the benchmark process. The enterprise needs to provide usage scenarios and specifications that will help establish the viability of the solution. The suppliers also need to have an opportunity to present the strengths of their solution (which might not be otherwise demonstrable from a benchmark that only features controlled specifications) and to demonstrate their technical and support capabilities.

Conditions

In its Benchmark Plan, the enterprise should clearly state the conditions under which the enterprise may elect not to continue with benchmark tests. For example:

- Supplier fails to demonstrate an item or items of tendered functionality to the satisfaction of the evaluation team.
- Solution fails to meet the performance requirements defined in the Benchmark Specification.

Benchmark Plan Template

A template for the Benchmark Plan is provided in Table 11.

VALIDATION CHECKLIST

The list in Table 12 is provided as a primer for enterprises that have not had the

Table 11: Sample Benchmark Plan Template

Benchmark Plan — Example Template

Document History
- Document Location/Revision History/Approvals/Distribution.

Glossary
- Terms/Description.

Part A: Introduction
- Purpose.
- Project aim and objectives.
- Scope of the requirement.
- Benchmark methodology.
- Logistics.
- Conditions.

Part B: Configuration Specification

Supplier will be required to provide a configuration environment that is essentially equivalent to the enterprise's technology operating environment (as defined in this specification) at its premises or premises of its choice in (nominate city). Specify the following types of requirements:
- Desktop environment (sufficient configured desktops to demonstrate all aspects of functionality).
- Server/network operating environment.
- Server/document/content management.
- Web publishing.
- Workflow.
- Recognition technologies (e.g., bar code, MICR, OCR, ICR).
- Scanner(s) — configured with imaging, recognition tools.
- Printer(s).
- Stipulate DBMS version/service release/patch numbers.

Part C: Business Usage Scenarios

---

opportunity to evaluate and benchmark IDCM solutions. It demonstrates the types of issues that might need to be considered when evaluating products. It is descriptive, not prescriptive, and it is by no means complete, because each instance of procurement for

Table 12: Evaluation Checklist Scenarios

Evaluation Checklist — A Primer

Architecture

- Does the system provide the capability of all modules to operate on the versions (including service release and patch release numbers, where relevant) of the desktop operating system and network operating system? What if there is a mix of desktop operating systems or network operating systems in the organization? Does the system support operating in a heterogeneous computing environment?

- What are the processes required for installing and configuring the IDCM software on desktop computers and servers? How easily is the software integrated with the operating system, and how easy is it to configure integration with desktop applications? What about nonstandard applications, such as CAD packages?

- Does the system provide for the capability of all modules within the integrated solution to operate on the version (including service release and patch release numbers) of the designated DBMS?

- What is the extent of transparency of integration between the modules that enable electronic documents to be registered as a "record"? Unless this functionality is offered as functionality inherent within the core DMS, the integration between modules or diverse products might be clumsy. During benchmark, was it necessary to switch between multiple products to achieve the required functionality?

Table 12: Evaluation Checklist Scenarios (continued)

Evaluation Checklist — A Primer

- Are benchmarks conducted using the precise version of software offered in a supplier's proposal?

- What strategies does the supplier propose to retrieve enterprise "corporate" documents and manage site-specific documents where remote sites may only have low telecommunications bandwidth? (What strategies does the enterprise need to put into place, if any, to upgrade the IT infrastructure at remote sites)? What assumptions have been made?

- Can the solution replicate metadata and content files between distributed servers, or does it only replicate metadata? If it only replicates metadata, then what impact might the inability to replicate content have on accessibility to (e.g., corporate policy) documents in decentralized locations?

Email

- What attribute data is captured directly from an email message when saved to a document repository? Does it meet the expectations of the enterprise?

- Can users save the same email (although it could be argued that it is a separate instance of the same email)? Can one user save the same email twice (assuming the same metadata)? What capabilities are provided to resolve?

- In what format(s) does the solution permit emails to be saved to a managed document repository? Will that format meet compliance with legal or regulatory requirements for evidence business transactions?

- How are email attachments saved? Does the system support any requirement to save email and attachments as a compound relationship, thus providing a context that may be suitable for recordkeeping requirements?

Digital Documents

- Is the system capable of supporting the management of templates so that the latest versions of templates are deployable to desktop computers or networks? What procedures and tools are recommended to update versions of templates on mobile devices such as laptops?

- Does the system support the integration of templates with metadata registration profiles, so that data keyed into a profile is automatically populated into a template, or vice versa, thus reducing the need for re-keying?

- How are templates and forms constructed for deployment of functionality on Web sites?

- Does the system support different capture scenarios for different types of documents? For example, more metadata might be required for important policy documents, than may be required for site-specific documents relating to a workgroup?

- How are documents migrated into the document repository? Does the supplier offer bulk load capabilities? If so, are they offered as part of the price?

- What are the license arrangements for a bulk loader? Is the use of the bulk loader restricted to a single network segment or can it be used simultaneously on multiple networks?

- Do you need a separate bulk loader to upload digital (CAD or image) drawings? If so, what are the licensing arrangements and cost implications?

- What alternatives exist to purchasing or leasing a bulk loader (e.g., development of scripts)?

- How are linked (compound) documents managed by the system? Link management might only be offered for specific formats, e.g., links between word-processing documents. During benchmark, establish a scenario where links are between parent and child spreadsheets, then a linked copy and paste into a word-processed document, and a link to a presentation diagram. Make sure that the links are managed during check-out and check-in processes.

- How are hyperlinks managed? What processes are required within the system to enable users to hyperlink between documents in the document repository?

Table 12: Evaluation Checklist Scenarios (continued)

Evaluation Checklist — A Primer

- Does the product integrate transparently with the folder structures offered in the desktop operating system? If not, is it important?

- Is the metadata of a document or content file maintained when it is updated to a new version, or is the metadata "lost"? Is it possible to synchronize metadata and versioning of objects, such that the metadata for a specific version is maintained with the specific version of the object?

Workflow

- How well is the workflow module integrated within the document or content repository management system? Is it an integral component of the system or a third-party product? If the latter, how well is it integrated — is it transparent to the user that the integration exists?

- During benchmark, is the integrity of documents participating in a workflow maintained at each step during the automated workflow processes?

- Does the workflow system require a separate license for each server (consider distributed sites) that has to support workflow processes? If so, has the cost of this requirement been considered in the budget?

Document Imaging

- How does the imaging system integrate with the document repository manager? Does the system integrate transparently, or are cumbersome step processes required to capture images and transfer to the document or Web content repository?

- Where does the user register metadata relating to an image? Is registration part of the imaging module or document repository application, or shared? If any metadata are captured via the imaging module, how are they transferred to the repository manager's database? (Validate all metadata transfer during benchmark.)

- How are images transferred between the imaging system and document or Web content repository manager? How does the system validate that all image objects have been successfully transferred, and how does it validate that the relevant metadata and image objects have been associated in the repository manager? (Validate object migration and metadata and object association during benchmark.)

System Administration

- How is offline storage managed by the system? Does the system generate a notification to the system administration to coordinate migration of documents or Web content to offline storage?

- Can the audit trail be configured? What facilities are available to the system administrator to invoke certain functions, or elect not to apply audit trail to other types of functions?

- Is it possible to manage all aspects of the system from the one system administration console?

- Can the system administrator access and manage multiple (e.g., distributed) repositories through the one instance of administration software?

Drawing Management

- Is the interface between the drawing module and the system for managing office documents (digital and physical) consistent?

- Does the drawing module enable a drawing user to capture an email direct to the repository, or is this capability only enabled to a user of the office document module? If so, how do users of the drawing module capture email into the repository?

- Does the drawing module integrate with the required version of the CAD authoring tools supported by the enterprise (or later versions, where the enterprise plans to upgrade its CAD tools)?

- If the drawing management system has its own integrated life cycle or workflow management regimes, can a nondrawing user view an instance of a life cycle or workflow? For example, viewing for recordkeeping and archival purposes?

Table 12: Evaluation Checklist Scenarios (continued)

Evaluation Checklist — A Primer

Search and Retrieval

- Does the system feature "recent documents" or "favorites" lists to help with search and retrieval?

- Does the system support "saved searches" to help the user easily locate documents required regularly using the same search criteria?

- Is the interface to the search tool such that it has a high degree of usability? What is the extent of navigation aids to facilitate end user access to documents and content?

- Is the system configurable to only search the content (full-text search) of the latest versions of document or Web content? If so, is it configurable to search all versions of a document? (What are the enterprise requirements?)

Web Publishing/Content

- How does the system render an office document to a Web format for publication? Is the output from the rendering process suitable from a usability perspective? How are the source and target formats managed if the source document is reversioned?

- How does the checkout procedure work? What happens if you check out two documents from the repository to a working file location and they are given the same filename during checkout? (This is a user problem, but not an unlikely occurrence.) Does the system attempt to resolve this conflict or enable check-in based on the latest check-out date?

- Does the system provide good visualization for documents or Web content that might be checked out for update?

- What capabilities are offered to publish content stored in the repository manager to the Web? Is the process such that it is not easily configurable, or can a system administrator invoke the process (manually) at any time?

- What type of staging strategy is supported such that content under review can be viewed before publication to the Web?

- How well does the workflow integrate with the system to invoke review and approval processes when new content is to be authorized for publication or old content is updated and submitted for review and authorization?

- Are content providers able to review the progress of a workflow to determine the status of content review, approval, and publishing?

- Does the system feature an expiry notification mechanism for content published to the Web?

System Performance

- During benchmark, when validating the performance of document retrieval from a server, was the cache on the desktop cleared to remove any previous instance of the same document? (Review performance tests again when in system acceptance testing in the enterprise operational environment.)

- During benchmark, when validating performance of retrievals of images from optical disk, was the cache on the server and on the desktop cleared to remove any previous instance of the image? (Review performance tests again when in system acceptance testing in the enterprise operational environment).

- During benchmark, test the actual throughput speed of the scanner by scanning a mix of documents and checking the resolution. If the enterprise requires scanning of 100 standard pages to be performed within "x" seconds, ensure that the required scanning resolution is specified and configured.

- During benchmark, was system administration of the integrated solution managed through a single interface that enables the administrator to perform functions relevant to all modules?

IDCM systems will have its own unique sets of issues that need to be addressed. It is meant as an aid to help organizations frame their own sets of questions and develop their own points of validation when assessing solutions and suppliers.

Table 12: Evaluation Checklist Scenarios (continued)

Evaluation Checklist — A Primer

Professional Services

- What are the capabilities of the technical support staff? Is knowledge vested in one or many individuals? Is knowledge about a specific aspect of the solution invested in too few technical support personnel, which might represent a risk to the project (i.e., technical resources leave the supplier's employ)? Does the supplier multiskill technical staff to reduce these types of risks?

- During benchmark, if functionality was not demonstrable or did not work, did the supplier offer excuses, or explain carefully why the error occurred, and the nature of the fix required?

- During benchmark, did the supplier demonstrate that it had a business focus as well as technology focus? Or was the main emphasis about selling the product, rather than trying to demonstrate how the product could be used to deliver a business solution?

- Was a discount offered on the licensed software that applies when determining the recurring maintenance costs of the system, and are these costs associated with the (higher) list price for the licensed software?

FINAL EVALUATION AND SELECTION

Approach

At the conclusion of steps 1 to 3 in the evaluation plan, the enterprise may need to continue to examine the advantages and disadvantages of the final shortlisted solution offerings in order to obtain a consensus view on the solution that is the best fit to the enterprise's requirements. This iteration may not be required if there is a clear candidate solution or supplier that can be recommended for contract award, but this is often not the case. One tool that might help enterprises to differentiate products and supplier capabilities is the gap analysis.

Gap Analysis

The gap analysis is used to identify shortcomings relating to specific issues and consider whether they can be worked around, which helps to determine whether a solution can be acceptable. There will, therefore, be a risk analysis component to gap analysis, for example, by assigning assessments such as:

- **Low,** which anticipates that the gap in requirements will not have a significant effect on the overall implementation of the project.

- **Medium,** which anticipates that the gap in requirements will have an impact on the overall implementation.

- **High,** which anticipates that the gap in requirements will have a significant impact on the overall implementation.

- **Extremely high,** which indicates that the gap in requirements presents a substantial risk to the project.

A risk factor with impact for different products can then be presented for consideration. It may take a form such as that which is excerpted in Table 13.

The analysis in Table 13 is particular to product functionality, but similar analysis may be carried out with respect to other factors. For example, in relation to supplier

Table 13: Example Extract from Gap Analysis Based upon Risk Factors

Impact	Risk Factor	Item	Comments	Follow-up Result
High	M	Check-in attribute screen	The check-in process presented a number of tabs. One of these tabs, containing the attributes required for check-in, was easy to miss or ignore unless it has mandatory fields.	Reference site visits have proved that this is configurable.
High	M	Level of customization required	Level of degree of customization versus configuration is not fully identified.	In follow up, it was identified that this is dependent on the desired outcomes of system operability required.
Medium	M	Email did not capture *From* and *To* details	Could not populate *From* and *To* in e-mail attributes. Neither application could successfully execute this without customization.	One reference site demonstrated that *From* and *To* details could be captured following customization during implementation.
Low	M	Define schemas	Definition of schemas required development of code. No tools were provided to assist in constructing the code, though existing code is reusable.	Customizable
Low	L	Data migration	Tool demonstrated required minor modification to code.	Customizable

capability, the supplier may not have submitted reference sites from the relevant industry sector. This may indicate a high impact (depending on the enterprise requirements), because the supplier lacks experience in the industry, and it may indicate that the product development path may not be sympathetic to the enterprise's needs. Similarly, analysis may show that a limited number of individuals responsible for implementation have prior experience in such work.

The enterprise needs to assess the manageability of the risks identified in the gap analysis. For example, a functional deficit might be customized at cost, which is manageable, but an architectural shortfall might be such that the solution represents high risk and might not be manageable.

Overall Assessment

At the conclusion of the gap analysis, or in conjunction with the development of the gap analysis, organizations may then review their overall assessment of products and solutions and derive an outcome. The overall assessment may involve reviewing all relevant steps in the evaluation plan and reviewing aspects such as capability of solution to meet the Requirements Specification, and the capability of the supplier to support the implementation (now and in the long term). The enterprise may also have to reconsider the fit of each proposal to the available budget, and the overall risk of each solution to the project.

Selection Report

The selection report produced as a consequence of the procurement process should be introduced by providing an overview of the process, the participants, and the reference documents used. The reference documents will typically be the RFP, the procurement plan, tender evaluation documents, benchmark specifications and assessment results, reference site reports, and any gap analysis taken as a consequence of examination of shortlisted solutions.

The selection report will need to present a compelling case why the selected system provides the best fit for an enterprise's requirements. For example, there may be points such as:

- The recommended solution offers a single suite of products (with the exception of the scanning software) managed by the vendor. This eliminates the risk of version synchronization problems when upgrades are implemented. Additional functionality available in new versions can be realized, without waiting for dependent or related applications to be upgraded as well.

- The recommended solution has the capability to render documents to multiple formats and manage synchronized version control over multiple formats. This capability was demonstrated during the benchmark assessment, where it was validated that version control over rendered formats was in fact managed by the solution.

- The supplier has implemented this particular solution (albeit one version earlier) in a distributed computing environment, with a similar size user base, in the same industry sector, using the resources that have been offered for this project. While the cited implementation is an earlier version of the products offered, thus being a risk to the organization, the benefit of the supplier's experience in this type of implementation is an advantage. Quality validation during development and system integration testing will help mitigate the risk that has been identified.

As with all information systems projects, the selection report that recommends a particular solution or outcome, should be formally presented to management, rather than just submitted. This enables the project team to have a face-to-face discussion with the management team to explain the outcomes of the evaluation, clarify any items regarding the process or recommendation solution, and demonstrate a positive and supportive view of the recommendation.

CONTRACT DEVELOPMENT
Importance of Contract

Another key to the successful implementation and ongoing relationship between an enterprise and its supplier of IDCM systems is the execution of an incontrovertible contract between the two parties.

Contracts are subject to the bounds of commercial law, and if the contract involves working with government parties, there will be additional regulatory requirements imposed to ensure public accountability. We made mention earlier in this chapter of such administrative guidelines for Australia. Another example, in this case for the United States, is the *Federal Acquisition Regulations* (United States Office of Federal Procurement Policy, 2002), which give guidance on the contractual frameworks employed with federal institutions in that country.

The legally binding documents will set out a statement of product specification along with work that is required. The relative proportion of product and service will influence whether the contract is fixed price, or involves compensation based upon costs. In the latter case, the contract will call for reimbursement for the work performed along with materials costs. In this case, it may also include a performance incentive.

If an organization stipulates that it proposes to enter into contract agreement with a prime contractor only, then the role of the prime contractor needs to be specifically defined, as a strategy to contain risk. The enterprise needs to scope and define the full responsibilities of the prime contractor, and this type of detail should have been elucidated in the RFP. The contract also needs to define the relationship between the prime contractor and any third parties that are subcontractors to the prime contractor.

The successful supplier may be asked to provide solutions and costs for a variety of different scenarios. For example, a particular environment may require consideration of buying licenses and implementing the IDCM solution for one site at a time, or alternatively, purchasing a corporate license and implementing levels of functionality across the enterprise. In a situation such as this, the contract might be constructed to indicate that the solution would be paid for on a project-by-project basis by individual business areas.

It is important that the ownership of intellectual property in any *customized applications* developed to integrate with the IDCM system be determined before the execution of a contract. For example, if there is a requirement of the supplier to build a customized application as part of an integrative solution, then such development might not be construed as part of the supplier's licensed software. The requirement to quell any doubts as to ownership of the intellectual property in the customized application will facilitate implementation.

Often, businesses and governments may waiver their rights to maintain intellectual property in return for benefits and assurances relating to the maintenance of the software. This type of arrangement is suitable if a supplier sees a marketing opportunity in the customized application, and the business and government organizations do not see the marketing of such applications as their core business. The supplier may wish to develop the customized application into one of its *products*, perhaps on a range of computing platforms, in which case, the enterprise may wish to seek an agreement on upgrading to the generic product.

It is important that the contract also define the requirements for the supplier to conduct systems testing. As indicated in Chapter 21, the testing process may involve three different aspects of testing, system testing, system integration testing, and system acceptance testing. The contract should be clear on the supplier's requirements for meeting the testing requirements of the organization.

The contract should also be quite clear on the project methodology that is to be adopted for the implementation process and the quality management system to be applied to the design, development, and implementation of software. The supplier should be able to elucidate the methodology applied to IDCM projects and the quality management systems supported. It is recommended that the enterprise validate the methodology and processes, the templates for the deliverables, and quality standards.

This validation may be made against its own methodology, or a general IS methodology, and against international standards for software development. The supplier might also be requested to provide a previous example of a specific type of deliverable, so that the enterprise and the supplier have a clear understanding of its nature. For example, the enterprise needs to understand the type of deliverable that it will be receiving for a "design specification," because there are wide interpretations on what constitutes a design specification. The same applies to a test specification, or a test plan, or the other many types of deliverables throughout the design, development, and implementation processes.

Negotiation of Terms

The enterprise needs to develop its negotiation strategy before commencing negotiations with a supplier. The negotiation strategy needs to represent an organizational consensus view on those items of the proposed agreement that are negotiable and those that are nonnegotiable. This strategy will provide the framework within which the enterprise can conduct its negotiations.

Remuneration is likely to be negotiated according to SLAs. Initially, SLAs will be negotiated based on accepted industry standards. However, it is possible that a contract may later be amended to reflect the SLAs required for the enterprise's established baseline.

The management of SLAs is likely to involve interaction between system managers, end users, and the vendor in order to establish realistic operational loads. Depending on the installation, the usage periods may be sectored into day and night or interactive and batch and backup. The mix of performance indicators may then include numbers of simultaneous users, transaction rates, work rates, and subsystems running. Reasonable downtimes and response times over specified periods will be derived. From this will ensue requirements such as "less than 5% of response times for check-in transactions will exceed 2 seconds when there are 250 concurrent users." These types of performance requirements should have already been defined in the *nonfunctional requirements* component of the Requirements Specification.

End users' subjective impressions of service levels may be difficult to secure — it is possible that problems affecting parts of a subsystem not made explicit in an SLA will be contributing to a function that is being measured. In a case like this, measurable systems performance may be fine, but the user impression will be poor.

Contract Structure

The structure of the contract is likely to be based on an enterprise's existing formats for information systems contracts. The contents of these contracts are generally aligned to the jurisdictional laws in which the enterprise operates, and the structure and terminology used may have been developed or reviewed by qualified legal practitioners.

In some cases in the public sector, standard contracts are developed at the central agency level for the procurement of information systems.[1]

It is *imperative* that enterprises develop contracts for the implementation of IDCM systems, because frequently, there are differences of opinion relating to the scope and the nature of work to be performed under the contract. It is also recommended that enterprises develop contracts in conjunction with legal practitioners with specific experience in the development of contracts for information systems and technology, and preferably in the domain of IDCM systems.

Table 14: Contract Checklist Excerpt

Contract Checklist — A Primer

- Which jurisdictional law applies to the execution of the contract? This might be relevant if the IDCM is to be deployed in multiple jurisdictions, even on a global basis.

- Who pays for the DBMS licenses? Are these offered as run-time versions of the software, or is it expected that the enterprise will fund the licenses?

- What are the acceptable ongoing costs for consultancy, software engineering, and system support in terms of daily or hourly rates?

- Who maintains intellectual property over custom-built applications?

- What are the levels of ongoing maintenance? Is this acceptable to the enterprise?

- Are service levels clearly defined?

- What are the professional services costs for implementation costs? Are costs offered under a time and materials or fixed price arrangement? If time and materials, are the time and materials costs capped?

Contract Issues

The issues that might need to be resolved in order to mold a generic information systems contract to an executed contract for an IDCM system are wide and varied. We give some examples in Table 14.

SUMMARY

Procurement procedures for all types of information systems have much in common. They will be influenced strongly by the regulatory domain within which an enterprise is functioning, so this will mold the strategy for evaluation.

We have shown how an evaluation strategy can be employed with specific reference to IDCM systems and provided examples of an evaluation plan and some components of it.

We provided excerpts from specific components, such as weighted scoring approaches, benchmarking, and gap analysis. Coupled with comment on reference site checking and contract development, we have shown how the procedures may be applied with respect to IDCM.

Also provided was a provisional checklist that business and government enterprises can use as a primer to mold their own questions and develop checklists of functionality and performance issues relating to their particular circumstances.

Once an organization has secured a watertight contract with its supplier, then the implementation of the IDCM system may proceed, and this aspect is discussed in the next chapter.

ENDNOTE

[1]   A case in point is the Queensland Government's *Government Information Technology Conditions*, which can be accessed on the Internet at http://www.gitc.qld.gov.au/.

Chapter 21

Implementation Planning

OVERVIEW

In this chapter, we provide guidelines for implementation planning, along with techniques that can be used during the implementation process to facilitate a successful project outcome. This includes satisfying the operational, technical, and financial objectives of the IDCM initiative, and providing guidelines for postimplementation review.

Our objectives in this chapter are as follows:

- Discuss the development of an Implementation Strategy.
- Discuss the requirements for a Project Execution Plan.
- Review the requirements for a Quality Plan to support the processes involved in development and implementation of an IDCM solution.
- Consider an initial set of risks that can be useful to capture at the commencement of an IDCM implementation, and discuss the requirements for an Issue Register and Risk Register.
- Review the requirement for the development of an effective Change Management Strategy and action plan.
- Consider the contents of an effective Communication Plan for an enterprise IDCM implementation.
- Discuss the typical requirements for a Data Migration Strategy to migrate existing (relevant) document registers and objects to the IDCM.
- Consider scenarios for backfile conversion of (relevant) hard-copy documents and the development of a Backfile Conversion Strategy.
- Consider the typical requirements for training and development of a Training Plan.

- Define a strategy for testing the configured IDCM, covering System Integration Testing and System Acceptance Testing strategies, and the development of Test Specifications and Test Plan(s).
- Review the importance of the Postimplementation Review study in the evolutionary deployment of an IDCM solution.

IMPLEMENTATION STRATEGY

This strategy defines the overall methodology by which the implementation stage of the IDCM product life-cycle will be achieved. The implementation strategy is typically defined (at least at an abstract level) at project initiation and incorporated in the Project Charter (refer to Chapter 6). The strategy needs to be aligned with the aim and objectives of the IDCM strategy, be complementary to the defined scope inclusions and exclusions, and be cognizant of the change and risk management strategies identified in the charter.

It is not unusual for an implementation strategy to have several iterations, particularly for complex IDCM solutions. The strategy may be changed when new knowledge is acquired about the implications of the implementation strategy, or there is a change of management direction. For example, as we mentioned in Chapter 11, the requirements of system changeover or data migration identified during the preliminary investigation of feasibility, or during detailed requirements analysis, may have implications for the implementation strategy. A final strategy may not be determined until a contract has been executed with a supplier.

An implementation strategy might be defined or iterated at the following key points in the product life-cycle:

- Project initiation —This is the initial abstract definition of the implementation strategy, aligned with aims, objectives, scope, change, and risk management.
- Preliminaries — The implementation strategy might need to be revised based on the operational, technical, and financial assessment of business and technology solution options.
- Requirements analysis and definition — The strategy might need to be reconsidered based on the nature of the functionality required and the likelihood of it being delivered successfully within the framework of the implementation strategy.
- Package selection/business case/contract negotiation — The knowledge acquired during the package selection, business case, and contract negotiations may have a bearing on the viability of the implementation strategy.

The final implementation strategy should be articulated in a Project Execution Plan (or Implementation Plan), the components of which we will now review.

PROJECT EXECUTION PLAN

The Project Execution Plan is a vital planning document that defines the implementation stage of a project. It draws on earlier project documents, such as the project charter, feasibility study reports, requirements specifications, and contract agreement executed

Table 1: Example of Project Execution Plan

Activity/Deliverable	Synopsis
Project Execution Plan	Like the project charter, the Project Execution Plan is a project management plan for the implementation of the IDCM solution, once package selection has been completed and a contract has been executed with a supplier or system integrator.
Project Schedule	The Project Schedule supports the Project Execution Plan and provides a definitive list of activities, tasks, and milestones, together with target dates, resource utilization, associated events, resource utilization, and costing details.
Risk Management Plan	This is the initial Risk Management Plan for the phase implementation. Risks identified in the Risk Management Plan are migrated to an Issues Register, which is also used to manage issues that emerge during the project.
System Changeover Plan	The plan should feature the legacy systems in operation and explain whether it is anticipated that they will be decommissioned, or the extent to which they may continue in use for a time or be modified to interface with the IDCM.
Data Migration Plan	The Data Migration Plan will define the scope, methodology, and deliverables for addressing the requirements for migration of data from registers or document stores.
Change Management Plan	This plan defines the change management strategies that will assure the successful involvement of all key stakeholders in the transition to the IDCM solution.
Training Plan	The Training Plan will define the scope, methodology, and deliverables necessary to meet the requirements of the Training Needs Analysis/Specification.
System Integration Test Plan	The System Integration Test Plan defines the testing requirements for client server architecture, network services, system integration (desktop/server), backup and recovery, and associated technical infrastructure.
System Acceptance Test Plan	The System Acceptance Test Plan will define the scope, methodology, and deliverables to meet the requirements of the System Acceptance Test Specification.
Postimplementation Review	This review takes place once the system has been in live operation to determine whether the IDCM solution met the operational, technical, and financial objectives identified for the implementation.

with the supplier(s) of the IDCM system solution. It normally begins with some scene setting that describes the environment for application, draws attention to scope and constraints, and expounds (or reiterates) the vision for what is to be achieved.

Enterprises are likely to have their own methodology and templates for project execution, so we do not propose to dwell on how to construct the Project Execution Plan. However, a snapshot of a planning template is provided in Table 1.

The planning template includes the requirement for a Postimplementation Review, outcomes of which may impact future directions for the development of the IDCM product.

The plan should include reconfirmation of the success factors for the project, as initially defined in the project charter. These are parameters that may be tested postimplementation. For example, an approach that identifies critical success factors may result in expression of indicators like those that appear in Table 2.

Table 2: Success Factor Identification

Success Factor	Key Performance Indicator
Meeting the business needs	- Match of solution with purpose - Extent of system use
Value for money	- High integrity of data and critical business documents - Contribution to business effectiveness
Executive commitment	- Shared vision is developed with all stakeholders - Resolve maintained during difficult assignments
Management support	- Projects initiated from business requirements - Line managers actively seek to sponsor projects - Successful project outcomes
Funding	- Funds meet capital, recurring, and professional service investments for IDCM
Expectation	- Expectations of the implementation time frames are realistic - Delivery of projects within an evolutionary planning model - Delivery of projects on time and within budget
Information quality	- Integrity, consistency, and currency of data

Table 3: Project Deliverables Extract

Deliverable Name	Outline	Author	Reviewer	Approval	Due Date
Software	All licensed software, as itemized in the contract, is delivered to the agency.	- Vendor	- Project manager - IT manager	- Project sponsor	
Project Execution Plan	This is the overall project management plan for IDCM Phase 1. It identifies key items such as scope, deliverables, assumptions and dependencies, project organization, key stakeholders, roles and responsibilities, risk and mitigation, quality assurance strategies, etc.	- Consultant - Project manager - Vendor	- Project steering group - Project reference group	- Project sponsor	
Communication Plan	This defines the communication strategies that are relevant for each of the key stakeholders identified in the Project Execution Plan.	- Project manager	- Key stakeholders - Vendor - Consultant	- Project sponsor	
Change Management Strategy	This defines strategies that will assure the successful involvement of all key stakeholders in the transition to the IDCM Phase 1 solution, It includes staff involvement in the joint application workshops.	- Project manager	- Key stakeholders - Vendor - Consultant	- Project sponsor	
Project Schedule	This supports the Execution Plan and provides a definitive list of activities, tasks, and milestones, together with target dates, resource utilization, associated events, and costing details.	- Vendor	- Project manager - Consultant	- Project manager	
Requirements Specification (for application interface)	This provides detailed user, functional, and technical requirements for accessing an inventory application.	- Vendor	- Key stakeholders - Project manager - Consultant	- Project manager	
Data Migration Requirements Specification	This specifies the data migration requirements for the migration of data from legacy systems.	- Project manager - Consultant	- Key stakeholders - Vendor	- Project sponsor	
Data Migration Plan	This define the scope, methodology, and deliverables for addressing the requirements for migration of data from the identified legacy systems.	- Vendor	- Key stakeholders - Project manager - Consultant	- Project manager	
Document Objects Migration Requirements Specification	The Data Objects Requirements Specification will specify the migration requirements for documentation objects and associated metadata.	- Vendor	- Key stakeholders - Project manager - Consultant	- Project sponsor	

Table 3: Project Deliverables Extract (continued)

Deliverable Name	Outline	Author	Reviewer	Approval	Due Date
Training needs analysis and specification	This defines the agency's requirements for IDCM Phase 1 training. It is based on an internal needs analysis, and will include user, functional, technical, and performance requirements.	- Project manager - Consultant	- Key stakeholders - Vendor	- Project sponsor	
Training plan	This defines the scope, methodology, and deliverables to meet the requirements of the training requirements specification.	- Vendor	- Project manager - Consultant	- Project manager	

The execution plan should also identify a set of deliverables, who is responsible for them, and which stakeholders should review what is provided. An example extract is presented in Table 3.

The execution plan should also identify objectives for the system (the product in its business environment), so it is appropriate for the objectives to relate to strategic and operational aspects. For example:

- Strategic objectives
  - Improve efficiency through reduction of business processes.
  - Provide consistent responses to customer inquiries.
  - Produce management reports that meet business needs.
  - Capture information assets and enable and promote information sharing as part of the strategy to develop a knowledge organization.
- Business — operation
  - Define business rules clearly.
  - Define ownership of data sets.
  - Capture data relevant to performance indicators.
  - Improve document control and security.
- System — operation
  - Provide architecture that has the following characteristics:
    - (a) Scalable and extensible for growth and wider deployment; and
    - (b) Flexible to cater to diverse business needs and emerging technologies.
  - Rationalize corporate data repositories and, where cost-effective, integrate corporate databases.
  - Decommission information systems that are not strategic to customer service needs.

The plan should also identify the scope of execution. This means that functionality that is to be included should be identified, for example, the extent to which the IDCM is to be interfaced with some existing software — it may be on a read-only basis. The scope should also identify exclusions where possible, for example, a decision may be made to exclude the incorporation of incoming facsimile messages or to avoid the use of certain types of documents in the initial phases.

QUALITY PLAN

Quality assurance has been referred to in a number of contexts in this book. Often, an IDCM solution has been referred to as being an integral part of quality management systems in general through support of documentation and record procedures for business processes. Naturally, an IDCM solution should also be subject to quality assurance, so it is important that requirements be identified as a fundamental aspect of implementation strategy. ISO 9001 principles (International Organization for Standardization, 2000) may be applied as a quality system for the implementation framework, requirements, design, and deliverables within a project execution.

Inclusions in an assurance approach may comprise the following:

- Statements of who is to conduct independent assessments and project reviews and when they are to be conducted;
- How assessment of project progress is to take place;
- Identification of relevant standards and procedures, and the extent to which there is adherence to these;
- Software quality analysis conducted according to established criteria; and
- Actions to be taken should there be inadequacies with particular data or functionality.

There may be specific assurance responsibilities required of the project participants, and these need to be identified along with milestones. Alternatively, it is possible that one person will have responsibility for quality assurance, but in either case, it will be necessary to identify skill requirements for testing quality.

It is likely that the strategy needs to provide for specific aspects of an IDCM. For example, Saffady (1996), when referring to document imaging procedures, points to quality control documentation that should indicate inspections, scanner test, and other procedures undertaken on specific dates. These may be complemented by written instructions prepared for operators of equipment employed for image inspection, index data entry, and scanning. In the case of scanning, these might indicate scanning resolution and compression requirements.

There are many evaluation techniques available for assessing information management. They may be grouped according to software evaluation, information evaluation, and evaluation of the interface between the user and information through the software. We will briefly summarize some criteria here that may be referred to in more detail in Middleton (2002).

For example, software quality may be assessed in terms of the following:

- Functionality — The operative characteristics of software expressed in terms of factors such as suitability for task and interoperability.
- Reliability — Measures of how dependable the software is expressed in terms of factors such as recoverability and fault tolerance.

- Usability — Characteristics that describe the ease with which software can be put to use and that measure the ease with which it is understood and learned.
- Efficiency — Measures of how economical the software is with respect to response and processing times.
- Maintainability — Attributes relating to upkeep of software, its stability, and the effort needed to analyze it and undertake development.
- Portability — Attributes that describe the extent to which the software is adaptable in different environments.

Information quality may be assessed in a number of ways, which, depending upon the way the IDCM is implemented, may include:
- Data dictionary evaluation that determines the extent to which entity-relationship attributes may be captured and documentation versioning and security support for data integrity is provided;
- Thesaurus evaluation that determines the extent of a controlled vocabulary that provides subject term metadata for documents; and
- Indexing evaluation that assesses the consistency with which indexing and classification metadata have been applied.

The interface between the user and the information has been defined in terms of many tests for human–computer interaction effectiveness. Among these is an ergonomics standard (International Organization for Standardization, 1992–2000) that considers presentation of information with respect to the following:
- Clarity — The information content is conveyed quickly and accurately.
- Discriminability — The displayed information can be distinguished accurately.
- Conciseness — Users are not overloaded with extraneous information.
- Consistency — The unique design conforms with the user's expectation.
- Detectability — The user's attention is drawn toward information required.
- Legibility — Information is easy to read.
- Comprehensibility — The meaning is clearly understandable, unambiguous, interpretable, and recognizable.

This ISO standard series also provides elsewhere specifically for evaluation of forms design, so that criteria are provided for assessing the effectiveness of templates established for data entry. These criteria are defined in terms of:
- Applicability — For example, workflow analysis may have shown that fields should be grouped in certain combinations, appropriate for when different users are entering their components of required data.
- Adherence — For example, institutional documentation may require that all data entry fields be displayed in reverse video.

RISK ASSESSMENT AND MITIGATION

The factors that may adversely influence the successful outcome of project execution are typically identified within a broader framework of assumptions and dependencies. It is therefore appropriate to identify operational assumptions that may include the following, for example:

- Key staff members are available for interviews.
- Project has full support of CEO, Chief Information Officer, and managers.
- Staff will be available for training sessions and testing of system.
- There is ready access to review current systems and relevant business documents.
- Project focus is customization with maximum adaptation of vendor software.

These may be complemented with technical assumptions, such as:

- The organization already has a server that is able to support the development environment for the IDCM.
- The IDCM will be functioning within a Unix operating environment.
- The organization will identify formats from legacy data for migration software development.

It is also likely that there will be funding assumptions, perhaps relating to staged allocation for finance or provision of support and training.

It may be appropriate to align assumptions with an expression of dependencies that shows which tasks are dependent upon prior or concurrent tasks and plans. These may be expressed in tabular form, or by using project management tools such as Gantt charts, Critical Path Method, or PERT (Program Evaluation and Review Technique) tools.

The software risk management process is a formalized approach to avoiding financial loss, time delay, and diminished performance. It involves identifying points in the project implementation where predicted goals may be unachievable within available resources, or because of circumstances, that although foreseeable are not expected to occur.

There are a number of structured approaches to undertaking risk management. For example, the model developed by the Software Engineering Institute (United States Department of Energy Quality Managers Software Quality Assurance Subcommittee, 2000) has the following stages:

- **Identify**

  This involves searching for and locating risks before they become problems adversely affecting the project. It assumes the establishment of an environment that encourages people to raise concerns and issues. The person undertaking the analysis conducts a process overview briefing and is able to do this with the aid of the taxonomy of risks itemized in the model.

  For example, the taxonomy uses classes for *product engineering*, *development environment*, and *program constraints*. Within the *work environment* area of *development*, the taxonomy lists *quality attitude, cooperation, communication,* and *morale.*

- **Analyze**

  At this stage, the risk data are processed into decision-making information. This will include reviewing, prioritizing, and selecting the most critical risks to address, with the facilitator looking for a consensus on consequence, severity, probability, and time frame for each risk. A risk matrix may be established to depict prioritized risks.

- **Plan**

  The risk information is translated into decisions and actions for implementation per medium of a Risk Management Plan. Risk action planning considers the future consequences of a decision made today. Risk plans aim to do the following:

  – Formulate risk aversion actions by changing the design or the process or by taking no further action, thus accepting the consequences if the risk occurs.

  – Mitigate the impact of the risk by reducing its risk level. For example, if contracting represents a significant part and risk for the project, then defining management practices that include formal methods for monitoring, evaluating, and controlling contractor performance would minimize that risk.

  – Develop contingency strategies, such as redesign, or redefined performance thresholds should the risk occur.

  The plan and analysis together may lead to matrices with actions, such as shown in Table 4.

- **Track**

  Monitor the risk indicators and actions taken against risks, making use of appropriate risk metrics that have been established in the plan.

Table 4: Risk Mitigation Plan for an "Asset Records" Project

Risk	Likelihood	Consequence	Severity	Mitigation
File migration software inadequate for task	Low	Major delays to asset records project	High	1. Vendor system engineer to validate capabilities and features offered by software to assure that the system will provide the required functionality
Partial data load extract not available as scheduled	Medium	Delays to Data Migration Plan and, hence, project	High	1. Project manager to coordinate delivery of partial data extract to meet scheduled time frame 2. Project manager to enable contingency in Project Management Plan
Full data migration fails	Low	Delays to go live implementation for asset records	High	1. Project manager to review outcomes of partial data load and determine further contingency planning requirements
Full data migration fails to transfer all data and objects	Medium	Potential delays to business processes	High	1. Project manager to review outcomes of partial data load and determine further contingency planning requirements
Conversion project does not meet time frames	Medium	Full migration will be delayed or be hampered to the extent that major delays occur	High	1. Agency project manager and the conversion project manager assure that activities for conversion occur in the time frames in the conversion plan

- **Control**

  Correct for deviations from planned risk actions by implementing contingency actions such as resource reallocation.

- **Communicate**

  Provide visibility and feedback data internal and external to your program on current and emerging risk activities, so that a conducive environment is provided for people to share their concerns regarding potential risks. The communication plan may be explicit about risk minimization by identifying possible risks along the lines of the following:

  - The project sponsor is unaware of project issues until it is too late to apply appropriate mitigating strategies.
  - The management team loses resolve to support the IDCM project.
  - The reference group established to contribute to the project feels that it has made insufficient contribution to development of the configured system and, therefore, undermines confidence in the IDCM and, in the worst-case, sabotages the implementation.
  - Employees are not adequately trained to use the IDCM at the point of go live.
  - Employees are not enthusiastic in wanting to use the IDCM, as they perceive that it is in conflict with efficient workflow.
  - User expectations have been raised beyond what is reasonably achievable.

Communication contingencies may be articulated in risk management and communication plans, so now we will turn to communication strategy.

COMMUNICATION STRATEGY

In Chapter 6, IDCM stakeholders were identified, and a communication plan is typically developed by the enterprise's IDCM project manager to express strategy for communication with project sponsor, project board, and key stakeholders. Objectives of the strategy may include identification of the following:

- Timing of project announcements;
- Nomination of personnel for communicating changes;
- Scheduling of review meetings for the duration of the project;
- Updating of stakeholders with status report; and
- Providing for personnel who are affected by implementation to be:
  - Successfully introduced to the project
  - Given the opportunity to express and resolve their concerns
  - Made aware of their anticipated role in the project
  - Provided the proper training to carry out their new or revised work functions.

Communication strategy may look like the example extract in Table 5.

Such a strategy may be accompanied by spelling out the specific actions as shown in the extract of Table 6.

Table 5: Extract from a Communication Strategy

Strategy	Implementation
Promote a positive outlook and perception of the IDCM project and the solution.	- Develop Project Issues Register that will include allocation of responsibilities, status, and outstanding actions required. - Develop a process to manage the Issues Register. - Protect project issues within the project as much as possible and escalate to project sponsor where necessary. - Release monthly bulletin to agency.
Provide adequate training "just-in-time" to **equip** employees to meet the expectations to be placed upon them.	- Develop a training strategy and training plan and interleave in the Phase 1 project plan.
Ensure information is delivered at the appropriate point in time to adequately **prepare** employees to meet the expectations to be placed upon them.	- Ensure that a key representative of each workgroup involved in the implementation is represented on the project team and attends project team meetings. - Minute project team meetings and circulate to workgroups during implementation. - Provide monthly bulletins to all members of the workgroup during the planning and development phases. - Provide fortnightly bulletins to all members of the workgroup during the testing and preparation for go live phases. - Continue bulletins until the implementation has "bedded down" to provide helpful hints, cheat sheets, etc.
Measure and monitor overall acceptance and perception of the IDCM and the project team by all staff.	- Upon completion of each Phase 1 workgroup implementation, conduct an anonymous survey to ascertain staff acceptance of the IDCM. - Use Whiteboard Sessions on Friday afternoons to encourage relaxed discussion on progress and corporate perceptions.

Table 6: Extract from Communication Plan

Communication Item	Target Audience	Medium for Release	Content	Frequency	Responsible Officer
Status report	Project sponsor	Written report	- Current status — tasks and milestones achieved in the preceding month - Planned activity — tasks and milestones to be achieved in the next month - Major project issues — resolved and unresolved - Project expenditure - Risk mitigation strategies and current status	Monthly	Project manager
Project team meetings	Project team workgroup user-base involved in implementation	Regular meetings held in person, through video, or by phone conference	- Project managers to allocate tasks - Each team member to report status on allocated tasks - Opportunity to verbalize any issues or concerns - Opportunity to provide feedback on reference group contact	Weekly	Project managers

Table 6: Extract from Communication Plan (continued)

Communication Item	Target Audience	Medium for Release	Content	Frequency	Responsible Officer
Project issues weekly report	Project team	Electronic report	- Issues with status of outstanding should be reviewed each week	Weekly	Change management officer
Project issues monthly report	Project sponsor	Electronic report	- Issues with status of outstanding with significant impact	Monthly	Project manager
Training strategy and plan	User-base A User-base B	Electronic reports	- Training needs analysis - Training strategy - Training deployment plan, including development of training courses, packs, and schedules	For the duration of the project	Training project officer
Workgroup bulletin	User-base A User-base B	Electronic PDF document published via the intranet	- More detailed and specific than corporate bulletin - Project status, including tasks achieved and timing of planned tasks - Project issues, as deemed appropriate - Helpful hints - Highlighting impact on user-base to adequately prepare them for changes and timing - Promotion of positive outcomes	Monthly during planning stage Fortnightly from beginning of execution	Change management officer
Head office whiteboard session	Corporate user-base	Verbal	- Provide information on milestones achieved and obtain feedback on current expectations and perceptions	At suitable milestones	Change management officer

CHANGE MANAGEMENT STRATEGY

The change management strategy is twofold:

1. Change management requirements documented by the enterprise as part of the Requirements Analysis and Definition stage, i.e., prior to RFP (Output is a change management specification.).
2. Change Management Plan typically developed by the enterprise or the solution provider to meet the Change Management Requirements Specification.

Organizational change concerns people (managers, employees, and customers) and their capacity to accommodate new ways of getting work done. An IDCM system can be expected to require changes to procedures, workload, workspace, skills, and the way the performance of them is measured.

The impact of these changes and how they are to be accommodated requires resolution of:

- Which groups or individuals will be affected by the change?
- How and when will information be communicated to various levels within divisions of the enterprise?
- What technical issues need to be resolved?
- What training will be needed for system users and administrators?

Therefore, change objectives should be established. They might be along the following lines:

- To involve staff in development and implementation of the new system in order to achieve ownership for the changes;
- To ensure that user needs have been identified and tested with an IDCM so that it is effectively aligned with workflow and business processes;
- To provide realistic expectations to users and stakeholders;
- To ensure that staff role in changes is made clear; and
- To ensure that staff members have the training for skills needed, and that the training is supported by effective documentation, in order to give them the assurance to carry out new tasks with appropriate tools.

Obviously, effective communication procedures supported by planning of the type outlined in the previous section, must help to achieve change management.

In some situations, software vendors may be keen to involve themselves in the change management process. However, it is incumbent upon the enterprise undergoing the change to drive this process. After all, they are the ones experiencing it.

DATA MIGRATION STRATEGY

Data migration requires the conversion of data used in legacy systems so that it may be effectively processed by the new system. In records management terms, it has been closely defined as moving records from one system to another, while maintaining the records' authenticity, integrity, reliability, and usability (International Organization for Standardization, 2001). For document and Web content management in general, these may be aspirations that should be planned for by:

- Migration requirements documented by the enterprise as part of the Requirements Analysis and Definition stage, i.e., prior to RFP (See Chapter 11); and
- A plan typically developed by the solution provider to meet a requirements specification for data migration (Refer to Chapter 11).

The plan should embody target dates and responsibilities for conversion that take into account hardware and software installation, along with workflow analysis, then provide specifically for:

- **Identification of data for migration**
  This will require establishment of an inventory of files with formats. The formats may range from hard-copy only, to digital formats that need to be rendered in formats compatible with the incoming system, to files that may require conversion programs written to have them available in compatible format with metadata.
  If schedules exist for records, then these should provide a basis for migration decisions.
- **Preparation of documents**
  This may include accumulation of hard copies to enable bulk processing, or relocation of archived digital data and testing of conversion software. It may

require decisions about the form of material to be used for conversion. For example, if the material to be converted is in original hard-copy form, along with a microfilm rendition, it may be preferable to go back to the original for higher definition following conversion, or to use the film version in order to assist workflow and the cost of conversion.

Documents may need to be identified within different classes, and these, in turn, may require the setting of different levels of security (see Table 7).

- **Conversion**

   Conversion may range from digitization of physical documents using scanning and OCR techniques, to conversion of data to new formats, at the same time adding metadata that are compatible with the new system. Particularly in the case of

Table 7: Sample Excerpt from Migration Strategy and Timetable for an Agency's "Assets" Records

- The data records to be loaded into the repository need to be supplied separately for each document class and location. Each set of data will be loaded into separate document classes.
- Each data set provided will be matched to a specified security model.
- If there is a requirement for a different security model for each document classification, then each set of records for each security model needs to be provided separately, along with the required security definition.
- The data records supplied will contain only the information required to be loaded into the system.
- Any assets document description that includes a required field in the repository specifications must have a value in that field. Any missing values will result in that data set being returned to the agency without being loaded into the system. Any records that do not meet the definition of the document properties in the specification will result in that data set being returned to the agency without being loaded into the system (i.e., character values for an integer field).
- The repository design is defined in the agency's *Assets Records Installation Specification*.
- Each data set is to be provided in a separate MS Access database file.
- A data loading script will be generated for each assets type, and each type will be loaded into separate folders.
- Data files will be loaded for each assets type into the IDCM using the nominated bulk loader tool. Errors will be logged and checked during the data loading process for any data items that were not loaded into the system.
- A report of data loaded versus items supplied by the agency will be generated to validate accuracy of the migration process.
- After the partial migration, the total number of successfully loaded assets records will be checked against the total number supplied by the agency. A Data Migration Report will be produced in the format described in an appended table.

Task	Responsibility	Target Date
Secure sign-off acceptance of Data Migration Plan.	Outsource project manager	24 June 02
Configure repository.	Outsource systems engineer	28 June 02–30 June 02
Deliver partial data extract.	Agency project manager	5 July 02
Test bulk loader.	Outsource system engineer	6 July 02
Configure the bulk loader and pretest migration.	Outsource system engineer	7 July 02
Validate data migration solution using partial data extract.	Outsource system engineer	8 July 02
Secure agency acceptance of partial data migration.	Agency project manager	12 July 02
Deliver full data extract.	Agency project manager	28 July 02
Perform final configuration and full data migration.	Outsource system engineer	23 July 02–2 August 02
Secure sign-off acceptance of final data migration.	Outsource project manager	4 August 02

graphical materials, it may require the provision of high-resolution images. Kenney and Rieger (2000) consider such imaging in some detail for the library and archives environment. They note the growing support for production of digitally rich images. This means that resolution requirements following conversion are set higher than necessary for immediate requirements.

Digital surrogates may then be used to produce lower resolution derivatives that may, for example, be used for presentation across networks. The high-resolution master may be retained as an archive for reuse as technology improves.

Consolidation of material from different sources may require the establishment of a unified classification scheme. For example, documents migrated from drawing, environmental, and property systems may be following different classification schemes in their legacy systems. A regime may need to be developed for concordance of their old classification with a new one.

- **Training and development**

  Training and development of manuals for these processes may be required. For example, with hard-copy material, it may be necessary to train for characterization of material into different types (manuscript, line-printer text, halftone artwork, photographs, mixed media) that will be diverted into different conversion processes.

  Training may be required in use of a controlled vocabulary for assigning metadata.

A developed migration strategy may contain statements along the lines of those shown in Table 7.

BACKFILE CONVERSION STRATEGY

Although we made some reference to digitization of hard-copy material above under data migration, our emphasis there was on material that was already electronic. For many enterprises, the introduction of an IDCM may be accompanied by a desire to convert paper-based documents to the new system.

In Chapter 15, we considered in some detail the mechanics of imaging processes. It will be evident from the variety and complexity of document digitization procedures that establishing a mechanism for incorporation of such material into an IDCM will be problematical and should be subject to stringent evaluation of worth. In fact, some have gone as far as to suggest that conversion is not usually a value-adding process and should be regarded as a necessary evil (Bielawski & Boyle, 1997, p. 92). However, as they concede, conversion into a format that enables quicker retrieval and access adds value.

Therefore, in contemplating plans for backfile conversion, we should take account of specific organizational requirements and examine the context of the requirements from the perspective of feasibility. For example:

- The variety of forms in which physical documents exist — Records that exist in manuscript form in bound volumes will not lend themselves to treatment in the same way as typewritten correspondence folios or maps in scroll form.
- The condition in which material exists — Some material may be in a fragile state and require specialized handling or even conservation procedures if it is to be digitized.

- The places in which it is stored — Remote storage may mean that scanning equipment should be taken to the documents, rather than the reverse.
- Intellectual property and rights management — Though the majority of the material may be internally generated (representing evidence of an organization's intellectual capital), there may be externally generated material on file that has restrictions imposed upon the wider dissemination that digitization makes possible, for example, "commercial in confidence" reports. The dividing line between internal availability with appropriate access restrictions and publishing to a wider audience, should be clearly drawn.
- The extent to which metadata are already available — For example, they may already be held in electronic form in digital finding aids, but it may be necessary to establish a process for indexing documents at the same time they are digitized.
- The extent to which hardware and software are already available — For example, hardware such as scanners, and software such as OCR, may already be available or may have to be introduced or developed in order to deal with the materials.

Clearly however, the most important criterion for selection of material for digitization is its subject matter. Strategy for conversion must, therefore, balance assessment of utility within an IDCM against cost and ease of digitization.

It may be found that a hybrid system is appropriate where physical records are maintained in that form, and that only metadata about them are introduced to the IDCM solution. This reflects the situation adopted in many library environments, where decisions are made to minimize digitization of older print material and retain metadata, in this case, catalog records, along with online full-text newer material (DeWitt, 1998).

If there is a justifiable requirement for converting physical documents to digital, film, or hybrid imaging systems, then it would be appropriate for these requirements to be documented in a specification, along the lines of those proposed in Chapter 11.

TRAINING STRATEGY

Training plans can be expected to document the business requirement for training, and to specify a training solution. They will be enhanced if they incorporate itemization of deliverables, identification of risks and contingency plans, and expression of methodology and management.

For example, risk mitigation may mean making provision to extend training periods for users who do not meet prerequisites, or to allow modification of training materials, or reconfiguration of hardware to emulate user environments.

Identification of training success factors within a particular environment may lead to specification of principles, such as:

- A test system must be accepted by the business prior to the commencement of training.
- A training environment must be established on the test system server.
- The training classrooms must be secured in sufficient time to schedule training and provide a safe and comfortable environment for training.

Table 8: Excerpt from a Training Plan

Group	Prerequisites	Session Content	Training Time
• Property group (owner/authors) • Repository administrator	Desktop SOE IE v5.0 preferred	• Overview/demonstration of IDCM Web client • Access levels • Application functionality • Adding or modifying a record • IDCM browse • IDCM search and retrieval	2 hours
• Property group (viewing) • Asset group (viewing)	IE v5.0 preferred	• Overview and demonstration of IDCM Web client • Access levels • IDCM browse • IDCM search	1 hour per group
• Repository administrator	Owner/author training	• Recap of IDCM Web client • Overview and demonstration of IDCM desktop client • Create folders • Add and modify user and group security levels • Change users and rename groups	½ day

- The equipment provided to facilitate training must be operational and configured with the agency's standard operating environment and relevant desktop software.
- The training consultant must have product and solution knowledge and the ability to communicate that knowledge in a classroom environment.
- Training materials must be:
  - Configured to the specific requirements for the IDCM subsystem
  - Structured for author/owner, viewer, and repository administrator
  - Visually presented in a format that is attractive to the participants
- Training must be timely and relevant. It should be scheduled as close as possible to when the participants will begin using the system.

Plans for a training group may therefore result in something along the lines of that shown in Table 8.

INSTALLATION PLAN

The strategy for installation should be established first by determining the scope of the installation, so that involved parties share agreement on what is included. It should also take account of the environment for installation, so that relevant sites are identified and described along with an understanding of accessibility, and information to be gathered relates to configuration requirements:

- Assumptions and risk dependency, such as identification of key people or activities to be performed;

- Resource requirements;
- An installation schedule including personnel involvement;
- Backup procedures; and
- Testing procedures including:
  - A checklist to see that stated functionality is available
  - Approval procedures for changes required following testing
  - Criteria for establishing prerequisites for installation and what must be attained for completion.

DEVELOPMENT SYSTEM

The development environment in which the IDCM solution is implemented will normally comprise a configuration stage along with production of guidelines and instructional and guidance materials.

The strategy for this may be expressed in the *project deliverables* and *training plan* for which extracts were provided in tabulations above.

The enterprise needs to consider the location of the development environment, which may depend on its physical location and accessibility to the supplier of the IDCM software. It would be incumbent on the enterprise to provide an environment consisting of client and server and communications to enable an effective development system.

It may be appropriate for development systems and object libraries to be maintained at a supplier site and also at a nominated enterprise site, in which case, development updates will need to be synchronized between parties.

The review process for the development deliverables will also need to be defined in the Project Execution Plan.

Configuration

For situations in which a vendor is establishing an IDCM system, configuration to the user's requirements may mean no more than installation on in-house hardware and loading and configuring software. However, it is likely, with the exception of the simplest implementations, that it will also include customization as defined through requirements analysis and definition. It may also require further configuration of bulk loading tools to deal with migration of data, or coding to develop interfaces with business systems complementary to the IDCM.

Testing

Testing usually involves three phases: (a) system testing, (b) system integration testing (SIT), and (c) system acceptance testing (SAT).

System Testing

System testing typically refers to unit testing, and the supplier of the system performs it before handing the IDCM system over to the enterprise for formal testing regimes.

System Integration Testing

The objectives of SIT are as follows:

- To verify that all nonfunctional and domain requirements defined in Requirements Specifications are satisfied by the system;
- To verify that all system interfaces, internal and external, are satisfied by the system; and
- To verify the operational aspects of the system, including regression testing, performance testing, and stress testing.

System Acceptance Testing

The objectives are as follows:

- To verify that all functional requirements defined in the Requirements Specifications are satisfied by the system;
- To confirm that all nonfunctional and domain requirements defined in Requirements Specifications are satisfied by the system; and
- To confirm that the configuration has been defined accurately and correctly in accordance with customer's requirements.

The requirements and strategies for SIT and SAT should be defined in a test plan, and this plan should be accompanied by test scripts that can be used to test the functional and operational aspects of the system at a detailed level.

POSTIMPLEMENTATION REVIEW

Following the implementation of the IDCM solution, and before further deployment of additional IDCM capabilities within an enterprise during a phased implementation, we recommend that the enterprise conduct a postimplementation review.

The objective of the postimplementation review is to assess objectively whether the IDCM implementation has satisfied the success criteria identified in project planning. The implementation needs to be reviewed in terms of meeting operational, technical, and financial objectives.

Project champions, IDCM suppliers, and systems integrators may be too closely involved in the project, and their impartiality may be impacted by career aspirations, further product sales, and similar behavioral issues. In order for management to obtain an untainted view, the postimplementation review might best be conducted by an external, independent third party to the project, ideally with experience in the implementation of IDCM, and preferably with relevant experience in the industry sector.

The postimplementation review should be an essential prerequisite to the progressive deployment of IDCM solutions throughout the enterprise and is a vital deliverable in helping an organization understand how information systems are helping to deliver real business benefits within the enterprise.

SUMMARY

The key to the successful implementation of an IDCM solution begins with planning, which is a technique that must be invoked from the commencement of product development, with the production of the Project Charter (refer to Chapter 6). At this point, there is a definition of an implementation strategy, a planning technique that may need to be iterated during the life-cycle of the product development.

Successful implementation strategies tend to be those that understand the complexities of deploying IDCM solutions and adopt an evolutionary rollout strategy for a definable set (or group) of business processes. The strategy should incorporate a program that features a progressive implementation of solutions designed to achieve a series of successful product deployments.

We recognize that an implementation strategy may need to be iterated during the product life-cycle based on new knowledge, and that the final strategy may not be decided upon until negotiations with suppliers have been concluded (before contract execution). The Project Execution Plan and an integrative range of planning documents that support the execution plan are designed to give effect to the implementation strategy. The plans developed during the implementation stage are designed to support a successful, quality implementation by managing expectations, change, and risk.

The postimplementation review is the final deliverable before an organization may wish to develop a Project Charter for a new deployment of IDCM functionality, and the life-cycle process recommences (refer to Chapter 6).

Chapter 22

Conclusion

Many enterprises in the commercial and business sectors are yet to address the inadequacies in their document and content management environment. Given the vital role that documents play in most business processes, the failure to implement management controls in this area is somewhat enigmatic. One might be forgiven for thinking that this failure is based on some wishful belief that the problem will disappear. However, many enterprises could not even adequately manage their documents in the "good old days," when mostly physical documents were used to support business processes and "life was easier." Perhaps some enterprises have the view that the new digitization of document formats will herald the long-awaited utopia of the "paperless office," and the problem of having to "manage documents" will magically vanish. We do not think so.

There may be a visualization aspect that impacts whether executives are able to discern that they may have a problem. With mismanaged physical document collections, executives have been able to *see* whether they had a problem, because they could observe collections of documents around offices, and notice volumes of documents waiting to be processed. However, millions of digital documents might be sitting mismanaged on network file systems, where it is difficult for executives to visualize the problem. Unless they care to browse the folder structures or arrange for scripts to detect the extent of document redundancy, inappropriate document naming and versioning, inadequate integrity constraints, and security issues, the disorder can remain hidden until a problem occurs. Then management's response is reactive rather than proactive.

Furthermore, the *digitization* of documents (or "putting them up on the intranet or Internet") does not equate with *management* of documents. We have always mismanaged documents. Those ancestors with their tortoise shells who were mentioned in earlier chapters, may have had them taken or destroyed by rival tribes. Their preservation technology was not all that satisfactory either. So, the requirement to manage information in containers in whatever form is not some "new problem," and it is not likely to be brought under control until it is addressed by executive management.

While on the topic of *disappearing*, we note that management of documents and Web content is not simply addressed by destroying documents without the legitimacy of approved disposal authorities. Those Roman citizens in Chapter 1 were lucky enough to have their leaders destroy their taxation records, which would no doubt be appealing to most citizens. It would virtually guarantee the return of any government looking to mobilize its electorate. On a more serious note, we as a society continue to witness reports of the willful and illegal destruction of documents by executives in some key business and government corporations. The types of actions have a significant impact on the ongoing viability of these organizations, their brands, products, and services, and indeed threaten their survivability.

Executives who turn a blind eye to the management of information as a resource are neglecting their responsibilities to their shareholders and the public. Busy executives may find it difficult to appreciate the scope and complexity of the problem, and quite often fail to realize that mismanaged document environments can have a detrimental impact on the efficiency and effectiveness of business processes. Business process redesign studies need to take into account the limiting effects that mismanaged document environments can have on business process efficiency. The alignment of business process redesign with innovation in practices and systems for managing documents and content might be a convincing way of addressing the problems identified in Chapter 3.

Professionals who practice in the information disciplines generally realize that their enterprises might have a problem with managing documents. However, they do not necessarily have a clear understanding of the problems their enterprises face with digitization of documents. We have heard the statements made that "if we could just get the physical documents managed properly, then we can address the digital documents." These types of statements tend to come from information disciples who may be uncomfortable with the complexities posed by the vast proliferation of digital documents, and the many different types of formats. Or, from consultants that have expertise in advising on the establishment of regimes for managing physical documents.

It is also difficult for some information professionals to come to terms with concepts such as "virtual documents" or "dynamic assembly of content," where structured units of information are created on the fly from digital fragments stored in repositories. However, it is incumbent on information disciplines to adopt a comprehensive view of the problem associated with managing documents and Web content files. We hope that this book helps to fill in gaps for those who do not have exposure to digital documents. After all, any suggestion to focus management initiatives on addressing physical documents may raise skepticism, e.g., "how long have organizations had to get their physical document collections in order? They have been dealing with them for the length of their corporate existence. If they haven't got it right yet, how much more time do they need?"

Problems are likely to become more evident in response to the expectations from a growing community of Internet savvy customers that transact business electronically. These customers want instantaneous access to services and information. They demand the same type of responsiveness from many channels, including call centers, responses to email, letters, and attending over-the-counter service centers. Enterprises will need to have their information assets (including those held as content in document containers) organized to provide the level of customer service that is and will be demanded in a customer service-centric market.

The challenge that enterprises face with managing information in digital format will become more critical with the planning and implementation of e-business initiatives, where digital transactions and documentation are the core elements of business activity. Therefore, enterprises will be faced with the requirement to manage more and more vital business information in digital format. Many enterprises are hardly in a position to implement effective e-business strategies, because concealed beneath the façade of attractive customer interface mechanisms are mismanaged document and Web content collections. Typically, these collections are identifiable by inadequately categorized information, redundant documentation (multiple users store variations on the same document many times over), and lack of contextual relationships between business processes, databases, documents, and records. (Such limitations were exemplified in Chapter 3.)

The requirement to manage email is a consistent problem with most enterprises. Aside from security concerns associated with inappropriate email messages and the potential for introduction of viruses via email systems, poor business practices exist for managing emails that are records of a business activity. Many organizations have no policy framework in place that enables users to identify business emails. They lack effective systems for managing such emails. Consequently, users may delete business-related emails. Or, they archive them to private stores, with the high likelihood that they will be deleted some time in the future. In these circumstances, an enterprise may have difficulty establishing that a transaction via email ever occurred.

There is also an ever-increasing requirement to support e-commerce and Internet-enabled customer service information publishing that relies on proliferation of content held on Web servers. The information presented via Internet channels is effectively a "record" — it is a record of information being presented to, and potentially acted upon, by customers. Content on active Web sites is regularly changed, and enterprises need to implement effective controls over the processes associated with authoring of new content, revision of existing content, review and approval, and publication processes.

The challenges with managing documents, email, and Web content are not new. The problem with managing digital information has been an imperative since the introduction of desktop authoring and messaging tools on networked computers. These enabled business users to generate messages and store digital objects in diverse formats without effective management regimes. The principles of recordkeeping must be applied to relevant digital documents, and enterprises have typically not applied best practice recordkeeping, including file classification schema, metadata standards, archival, and disposal authorities to electronic documents.

These fragmented document and Web content environments represent a high risk to enterprises in terms of effective compliance with regulatory requirements. It is more than a technology issue. These environments are generally an outcome of a volatile cocktail that contains a mix of poor information policies, practices, and management systems. There may also be issues of lack of executive support, low management priority for information best practice, lack of a project champion, and the failure of management to recognize that information is a resource that needs to be managed.

Unless the information challenges are addressed, business planning imperatives and operational schedules may continue to be impacted negatively due to fragmented information, regardless of the adoption of e-business or related Web-based ("e-Everything") strategies. An intuitive interface to the e-community helps with usability, but the back-end information processes need to be optimized and managed to support any Internet enabling strategies. Products (or services) may be consistently late due to mismanaged information or simply affected by delays in decision making due to the inability of users to find appropriate content in documentation upon which to make decisions.

Often, users simply do not have the confidence to make decisions on digital documents, as they cannot be assured that they are accessing the latest version of a document. Consequently, paper copies of the same digital document proliferate in departmental and local filing systems, frequently unmanaged, because users are more confident in viewing a copy of a physical document (often because it is the "signed original"). Leaving aside the capabilities of trusted systems and digital signatures to address the requirements for authenticating digital documents, there is still a high degree of reliance on physical documents for decision making, so that the concept of the much venerated (but demonstrably unachieved) "paperless office" remains utopia.

A fragmented information environment is also a hindrance for organizations wishing to develop and implement effective knowledge strategies. In this respect, while many enterprises are in the process of developing knowledge management strategies, the challenge they face is that *users cannot even find information, let alone share information*.

Consequently, enterprises in the private sector and government need to marshal their organizational resources to assure that the correct information is provided to end users and customers in a timely manner. Enterprises in both sectors are seeking new solutions to meet the challenge of processing the digital information deluge. The requirement to implement effective management controls over business documentation and Web content (regardless of format) should be an effective component of any information policy and associated implementation strategy.

If the conditions are right within an enterprise, information champions may be able to argue the case for enabling technologies to support better management of documents and Web content. This assumes there is excellent support at an executive management level for the concepts, and an appreciation of the resources (human and financial) that will need to be allocated to achieving well-managed solutions at an enterprise level. However, these types of conditions are often utopian, and it can be too simplistic to mount a business case based merely on technology concepts when trying to address the problems associated with managing so-called *unstructured* information.

The reality more often than not appears to be that business cases are difficult to develop based on the notion that an enterprise "needs a DMS" or "needs Web content management." It is akin to saying, "we need a DBMS." We ask: "what for?" Our view is that project champions might be best able to acquire budget funding for document and Web content management projects by identifying a series of specific business processes that will be improved by integrative document and Web-content-enabled solutions.

Business case development should be aligned to important strategic planning imperatives and deliver real business process improvements where performance can be more easily measured. In this way, the business case for systems required to support IDCM is more easily justifiable, by defining tangible benefits associated with business outcomes in their entirety, rather than trying to justify based on notions of "better managing documents." These notions, while well intended, are difficult to qualify when competing against other priority projects and difficult to quantify in terms of realizing tangible benefits. Implementation of "fit-for-purpose" solutions can be managed within an overall program that enables an evolutionary deployment of products over a period of time. The integrative approach combines an IDCM management framework and IDCM systems architecture to help organizations deliver professional solutions for managing different forms of information.

Many organizations have had experience with implementing single-purpose solutions for managing hard-copy documents (records), or a specific application of electronic document management, or perhaps a site-specific content application for Internet and intranet implementations. In these situations, the scope of the requirement can be contained to a specific application or business function, and there is a reasonable degree of likelihood that a fit-for-purpose technology solution can be selected and implemented.

The problem of finding a fit-for-purpose solution when trying to address the document and Web content management requirements at an enterprise level is challenging. While many technologies are available, enterprises need to plan and implement integrated solutions, which may cover a wide range of specific business applications, and cover a diversity of document types, recordkeeping requirements, and arrangements for publishing Web content. There is also the drawback that technologies evolving from an initial point of strength in one information management domain, may be yet to develop adequate capabilities to manage functionality outside a product's original domain.

For example, a product may have a functional heritage in the traditional environment for managing physical documents (records management) and have developed new functionality for managing digital documents. However, the product may not yet offer functionality for managing complex document relationships (e.g., compound documents). Another example is a product may have been developed in the drawing management domain with functionality to manage digital office documents, but may not yet manage email (or physical office documents) very well.

When reviewing technology options from the enterprise perspective, organizations may need to consider the capability of solutions that provide a managed repository for all types of documents. These types of objects include digital office documents, email, drawings and technical specifications, Web content, tracking physical documents, and applying recordkeeping and archival rules to relevant documentation. There may be a requirement to manage complex document relationships, such as exist between linked digital office documents, or drawings that reference other drawings.

They may also have a requirement for integration with different types of workflow (e.g., document-centric and process-centric), ad hoc, administrative, or production-level imaging systems, enterprise report management (or COLD) systems, and trust service systems, such as single sign-on, user authentication, digital signatures, and similar tools. Furthermore, at an enterprise level, organizations may wish to achieve productivity benefits by integrating an IDCM solution with strategic business systems, such as ERP, CRM, and GIS.

The technology solution becomes more complex when the enterprise exists in a distributed computing environment, featuring multiple geographical locations, probably interconnected by a WAN, or perhaps campus-style networks that support multiple LAN segments. Enterprises may also have the requirement to support highly mobile users who need to interconnect to information systems via low-speed modems from remote locations, such as temporary offices, motels, or home locations. There may also be a need to support portable computing users via wireless technology. Detailed consideration to the type of architecture supported by the technology solution is required in such circumstances.

Architectural considerations may include the requirement for thin or fat clients (depending on different types of document and Web content functions, such as authoring, review and approval, search and retrieval, compound document management), and the requirements for three-tier (or "n-tier") client server architecture. The three-tier architecture typically features a first tier that acts as the user interface, a second tier that provides document and content repository services executed at the application server level, and a third tier that is the DBMS, which is generally invoked directly from the second tier. There is also a requirement to consider centralized or decentralized databases, centralized or decentralized document and content services, and analysis of the requirement for replication services.

The overall architectural considerations need to include the provision of secondary storage capacity for documents and records that do not need to be directly accessed, but which are required for temporary or permanent (archival) storage. The requirements for this type of solution may need to include interaction with enterprise resources involved in managing database-centric information, including ERP systems, CRM systems, and similar requirements for managing transactional and administrative digital documents, as well as superseded content, within a recordkeeping and archival framework.

The means of addressing the information management challenges facing enterprises typically consist of a mix of business and technology solutions designed to eliminate fragmentation and redundancy and provide a cohesive, managed environment for information resources. This integrative approach helps to resolve the threats associated with a fragmented information environment and assist enterprises in planning and implementing new initiatives such as e-business strategies in an effective manner.

The challenges need to be addressed at the enterprise level, and the way forward can begin with an effective information policy, supported by associated document, content, records, and archival policies. An examination of processes and the use of documents and records within the business context may offer opportunities for business process improvement. This analysis will also identify the document types and record classes and help to develop the overall requirements for the system.

In addition to the risks relating to noncompliance, and associated with legal discovery, there are risks connected with information security, particularly in regard to business imperatives for disaster recovery and business continuity. These imperatives for effective information resource planning require communication by an information champion, supported by the framework of an integrative program. The specific aim should be to deliver the necessary synergy of business and technology solutions to provide a well-managed document and Web content environment to support information policy.

Unfortunately, organizations believing that the problems associated with managing documents might magically "disappear" are not helped by the information industry. Some so-called experts claimed that document management as a technology was not a viable proposition. Pundits derived this outcome from observations that the expected take-up of DMS never reached the zenith levels prophesized by industry analysts. They also commented that organizations found it difficult to develop compelling business cases for implementing DMS. Consequently, the latest industry reinvention of itself is the hyperbole associated with marketing *content management solutions*. (The fact that content published to Web sites, except content derived from structured databases, is created or acquired, managed, and published in digital document formats does not elude the awareness of skeptical observers.) If one looks at a range of industry trade journals and visits many vendor Web sites, one would be forgiven for thinking that the requirement to manage documents has actually vanished. The industry seemingly tries to reinvent itself, primarily to associate marketing with new technology capabilities, but perhaps there is a need to adopt a longer-term view of its customers' requirements, rather than associating marketing strategies only with the latest technology developments and short-term gains. The learning and assimilation requirements associated with take up of new technology must be factored in.

Despite the hyperbole that accompanies each step forward in IT, or software evolution, effective business application of the technology, in many cases, falls far short of predictions. There are many reasons for this, not least of which is an optimistic "silver bullet" approach that is often hopefully employed with business solutions. Sustained business improvement is more likely to be associated with the transformation that accompanies long-term assimilation of technology. Businesses first need to put the effort into understanding the implications in relation to their objectives, then realign themselves to employ the technology where appropriate. It takes time and fundamental restructuring to take full advantage. Thorp (1998) referenced the learning lag. He gave the example of an earlier technology, the electric motor, which took more than 40 years to realize business productivity gains in the United States, as manufacturing plants reorganized production lines to deal with its capabilities. Consequently, the information industry might be better off stabilizing its efforts to educate government and business enterprises rather than trying to constantly reinvent itself for "quick win" sales opportunities, many of which do not prove sustainable.

There are compelling reasons for organizations to plan and implement an IDCM strategy, which may need to embrace a development program that identifies the outcome as a product, with a specific product description, and that is managed as a project. The project life-cycle methodology generally needs to cover the planning, policy development, specification, procurement and selection processes, and project execution plan that typically embraces a planned evolutionary deployment strategy to assist with a successful implementation. Critical keys to success will include management commitment, user involvement, effective change and project management, and the selection of the right strategic business and technology solution.

Integrative systems (refer to Chapters 1 and 4) can provide the controlled repository, business process support, and authentication tools for managing all types of digital documents and their content within an enterprise. They should also manage physical documents and can provide indexing and search capabilities for images stored on microfilm. The solution should have the capability to apply recordkeeping and archival rules to those documents and Web content files that represent a record of business transaction or activity.

Good luck with addressing your organization's document and Web content management requirements. We hope that you enjoy the challenges of developing synergies between policies, processes, software, technology, and most of all, *people*, in helping your organization define and implement integrative document and Web content strategies for exploiting enterprise knowledge. The appendices provide some further resource information.

PART 5

Appendices

Appendix 1

Glossary

The terminology used in the book draws from the disciplines of systems analysis and design, document management, and records and archives systems, and there is some variation in the use of terms between these approaches. Where possible, we consolidated the terminology, but in some cases, we resorted to multiple definitions. Definitions that have been used based upon those given in the records management standard ISO 15489-1 (International Organization for Standardization, 2001) are indicated.

Where superscripted numbers are used, e.g., record[1], record[2], this indicates alternative definitions of a term.

Acronyms are used in preference to spelled out names for entry points, but their description includes the equivalent spelled-out version. Acronyms that represent organizations have been excluded, and those that represent equipment have been limited.

For more wide-ranging terminology with respect to imaging, refer to the dictionary of Moore (1995). Online dictionaries that cover some of this terminology, but have an emphasis on technology, include *FOLDOC* (Howe, 1993–2002), *Techencyclopedia* (CMP Media Inc., 1981–2002), *Whatis?com* (TechTarget, 2002), and *High-Tech Dictionary* (ComputerUser.com Inc., 2002).

Term	Description
Accountability	The principle of explaining one's actions to another. It may be required at an organizational level for statutory, regulatory, or audit requirements, or to satisfy codes of practice or community expectations.
	The principle that individuals, organizations, and the community are responsible for their actions and may be required to explain them to others (ISO 15489-1–2001).
Active records	Frequently consulted records[2] that include material of immediate relevance to an enterprise's current activity.
Adequacy	How well an enterprise initiative is documented to the extent of requirements. A major initiative should be extensively documented; a routine administrative action requires minimal information.
Anchor	The representation of a hypertext link.
Aperture card	A card containing an engineering drawing on a film clip, typically 35 mm. The card may be coded with identifying metainformation.

API	Applications Programming Interface. An API is the specific method prescribed by a computer operating system or by another application program by which a programmer writing an application program can make requests of the operating system or another application.
Appraisal	The process of evaluating business activities to determine the records[2] that need to be captured, and how long the records need to be kept, to meet business needs, the requirements of organizational accountability, and community expectations.
Archive	The whole body of records[2] (or "corporate memory") that is of continuing value to an organization or individual or a repository for such records; used in the plural form, "archives," it may more specifically mean those records that are appraised as having continuing value.
ASCII	American Standard Code for Information Interchange; the binary code for representation of a basic character set of letters and numerals, which is interpreted by most software.
ASP[1]	Active Server Page; a means of dynamically creating WWW pages by combining HTML with scripting facility to provide pages that are interactive with databases. Therefore, information on a page is tailored by the user interaction.
ASP[2]	Application Service Provider; a company providing outsourcing requirements.
Audit trail	Systematic recording of evidence of transactions and activities for accountability purposes.
Authoring	Creating a document by providing the substantive content and the formatting.
Authority file	A file[1] of the allowed contents of a controlled data field; it contains the established forms of terms that are to be used as values, for example, the names of people or mechanical parts, or names of organizations, stored in a standard manner.
AutoCAD	A software package marked by Autodesk Inc., which enables creation of drawings that are saved with a DWG filename extension.
Automatic indexing	Creation of index files[1] using software for extracting terms from text.
AVI	Audio Video Interleave; a file format for *Microsoft*'s *Windows* standard.
Backup	Procedures for creating and maintaining additional copies of the information in documents.
Bar code	A mechanism for coding data using a series of lines of varying width that may be read electronically. Physical documents may be given unique identification with bar codes that enable reading by devices such as wands to enable document tracking.
Bit mapping	Using individual pixels (or dots) to represent binary coded data for graphical display. The dots may be a simple on or off representation, or may represent colors with a variety that depends upon how many bits (binary digits) are assigned to a byte that corresponds to a pixel. Compare with raster.
BMP	Bit-Mapped Graphics; an application of raster coding for compression; each pixel is assigned a specific location and color value.

Boolean searching	Formulation of a search query for information retrieval using concepts linked by logical connectors, typically *AND* or *OR*.
BPR (or BPE)	Business Process Re-engineering; analysis and redesign of existing workflows and processes using a radical redesign approach to improvements in performance in contrast to the incremental approach of TQM.
Browser	A program that permits a searcher to navigate through information that is typically associated with links, as on the WWW.
Byte	A combination of bits (binary digits) that together represent a character such as a letter or numeral; often expressed as multiples such as kilobyte (KB) for 10^3 bytes, megabyte (MB) for 10^6 bytes, gigabyte (GB) for 10^9 bytes, and terabyte (TB) for 10^{12} bytes.
CAD	Computer Aided (or Assisted) Drawing (or Design or Drafting), for physical layout steps of engineering design, often used as CAD/CAM in association with Computer Aided Manufacturing.
Capture	An action that results in the registration of a record[2] into a recordkeeping system; in digital systems, this should be concurrent with document creation.
CAR	Computer-Assisted Retrieval.
Case files	Files[2] such as those recording information for insurance, personnel, or medical purposes, where the name of a person or an organization is the subject.
Catalog	An organized description of a collection of documents; in some contexts, is referred to as a finding aid or index.
CD	Compact Disk; an optically encoded digital disk for data storage.
CD-R	Compact Disk — Recordable; a CD to which data may be added, but on which existing data may not be edited.
CD-ROM	Compact Disk Read-Only Memory; a CD recorded from a master; once multiple copies have been produced, they may not be edited or further recorded.
CD-RW	Compact Disk — Rewritable; a CD that may be edited and rerecorded.
CGM	Computer Graphics Metafile; a standard vector graphic compression format used by many word processors.
Classification	Organization by categories in a systematic manner; this may involve grouping by subject, function, or other criteria, or determining document naming conventions. Systematic identification and arrangement of business activities and records[2] into categories according to logically structured conventions, methods, and procedural rules represented in a classification system (ISO 15489-1–2001).
CMS	Content Management System; software support for creation, organization, and presentation of information, usually for delivery via WWW.
COLD	Computer Output to Laser Disk; production of images directly from computer by optical writing, typically used for computer-produced reports.
COM[1]	Component Object Model; a general concept that succeeded OLE and supports the development of "plug-and-play" pro-

	grams that can be written in any language and used dynamically by any application in the Windows operating system.
COM[2]	Computer Output Microfilm; movement of data by a recording device to microfilm directly from computer, or using digital transmission, typically via magnetic tape or disk.
Compliance	The way in which records[2] fulfill the regulatory and accountability requirements imposed upon an enterprise.
Compound document	A document, created at the time of viewing, that may comprise components from several digital sources in different formats brought together for display.
Compression	The use of an algorithm to reduce the storage space required for the representation of a digital object.
Content management	The procedures for handling the authoring, organization, and dissemination of digital documents in an enterprise, often used specifically in relation to Web-based documents. (See also ECM.)
Continuum	The coherent context of the existence of a record[2] and the processes affecting it from time of creation through to preservation, archiving, or destruction.
Controlled vocabulary	An allowed list of terms, such as an authority file, but usually also containing semantic relationships and rules for creating terms and their relationships, which, if they are subject terms, makes the vocabulary a thesaurus.
CORBA	Common Object Request Broker Architecture; a specification for creating, distributing, and managing distributed programs by allowing different vendor programs at different locations to communicate.
Correspondence	Recorded communication to and from the personnel of an enterprise, typically on policy, market, and administrative matters.
CRM	Customer Relationship Management; management by an enterprise of all interactions that it has with its customers.
CSV	Comma Separated Values; a CSV file[1] contains the values in a table as a series of ASCII text lines organized so that each column value is separated by a comma from the next column's value, and each row starts a new line.
Data	Encoded representation of information.
Database	Data that have been organized systematically for information retrieval in a structured manner in a file,[1] or more likely an interrelated group of files.
DBMS	Database Management System.
DCOM	Distributed Component Object Model. (See OCX.)
DDL	Document Description Language; provides the framework within which a document may be created and stored in a specified rendition.
Descriptor	Index term that has been created by precoordinate indexing.
Destruction	The process of eliminating documents so that they are beyond reconstruction.
Digital imaging	See imaging and imaging systems.
Digital signatures	A digital means of identification that may be interpreted by software to match different documents, typically in imaging systems.

Disaster planning	Provision for backup procedures in the event of major destruction of documents, typically to identify protection for vital records.
Disposal schedule	See Schedule.[2]
Disposition	The range of processes associated with implementing records[2] retention, destruction, or transfer[1,2] decisions documented in disposition authorities or other instruments (ISO 15489-1–2001).
DLL	Dynamic Link Library; a collection of small programs, any of which can be called when needed by a larger program that is running in the computer.
DMS	Document Management System; software support for organization and control of enterprise documents.
DOC	The filename extension and format for MS Word.
Document	Any medium that carries symbolic representation of human thought; recorded information on paper such as a form, report, directive, correspondence, book, or map, or its equivalent created and used on another medium such as film or disk. (A document, to be a record,[2] must have evidentiary value.)Recorded information or object that can be treated as a unit (ISO 15489-1–2001).
DOS	Disk Operating System.
DOT	An MS Word template document.
DPI	Dots per Inch; a measurement of resolution, usually referring to the number of discrete dots that a printer can print vertically or horizontally.
DTD	Document Type Definition; the set of rules that govern the structure of a marked-up document using markup such as HTML or XML.
DVD	Digital Versatile Disc (often also termed Digital Videodisc); a development of the CD to provide for audio, video, and data storage on one disk.
DWG	The filename extension and format for a standard AutoCAD drawing.
ECM	Enterprise Content Management; the aspiration that an enterprise's intellectual assets (content) and document systems can be effectively linked to business processes for effective utilization.
EDI	Electronic Data Interchange; generically, the transport of data between computers, and specifically, the international standard protocol for supporting trade transactions.
EJB	Enterprise JavaBeans; software support for writing reusable and transferable enterprise applications. It uses Java software to provide the basis for J2EE.
Electronic imaging	See imaging and imaging systems.
Email	Electronic mail; the software that enables transport of messages between computers that have unique addresses on a telecommunications network.
Encryption	The process of applying a complex transformation to a digital object so that it cannot be rendered by an application in an understandable form unless a corresponding decryption transformation is applied.

ERM	Enterprise Report Management; an aspect of document management used to describe an integrated approach to dealing with reports for application with COLD technology.
ERP	Enterprise Resource Planning; an industry term for the broad set of activities supported by multimodule application software that helps a manufacturer or other business manage the important parts of its business, including planning product, purchasing parts, maintaining inventories, interacting with suppliers, providing customer service, and tracking orders. ERP can also include application modules for the finance and human resources aspects.
Evidence	Information that substantiates a fact; not necessarily in the legal sense.
FAQ	Frequently Asked Questions; often stored with answers in a publicly available database as an element of content management or to support knowledge management.
FAX	Facsimile transmission; the procedures for supporting transport of images of documents across telecommunications lines, typically by creating images of printed documents.
FCS	File Classification Scheme (or File Plan); an outline of the way in which files are classified.
Feature extraction	An OCR technique that seeks the features of individual characters to distinguish and then recognize handwriting.
Field	A defined component of data within a record[1] within a logical model of a database.
File[1] (database)	A collection of related records[1] that may stand alone or comprise a logically consistent part of a database.
File[2] (document)	A group of related documents usually combined physically within one container or a series of related containers, such as folders or binders.
File system	The way in which files[1] are named and where they are placed logically for storage and retrieval. The DOS, Windows, OS/2, Macintosh, and UNIX-based operating systems all have file systems in which files are placed somewhere in an hierarchical (tree) structure. A file is placed in a directory (folder in Windows) or subdirectory at the desired place in the tree structure.
Filing	The process of storing in sequence, physical files[2].
Finding aid	See Catalog.
FLO	The filename extension and format for ABC Flow Charter version 7.
Forms management	The procedures for controlling establishment, formatting, and standardization of physical or digital forms.
Free text search	See Full-text search.
FTP	File Transfer Protocol.
Full-text search	Information retrieval from a document using the complete text other than stop words held in a stoplist.
Function	An umbrella unit of business activity in an organization or jurisdiction.
GIF	Graphic Interchange Format; a common format for a graphic image on the WWW, the other being JPG. Along with JPG, the

	GIF has become a de facto standard form of image for the WWW and elsewhere on the Internet, such as bulletin board services.
GIS	Geographical Information System; a GIS returns results from a database query explicitly in terms of geographic coordinates (latitude and longitude or some national grid coordinates) or implicitly in terms of a street address, postal code, or map.
GML	Geographic Markup Language; standard for geospatial object description.
Grayscale	The spectrum or shades of black possessed by an image, the extent of which will depend upon the number of bits in a byte used for bit mapping.
Groupware	Software that supports the concept of people working jointly on tasks, typically report writing.
GUI	Graphical User Interface; an interface that permits use of images.
Half-tone	An image that uses dots to represent variations in tone, according to the density of the dots.
Hard copy	Representation on a medium readable by a person, typically paper.
Hardware	Computer components and peripheral equipment.
HDD	Hard Disk Drive; equipment for interacting with a magnetic disk with high storage capacity.
HTML	Hypertext Markup Language; the scripting language used for most of the WWW pages produced to date. It describes the contents of a Web page (mainly text and graphic images) in terms of how it is to be displayed.
HTTP	Hypertext Transfer Protocol; the set of rules (application protocol) for exchanging files[1] (text, graphic images, sound, video, and other multimedia files) for use with HTML on the WWW.
Hypertext	Text that is marked up using a language such as HTML or XML to enable associations between different parts of the text or to files[1] external to the text.
ICR	Intelligent Character Recognition; a form of OCR that includes using context to improve the possibility of correct recognition of characters.
IDCM	Integrative Document and Content Management; used throughout this book to represent a systematic integrative approach to implementation and management of DMS, CMS, and RMS and how these systems are associated with workflow.
IDEF	Integrated Computer Aided Manufacturing DEFinition; a method of modeling decisions, actions, and activities of an organization.
Image	Representation of information using radiation or digitization.
Imaging	Process of capturing, storing, and retrieving documents, regardless of original physical format, using micrographics or digitizing techniques.
Imaging systems	Systems designed to obtain documents or images that are not already in computer-based form. At its simplest, a system may comprise devices for acquisition, such as scanner or camera, for output, such as a printer or microform writer, and an intermediate image processor.

Inactive records	Records that are rarely required for information retrieval, but which must be retained for archival or legal reasons, in case of occasional use.
Indexing[1] (database)	The use of software to create, from key data attributes, additional files in alternate sequences, sometimes called inverted files.[1]
Indexing[2] (bibliographic)	The use of keywords to create ways of looking up subject matter in text.
Indexing[3] (document)	The process of establishing access points to facilitate retrieval of records[2] and information.
Information	Data that have been organized or signs capable of interpretation within a context that may be assimilated into knowledge.
Information management	Procedures, which may be technical, analytical, or strategic, for optimizing the use of information.
Information retrieval	The procedure of searching for and extracting records[1] or parts of records from databases and presenting them to the searcher as information.
Internet	A worldwide system of computer networks — a network of networks — in which users at any one computer can, with access permission, get information from any other computer.
Intranet	A private network contained within an enterprise. It may consist of many interlinked LANs and also use leased lines in a WAN.
Inventory	A complete and detailed summary of records[2] and their storage in an enterprise; see also Catalog.
IT	Information Technology.
J2EE	Java 2 Platform, Enterprise Edition; a platform for multiple-level server-oriented enterprise applications using Java software.
JPEG or JPG	Joint Photographics Experts Group; which established the digital compression standard JPEG (or JPG), a graphic image created by choosing from a suite of compression algorithms. It is a file[1] type supported by the WWW protocol.
Keyword	An indexing term used as an access point for manually assigned indexing[2,3] or automatic indexing.
Knowledge	Information that has been cognitively assimilated.
Knowledge management	Information management that takes into account unrecorded information or knowledge retained by an enterprise's personnel.
LAN	Local Area Network; a computer network within a constrained area, typically an office.
Legacy system	An earlier generation of a computer system, from which data may have to be transferred, or procedures adapted, for interfacing or supplanting by a new system.
Life cycle	Sometimes used to represent the stages of existence of a record,[2] but also see continuum.
Link	A facility that enables a browser to navigate within hypertext to another idea or concept using an anchor.
Magnetic ink	Ink that may be recognized by a magnetic scanner for interpreting characters, typically on checks.
MAPI	Messaging Application Program Interface; a Microsoft Windows program interface that enables email to be sent from within

a Windows application, at which point the document is attached to the email.

Markup
Tagged text codes included in a document in order to convey information about its structure and form.

MDB
The filename extension and format for MS Access.

Memory
The hardware in a computer that holds data for processing.

Metainformation or metadata
Information about information that improves the ability to understand the information by providing context, content, structural, or management information. For example, the layout of a form to be completed, the definition of fields in a database, or the identification of parts of the description of a document. Information included within markup is often referred to as metadata rather than metainformation.

Microforms
Documents on which information is recorded photographically in reduced form that requires magnification for reading, typically microfilm, microfiche, or microcards.

Micrographics
The discipline concerned with producing microforms.

Migration
The act of moving records[2] from one system to another, while maintaining the records' authenticity, integrity, reliability, and usability (ISO 15489-1–2001).

MIME
Multipurpose Internet Mail Extensions; a standard for multimedia email messages in multiple parts on the Internet that provides for graphics, FAX, and audio, in addition to text.

MIS
Management Information System; a computer-based system that provides consolidated information to management from several subsystems, such as accounting and human resources.

MODEM
MOdulator–DEModulator; device for encoding data for telephonic transmission.

MPEG or MPG
A video compression format developed by the Motion Picture Expert Group that uses lossy compression by storing only the changes in successive video frames, rather than each entire frame.

MPP
The filename extension and format for MS Project.

MS
Microsoft Corporation.

MSG
The filename extension and format for a MS Outlook mail message.

MW
Megawatt.

NAP
Normal Administrative Practice.

Natural language processing
The process of using automatic means of analyzing the text of documents so that they may be indexed or characterized for information retrieval, without use of a controlled vocabulary.

Notation
The set of signs used to represent a classification scheme.

NT
A computer operating system developed by Microsoft.

Object modeling
The use of objects to represent what is being modeled for a computer system.

OCM
Organizational Change Management.

OCR
Optical Character Recognition; the procedure for using a scanner to recognize printed alphanumerical characters and digitize them.

OCX
An OLE custom control, a special-purpose program that can be created for use by applications running on Windows systems, called by Microsoft an ActiveX control.

ODBC	Open Database Connectivity; a standard or open API for accessing a database.
ODMA	Open Document Management API; an industry standard for managing documents that allows users to store, retrieve, and share them with security and version control.
OEM	Original Equipment Manufacturer; an enterprise that repackages equipment, such as computers, made by other companies.
OH&S	Occupational Health and Safety.
OLE	Object Linking and Embedding; a framework for a compound document technology; and a mechanism for maintenance of links between versions so that changes to an original may be reflected subsequently.
OMR	Optical Mark Recognition; use of scanner for interpreting pencil marks on specially designed documents, such as forms, surveys, and answer sheets.
Operating system	The computer programs that jointly manage the computer hardware and software and make it possible for applications to interact with a computer.
Optical disk	Medium that includes a recording layer onto which data may be encoded and read by optical beams.
Orientation	The way in which a printer page is aligned, often expressed as landscape for horizontal orientation or portrait for vertical orientation.
PDA	Personal Digital Assistant; a handheld computer used for appointment tracking and note taking using character recognition software combined with input from a "pen."
PDF	Portable Document Format; a format developed by Adobe Systems for document publication.
PICS	Platform for Internet Content Selection; a WWW Consortium standard for metainformation that makes it possible for authors to describe their WWW sites in such a way that filtering software may be used to decide upon access to the sites.
Pitch	Horizontal measurement of how many characters fit into a particular space, typically an inch.
Pixel	A basic picture element for display.
PKI	Public Key Infrastructure; it enables users of a basically unsecured public network such as the Internet to securely and privately exchange data through the use of a public and a private cryptographic key pair that is obtained and shared through a trusted authority.
PNG	Portable Network Graphic; a bit-mapped format for compressed graphic images that, in time, is expected to replace the GIF format that is widely used on the Internet; it includes features such as built-in color correction, 48-bit color, and the capacity to print at a different resolution from that displayed.
Portal	A gateway for an Internet/intranet site that represents itself as a major starting site for users when they get connected to the WWW, or that users tend to visit as an anchor site. The portal provides users with a single point of entry to information holdings. There are general portals and specialized or niche portals.

Postcoordinate indexing	An approach to indexing[2] that assumes no coordination of index terms syntactically, assuming that any term combination will occur as part of information retrieval.
Postscript	A programming language that describes the appearance of a printed page. Developed by Adobe in 1985, it has become an industry standard for printing and imaging.
PPT	The filename extension and format for MS PowerPoint.
Precoordinate indexing	Assigned indexing[2] in which individual index terms are associated in strings of descriptors by the indexer, so that they may be used as term strings for information retrieval or display.
Preservation	Procedures for minimizing the deterioration of documents. Processes and operations involved in ensuring the technical and intellectual survival of authentic records[2] through time (ISO 15489-1–2001).
Provenance	The origination of records[2] and their ownership.
Proximity operator	An indication within a search strategy for information retrieval of the permitted distance between search terms within the searched text.
PRX	The filename extension and format for a single project created by Primavera Expedition.
Public office	A government instrumentality.
QBE	Query By Example; information retrieval by an interface that requires the user to present a query by completing or partially completing a table or formatted screen. The results are usually presented in the same format as the query.
Quality records	Records[2] used to demonstrate conformance to specified requirements, and effective operation of quality systems.
Raster	The description of a line pattern by means of an array comprising a horizontal and vertical dimension, in contrast to a bitmap, in which images are created by individual pixels.
Record[1] (database)	A data entity that may consist of one or more data elements or attributes.
Record[2] (document)	Any information captured in reproducible form that is available for conducting business. In this sense, it is a document that has evidence value. Information created, received, and maintained as evidence and information by an organization or person in pursuance of legal obligations or in the transaction of business (ISO 15489-1–2001).
Record[3] (bibliographic)	Reference information such as a catalog or an indexing[2,3] entry that acts as a pointer to other information.
Record series	See Series.
Recordkeeping	Systematic creation and maintenance of complete, accurate, and reliable evidence of and information about business activities in the form of recorded information.
Reference file	Earlier design files that are overlaid to provide a new version of a digital drawing in CAD.
Registration	The act of providing a document with an identity; in a recordkeeping system, this will mean giving a record[2] a unique identity.
Registry	The section in an enterprise that is responsible for mail handling, including registration, distribution, and filing; typically used in government departments.

Relational database	A database containing fields within two-dimensional arrays or tables that are defined logically with respect to each other.
Rendition	A specific, usually digital, manifestation of a document, for example, it may be produced in .rtf and .htm renditions.
Repository	The database or combination of files and databases that store an enterprise's documents; the term may also be used to represent a collection of physical documents.
Requirements analysis	The practice of reviewing the processes in an enterprise to determine business requirements, and how a system must function in order to meet those requirements.
Requirements specification	The expression of the requirements analysis into a form that spells out conditions from the viewpoints of the users, of functional capabilities, of administrative or technical constraints, or a combination of these.
Resolution	The capacity to be able to distinguish parts of images that are close together.
Retention schedule	See Schedule.[2]
RFI	Request for Information; generally used as a preliminary to establish from potential vendors the general capabilities of their systems.
RFP (or RFT)	Request for Proposal (or Tender); generally used to obtain formal proposals and costing of a system from potential vendors.
RM	Records Management; the field of management responsible for the efficient and systematic control of the creation, receipt, maintenance, use, and disposition of records,[2] including processes for capturing and maintaining evidence of and information about business activities and transactions in the form of records (ISO 15489-1–2001).
RMS	Records Management System; software support RM.
ROI	Return on Investment.
ROM	Read Only Memory.
RTF	Rich Text Format; a file[1] format that enables text files to be exchanged between different word processors in different operating systems.
Scaling	Increasing or decreasing the size of an image by manipulating the bit-mapping density.
Scanner	A device that converts an eye-legible document into digital code, typically used in an imaging system or for OCR.
Schedule[1] (bibliographic)	The systematic listing of subjects in an index vocabulary, usually classification scheme, showing their relationships.
Schedule[2] (document)	A guide used in recordkeeping that for an inventory of records[2] registers the appraisal of the records and specifies the extent of activity of groups of records.
SCM	Supply Chain Management; business process attention to profitable transformation of raw materials into finished products with timely distribution to customers.
SDI	Selective Dissemination of Information; a process by which information seekers are provided periodically with information retrieved from new additions to databases by a search strategy that matches their interests.

SDML	Signed Document Markup Language; a language proposed by the Financial Services Technology Consortium to enable signing, endorsing, or witnessing of documents or parts of documents using public key cryptography.
Secondary storage	Storage of inactive records, often in physical facilities remote from and cheaper than those used for active records.
Security	Safekeeping and integrity procedures.
Sentencing	Deciding how records[2] should be stored and for how long, so that this may be recorded in a disposal schedule.[2]
Series	A group of related records[2] that are normally treated collectively as a unit.
Server	Hardware that makes files[1] available to users of a network to which it is connected.
SGML	Standard Generalized Markup Language; an international comprehensive standard for markup of documents.
SLA	Service Level Agreement; a contract in which a basic level of service is defined and agreed upon by negotiating parties.
SMS	Short Messaging Service; brief alphanumeric message that may be buffered by a network and sent to a mobile phone when it is activated.
SOE	Standard Operating Environment; a set of software recommended by an organization and available for installation on staff workstations, typically comprising an operating system and standard office and corporate applications.
Software	The programs and associated documentation of procedures for operation of computers and applications on them.
SOP	Standard Operating Procedure; the business rules and procedures that apply, particularly in a regulated environment.
SQL	Structured Query Language; a standardized protocol for expressing information retrieval queries.
SRS	System Requirements Specification; a detailed expression of what is required in a particular system.
Stoplist	A list of common terms provided to software to avoid their use in automatic indexing.
Storage capacity	The extent to which data may be stored on a particular device, typically expressed in bytes.
SVG	Scalable Vector Graphics standard; an open standard language for describing two-dimensional vector graphics in XML.
System administrator	Person responsible for following procedures and maintaining a computer system, its operating system, and applications.
TCP/IP	Transmission Control Protocol/Internet Protocol. The de facto Ethernet standard protocols incorporated into Unix and used to support Internet data communication.
Telnet	An Internet protocol that permits connection to a remote system and direct interaction with its applications, typically a database.
Template	A file[1] that contains outline text and formatting to enable creation of a document for a specific function and form, such as a memorandum, an application form, or an agenda.
Terminal digit filing	Filing using sequencing from right to left of numbers assigned to physical documents.

Thesaurus	The controlled vocabulary of an indexing[2,3] language formally organized so that connections between concepts are made explicit in the form of a priori equivalence, hierarchy, and associative relationships.
TIF or TIFF	Tag Image File Format; a common format for exchanging raster images between application programs, including those used for scanning images.
TQM	Total Quality Management; a structured process development approach that takes account of organizational culture to achieve continuous improvement in business functions.
Tracking systems	Systems for capturing and maintaining information about the movement and uses of records.[2]
Transaction	The smallest unit of business activity; the use of a record[2] is a transaction.
Tranfer[1]	Change of custody, ownership, or responsibility of documents.
Tranfer[2]	Movement of documents to another location.
Truncation	Information retrieval using "wildcard" symbols to look for fragments of words.
URL	Uniform Resource Locator; a WWW address consisting of computer domain name and file location.
Vault	See Repository.
Vector graphics	Digital description of an image comprising functions identifying geometrical relationships of parts of the image; the images are digitized by an algorithm that uses a mathematical expression of shapes, such as curves and lines, and may be reconstituted for representation, by application of the same algorithm.
Version control	Procedures for identifying unequivocally the authorship and sequence of different drafts or editions of a document.
Vital records	Records[2] without which an enterprise could not continue to function, typically those needed to reestablish it if there is a disaster.
WAN	Wide Area Network; a telecommunications network across a broad geographic area, in contrast with a LAN.
WAP	Wireless Application Protocol; it is a specification for a set of communication protocols to standardize the way that wireless devices, such as cellular telephones and radio transceivers, can be used for Internet access, including email, the WWW, newsgroups, etc.
Wildcard searching	See Truncation.
Workflow	The way that business transactions proceed; more specifically, software for tracking documents as they progress.
WORM	Write One Read Many; a type of optical disk that may be written on just once, and then read from indefinitely.
WWW	World Wide Web (often shortened to Web); it is the most widely used part of the Internet. It features hypertext, which is a method for instant cross-referencing.
XLS	The filename extension and format for MS Excel.
XML	eXtensible Markup Language; it is similar to the language of most WWW pages, HTML. Both XML and HTML contain mark-up symbols to describe the contents of a page or file.[1] XML is a simplified version of SGML, that being a metalanguage, permits much greater flexibility of document definition than HTML.

Appendix 2

Bibliography

References are listed alphabetically by author and date. Where references have been cited, an indication of the applicable chapter(s) is given in brackets, at the end of the reference.

Aaker, D. A. (2001). *Developing business strategies*. New York: Wiley.

Advanced Distributed Learning. (2002). *SCORM overview*. Retrieved on July 11, 2002 from the World Wide Web: http://www.adlnet.org/index.cfm?fuseaction=scormabt [Chap. 1].

American National Standards Institute, & Association for Information and Image Management International. (1998). *Glossary of document technologies* (ANSI/AIIM TR2-1998). [Chaps. 4, 15].

Arthur Andersen. (2000). *Practice administration: client engagement information — organization, retention and destruction, statement No. 760*. Retrieved on July 31, 2002 from the World Wide Web: http://www.andersen.com/resource2.nsf/vAttachLU/PDF_ PracticeAdministrationClientEngagementInformation/$File/PDF_PracticeAdministration-ClientEngagementInformation.pdf [Chap. 1].

Asprey, L. G. (2000). *An extension to system development methodologies for successful production imaging systems*. Masters thesis, QUT, Brisbane. [Chap. 15].

Association for Information and Image Management International. (2001). *AIIM recommended practice — implementation guidelines and standards associated with Web-based document management technologies*. AIIM. Retrieved on July 4, 2002 from the World Wide Web: http://stnds.aiim.wegov2.com /file_depot/ 0-10000000/0-10000/1462/folder/10666/ AIIM+ARP1+2000.pdf [Chap. 7].

Auer, N. J. (2002). *Bibliography on evaluating Web information*. Retrieved July 31, 2002 from the Web site of Virginia Tech University Libraries: http://www.lib.vt.edu/research/ evaluate/evalbiblio.html [Chap. 18].

Australia. Department of Finance and Administration. (2001). *Commonwealth procurement guidelines and best practice guidance*. Retrieved on February 7, 2002 from the World Wide Web: http://www.finance.gov.au/ctc/publications/purchasing/cpg/commonwealth_ procurement_guide.html [Chap. 20].

Australia. Information Exchange Steering Committee. Electronic Data Management Sub-Committee. (1993). *Management of electronic documents in the Australian Public Service*. Parkes, ACT: Australian Department of Finance. [Chap. 11].

Avedon, D. M. (1995). *Introduction to electronic imaging* (3rd ed.). Silver Spring, MD, USA: AIIM International.

Barnett, R. (1996). *Managing business forms* (4th ed.). Canberra, ACT: Robert Barnett and Associates. [Chaps. 2, 3].

Bentley, C. (2000). *Managing projects the PRINCE2 way*. Waterlooville, UK: Hampshire Training Consultants. [Chap. 6].

Bielawski, L., & Boyle, J. (1997). *Electronic document management systems: a user centered approach for creating, distributing and managing online publications*. Upper Saddle River, NJ, USA: Prentice Hall. [Chap. 21].

Birnbauer, W. (2002). *Smoker awarded $700,000 after evidence was destroyed*. ICIJ member report. Retrieved on July 13, 2002 from the World Wide Web: http://www.icij.org/investigate/birnbauer_042502.html [Chap. 9].

Black, D. B. (1996). *Document capture for document imaging systems*. Silver Spring, MD, USA: AIIM International.

Boisot, M. H. (1998). *Knowledge assets: securing competitive advantage in the information economy*. Oxford, UK: Oxford University Press. [Chap. 2].

Boston Consulting Group. (2000). *Getting value from enterprise initiatives: a survey of executives*. Boston Consulting Group. Retrieved on February 27, 2002 from the World Wide Web: http://www.bcg.com/publications /files/Enterprise_ Computing_report.pdf [Chap. 1].

Brackett, M. H. (1994). *Data sharing using a common data architecture*. New York: Wiley. [Chap. 3].

BRE Centre for Construction IT & Construction Industry Computing Association. (1999). *BRE/CICA case study: document management at Ove Arup & Partners*. Retrieved on May 28, 2002 from the World Wide Web: http://www.cica.org.uk/ arup_columbus_edm_case_study/arup_columbus_edm_case_ study.htm [Chap. 5].

Brooking, A. (1999). *Corporate memory: strategies for knowledge management*. London: International Thomson Business Press. [Chap. 2].

Browning, P., & Lowndes, M. (2001). *JISC TechWatch report: Content Management Systems*. (TSW 01-02). Retrieved on July 21, 2002 from the World Wide Web: http://www.jisc.ac.uk/techwatch/reports/tsw_01-02.pdf [Chap. 4].

Buckland, M. K. (1997). What is a "document"? *Journal of the American Society for Information Science, 48*(9), 804–809. [Chap. 1].

Burns, N. (1994). Workflow automation: a methodology for change. In *The Workflow CD-ROM Sampler* (CD-ROM). Palo Alto, CA, USA:Creative Networks [Chap. 4].

CCTA. (1994). *Data management*. London: HMSO for Central Computer and Telecommunications Agency.

Chatelain, J., & Yen, M. O. (2000). The politics of content: ownership, relevance and access. In Keyes, J. (Ed.) *Internet management* (pp. 99–108). Boca Raton, FL, USA: Auerbach/CRC Press LLC. [Chap. 3, 18].

CMP Media Inc. (1981–2002). *Techencyclopedia*. Retrieved on May 2, 2001 from the World Wide Web: http://www.techweb.com/encyclopedia/ [Appendix 1].

ComputerUser.com Inc. (2002). *High-tech dictionary*. Retrieved on January 10, 2002 from the World Wide Web: http://www.computeruser.com/resources/dictionary/dictionary.html [Appendix 1].

Consultative Committee for Space Data Systems. (1999). *Reference model for an Open Archival Information System (OAIS)*. Red Book. CCSDS 650.0-R-1 (Issue 1). Retrieved on April 24, 2002 from the World Wide Web: http://www.ccsds.org/documents/pdf/CCSDS-650.0-R-1.pdf [Chap. 11].

Cornell University. Department of Preservation and Conservation. (2002). *Moving theory into practice: digital imaging tutorial*. Retrieved on June 27, 2001 from the World Wide Web: http://www.library.cornell.edu/preservation/tutorial/index.html [Appendix 5].

Dailey Jr., F. E. (1995). *Electronic document management systems*. Charleston, SC, USA: Computer Technology Research Corp.

Davenport, T. H., & Prusak, L. (1998). *Working knowledge: how organizations manage what they know*. Boston, MA, USA: Harvard Business School Press. [Chap. 1].

Deloitte Touche Tohmatsu. (1993). *Imaging survey, the state of the industry 1993, Australia and New Zealand*. Melbourne, Deloitte Touche Tohmatsu International. [Chap. 11].

Deloitte Touche Tohmatsu. (1997). *Imaging & workflow survey, the state of the industry 1997, Australia and New Zealand*. Melbourne, Deloitte Touche Tohmatsu International. [Chap. 11].

DeWitt, D. L. (Ed.). (1998). *Going digital: strategies for access, preservation and conversion of collections to a digital format*. NY: Haworth. [Chap. 21].

Distributed Systems Technology Centre. Resource Discovery Unit. (2002). *Metadata.Net*. Retrieved on January 6, 2002 from the World Wide Web: http://metadata.net/ [Chap. 7]

Document management solution cures hospital ills. (2001). *Today, 23*(5), 28–30. Available online through ABI/Inform. [Chap. 5].

Drucker, P. (1998). The coming of the new organization. In *Harvard business review on knowledge management* (pp. 1–19). Boston, MA, USA: Harvard Business School Press. [Chap. 2].

Drucker, P. (1999*)*. Beyond the information revolution. *Atlantic Monthly, 284*(4), 47–57. [Chap. 2].

Duyshart, B. (1997). *The digital document: a reference for architects, engineers and design professionals*. Oxford, UK: Architectural Press. [Chap. 12].

Ellis, J. (Ed.). (1993). *Keeping archives* (2nd ed.). Port Melbourne, Vic: Thorpe in association with Australian Society of Archivists.

European Communities IDA Programme. (2001). *Model requirements for the management of electronic records: MoReq specification*. Cornwell Affiliates plc. Retrieved on January 15, 2002 from the World Wide Web: http://europa.eu.int/ISPO/ida/ [Chap. 4].

European Software Institute. (2002). *Models and tools*. Retrieved on January 20, 2002 from the World Wide Web: http://www.esi.es/Projects/models-tools.html [Chap. 6].

Financial Services Technology Consortium. (1998). *SDML — Signed Document Markup Language: draft submission to W3C* (W3C Note 19-June-1998). Retrieved on January 15, 2002 from the World Wide Web: http://www.w3.org/TR/NOTE-SDML/ [Chap. 4].

Fincham, R., & Rhodes, P. (1999). *Principles of organizational behaviour* (3rd ed.). Oxford: Oxford University Press. [Chap. 4].

Fink, R. A., & Fisher, B. (2000). How to save time and money in a less papered office. *Corporate Legal Times, 10*(98), 31–33. [Chap. 5].

Fischer, L. (Ed.) (2002). *Workflow handbook 2002*. Lighthouse Point, FL, USA: Future Strategies Inc. Retrieved on July 5, 2002 from the World Wide Web: http://www.wfmc.org. [Chap. 4].

Flynn, D. J. (1998). *Information systems requirements: determination and analysis* (2nd ed.). London: McGraw-Hill. [Chaps. 6, 8].

Fruscione, J. (1995). *Outsourcing document conversion and indexing services*. Silver Spring, MD, USA: AIIM International. [Chaps. 11, 15].

Gartner Group. (1997). *Strategic analysis report*. [Chap. 1].

GILS: Global Information Locator Service. (2002). Retrieved on February 14, 2002 from the World Wide Web: http://www.gils.net/index.html [Chap. 7].

Green, W. B. (1993). *Introduction to electronic document management systems*. Boston, MA: Academic Press.

Grigsby, M. (1999). *Computer output to laser disk (COLD): an AIIM COLD study group white paper*. Silver Spring, MD, USA: AIIM International.

Hackos, J. (2002). *Content management for dynamic Web delivery*. New York: Wiley. [Chap. 4]

Hall, G. M. (1991). *Image processing: a management perspective*. New York: McGraw-Hill. [Chap. 15].

Hammer, M., & Champy, J. (1994). *Reengineering the corporation: a manifesto for business revolution* (rev. ed.). London: Brealey. [Chap. 16].

Hawryszkiewycz, I. (2000). Knowledge networks in administrative systems. In *Preprints* (pp. 59–76). Working Conference on Advances in Electronic Government, Zaragoza, Spain. [Chaps. 5, 9].

Herschmann, D. (1996). *Designing effective user interfaces for business applications.* Silver Spring, MD, USA: AIIM International.

Hollingsworth, D. (1995). *The workflow reference model.* (TC00-1003; Issue 1.1). Hampshire, UK: Workflow Management Coalition. [Chap. 4].

Howe, D. (Ed.). (1993–2002). *FOLDOC: Free on-line dictionary of computing.* [Appendix 1].

Howe, T. (1998). *Developing document management systems with Microsoft Word.* Paper presented at the Microsoft Office and VBA Solutions Conference and Exposition, London, England.

Hoyle, D. (1994). *ISO9000 quality systems handbook* (2nd ed.). Oxford, UK: Butterworth-Heinemann. [Chap. 7].

IETF WEBDAV Working Group. (2002). *World Wide Web distributed authoring and versioning.* Retrieved on July 29, 2002 from the World Wide Web: http://www.ics.uci.edu/~ejw/authoring/[Chap. 18].

International Electrotechnical Commission. (2001a). *Specifications for document management systems — Part 1: principles and methods.* (IEC-82045-1: 2001). [Chap. 7].

International Electrotechnical Commission. (2001b). *Specifications for document management systems — Part 2: reference collection of metadata and reference models* (In preparation). [IEC-82045-2 (draft)]. [Chaps. 3, 7].

International Electrotechnical Commission. (2001c). *Project risk management — Application guidelines.* (IEC-62198: 2001). [Chap. 2].

International Federation of Library Associations and Institutions. (2002). *Digital libraries: metadata resources.* Retrieved on July 5, 2002 from the World Wide Web: http://www.ifla.org/II/metadata.htm [Chap. 3].

International Organization for Standardization. (1992–2000). *Ergonomic requirements for office work with visual display terminals (VDTs).* (ISO 9241: 1-17). Geneva, Switzerland: ISO. [Chap. 21].

International Organization for Standardization. (1996). *Environmental management systems — Specification with guidance for use.* (ISO 14001:1996). Geneva, Switzerland: ISO. [Chaps. 2, 7].

International Organization for Standardization. (2000). *Quality management systems — Requirements.* (ISO 9001:2000). Geneva, Switzerland: ISO. [Chaps. 2, 7, 21].

International Organization for Standardization. (2001). *Information and documentation — Records management.* (ISO 15489:2001). Geneva, Switzerland: ISO. [Chaps. 1, 5, 6, 7, 21].

International Organization for Standardization, & International Electrotechnical Commission. (1995). *Information technology — Software life cycle processes.* (ISO/IEC 12207: 1995). Geneva, Switzerland: ISO. [Chap. 6].

International Organization for Standardization, & International Electrotechnical Commission. (1998). *Information technology — Software process assessment.* (ISO/IEC 15504: 1-9). Geneva, Switzerland: ISO. [Chap. 6].

International Organization for Standardization, & International Electrotechnical Commission. (2000). *Information technology — Guidelines for the documentation of computer-based application systems.* (ISO/IEC 6592:2000). Geneva, Switzerland: ISO. [Chap. 6].

Jones, J. I. (1999). *The document methodology.* Rochester, MI, USA: Priority Process Associates.

Kaplan, R. S., & Norton, D. P. (2001). *The strategy-focused organization: how balanced scorecard companies thrive in the new business environment.* Boston, MA: Harvard Business School Press. [Chap. 9].

Kendall, K. E., & Kendall, J. E. (2002). *Systems analysis and design* (5th ed.). Upper Saddle River, NJ, USA: Prentice Hall. [Chap. 8, 10].

Kennedy, J., & Schauder, C. (1998). *Records management: a guide to corporate record keeping* (2nd ed.). South Melbourne, Vic: Addison Wesley Longman. [Chap. 4].

Kenney, A. R., & Rieger, O. Y. (Eds.). (2000). *Moving theory into practice: digital imaging for libraries and archives*. Mountain View, CA: Research Libraries Group. [Chap. 21].

Keown, J. (2000). Case study: document management for a SONGS. *Inform, 14*(1), 48–52. [Chap. 5].

Kotter, J. P. (1996). *Leading change*. Boston, MA, USA: Harvard Business School Press. [Chap. 6].

Koulopoulos, T. (1995). *The workflow imperative: building real world business solutions*. New York: Van Nostrand Reinhold. [Chap. 4].

Leymann, F., & Roller, D. (2000). *Production workflow: concepts and techniques*. Upper Saddle River, NJ, USA: Prentice Hall. [Chaps. 4, 16].

Lyman, P. et al. (2000). *How much information?* University of California. School of Information Management and Systems. Retrieved on July 18, 2002 from the World Wide Web: http://www.sims.berkeley.edu/how-much-info/index.html [Chap. 1].

McLain-Smith, R. (1998). Document issues in the pharmaceutical industry. *Document World, 3*(5), 49–51. [Chap. 2].

Mcleod Jr., R. (2000). *Management information systems*. (8th ed.). Upper Saddle River, NJ, USA: Prentice Hall. [Chap. 9].

Megill, K. A. (1997). *The corporate memory: information management in the electronic age*. London: Bowker Saur. [Chap. 2].

Megill, K. A., & Schantz, H. F. (1999). *Document management: new technologies for the information services manager*. East Grinstead, UK: Bowker-Saur. [Chap. 2].

Middleton, M. (2002). *Information management*. Wagga Wagga, Australia: Charles Sturt University. [Chaps. 1, 7, 11, 12].

Moore, A. (1995). *Moore's imaging dictionary: the official dictionary of electronic document and image processing* (2nd ed.). New York: Flatiron Publishing. [Appendix 1].

Muller, N. J. (1993). *Computerized document imaging systems: technology and applications*. Boston, MA: Artech House.

National Archives of Australia. (1999). *Recordkeeping metadata standard for Commonwealth agencies*. Retrieved on July 11, 2002 from the World Wide Web: http://www.naa.gov.au/recordkeeping/control/rkms /summary.htm [Chap. 7].

National Archives of Australia. (2000*). DIRKS: Designing and implementing recordkeeping systems*. Retrieved on November 14, 2000 from the World Wide Web: http://www.naa.gov.au/recordkeeping/dirks /dirksman/contents.html [Chaps. 2, 6, 11].

National Library of Australia. (2002). *Pandora archive*. Retrieved on January 14, 2002 from the World Wide Web: http://pandora.nla.gov.au/index.html [Chap. 3].

Parker, E. (1999). *Managing your organizations' records*. London: Library Association.

Popkin, J. (1996). *Introducing third generation enterprise IDM architectures*. (Research Note T-620-177): Gartner Group. [Chap. 1].

Popkin, J., & McCoy, D. (1998). *Ten hot reasons for seeking a single IDM system*. (Research Note TU-04-0875): Gartner Group. [Chap. 1].

Public Record Office of Victoria. (2000). *VERS metadata scheme PROS 99/007 specification 2*. Retrieved on May 3, 2002 from the World Wide Web: http://www.prov.vic.gov.au/vers/standards/pros9907/99-7-2.pdf [Chap. 7].

Remenyi, D., Sherwood-Smith, M., & White, T. (1997). *Achieving maximum value from information systems: a process approach*. Chichester, UK: Wiley.

Robek, M. F., Brown, G. F., & Stephens, D. O. (1995). *Information and records management: document-based information systems* (4th ed.). New York: GLENCOE/McGraw-Hill.

Rollo, C., & Clarke, T. (2001). *International best practice: case studies in knowledge management.* (SAA HB 275 Supplement 1-2001.). Sydney, Australia: Standards Australia International. [Chap. 2].

Rosencrance, L. (2001). FedEx imaging systems to boost access to shipping information. *Computerworld.* Retrieved on July 7, 2002 from the World Wide Web: http://www.computerworld.com /managementtopics/ebusiness/story/0,10801,63375,00.html [Chap. 5].

Rosenfeld, L., & Morville, P. (1998). *Information architecture for the Word Wide Web.* Cambridge, MA, USA: O'Reilly. [Chaps. 4, 18].

Saffady, W. (1978). *Micrographics.* Littleton, CO, USA: Libraries Unlimited. [Chaps. 1, 4]

Saffady, W. (1996). *Electronic document imaging: a state of the art report.* Prairie Village, KS: ARMA International. [Chaps. 2, 21].

Schäl, T. (1998). *Workflow management systems for process organizations* (2nd ed.). Berlin, Germany: Springer. [Chaps. 2, 4].

Seattle City Clerk. (2002). *Thesaurus.* Retrieved on July 20, 2002 from the World Wide Web: http://clerk.ci.seattle.wa.us/~public/thesintr.htm [Chap. 12].

Sharp, A., & McDermott, P. (2001). *Workflow modeling: tools for process improvement and application development.* Boston, MA, USA: Artech House. [Chaps. 4, 10].

Shelly, G. B., Cashman, T. J., & Rosenblatt, H. J. (2001). *Systems analysis and design* (4th ed.). Boston, MA, USA: Course Technology. [Chaps. 8, 9, 10].

Skyrme, D. (1998). *Measuring the value of knowledge: metrics for the knowledge-based business.* London: Business Intelligence Ltd. [Chap. 2].

Smith, C. (1978). *Micrographics handbook.* Dedham, MA, USA: Artech House. [Chaps. 1, 4].

Sommerville, I. (2001). *Software engineering* (6th ed.). Harlow, UK: Pearson Education. [Chaps. 10, 16, 19].

Spencer, H. (2001). E-forms. *e-doc, 15*(6), 46–51. [Chap. 5].

State Records of New South Wales. (1997). *Desktop management — Guidelines for managing electronic documents and directories.* Retrieved on May 22, 2002 from the World Wide Web: http://www.records.nsw.gov.au/publicsector/erk /desktop/desktop.htm [Chap. 3].

Sutton, M. J. D. (1996). *Document management for the enterprise: principles, techniques and applications.* New York: Wiley. [Chaps. 1, 7].

Synnott, W. R. (1987). *The information weapon; winning customers and markets with technology.* New York: Wiley. [Chap. 7].

Task Force on Archiving of Digital Information. (1996). *Preserving digital information: final report and recommendations.* Retrieved on March 4, 2002 from the World Wide Web: http://www.rlg.org/ArchTF/ [Chap. 11].

Tauber, J., & van den Brink, L. (2000). *XMLSoftware Document/content management systems.* Retrieved on November 14, 2000 from the World Wide Web: http://www.xmlsoftware.com/dms/.

Taylor, F. W. (1919). *The principles of scientific management.* New York: Harper. [Chap. 4].

TechTarget. (2002). *Whatis?com.* TechTarget.com. Retrieved on July 27, 2002 from the World Wide Web: http://whatis.techtarget.com/ [Appendix 1].

Thorp, J. (1998). *The information paradox.* Toronto, Canada: McGraw-Hill. [Chap. 22].

Toigo, J. W. (2000). *Disaster recovery planning: strategies for protecting critical information* (2nd ed.). Upper Saddle River, NJ, USA: Prentice Hall. [Chap. 11].

Tudor, D. J., & Tudor, I. J. (1997). *Systems analysis and design: a comparison of structured methods.* Hampshire, UK: Macmillan. [Chap. 6].

United Kingdom Office of Government Commerce. (2002). *PRINCE2.* Retrieved on February 4, 2002 from the World Wide Web: http://www.ogc.gov.uk/prince/index.htm [Chaps. 6, 8].

United States Department of Energy Quality Managers Software Quality Assurance Subcommittee. (2000). *Software risk management: a practical guide.* Retrieved on February 5, 2002 from the World Wide Web: http://cio.doe.gov/sqas /sqas21_01.doc [Chap. 21].

United States Office of Federal Procurement Policy. (2002). *Acquisition Reform Network federal acquisition regulation*. Retrieved on May 10, 2002 from the World Wide Web: http://www.arnet.gov/far/ [Chap. 20].

Verzuh, E. (1999). *The fast forward MBA in project management*. New York: Wiley. [Chap. 6].

Wasner, R. (1998). *Implementing document imaging systems*. Hingham, MA, USA: KM World. [Chap. 15].

Wiggins, B. (1994). *Document imaging: a management guide*. Westport, CT, USA: Meckler. [Chap. 15].

Wiggins, B. (2000). *Effective document management: unlocking corporate knowledge*. Aldershot, UK: Gower. [Chap. 4].

Wilkinson, R. et al. (1998). *Document computing: technologies for managing electronic document collections*. Boston, MA, USA: Kluwer Academic. [Chap. 4].

Witten, I. H., Moffat, A., & Bell, T. (1999). *Managing gigabytes: compressing and indexing documents and images* (2nd ed.). San Francisco, CA: Morgan Kaufmann.

Young, T. (1998). *The handbook of project management: a practical guide to effective policies and procedures*. London: Kogan Page. [Chap. 6].

Appendix 3

Sites

WEB RESOURCES OF INTEREST FOR IDCM

The following sites are relevant to IDCM for a number of reasons, such as the following:

- Industry magazines and ongoing literature
- Consultancies that also publish material on document management
- Professional associations
- Resource guides to Web material
- Specialist information sources

An up-to-date version of this list with links is maintained at http://www.pims.com.au.

Web sites, in most cases, provide detailed contact information, activities, and objectives. Links to specific software sites are listed separately in Appendix 4.

Web Resources

Resource	Location
ACM Siggraph Organization for generation and dissemination of information on computer graphics and interactive techniques; publishes *Computer Graphics Quarterly* and runs the annual SIGGRAPH Conference	http://www.siggraph.org/
Advanced Imaging Magazine Information on imaging products and services: hardware, software, and peripherals	http://www.advancedimagingmag.com/
AIIM International Promotes itself as a global industry association that connects the communities of users and suppliers of Enterprise Content Management- the technologies used to create, capture, customize, deliver, and manage enterprise content to support business processes.	http://www.aiim.org/
Aproged The Association of the PROfessionals of the GEiDe (Gestion Electronique d'Informations et de Documents pour l'Entreprise)	http://www.aproged.org/

ARMA: Association of information management professionals An international not-for-profit association serving information management professionals including records and information managers, MIS and ADP professionals, imaging specialists, archivists, hospital and legal administrators, and librarians	http://www.arma.org/
Aslib: the Association for Information Management Aslib has about 2000 private and public-sector companies and organizations as members internationally; it is concerned with managing information resources efficiently	http://www.aslib.co.uk/
The Association for Work Process Improvement (TAWPI) Its mission is to enhance the performance of organizations and strengthen the value of professionals that employ emerging technologies in mail, remittance, document, and forms processing	http://www.tawpi.org
Belgian AIIM	http://www.belaiim.org/

brint.com
 	
Provides research portals to:
 	
   • Content management
   • Document management
   • Knowledge management
	http://www.brint.com/

CIMdata Inc. This company provides technical consulting and market research and Product Data Management; it produces the *PDM Buyer's Guide* that reviews vendor systems, and a case studies subscription service; it now promotes collaborative Product Definition management (cPDm)	http://www.cimdata.com/index.htm
Cimtech A consultancy service based at the University of Hertfordshire that advises clients on re-engineering and process modeling of business processes, with an emphasis on digital document management, records management, and workflow management	http://www.cimtech.co.uk/
CompInfo – The Computer Information Center Directory on document management and imaging, including terminology, literature, and suppliers	http://www.compinfo-center.com/tpdcmn-t.htm
Computing Suppliers Federation A UK not-for-profit trade association with the aim to educate business users and help increase their understanding of the ICT industry and the applications available; independent publications are provided	http://www.csf.org.uk/
Dansk Image Management Organisation	http://www.dimo.dk/
Delphi Group This organization provides strategic business advice and training with a focus on what they see as emerging markets, where business and technology intersect	http://www.delphigroup.com/

DMware	http://www.dmware.org/
AIIM's Document-Management Interoperability Exchange; includes links to *DM Reference Model* for integrated use of standards; DMA, the Document Management Alliance Specification; and ODMA, the Open Document Management API	
Doculabs	http://www.doculabs.com/index.html
This North-American-based industry analyst undertakes applied product assessments to differentiate between products in emerging technology segments and evaluate their impact on business requirements	
Document Boss	http://www.documentboss.com/
This company focuses on human resources and company acquisitions in the European and U.S. electronic document management technologies sectors and provides free information services to senior management	
Document Management Avenue	http://www.documentmanagement.org.uk/index.htm
An independent site for those involved in document and content management, such as IT professionals or executives interested in content strategy; links are provided to vendors and other related sites, white papers, and news about the market	
Document Management Industries Association	http://www.dmia.org/
Association based in the United States for increasing the knowledge and professionalism of forms, business printing, and document management professionals	
Document Manager	http://www.document-manager.com/
DM magazine and resource guide	
E-Doc Magazine	http://www.edocmagazine.com/
A product of AIIM	
Econtent	http://www.econtentmag.com/
Produced by *Online Inc.,* this is the Web version of *EcontentMagazine,* a print publication delivering trend and strategy analysis in the Internet and enterprise content industry	
Gartner	http://www.gartner.com
IT consultancy and training group that also sells documents that, for example, provide comparisons of document management software and strategic analysis of IDMS	
IDC	http://www.idc.com
IT forecasting and market reviews based upon industry surveys with some content and document management analysis	
idm.net.au	http://www.idm.net.au/home.asp
An Asia-Pacific information management source and online publisher of *Image and Data Manager Magazine*	

IIM: Institute for Information Management Ltd.	http://www.iim.org.au/national/html/
An Australasian industry group with objectives to provide an information management forum and source, award excellence, improve service, and promote social responsibility in the industry	
Imaging Magazine	http://www.imagingmagazine.com
Information Management Internet Directory	http://www.dm-kmdirectory.com/
DocuMation Decisions Ltd Guide to software, hardware, consulting, and education resources on the Web in categorized areas of information, knowledge, and document management	
International Records Management Trust	http://www.irmt.org/
UK-based charity that aims to improve public resource management through consultancy services, educational materials, and research and development programs	
iTx Marketing Services	http://www.itx.co.uk/
UK group that provides educational resources and events for senior executives concerned with information management, including document and records management; publishes *Info Bulletin*	
Japan Image and Information Management Association	http://www.jiima.or.jp/
Ovum	http://www.ovum.com
IT research and consulting organization that makes available many evaluation reports on content and document management	
Records Management Association of Australia	http://www.rmaa.com.au/
Records Management Society of Great Britain	http://www.rms-gb.org.uk/
Strategy Partners International	http://www.strategypartners.com/
Consultancy company that undertakes market forecasting and research, company assessments, and technology evaluations with particular reference to document management, ERP, and knowledge management	
Unesco Archives portal	http://www.unesco.org/webworld/portal_archives/
This site provides links to archives institutions and societies internationally	
Workflow Management Coalition	http://www.wfmc.org/
This group has an international membership in business and academia and promotes workflow technology through the establishment of standards for software terminology, interoperability, and connectivity between workflow products	
The XML Cover pages	http://www.oasis-open.org/cover/sgml-xml.html
An online reference work on the eXtensible Markup Language, and its parent SGML. It derives from work of Robin Cover, and is sponsored by the Organization for Advancement of Structured Information Standards	

Appendix 4

Software

VENDOR SITES FOR DOCUMENT, CONTENT, AND ASSOCIATED SOFTWARE

The following site information has been compiled in good faith by the authors as a reference for readers. It is intended to provide referral information only. We do not claim that this list is conclusive and do not give any representation as to the accuracy, reliability, completeness, or timeliness of the information that is provided at the sites.

Sites that provide directories for content, document and records management software include the following:

- *Open Directory Project* at:
  http://dmoz.org/Computers/Software/Document_Management/
  http://dmoz.org/Computers/Software/Internet/Site_Management/
     ~Content_Management/
  http://dmoz.org/Reference/Archives/Records_Management/

- *Yahoo* at:
  http://dir.yahoo.com/Business_and_Economy/Business_to_Business
     ~/Computers/Software/Business_Applications/Document_Management/
     ~/Communications_and_Networking/Internet_and_World_Wide_Web/
        Software/Development/Content_Management_Systems__CMS_/
     ~/Information/Records_Management/Software/

We avoided categorizing the software into records, document or content management because of the overlapping functionality of many products.

All links were checked and active on October 10, 2002.

Updates and additions to this list, along with links, may be found at http://www.pims.com.au.

Representative List of Software Sites

Vendor	Package Example	Internet Reference Site
A2iA	FieldReader™	http://www.a2ia.com
Accusoft®	DocsNow™	http://www.accusoft.com
Advanced Data Integration	DataWorks	http://www.advdata.com.au
Appolis	eElement	http://www.appolis.com/
Atrove Systems	InfoTrove	http://www.atrove.com/index.htm
BancTec®	eFIRST Solution Suite	http://www.banctec.com/
Bentley Systems	ProjectWise	http://www.bentley.com
Broadvision®	One-To-One® Content™ Publishing Center™ QuickSilver™	http://www.broadvision.com
Captiva	FormWare	http://www.captivasoftware.com/index.htm
Cardiff Software	LiquidOffice TELEform®	http://www.cardiff.com
CD Dimensions eDOC Technologies	Internet File Room	http://www.internetfileroom.com/cddi.asp
Centra 2000, Inc	CENTRA 2000®	http://www.centra2000.com/
centricMinds	centricMinds	http://www.centricminds.com/public.asp
Cimage	e3-RMS	http://www.cimagenovasoft.com/index.htm
Computer Data Solutions	IMR Alchemy	http://www.goodbyepaper.com
Cyco Software	Auto Manager Team Work	http://www.cyco.com/
Cypress	Cypress®	http://www.cypressdelivers.com/
Day Software Holding AG	Communiqué Unify	http://www.dayinteractive.com/
Dejevu	Dejevu edms	http://www.dejevu.com
Dexmar Ltd	KnowPro	http://www.dexmar.com/
Diagonal Solutions	Wisdom	http://www.diagonal-solutions.co.uk/
divine™	Content server	http://www.divine.com
Docassist	OMT Office OMT Engineering	http://www.docassist.se/
Documentum	Documentum 4i	http://www.documentum.com
DocuWare AG	DocuWare	http://www.docuware.com
EASY SOFTWARE	EASY WARE	http://www.easysoftware.net/
80-20 Software	80-20 DME	http://www.80-20.com
eiStream WMS Inc.	ERM	http://www2.eistream.com
eManage Inc	eManage	http://www.emanagecorp.com/index.html
ePaperlessOffice.com	CabinetNG©	http://www.cabinetng.com
Excosoft	ExcoConf XML client	http://www.excosoft.se/sweb/site/home.html
Fabasoft	eGov-Suite	http://www.fabasoft.com/html/layout/mainpage.htm
Feith Systems and Software	Feith Document Database	http://www.feith.com/
FileNET	Panagon	http://www.filenet.com
Focal Point Systems	EDMS	http://www.focalpointsys.co.uk/
Fuji Xerox	DocuShare	http://www.fujixerox.com
Gauss	VIP Enterprise 8™	http://www.magellan.com/
Global Management Systems Inc	Enterprise document management system	http://www.gmsi.com/dms/index.shtml
GMB Knowledge Management Inc	GEM RecFind Corporate	http://www.gmb.com.au
Green Pasture Software	G5	http://www.greenpasture.com
HarvestRoad	Hive	http://www.harvestroad.com.au

Hummingbird	DOCS Open®	http://www.hummingbird.com
	CyberDOCS, PowerDOCS, DOCSFusion	http://www.mdy.com
Hyland software	OnBase	http://www.onbase.com
IBM	Content Manager	http://www.ibm.com/us/
IBM/Lotus	Lotus Domino™	http://www.lotus.com/dominodoc
Identitech	FYI®	http://www.identitech.com/index2.aspx
IDOCSystem.COM	IDOCS Document Control System	http://www.idocsystem.com/index.shtml
Igatech	FileCM©	http://www.igatech.com/filecm/index.html
Imanage	WorkDocs	http://www.imanage.com
InfoVision	AUSinfo DMS	http://www.infovision.com.au
Intergraph AIM		http://www.intergraph.com
Interwoven	TeamDoc™	http://www.interwoven.com/
IQMS	i know	http://www.iqms.com.au
IXOS®	eCON	http://www.ixos.com
LaserFiche	LaserFiche United	http://www.laserfiche.com/
Legato	ApplicationXtender®	http://www.legato.com
Lotus Domino	Domino™	http://www.lotus.com/dominodoc
Macromedia	Spectra	http://www.macromedia.com/
MDY Advanced Technologies	FileSurf™	http://www.mdy.com
Meridio	Meridio RM	http://www.meridio.com/
Meticulus	Meticulist	http://www.meticulus.com
Microsoft	Sharepoint™ Portal Server	http://www.microsoft.com/sharepoint/techinfo/planning/introducing.asp
Mindwrap	Optix®	http://www.mindwrap.com
Neurascript	Neurascript	http://www.neurascript.com
Objective	Objective EDM	http://www.objective.com
Obtree	C4	http://www.obtree.com/
Open Text	Livelink BASIS® iRIMS™	http://www.opentext.com
Optika	Acorde™	http://www.optika.com
Oracle	Oracle9iDB Content Management	http://www.oracle.com
Oxford Computer Consultants	inQuire2™	http://www.oxfordcc.co.uk
Qumas	Qumas	http://www.qumas.com
Scansoft	OmniPage OmniForm	http://www.caere.com
SER Solutions Inc.	SERsynergy™	http://www.ser.com
Silent One Ltd	SilentOne	http://www.silentone.com
Spescom	eB® Fastrack	http://www.spescom.com/
Stellent	Content Management	http://www.stellent.com/
Tarian Software	eRecordsEngine	http://www.tariansoftware.com/
3Tier Technology	Pasidium 2000	http://www.3tt.com.au
3rdmill	3rdgen	http://www.3rdmill.com.au
Tower Software	TRIM Captura™ TRIM PA™ TRIM eDrawer™ TRIM Context™	http://www.towersoft.com.au

Tower Technology	IDM™	http://www.towertech.com/
Tracker Software	Docutrak	http://www.docu-track.com
Tridion	DialogServer	http://www.tridion.com/com/
TrueArc	ForeMost® Enterprise	http://www.truearc.com/
Valid Information Systems	R/KYV	http://www.valinf.com/
Vignette	Vignette V6	http://www.vignette.com/
Watson Consulting	Active Publisher	http://watson-net.com/main.asp
Westbrook	File Magic Fortis	http://www.filemagic.com
World Software Corporation	Worldox	http://www.worldox.com

Appendix 5

Storage Media

In 1965, Gordon Moore of Intel noted that the memory capacity of new integrated circuit memory chips being developed was doubling approximately annually (later revised to about 18 months). This came to be known as Moore's Law and was appropriated to describe a variety of areas of exponential increases or improvements in information technology. Development of the capacity of magnetic and optical disks has, for a period, been doubling in periods of less than a year. The gargantuan storage capacity now available encourages the further digitization of content. However, this capacity places greater strains on the ability of individuals to organize and assimilate the consequent "data glut."

The rate of increase in existing commercial media is unlikely to continue in this fashion because of technical limitations, and because access speeds to the data are not increasing at the same rate. However, alternative technologies under development, such as the long-anticipated holographic storage, hold the promise of capacities beyond the largest physical repositories, including text and images. Even now, there are Web archiving machines, such as the *Internet Archive* at http://www.archive.org/, that hold over 100 terabytes (a terabyte is a million megabytes or approximately 10^{12} bytes) of data. This is well in excess of what has been estimated to be within the texts of the U.S. Library of Congress.

Microform in formats such as microcard, microfilm, and microfiche, have long been used to archive information in compact form. It is relatively cost-effective, and its permanence is more proven than digital imaging. However, access to microforms has always been constrained by location of the material and readers for it. In contrast, digital imagery may easily be replicated and distributed through networks. Because of its archival qualities, microform is regularly used for backup permanent copies of digital material.

Digital Storage Media

Magnetic media are the basic secondary storage media used for computer systems. Digitization to represent the basic code, a bit, is achieved by varying the polarity (direction of magnetization) of the magnetizable coating used. Formats include the following:

- Tape — On reels or in cartridges, with varying numbers of parallel tracks, typically nine, and capacity according to length and packing density of tape, usually expressed in bpi (bits per inch) [A typical packing density is 1600 bpi. Among current configurations are QIC (Quarter Inch Cartridge), 4 millimeter DAT (Digital Audio Tapes utilized for data storage), DLT (Digital Linear Tape), and 8 millimeter Exabyte.]

- Disk — May include hard disk in various forms, such as floating head "Winchester" disks on mainframe machines, down to floppy disks developed for low-capacity storage on personal computers (Data are stored on either or both surfaces in concentric rings (tracks), which in turn, are divided into sectors.)

  Multiple rigid disks may be mounted on the same axle for a disk drive with the set of tracks at the corresponding points on each of their surfaces comprising a cylinder. Multiple arrays of diskettes arranged in devices to provide greater storage capacities have also been developed.

- Drum — Now outmoded cylindrical partitioned devices on mainframe computers

Optical storage media are disks where encoding of data and subsequent retrieval are achieved with lasers. The data encoding takes place in pits or bubbles within the tracks through a substrate in the medium. A disk may have a single track that is a continuous spiral on which the data are recorded at a constant density, meaning that it must be read using heads of variable speed, depending on where on the disk the data reside, so that a Constant Linear Velocity (CLV) is maintained. Alternatively, it may be encoded like magnetic disks with concentric circles, and data are less densely packed on outside tracks, so that it may be read at CAV (Constant Angular Velocity).

Optical media are often characterized according to use by the terms read-only, write-once, or rewritable:

- Read-Only Memory (ROM) — Initially developed on compact disks as CD-ROM to enable mass reproduction from master disks in a common 4.75 inch format. Recording occurs prior to distribution to users. As CD-audio, it constituted the consumer phenomenon that largely supplanted vinyl recordings. It has also been widely used for information storage. This has been principally because the 650 megabyte capacity CD-ROM has been based upon standards that have been generally adopted, to the extent that most PCs make provision for CD-ROM. The OROMs (Optical disks Read-Only Memory) are versions that use concentric encoding and CAV access.

  Interactive versions of CD-ROM are known as CDI. They contain video, audio, and data with built-in decoding mechanisms for the respective signals.

  DVD (Digital versatile or digital video disks) are a more recent format developed principally to cater to audio and video. They may have several readable layers. DVDROMs start in excess of 4 gigabytes. They have at least seven times the capacity of CD-ROMs and are, for example, capable of storing a 2-hour motion picture. Multiple-layer DVDROMs can store the equivalent of hundreds of thousands of pages of text.

- Write Once — This makes provision for direct data storage. It functions by the laser writing directly to individual disks in the user's own situation (unlike the reproduction from a master approach). The most usual acronym used is WORM (Write-Once Read Many), although ODD (Optical digital Data Disk) and CD-R (Recordable) are also in use. WORMs have found favor in legal circles, the inability to alter, and their permanence providing admissible evidence.

  DRAW (Direct Read After Write) is a form of WORM that includes verification of record blocks for error-checking purposes as soon as they have been encoded. DVD allows for write-once provision through the recordable version, DVD-R or DVD-WORM. These may be recorded on two sides, though much of the reading equipment will read only from one side, meaning that disks must be manually reversed for reading both sides.

- Erasable — As with magnetic disks, these provide for repeated rewriting over previously stored data. One way in which this is achieved is by using a combination of magnetic and laser technology. A laser is used to heat areas of a disk coated with transition metals. When a magnetic field is applied, their polarity is reversed to other material on the disk. The reading laser detects polarization differences. Data may be rewritten using a stronger laser that is able to reverse polarity.

  An alternative encoding technique is phase-change technology, where the equivalent of polarity reversal is achieved using materials that may be in crystalline or amorphous states that can be altered by laser.

  The erasable CD manifestation is CD-EPROM (Compact Disk-Erasable Programmable Read-Only Memory), and DVD versions include DVD/RW (for Read-Write) and DVD-RAM. These may be recorded on two sides with a single layer per side with a total in excess of 9 Gigabytes.

Magnetic and other digital storage technologies suggest a step forward in the preservation of information. The information may be text, graphics, photographs, or other images, such as slides or motion pictures. It may be transferred from source document or be digital original. However, the life expectancy of optical media still must be proven beyond the laboratory environment. Rigorous management programs must be employed to manage longer-term use. For example, application of open system formats enables replication of data from legacy systems, and retention and maintenance of hardware and retrieval software enables continuing access to archival information.

The extent to which different media will accommodate organizational needs may be determined with the assistance of guides that give comparisons of storage capabilities and relate these to different types of originating physical material. For example, Cornell University's Department of Preservation and Conservation (2002) provides a digital imaging tutorial that includes estimates of storage requirements.

About the Authors

Len Asprey

Len is a Principal Consultant with Practical Information Management Solutions Pty Ltd, Australia, and provides professional information management and technology consulting services to corporations, businesses and government departments. His consultancy services include a wide range of assignments related to document management, content management, document imaging, workflow and business process analysis and re-design. Len was the founding Chair and is a Life Member of the Institute for Information Management (IIM), and is a member of the Association for Information and Image Management (AIIM International), affiliated through the Aloha Chapter in Hawaii. He is a recognised speaker in the information management and technology domain on the international circuit.

Michael Middleton

Michael Middleton is a Senior Lecturer in the School of Information Systems at Queensland University of Technology, Brisbane, Australia. During the last 10 years his academic experience has been augmented with numerous consultancy assignments in the field of information management and services. Michael's previous employment includes services at Edith Cowan University and the University of New South Wales as an academic, and in management positions at Edith Cowan University, National Library of Australia and the Australian Atomic Energy Commission.

Index

D

data administrators 5

data migration, *see migration*

database application reports 76

database management systems (DBMSs) 15, 17–18, 423

designing and implementing recordkeeping systems (DIRKS) 43

desktop environment 9, 16, 112, 390, 422

development systems 478–479

digital cameras 65, 352–353

digital imaging, *see imaging*

digital office documents 48, 54, 305–329

digital signatures 23, 128, 397

disaster preparedness 298

disk setting 366

disposal 43, 54, 58, 63, 73, 82, 99, 326, 340, 342

document capture, *see capture*

document characteristics 2, 11, 21, 233

document classification, *see classification*

document creation 48, 55, 59, 74

document description language (DDL) 12, 92

document destruction 3

document imaging, *see imaging*

document inspection 362

document management standards 203–212

document managers 5

document preparation 356

document profiles 354

document receipt 48, 77

document registration, *see registration*

document review 97

document routing 52

document volumes 307–308, 346

documentation production 13

domain requirements 278, 415, 420–430

drawing conversion 401

drawing history 398

drawing management 87, 102, 104–109, 120, 146, 381, 388–391, 395, 397, 403–408

drawing number schemas 390–392

drawing registers 398

drawing registry systems 104–105

drawing transmission 62, 394–396

drawings 17, 59–63, 102–109, 147, 388–408

Dublin Core 208, 210

E

email 55, 58, 100, 330–335, 380–381, 483

employee relations management 140

engineering industries 34, 160–161

enterprise report management (ERM) 9, 130

enterprise resource planning (ERP) 17, 45, 126, 135, 399

environmental management 41, 202

evaluation 441–457

evidence 11, 37, 199

executive commitment 227

eXtensible markup language (XML) 10, 68, 70–71

F

facsimile transmission 65, 76–78, 352

feasibility study 217–239, 274, 350

file registration, *see registration*

filing 4

financial feasibility 236

financial management systems 139

financial services industries 32, 156

forms 12, 42, 75, 150

full-text indexing, *see indexing*

functional requirements 278, 305–414, *see also under document types, e.g., email*

G

gap analysis 455–456

geographical information systems (GISs) 138–139, 164

S